KENNETH TYNAN was born in 1927 and educated at Magdalen College, Oxford. His chief reputation is as a drama critic, but he was also a theatrical producer (of shows ranging from *Oh! Calcutta!* to *Soldiers*) and, from 1963, Literary Manager – later Consultant – to the National Theatre in London.

His books include *He That Plays the King, Persona Grata, Alec Guinness, Bull Fever, Curtains, Tynan Right and Left, A View of the English Stage 1944-63, The Sound of Two Hands Clapping* and *Show People.* Published scripts include *The Quest for Corbett* and *Oh! Calcutta!*

Kenneth Tynan died in July 1980.

KATHLEEN TYNAN is a novelist, journalist and screenwriter. She is the author of *The Summer Aeroplane, Agatha* and *The Life of Kenneth Tynan.* She was married to Kenneth Tynan in 1967. She lives in London with her children, Roxana and Matthew.

ERNIE EBAN is a former investigative journalist for *World In Action*, a feature writer on *The Village Voice*, video critic of *The Listener* and consultant to The Open University on computer-based training. He is presently producing digital sound documentaries on various subjects.

P35

£4

To William Shawn

Kenneth Tynan

PROFILES

Selected and edited by
Kathleen Tynan and Ernie Eban

Preface by Simon Callow

Nick Hern Books
A division of Walker Books Limited

A Nick Hern Book

Profiles first published in 1989 by Nick Hern Books.
a division of Walker Books Limited.
87 Vauxhall Walk, London SE11 5HJ

This paperback edition first published in 1990

British Library Cataloguing in Publication Data
Tynan, Kenneth, *1927-1980*
Profiles
1. Great Britain. Theatre. Actors & actresses
1925-1982 – Biographies
I.Title II. Tynan, Kathleen III. Eban, Ernie
792.0280922

ISBN 1-85459-028-6

Typeset by L. Anderson Typesetting. Woodchurch, Kent
TN26 3TB
Printed and bound by Billings of Worcester

Publisher's Note
Due acknowledgment of the books, journals or newspapers in
which these pieces first appeared, along with their respective
date of first publication, is given at the end of each profile.

Contents

Preface by Simon Callow
Introduction by Kathleen Tynan

Preface

Like many people of my age, I did my formative theatregoing not in the West End or down the Waterloo Road, still less in a repertory theatre or on the fringe, but in my own front room, with a copy of Kenneth Tynan's *Curtains* in my hands. Its chance discovery on a bookstall was the epiphany that revealed to me the existence of a fabled, exotic, distant world, that became my goal: the world of theatre. Reading and re-reading the reviews, I felt that I had seen the productions so enticingly described; that I had been there when Olivier's entrance as Titus had 'ushered us into the presence of the man who is, pound for pound, our greatest living actor'; had seen Orson Welles's false nose part company with his real one as he became – unlike Olivier's Hamlet ('a man who could not make up his mind') – 'a man who could not make up his nose'. Visits to the theatre itself – to the Old Vic, for instance, in its grey final days before the National Theatre moved in, or the dull West End of the early sixties – were poor competition for the productions I had seen in Tynan's pages. Tynan's theatre was a place of glamour, intellectual glamour, above all, a place where ideas were thrillingly incarnated by exceptional human beings. It was not until Olivier's first season at the Vic in 1963 that I saw with my own eyes what he had been talking about; and it was Tynan of course, who, as Literary Manager, was part architect of that thrilling succession of performances and productions.

At the heart of his work as a critic was a sense of the individual achievement: the writer's, the director's, and, supremely, the actor's. His reviews have less to do with judgement than with evocation; the element of performance was the crucial one for him. He writes about acting and the theatre as if he were a sports commentator: knowing the form, following every turn of the game, submitting to the physical excitement of it. Roaring with the crowd and dismayed at reverses, he never for a moment forgets that it is a game he's involved in. He brought the same approach to life, and it underlies all his writing: *Bull Fever*, obviously, but equally the profiles which throughout his career he wrote alongside his formal reviewing. They focus on people of many kinds, by no means all connected with show business; but the theme, from the earliest profile of his Oxford friend Alan Beesley to the full-scale study of Ralph Richardson, is always Life as a Performance, embodied in prose which is Writing as a Performance.

A wonderful performance it is, too. Simply as journalism, the pieces here collected are masterly. The curricula vitae are elegantly and accurately despatched, a physical portrait, often of great virtuosity, is limned, and the subject's conversation recorded. As a reporter his ear and eye are first-rate, and in the use of simile he is among the funniest and most arresting writers of the century. Charles Laughton looks like 'a fish standing on its tail'; he leaves the room 'with a furtive air like an absconding banker'. Edith Evans' acting is 'a succession of tremendous waves, with caps of pure fun bursting above them.' He constantly surprises with unexpected conjunctions, as when, for example, he illuminates Humphrey Bogart by reference to Seneca. The longer profiles, less hectically brilliant than the sketches, are sustained examples of analysis and assessment worth more than whole volumes of biography. But beyond the sheer skill of the writing, its achievement is to make one long to have been around these people, just as one longed to have seen the productions Tynan reviewed. His love of the egregious, his sense of 'these great ones', is not snobbery: it is an affirmation of style as a form of courage. In this he rather resembles Cocteau; like Cocteau too he has a fine sense of the loneliness of those who invent and perform themselves. He never quite loses his posture of amused admiration, presenting himself as a dandy delicately negotiating the rim of a volcano; but his seriousness is none the less real for lacking any moral dimension. He doesn't judge, he has no lesson to draw. His philosophy is, rather, a perfumed existentialism, a flamboyant stoicism. He admires the man or woman who lives his or her life exactly as they mean to, and then picks up the bill – as he did himself, weighing the pleasure of cigarettes against the price of death. In this sense, his profile of Antonio Ordóñez, the matador he admired above all others, is essential Tynan. Whether the chosen arena is the cabaret, the theatre, the drawing room or the corrida, the dangerous giving of oneself is the distinguishing mark of all these people.

In addition, there is his central perception of the bi-sexuality of the greatest performers. He discerns it in Bea Lillie, in Laurence Olivier, in Dietrich of course ('she has sex but no particular gender') – even, more surprisingly, in Sid Field: 'A certain girlishness seeps through the silly male bulk of the man, a certain feminine intensity on the emphatic words.' Antonio Ordóñez is unexpectedly gentle, sweet, and slight, not the machismo figure of ignorant fantasy. Coupled with this insight is a sense, also insistently noted, of a transcendence of the physical moment. The great hedonist and prophet of the flesh discovers something quite different at the heart of many of his subjects. Bea Lillie has some attributes of the Zen master; in Garbo, there is 'something wanting, something cheated of fulfilment ... but whatever it may be, the condition is one which could not be cured in a film studio. It has to do with her whole life.' Orson Welles 'is a connoisseur – that social, wine-wise, stomach-sensitive creature without whom art could never be understood, but by whom it is so rarely hammered out.' The act of theatre, the production of art, are in the end secondary to the fact of being. The mystery of personality and the concentrated embodiment of certain essences of the human condition were, for him, sufficient contribution to the brave evasion of mortality that he celebrated. His blow-by-blow account of Olivier's Othello is an invaluable record of a great performance; but what sticks in the mind is the account of the actor's heroic struggle with his own body and temperament. We know too where his priorities lie in his unforgettable assessment of one of his subjects (Welles again); 'A superb bravura director, a fair bravura actor and a limited bravura writer; but an incomparable bravura personality.'

In the thirty years during which he wrote, the theatre and the world changed almost out of recognition, and his style modified accordingly. From the peacockery of his celebration of Beesley, through the fanfares and gavottes of his *monstres sacrés* pieces to the extended reflections in the essays on Louise Brooks, Tom Stoppard and Nicol Williamson, he ceased to mythologise and began instead to explore his subjects and their relationship to their world with a novelist's complexity. As a stylist Tynan came less and less to live up to his middle – his *real* – name.

The group portrait of the theatrical beau monde that this collection of profiles provides, written by a fan who was also an insider, and whose enthusiasm was matched by his wit and his verbal brilliance, celebrates a vanished world of outsize personalities. It is also a glittering memorial to Tynan himself.

Simon Callow
July 1989

Introduction

It comes as no surprise that a journalist who described himself as 'a drama critic at large ... in the lives of other people' chose to write profiles of highly dramatic subjects. Ken revered larger-than-life men and women of exceptional talent, craftsmanship, elegance and wit. If to these qualities was added the spice of a dangerous or eccentric temperament, he would rejoice.

Though most of the pieces in this collection were written on commission, they unabashedly reflect his taste and bias: actors, directors and writers dominate the cast. A bunch of comics perform. Four critics make their appearance, along with two jazz musicians, two obscure eccentrics, a dancer and a bullfighter.

Ken knew two thirds of the people chosen, and enjoyed more than a passing friendship with the rest (with the exception of the three who died before he could make their acquaintance). He often makes a personal appearance, and this backstage intimacy enlivens the encounters. His absence is felt in the two anonymous profiles written for the *Observer*, on Thornton Wilder and Arthur Miller.

The genesis of the book is as follows: Nick Hern agreed to publish three volumes of Ken's theatre criticism in chronological order and with proper annotation. As an overture to these volumes we decided to publish a collection of profiles, offered more for entertainment than scholarship.

Our original plan was to put together an alphabetical assembly, in the manner of Ken's collaboration with Cecil Beaton, *Persona Grata*. But that frivolous arrangement of short impressions, largely written for the occasion (1953), could not be repeated; not when we had in hand material that varied so much in technique and length. A chronological presentation seemed more suitable. One could travel fairly comfortably from the schoolboy's homage to Alexander Woollcott of 1943, to his *New Yorker* profile of Louise Brooks, written 36 years later. The variations in style and perspective would reflect the development even while Ken was making concessions – on hindsight very few – to the marketplace, to magazines as different as the specialist film journal *Sight and Sound*, the popular *Everybody's* and the inimitable *New Yorker*.

Having decided on a chronological approach, we had next to make our selection. What to choose from some 170 pieces which, whatever their form, could justly be described as portraits of people? We were counselled to go for new material, not previously published in book form, to seek out useful stuff for biographers, and nostalgia for the aged. We rejected this advice in favour of pieces that could only have been written by Ken, on subjects most dear to him. Our guide was his own standard for good drama criticism, that it is not the opinion that counts so much as the art with which it is expressed. Only 17 of the pieces are appearing in book form for the first time. (Though we should add that all the Tynan collections are now out of print.)

We reduced the pile, by chance, to 50. Nick Hern liked the round number and we've stuck to it. The material falls roughly into two categories, the profile in which both a subject's work and his biography are treated (Peter Brook, Alec Guinness), and the piece which celebrates and explains a particular artist at work (Sid Field, James Cagney). A couple simply celebrate a unique human being, such as Alan Beesley.

We start the first part of the book with two contributions by Ken to the King Edward School Chronicle, on Alexander Woollcott and Orson Welles; followed by studies in *Isis* and *Cherwell* of two eccentrics he met as an Oxford undergraduate: Alan Beesley, a precursor of Jimmy Porter, and Stanley Parker, a 'Savoy Grill Falstaff'. The great comic, Sid Field, appeared in *He That Plays the King*, Ken's first book, published in 1950. W.C. Fields, James Cagney, and Greta Garbo were commissioned by Penelope Houston for *Sight and Sound*. The interview with Charles Laughton, conducted in 1951, is our sole selection from the *Evening Standard*, where Ken worked as drama critic. The first of the two pieces on Noël Coward is from the short-lived arts magazine, *Panorama*, edited by Daniel Farson. Alec Guinness, John Gielgud, Peter Brook and Cyril Connolly are among the many profiles Ken wrote for *Harper's Bazaar* (U.S.) under the editorship of Carmel Snow. Katharine Hepburn and Judy Holliday appeared in the now defunct picture magazine, *Everybody's*, Edith Evans in *Woman's Journal*, under the pseudonym 'Georgian'.The Crazy Gang, C.S. Lewis, George Jean Nathan, James Thurber and the second of our offerings on Orson Welles all appear in *Persona Grata*.

Contributions to the *Observer* published between 1954 and 1973 include Thornton Wilder, Arthur Miller, George Bernard Shaw, Gordon Craig, Paul Léautaud, Martha Graham, our second on Noël Coward, Harry Kurnitz and Eric Morecambe.

From American magazines: Tennessee Williams (*Mademoiselle*), Antonio Ordóñez (*Sports Illustrated*); George Cukor, Miles Davis, Beatrice Lillie and Joan Littlewood (*Holiday*).

Orson Welles – our third profile, justified, we believe, by Ken's life-long fascination for the man – appeared in *Show* and Humphrey Bogart was originally published in *Playboy*.

The piece on Lenny Bruce was written as an introduction to Bruce's autobiography, *How to Talk Dirty and Influence People*; the homage to Marlene Dietrich for *Playbill*.

Although Ken interviewed Laurence Olivier in a question-and-answer format, reviewed many of his great performances, and wrote extensively about him in unpublished journals, his only profile is the one we include, which is also a backstage study of Olivier at work on the part of Othello (included in a 1966 National Theatre book).

In the case of Bertolt Brecht, we have taken the liberty of excerpting a section from a *New Yorker* article on the German theatre (1959), since this is the best available material.

The second half of the collection is exclusively from the *New Yorker* : Nicol Williamson, Ralph Richardson, Tom Stoppard, Mel Brooks and Louise Brooks. Ken described the *New Yorker* prose style as 'pungent and artless, innocently sly, superbly explicit: what one would call low-falutin'. Despite the magazine's prudish censorship and editorial quirkiness, he readily submitted to its dictates. In William Shawn he found an ideal editor.

For his early profiles he worked often from memory, and with speed, using interview quotes, or ideas, or fully formed phrases, which he had jotted down on scraps of paper, or in his pocket diary, or on the back of a cigarette box. Because of the demanding length of the *New Yorker* profiles, however, Ken found himself doing much more research than he considered was good for him: he felt quite simply burdened by the bulk of his notes.

We have chosen to print the versions of these profiles as amended by Ken for their appearance in book form. Our principle has been not to cut. Although the Brecht piece is an excerpt, we have not tampered with it internally.

The editorial 'we' consists of myself and of Ernie Eban, who prepared an extensive chronology of Ken's works and papers for my 1987 biography, *The Life of Kenneth Tynan*. The third part of the editorial 'we' is our publisher Nick Hern whose enthusiasm, imaginative know-how and publishing house made this collection possible.

Kathleen Tynan, 1989.

ALEXANDER WOOLLCOTT

In the month of January 1943, those of us who probe and appreciate received a darkening shock; many, I among them, sought out emblems of mourning; and I, for one, decided finally not to go to America. We heard a voice, a maddening and impartial voice, telling us calmly and reservedly that a dynasty had collapsed, an era had passed — in short, that Alexander Woollcott was dead. That strange, errant, erudite, and immensely lovable mountebank; that questing, querulous spirit, with all its forthrightness and ingenuity, had flitted off into some odd corner in limbo, there to comment and chuckle and be malign; to dart unseen rapiers at that mortal race that once and ever he had loved.

Alexander Woollcott was an all-embracing, non-respecting, joy-loving genius; a great dramatic critic, a brilliant wit, 'full of subtile flame,' a teller of unmatched short stories, and the most expert of feuilletonists, he was the omnipresent pivot of literary and theatrical life in the seething, sky-scraping metropolis that is New York City. His fine and illuminated intellect grasped, held, and assessed; little indeed was beyond his wit, the wise and jetting laughter of a corkscrew of a brain.

We may here thank God for the foresight of those responsible for the publication over here of *While Rome Burns*, his intense and widespread vision of humanity. This jumbled jostling mosaic of criticisms, portraits, journals, and those glittering and unforgettable anecdotes, now suspended in a frenzy of expectation, now pervading our thoughts suggestively and unpleasantly — all these we loved, and we turned to America for more of this versatile and providential commentator of his times — for more of that 'gaiety which might be mere gaiety and would be pretty good at that, but which is backed by a profound knowledge of human nature and history, and the soundest of values.' I quote from one of his English disciples, Rebecca West.

Yes, the people of New York had an inestimable advantage in those years between the wars; they had the platinum, the ruby-encrusted joy of dramatic criticism from the gilding pen of Alec Woollcott. People — the best people — made pilgrimages to see this fantastic creature on his flamboyant and piquant eminence; and people — the best people — respected him. And sometimes (let us be frank) feared him; listen to Noël Coward:

Alexander Woollcott in a rage has all the tenderness and restraint of a newly-caged cobra; and, when striking, much the same admirable precision. There was always a sly, rococo twist to Woollcott; he was indubitably a character; in its highest sense he was what the French call an 'original'.

As *maître de salon,* too, he was supreme. Clad in insecure egg-stained pyjamas, he would preside over an animated crowd of backgammon playing, talking and eating guests. There would be Dorothy Parker, the Kaufmans, Charles MacArthur, Marc Connelly, Kathleen Norris, and even Alec's old adversary, Edna Ferber — in fact, all playwriting New York, and the cream of the wit of a continent. They were noisy, joyful assemblies; and memorable, too, even if only for Alec himself, crooning in some ghastly baby language: 'EVWY day my pwayers I say, I learn my lessons EVWY day' — until his opponent happened to throw double sixes, whereupon he would scream a shrill and profane imprecation in tones of apparently ungovernable fury.

This, then, was their Woollcott. We came gradually to know him; half a dozen broadcasts he did for us remain like beacons in the misty, fretful first year of war. His spirit, too, has been perpetuated, somewhat wryly, by his cronies, George Kaufman and Moss Hart, in their journalistic tour de force, 'The Man Who Came to Dinner', whose central character — but let Alan Dent describe him:

> Sheridan Whiteside is a roaring, tearing monster of a petted and pampered dramatic critic . . . His friends dread him, and his enemies make allowances for him . . . He somehow obtains everything in life — nay, life itself, at a considerable discount. . . . He is a living, breathing, writing, talking paradox, a pet and a menace, a pest and a delight . . .

It needed an idiosyncrasy like that of Woollcott to reconcile this description to the writing of this golden fragment; here is Woollcott on Lilian Gish's *Marguerite Gautier*:

> It is the immaturity of a pressed flower — sweet, cherishable, withered. It has a gnome-like unrelation to the processes of life and death. It has the pathos of little bronze dancing boots, come upon suddenly in an old trunk. It is the ghost of something that has passed this way — the exquisite print of a fern in an immemorial rock.

And it was thus, quietly and suddenly, that this mountainous cavalier left his company of cynical worldlings. He was stricken in the course of a broadcast discussion; he was removed to hospital, and died there, just before midnight, on the evening of January 23, 1943.

I like to think that now, whenever I chuckle in my inmost heart, something of Alexander Woollcott, in my very presence, is chuckling with me; that somewhere, in a shady vantage-point in paradise, a crashing lost chord is quietly resolving itself.

King Edward's School Chronicle: July 1943

Orson Welles

There is a man flourishing now and being mighty on the other side of the Atlantic. He has a lovely wife and twenty odd years of flamboyant youth — but his accomplishments do not end here. Betraying the smoke-ring silence of artistic achievement, he has burst upon the American scene with a heavy gesture of ineffable superiority; he is the saviour of a broad land, and he knows it. For Orson Welles is a self-made man, and how he loves his Maker; he has become a legend, lurid and bruited in his own lifetime.

What does he do, this finest and most lordly? He plays the piano with a new harshness; he is a writer of the most brittle poetry, shot with the superficial majesty of sorcery; he moulds art out of radio, the scourge of art; he is a wit as only Americans can be wits; and he is a dandy among impromptu speakers. He is a producer of plays in kingly fashion, independent as a signpost in all he does; and he has carved out of a face of massy granite the subtle likeness of a great actor. He is a gross and glorious director of motion pictures, the like of which we have not seen since the great days of the German cinema; he reproduces life as it is sometimes seen in winged dreams.

He is all these things, vastly exaggerated and blown up into the balloon of bald promise and brash achievement that is Welles. Yet with all his many-sidedness he has no dignity. 'I have,' he once said, 'the dignity of a nude at high noon on Fifth Avenue.'

One perquisite of greatness he lacks; artistic integrity. Perhaps he has burgeoned too early and too wildly; at present he is too cynical to be true even to himself. But it will come with praise and age; and then we shall behold a gorgeous, patriarchal figure, worthy of the Old Testament. Until then — watch him, watch him well, for he is a major prophet, with the hopes of a generation clinging to his heels.

King Edward's School Chronicle: December 1943

ALAN BEESLEY

He was born in 1923, but isn't sure where. Somewhere in London, he thinks. From 1942 to 1945 he served in Canada with the R.A.F., and in Michaelmas, 1945 came up to Pembroke. There are one or two other facts about Alan Beesley, but they are swallowed up and made trivial in the pungency and valour of his personality. It would be easy to dart cool gibes at him: the sick-brained, tail-chasing idealist; the penniless, raving introvert who makes life a medley of mad error and soaring abandon. It would be easy; but dishonest, and pointless.

Alan Beesley thrust and bored into Oxford in October, 1945, and it was like a kick in the midriff. Amongst other things he founded the Author-Critic Club, and made about five hundred friends. He published two anthologies, swam, drank, and played rugger. In Trinity, 1946, Ken Tynan, speaking for a roomful of enthusiasts, offered him the Editorship of a new *Cherwell*, and he took it. *Cherwell* 1946 was an unhappy, excitable paper, pitched high in brilliant zanyism, at times almost Evangelical, always brittle and collapsible. *Cherwell* 1947, a smoother job, smeared him unnecessarily across the headlines. He was in the news, but disastrously out of pocket. That was anguish, and calamity. The matter is now closed, and Alan sits firmly on the lid of what might have been a Pandora's box.

He is small, compactly tough, and urgent; as well as being sinuous. He says he is 'a booly and a thug,' and externally he may be right: He smokes continuously with dazed nonchalance, and carries his shoulders in an aggressive-defensive bunch about his neck. His face is wan and puckered, bitten and polished by the diligence of hard circumstance. And he has a sad child's eyes, of extraordinary beauty and despair. He moves in quick spasms, as if shaking off a succession of oppressive burdens. His talk is a flood, and he keys himself precariously to cling to the crests of its waves. His voice is flat tenor, very high but never shrill; he calls it 'ruggedly effeminate.' His ideas are of the moment: mood-creatures who swamp his whole self and possess it. And then a new dawn cracks round his horizon, and it is a new moment, and a new personality. He sheds his notions daily, like a slough, leaving only a residue of conviction that the world is insane, pathetic, and bad. He wrings each minute dry, and then discards it; for the thought of age terrifies him. The future is shut out permanently from his mind. He will not speak of it.

In conversation he can communicate complex ideas by sheer emotional verve and a bounding pulse of exposition. When he is bright, there is no more sensitive or responsive company in Oxford. He has more personality and less egotism than you would think possible: his humility is overwhelming. Yet he can dominate a room by brooding, crook-backed and silent, in a far corner. Suddenly some intolerable opinion will wound him, and he will leap upon it, and tear it with his talk and incisive teeth to a tattered death. He has catch-phrases: for Alan, the epithet 'gay' applies with utter abandon to anything from envelopes to omnibuses, and it means precisely what he makes it mean. 'Gaiety! Gaiety!' (pronounced 'Gairty') is his social rallying-call. Compare him, it you wish, to some odd, exulting rodent, some nipping, eager quadruped with bright eyes — a sort of intellectual Sredni Vashtar.

He is probably the only genuine neurotic in Oxford. You get a sense of *rapport* with the Life-Force, an insane drive granted, they say, only to idiots and prophets. His nails are bitten to the quick, and his finger-tips raw. But this is not an inert, lounger's neurosis: it is dynamic, and can explode the most resilient mental fabrics away to rubble. To discuss his politics and opinions would be silly. These things are tiny trappings, which jingle cleverly for an hour, and are then renewed. Alan wears things out quickly, including himself. He lights his candle at both ends: tremulous, hypnotic flames which he snuffs regretfully, always just before both ends meet. While it burns, and you are with the subjective, not the objective Alan, you are mesmerized by that relentless personality — so shaming and humiliating that it might be tangible. You even put out a wary hand. But then the reverie ends, and you see that Alan is yards away from you, staring past the fire into his thoughts.

To his confusion, he finds himself constantly attended by friends, willing and hoping to help him through the imbranglements which string his moods together into a life story. Women invariably appoint themselves his confessor or foster-mother. He is, then, a tight parcel of busy energy, living dangerously beyond its means, both financially and nervously; paring all creeds and customs to the bone with the sharp knife in his mind. Simple existence for Alan is a full-time responsibility, involving endless repairs, overhauls, injections, and works of preservation to his selfhood.

What does he do? He is a writer. He writes as he talks — in crisp nodules, fired point-blank into print. He has the novelist's, or marksman's eye for words. His short stories are devastating, and he will soon write a great novel. If he is not pushed along the dirty path of the forgotten martyr; if he can be fed occasionally, and given paper, cigarettes, and typewriter, Alan Beesley will write several great novels.

Canonized or crucified, ignored, or loathed, or loved, Alan is hard, unmistakable diamond, and his setting is an inconsiderable *petit-rien*. He dresses badly (by accident, not affectation); he is mostly broke (again, by accident) — but these are slight matters. About them he could not care less, and when he says that, it is with the candour of complete intellectual honesty. He is really out of touch with and bored by this world; like a bad mystic, he is always leaping for a halo of self-realization, but circumstances and 'extraneous detail' (his favourite phrase) anchor him to earth. In a sense, he *is* the disease of this generation; in much the same sense, a pearl is a disease of the oyster. This modern world, given luck and frequent solace, may be Alan's oyster.

The Isis: 12th February 1947

STANLEY PARKER

I deserve, I think, a little space for a clown so intimately bound up with a sky-rocketingly delightful part of my life that his image is magnified for me beyond all reasonable proportions. He is not a professional humourist; his audiences must never exceed half a dozen, and those preferably tipsy; and it may be that in writing about him I am being as blind as the people in Thurber's savage little story, who thought Jack Klohman the funniest man they had ever seen. Nevertheless, I want to write about Stanley Parker, because it is quite possible that nobody else ever will.

This is a sane thanksgiving and a farewell to Stanley, and I write it because he is centrally tangled and embedded in what I like to remember of Oxford, and because I have laughed with him more clamorously, more forgetfully of time and station, more recklessly, than with anyone else. I hope the years are so generous and joy-spawning to him as he has been to me.

Stanley Parker came to Oxford in 1942 to goad the sleeping demons of gaiety from their frozen dens in a grey and warlike city. He brought with him his mother, his brother, a flossy and glossy journalistic reputation in Australia and London, and the buoyancy of twenty-eight spendthrift years. It was rather like letting a rogue elephant loose in a mausoleum. Stanley's friendship with Oxford began, like many of his attachments, by unpremeditated assault. He was never very good at premeditation; I see him rather as an impulsive explorer of sunny moments, which he can inflate into big gleaming bubbles, and deck his day withal, as if they were so many Chinese lanterns. In Stanley's company motives and means and ends and all things aforethought seem tiny and squalid, fit only for page three of the *Oxford Mail*. He is the safest person I know in whom to invest the next ten minutes of one's life; you will be gladdened, if not enriched. He will be a sort of Ronald Searle schoolboy, yet jocund, and plumply droll, and his laughter will be the heart's laughter, which is ease.

I met him some years ago at a party in Trinity College; we sat on the lawn drinking wine, and I thought, here is a fat lizard. I now propose to give up fifteen hundred words to explaining how wrong I was.

Stanley is the Vulgar One, the Big Imp, a laughing buddha sculpted in lava; a Savoy Grill Falstaff; a sophisticated Billy Bunter, a demoniacal and uproarious Owl of the Remove who flies hooting by night. In the same way as Noël Coward looks like an Oriental butler, Stanley looks like a Filipino houseboy. Observe the quick fastidious step, hips held high, shoulders almost in flight: he moves with all the wobble and purpose of a blanc-mange disdainfully deserting Lyons for Claridges, high tea for theatre supper. 'It's no good your saying a *word*,' his face tells us, 'I will *not* be eaten with plastic spoons.' The forehead wryly bulging, betokens deter-mination. His sandals fussily brush the pavement; just as fussily, words brush against his lips as he speaks. It is not a juicy voice, but dry and florid, save when it swoops down to emphasise and point a phrase, and is bolstered up again with a rose-red intestinal chuckle. Then the whole body becomes a madcap jelly, thunderously quaking, and the voice a squelching roar. There is an epic quality about Stanley's smallest mischief, an animal capering; in Oxford he has the loony unexpectedness of a giant panda at the Algonquin. Rococo black finger-curls crowd over a merry sleazy face; in his bustling mock-pomp he sees every party as a gladiatorial arena, and if there is not blood and sand on the floor there ought to be. Yet I would not call him flamboyant; by comparison with his own Lupercalian standards of gaiety he works with a splendid economy and is almost a miniaturist. He rarely makes huge gestures, but when he does, he will probably knock a table over, so tremendous and unlooked-for is his physical strength. He dances with amazing lightness and deftness, bouncing like a rubber puppet and never missing a beat; at parties he has the authority and agility of an orien-tal nabob in whose body the soul of a marmoset has found temporary refuge.

He lives a life of exuberant exclamation marks, vast eyebrow-raising question-marks, and curiously inverted commas; he sees everything heavily italicised, and has no time for anything as half-hearted as a semi-colon. I doubt whether he believes in the existence of full stops. If the things around him are not on a gargantuan scale, he will strive to make them so. Introduce him to a man with a strong laugh, and a moment later you will find him telling everyone that the man has not stopped laughing in fifteen years, that he has been laughing at the sheer absurdity of living, with tears streaming down his face. (Stanley once came within an ace of holding a Laughing Party for all the professional laughers in the University.) Everything Stanley cherishes is anti-realistic; his world is peopled with that which is against or beyond reality. This is his compensation for the fruitlessness of everyday; with wild verbal felicity he spends his time retouching the dull succession of blurred half-tone prints which add up to being alive. Like a lightning telescope, his mind exaggerates drab fact; and all words, fair or foul, are his legitimate meat.

Yet he never swears, not even to say 'hell' or 'damn'. It has been sug-gested that his profound belief in the existence of evil is akin to that of the provincial spinster; it is probably nearer to that of the Catholic martyr. He explained one bout of self-mortification by telling me sombrely: 'I don't think I could survive a sudden death.' Once he refused point-blank to go to a party, because he heard that a hypnotist was to be present; he said he was appalled that such men should be fêted and encouraged. Even in their most frenzied lubricities, the men of the High Renaissance kept their awe of God, and so does Stanley. As Shaw said of Stalin: 'You might guess him to be the illegitimate soldier-son of a cardinal.' In his most elastic party-moods, he retains a certain perspiring holiness, like a Papal bull in a blue china shop; and, like most pontiffs, in addition to knowing good from evil, he knows instinctively which of two photographers represents *The Tatler*, and which the *Daily Mirror*.

He has drawn and written about nearly everybody who *is* everybody; but he will agree that his finest gift is talk. He is the funniest talker I have ever heard, and yet his conversation springs largely from two sources — one, a marvellous eye for physiognomical peculiarity, and two, a marvellous ear for verbal bric-à-brac. He dips, swallow-like, into a sea of words, and comes up dripping and diffuse. His methods are those of snowball accumulation; it is thus that he creates legends where no legend was. The Curator of a zoo once gave him an owl for a birthday present; it was beautifully stuffed, he thought, and he had it put on the mantelpiece beside the stuffed canary. Later, as the party raged into the night, he returned to admire it. It immediately screamed in his face TOO WOOO TOO WOOO and 'began flapping round the room, drinking all the drink, making love to everybody . . .'. It was too much. Ashen, Stanley gathered his shaken dignity about him. 'Either the owl goes, or I go,' he said steadily; '*The owl must leave.*' The owl left.

Stanley is the great escapist; he will never admit that reality is anything more than the unfinished sketch of a careless and indolent creator. It is Stanley's mission to finish the job; he will be the *reductor ad absurdum* of the commonplace. Show him a smallish nose, and he will describe it as 'just two holes in the face', and finally, by almost skull-splitting extension, it will become *concave*. The extremeness of his vision reminds me of a passage in Max Beerbohm:

> The jester must be able to grapple his theme and hang on to it, twisting it this way and that, and making it yield magically all manner of strange and precious things, one after another, without pause. He must have invention keeping pace with utterance. He must be inexhaustible. Only so can he exhaust us.

A favourite theme has to do with a headline which he saw years ago in an Australian daily. 'BEAR IN COURT' it said; and Stanley can still relive the joy of the first image that occurred to him — could it be that 'the bruin in question' had swept into the throne-room with three feathers on its head, and curtsied? The page proved to be the story of a Mrs. Bear, whose psychiatrist reported on her in a sentence which Stanley has never quite got over: 'She was quite normal, *except* that whenever the phrase "point of pin" was mentioned, she thought the word "toe" was indicated.' It is upon such baffled blind alleys of meaning as this that Stanley really lets go. When his brother dreamt of an apocryphal best-seller called *The Whist Between Us*, Stanley spent a morning explaining exactly how it was going to be turned into a film with Anna Neagle and Michael Wilding; he can devote hours of orgiastic talk to deciding just what sort of a woman would have a name like Enid Sharp-Bolster or Didi de Pledge. And you would have to know Stanley very well to understand why the mere mention of concrete floors nowadays gives me hysterics. Set him dithyrambing on a malleable theme, and its changing lights will lure him on into visions in which frogs, frigates, fire hydrants and incantations to the moon will all have a perfectly reasonable place. He never tells jokes or laughs when they are told him. 'Jokes *happen*,' he will say: and his business is to make them happen near him, not to collect them at second hand.

Sometimes ecstasy ties his tongue; as when he thrice insisted to a sloe-eyed Piccadilly bus conductress that he wanted a ticket to 'H-H-Hard Pike — H-H-H-Hard Pike Corner'. Even more attractively confused was his gauche farewell, many years ago, to Athene Seyler. 'Well,' he said, shifting from foot to foot, 'better be get alonging.'

He can be a very hard worker when the fit seizes him; when I first knew him, he could talk of nothing but his new pictures of Gigli and T. S. Eliot. His very holidays and truancies from work are athletic and prostrating; I can think of no one who can better communicate the glow of knowing (in the words that open *The Lost Weekend*) that 'the barometer of his emotional nature is set for a spell of riot'. I do not think he writes particularly well, and his drawings, though Shaw called them 'dramatic criticisms', are very much of the thirties — nearly all represent a left profile staring glumly and intently into mist. But as a *boulevardier* he is unique in Oxford, perhaps in England; and to stoke up that indomitable personality is a full-time job, involving endless night-shifts. Oddly, he is full of love; Max Beerbohm's phrase for him was 'potent in pencil as in pen, but not, I think, in poison'. He still takes his mother to every first-night he attends, and he loves his friends with the pertinacity of an anaconda. I once asked him for an epithet to sum up his whole being, and he proudly replied: 'Wholesome.' He likes piggy pleasures ('I adore food and bacon and things'); and I have often reflected that his existence might be divided into three parts — pork, apple sauce, and stuffing. His most beloved book is *Zuleika Dobson*; he reads the Greeks and the Decadents avidly, and sometimes wonders idly what happened to literature between the death of Pindar and the birth of Whistler. The best acting he has ever seen was Sybil Thorndike's Medea, which he saw sixteen times; and the most humbling genius he ever met was, he says, Pavlova. His proudest recent memory is of a letter Frances Day wrote him addressed to 'Stanley Parker, Oxford'. It was instantly delivered.

For Stanley, laughter is god-like, and despair the ultimate evil. I have heard him say, after a bright evening at the theatre: 'God was with me all evening; he was on my knee.' He detests solitude and cannot remember being alone; except voluntarily, once a week, when he goes to church in mid-afternoon and meditates wasted days. It is 'a very un-smart church' and if interrupted, he pretends to be an ikon.

He especially warms to Mae West and all that drapes itself about her — sequins, ostrich feathers, pink spotlights; all that is deliberately artificial, faintly funny, and nostalgic of the middle thirties. One of his favourite lines comes from a minor triumph of Miss West's in which, cocooned in silk and lace, she turned to her coloured maid and said with almost feudal scorn: 'Beulah — peel me a grape.' This is the life Stanley thirsts after, and it is a sad truth that he has never even aspired to a recognisable pair of shoes.

Never, while you live, permit him to be serious; the brow wrinkles, the lips purse up with affected boredom, and he will talk endlessly in a flurry of furtive platitude. But when a fat woman enters a room, garish under a pumpkin hat, Stanley's face will collapse into a comic mask and you can relax again. He may be going to fall in love with her, or to make outrageous suggestions about her; it matters little; he will be funny. His humorous reflexes are hair-triggered: one afternoon, by sheer loquacity, he persuaded me that Woodstock Road (which telescopes away northwards to the suburbs of hell) was Europe's playground. And he can make the Randolph bar at midday seem as innocent and sunlit and sensual as Hieronymus Bosch's Garden of Delights. Neurosis in his presence becomes a laughable fiction; he is Edward Lear and Lewis Carroll stripped of frailty and whimsey and dipped thoroughly in beer and bacon-fat. There is an almost Chinese imperturbability about him ('I worship everything that is Ping'): often he reminds me of a dissolute old mandarin with a gourmet's love of peacock's tongues and a hatchet up either sleeve.

Sometimes I decide he is a pernicious rascal, a wicked vagabond, and I argue hotly against him, and call him a pantaloon Micawber. It is easy to despise, easier still to pity him: the frightful thing is that he remains full of laughter, knowing your motives better than you do yourself. We do not always see eye to eye. But we invariably see ego to ego.

Cherwell: 14th June 1948; *He That Plays The King*, 1950

SID FIELD

Very occasionally, after long and painful intervals, there emerges from a provincial city a clean comedian. The consequent fracas is always heartening: a boisterous quarterstaff is giving battle to the jagged razors of innuendo, and putting the nasty rout to flight. Late years have granted us but one theme for such talk as this: the munificent clowning of the late Sid Field, the bumpkin droll. It is wrong to be precious in speaking of a man so burly; to fantasticate one whose renown was built upon blunt ways and broad gestures. But there was a finical subtlety to Mr. Field that deserves writing about. I cannot do it: yet I'll hammer it out.

With him, comparison, the critic's upholstery, must retire defeated: nobody has done such things before on our stages. He was enchanted as Bottom was, but he knew it: he was a soul in bliss. There can be no explaining that angelic relaxedness, no dissecting that contentment. He was in permanent possession of some rare and delectable secret, the radiance in the blear eyes told you: yet what he said was serenely, even pugnaciously usual. He could be very nearly a rudesby. I cannot fathom by what alchemy this blend of celestial stance and mundane observation, of nectar and beer, was contrived. You would not guess, from the moonstruck words that eased out of him, that this man would appear in guise and circumstance as other men. Yet I dare insist that no more naturalistic clown walked the land. He employed no barb of repartee, he had no niceness in returning phrase for phrase: his ordinary situation was confusion, or at best mild bafflement. The sketches he animated have, when you think about it, no intrinsic humour of line about them; and if they have, it is generally something trite beyond words (in his golfing sketch, for instance, the instructor would tell him to make the tee with sand; and Mr. Field, mistaking him, would make a slightly hurt, recoiling movement and then venture defensively: 'I'm not drinking that *sterf*': his voice climbing to a pained shrillness, and then, after a moment's consideration: 'More like *co-coa*.'). He had no use at all for pathos, or for the poignant eyes of the quick, ferret comic; to be honest, his face was sadly flat and slab-shaped. Apart from the habit of stage ease and peace, he had none of the marks of his contemporary drolls. He was elephantine. And though he did it delicately, he lumbered. His style was amorphous: he was like a man carrying about with him a number of inexplicable parcels, which he couldn't remember buying, and certainly didn't want. Yet whenever he opened one of them, something wildly funny flew out.

He was most recently seen in the American play *Harvey*, in which he played a dipsomaniac whose *fidus Achates* is a six-foot rabbit, which we cannot see. It was his first straight part, and it was not pleasant to hear: he took all the easy spontaneity out of his voice, and turned it into a carefully modulated tenor with about as much personality as a cod: he dropped the faint Midland accent, the soft uncouthness which was his birthright, and the loss was irrecoverable. His miming was still perfect, though: jocose, flaccid, topful of indiscriminate *bonhomie*, he would nudge and nod confidingly at the rabbit by his side; he would trip and turn to stare reproachfully at the invisible foot that had toppled him, and then, with a wink, extend his own foot to return the trick. Touches like this, and the scene in which he dialled a telephone number with hand movements appropriate to a man painting a picture, made the play bearable.

But he must not be judged on this rash adventure: he was too solitary, like all great comics, for the interactions and cross-stresses of drama. I want us to remember him with a blaze of footlights before him, in small and simple sketches. Picture, to begin with, a pair of drunks, veering with no great determination, around a lamp-post. One of them is portly and has the constricted look of a man about to vomit. That is Mr. Field. The other is very tiny, and from time to time he supports his little frame by clutching at Mr. Field's middle. This, on the fourth or fifth occasion (these things happen gradually) shakes Mr. Field's equanimity. He surveys his partner from above in slow wonder — wonder, perhaps, that there should be men so much smaller than himself. Then, in weary exasperation: 'Get-tout-from-mund-der-neath-me-Ver*non*!' — the last word with unmistakably effeminate emphasis. How print, the great leveller, flattens that line! and how unfairly it robs Mr. Field of the convulsive squirms of dismissal which accompanied it! The written word is untender to comedians, whose every inflexion must have its record if it is to survive. Mr. Field's more wayward triumphs are almost impossible to pin down. How should you see that it was, for example, very funny when he tried to be intimidating; when, after a few threatening starts and a clouded warning glance, he decided to assault his provoker. This he did, mind you, not with fist or foot, but by removing the cloth cap from his head, folding it neatly, and making curious little dabs and pokes with it, shadow-boxing the while. I asked him once how he knew that the only fitting weapon was the cap. He thought it over. Finally: 'It relieves my feelings,' he said, 'without being brutal.'

I liked him, too, when he 'put it on'. His normal accents were, as I have said, those of the suspicious West Midlander; but he could, if he wished, persuade us that he was born within sight of the Victoria and Albert Museum. He would incline, with earnest benignity, to the members of the pit orchestra, and inquire politely: 'And how are yooo to-day? R-r-r-reasonably well, I hoop?' The incongruity of all this, proceeding from those stolid peasant lips, was irresistible. He always revelled in these elocutionary achievements. I once heard him successfully pronounce that formidable word 'Shostakovitch'. At first the magnitude of what he had done escaped him; he passed on, and would have finished the sentence. But all at once glorious consciousness of it overtook him, and he stopped, enthralled in recollection. After a moment's rapture, slow irradiation broke across his face, until it became a huge, blushing, beaming rose. Impulsively he turned towards the wings, and sang out: 'Did you heah *me*, Whittaker?' I do not know who Whittaker was.

Then there was the sketch in which he played all the male parts, making rushed exits which nearly tore the scenery down; one of these character studies was an aged sire, decrepitude being suggested by an uncombed white wig. The character had a paralysed hand which rotated regularly as if preparing to roll dice; it dangled over the edge of the table at which he sat. As I remember it, Mr. Field was talking about the awful state of everything. 'The chimneys haven't been swept,' he complained, 'the windows won't open, the floor's dirty, the wallpaper's coming off.' Then, his gaze wandering to his infirmity, he watched it with gloomy interest and, indicating with his good hand this final item in the catalogue of decay, added mournfully: 'And *this'll* have to be seen to.' And there was his impetuous, cavorting, velvet-clad photographer, welcoming an old friend as a sitter, and making tea for him. Having drunk it, he sets the man in position, chatting cosily, paces out the correct number of steps for the camera, then turns and, in a flash of quiet aberration, runs up as if to bowl. Seeing his blunder, he blushes gauchely and fumbles out an apology. Actually, Mr. Field running up to do anything was fanciful enough: in his Slasher Greene sketch, which involved his wearing a vastly beshouldered overcoat, a pencilled moustache, and all the wily self-confidence of the local boy cutting a shady dash in the city, he was constantly threatening to run up and do something. 'Stand well back, Harry,' he would warn his partner, 'stand well back, boy. I don't know what I might do.' You felt that this was quite true; squinting with determination, he pawed the ground, and was about to set off, when the inadequacy of a stage for his giant exploit hit him: 'Not enough room really. I ought to be in a *field*.' And so we never knew just what it was that he didn't know what he might do.

He was often a prey to stage children. I am thinking of one especially, a gay and omniscient little fright, who took a hellish delight in carping at his brushwork. (For some reason he was painting a landscape.) By and by he suggested that she might like to go away and peddle her papers: 'Why,' as he put it, 'don't you go and play a nice game on the railway track — with your *back* to the *oncoming engines*?' He tried to soothe her with a drink of lemonade ('Get the bottle well down your throat'). But nothing availed him, and at last the crash came. She was telling him about the difference between ultramarine (which he was using) and Prussian blue (which she would have preferred), and it was here that he went to pieces. He rounded on her, fixed her with a moistly aggressive eye, and began a terrible verbal attack on Prussian blue, speaking at great speed and in devastating fury. As the rage seized him, he started to sag at the knees: his legs wilted, and he collapsed to the ground in a lump. The little girl, stunned, helped him to his feet, and waited, with an odd and worried look. We waited, too. At last, between gulps, and in tones of the utmost deprecation and shame, he explained. 'I am a *fool*,' he said petulantly; 'I *must* remember to *breathe* when I speak.' If that is not good enough for Lewis Carroll, I have misunderstood him badly.

His great golfing sketch was full of these things, and we have not space for them all. How would you reply to a pro who said: 'When I say "slowly back", I don't mean "slowly back", I mean "slowly back"'? Mr. Field just stopped in his tracks and thought; and then: 'Let's pick flowers,' he urged hopefully. He made no attempt to reply to the pro's heavy sarcasm in its own vulgar kind; instead, he affected sublime indifference. 'I could have been having my music lesson — with Miss Bollinger,' he explained with careful scorn; 'Miss Bollinger is nice and kind. She can play the piano.' An afterthought occurred to him: '— and the flute.' He flipped out his tongue elaborately in making the 'the' sound. I would enjoy writing about how he looked when his mentor told him to get behind the ball, and he screamed back: '*It's behind all round it!*' But the others have noticed that, and the ground is covered.

I do not pretend to account for these strokes: I can only point vaguely to the quality most of them share — a certain girlishness that seeps through the silly male bulk of the man, a certain feminine intensity on the emphatic words. But Mr. Field was even more bewildered. 'I suppose,' he replied laboriously when I asked him to explain some of the things he said: 'I suppose I'm just peculiar altogether.' It might be possible, in some sort, to trace his genealogy from the names of his three favourite comedians, Bob Hope, Bud Flanagan and Jimmy James. Particularly from the last-named buffoon, with whose genius he had many affinities. He is certainly not explicable in terms of scripts, a fact which ought to be clear by now: nearly all his sketches were originally 'ad-libbed' around an inconsiderable nucleus of ideas, and many affecting tales are told of the anguish of those who tried to tie him down to what they had written for him. He never, he said, forced a laugh in his life; it embarrassed him physically to have to utter a line he did not think funny. 'Makes me perspire all over,' he would mutter. Not many comedians have that discretion. I think a saint would have laughed at Sid Field without shame or condescension.

He That Plays The King, 1950

W.C. FIELDS

If you had been visiting Philadelphia in the winter of 1892 and had wanted to buy a newspaper, you would have stood a good chance of having mild hysterics and a story to dine out on in after years. W. C. Fields, then a frowning urchin of thirteen, was spending a few halcyon months peddling papers; and his manner of vending contained already the germs of a technique which later made him one of the two or three funniest men in the world. While other lads piped about wars and football, Fields would pick on a five-line fill-in at the bottom of a page and, quite disenchantedly, hawk it at the top of his voice. 'Bronislaw Gimp acquires licence for two-year-old sheepdog!' he would bellow at passers-by, adding unnecessarily: 'Details on page 26!' And by the tone of his voice, his latest biographer tells us, you would gather that Gimp was an arch-criminal, for Fields trusted no one. A flabby scowl sat squarely on his face — the same scowl that we see in the curious portrait with which John Decker celebrated the comedian's sixtieth birthday: with a doily on his head and a silver salt-cellar balanced on top of that, he sits, squinting dyspeptically at the camera, perfectly well aware of the profanity of the caption: 'Sixty Years a Queen.' Fields disliked and suspected most of his fellow-creatures to the end of his life; his face would work in convulsive tics as he spoke of them. For sixty-seven years he played duck's back to their water, until on Christmas Day 1946, the 'fellow in the bright nightgown' (as he always referred to death) sneaked up on him and sapped him for good.

W. C. Fields: His Follies and Fortunes is certainly the best book we are likely to see about this droll and grandiose comic. Robert Lewis Taylor is a graduate of the *New Yorker*, and thus a master of the Harold Ross prose style — pungent and artless, innocently sly, superbly explicit: what one would call low-falutin'. Like all the *New Yorker*'s best profiles, this picture of Fields is composed with a sort of childish unsentimentality, the candour of a liquorous quiz kid. Taylor, having inscribed Fields' name glowingly on the roll of fame, beats him over the head with it. Except that he sometimes calls a mistress a 'friend', he spares us little. We learn of Fields' astonishing consumption of alcohol (two quarts of gin a day, apart from wines and whisky); of his quite sincere cruelty (his favourite sequence was one in which he took his small niece to a fun fair and parked her 'for safety' in the shooting gallery); of his never wholly cured habit of pilfering (on his first visit to England he strolled around stealing poultry hanging out in front of shops; it was his tribute to the salesmanship of the proprietors and, as he indignantly added: 'You don't think I'd have stolen chickens in the Balkans, do you?'); of his jovial callousness towards his friends, towards most women, and towards the clergy. One rainy night Fields, fairly far gone, was driving home waving a gin bottle in his free hand, and generously gave a lift to a hitch-hiker. The man was outraged when Fields offered him a drink and, explaining that he was a clergyman, went on to deliver a free sermon to the comedian — 'I'll give you my number four,' he said, 'called "The Evils of Alcohol."' He was well into his stride when Fields nonchalantly pulled up alongside a hedge, kicked the man out, dropped a bottle of gin after him, and roared: 'That's my number three — "How to keep warm in a ditch"!' Equally savage was his exchange with a bartender in *My Little Chickadee*. 'You remember the time I knocked down Waterfront Nell?' he said. The barman, pretty angrily, replied: 'Why, you didn't knock her down, *I* did.' 'Well,' Fields went on, unperturbed, 'I started kicking her first.' He once genially condescended to teach an acquaintance of his, against whom he bore some slight grudge, a simple juggling trick requiring two paring knives. 'I hope he worked at it,' said Fields afterwards, 'because if he did, he was almost certain to cut himself very painfully.' Some of the managements for whom he worked complained about such jests as these. Fields never lost his temper on such occasions. 'We must strive,' he would say thoughtfully, 'to instruct and uplift as well as entertain.' And eyeing them carefully, he would light a cigar.

About all this Mr. Taylor is quaintly frank; and he is even better at describing (for nobody could ever explain) the mysterious caverns of private humour in which Fields delighted. There was the two-reeler entitled *The Fatal Glass of Beer* which he did for Mack Sennett: it opened with Fields sitting on a campstool in a far Northern shack, wearing a coonskin coat and crooning to himself. From time to time he would get up, open the door, and cry: ' 'Tain't a fit night out for man nor beast!' whereupon an extra would pelt him in the face with a handful of snow. There was hardly any other dialogue in the film.

Fields nearly always wrote his own stories (under pen-names such as Mahatma Kane Jeeves), and would drive studio chiefs to despair by his failure to understand that the fact that he appeared in every shot did not necessarily ensure continuity of plot-line. Still, he continued to scrawl plots on the backs of old laundry bills and to get $25,000 a time for them. Often he would wander through the streets wearing a false beard, a repulsive clip-on moustache and an opera cape, and amble into any party he saw in progress, introducing himself as 'Doctor Hugo Sternhammer, the Viennese anthropologist.' He first did this during the First World War. 'I remember telling one woman that the Kaiser was my third cousin,' he mused: 'she gave a little scream and ran like hell.' His treatment of women often bordered on the fantastic: finding strange, unaccountable depths of hilarity in the Chinese, he made one of his mistresses dress in satin slippers and a split black skirt and always called her 'The Chinaman.' Many of his letters to his last mistress and devoted nurse, Carlotta Monti, start out 'Dear Chinese People,' and are signed, even more bewilderingly, 'Continental Person,' or 'Ampico J. Steinway.' He liked ordering Chinese meals in his films; in *International House* (for Paramount in 1932), he called up room service and blandly asked for: 'A couple of hundred-year-old eggs boiled in perfume.'

Fields enraged most people he worked with. Mae West still remembers how stunned she was when, in the middle of a take, he benignly ad-libbed: 'And how is my little brood mare?' He worked first for Mack Sennett and later for Universal and MGM (most notoriously in *David Copperfield*, in which he was narrowly restrained from doing his entire juggling routine); but after he left Ziegfeld's *Follies* in 1921 we are probably most indebted to Paramount, who suffered under him through twenty-one movies, including *Tilly and Gus*, *If I Had a Million*, *Six of a Kind*, *Mrs. Wiggs of the Cabbage Patch*, *Mississippi* and *The Man on the Flying Trapeze*. Much of the time they had to fight to keep him from cursing during takes: in retaliation he devised two expressions — 'Godfrey Daniel!' and 'Mother of Pearl!' — with which he baffled the Hays Office for more than a decade. They granted him a salary so spectacular that even Bing Crosby raised his eyebrows and, by their unearthly tolerance, they allowed him to turn out a series of films which must rank amongst the least money-making comedy classics in cinema history. At last he left them, his powers quite unimpaired, and went to Universal for his last four pictures, *You Can't Cheat an Honest Man*, *My Little Chickadee*, *The Bank Dick*, and the amazing *Never Give a Sucker an Even Break* — the last two of which probably represent the height of his achievement. They were made between 1938 and 1942, when Fields was moving reluctantly into his sixties. Someday they should be revived by the film societies, for in addition to being amongst the funniest films of a good period, they are splendid illustrations of the art of film-making without portfolio, or cinematic actor-management.

The function of a director in a Fields movie was clear right from the start. He either fought with or ignored them. He would reduce such men as Leo McCarey, Norman McLeod, George Marshall and even George Cukor to impotent hysterics of rage by his incorrigible ad-libbing, his affectation of deafness whenever they suggested the slightest alteration in any of his lines or routines, and by his jubilant rudeness to anyone else who happened to be working in the neighbourhood. (Once, when it became known that Deanna Durbin was on a nearby lot and might be audible on clear days, Fields threatened 'to get a good bead from the upstairs balcony and shoot her.') The only director to whose advice he ever paid attention was Gregory

La Cava. 'Dago bastard!' he would growl as, fretfully, he listened to La Cava's analyses of his gifts: yet he admitted that the director was in the right when he implored Fields not to work too hard for his laughs. What La Cava said is worth quoting, for it is acute and provides some sort of key to Fields' later methods. 'You're not a natural comedian, Bill,' he said. 'You're a counter-puncher. You're the greatest straight man that ever lived. It's a mistake for you ever to do the leading. When you start to bawl out and ham around and trip over things, you're pushing. I hate to see it.' He said that in 1934.

La Cava was correct, as Fields' maturer films show. Fields quiescent and smouldering is funnier than Fields rampant and yelling. He played straight man to a malevolent universe which had singled him out for siege and destruction. He regarded the conspiracy of fate through a pair of frosty little blue eyes, an arm flung up to ward off an imminent blow, and his shoulders instinctively hunched in self-protection. It is hard to imagine him without the 'As I suspected' look with which he anticipates disaster. Always his face looked injured (as indeed it was: the nose was ruddy and misshapen not through drink, but from the beatings he received in his youth); he would talk like an old lag, watchfully, using his antic cigar almost as a cudgel. Puffy, gimlet-eyed, and magnificently alarmed, he would try to outwit the agents of calamity with sheer pomp, and invariably fail. Everything he says, even the most crushing insult, is uttered as if it were a closely guarded secret: he *admits* a line rather than speaks it. Only his alcoholic aplomb remains unpersecuted: that they cannot touch, these imps who plague him. Fields breakfasting with his screen family behaves with all the wariness of Micawber unexpectedly trapped in Fagin's thieves' kitchen. His face lights up only rarely, at the sight of something irresistibly and universally ludicrous, like a blind man. One remembers his efforts, in the general-store sequence of *It's a Gift*, to prevent a deaf and blind customer from knocking over things with his stick while Fields is attending to other clients. It was unforgettable, the mechanical enthusiasm of those brave, happy cries: 'Sit down, Mr. Muckle, Mr. Muckle, please sit down!' (a stack of electric light bulbs crashes to the floor.) 'Mr. Muckle, honey, *please sit down!*'

His nose, resembling a doughnut pickled in vinegar or an eroded squash ball, was unique; so, too, was his voice. He both looked and sounded like a cement-mixer. He would screw up his lips to one side and purse his eyes before committing himself to speech; and then he would roll vowels around his palate as if it were a sieve with which he was prospecting for nuggets. The noise that finally emerged was something quietly raucous, like the crowing of a very lazy cock. (If you substitute 'Naw' for 'No, sir,' and cast Fields as Johnson, most of Boswell becomes wildly amusing, as well as curiously characteristic.) Fields' voice, nasal, tinny, and massively bored, is that of a prisoner who has been uselessly affirming his innocence in the same court for centuries: when, in *It's a Gift*, he drives a carload of people straight into a large reproduction of the Venus de Milo, his response as he surveys the fragments is unhesitating. 'Ran right in front of the car,' he murmurs, a little wearily.

The recent revival of *It's a Gift* (Norman McLeod for Paramount, 1934) was received gratefully by students of Fields' middle period. He does little heavy wooing in it, and robs surprisingly few people, but most of his other traits are well represented. The cigar is there; so is the straw hat, which nervously deserts him at moments of crisis and has to be retrieved and jammed back on to the large, round head which squats, Humpty-Dumpty-like, on the oddly boyish shoulders. There is Fields' old rival, Baby LeRoy, to spill a barrel of molasses, described by the comedian in a famous line as the 'spreadingest stuff I ever saw in m'life'. (To a friend who enquired the name of his new co-star, Fields replied: 'Fellow named LeRoy. Says he's a baby.') There is Kathleen Howard, the Fieldsian equivalent of Margaret Dumont, sneering with her wonderful baritone clarity at his 'scheme to revive the celluloid collar.' And there is the long and savoury sequence in which Fields, driven by Miss Howard's nocturnal scolding to seek sleep on the verandah, is kept awake by such things as a coconut rolling down a fire-escape, a squeaking clothes-line, an insurance salesman (who asks 'Are you a Mr. Karl Lafong, capital K small A small R small L capital L small A capital F small O small N small G?'), the whirr of bottles in a milk-crate, a 'vegetable gentleman' selling calabashes, and, of course, by Master LeRoy, who drops grapes from above into the comedian's mouth. 'Shades of Bacchus!' mutters Fields, removing the eleventh.

In the same programme as *It's a Gift* was a revival of *Monkey Business*, which the Fields section of the audience took in glacial silence, because this is script-bound comedy, the comedy of quotability. Groucho owes much to Perelman: Fields owes nothing to anyone, except dubiously Harry Tate. Fields strolls out of the frame into the theatre, while the Brothers remain silhouettes. Fields' fantasy has its roots in the robust soil of drunken reverie: theirs are in the hothouse of nightmare. They will resort to razors and thumbscrews to get laughs that Fields would have got with a rolled-up newspaper. Their comic style is comparable with his only in that, as Mr. Taylor notes, 'most people harbour a secret affection for anyone with a low opinion of humanity.' It is nowhere recorded what Fields thought of the Marx Brothers, but it is permissible to guess. Hearing them described: 'Possibly a squad of gypsies,' he might have grunted, pronouncing the 'g' hard, as in gruesome.

Fields is pre-eminently a man's comedian. Women seldom become addicts of his pictures, and it is no coincidence that his closest friends (John Barrymore, Ben Hecht, Gene Fowler, Dave Chasen, Grantland Rice) were all men. He belongs inseparably to the poolroom and the barroom — though rarely to the smoking-room; and while he looked like a brimming Toby Jug, it was always clear that no mantelpiece would hold him. Few wives drag their husbands to see his films, which may partly explain their persistently low profits. Like Sid Field, he rejected pathos to the last, even when working with child stars: he refused to tap the feminine audience by the means that Chaplin used in *The Kid*. It is appalling, indeed, to reflect what Fields might have done to Jackie Coogan, a less resilient youth than LeRoy. Perhaps it is a final judgement on him that no self-respecting mother will ever allow her children to read Mr. Taylor's brilliant book — a chronicle of meanness, fraud, arrogance and alcoholism.

We know, by the way, Fields' opinion of Chaplin. Late in life he was lured to a cinema where some of the little man's early two-reelers were being shown. The laughter inside was deafening, and halfway through Fields uneasily left. His companion found him outside in the car at the end of the show, and asked what he thought of Chaplin's work. 'The son of a bitch is a ballet dancer,' said Fields. 'He's pretty funny, don't you think?' his friend went on doggedly. 'He's the best ballet dancer that ever lived,' said Fields, 'and if I get a good chance I'll kill him with my bare hands.'

Sight and Sound: February 1951; *Curtains*, 1961

JAMES CAGNEY

Twenty-one years ago James Cagney, playing in his first film, invented a new kind of screen character. In more than fifty subsequent appearances he has polished and complicated it, but the type has remained substantially unchanged; and it may now be time to investigate its extraordinary influence. Morally and psychologically, it could be maintained that the Cagney code and manners have come to dominate a whole tradition of American melodrama.

Before Cagney boffed Mae Clark with a grapefruit in *Public Enemy*, Hollywood had adhered to what was, by general consent, a reasonably stringent set of moral principles. The film is no exception to the other popular narrative arts: in its infancy it clings to a broad and exaggerated ethical system, based on pure blacks and whites. In the theatre this period is represented by the morality play, and was superseded by Marlowe, whose heroes were noble and wicked, fraudulent and pious, cruel and idealistic, at the same time. In the novel the period of over-simplification ended with the Romantics; and in the film it ended with Cagney.

This is not to say that the American movie before 1930 was never immoral: the very urgency of the need for a Hays Office demonstrates the contrary. But its immorality, however blatant, was always incidental and subordinate: a sheikh might flay his wives with scorpions to enliven the curious, but he would be sure to be trampled on, baked, or impaled in the last reel. He was always transparently evil, and the flayee transparently innocent. In the early Westerns there is no doubt who is the villain; he is the man leaning against the bar in black frock-coat, ribbon bow-tie and pencilled moustache. He is a killer, charmless and unfunny, and suffers dreadfully by comparison with the bronzed hero on the white horse; his part, too, is much shorter than the star's. In the twenties there was not only a rigid distinction between the good characters and bad; they were also evenly balanced in numbers and fame. Vice and virtue proclaimed themselves irrevocably within the first hundred feet, or the director was failing at his job.

Cagney changed all this. In *Public Enemy* he presented, for the first time, a hero who was callous and evil, while being simultaneously equipped with charm, courage and a sense of fun. Even more significantly, he was co-starred not with the grave young district attorney who would finally ensnare him, but with a bright, callow moll for him to slap. The result was that in one stroke Cagney abolished both the convention of the pure hero and that of approximate equipoise between vice and virtue. The full impact of this minor revolution was manifested in the 1942-47 period, when Ladd, Widmark, Duryea and Bogart were able to cash in on Cagney's strenuous pioneering. It now becomes fascinating to trace the stages of development by which the Cagney villain (lover, brute, humorist and killer) was translated into the Bogart hero (lover, brute, humorist, but non-killer). It is an involved story.

Probably it begins with the physical attributes of Cagney himself. One finds it hard to take such a small man seriously: how, after all, can a playful redhead of five feet eight inches really be a baron of vice? It is safe to say that if Cagney had been four inches taller, his popularity would be fathoms less than it is. Villains before him had tended to be huge; they loomed and slobbered, bellowed and shambled; you could see them coming. Cagney was and is spruce, dapper and grinning: when he hits a friend over the ear with a revolver-butt, he does it as casually as he will presently press the elevator button on his way out. By retaining his brisk little smile throughout he makes one react warmly, with a grin, not coldly and aghast. Nobody in 1930, the year after Chicago's St. Valentine's Day massacre, at which Capone's lieutenants slaughtered nine men in a disused garage, would have tolerated any romanticisation of the gangster legend. When Muni played *Scarface* for Howard Hawks two years later, he presented the mob leader as an unhealthy, ungainly lout, a conception clearly in key with contemporary taste. Cagney unconsciously paved the way for the advent of the smooth, romantic gangster of the late thirties; he softened public opinion by sneaking up on it through a forgotten and unguarded loophole. He was never a romantic figure himself — at his height you can't be — nor was he sentimental —Cheshire cats never are — but he possessed, possibly in greater abundance than any other name star of the time, irresistible charm. It was a cocky, picaresque charm, the charm of pert urchins, the *gaminerie* of unlicked juvenile delinquents. Cagney, even with sub-machine gun hot in hand and corpses piling at his ankles, can still persuade many people that it was not his fault. By such means he made gang law acceptable to the screen, and became by accident one of the most genuinely corrupting influences Hollywood has ever sent us. Cagney brought organised crime within the mental horizon of errand-boys, who saw him as a cavalier of the gutters — their stocky patron saint.

But before the actor comes the script. What literary circumstances were conspiring to produce a climate in which the brutal hero could flourish? It would be superficial to neglect Hemingway, who was beginning to project on to the American mind his own ideal of manhood — a noble savage, idly smoking, silhouetted against a background of dead illusions. Surveyed impartially, the Hemingway hero numbers among his principal characteristics that of extreme dumbness: he is the sincere fool who walks phlegmatically off the end of the pier. He is honourable, charmless, tough and laconic; and he is always, in some sense, a pirate or an adventurer. What Cagney did was to extract the moral core from Hemingway's creation and put smartness in its place. The result was a character charmingly dishonourable, but saved from suavity or smugness by his brute energy and swift, impetuous speech. Perhaps the simplest point of departure is that, whereas the Hemingway man never hits a woman for fun, Cagney made a secure living out of doing just that.

The success of Cagney's methods made all sorts of variations possible, chief among them the *genre* popularised in the novels and films of Raymond Chandler. Here the central character is tough, cynically courageous, and predisposed towards brutality; he is in fact identical with the Cagney version in all save one vital respect — he is on the side of the law. The process is thus completed: the problem of how to retain the glamour of the killer without the moral obloquy of murder has been solved. Let your hero be a private eye, and he can slaughter just as insensitively in the name of self-defence.

Cagney himself has rarely compromised; at the height of his career he never lined up with the police or made any concessions to public morals beyond the token one of allowing himself to be killed at the end, as an indispensable but tiresome rubric. At his best (*Public Enemy*, *The Mayor of Hell*, *The G-Men*, *White Heat*) he flouts every standard of social behaviour with a disarming Irish pungency that makes murder look like an athletic exercise of high spirits and not a mean and easy transgression. He sweetened killing; and to have done this immediately after the Capone regime, during the era of the concentration camp and between two lacerating wars, is something of an achievement.

He was born in New York in 1904 and educated at Stuyvesant High School and Columbia University; his background was East Side, but not the slum and tenement area. He began his stage career, mysteriously, as a female impersonator in 1923, and thereafter for six years danced and understudied in vaudeville. He was mostly penniless. In 1929 William Keighley, then a Broadway director, saw Cagney and Joan Blondell in a romp called *Maggie the Magnificent* and starred them in *Penny Arcade*; the play was bought by First National and all three went to Hollywood with it. Retitled *Sinners' Holiday*, it was released in 1930. Cagney made eight pictures with Joan Blondell in less than four years, and she proved a perfect punch-bag for his clenched, explosive talent; the best of the series, *Steel Highway*, started a revealing vogue for stories about men who work in dangerous proximity to death-dealing machines. These films invariably centred on a character who was happy only when close to sudden extinction, who enjoyed tight-roping along telegraph wires or lighting cigarettes around kegs of dynamite. For such parts Cagney was a natural, and Wellman, who directed *Steel Highway*, quickly exploited the new star's edgy gameness by putting him into *Public Enemy*, with Blondell and Mae Clark. When the film appeared in 1931, the age of the screen gangster had officially begun. Howard Hawks followed in 1932 with *Scarface*, which, though it had the advantage of one of Ben Hecht's best scripts, lacked Cagney's spearhead precision to hold it together. For ten years afterwards he led the gangster film to extraordinary box-office eminence, and four times appeared in the annual list of the ten top money-making stars. In 1932 Hawks made *The Crowd Roars* with Cagney and Blondell; in 1933 came *The Mayor of Hell*; in 1934 Michael Curtiz' *Jimmy the Gent*; in 1935 Keighley's expert and sombre *The G-Men*; and finally, feeling that things were becoming too easy for him, Warners teamed Cagney with Bogart in *Angels With Dirty Faces* (1938) and *The Roaring Twenties* (1939). At this point he had made thirty-two films in nine years; the association with Blondell had dissolved, and his most frequent sparring partner was Pat O'Brien.

Cagney was now maturely at his best. Even the most ascetic *cinéaste* will admit that it is impossible to forget how he looked and talked at the height of his popularity. The spring-heeled walk, poised forward on the toes; the fists clenched, the arms loosely swinging; the keen, roving eyes; the upper lip curling back in defiance and derision; the rich, high-pitched, hectoring voice; the stubby, stabbing index finger; the smug purr with which he accepts female attention — Cagney's women always had to duck under his guard before he would permit them to make love to him. He was practically unkillable; it would generally take a dozen Thompson guns and a bomb or two to bring him to his knees; and he would always die running at, not away from, his pursuers, in a spluttering, staggering zig-zag, ending with a solid and satisfying thump. He moved more gracefully than any other actor in Hollywood. And he had a beguiling capacity for reassuring while he murdered: he would wrinkle up his face into a chubby mask of sympathy and then let you have it in the stomach. His relaxation, even when springing, was absolute; he released his compact energy quite without effort. When circumstances forced him to shout, his face would register how distasteful he found it.

Cagney's first rival in the game of romantic murder appeared in 1936. Humphrey Bogart, five years Cagney's senior, had made half a dozen mediocre pictures since 1932, and had returned to the stage to play the escaping gangster, Duke Mantee, in *The Petrified Forest*. In 1936 the play was filmed and Bogart was established. It was a new style; speculative, sardonic, sourly lisping, he stood out in direct contrast to Cagney, who was agile, clean-cut, and totally unreflective. Bogart frequently appeared unshaven; Cagney, never; but the challenge was clear, for both men specialised in whimsical law-breaking and both commanded alarming sex-appeal. Cagney, who had captured several million infant hearts with pictures like *Here Comes the Navy*, *Devil Dogs of the Air*, and Howard

Hawks' *Ceiling Zero*, had access to an audience to which Bogart never appealed; but Bogart split Cagney's female admirers, and was usually featured with bigger stars and better directors than Warners could offer Cagney. *Bullets or Ballots* (1936) followed *The Petrified Forest*; in 1937, after a brief and unsuccessful venture into legality as the DA in *Marked Woman*, Bogart made *San Quentin* and *Kid Galahad*; and he breasted the year with his superbly metallic playing of Baby-Face Morgan in Wyler's *Dead End*. He had added to the gangster film something which Cagney always avoided: the dimension of squalor. In Cagney's looting there had been an atmosphere, almost, of knight-errantry; Bogart, tired, creased and gnarled, effectively debunked it. The two films they made together for Warners made an absorbing conflict of styles — with Cagney throwing his hard, twisting punches and Bogart lazily ducking them. Cagney's was the more accomplished exhibition of ringcraft, but Bogart's sewage snarl won him the decision. At times both men found themselves using the same tricks; each had perfected his own version of the fanged killer's smile, and a good deal of *The Roaring Twenties* developed into a sort of grinning contest.

The experience must have proved something to both Cagney and Warners, because he made no more gangster films for ten years. By then the war had begun, the mob was very small beer, and the echo of machine-guns across deserted lots had lost its fascination for movie audiences. Bogart graduated to the side of justice, and the second important change in the history of filmed mayhem had taken place. In 1941 he played Sam Spade for Huston in *The Maltese Falcon* — still the same wry brute, but more insidiously immoral, since now there was a righteous justification for his savagery. He repeated this performance in *Across the Pacific*, and when *The Big Sleep* appeared in 1945 it looked as if the pure gangster film was dead. In 1942, Paramount produced their answer to Bogart in *This Gun for Hire* — the soft and silky thuggishness of Alan Ladd; and Dick Powell entered what was by now a very competitive market with *Farewell My Lovely* (1944) and *Cornered* (1945). Screen melodrama in this period was filled with ageing bandits, battering their way to glory under police protection. Meanwhile Cagney had not been idle, though films like *The Strawberry Blonde*, *Captains of the Clouds*, and *The Bride Came C.O.D.* (in which he daintily plucked cactus needles from Bette Davis' behind) were not materially helping his reputation. In 1942, Curtiz made *Yankee Doodle Dandy*, a masterpiece of heartfelt hokum, and Cagney won an Academy Award with his sturdy, chirpy pirouetting; but the shamelessness of his early days seemed to have vanished. The woman-slapping outlaws of the forties were performed by feature players, not by stars, and they were mostly in the hands of Dan Duryea, the impact of whose rancid and lascivious unpleasantness in *The Little Foxes* had been confirmed by his straw-hatted blackmailer in Lang's *Woman in the Window* (1944) and his raucous pimp in *Scarlet Street* (1945). The courage of nastiness had gone.

In 1942 Cagney formed his own production unit with his brother William, and in seven years made only four films — *Johnny Vagabond*, a philosophical failure; *Blood on the Sun*, a commonplace espionage thriller; *13 Rue Madeleine*, a documentary-style spy story; and *The Time of Your Life* — a shrug of a film, charmingly aimless and inexpensive, in which Cagney, as a talkative drinker, gave his best performance since *Yankee Doodle Dandy*. The critics were suggesting that Cagney had agreed to accept middle age and abandoned the orgiastic killing of his youth. Then, in 1950, he suddenly returned to Warners and, with Raoul Walsh, made *White Heat*.

The style in that amazing film was the man himself: Cagney had never been more characteristic — flamboyant, serio-comic, and tricky as a menagerie. It is not easy to decide why he came back to straight gangster vehicles, though I have the impression that Twentieth Century had much to do with it; they had begun, in 1947, an ambitious campaign to sell Richard Widmark to the public. His weedy, snickering murderer in *Kiss of Death* gave an unexpected lease of life to the gangster film. Playing within the semi-documentary convention, he could not be permitted to dominate his films as Cagney had in the lawless thirties, but he had the same gimlet appeal and was tapping the same love of clever violence. By 1949, his popularity was such that it must have persuaded Warners to disturb the retirement of their senior hoodlum.

Walsh and Cagney reverted in *White Heat* to the frankly artificial framework of *Public Enemy*: there were a few location sequences, but the main burden fell on the star's personality. The scenario made a genuflection to contemporary demand by giving its hero a mother-complex, and Cagney staggered even his devotees by acting it up to the hilt with a blind conviction which was often terrifying: he never let up. The film dealt with the breakdown of a killer's mind and his slow, unwitting, unadmitting approach to the long tunnel of insanity. Cagney never indulged in self-pity for a moment: if the script called for a fit, he would throw one, outrageous and full-blooded; and by a miracle his integrity never gave out. The result was a lesson in neurosis which ranks, in recent memory, only with Richard Basehart's in *Fourteen Hours*. One cannot unlearn the sequence in which Cagney, attempting to ward off a mutiny in the mob, succumbs to one of his recurring blackouts and drags himself to the cover of a bedroom, moaning in deep thick sighs like a wounded animal. And, above all, the scene in the prison refectory. Word is passed down the table to Cagney that his mother has been killed: he stops eating, grins spasmodically, murmuring to himself, and then goes berserk, letting out strange, bestial cries and punching, punching at everyone with a compulsive defiance as he scampers the length of the hall. No other actor in Hollywood could have got away with that.

The older, crisper Cagney was there too; even he has never outdone, for sheer casualness, the murder of the stool-pigeon, whom he has locked up in the luggage-trap of his car. 'Kinda stuffy in here,' the prisoner complains. 'Like some air?' says Cagney, cocking a wicked eyebrow; and, stopping only to pop a hot dog in his mouth, fires six shots into him through the body of the car. The climax was nerve-wracking: cornered, he takes refuge in an explosives plant and is chased to the top of a huge circular vat of, presumably, TNT. Yelling: 'On top of the world, Ma, on top of the world!' he sends his last bullet into it, and is blown sky-high. It was audacious and incredible in retrospect, but such was the intensity of Cagney's playing that one refused to laugh. It is seldom easy to deride perfect stylists, even if one disapproves of the ends to which the style is being put. There could be no question, in this sequence, that a very remarkable actor had hit his full stride and was carrying his audience with him.

I do not mean, by all this, to suggest that the crime film deserves over-serious analysis: it has always been openly unreal in structure, depending for its excitement on jazzed dialogue and overstated photography. But its influence on scripting and camera-work has been incalculable, involving many of the most expert and adult intelligences in Hollywood — Hecht, Hawks, Wyler, Toland, Huston, Wellman, Lang, Chandler, and Hellinger among them — and it has provided an incomparable outlet for at least one unique acting talent. If it has had a pernicious social influence, that is probably Cagney's fault, and there is no space here to balance the old scales between art and morality. For myself, I do not mind walking the Edgware Road in peril as long as there is a Cagney picture at Marble Arch. A great deal of desperate urgency and attack would have been lost to the cinema if the gang film had not arrived, making fantastic technical demands on cameraman and electrician and recording engineer, with Cagney, safe and exulting, at the wheel of a bullet-riddled Cadillac.

Sight and Sound: May 1951; *Curtains*, 1961

CHARLES LAUGHTON

A few weeks ago Charles Laughton returned to England: a prodigal son
bearing a strong resemblance to the fatted calf. Laughton, a fifty-two-year-
old son of Scarborough, has not appeared in this country since 1936, when
he played Captain Hook in *Peter Pan* at the Palladium. Now, in company
with Agnes Moorehead, Cedric Hardwicke and Charles Boyer, he is touring
the provinces in Shaw's *Don Juan in Hell*, playing the Devil — a study in
sly villainy which differs from Hook only in being mellower and more
disillusioned.

Laughton has spent the prime of his exile in Hollywood. There exists a
photograph of his arrival there: on the footboard of the train behind him are
written the words: 'Watch Your Step'. During what promised to be the
most productive decade of his career he stayed, watchfully, on the same
step; meeting him today, one is amazed that he still feels any
responsibilities at all towards the theatre.

He was rushed to fame in one sudden startled jump — in 1926 a student,
in 1928 playing leads in the West End. He had a gift — rare, in young
actors — for seeming to be forty on stage: youth and old age, the juvenile's
usual province, were both beyond him. At the age of twenty-eight, he was
using this gift in a play called *The Happy Family*, when the New York
producer Gilbert Miller cabled to London: GET IN TOUCH WITH MIDDLE-AGED
AMERICAN ACTOR NOW APPEARING IN PRODUCTION OF HAPPY FAMILY.
Ironically, Miller was a prophet: now successfully naturalised, Laughton
has become a middle-aged American actor.

From his early thirties movies have captivated him. He was constantly
being spurred to make the stage his home; but of the parts most frequently
suggested to him — Doctor Johnson, Cagliostro, Falstaff, Columbus,
Pepys, and the Devil — he has played only the last. His film triumphs —
Henry VIII, Ruggles of Red Gap, Mutiny on the Bounty and *The Barretts of
Wimpole Street* — were all finished before his fortieth year; and in the last
decade his reputation has suffered a slow sag.

I asked him yesterday why he chose Hollywood. From the depths of his
face he said: 'I'm far less scared of the camera and American audiences than I am of English ones. They terrify me.' He sat slumped in his
hotel room; the collar of his blue shirt protruded unmanageably over his
sports-jacket. The chasm between his jowls is bridged by slack, surly lips,
on which words sit lovingly. His voice, which has no trace of American

accent, flabbily nudges your ear; it has acquired a pedagogic note, the dry authority of a teacher.

'Have you ever had any interests outside acting?' I said. 'Acting,' he murmured, and smiled. His smile is that of a small boy jovially peeping at life in a nudist colony. In repose his face is a blank: it belongs to a mooncalf, perhaps to the moon itself. You might cast him, on its evidence, as Cloten in *Cymbeline*, or, more appropriately, as that tireless organiser of amateur theatricals, Bottom, in *A Midsummer Night's Dream*; or even as Caliban in *The Tempest*, for, with his large watery eyes, he sometimes has the look of an undersea monster aground on a fishmonger's slab. In one of his first films, *The Devil and the Deep*, he played a submarine commander; and he still reminds me of an angel-fish, if that is the one that inflates when it scents trouble.

A waiter brought his breakfast. 'Thank you,' he said, with the air of a man quietly closing a distasteful subject. We talked about Hollywood; except for the late Irving Thalberg and the early Alexander Korda, he loathes all film producers ('They are thugs') with the intensity of a chubbier Sheridan Whiteside.

He has abandoned his pipe-dream of working with a permanent repertory company of film actors; recently he has taken to solo dramatic recitals. In a two-and-a-half hour programme he reads excerpts from the Bible, Dickens, Thomas Woolf and James Thurber, and the success of these monologues has inspired the idea that he should read the whole of *King Lear* with the movie cameras turning. He will probably never appear again on the commercial West End stage; but he has a recurrent hankering to play a season at the Old Vic, as he did in 1933-34, especially since his old producer, Tyrone Guthrie, is back. 'I'm too old for long runs,' he said. 'I only want limited engagements.'

He has been told that Alec Guinness is the only contemporary classical actor whose approach is thoroughly modern: 'They tell me he does the one vital thing — he brings old plays in touch with what's happening right outside the theatre. You've got to bring *today* into Shakespeare. That's what Olivier never does; he's the apotheosis of the nineteenth-century romantic actor.' Richly sour his voice continued. I reflected how much the London theatre had missed its odd affectations and its special seedy kind of pomp. Though it strikes drily on the ear, he salivates prodigiously to produce it. You get the impression that butter is for ever melting in his mouth.

Laughton today looks the reverse of tired and disenchanted; Captain Hook has returned in the character of Peter Pan. The man of fifty looks like a mere boy of forty, a lordly urchin playing a hard game of marbles with his own talents. He is as ageless as Humpty-Dumpty. The secret of his freshness possibly lies in his boredom with anything that has ever been done before. As actor, he goes to fantastic lengths to avoid the obvious:

called upon to express simple love or hatred, he will offer instead lechery or disgust. His style is circuitous, and rarely steps on to the direct highroad to an audience's heart. In this he is like the man in Chesterton's poem, who would travel to John O'Groats by way of Beachy Head. Laughton arrives at his characterisations panting, having picked up a hundred assorted odd-ments on the way; and the result is always a fascinating and unique mosaic.

Soon he rose to leave, donning a hat whose brim turned up back and front, and moved fastidiously to the door. He walks top-heavily, like a salmon standing on its tail. Laughton invests his simplest exit with an atmosphere of furtive flamboyance; he left the hotel for all the world like an absconding banker. He took leave of me in the manner of a butler begging an afternoon off. As a friend of his once commented: 'Considering he's a great man, Charles makes his voice do an awful lot of bowing and scraping.'

Evening Standard: 2nd July 1951

NOËL COWARD

Benign, yet flustered, as a cardinal might be at some particularly dismaying tribal rite; exuberant, replete to the brim with a burning, bright *nostalgie de la boo-hoo;* taut, facially, as an appalled monolith; gracious, socially, as a royal bastard; tart, vocally, as a hollowed lemon — so Noël Coward appeared for us at the Café de Paris, in a limited season of cabaret. Its limits were his limits, for he sang none but his own songs, in none but his own key (it was not always the pianist's) and in none but his own period manner. In large, cosmic terms, of course, his vision and scope are no better than a squint, his references to time and tide and the gay enchantment of an evening would hardly fill out a medieval *envoi,* and as he puts our epoch through his hoop, we cannot but feel painfully straitened, like the camel in the needle's eye. He is, if I may test the trope, the monocle of all he surveys. His graces are hard won, his ease careworn; his aplomb is gnarled, made smooth by the sandpapering of a hundred corners. He was born, fifty-one years ago, with simply a voice and a magnetism; born, you might say, to the purr and the pull rather than to the purple; and his soul is, for him, very much an acquired taste.

We had last seen him a few days after Elsa Lanchester, coaxed like a performing poodle, had opened her sad little stay at the same *boîte:* shy and nauseating, she had slowly gambolled through a routine of *double entendres* which, as a friend said, 'simultaneously brought a blush to my cheek and a yawn to my jaw.' The question, how he had enjoyed her performance, must needs be put to Coward. With a take-it-or-leave-it stare, at once challenging, flippant and stark, he had hissed: 'Sauce! Sheer sauce!' Now it was his turn, and, after careful and minute rehearsal, he thudded briskly down to the dance-floor and, with not a hair out of place, rose toweringly above it.

A part of Coward's uniqueness is that, unlike nearly all our contemporary giants, he was not born out of his time. One of the most frequent excuses for Orson Welles is that, after all, he never met Lorenzo de'Medici, and that he was launched into a world of shallows. Coward's triumph is to have been born into his own era; he belongs to it as ineradicably as the five-piece jazz band and the electric razor, and he has met everybody he needs to meet. This was the era in which matinée idols were just ceasing to take themselves pompously; in which society, bereft of its glamorous Princes Regent, was open to the witty provincial; in which the intelligentsia, having outgrown the scandal of being cynical, were ready to enjoy the sheer fun of it. Where previous wits were stealthy and crept, Coward is bluff and romps: his sense of humour is as ebullient as a paying oil-well. A certain fastidiousness of tone and gesture is Coward's only legacy from the earlier kind of witty man — the Wilde or the Labouchère; and he has transmuted even that. Coward's fastidiousness, outrageously enough, is that of a first-rate male impersonator.

He habitually refers to himself — especially when there is talk of his performance in the film of *The Astonished Heart* — as 'that splendid old Chinese character actress.' It is true that his hunched, obsequious shoulders, prowling gait, and totemesque face suggested Charlie Chan turned major-domo: his playing had some remarkable backstairs overtones. Nowadays, running its intense but oddly undifferentiated gamut from repose to agony, his face has more creases, and brings to mind what Robert Benchley once labelled the 'look of a dead albatross'; but one would still not start at its apparition at the helm of a dhow navigating the sandbars of the lower Yangtze-Kiang.

Theatrically speaking, it was Coward who took sophistication out of the refrigerator and put it on the hob. If we are not to malign him, it is important to have this understood, for it has often been imputed to him that he made comedy acting a fatigued and enervated thing; that he taught English actors the trick of boredom. Here he is the victim of his imitators, for his own style contradicts them. His 'too, too's emerge with the staccato blind enthusiasm of a machine-gun. So far from being arid, he overflows. His stage expression of boredom is vivacious; he is mask-like and supercilious, but raffishly, eagerly so. He never less than glows; there are no ashes in his work.

Tight lines of pain and worry stretch across his forehead, and others again appear to suspend, like a chinstrap, his leathery, jutting, jolly jaw. His skin is drawn like a drum, too tough for sweat. Before the cabaret microphone he balances on black-suede-clad feet, leaning forwards, hands upraised in a gesture which one associates with Irene Vanbrugh saying: 'Ah, Emma, so it is you at last!' These hands, which appear, long before he starts singing, to be already affectionately calming your too-kind enthusiasm, are a vital part of the delicious act. The head tilts back, the eyes narrow confidingly; they will flash white only when an 'r' is to be rolled, as in words like 'Frrrrantic' or 'Digby-Frrrrrobisher.' Baffled and amused by his own frolicsomeness, he sways as he sings from side to side, occasionally wagging a finger if our attention wanders. I do not know whether or not he has false teeth, but if pressed, I would plump for the affirmative.

What he sings is all old. Songs like the bravely indulgent 'London Pride,' with its dependence on bombs and blackouts, he sings as if they were still significant and apposite. 'Don't put your daughter on the stage,

Mrs. Worthington' is put over with a venom redoubled by the years —
'That sufficed, Mrs. Worthington; *Christ*, Mrs. Worthington! . . .'
Listening, it struck me that he had done what no other actor or playwright
of our time had done: invented, not only a new acting style, but a new life.
Not merely a new character, the result of grease and skill, but the instant
projection of a new kind of human being, which had never before existed in
print or paint. Naturally, it is useless outside his own writings — since his
success, he has never (another mark of uniqueness) sung or spoken on a
stage anything that he had not written — but it is intensely personal, and
rare. At his worst, Coward is idiosyncratically bad.

Baring his teeth as if unveiling a grotesque memorial, and cooing like a
baritone dove, he displays his two weapons — wit and sentimentality. He
can move from one to another without a change of costume, or of position. I
have heard it objected to Coward that what he peddles is not sophistication
at all, but a facile poor relation, lacking the tact and grace and wisdom of
the real thing. Such complaints miss the point. He has added a new
subdivision to the dictionary meaning of the word; we have pigeon-holed
him there because nothing else would cover him; and everything he does,
by definition, extends its field of application. He would not, I think, claim
to be much more than a troubadour askew, a contemporary minstrel with
bloodshot eye and a touch of liver: he has never hoped for anything in the
artistic hierarchy more distinguished than mere uniqueness. Inside him, a
poet and a philosopher are shrieking to be kept in. On the few occasions
when they have escaped (parts of *In Which We Serve*, parts of *This Happy
Breed*), they have died horribly within minutes.

His house in Kensington is like a smart tavern in a market-town: hidden
in a mews, with doors of glass and wrought-iron, and new-smelling
panelling on the walls. A chic but quiet rendezvous, with a good cellar, you
might judge, until you enter the studio — a high, airy room which might
belong to a landscape painter with a rich Italian mistress. There are
paintings everywhere except on the floor, which is board as often as it is
carpet; over the door, an excellent oil of the owner by Clemence Dane;
deep, snug and unshowy armchairs; and two grand pianos on rostrums in
opposite corners. I had, on my first visit, hoped to interview him, but he
bustled in and boomed questions at me — what was I doing, and for whom,
and for how much, and had I met *that* bloody man and his bloody awful
daughter, and how could I bear them. And my writing sounded genuine,
and affectionate, which was so important in a critic; and (for he doses his
sentences with pauses as you dose epileptics with drugs): 'You must
understand' (blank, compelling glare) 'Daphne began with nothing — but
nothing!' (another glare) 'and it's amazing' (another glare) 'that she can
speak!' Everything is final, and indisputable, and followed by a gauntlet-
hurling, cards-on-the-table, popeyed stare; a sort of facial shrug. Coward's
loyalties are rapidly formed and permanent; most of his failures in recent

years are directly attributable to elephantiasis in this virtue. Yet he is warming; a superb thawer.

We discussed, I remember, star quality, which is his grail. 'I don't know what it is, but I know I've got it.' He asked me which moment in his last West End play, *Present Laughter*, I had thought most star-quality-studded. I decided, though it was neither the funniest nor the most original, on the moment when he (playing Garry Essendine, the egotistical actor) reviled his friends for their ingratitude, and then threw himself headlong on to the floor, pounding it with fists and feet and sobbing. Only he, I implied, could have carried that off. For a minute he looked interestedly aghast, and then burst out. 'My God, Mr. T.', he said urgently, 'but how astounding! All that was improvised. We'd been on tour for a long, long time before coming in to town, and I'd never been happy about that last act. It needed a firework. One evening we were playing in Cardiff to an audience of deaf mutes, and I knew they weren't caring. So I flung myself into the dike. I marched down to the footlights and screamed: "I gave you my youth! Where is it now? Whistling down the wind! *Ou sont les neiges d'antan? Ici!* (jabbing at his temples) *Ici!* . . ." And I went madly on in French and Italian, and finally hurled myself in a stretcher-case at their feet, rather putting out everyone else on stage. When the curtain came down I dived into the wings and asked the stage manager if he'd got any of it, and he said not a bloody word, so I dashed upstairs and typed away like bloody hell!'

To most casual students, Coward's reputation is based on wit, convention-flouting, and an honestly vulgar command of middle-class idiom (which began a vogue of 'common small-talk', still among us in the shape of Mayfair Cockneyisms); and you will find others who further revere his melodic sense, with its bat's-wing lightness of touch. But above all these, he has energy, and as long as that lasts, the reputation is unlikely to dim. Even the youngest of us will know, in fifty years' time, precisely what is meant by 'a very Noël Coward sort of person.'

Panorama: Spring 1952

ALEC GUINNESS

Until quite recently Alec Guinness was one of the most unrecognised of actors; and he remains, even now, one of the most unrecognisable. Few people stop him in the street to shake his hand. Facially, he is akin to what John Locke imagined the mind of a newborn child to be — an unmarked blank, on which circumstances leave their casual trace. Guinness looks bland and unmemorable, and will never be the average man's idea of an actor. Mr. Partridge, in Fielding's *Tom Jones*, went to see Garrick as Hamlet and liked the King best, because 'He speaks all his words distinctly — Any Body may see he is an Actor.' And G. H. Lewes, a century later, was tacitly echoing him when he said, 'The naturalness required from Hamlet is very different from the naturalness of a Partridge' — meaning that the simulation of Hamlet, or of any grandly rhetorical personage, had little to do with the simulation of life. The point is that neither Lewes nor Partridge, neither the nineteenth century nor the eighteenth, would have understood Alec Guinness. For better or worse, he is tethered to his own epoch: he embodies, as no one else does, the modern-dress style of acting, which works quietly within itself for its own strictly contemporary purposes. Guinness is a master of anonymity; one thinks of him as an industriously receptive cipher, a judicious and unbroken code — the inventor of an obsequious magic which obtains its results — such is the modern way — by spells. He has banished from his artistic vocabulary what Hazlitt would called called 'the striking effect.'

He lives in West London, in St. Peter's Square, near Hammersmith; a nobly stagnant recess, untouched since the Regency, when it was built to house the survivors of Waterloo. His wife and son are there, and a parrot, Percy, who can recite (with grisly retchings) the greater part of 'O, what a rogue and peasant slave am I!' Guinness' climb to this social peace has been tricky. He was born thirty-seven years ago in Maida Vale, a rusty London suburb, and left school early for eighteen months' unwilling employment in an advertising firm. Here his incompetence was staggering in its scope and variety, and, at sixteen, he was happily translated to the Fay Compton School of Dramatic Art. At the Public Show he performed a bold snippet of Mercutio, sang 'Waiting at the Gate for Katie,' and dominated a mime play by Compton Mackenzie about the proprietor of a Punch-and-Judy show who beat his wife to death. The judges, among whom was John Gielgud, awarded him first prize — a leather-bound Shakespeare — and sent him out into the world, where he almost starved. He was nineteen, and owned two shillings and sixpence.

For a while his quondam fellow-students kept him, barely subsisting, in a grubby Bayswater attic. Each week he set aside a luxury sixpence, to be spent on a gallery seat at the Old Vic. Repeatedly and fruitlessly he bearded Gielgud, his benefactor, but had to wait until his twentieth birthday — April 2, 1934 — for his first speaking part. This was in *Queer Cargo* at the Piccadilly Theatre, in which he played, with prophetic versatility, a Chinese coolie in Act I, a French pirate in Act II and a British *matelot* in Act III. In November of the same year Gielgud beckoned him to the New Theatre, where he doubled Osric and the Third Player in *Hamlet* for seven pounds a week.

He found Gielgud a great ringmaster and trainer, but a cowing influence: here, in full cry, was the final representative in England of the romantic tradition, with all its anguished disciplines. Gielgud may have made Guinness self-conscious; he stiffened many a young actor with his exactions and rebukes; but with him Guinness stayed, spongelike under Niagara, until the summer of 1936. Then began a long period of shuttling, which lasted until the outbreak of war, between Gielgud, the actor's actor, and Tyrone Guthrie, the producer's producer, who was then in command at the Old Vic.

He soon discovered that Guthrie's approach was the precise antithesis of Gielgud's: it offered him elbow-room and freedom, relaxation and abandon, but also, and more perilously, opportunities for inspired carelessness. The next season whisked him back to Gielgud; the next, back to Guthrie; and it was then, in 1938, that he became critically considerable, playing a modern-dress Hamlet which bestowed on his name an aura of civilised controversy which it has never wholly lost. That winter he saw the signposts — Gielgud pointing one way, Guthrie another, and the captious, cud-chewing finesse of Michel Saint-Denis a third. He took stock, and, offending nobody, eluded their shadows to carve out a separate route for himself.

Where that route was taking him first began to be clear in December, 1939, when he played Herbert Pocket in his own stage adaptation of *Great Expectations*. In 1940 he toured the country in the peculiarly apt role of the lighthouse-keeper in *Thunder Rock*; apt, because all his subsequent successes have been in characters cut off, benighted, rejected, or sequestered. Michael Redgrave had created the part in London, another actor who is beloved of solitariness and prefers islands on stage to peninsulas. Both of them have since had to adjust their natural isolation to the spectator's insatiable demand for intimacy. Guinness' answer was to hood himself yet more raptly: he became a kind of sympathetic enigma.

He was called up for the Navy in 1941 and, having gained a commission within a year, spent most of the war ferrying hay and butter to the Yugoslavs. Accidentally, he was the first man ashore in the invasion of

Sicily. The time of the landing had, unknown to him, been postponed, and he arrived on the beach an hour early, at the helm of a lonely landing craft. Later, with understandable petulance, he confronted the admiral with the curt but ill-advised assertion that such tardiness would never be tolerated in the West End theatre.

Since 1945 his career has been public property. He reappeared on the London stage as Mitya in his own version of *The Brothers Karamazov* — a nail-biting, scorn-darting, recluse performance — and thereafter passed two razor-edged seasons at the Old Vic. From these there is much to be remembered: his Abel Drugger in *The Alchemist*, hopeful and helplessly ruddy, his stricken fool to Olivier's King Lear, his Dauphin in *Saint Joan*, and a Richard II fashioned out of trembling ice. Between whiles he removed his *toupée* and summed up for us the shame of France in his Garcin, the disgraced cynic of Sartre's *No Exit*.

There followed a series, almost a glut, of films: he played Herbert Pocket in David Lean's *Great Expectations*, made a harrowing but not unlikeable sketch of Fagin in *Oliver Twist*, and then crowned all with his great trio of Ealing comedies: *Kind Hearts and Coronets*, *The Lavender Hill Mob* (a role which, relishing such words, he describes as 'fubsy') and *The Man in the White Suit* (to be released in the United States this month). He would cheerfully, I know, have exchanged all three for success in his Festival production of *Hamlet*, but this is a wound over which new tissue is steadily forming, and some day he will attempt the part again. For the moment he must be content with one critic's description of him as 'the waxen, poker-faced Chaplin of British movies,' and reflect that nobody has ever demonstrated so fully how bizarre and unpredictable little men can be.

His last film, as yet unreleased, is *The Card*, adapted from Arnold Bennett's novel. He chose it partly in an effort to conquer the hitherto unresponsive provincial audience; partly because the central character is an extrovert opportunist — a new departure for him; and partly because in it, for the first time since he appeared in *Cousin Muriel* with Peggy Ashcroft twelve years ago, he gets the girl. Guinness' absorbed, ingrowing style does not merge readily into love-making, and this, the touchstone of a popular favourite, he has always been careful to skirt.

He wants more than anything, to play opposite Edwige Feuillère or Tallulah Bankhead; at present, for want of a congenial human subject, he is making do with the leading role of an ant in Sam Spewack's insect comedy, *Under the Sycamore Tree*, which will be seen in London later this spring. To Guinness the choice of play has always been an exasperating obstacle: like all versatile actors, he constantly finds that nothing seems to have been written especially for him. Perhaps, in tragedy, he might hit his full stride as one of Chapman's stony Jacobean heroes, who say to their priest at shriving-time, 'Leave my soul to me, whom it concerns . . .'; or, in comedy, he might turn to the self-intoxicated Boswell of the *Journal*. His private ambition, curiously, is to play national leaders: Nelson, for one, and Gordon, Wolfe, and Captain Cook — above all the last-named, whom he regards as the greatest Englishman, Shakespeare apart, that ever lived. It may be that he is temperamentally incapable of conveying the rough core of such prosperous pioneers as these; for Guinness' strength is his softness, his pliability, the tactful grace with which he pours himself into awkward moulds.

Offstage he is a slight man, balding and rakishly modest, with an impulsive snicker, deprecating shoulders and a twitch of a smile like a crescent moon; the eyes are guileless, but they are also sly, and his manner communicates intimacy as if from a great distance. He might be mistaken for a slightly tipsy monk, and is certainly very far from the austere intellectual which some of his admirers envisage. He can be the most impetuous of actors, and the least premeditated: at one performance of *Hamlet*, stung by the unwonted peremptoriness with which a colleague delivered the line, 'My Lord, you must tell us where the body is and come with us to seek the King,' he strode the width of the stage and slapped the offender across the right ear, nearly knocking him into the pit. It was a purely automatic reaction: 'I felt I had to,' he murmured afterward, his eyes moist with apology.

He can — and this is rare — act *mind*, and may be the only actor alive who could play a genius convincingly: Donne, for instance, Milton, Pope, or even Shakespeare (the idea has often occurred to him) would be comfortably within his grasp. But he is not, and never will be a star, in the sense that Coward and Olivier are stars. Olivier, one might say, ransacks the vaults of a part with blowlamp, crowbar and gun-powder; Guiness is the nocturnal burglar, the humble Houdini who knows the combination. He does everything by stealth. Whatever he may do in the future, he will leave no theatrical descendants, as Gielgud will. He has, illumined many a hitherto blind alley of subtlety, but blazed no trails. Irving, we read, was rapt, too: but it was a weird, thunderous raptness that shook its fist at the gods. Guinness waves away awe with a witty fingertip and deflects the impending holocaust with a shrug. His stage presence is quite without amplitude, and his face, bereft of its virtuosity of make-up, is a signless zero. His special gift is to imply the presence of little fixed ideas, gambolling about behind the deferential mask of normality. The characters he plays are injected hypodermically, not tattooed all over him; the latter is the star's way and Guinness shrinks from it. Like Buckingham in *Richard III* he is 'deep-revolving, witty'; the clay image on whom the witches work. An innocence, as of the womb, makes his face placid even when he plays murderers.

Whether he likes it or not (and I suspect he does), his true métier will continue to be eccentrics — men reserved, blinkered, shut off from their fellows, and obsessed. Within such minority men there is a hidden glee, an inward fanatical glow; and in their souls Guinness is at ease. Thankfully, in life as in the theatre, they are many. We are still grateful for nonconformity, and warm to the oddments, the outcasts and the loons. To watch Guinness playing them, and doing them as proud as only he can, is to recall Lamb's tribute to a well-loved old actor: 'He is not one, but legion. Not so much a comedian, as a company.' But there cannot be, just yet, or for many seasons more, a last word on Guinness. There will always be those who smile, finding him quaint, and these will be his enemies; while on the other side, a much quieter throng, there will be those who stare, finding him unique.

Harper's Bazaar, US: April 1952

KATHARINE HEPBURN

The spectacle of a forthright, unleashed and obviously very happy human being has always annoyed as many people as it has delighted, and that is why it is possible to dislike Katharine Hepburn without ever having met her. Bright, barefaced, scandalously bold, she begets excitement wherever she travels. Her very nerve-ends tingle with glee: she is an affirmation of life, and especially of the part of it which is called fun. Hepburn is a gay by-product of female emancipation, wearing the pants and using the vote, and her aggressiveness is that of the sun at high noon.

Twenty years ago, almost to the day, an article appeared in an English daily, headed: 'Stop This Nonsense, Miss Hepburn!' The writer was riled because Miss Hepburn had decided that she could get along, prosperously enough, without going out of her way to meet the press; and he accused her of being a neurotic egoist. It is a shame he never knew her. Her smile, which is about as egotistically neurotic as a wild orchid, has a way of testing your heart; it makes small, dry people shrivel. Her vitality is deafening. If anything, she has a Huckleberry Finn complex, a sheer love of truancy, which never fails to worry those whose view of life is impaired by the grindstones in front of their noses.

She was born, forty-three years ago, in Hartford, Connecticut; the home state, significantly enough, of the young girl in the limerick, who had such a Deplorable Absence of Etiquette. Her father was a surgeon, and her mother a strident and unpredictable champion of woman's rights. Dr. Hepburn had six children, an unwieldy nestful whose juvenile activities were almost Chekhovian in their variety and futility. 'In the house in which we were brought up, it was terrible,' claims Miss Hepburn, 'tears and rows the whole time; but nobody seemed to want to get away. It was home and it was so darned nice.'

She was educated at Bryn Mawr College, where brows run high, and for four years studied psychology, learning in the process enough about herself to marry, in 1928, a Wall Street financial adviser named Ludlow Ogden Smith. In the same year, for no very good reason, the stage claimed her. She took to it, at first, like a duck to walking; a little college experience as an amateur, an inborn love of the up-and-down life, and, above all, a growing impatience with everybody else's opinion of her talents were all that she had to set her ambition flaming. It backfired almost immediately: just after her marriage she made her Broadway debut in a drama about girls who work in dance-halls, which was a flop. The actor George Coulouris remembers her, with distant acrimony, at this period, lunching in slacks with her feet on the table, and reading French symbolist poetry between forkfuls. As no doubt she knew, he was feeling a strange impulse to slap her. It was around this time, too, that she became a serious advocate of trousers for women, a whim which she did much to popularise and which she has never foregone.

She had to wait four years for stage success: it came in 1932, and the play this time was one about Amazons. George Cukor, the film director, at once sought to trap her for Hollywood, and was shocked by the effrontery with which, her Scots ancestry emerging, she demanded a salary of $1,500 a week, to begin with. 'The way she talks,' sighed a friend, 'they'll have to strap her down to comb her hair.' However, she got the money, and the film was *A Bill of Divorcement*. It made her, as no other actress has been made in film history. Phrases about her 'rocking-horse nostrils,' references to 'the hard dialling tone' of her voice began to pepper the columns: a new myth was now in the making. In 1933 she played a lady flyer in *Christopher Strong*, and followed it with *Morning Glory*, which won her the Hollywood Gold Medal for the best actress of the year. By now she was being hailed as Garbo's only rival, and already the critics were likening her, in their search for similes, to swans and rare flamingoes. That she was unique, and proficient at putting across her uniqueness, there was no doubt at all.

Lately we have known her chiefly as a shrewd and stirring comedienne, but at the beginning her film career was a mixture of starkness and whimsy. Guided by the tactful Cukor, her first ring-master, she made *Little Women*; cropped her hair and dressed as a boy for *Sylvia Scarlett*; and went on to *The Little Minister*, *Mary of Scotland* and *Quality Street* — all of them striking, sentimental, and a little immature.

Greeted by her indignantly raised eyebrows, the press now began to invade her private life. Almost every week in 1935, some newspaper or other was running the headline: 'Is Hepburn married to Leland Hayward?' She had just obtained a divorce from her husband, whose work in New York kept him a continent away from her, and Hayward, who has since become the producer of such successes as *South Pacific*, *Mister Roberts* and *Call Me Madam*, was then her agent. He was also an amateur aviator, and the reporters went to work when he and Hepburn flew into St. Louis, sharing a two-seater plane. 'Aren't you Miss Hepburn's agent?' said a local journalist. 'No,' said Hayward outrageously and untruthfully, 'I'm only her husband.' Their next stop was a forced landing at Pittsburgh, where a mob of pressmen flooded across the tarmac. 'Are you Miss Hepburn's husband?' shouted seven of them. 'No,' said Hayward, repentant but still debonair, 'I'm only her agent.' By now it was too late, and the news of an elopement hit every front page. Hayward, to stifle the story, was afterwards forced to adopt more direct methods. 'Do you think,' he replied quizzically when asked whether or not Hepburn was his bride, 'that I am some kind of sap?'

In 1936 the cry was: 'Hepburn and Howard Hughes Wed?' Hughes, the millionaire sportsman who made *Hell's Angels* and with it Jean Harlow, was widely touted as Hayward's successor, and for several months Hepburn lived in a state of siege, mostly locked in hotel rooms; on one occasion she eluded the reporters by scrambling down a fire escape, having equipped her maid with a disguise of dark glasses, slacks and mink coat, and instructions to give herself up.

There were other stories, too: of how Francis Lederer, cast opposite her in *Break of Hearts*, walked out after one day's shooting, vividly complaining that the cameras never seemed to be pointing in his direction. Hepburn's violent outdoor proclivities were meanwhile helping to eke out a legend: she rode, swam and played tennis exhaustingly and daily, and her golf professional drove himself into print by announcing that she rarely went round in more than eighty.

Her screen ambitions swelled; in one year, 1936, it was publicly stated that she would appear in *Peter Pan*, *The Forsyte Saga*, and *Saint Joan*. And of this last project Cecil Beaton has left a phonetic record. 'I shall shive my head,' she said to him, 'and wear no mike-up, only grease.' She never of course, played the part.

Hepburn was probably the first native-born American film star who never fell dangerously in love with Hollywood. She kept her enthusiasm, her rapacity, her recklessness and her energy quite unspoilt, and the press seized upon this rapturous normality as if it were somehow mysterious and eccentric. She learned quickly to beware of interviewers, and ever since the Howard Hughes fiasco, all questions about marriage have been countered with a bleak and blithe: 'Yes, I am married. I have six children, three of them coloured.'

By 1938 she had made fourteen films in a career that had lasted five years. Most of them were good (the last two had been *Stage Door* and the witty uproar called *Bringing Up Baby*); but saturation point was dangerously near. Late that year a conclave of the Independent Motion Picture Theatre proprietors, never a notable hotbed of chivalry, dubbed her 'Box-Office Poison.' Soon afterwards, and to nobody's surprise, she walked out of her contract with Radio Pictures. It was a decision which cost her $200,000 in salary for two unmade films, but the gamble paid off handsomely. Unquiet and hyperthyroid as ever, she marched back to Broadway and the theatre; and, almost without thinking, leapt back into the headlines with her treatment of a burglar, whom she surprised at work on her jewel-case and sent screaming into the night by yelling into his face: 'Just what the hell are *you* doing?'

She went into what proved to be her greatest success: Philip Barry's comedy, *The Philadelphia Story*. She bought the film rights from the author, before rehearsals began, for $30,000 and later sold them to MGM for five times that amount. She played the part of Tracy Lord for two years, one year on Broadway, one year on tour, and she loved it. On the play's last night — appropriately in a Philadelphia theatre — she begged the stage manager not to ring the curtain down before the theatre had emptied. 'I'd just hate to think,' she said, tears streaming down into her smile, 'that the curtain ever fell on our play.'

Philip Barry wisely went on writing for her, and in 1942 she appeared on Broadway in his *Without Love*, the story of two indefatigable careerists who try to make marriage work without sharing a bedroom. MGM filmed it with Hepburn and Spencer Tracy, and George Cukor directed it, still faithful to the woman whom he had described, only a few months before, as 'an artistic bully.' The result was what history may describe as the coming-of-age of Hollywood comedy, a really adult and mellow piece of filmic wit, and the nearest screen equivalent to the stage technique of the Lunts. It was Hepburn's completest retort to Dorothy Parker, who had hauntingly written of her performance in a play called *The Lake* that: 'She runs the gamut of emotion from A to B.'

Hepburn and Tracy, who are now as close as friends can reasonably be, have embodied over the last ten years a whole tradition of American sophistication. It is not the European sort, poised and glittering; it unbends, wears sneakers about the house, and relaxes, chuckling, on sofas. Tracy, the placid, sensible panda, and Hepburn, the gracious, dead-pan albatross, have joined together successfully in such festivities as *Woman of the Year*, *The World and His Wife*, *Adam's Rib*, and (as yet unseen) *Pat and Mike*. What they have done for screen values is to replace the crude comedy of flirtation with the subtler, warmer comedy of marriage; and it was about time.

'Spence and I have an agreement when we're working,' she once told me. 'If we fluff a line, we won't stop. In *Adam's Rib*, there was a scene with us dressing to go out, and I had to put on a hat and say: "How do I look?" and he was supposed to say something good and flattering. What happened was, he stepped back and said: "You look like Grandma Moses!" I stamped my foot and sort of yelped — but they printed it.' Grandma Moses, apart from being a hat-wearer, is a nonagenarian.

Last year Hepburn played Rosalind in *As You Like It* on Broadway, and then narrowly missed an Academy Award for her performance as the missionary in *The African Queen*, during the filming of which I first met her. She looks, at once, as if she would be warm to the touch, ready and eager to communicate. To the tip of her nose, she is pink; her nostrils shine as if oiled, and the bright bone of her face stretches the skin. Rangily she paced the studio floor, swinging her fancy hips, with freckles dotting her face like a cloud of locusts. At close quarters you can see wrinkles round her eyes, but the sun's dazzle has put them there; they enclose the alertness, the appetite for life which we prize. Her build is pencil-slim and capable, and she has practical hands; her hair, a wiry flourish of chestnut, was dragged back into a knot.

She talked about that generation of Hollywood which time seems to have overlooked. 'Cagney and Bogart and Tracy and Bette Davis — they're all *invulnerable*, is that the word I mean?' I said it was. She found in them a certainty, a diamond core which could not be dimmed or devalued: they were stars. 'And why,' she said, suddenly mad, 'should actors pretend that they're like other people? They're not. Take me: I *like* driving up to theatres in golden chariots, and not doing my own cooking. . . .'

Invulnerable, I thought afterwards, was a word which fitted Hepburn too. And defenceless. Wide open, yet with no breaches in her armour. It is the paradox which makes stars. To complain about her frank self-exposure would be like bombing an open city. I recalled the occasion in 1950 when her chauffeur was brought into court on a speeding charge, and she insisted on defending him herself, getting so carried away by her theme that she backed, still arguing, into a hot stove, unaware that it was scorching beyond repair a mink coat worth $5,500. It took Hepburn, unprotected and invincible, to do that without looking plain silly.

This week she makes her first appearance on the London stage, playing the title-role in Shaw's comedy, *The Millionairess*, at the New Theatre. The part was written for Edith Evans in 1936, but so far London has never seen it. Hepburn has taken it on a six-week tour, and has already dislocated the right knee of Cyril Ritchard, with whom, in the first act, she has a short wrestling bout. Robert Helpmann, who plays the ascetic Egyptian doctor whom she finally selects as her mate, says that acting with her is like dancing with Margot Fonteyn, and like nothing else that has ever happened to him.

The play contains one particularly revealing speech, in which the doctor explains what it is that draws him irresistibly towards Epifania, the girl with £30,000,000 and no scruples. He has fallen in love, he says, with the feel of her pulse, because it is the pulse of life itself. Whether what Hepburn does is acting in the strict sense of the word, I do not know; but whatever it is, and wherever you are sitting, you cannot deny the throb and the urgency of that magnificent pulse.

Everybody's: 28th June 1952

JOHN GIELGUD

Arthur John Gielgud, of London, who is forty-eight years old, made his first stage appearance at the Old Vic in 1921, when he played the Herald in *Henry V*. So much is ascertainably true; and it would be equally true to say that fish, given a measurable degree of sea-worthiness, want to swim, and birds to fly; equally true, and equally otiose. For Gielgud is not so much an actor, as *the* actor; his uniqueness lies in the fact that he is greater than the sum of his parts. Gielgud is a theatrical possession; an inscription, a figurehead and a touchstone; and he bears roughly the same relationship to the everyday traffic of acting that a helmsman bears to a galley-slave. He is the guarantee, rather than the product; the seal and the signature, rather than the proclamation. It is as patron, not merely as participant, that he lends what dignity it possesses to the ramshackle and transient business of stage pretence.

Yet — watch his style. It is eclectic, it joins hands across epochs, it is not wholly of its century; but its stamp stays on the mind, as a dainty-stepping *haute-école* pony leaves its careful print on circus sand. Gielgud's acting is a tourney between body and soul, which soul invariably wins. It is a troubled soul, even in comedy, where its best moments come from discomfiture, from dignity dislodged. What is certain is that Gielgud's style lacks heart and stomach. When Olivier enters, lions pounce into the ring, and the stage becomes an arena. Gielgud, on the other hand, appears; he does not 'make an entrance'; and he looks like one who has an appointment with the brush of Gainsborough or Reynolds. The face is reposeful, save when emotion convulses it, and then it twitches, suddenly constricted, working intensely, as if a bowl of ammonia had been thrust beneath its nostrils. It is a teacher's face, noblest in rebuke, which has never known the thud of a quarterstaff, but only the sting of the cane. Its very smile is whipped. In the lips, sombrely pursed, and the cheeks, sedately sunken, there is a defiant melancholy, overcast by a perfect and traditional poet's sadness, like that of Arnold's Scholar Gypsy. The voice thrills like an arrow, rising to its inflections in the manner of a charmed snake, and bears witness to great suffering. The east wind has blown through it. It is intemperate in scorn and malice, and has rarely brushed the gruff phrase of earth. Now, as we listen, the voice flies higher still, striking a resonant and febrile alto head-note. This is its climax. It has not yet struck us below the belt, where mundane excitement is, and probably it never will.

The contrast with Olivier betrays both men's secrets. To Olivier we look for the large, shattering effects of passion; to Gielgud, in his 'tempest-proof pavilion,' for the smaller, more exquisite effects of temper. Hereabouts I can slip into a an older critical terminology, for this is the ancient antithesis between Nature and Art. For the best-ordered idealisations (as Hazlitt might have put it) of that with which we are familiar, Gielgud is our mentor; but if we would explore alien territory, axe and compass in hand, Olivier must be our guide.

It is rather like the contrast between what was known as 'beautiful' and what was known as 'sublime.' As Gielgud says, when you quiz him on the point: 'It's obvious, isn't it? I'm Macready, and Larry's Edmund Kean.'

Gielgud's sheer technocratic art is transparent, and shows through his skin. You may watch it, writhing within him to overcome what he imagines to be the obstacles inherent in his face — especially the dominant nose, of which, as a victim of sinus blockages, he is far more conscious than his audiences. His work looks calculated, like that of a bullfighter to whom, after a good afternoon in the ring, I once dashed up and exclaimed: 'Maestro!' (his first name was a sibilant blank in my mind) 'Your wrists were impeccable today! And your profiling! And the timing of your *reboleras*! And . . .' I paused to inhale. The matador grumbled, wagged his head, and spat. 'If you noticed all those things, one at a time,' he said, 'then I have been a failure.' But with Gielgud you do notice these things, one at a time: to surprise and overwhelm is not within him, and to that extent he is cut off from the urgent, all-of-a-piece declaration of selfhood on which the most memorable acting is based.

Like Irving, Gielgud is not really a tragedian, but a romantic, ductile and aloof. His inherited task is to preserve tradition, which has seldom had a more jealous custodian. Both as director and as actor, he may take few risks, and thus becomes, in time, predictable, as only the dedicated and single-minded can be. He must be above the tumult, unswervingly right. He is a Puritan among directors, astringent and deft, who handles plays with kid gloves, and is wary to leave no fingerprints; a cardinal, taking the long view, in a profession mostly made up of ravishing but short-sighted heretics. It was not by accident that my pen, in search of a comparison, strayed to the bullfight. In the serenity of his pride, in his sure-footed assumption of poise and authority, Gielgud is something of a matador himself, particularly in his attitude towards his audiences. He avoids moving them too drastically, as might happen if he surrendered himself, and permitted his intestines to be gouged out in their sight. He gazes at them, instead, with a prudent coolness, controlling them by skill rather than strength. What he projects is, in the main, a mixture of glamour and remoteness.

For Gielgud is a Terry, of the stock that produced Ellen Terry and Gordon Craig, and he speaks, freely and genially, of his lineage. He will tell you of Julia Neilson and Fred Terry, dancing the minuet in *The Scarlet Pimpernel*: and, with amused pride, of how, when they had aged past dancing it, they sat it out on stage, and everyone cheered. Gielgud cannot, and would not, forget his ancestry. He refuses nowadays to play Malvolio in *Twelfth Night* because he feels the part should have the impact of an uppish vulgarian; and, as he says: 'I am quite unable to act without suggesting good breeding.'

His smile, as he says such things, is a benevolent wince, which deepens the vertical furrows between his eyebrows. His hands are loosely embraced, and his frame sits sleek and angular; he looks like a sophisticated don. He knows, his posture confesses, that he is a cynosure. 'Egotism in an imbecile,' said Sarah Bernhardt, 'is a vice: in an intelligent spirit, a virtue.' Eager, unleashed and unstraining, he is communicative about himself (it is like a *causerie* with an archive); and he talks with a speed and a cogency which no sports-commentator could rival. Of his Shylock, which was deliberately grubby and realistic, he says: 'It was a failure, most of all because I find it practically impossible to be disliked on stage.' For the same reason, he continues, he will never play Iago. Iago, remember, is an unflattering close-up of a man, a candid-camera shot, and Gielgud, with the superstition of his kind, mistrusts photographers.

He is about the only English actor of any eminence who has consistently disregarded films — his last, *The Great Disraeli*, is more than ten years old. Nobody would cast him, he explains, as anything but 'an ambassador, a hypocrite, or a poet'; and he bears, anyway, a mild resentment towards having himself perpetuated in any form. 'Acting should always be an ephemeral business,' he says (embodying in the words how much of the romantic's love of impermanence!); 'It must be passed on by word of mouth if it's to survive.' Bernhardt's films, with their 'flingings and wailings,' will, he feels, always be held unjustly against her when compared to those of Duse ('an older Garbo'), who managed instinctively to adapt her style to that of the movie camera. 'It's very flattering to be enshrined in celluloid,' he says, 'but it isn't essential. My job is to be successful on the stages of two cities — London and New York. People tell me I should make films, just as they tell me I should tour Australia. I think it's superfluous. It's an irrelevant risk.'

Gielgud's conversation, like his library, bulges with theatre history and histoires. His mind dwells on the days when play-going was a long-awaited act of homage and self-indulgence; when actors performed only as often as, for instance, Flagstad sings. About the contemporary theatre and its inhabitants he is blandly outspoken, with only the barest patina of tact (he has dropped, in his time, bricks enough to rebuild the Globe Theatre); and his malice is authoritative, reinforced by an ex-cathedra delivery and a high forehead, which time has dilated into a dome. Were he not so clearly saintly, you might be tempted to call him glib.

'Acting,' he declares, 'is half shame, half glory. Shame, at exhibiting yourself; glory, when you can forget yourself.' An actor's growth, as he sees it, takes place in two stages: the first being self-revelation, pure and simple, and the second, purer but not so simple, self-presentation — which demands detachment. At the beginning of his career, Gielgud delighted in mere strutting and preening, and wondered why he felt dissatisfied; next, moving to another extreme, he formed a habit of 'novelistic absorption' in the people he was playing, and gave himself over to heavy, self-concealing, mask-like make-ups, through which he would peer, hopefully but not yet quite convinced. Late in the nineteen-twenties, with the problem still unsolved, he was forced to conclude that he could be defined only as a star; and that his responsibility was to no theory of acting, no producer and no management, but to himself, and through himself, to his authors. This moment of decision comes, sooner or later, to every actor; the moment at which, consciously or unconsciously, he takes stock, and says to himself; 'I know my powers; I have tested them thoroughly. And I am fairly sure that some of them are unique, and theatrically valid quite apart form the roles I play. These qualities will not survive me, as *Hamlet* or *Peer Gynt* will survive me. My job, therefore, is to concentrate on putting them over while I still have my looks.' This is what, with the utmost circumspection, Gielgud has done and is doing, and it represents an attitude far closer to humility than that of the actor who says: 'I can play anything moderately well.' Gielgud is a virtuoso, and virtuosi, since the Renaissance, have rarely aspired to versatility.

Like Coward and Olivier, Gielgud became a star during what, in an earlier theatrical tradition, would have been his time of apprenticeship. 'Noël and Larry and I were famous too early,' he says, meaning it; 'we had no oracles — there were hardly any elder statesmen about to bring us up slowly. Older men, you notice, tend to die not during wars, but a year or so afterwards, from the shock of conforming to a new era. Most of the pillars of the Edwardian stage were dying off between 1923 and 1925.' The hurdles were cleared for the newcomers. There was but one remaining sage, the brilliant and pertinacious Harley Granville-Barker; whom the aftermath of another war carried off, to Gielgud's great sorrow, in 1949.

Among living actors and actresses, he reserves his keenest eulogies for Edith Evans, whom he quotes constantly, and whose gaudy disembroguings into the theatre still fascinate him. 'Edith has a weird, earthly sense of stagecraft,' he says, 'she's got a *badger's* way of sniffing out things, of isolating what's best and most actable in a part.' Of modern directors, he most admires Peter Brook, with whom he has worked in *Measure for Measure* (1950) and *The Winter's Tale* (1951). His Angelo, in the former play, a fumbling, nerve-wracked spinster of a man, was a frank and risky excursion on Gielgud's part into middle age, and a profoundly touching success; perhaps his best work since before the war. His contorted kings, his elegant swaggerers, we had seen before and have seen since; Leontes and Benedick, the latest pair, fit snugly into his already familiar tragic and comic masks; but Angelo was new, new and painfully fine.

Gielgud muses, so intently that you can almost hear the beads click; it is as if a gyroscope whirred within his head. Then, at last, his voice issues. It is aromatic, tinted like a good artificial flower, but there is sinew and purpose behind its prettiness. 'The stage is like an unfinished canvas,' he says: 'I get impulses, during rehearsals, that I could explain to no one. I see an empty space — downstage, perhaps, to the right — and I feel: that space needs me to fill it, *now*.' Filling it, he fills theatres (at present the Phoenix), and has a way of sanctifying all that goes on in them. His presence in a cast obscurely reminds the playgoer of his kinship with the pilgrim. Alone of his contemporaries, Gielgud has the secure, lamp-lit blaze, deep in his eyes, which is the mark of the high priest.

His energy is unwaning, and his hold on the reins of rhetorical acting unchallenged in Europe. The English theatre has accepted him as its ringmaster, and I think it unlikely that it will grow flabby under the flick of that fanatic, magisterial whip. Like Wordsworth's Happy Warrior, Gielgud's grace is peculiar; and his influence, constant.

Harper's Bazaar, US: July 1952

GRAHAM GREENE

Some people are able, over the years, to build up a fairly secure resistance to alcohol. Graham Greene has never been able to build up a resistance to sin: no sooner has a nip of it reached his stomach than the hangover begins. This prompt and unfailing reaction has moved him to undertake, over the last two decades, an exhaustive examination of sin in all its forms: but especially sin the pleasure-giver, sin the pain-inflictor and sin the unholy paradox. Like several other modern Catholics who have been articulate on the subject, Greene believes that sin holds within it the seeds of virtue, and the paradox of evil breeding sanctity, of dunghills sprouting daisies, has become one of the trademarks of his work. William Blake found eternity in a grain of sand; a Graham Greene character is more likely to find it in ten grains of cocaine. Greene finds it easier to share his sympathies with sinners than with the moderate, diurnally good people, who, with their self-confidence and blunt certainties, manage to repel him, making him glad to return to the shy, guilt-riven souls whose reticence and loneliness he shares.

He was converted to Catholicism in 1926, when he was twenty-two. His subsequent explorations into the problems of the soul-racked have rewarded him in no beggarly fashion: his business sense, as everyone concedes, is as highly organised as his sense of sin. Although he is rich, he remains lonely, a sequestered, roaming man who can now afford to travel where he likes and avoid whom he wishes. At present he writes for only ten weeks in each year, and his purposes are nearly always strictly didactic. As he admits, his aim is the single and unmistakable one of demonstrating, as graphically as he can, the truths of his religion; but, unlike most didactic writers, he could never be called a demagogue. Greene is the most notable case in recent literary history of the unhealed physician. Self-accusation, amounting almost to self-flagellation, is second nature to him, a trait in which many of his detractors have smelled morbidity. For Greene, said one of them, 'time not wasted is time misspent — an opportunity for remorse needlessly foregone.' Mauriac, his closest contemporary equivalent, shows little of Greene's stricken, compulsive conscience; his tone is calmer, more magisterial; whereas in Greene's work you can catch, between the tautness of the lines, something of the shuddering ardour of Dostoevski. It is one of his most extraordinary technical achievements to have written on his nerves for so long without ever getting on ours. Hate as a springboard for love, as in *The End of the Affair*; sin as an incitement to salvation, as in *The Heart of the Matter* — these are his special business, and he recoils stuttering with horror from the gusty, knockdown Christianity of men like C. S. Lewis. Greene dislikes what he calls 'Lewis's domesticated Devil,' preferring always the internal kind, the cancer carried within; and if Satan must be allegorised, Greene would make him a sedate and bowler-hatted civil servant rather than a hairy, brimstone-gorged eye-roller.

His beliefs, however deep their roots, are beyond question violent and uncompromising. Indeed, he has devoted much of his time to making religion difficult enough for himself; to uncovering those thorns and snares in its path which made it hard even for the saints. His acceptance of miracles is the result of no sudden, blinding flash of revelation: it is hard-won, toughly argued and jealously tested against flaws and heresies. He was amazed, last year, to find that his readers were having trouble swallowing the miracles in *The End of the Affair*. 'Leaving the miraculous out of life,' he wanly protests, 'is rather like leaving out the lavatory or dreams or breakfast.'

Your interpretation of Greene's life depends simply upon your allegiances. It is either a Catholic pilgrim's progress, or it is the tale of a man diseased, who has come to define his sickness as health. There is no third conclusion, nor would Greene wish there to be: he wants to challenge our powers of choice, to remind us that all decisions are decisions between absolute good and absolute evil, to point out that there is a theological element even in ordering lunch. For every minute of our lives we are, to his mind, oscillating between salvation and damnation, and not, as most of us would say, between ease and unease, satisfaction and discontent. The object of psychiatry being to remove the unease and the discontent, Greene regards it coolly, wondering whether it may not be designed to pour the baby of creativeness away with the bath water of neurosis.

He was born forty-eight years ago, one of four brothers, all of whom have since telescoped up to heights of more than six feet. At six-feet-three, he comes a poor second to brother Hugh, who is six-feet-seven and the head of the BBC Eastern European Service. His father was the headmaster of Berkhamsted School, near London, where all the boys were educated, and it is no coincidence that Greene's loathing of authority extends with particular venom to the public school system. He hated most of of his youth; and when, on an early journey to Africa, he saw his first masked Devil-Man, his instinctive response was to liken him to Dr. Arnold of Rugby. It was at this period that Greene took up Russian roulette, the sport in which you load one bullet into a revolver, spin the chamber, put the barrel in your mouth and press the trigger, giving yourself what he has since described (a little carelessly) as a six-to-one chance. By the time he left school he had become a connoisseur of oppression. Or so he felt; the sense of victimization is not uncommon. Greene's uncanny distinction is that he can express it with no concessions to self-pity.

He won an Exhibition — a sort of junior Scholarship — to Balliol College, Oxford, where he took second-class honours in history and edited a mushroom magazine called *Oxford Outlook*. In his first year he became a probationary member of the Communist Party, into whose funds he paid two shillings, and under whose wing he remained for exactly four weeks. This first, brief loyalty to anything outside himself recoiled on him when, twenty-nine years later, he was classed as undesirable on the strength of it and refused admission to the United States. Greene, who was left kicking his heels at Saigon, was irritated, but not wholly dismayed at a chance to pour scorn on what he now calls the US's 'cellophane curtain.' He reminded the press of the fact that most of his books had been banned in Russia, and added tartly that the atmosphere of panic he found in New York on his last visit recalled to him nothing so strongly as that of England in the late seventeenth century, when the persecution of Catholics was at its height. Greene is still perfectly willing to 'rob the robber barons,' as he puts it, by writing for the richer American magazines; his two consciences, the craftsman's and the moralist's, function with a quite magnificent independence.

His search for external loyalties came to a second and final halt in 1926, when he was admitted to the Catholic Church. In the next year he married Vivien Dayrell-Browning at St. Mary's in Hampstead, and left Oxford a settled dogmatist on most of the larger questions of human existence. They were soluble not through politics, he was sure, but through God; and they were to be understood not in terms of right and wrong, which are expedient and alterable, but in terms of good and evil, which are absolute. This distinction puzzled a good many people when he introduced it, more than a decade later, into *Brighton Rock*: the beery, well-meaning woman who only 'knows right from wrong' is unfavourably contrasted with the race-gang murderer Pinkie, who knows the meaning of evil. Greene's attitude is not unlike that of a prisoner who insists that no aristocrat can be judged by middle-class standards; which was Evelyn Waugh's attitude, too, until he discovered, in *Brideshead Revisited*, that the Church's way of putting these things somehow carries more weight. Waugh's Sebastian, for all his saplessness and debaucheries, has the gift of grace, which accommodatingly sets him outside human jurisdiction.

Greene's Oxford years had proved to him that the best of English literature, from Shakespeare to James Joyce, had always been produced from a Christian standpoint. It infuriated him to hear men like Stephen Spender deploring the dearth of politically conscious novelists in England. Political novels, said Greene in the course of a public wrangle with Spender, were aimed at an attainable objective, and once that objective had been gained, all passion died. Look, he exhorted his audience, at the later Russian cinema. Religious novelists, on the other hand, could never gain their objective, and accordingly their care and passion never diminished.

Greene has always preferred a sense of passionate inadequacy to a sense of fulfilment, and this debate with Spender (which ended in the latter's rout) helped to explain why. It also explained the basis of his bitter contempt for the gentler, unaspiring, jog-trot English novels of the thirties: he is still fond of quoting one contemporary critic, who spoke approvingly of them as 'good, wholesome books that leave no taste in the mouth.'

After Oxford Greene listlessly sought work with the British Imperial Tobacco Company, whom he deserted after ten bewildered days. He then spent three months sub-editing a provincial daily, from which he graduated to *The Times*, his solid bower for nearly four years. In 1930 the success of his first novel, the elaborate study of fear called *The Man Within*, opened a decade of astonishing industry on Greene's part: in ten years he produced thirteen books, most of them crisp and pungent 'entertainments' like *This Gun for Hire*, *Stamboul Train* and *The Ministry of Fear*. Up to the outbreak of war, his best (apart from *The Man Within*) was probably *Brighton Rock*, which was received by the citizens of Brighton as a personal affront. 'Mr. Greene has stuck a knife in our backs,' wrote one romantic; another, thrashing wildly about in search of epithets, finally came out with: 'this *so-called* book is a gross calumny.' There were other controversies, too: as film critic of *Night and Day*, the short-lived English answer to *The New Yorker*, Greene wrote, in 1938, a review of Shirley Temple in *Wee Willie Winkie* so blisteringly unpleasant in its implications about the sources of the nine-year-old star's appeal that the editor was thankful to settle, out of court, for £3,500. Twentieth Century-Fox's libel action closed the magazine down, and only one copy of the offending issue is known to exist. It is in the vaults of the British Museum, and it contains one of the few things Graham Greene has written which he will never reprint.

When, in 1949, the *New Statesman* announced a competition with a prize for the best parody of Graham Greene, it attracted a record entry: the winner, under a pseudonym, was Greene himself, who published a demure letter of thanks in the next number. Ten years earlier, his style was already widely imitated and quite easily imitable. 'He hated the world' — so runs an extract from a novel Greene began in 1938 and wisely left unfinished — 'that was the permanent, the first article of his creed — you couldn't help drinking, you couldn't help moving on, but the emotion that made every departure a sad one suggested the somewhere — something — he had no terms for it — there existed. . . . He pushed his coins across the counter and went out into the cool and grimy night.' Later, in the same unwary fragment: 'He stood there in the tin-roofed church and looked around — the small bare crossless altar, the yellow pitchpine benches, the big tin tank for total immersion. It was a kind of home . . .' The definite article, used to inspire a false sense of recognition, is a favourite trick: each item is numbered, tagged and ironically isolated. The people in Greene's lesser books undeniably evoke our pity; but pity, as Max Beerbohm said, is little sister to contempt. No resource of phrase or rhythm could conceal the fact that Greene had a warm and informed dislike for most of the people he was writing about, and he carved them up with a sort of sorry relish. 'Emotion recollected in hostility' was someone's stinging description of his method.

Tranquillity, and a fuller adherence to the old Wordsworthian gambit, came only in 1940, when he published *The Power and the Glory*; in following the adventures of the disgraced whisky-priest across Mexico, Greene made for the first time a mature and humane statement of his spiritual position. The book won the Hawthornden Prize for 1940, which it deserved; but the film treatment it deserved it never got, as anyone who saw *The Fugitive*, John Ford's version of it, must be rancorously aware. Greene's wartime stay at the Foreign Office, coupled with certain domestic mishaps, kept him silent until 1948, when *The Heart of the Matter* appeared — Greene's compassionate analysis of Scobie, the man forced to choose between divorce and suicide. It was instantly banned, of all places, in Southern Ireland; but Greene's new power was there, as it had been in *The Power and the Glory*, the power of endowing the mundane and the wretchedly commonplace with celestial repercussions, the power of warning us that little things are sent not only to try us, but to put us on trial for our lives. Greene could now communicate a thing vital to all Christian literature: a sense of shame. It is a quality he shares with Conrad, and very few others. Greene makes us shiver by sealing his events up in a kind of eternal echo chamber; he can make us feel the heat of the neck on which the hounds of heaven have breathed.

Meanwhile the films had been enriching him: he scripted *Brighton Rock*, *The Fallen Idol* and, most recently, *The Third Man* — all of them dealing with the same basic subject; the way in which ordinariness, casual, complacent and corrupting, conducts youth on to the threshold, if not into the presence, of mortal sin. Out of his cautionary tales about Pinkie, Harry Lime and the child Philip, Greene earned enough to buy a nine-ton yacht and a villa at Anacapri. By now his distrust of America had found a rival in his detestation of Britain, which was intensified by a squabble with the Bank of England, who refused him the businessman's £10-a-day allowance when he was invited, in 1949, to go to New York and adapt *The Heart of the Matter* for the stage. The dispute rankles still in Greene's mind, as a further proof that earthly as well as celestial authority is out to get him.

In *The End of the Affair*, which appeared last year, Greene is at his most doctrinal and also his most hypnotic. He insists on full acceptance of the nails and the pain of the Cross, and completes, in his treatment of Sarah, the only full-length portrait of a saint in contemporary literature. The hero of *The End of the Affair* is 'I,' a much less detached choice than Greene's familiar and clinical third person, and he still hopes that when the book is filmed, it will be in the style used by Robert Montgomery in *Lady in the Lake* — the style in which the camera stands for the eyes of the narrator, whom we hear but do not see. This technique would be reversed for the excerpts from Sarah's diary: here we should see Bendrix for the first time, and Sarah would become invisible. It seems unlikely that Greene and Louis B. Mayer, with whom he is at present negotiating, will readily see eye to eye, or lens to lens, on these contentious points.

He has just finished his first play, but beyond the facts that it has one set, seven characters and is called *The Living-Room*, he will reveal nothing about it — except that he trusts it will not turn out to be a comedy. Anyone acquainted with Greene's love of paradoxes might reasonably guess, after a glance at the title, that the action will have a good deal to do with dying. And afterward: he promises no more novels until 1954, when he will make a second attempt at self-commitment in the first person.

Greene's story sounds like one of success, but to meet him you would think it represented failure. He looks retiringly pedantic, and sits hunched, with hands and knees crossed, peering out at the grey flux of circumstance with bright, moist, hopeless eyes. His face is pouchy and veined pink, and he will rouse himself from time to time to venture some little riposte in a petulant, time-stained voice which still has trouble with its *r*'s. A man, you might suppose, who feels he has disappointed life as much as life has disappointed him: the impression he leaves, as he wanders rangily off along a crowded street, is one of acute solitariness. His talk is not so much kindly as commiserating, and his demeanour is that of a scholar at a jam session, rather than a saint in the market place.

His only hobby is a sad one, a cheerless atonement for his existence; in it there can be no fulfilment, and only the least, most momentary shreds of triumph. It takes a compulsive form: like Bendrix in *The End of the Affair*, Greene collects car numbers. You must spot first the figure 1 by itself, and then work numerically upward: the first hundred are the hardest. It demands the utmost honesty, this treadmill pastime, since it leads nowhere save toward an ever stronger temptation to cheat. After a few hours in his flat, Greene goes out to stare intently past car headlights. God knows what, if anything, he is expiating; some day, perhaps, we all will; meanwhile the speed and zest of his story telling will continue to bustle us past the question. To have brought together spite, sensuality and saintliness in one novel (as Greene has), and then to have cemented them with an awareness of sin unparalleled since Hopkins's Holy Sonnets (his favourite poems) is to have dignified beyond measure the history of contemporary fiction.

And if the process has involved a shunning of song and fruitful laughter — qualities all his writing lacks — that is because, after all, 'Hell is murky'; and Dante, remember, escorted us through a long purgatory and a still longer inferno before, in the last Cantos of the *Paradiso*, he unfolded joy. The final test of a man's stature is his capacity for proper exultation: but we must wait ten years or more before deciding whether Greene's literary journey is going to bring him back across the Styx. It may be that he will choose to linger unconvinced and a little pallid, within earshot of Charon and the depth, hesitating to face redemption lest he should find, among the saved multitudes, a swarming majority of the shiny, shallow, untormented creatures whose strange simplicity has irked him for so long. I doubt whether their kind of bliss could ever be much fun for Graham Greene.

Harper's Bazaar, US: February 1953

THE CRAZY GANG

The Crazy Gang, all five of them, are automatic choices for any dream-banquet, or indeed for any dream; these elderly rascals haunt the climaxes of my nightmares, welling up out of my subconscious in red wigs and attempting to pass themselves off as the Sugar Delegation from Madagascar. I can imagine how they would divert themselves at a formal feast. One of them, dressed in livery and powder-wig and holding a flaming candelabrum, would carefully trip up the guests at the top of the stairs; another would be distributing hot spoons, for reasons which would not become evident until much later on; a third would be needling the champagne with equal parts of vinegar and alka-seltzer; while the other two, attired as members of the royal family, would throw handfuls of birdseed from the balcony to the waiting mob beneath. At some point in the evening there would be a fall of soot in the fireplace, and Jack Hylton, gagged and bound, would be discovered half way up the chimney. The uneasy silence would be broken by (probably) Flanagan. 'I don't know why he does it', he would say, pityingly; 'I've told him a hundred times it's not funny.'

A stubborner quintet of rude uncles can never have existed than the Crazy Gang: they refuse to acknowledge that humour has developed in any way since Mr. Punch first murdered his wife with a mallet. They remind me of the distinction Groucho Marx once drew between amateur and professional senses of humour: for the amateur, he said, the funniest thing in the world is the sight of a man dressed up as an old woman rolling down a steep hill in a wheel-chair and crashing into a wall at the bottom of it. 'But to make a pro laugh', he went on, 'it would have to be a real old woman.' The Crazy Gang, by this definition, are amateur and professional at the same time. For them the upper slopes of hilarity are dotted with major and minor cruelties, with flea-powder and disinfectant sprays; and the mere suggestion of masquerading as women fills them with unabashed delight. When (as in their present show, *Ring Out the Bells*) they borrow snatches of routines from Chaplin, or Olsen and Johnson, you can feel their pulses racing at the thought of being so outrageously modern. Slapping and shoving each other, swapping puns and laying traps, they belong to the archaeology of farce.

If it were not for Teddy Knox and Bud Flanagan, I would in all likelihood have given them up long ago; but when these two are at large, the antics of the rest take on an unearthly, subliminal glow. Mr. Knox, you remember, is the shrewd one with the moustache who looks like a bookmaker, raffishly absconding; while Mr. Flanagan is a straightforward caricature of the man in the moon, provided always that the moon is made of green cheese. They take it in turns to shepherd the others and deploy them for combat; and when battle is joined, it is usually Mr. Knox or Mr. Flanagan who leads the dash into the breach, routing all defences with some loud, fantastic war-cry. 'Who's dirty?' bellows Mr. Knox, early in the evening, as he pelts the audience with cakes of soap: he starts on the right note, bent on affronting us if he can. Later in *Ring Out the Bells* we find Mr. Flanagan, lurid and gross in a cotton frock, playing one of four appalling baby-sitters. Spying the tot in an adjoining pram: 'What an ugly child!' he says charmingly, fetching it a tremendous crack over the head with a hammer.

As the show buckets along towards its close, Messrs. Knox and Flanagan come together in a drama of love and hate on a rubber plantation (rubber, like kitchen china, unfailingly amuses them). Here Mr. Knox affects a monocle, and Mr. Flanagan a sjambok, with which he lashes out from time to time in an effort to coax Mr. Knox's wife into submission. 'And if that won't work,' he growls, 'I'll give her the *Chunk'hara!*' It is a dreadful threat, fraught with the horrors of the unknown; though I would be prepared to bet that red ink and flour would lie somewhere at the heart of it.

Time was when nobody on stage and few people in the house were safe from the Gang. In their early days, twenty years ago, they used to welcome the customers at the door, sell them inaccurate programmes at inflated prices, and direct them with killing politeness to the wrong seats. Harmless sopranos would suddenly be whisked up to the roof with anchors cunningly hooked into their belts. Nowadays, I am afraid, the boys have gone a little soft; and I pray that they may shortly recover their old grip on the secret of comedy — man's inhumanity to man, and his positive bestiality towards woman.

I carry with me one particularly cryptic memory of Mr. Flanagan. On the occasion of the Gang's twenty-first anniversary, which fell in the autumn of 1952, he made a brief, nostalgic speech, the opening words of which are fixed in my mind. 'We used to be a rough-and-ready lot', he began, his large eyes brimming '— always running up and down corridors . . .' I wondered, and I still wonder, what corridors, and why, but he did not pursue the matter; I suppose he thought the point was clear. And thus it comes about that whenever the Crazy Gang are mentioned, I hear heavy boots clattering along a corridor and waking echoes all the way. It is a school corridor, and the wearers of the boots, having escaped from the classroom, are bound for the locker-room, where they will puff cigarettes and meditate blowing up the gym.

Persona Grata, 1953

C.S.LEWIS

C.S. Lewis is a legislator, a direct descendant of the robust Macaulay school of literary criticism: it is in this capacity, rather than as a Christian apologist, that I chiefly revere him. His principal intellectual weapon is gusto. He argues flamboyantly, in a vein of outrageous paradox, demolishing premise with counter-premise and sealing the subject with a knock-down QED. He has revivified the Middle Ages for many generations of Oxford undergraduates by presenting medieval studies as a controversial topic for immediate debate, on which the closure has not yet been enforced. His faults, like those of Sarah Bernhardt, cry to Heaven, when he is not there. For one thing, too many of his arguments depend on crafty analogy; for another, his passion for ritual art ('applied art', as he calls it) is such that one sometimes wonders by what right lyric poetry ever came into existence at all; and for a third, he is likely to spend so long explaining what Statius was *not* trying to do in *The Thebaïd* that the poem's positive virtues became clouded in an impenetrable smoke-screen of negatives. But in a non-stop intellectual circus a few bad turns can be excused. When he is talking about something he loves (Milton, perhaps, or Amanda Ros), his erudition never fails to coruscate. He has more knowledge available at his finger-tips than anyone I have ever known, and probably more than anyone else who has appeared on the cover of *Time* magazine. After an hour's tutorial session, he will enquire of his pupil, in a voice juicy and measured, whether he feels any 'new acquist of true experience from this great event'. If the pupil's assent is too fulsome, he is displeased. 'Keep a strict eye', he will say, 'on eulogistic and dyslogistic adjectives. They should *diagnose* — not merely blame — and *distinguish* — not merely praise.' Lewis talks, as he writes and thinks, in italics.

As a man, he combines the manner of Friar Tuck with the mind of St. Augustine. His Christian consciousness of sin does not appear to have affected his digestion or made him less rubicund and jolly than in agnostic days. Lewis is vaguely reminiscent of the 'man of a very stout countenance' in Bunyan, who bellowed at the keeper of the book of life: 'Set down my name, Sir!', and hacked his way thereafter through an army into Heaven.

Persona Grata, 1953

George Jean Nathan

George Jean Nathan, who is over seventy and probably the oldest practising dramatic critic since Aristotle, once said: 'Show me a critic without prejudices, and I'll show you an arrested cretin.' For clarifications like that, generations of reviewers stand in his debt. One would have thought that the notion of an impersonal critic was as patently absurd as that of an impersonal person: yet playwrights still cherish it as a sort of holy ideal. Admittedly, we all make *mystiques*: but this one is particularly wishful. The man who asks for anonymous, impartial criticism is trying to elevate criticism to the status of a science; whereas it is, I am afraid, only an art. The critic's business is to write readable English: the playwright's to write speakable English. Beyond that it is every man for himself.

Nathan, being a congenitally mischievous person, would probably go further: I can imagine his arguing that the critic is performing a function in some respects higher than that of the dramatist. Put the case like this: the playwright scans life, selects from it, and organises his findings into dialogue. Might it not be held that he is acting as the critic's scavenger, sieving away the waste, the trivialities and the redundancies, and offering up the essence? That he is sub-editing life, skimming the cream from the milk, and passing it on to the critic for further analysis and final condensation? At this point, breathing heavily, the defence rests.

After nearly half a century of alternately sighing and enthusing over the American theatre, Nathan's vivacity is quite unimpaired: he can still write with the same vigour about Eugene O'Neill and the Decline of Burlesque, nor has he lost his skill when it comes to constructing knock-down sentences such as this, written in 1940: 'Much of the contemporary English polite comedy writing suggests a highly polished and very smooth billiard table with all the necessary brightly poised cues, but without balls.'

Nathan has not succumbed to the critic's scourge — atrophy of love: or, to use a blunter expression, cynicism. Critics are for ever complaining that the constant effort of dissecting other men's work leads to over-punctilious self-criticism, and thence to paralysis. Schiller made the point well in a letter to a friend who was worried because his writing, after years spent as a critic, was growing dry and inhibited. 'Apparently it is not good', said Schiller, '— and indeed it hinders the creative work of the mind — if the intellect examine too closely the ideas already pouring in, as it were, at the gates. . . . In the case of a creative mind, it seems to me, the intellect has withdrawn its watchers from the gates, and the ideas rush in pell-mell; and only then does it review and inspect the multitude. You worthy critics . . . are ashamed or afraid of the momentary and passing madness which is found in all real creators, the longer or shorter duration of which distinguishes the thinking artist from the dreamer. . . . You reject too soon and discriminate too severely.'

Which seems to close the subject: and *vae victis*! That is why I am thankful for Nathan; one can open him (as one used to open Shaw or Beerbohm) and be reassured that criticism is not a desert of dry bones, but a real, fleshly, shapely minor art.

Once, perhaps, in a generation, a truce is called between artist and critic. This is when an over-riding genius lands, as it were, by parachute on the very tip of Parnassus, making the land quake, shivering our yardsticks to splinters, and dislodging everyone, authors and reviewers alike, from their several footholds. Standards then rise abruptly on all sides, as they rose seventy years ago when Ibsen thundered down on us and showed us what we had all been driving at. At such times feuding ceases, and everybody gets down to work.

Persona Grata, 1953

JAMES THURBER

James Thurber is four-fifths blind, a misfortune which may have helped to make him one of the funniest writers in the world. (The word 'humorist', in his context, has a horrid ring of cliché.) Like Milton and Mister Magoo, he lives in a true world of comedy, a world dimly discerned, private and remote, peopled with exaggerations: furtive, apprehensive men, women prophetic and horrific, and animals beyond the strangest imaginings of Edward Lear. The Common Thome, Hackett's Gorm, the Whited Sepulchre and the Tantamount are some of the animals: he draws them either peering aghast over their shoulders or asleep. These two conditions — acute fright and deep coma — are the most prevalent in Thurber's universe. Tangible reality oppresses him: domestic articles like telephones, overcoats and needles constantly get in his way, tripping him up and baffling him by their reluctance to compromise with his vision. The people in his stories live in a state of lymphatic apathy until they have had a few drinks; then, suddenly, they light up, and pierce through his twilight. Potted, they exult; sober, they grumble, half-heard. The only temperate people who attract him (I am speaking of the writer, of course, not the man) are either eccentric or insane. People like the maid Della, who said that the men had come with the 'reeves'; or the hired man Barney Haller, who invited Thurber to come up to the attic and hunt 'warbs' — these departures from verbal conformity fill him with a fearful glee, and he becomes downright moody when he finds that the reeves were merely Christmas wreaths and the warbs nothing more abnormal than wasps.

In a letter to Wolcott Gibbs, his colleague on the *New Yorker*, he once explained some of the perils involved in getting a play produced on Broadway. Gibbs' comedy, *Season in the Sun*, was about to go into rehearsal, and Thurber felt it only comradely to advise the author, on opening night, to spend the third act in a neighbouring bar. 'You will get back to the theatre', he went on, 'in time to see Dick Watts (the critic of the *New York Post*) running for his typewriter. He will say something to you that sounds like "Organ recital. Vested fever" . . .' These words have clearly haunted Thurber; they wander past the guards into the underground vaults of his mind, which are protected by an electric eye so designed that it sounds the alarm whenever reality tries to intrude. Behind his astigmatism, a distorting veil, he sits secure. World events occasionally penetrate it, and reduce him to solemn panic. He once said, on what pretext I cannot recall, that he and George Kaufman 'might make a striking pair of book-ends in Brentano's window — for a display, say, of books about the precarious nature of the world situation'.

If you want a story about a dull, nagging wife driving her dull, nagged husband to a cocktail party, you must go to John O'Hara. But after the party, when the wife, still dull and nagging, is driving home a husband agog with alcohol and breaking loose — to exploit this situation, this contrast between (as Hazlitt said, defining humour) what is and what ought to be, the only man is Thurber.

Concluding an exhaustive survey of the extinct animals of Bermuda, he once wrote: 'I am sorry that I could not include a picture of Thompson's snab. But I couldn't. I can't do everything.' I am sorry, for my part, that we cannot include a picture of Thurber: it proved geographically impossible to pin him down. He did, however, write us a letter recounting his own experiences as a photographer. 'I used to be a 3-A man, and a pretty good one', he told us, 'but I'm too blind to use a Kodak any longer. I had a knack of making a woman subject angry and proud at the same moment, which gave me extraordinary results.' Here unreality crept in: 'I would start to leave the room saying, "Go to hell, you most beautiful of creatures." Then I would snap her.'

Persona Grata, 1953

ORSON WELLES

Nobody in the entertainment industry has been more generally teased and maligned than Orson Welles. He is thought weird. Yet Rousseau might have described him as an average man, fit for election to a community of noble savages, sun-burnt, nomadic and Whitmanesque. Welles is at once as abnormal and as natural as Niagara Falls. He outgrew the playboy legend about eight years ago: confronted with it nowadays, with the grey invasion of thirty-seven years at each temple, he sulks. Then: 'Hell, Barrymore died', he says, embracing your eyes with his smile: 'and I took over. It's time someone relieved me.' Honestly, and much more rapidly than his apologists, he has forgotten his past. 'The bee is always making honey', he explains, making a happy gesture as of wings flapping; 'Progress continues!' Vanquishingly, he laughs, hunching his blubber shoulders and perhaps even pounding the table. Welles is always open to inspection: he hides nothing. His mind is a bazaar, his case-book a best-seller.

He has genially detested Hollywood ever since, as he puts it, '*The Magnificent Ambersons* was cut in my absence by the studio janitor'. He is one of the tribe of Americans who have forsworn their upbringing since hitting Europe: for our dishevelled civilisation he has acquired a reverence which is dismayingly far from the keen, caustic iconoclasm of *Citizen Kane*. Welles belongs to the Hemingway breed of burly buccaneers, whose eclecticism is their pride. The aromas of wines have grown treasurable to him; bullfights are to be discussed with brows properly knitted — so many venerable things are new. In growing up, he has developed a perilous humility towards his own talents: he shakes with laughter at his weaknesses. Art, with him, has become a last resort, a final alternative to living. The new changed Welles is a connoisseur — that social, wine-wise, stomach-sensitive creature without whom art could never be understood, but by whom it is so rarely hammered out. In broadening, he may have become flattened: possibly the swift uppercut of theatrical or filmic effectiveness is even now beyond him.

He remains immense. No one offers more verbal largesse, for example, over luncheon, or offers it with less reticence to everyone in the restaurant. In these lean years he has fattened and, in repose, now resembles a landed whale. The body slumps like an inflated embryo; the eyes glower without meaning; the nose is a button; and the head tilts sumptuously back as if reclining on a houri's shoulder. But speech transforms him. The mane of the fighting bull bristles, and he lunges forward, breasting his paragraphs like a surf-rider, bouncing over your interpolated breakers of 'But perhaps —' and 'Don't you think —' His punctuation is laughter, with him an effortless cachinnation. He chokes over his own good humour like a fat boy at a feast. Time, meanwhile, slides by. They say that drunken men never look at their watches; Welles's inebriation is verbal, a gesture of ease, a great coherent chuckle with echoes everywhere.

People have compared him to Thurber's Eliot Vereker, the explosive intellectual whose trick it was to throw hard-boiled eggs into electric fans, and who would loudly toss off aphorisms such as: 'Santayana? He's a ton of feathers', or: 'When you have said Proust was sick, you have said everything'. Welles's opinions are equally sweeping, but a trifle more amiable. 'Negro actors are all untalented', he may assert: 'Paul Robeson was just Brian Aherne in black-face'. A moment later: 'What's the problem about *The Cocktail Party*? It's a straight commercial play with a traditional comic climax that Saki used and Evelyn Waugh used — surprising martyrdom of well-bred lady in exotic surroundings.' What does he read most? 'You'll think me pompous, but P. G. Wodehouse. Imagine it! A *benign* comic artist in the twentieth century! Nothing about personal irritations, the stuff Benchley and Dorothy Parker wrote about — simply a perfect, impersonal, benevolent style.' Shakespeare: 'I think Oxford wrote Shakespeare. If you don't agree, there are some awful funny coincidences to explain away. . . .' Welles's conversation has the enlivening sciolism of Ripley's *Believe it or Not*. His library of snap judgments is magnificently catalogued.

He was an onlooker at the clumsy, poignant suicide of 'The Man on the Ledge', which took place in New York in 1938, when a boy perched for fourteen hours on a window-sill of the Gotham Hotel before plunging into the street. 'I stood in the crowd outside for a long time', Welles says pensively, 'and wanted to make a film of it all. But they tell me that in the Hollywood version they gave the boy a *reason* for what he did. That's crazy. It's the crowd that needs explaining.' It is worth recalling that Welles gave Chaplin the germinal idea for *Monsieur Verdoux*, which was based on the theory that it is our society, and not the individual lawbreaker, which needs excuses. From Welles's point of view we are the crowd, gaping and giggling and laying bets: and he, balanced, exposed, relaxed and taking the air, is the man on the ledge. He is baffled by the fact that, after fourteen years of notoriety, we continue to stare at him.

Welles is a versatile, centrifugal, all-round talent in eclipse; but even in eclipse, unique. Would you hear the perfect *aperçu* about the relationship between such an artist and his audience? It is contained in a tale about Welles. Arriving, some years ago, to deliver a lecture in a small mid-Western town, he was faced with a tiny handful of listeners and no one to introduce him. He decided to introduce himself.

'Ladies and gentlemen', he began, 'I will tell you the highlights of my life. I am a director of plays. I am a producer of plays. I am an actor on the legitimate stage. I am a writer of motion pictures. I am a motion-picture actor. I write, direct and act on the radio. I am a magician. I also paint and sketch, and I am a book-publisher. I am a violinist and a pianist.' Here he paused, and rested his chin on his hands, surveying the sparse congregation. 'Isn't it strange', he said, quizzically but with clinching emphasis, 'that there are so many of me — and so few of you?'

Persona Grata, 1953

CYRIL CONNOLLY

Cyril Connolly is either a bon viveur with a passion for literature, or a *littérateur* with a passion for high living. He has never quite made up his mind, and his biography will be the story of his indecision. It is a conflict of extremes, because his standards of living and writing are both immensely high, too high for comfortable co-existence within the same very self-critical human being: Brillat-Savarin and a fasting friar might sooner inhabit the same cell. Whenever he revisits the *grands restaurants* a nagging voice keeps reminding him of his own dictum: 'The true function of a writer is to produce a masterpiece; no other task is of any conse-quence.' Fancifully, one can picture him echoing Ben Jonson's cry; 'O! If a man could restrain the fury of his gullet and groin!' Only the best in food or art is good enough for him: only what he calls 'alpha people' interest him, and nothing depresses him more than an encounter with a thriving, contented, beta-plus, best-selling novelist. Mediocre writing strikes him as several degrees worse than no writing: 'The books I haven't written,' he once said, 'are better than the books other people have.' For over twenty years he has been pressing on his contemporaries the information that art is a ferocious taskmistress, that the muses do not welcome novices, but (as Cocteau said) simply open the door and silently point at the tightrope.

Immoderate faith in Connolly's pronouncements might persuade any young author that literature was almost an impossibility: his glum, lapidary admonitions produce an effect like that of reading a medical textbook on the use of dangerous drugs, and it has been said that the idea of modern English literature without him is as inconceivable as the idea of *Hamlet* without the Ghost. For him the test of a piece of writing is: 'Would it amuse Horace or Milton or Swift or Leopardi? Could it be read to Flaubert?' Writing under the shadow of these appalling questions is naturally an exacting occupation, and it is no wonder that Connolly has been a miser of words, publishing only five books of his own work in a lifetime of fifty years.

Horizon, the literary monthly which he ran from 1939 until 1950, established him as a great editor, carrying on a rearguard action in the service of letters at a time when art and frivolity were all but equated in the public mind. His anthology *The Golden Horizon* contains only one item, a brief questionnaire, written by himself, but the book bears his trademark on every page. Its flavour is wry, pungent and personal; the choice is that of a man to whom pomp, lushness and slogans are uniformly hateful. In *Ideas and Places*, a collection of his *Horizon* editorials, and in *The Unquiet Grave*, a quotation-peppered stew in which the modern intellectual's predicament is sadly anatomized, Connolly has stated his case against twentieth-century culture. The onlooker sees most of the game, but to Connolly the game is a war, with literature an open city being saturation-bombed by economic stress and betrayed from within by *Angst* — a cult word which he did more than anyone to popularise. Sometimes one suspects that Connolly the physician is merely diagnosing his own ailment, and that the x-rays have been rigged to show only the cancers of guilt and indolence. He has tried and failed to cultivate what Lamb called 'a brawny defiance to the needles of a thrusting-in conscience.'

'His virtue as a critic,' said one observer, 'has always been the directness that comes from treating all writing as the personal expression of a particular human being in particular circumstances . . .' How late did Baudelaire lie abed? What was Voltaire's digestion like? How important was sex to La Rochefoucauld? These are the questions which fascinate Connolly: in answering them, he has become the greatest living authority on good reasons for not writing. His lifework is a series of attempts to define the material and spiritual circumstances most propitious to the creation of good art. What pressures and solaces, how much drink, how much money, how much of the hermit's barrel and how much of the marriage bed, conduce to the nourishment of the creative mood? He has spent most of his career in search of the right solution.

'I have always disliked myself at any given moment,' he has written: 'the sum total of such moments is my life.' It began in England on 10 September 1903. Much later, in a completely un-autobiographical context, he said: 'Thus astrologers find this love of perfection in those born under the sign of Virgo . . . between the end of August and end of September.' His father was a soldier, of naval and military ancestry, and a collector of shells, a trait which has reproduced itself in Connolly's abiding love of hoarding exotic objects. His mother sprang from a line of gay Irish squirearchs, and in extreme youth, he says, 'I became a snob. The discovery that I was an earl's great-nephew was important to me. . .' He had a conventional English writer's childhood, which is to say, one that was geographically and genealogically bizarre, involving exposure to good books, the minor aristocracy and outposts of Empire — he twice visited South Africa before he was seven.

From private school, where his best friends were Cecil Beaton ('prettiness') and George Orwell ('intellect'), he went to Eton with a scholarship. He read intensively, became known as a wit, and suffered abominably. The evasiveness, the shrillness, the tendency to blink and stammer, which are to be found in most English intellectuals, can be traced directly to their public schools; and Connolly's account of the cliques and cruelty of Eton is characteristically alarming, as much in what it condones as in what it condemns. 'To this day,' he wrote 'I cannot bear to be sent for or to hear of anyone's wanting to see me about something without acute nervous dread.' He rejoiced when he was admitted to Pop, the Eton Society, much as he rejoiced when, years later, he was elected to White's Club, the Pop of St. James's Street.

He took a degree in history at Oxford, and from this period dates his vision of himself as 'the boy who let the side down, the coming man who never came.' In 1926 he found a patron: the London refugee from Philadelphia, Logan Pearsall Smith, author of *Trivia* and like minor works, apprised of his brightness, offered him a secretarial job which proved to be less than exacting. *Chez* Pearsall Smith, he would rise at ten, spending the morning in a constantly replenished hot bath: at luncheon he would grumble politely if the wine insulted his palate; the afternoon might be occupied with yachting on the Solent; and then dinner, after which he customarily fell into a deep sleep.

He likens his subsequent career to a tree that has its destined shape but takes time to decide which branch is the main artery. He flourished ephemerally as a conversationalist, and more lastingly in the pages of the *New Statesman*, where his mentors were Raymond Mortimer and Desmond MacCarthy, who managed to rouse him from fits of what he calls 'mutinous and iconoclastic sloth'. His thirties' journalism is vivid, erudite, sharply metaphoric and only slightly cliquey: the best of it includes half a dozen lacerating burlesques, one of which, the playful demolition of Aldous Huxley entitled 'Told in Gath', has been described as the most brilliant parody of the twentieth century. He also published a novel, *The Rock Pool*, which encapsulated the seedy, sub-Bohemian side of the French Riviera in the twenties, drably shivering under the blast of the mistral.

In 1930 he had married a not ill-heeled American, and was spared the necessity of sinking to the cheaper varieties of journalism. Analysing the blights afflicting the twentieth-century artist, he said, '. . . broadcasting, advertising, journalism and lecturing all pluck feathers from the blue bird of inspiration and cast them on the wind'. He more or less resisted all four, achieving instead considerable standing as guest, host, mimic, and Guardian of Values. Even now, it is difficult to leave his company without feeling determined to repel all forms of literary prostitution, a determination which can easily lead to inertia. He travelled, found acolytes, made friends and entertained them in Chelsea on champagne and sucking-pig.

'Favourite daydream' he wrote in 1933, 'to edit a monthly magazine entirely subsidised by self. No advertisements. Harmless title. Deleterious contents.' In 1939 war broke out, and with it, like the rash sometimes produced by vaccination, *Horizon*, backed by Connolly's friend Peter Watson. From a chrysalis of journalism, fiction-writing and marriage (he was separated from his wife in 1939), an editor emerged, with views that were perfectionist without being pontifical, and for ten years the magazine spread its name around the world. In 1950, faced with a diminishing circulation, *Horizon* sank: 'only contributions continued inexorably to be delivered, like a suicide's milk,' Connolly wrote recently, 'and keep on coming'. He had lived lavishly during the forties, overspending on furniture, china and food; now he was jobless and in debt. A new self was called for.

'Stoic in adversity, Epicurean in prosperity': thus he epitomised himself; now, obviously, was the Stoic's chance. 1950 was a cashless year. He had just remarried, his new wife being the long, catlike, amazingly slim Barbara Skelton, whose circle of friends had formerly ranged from Peter Quennell to King Farouk. With her companionship, Connolly withdrew from London literary life, took an isolated cottage in Kent, acridly illuminated by oil lamps, and became an ascetic. The Spartan, antiseptic life of Oak Cottage was intended to sharpen his creative wits for the twenty years of literary activity which he believed were left to him: two decades to turn out the masterpiece to put immortal flesh on the Ghost. 'I am,' he said, 'a refugee from the business lunch and the *couche-tard* principle.'

The fleshed Ghost was and is a baggy, besandalled Buddha, with a pink child's face, slack jowls, a receding fuzz of hair skirmishing across his scalp, and somewhat sour, blank eyes which express the resignation of one who envisaged himself in a sedan chair sucking on a hubble-bubble and was fobbed off with secondhand Sheraton and cigars. Physically, a part for Charles Laughton at his driest and least expostulatory; intellectually, a logbook of his generation's voyages and discoveries — Freud in the twenties, the left in the thirties, the preservative artistic right in the late forties. In 1951 Connolly took a post as literary critic on *The Sunday Times*, a retreat to journalism but a concession to security. His vocation was still 'to make books', but his new job enabled him to vary the hermitage routine by spending one night a week at the Ritz, if only to get his pants pressed.

Last winter he concluded that his programme was 'to shed ballast, to cast off some of my selves — the Editor, the International Journalist, the Romantic Adolescent and the Diner-Out'. This last self was hastened to oblivion partly by Virginia Woolf's reference to him in her notebooks as 'that cocktail critic, C. Connolly', but more by Nancy Mitford's gentle parody of him in *The Blessing*, where he figures as the Captain, with a circle of handmaidens, sudden infatuations, and helplessly expensive tastes. 'I want to write myself out of journalism,' he says, 'as I have journalized myself out of editing.' His publications since his rural retirement have been three anthologies, two from *Horizon* and one of *Great English Short Novels*. 'I have read or reread about sixty or seventy novels for this selection,' he told his publishers. 'It has been a revelation to me and freed me at last from the bondage to French nineteenth-century writers, which has been holding me up for years and prevented me from writing more myself. . . . I should like those who read this anthology to find all long books rather absurd.' He is now, not unexpectedly, working on a short novel ('form and shape and rapidity') about the murder of a man of letters. 'I write as a rule in the afternoons, using the mornings to rev up the engine,' he explains. 'I can go for long spells without working.' Sir Max Beerbohm has attested, among many others, that no writer enjoys writing. Connolly is reluctant to face the typewriter because, he says, the sheer *jouissance* of creation always burdens him with a profound, hungover sense of guilt. He cites, as a parallel, a fellow-critic who was told by a psychiatrist that his literary blockage was due to a subconscious identification of the desire to write with the desire to sleep with his mother.

Connolly fills the pre-lunch revving-up period with his other interests. He must feed his pet coati (a replacement for the lemurs whose distinctive stench pervaded most of his earlier homes); he must attend to his two Chinese ducks and his lovingly fattened guinea fowl. He gardens assiduously and adventurously, and next year he plans a 'Poison Corner'. His own list of hobbies runs: 'READING, travelling, talking, eating, drinking, motoring, gardening, thinking, planting shrubs and watching fishes, architecture, china, silver, paintings, furniture, reading. READING, READING.' His acquisitiveness is violent and endless: 'I am,' he once said, 'one of nature's Rothschilds.' His afternoon bouts of creativeness produce the same concise, elegant, informal results as ever, laced with nodules of venom: he recently dismissed a volume of expendable memoirs with the phrase: 'wanly recommended'. He dines out seldom, but when he does he is ruthlessly critical of the food ('But the mashed potatoes were the best I've ever tasted,' or 'When will X learn that the champagne should *keep on coming*?') and more anxious than of old to get back home and read. Horace, Catullus, Flaubert, Lucretius, Stendhal, Molière, Firbank, Rabelais and Lamb are all within arm's length of his bed, the beloved collaborators on his 'culture picture'. 'A writer has to construct his shell, like the caddis worm, from the debris of the past.' The French finality of Connolly's style, at once supple and bleak, is one of the most glittering of English literary possessions, among which it shines like a crown jewel in a pawnbroker's shop.

It is hard to explain his influence to anyone who has not felt the impact of his personality. One might say that Alexander Woollcott was a vulgar, eunuchoid, ragtime caricature of Connolly, except that Connolly's earlier waspishness has mellowed with time. Nowadays, he says, 'things do not annoy me unless they are very badly made'. It is the making that worries him, the solitary toil of turning out a perfect sentence: but the hedonist in him forever militates against the anchorite. He wants to move up 'from the cottage class to the country-house class'; and thus, when his American publishers sent him a questionnaire with a final request for 'any other information about yourself . . . please do not be modest', his response was immediate: 'I could use a million dollars.' He loathes hearty, county people, but relishes the food they can afford. He is a journalist, but takes no newspapers. He detests easy fame, but wants to get rich quick. A fair description of Horace, Connolly's idol, might almost be a description of the idolater himself, but there is something irremediably comic about an English Horace in the 1950s. It conjures up a picture I cannot expunge from my mind: a drafty old Sunbeam Talbot being driven across country at breakneck speed in a rainstorm, Mrs. Connolly furiously at the wheel, moodily grinding her teeth, and Connolly himself squatting in the back seat on what appeared to be a spare tire and murmuring to me, in his fussy, tentative voice, 'By habit, of course, I am an Epicurean,' as the needle touched seventy, the car lurched on a bend and an ominous banging was heard, as I remember, from the neighbourhood of the back axle.

Harper's Bazaar, US: March 1954; *Tynan Right and Left*, 1967

PETER BROOK

He has just staged the London production of Christopher Fry's new play *The Dark is Light Enough*, and he is twenty-nine years old. Peter Brook is a prodigy all right. He seems to have been born middle-aged with no illusions left. Meeting him, a sure, sage little man who listens as intently as a dictaphone, you would say that his métier was music, an art less gregarious than the drama. For Brook is not the extrovert, Orson Welles, *monstre sacré* kind of boy-genius: nonconformity does not tempt him, he was never a crusader, and he looks about as neurotic as a chipmunk. Snub, stubby and self-contained, he radiates nothing more alarming than confidence. Talking, he leans back on his heels, gesturing (like a pianist) with short, soft fingers; his veiled eyes blink and twinkle, and he smickers secretly, watching you in a cat-mouse way which can be extremely discomfiting. It seems incredible that a personality so private should thrive on anything as public as the business of stagecraft. Yet in ten professional years Brook has directed twenty plays, six operas, a film and a TV show.

His power resides in concentration, and in an egotism so cautious that it forbids him ever to lose his temper. Nothing disconcerts him, everything amuses him, and he is not even on nodding terms with doubt. His guiding principle is that there is no technique which cannot be mastered overnight. Art, he feels, should be like jujitsu, the maximum effect with the minimum strain. In his time he has handled Robert Morley, Orson Welles, John Gielgud and Laurence Olivier, flipping each blandly over his shoulder, and emerging chubbily unscarred, except that he is balding perceptibly. Brook has the true director's sadism, a sadism without cruelty, which delights in changing the face of things to fit a personal pattern.

'Peter wasn't born to the purple,' said an actress; 'he was born to the 36 pink gelatine and the 18 blue.' He comes of Asiatic, non-theatrical stock: his parents, both Russian-born, emigrated to England early in life. He has an elder brother, Alexis, who is now a psychiatrist: 'Alexis,' says his father, 'is the classicist of the family — Peter is the romantic.' Aged five, Peter inherited his brother's teddy bear, an obese animal much prized for its ability to growl. Within an afternoon he had ripped it apart to find out where the noise came from: it never growled again, but at least he knew how it had growled. In the same year he was given a fully equipped model theatre, and his childhood abruptly ended. Free from the distraction of live actors, he learned the rudiments of his craft, forming a conception of theatre which time has modified only slightly, a conception in which individual performers were intruders, wilful aliens for whom, somehow, a place must be made. Before long his father came across a manuscript headed: '*Hamlet*, by P. Brook and W. Shakespeare.' Obviously, a career had begun.

He switched schools frequently, partly because of a recurrent glandular infection, but chiefly because of a tendency to treat his teachers with the *dégagé* compassion usually reserved for idiot children. He became an accomplished pianist, a lecturer ('P. S. P. Brook delivered a speech on Art, Music and Democracy'), and a debater ('P. S. P. Brook regarded the existence of women as an unfortunate accident'); but he was also a prizewinning linguist, fluent in French, Russian and German. At sixteen he shook the dust of secondary education from his feet and toddled into films, spending a year as assistant director of documentaries and advertising shorts.

In 1942 he went up to Oxford. His impact on the university is described by a contemporary: 'It was as if he'd come up by public request. Rather like a high-pressure executive arriving to take over a dying business. His mental age, I should say, was around thirty-five.' Impatient with existing theatre groups, he formed his own company and took a small theatre in Knightsbridge, where he staged a production of *Doctor Faustus* in which Mephistopheles played all seven of the Deadly Sins. In 1943, by a dazzling coup d'état, he gained control of the University Film Society and, armed with £250, set out to shoot his own adaptation of Sterne's *Sentimental Journey*. His college, resentful at being used simply as a location, decided to send him down, imparting the news in a letter which Brook, engrossed in filming, omitted to answer. 'A rope fire escape has disappeared from your rooms,' sighed a postscript. 'I presume you are responsible.' Brook's father contrived to secure his reinstatement, on a promise that shooting would be suspended during term time, but nobody ever found the rope ladder.

Having left Oxford with a wartime degree and achieved a C4 medical grade from the army, Brook assembled *Sentimental Journey* ('A Film by Peter Brook') and showed it to the London critics. Some applauded: one thought he must be going blind; and Dilys Powell spoke for the majority when she wrote: 'The direction and playing have a certain freshness, but there is no denying that the cinema is a highly technical business.' Unteachable as ever, Brook launched his first professional production, Cocteau's *Infernal Machine*, at a now defunct neighbourhood playhouse. Its instant success reassured him: one toy, anyway, was mastered; and, impervious to rebuffs from experienced actors, he went on to direct *Pygmalion*. As a result, he found his Maecenas: Sir Barry Jackson, founder of the famous Birmingham Repertory Theatre and the nearest approach to a complete *homme du théâtre* that England has had since Harley Granville-Barker, heard of the production, and invited Brook to Birmingham to direct *King John*. He stayed on to capture a national press with *Man and*

Superman and Ibsen's *Lady from the Sea*, and it was by natural consequence that Jackson, who had just assumed control of the Stratford Memorial Theatre, summoned Brook to stage *Love's Labour's Lost* there in the spring of 1946.

That spring was his springboard. The production, in which the shadow and sunlight of Watteau were miraculously distilled, caused a sensation. Brook was hailed as 'the legitimate successor to Komisarjevsky,' and to my generation at Oxford he was the *Wunderkind*. Moving to London, he directed Alec Guinness in *The Brothers Karamazov* and Sartre's *No Exit:* by now the comparisons were with Meyerhold. In a theatrical magazine Brook quoted Gaston Baty: '*C'est au metteur-en-scène qu'il appartiendra de restituer à l'oeuvre ce qui s'en est perdu dans le chemin du rêve au manuscrit.*' Here Brook stood, between the dream and the text, subtly influencing both. He returned to Stratford in 1947 with a torrid, blood-feuding production of *Romeo and Juliet*, conceived during a holiday in Tangier. The critics, warned of his youth, allowed faint smiles to play around their lips: but for all its Arabic excesses, the production was sudorifically exciting.

His talents had started to define themselves: he was best at extremes, either the firework realism of *Karamazov* or the filigree enchantment of *Love's Labour's*. Before we could see more, Sir Barry stepped in, as a potent member of the governing body at Covent Garden, to offer Brook a job as director of productions. It kept him out of the legitimate theatre for two years. His operatic joyride began with a gaudy, Byzantine *Boris Godunov*, and continued with less tendentious productions of *La Bohème* and *Figaro*. The critics, as is their way, complimented themselves on his having 'settled down': it must be remembered that in the English theatre experiment is as much of a joke as tradition is in the French theatre. London critics derive an obscure pleasure from the spectacle of an 'amusing' revolutionary developing into a 'reliable' conservative. And just as I had begun to fear that Brook had become absorbed in 'the tradition,' he burst upon us with his masterpiece.

It was early 1949, and the play was *Dark of the Moon*, a backwoods melodrama of witchcraft and revivalism: with a youthful company, Brook worked a lurid wonder, throat-gripping as a three-engine fire, with every scene held as in a magnesium flare, full of flickering life. Postwar London has seen nothing so totally, uncompromisingly theatrical. He followed it with *Salome* at Covent Garden, designed by Salvador Dali. Buoyantly returning from conference with his surrealist confrere, Brook announced: 'We are determined to do more things together. Our next will be in the open air, with armies and airplanes.' Ljuba Welitsch, who sang Salome, bellowed her concession: 'For you, Peter *mein Kind*, I sing it back to front.' But Dali's settings were nerve-rackingly clumsy, and Brook was briefly booed on opening night.

1950 was his annus mirabilis. He directed *Ring Round the Moon*, by Fry out of Anouilh; Nancy Mitford's adaptation of *The Little Hut*; and the great, bleak Stratford production of *Measure for Measure*, with Gielgud as Angelo, which later toured Germany, where the critics acclaimed it in terms of Bosch and Brueghel. Happily, Brook resigned his post at Covent Garden: 'After two years' slogging,' he said, 'I came to the conclusion that opera as an artistic form was dead.' The aesthetic gyroscopes whirling within him slackened for a while, and 1951 was a drab year, lightened only by his marriage to a raven-haired, mockingly beautiful starlet named Natasha Parry. He took a wan, witty satire called *A Penny for a Song* and over-embellished it into a flop. He pursued his collaboration with Gielgud in *The Winter's Tale*, turning the hot-blooded pagan fairy-tale into a chilly domestic *drame*. And he staged an emasculated version of Anouilh's *Colombe* which played all out for prettiness and sniggers. I despaired: and the critics buzzed with joy, hinting that Brook had learned his lesson, that he had come to terms with the limited, formal, elegant requirements of West End theatre.

The Beggar's Opera, which kept him in the film studios throughout 1952, did not silence my qualms. It was soon whispered that things were going less than smoothly, that Olivier, star and part-financier of the film, was getting too much of his knightly way. His idea of Macheath was a gentleman highwayman, spruce and gay; Brook's was a Hogarthian rake-hell, lusty and begrimed; and Olivier noticeably prevailed. Gay's work lost its satiric teeth, and what was screened was a jolly tale of a gallant in love with two rather smart, pallid girls. From this misfire Brook recovered with a pure classical production of Otway's *Venice Preserv'd*, in which Gielgud permitted himself to be overshadowed by a bravura performance from Paul Scofield and bravura direction which packed the lines with conspiracy and threat. Thus revived, Brook crossed the Atlantic to brave Broadway.

The trip was ill-planned. *The Little Hut,* with a second-best cast, was quickly guillotined. The televised *King Lear*, with Orson Welles, was under-rehearsed on the technical side: as with *Sentimental Journey*, Brook attempted marvels and achieved near-competence. He recouped with his nineteenth-century staging of Gounod's *Faust* at the Metropolitan — another version of the story with which, eleven years before, he had begun his career: the story of a man who learns to love the devil.

Which brings us to the Fry play: after which Brook will probably direct *L'Alouette*, Anouilh's version of St. Joan's martyrdom. I cannot guess what comes next. The urgency of Brook's teens has left him; if he were rich enough, he tells me, he would give up everything in order to travel and 'live in widening spirals.' For the moment his mission is completed. In England, depressingly, there is a limit to what one can accomplish in the theatre. There is no state-run playhouse in which to create a permanent tradition: in France, Brook would have joined the Comédie Française and, by now, seceded to form his own company. In the West End he must jump from play to play, cast to cast, without a chance to consolidate his gains or to move the front line forward.

He has in fact flourished in the wrong country, though he has often shown it the right theatrical way — on postwar achievement he is the best director in London. But, more than that, he was born in the wrong epoch. He belongs to the future, because he is obsessed not by words but by sights and sensations. We are living at the end of the era of the word: soon, the quicker responses of the eye may be officially paramount. Brook, who 'sees' plays with a deep-focus clarity which few contemporaries can rival, is the prophet of that unborn time, when to show in images will be more than to tell in phrases, when to demonstrate will be more than to speak. At present he is an enforced renegade, who has surrendered to literature, to Fry and Gielgud, without really, fully, finally loving it. 'The guy works like a God damn photographer,' said one disgusted actor in a Brook production, ' "Move a few steps left, Freddie," "Climb on that stair, Freddie," "Stand on your head, Freddie" — you get jumpy waiting for the flash.' The same actor was at the time, quite unknown to himself, giving the best performance of his life.

Harper's Bazaar, US: April 1954

GRETA GARBO

What, when drunk, one sees in other women, one sees in Garbo sober. She is woman apprehended with all the pulsating clarity of one of Aldous Huxley's mescalin jags. To watch her is to achieve direct, cleansed perception of something which, like a flower or a fold of silk, is raptly, unassertively and beautifully itself. Nothing intrudes between her and the observer except the observer's neuroses: her contribution is calm and receptiveness, an absorbent repose which normally, in women, coexists only with the utmost vanity. Tranced by the ecstasy of existing, she gives to each onlooker what he needs: her largesse is *intarissable*. Most actresses in action live only to look at men, but Garbo looks at flowers, clouds and furniture with the same admiring compassion, like Eve on the morning of creation, and better cast than Mr. Huxley as Adam. Fame, by insulating her against a multitude of experiences which we take for granted, has increased rather than diminished her capacity for wonder. In England two years ago she visited Westminster Abbey, early one morning when no one was about, and in this most public of places found a source of enormous private enchantment. A walk along a busy street is for her a semi-mystical adventure. Like a Martian guest, she questions you about your everyday life, infecting you with her eagerness, shaming you into a heightened sensitivity. Conversing with her, you feel like Ramon Novarro, blinded in *Mata Hari*, to whom she said: 'Here are your eyes,' and touched her own.

I half-believed, until I met her, the old hilarious slander which whispered that she was a brilliant Swedish female impersonator who had kept up the pretence too long; behind the dark glasses, it was hinted, beneath the wild brown hair, there lurked the features of a proud Scandinavian diplomat, now proclaiming their masculinity so stridently that exposure to cameras was out of the question. This idle fabrication was demolished within seconds of her entering the room; sidelong, a little tentative, like an animal thrust under a searchlight, she advanced, put out a hand in greeting, murmured something muted and sibilant to express her pleasure, and then, gashing her mouth into a grin, expunged all doubt. This was a girl, all right. It is an indication of the mystery which surrounds her that I felt pleased even to have ascertained her sex.

'Are you all things to all men?' someone asks her in *Two-Faced Woman*; to which the honest reply (I forget the scripted one) would be: 'To all men, women and children.' Garbo, Hepburn and Dietrich are perhaps the only screen personalities for whom such a claim could seriously be made. 'She has sex, but no particular gender,' I once wrote of Dietrich, 'her masculinity appeals to women, and her sexuality to men'; which is also true of Hepburn. Yet Garbo transcends both of them. Neither Hepburn nor Dietrich could have played Garbo's scenes with her son in *Anna Karenina*; something predatory in them would have forbidden such selfless maternal raptures. Garbo alone can be intoxicated by innocence. She turns her coevals into her children, taking them under her wing like a great, sailing swan. Her love is thus larger than Hepburn's or Dietrich's, which does not extend beyond the immediately desired object. It was Alistair Cooke who pointed out that in her films she seemed to see life in reverse, and, because she was aware of the fate in store for them, offered the shelter of her sympathy to all around her.

Through the cellophane kitsch (how it dates!) of the Lubitsch Touch she pierced, in *Ninotchka*, to affirm her pity for the human condition. The words were addressed to Melvyn Douglas, but we all knew for whom they were really intended, and glowed in the knowledge: 'Bomps will fall, civilisations will crumble — but *not yet*. . . . *Give us our moment!*' She seemed to be pleading the world's cause, and to be winning, too. Often, during the decade in which she talked to us, she gave signs that she was on the side of life against darkness: they seeped through a series of banal, barrel-scraping scripts like code messages borne through enemy lines. Sometimes, uttering sentences which were plainly designed to speed the end of literature, she could convey her universal charity only in glimpses, such as, for instance, a half-mocking, half-despairing catch in the wine-dark voice. Round the militant bluster of MGM dialogue she wrapped a Red Cross bandage of humanity.

It is likely that too many volumes have been read into and written about her, and that every additional adulatory word reinforces the terror I am sure she feels at the thought of having to face us again and measure up to the legend. Possibly we exaggerated her intelligence from the beginning; perhaps she was perfectly happy with the velvet-hung, musk-scented tin lizzies which Salka Viertel and S. N. Behrman (among others) turned out as vehicles for her. Perhaps association with Lewis Stone and Reginald Owen, a stout pair of uncle-substitutes who crop up, variously bewigged, in many of her films, was vitally necessary to inspire her. Recall, too, that Carl Brisson and John Gilbert are known to have been high on her list of ideal men; and that we have no evidence that she has ever read a book. Except physically, we know little more about Garbo than we know about Shakespeare. She looks, in fact, about thirty-four, but her date of birth is disputable; the textbooks oscillate between 1905 and 1906, and one biography ungallantly plumps for 1903, which may, of course, be a wound left by an embittered typesetter. Stockholm cradled her, and, like Anna Christie, she was the daughter of an impoverished sailor. She had a brother and two sisters, left school at fourteen, entered the newly expanding Swedish film industry, and was discovered by Mauritz Stiller. After the completion of *Gösta Berling* in 1924, her life is a list of movies, twelve silent, fourteen talking, and a file of newspaper pictures, catching her aghast and rain-coated, grey-faced and weirdly hatted, on the gangplanks of ships or the stairways to planes. We often know where she is going, but never why. Occasionally a man is with her, a sort of Kafkaesque guard, employed to escort her to her next inscrutable rendezvous. Baffled, we consult the astrologers, who tell us that those born, as she was, between the end of August and the end of September are almost bound to be perfectionists; but what, we are left sighing, is she perfecting?

She changed her name from Gustaffson to Garbo, the Swedish word for a sprite. I used to think the Spanish 'garbo' an insult to her, having heard it applied to matadors whose work seemed to me no more than pretty or neat. A Hispanophile friend has lately corrected me: 'garbo,' he writes, 'is animal grace sublimated — the flaunting of an assured natural charm, poise infected by *joie de vivre*, innate, high-spirited, controlled, the essentially female attribute (even in bullfighters). . . .' In short, 'garbo' is Garbo without the melancholy, with no intimations of mortality. The word describes the embryo, the capital letter invests it with a soul. It is the difference between *Gösta Berling* and *Anna Karenina*.

But here again I am acquiescing in the myth of gloom. Long before the fit of hoarse hysterics which convulsed her when Melvyn Douglas fell off his chair, Garbo had laughed, even if it was only 'wild laughter in the throat of death,' and made us laugh too. She was never wholly austere. Posing as a man in the tavern scene of *Queen Christina*, how blithely she made us smile at her awkwardness when asked to share a bedroom with the Spanish ambassador! A secret heart-smile, with the lips drawn back as if bobbing for apples, was always her least resistible weapon. Her gaiety coalesced, to the dismay of academic distinctions, with plangency. Her retirement is unforgivable if only because it means that now we shall never see her as Masha in *The Three Sisters*, a part Chekhov might have written for her. It takes lesser actresses to express a single emotion, mirth or mirthlessness. Garbo's most radiant grins were belied always by the anxiety in the antennae-like eyebrows; and by the angle of her head she could effect a transition, not alone of mood, but of age. When it was tilted back, with the mouth sagging open, she was a child joyously anticipating a sweet; when it was tipped forward, the mouth still agape, she became a parent wide-eyed at her child's newest exploit.

Some of her impact, certainly, was derived from the exoticism of her accent; hers was probably the first Swedish voice that many a million filmgoers had ever heard. Anglo-Saxons are notoriously prone to ascribe messianic characteristics to any stranger with a Slavic, Teutonic or Nordic intonation; Bergner and Bergman are examples that come to mind, and the history of the London stage is punctuated with shrieks of exultation over long-forgotten soubrettes with names like Marta Kling, Svenda Stellmar or Ljuba Van Strusi. Garbo was unquestionably assisted by the fact that she had to be cast, more often than not, as an exile: how often, to go about her business of home-wrecking, she arrives by train from afar! The smoke clears, revealing the emissary of fate, hungrily licking her lips. The displaced person always inspires curiosity: who displaced her, what forces drove her from her native land? If it was Garbo's luck to provoke these enquiries, it was her gift which answered them. The impulse behind her voyages was romantic passion. Bergner might have left home to collect Pekes, Bergman to go on a hiking tour; Garbo could only have journeyed to escape or to seek a lover. Which is, as a line in *Ninotchka* has it, 'a netchul impulse common to all.'

Superficially, she changed very little in the course of her career; a certain solidity in her aspect suggested, at the very end, a spiritualised reworking of Irene Dunne, but that was all. She could still (and often did) fling her head flexibly back at right angles to her spine, and she kissed as thirstily as ever, cupping her man's head in both hands and seeming very nearly to drink from it. And her appeal never lost its ambiguity. The after-dinner cooch-dance which drives Lionel Barrymore to hit the bottle in *Mata Hari* reveals an oddly androgynous physique, with strong-kneed legs as 'capable,' in their way, as the spatulate fingers: nothing is here of Herrick's 'fleshie Principalities.' Pectorally, the eye notes a subsidence hardly distinguishable from concavity: the art that conceals art could scarcely go further. If this undenominational temple-dance is seductive (and, like the swimming-pool sequence in *Two-Faced Woman*, it is), the explanation lies in our awareness that we are watching a real, imperfectly shaped human being, and not a market-fattened glamour-symbol.

I dwell on Garbo's physical attributes because I think the sensual side of acting is too often under-rated: too much is written about how actors feel, too little about how they look. Garbo's looks, and especially her carriage, always set up a marvellous dissonance with what she was saying. The broad ivory yoke of her shoulders belonged to a javelin-thrower; she walked obliquely, seeming to sidle even when she strode, like a middle-weight boxer approaching an opponent: how could this athletic port enshrine so frail and suppliant a spirit? Queen Christina, reputedly her favourite character, is encased for several reels in masculine garb, and when besought by her counsellors to marry, she replies: 'I shall die a bachelor!' And think of: 'I am Mata Hari — I am my own master!' To lines like these Garbo could impart an enigmatic wit which nobody else could have carried off. Deficient in all the surface frills of femininity, she replaced them with a male directness. Her Marie Walewska was as lion-hearted as Napoleon himself, and I have heard her described as 'Charlemagne's Aunt.' Her independence (in the last analysis) of either sex is responsible for the cryptic amorality of her performances. In most of the characters she played the only discernible moral imperative is loyalty, an animal rather than a human virtue — that 'natural sense of honour' which, as Shaw says, 'is nowhere mentioned in the Bible.'

'Animal grace sublimated': I return to my correspondent's phrase. If it is true (as I think it is) that none of Garbo's clothes ever appear to be meant for her, much less to fit her, that is because her real state is not in clothes at all. Her costumes hamper her, whether they are stoles or redingotes, or (as on one occasion) moiré, sequinned, principal-boy tights. She implies a nakedness which is bodily as well as spiritual. It is foolish to complain that, basically, she gave but one performance throughout her life. She has only one body, and in this incarnation that is all we can expect.

Through what hoops, when all is said and done, she has been put by Seastrom, Cukor, Clarence Brown and the rest of her mentors! She has gone blonde for them, danced 'La Chica-Choca' for them, played a travesty of Sarah Bernhardt for them, stood straight-faced by for them as Lewis Stone warned her of 'a new weapon called The Tank.' Can we ask for more self-abnegation? A life of Duse was once mooted for her — what an *éducation sentimentale*, one guesses, she would have supplied for D'Annunzio! Later she hovered over, but did not settle on, a mimed role in Lifar's ballet version of *Phèdre*. And at the last moment, when all seemed fixed, she sidestepped the leading part in Balzac's *La Duchesse de Langeais*. The most recent, least plausible rumour of all insisted that she would film *La Folle de Chaillot*, with Chaplin as the Rag-Picker. . . .

So it looks as if we were never to know whether or not she was a great actress. Do I not find the death scene of *Camille* or the bedroom-stroking scene of *Queen Christina* commensurate with the demands of great acting? On balance, no. The great actress, as G. H. Lewes declared, must show her greatness in the highest reaches of her art; and it must strictly be counted against Garbo that she never attempted Hedda, or Masha, or St. Joan, or Medea. We must acclaim a glorious woman who exhibited herself more profoundly to the camera than any of her contemporaries; but the final accolade must, if we are honest, be withheld.

Sight and Sound: April 1954; *Curtains*, 1961

JUDY HOLLIDAY

Judy Holliday's secret, when you come right down to it, is that she symbolises something which might be called 'The Moron's Revenge.' There comes a moment in each of her five films when, goaded beyond endurance by the blind, unreasoning intelligence of those around her, she explodes in protest, turning on her persecutors with a terrible cry of 'Bluarrgh!'

Most of us secretly resent the smugness of perfectly articulate people. Judy takes revenge for us by throwing a spanner into the works of logic. According to Garson Kanin, who, with his wife Ruth Gordon, has written nearly everything Judy Holliday has ever played, the basic Holliday gambit is to face all life's problems with 'a plain statement of fact.' In *Adam's Rib*, for example, when asked how she felt after shooting her husband, she makes the truthful but utterly confusing reply: 'I felt hungry.'

Rational conversation demoralises her; she regards it as a plot to 'get at' her. To preserve her dignity, she puts on a broad, meaningless smile which conceals total incomprehension and lasts until the pressure on her brain is removed. Then, like a child let out of school, she is her chaotic self again, a supreme vindication of Wilde's epigram: 'Ignorance is like a delicate, exotic fruit; touch it, and the bloom is gone.'

The bloom has not gone from Judy Holliday. She is now perhaps the subtlest comedienne in America, and an Academy Award winner to boot, which is curious, because she is not, so to speak, a career clown.

Her early ambition was something quite different. She was born about thirty-five years ago in New York, the only child of parents untainted by any trace of theatrical blood; yet she left high school determined to become a theatrical director. She changed her name from Judith Tuvim to Judy Holliday and, hoping to be infected by the genius of Orson Welles, got a job as switchboard operator at his Mercury Theatre. After a hard day at the plugs, she would visit the cafés of Greenwich Village and commiserate with other frustrated theatricals. At one, which specialised in broken-down poets and encouraged its clients to provide their own floor show, she met, in 1939, Adolph Green and Betty Comden, later to become successful lyric writers. With two others they worked out a comedy routine, billed themselves 'The Revuers,' and even achieved the miracle of payment: $15 each for three performances a week.

From then on nothing could hold them. The Revuers became fashionable, moved up-town to the smart supper-clubs, and broadcast a weekly radio programme; but all the time, it was noticed, Judy was growing sadder and more pensive. She now wanted to be a writer as well as a director, and both ambitions were being thwarted. The moment of decision came in 1943; the team was appearing in Hollywood for the first time, and Twentieth-Century Fox offered Judy a contract. 'So we played a stock scene out of a million movies,' explains Adolph Green. 'The one where she says: "I'll stick with you, fellers," and we say: "Go ahead, kid. We won't stand in your way. That's — show business." And she signed the contract.' But it proved to be a false dawn. In two years she was given only one small part.

She returned to New York in 1945 and snapped up an engagement in a comedy called *Kiss Them For Me*. During rehearsals she dumbfounded the director by insisting on making a smallish role smaller. With shorter speeches, she said, she could get bigger laughs. She was right: her performance won her an award as the best supporting player of the season. But it seemed to lead nowhere; soon after the play closed she was within measurable distance of starving. Then Garson Kanin interviewed her as a possible understudy for Jean Arthur, the star of his new play *Born Yesterday*, which had just opened in Boston. Finding her stout and rather sullen, he turned her down; but a week later, when Miss Arthur collapsed in Philadelphia, he begged Judy to take over the part at three days' notice. She arrived, still too plump — when not working she is a compulsive eater — but three days of agonised rehearsal satisfactorily dwindled her. Broadway embraced her, and *Born Yesterday* ran for four years.

During the run she warily admitted two more candidates to the small circle of her intimate friends. One was David Oppenheim, a brilliant clarinettist and record-company executive, whom she married in 1948. The other was George Cukor, whose adroitness in handling such prima donnas as Garbo, Crawford and Hepburn had long since established him as the best woman's director in Hollywood. Cukor offered her a part in his film *Adam's Rib*. The resulting sketch of a baffled brunette was exquisitely funny, but it did not persuade the film company, as Cukor had hoped, that she was ripe to star in the film of *Born Yesterday*. The studio tested thirty-six other actresses in rising desperation before considering Cukor's choice, who promptly won them the Academy Award.

In the spring of 1951 a slice of Judy's past loomed up to threaten her future. She was named by the Un-American Activities Committee as having associated with 'Communist-front organisations.' Her employers instantly panicked, and for more than a year, until she was called to answer the charges, no publicity went out on her from the studios. What emerged from her testimony was that she had sent a telegram congratulating the Moscow Art Theatre on its fiftieth anniversary; that she had sympathised with the famous 'Hollywood Ten' who were imprisoned for refusing to answer the Committee's questions; and that she had signed a peace petition. Although she made an abject apology, saying that she had been 'irresponsible and more than slightly stupid,' and even though there was no suggestion that she had ever been a communist, her films were widely picketed, and it was hinted that the studio had to spend large sums of money to get the pressure group called off.

Her next film, *The Marrying Kind*, appeared in 1953, when the stir died down. Both it, and its successor, *It Should Happen to You*, were hilarious on a pretty intelligent level. Hollywood comedy had acquired, almost for the first time, a broadly funny woman whose technique did not depend on man-chasing. The Kanins' sly, elliptical style, with its half-thoughts and hesitations, suited her to perfection.

The prospect of making *Phffft*, her current film, threw her into a fit (or phffftl) of terror, because for nearly ten years every word she had uttered on the screen had been written by the Kanins and directed by Cukor. But George Axelrod and Mark Robson turned out to be admirable replacements, and her first solo flight was a reassuring success. The nervous laugh, the fugitive smile and the divine innocence were as peerless as ever.

She still regards Hollywood as foreign territory, and spends most of her time in New York with her husband and Jonathan, their two-year-old child. Chess, books and chamber music take up much of her leisure, and the rest is mostly divided between playing the horses, playing word-games and buying second-hand furniture. Domesticity appeals to her, not least because it allows her to eat interminably, and some think she would like to devote her life to it. But at present she is too valuable an investment for that to be possible. She will shortly start work on a new film, and after that there is talk of a play in London.

However, her intelligence, a sharp and intuitive organ, has lately been warning her that the middle thirties are a dangerous period for an actress to survive. Will she be able to make the transition, which Lynn Fontanne, Ruth Gordon and Shirley Booth have all had to make before her, from comedy to serious drama? Can her talent live without constant infusions of laughter? Almost certainly the problem will solve itself, for she is a born fretter, who bites her fingernails with a sustained voracity given to few. 'And if you keep that up,' Garson Kanin once said to her, 'the only part you'll be fit for will be the Venus de Milo.'

Everybody's: 29th January 1955

THORNTON WILDER

Thornton Niven Wilder, whose new play, *A Life in the Sun*, has its world première at the Edinburgh Festival tomorrow, is often asked whether he thinks of himself primarily as a novelist, a playwright or a scholar. His evasive habit is to reply that he is merely 'a schoolteacher who would like to be a poet,' a description which does not compare in accuracy with that given by a London friend of his, of whom he recently inquired what plays — 'as a visiting fireman' — he should see. 'You're not a visiting fireman,' said the friend, 'you're a visiting fire.'

The remark was just: Wilder is perpetually aflame with ideas, and his true vocation is that of cultural evangelist. Faced with the variety of human knowledge, he licks his lips, eats omnivorously and transmits his delight in letters and lectures to fellow-writers all over the world. Few men learn more hungrily or teach more generously. Wilder's own output inevitably suffers: in thirty years of literary activity he has published little beyond five novels and five plays. What distinguishes his work is its loyalty to a conviction he first uttered in *The Bridge of San Luis Rey*, that 'the whole purport of literature . . . is the notation of the heart.'

He is the survivor of a pair of identical twins born in Wisconsin on 17 April 1897, to the wife of Amos Parker Wilder, then editor of the *Wisconsin State Journal*. He had a polyglot upbringing. In 1906 he spent a year at a German school in Hong Kong, where his father was Consul-General; later the family moved to Shanghai; and in 1913 he was sent to continue his studies in California. His father, who came of New England stock, had firm ideas about child care: Wilder had worked on a farm and passed two years at a co-educational college in Ohio before he was permitted to enter Yale. But Amos' plans bore abundant fruit: all his five children grew up to be writers.

Interrupted by a year's military service in the Coast Artillery Corps, Wilder's stay at Yale ended in 1920 and left him a confirmed bachelor, ready for the mental gymnastics through which, over the years, he has managed to keep his intellectual reflexes as fit and fresh as a child's. In 1921 he joined the staff of a school in New Jersey where he taught French (one of the four languages in which he is fluent) for seven years. A first novel appeared, and a first play, neither of them much praised.

His curious blend of innocence and erudition found its audience in 1927: *The Bridge of San Luis Rey* won a Pulitzer Prize and offered to a swarm of

imitators that ultimate rarity, a new narrative technique. Wilder brought five
human beings together in a crisis — the collapse of a bridge — and then ran
back over their lives up to that moment. No literary device in this century
has earned so much for so many people. Unite a group of people in artificial
surroundings — a hotel, a life-boat, an airliner — and, almost
automatically, you have a success on your hands.

For two years afterwards Wilder gorged himself on European travel.
Feeling the tug of vocation, he then joined the English Department of the
University of Chicago, on the understanding that he would be free for six
months of the year to write and lecture elsewhere. This arrangement lasted
for six years and produced a volume of one-act plays and a new novel; but
when Wilder left Chicago in 1936 to settle in Connecticut, he was widely
regarded as a minor literary figure — 'a faint shadow,' he was called, 'of
James Branch Cabell.'

He shook off that taunt by intensifying his courtship of the theatre. But
not the theatre as most of his contemporaries understood it: Wilder had a
dream, large and ingenuous, of theatre 'as magnificence, as eloquence . . .
as religious power, as social commentary.' To be fully realised, it would
need new architects as well as new dramatists. He went as far towards it as
he could with *Our Town*, which took the Broadway stage in February 1938,
and stayed there for a year. With a few chairs as scenery and a philosophic
Stage Manager as chorus, he evoked the seasonal rhythm of small-town life
so perfectly that Grover's Corners, New Hampshire, was placed not only
geographically but cosmically: at times one seemed, as Wilder says, 'to be
looking at the town through the wrong end of a lunar telescope.' Like
Turgenev, he hit his full stride as the scholar-poet of provincial life.

His next play, *The Merchant of Yonkers*, was a failure for fifteen years
until, rewritten as a scampering farce, it arrived in London last season at the
Haymarket Theatre, newly entitled *The Match-Maker*. After its Broadway
débâcle, he lectured in Britain and South America throughout 1941. No one
who heard him could deny his mastery of the spoken word. Bold, eager and
emphatic, his lecturing style combines *gentillesse* and jauntiness, its
English derivative; it is not surprising to learn that more than once, after
token protests, he has been persuaded to act in his own plays.

In 1942, after Wilder had accepted a commission in the Air Intelligence
Combat Force, the most ambitious and aberrant of his plays opened in New
York. *The Skin of Our Teeth* embodied all of his impatience with dramatic
convention; with impish nonchalance, he set a modern American family
struggling against the cataclysms of prehistory, and at one point begged the
audience to chop up its seats to feed the fire necessary to ward off the Ice
Age. Whenever serious discussion loomed up, Wilder would scare it away
with a slapstick. The critical reaction in New York ranged from Alexander
Woollcott's assurance that the play was 'head and shoulders above anything
else ever written for our stage' to the accusation made by the *Saturday*

Review of Literature that it had been plagiarised wholesale from James Joyce's *Finnegans Wake*.

Wilder never answered the latter charge, but he does not deny that much of his inspiration comes from literature: 'I frequently take off from a masterpiece.' To take a masterpiece and spin around it a modern, idiomatic fantasy is his greatest joy; like Cocteau, he works in no tradition, and is content to be called sage, stimulant or irritant. *The Match-Maker* owes its plot to an eighteenth-century comedy; *The Ides of March*, his last novel, sprang from Cicero, Catullus and Suetonius; and *A Life in the Sun* has its origins in Euripides' *Alcestis*. His work draws on multiple sources, which may explain why English audiences have frequently fought shy of it.

He is a polymath playwright and a polymath conversationalist. His talk is a bumpy ride on an intellectual roundabout: his stocky body bent forward with wonder at the size and scope of human achievement, he lovingly enlarges on anything that fascinates him. On music, for example, of which he has a technical knowledge which few executants could rival. On the regrettable displacement of the 'omniscient novelist' by the novelist who coyly writes: 'Who knows what was passing through Harriet's mind when she entered the convent?' On Freud, with whom he was 'on teasing terms,' and on Aeschylus as humorist — 'all antiquity rang with his fame as a comic poet.' After a ribald quotation from Tallulah Bankhead, one awaits the unavoidable reference to Lope de Vega, all of whose 470 extant plays Wilder has read.

Yet there is no pedantry in him; he always obeys Ezra Pound's advice to 'make it new.' Above all, he is a historian of the heart. 'Consciousness,' he once exclaimed, 'means a sense of the uniqueness of occasion.' He lives up to his own dictum: for Wilder, every occasion is unique and treasurable. Sometimes his exuberance verges on the naïve. A few months ago he was out walking with one of his acolytes, who confessed that lately he had found writing so difficult a chore that he had become ashamed of the page in his passport which read: 'Occupation — Writer.' Wilder stopped, transfixed, refusing to believe that passports contained such definitions. Bounding back to his hotel, he opened his passport and read the appropriate page. His eyes shone with pride and astonishment. 'Think of that!' he said: 'Think of that!' The entry read: 'Occupation — Playwright.' At last, he must have felt, and glowed to feel, it was official.

Observer: 21st August 1955

PAUL LÉAUTAUD

In an age when there are more successful commentators than important events to be commented on, the temptation to become a critic is enormous. Ours is a minuscule era with a million microscopes trained on it: and the natural tendency is to become one of the watchers rather than one of the watched. After all, why bother to make history if you can earn a better living as a non-combatant observer? The argument is powerful but specious. Those whom it has seduced into espousing criticism as a career should study the case of M. Paul Léautaud, the second volume of whose *Journal Littéraire* has just appeared in Paris.

M. Léautaud, now eighty-three, was the illegitimate son of a prompter at the Comédie Française. He became a critic in 1907 under the name of Maurice Boissard: witty, hawk-eyed, vehement and a master of paradox. In matters of style he revered the swiftness and nonchalance of Stendhal; of prettiness, and style for style's sake, he had a horror, and said that one read Anatole France simply to find out what Anatole France had been reading. Shrewdly and sternly, he reviled the excesses of French classical acting, and became quickly notorious.

He loathed tragedy above all things, and quoted with approval the remark of Crébillon *fils* that French tragic drama, as exemplified by Corneille and Racine, was the most perfect farce ever invented by the wit of man. (*Andromaque*, which he liked, he defined as a brilliant psychological comedy.) 'Il n'y a de théâtre,' he cried, 'que le théâtre comique,' by which he meant to endorse the tragi-comic while excluding for ever the purely, relentlessly tragic. On and off, he flourished for more than thirty years, always candid and often querulous, in the best traditions of French polemic. Yet in 1941 he abandoned his craft and fled. Why?

His enemies say that his egotism had grown so unbridled that to sit in silence for three hours while actors declaimed had become a torture to him. Others hold that he took fright when a rancorous tragedian, sitting behind him at the Comédie Française, set fire to his coat-tails. Whatever the reason, he retired with an army of pet cats to a tumbledown suburban house and locked himself in, like a wounded hermit crab. Warily, five years ago, he crept out to give a devastating series of broadcast talks about his private life: for a while he became fashionable, and no salon was complete without this dwarf cactus of a man, with his pockets full of cat's-meat and his mouth full of insults. Soon afterwards he shuffled back to his retreat; and nowadays to visit him is to court annihilation.

At your approach an outpost or sentinel cat dashes indoors, presumably to warn its brethren to make the air hideous for your arrival. The door hangs on a rusted hinge, and the windows are broken and grey with dust. With a shout you announce yourself, and the response, from a high and smelly landing, is a strangled cry of grief. It comes from one who knew Zola, Huysmans, Péguy, Verlaine and Rémy de Gourmont; it is the sound made by a critic at the end of his life. Do not mount the staircase: M. Léautaud lives at the top of it purely, they say, for the joy of kicking you down. He exists in imminent expectation of being blown to pieces. In this he sees no pathos. He wants no sympathy save that of his cats; it is only when human beings invade his hermitage that he grows petulant. And this is his chosen fate: logically, for his kind, there is no other. You would become a critic? Consider M. Léautaud: and think again.

Observer: 9th October 1955

EDITH EVANS

Of many actresses it is the face that we first remember — smiling or sad, enraged or impassioned; of many more it is the figure, or the carriage of the limbs. With Edith Evans the case is different.

How she looks runs second to how she sounds: it is in the ear of memory that she chiefly lingers. Her great instrument is the voice. She once said that her greatest fault was that when she got a beautiful word into her mouth she could not bear to let go of it; it is a fault which, to our infinite pleasure, seems past curing.

How many images, how many adjectives have been summoned to evoke the wonderful noise Dame Edith makes! Her voice has been said to caress, to ripple and to cascade; it has been likened to silk, satin and even bombasine; it has been compared to a river in flood and the sea in a Cornish cove, not to mention lark-song and the music of the nightingale. What is certain is that her cadences and arpeggios have been mimicked by a whole generation of younger players, and not always wisely. The Evans voice has helped to form what has been unkindly called 'the hostess style' of English acting, whereby the actress behaves as if every play in which she appears were a house-party at which she was the gracious *châtelaine*. But Dame Edith must not be blamed for the shortcomings of her imitators any more than Shakespeare must be blamed for the hordes of lesser playwrights who aped him and whom he dwarfed. In an age more and more dependent on the eye, she has always held that drama is an art of words, addressed primarily to the ear. She makes pictures but above all she makes music.

Hers is not the harsh, discordant music of tragedy, but a subtler, gentler kind, unrivalled in high comedy and sentimental drama, in *The Way of the World* or *Waters of the Moon*. Dame Edith is among the tiny handful of modern players who have never had to rely on the cinema for a living. The others include Sir John Gielgud, Alfred Lunt and Lynn Fontanne, all of them artists for whom the ear is paramount and who know that, although film audiences are prepared to stop and look, they seldom listen. Dame Edith has appeared in three films — *The Queen of Spades*, *The Last Days of Dolwyn* and *The Importance of Being Earnest* — but they all came late in her career, when she was already fully established. She has never needed the cinema half as much as it has needed her.

In a sense she has never needed anything very much outside her job. A theatre, a costume or two, and a few hundred speeches to utter: these have always been enough. She lives unflamboyantly. Her home is a quiet apartment in Albany, sheltered from the roar of Piccadilly. Occasionally, looking *formidablement gaie*, she goes to parties, but rarely stays long: her private life has none of the extravagances associated in the public mind with Great Ladies of the Stage. She has enough spiritual strength not to need crowds of people around her, and her religious conviction is a reflection of this.

She was not — far from it — a success overnight. Hers was a slow rise, step by careful step, a classic example of a career which began by conquering the critics and then went on to conquer the public as a whole. No one in her family had any interest in, or talent for, the stage. Her father, a civil servant, lived in Westminster, where she was born in 1888. There is no sign in her background of the emotional problems and domestic tempests which so often, for good or ill, seem to drive people into the arts. She attended St. Michael's School in Chester Square, and left at the age of fifteen to become a milliner's apprentice, working hard all day on her ribbons and spending most of her evenings at night-school.

Her first lunge towards the theatre took her into the amateur movement, at first purely for fun. Edith Evans is one of the few amateurs who have successfully made the awkward transition to professionalism. I have heard people say that amateurs, who work for nothing, have a more genuine and disinterested love of the drama than professionals, but this can scarcely be true. How can a man who devotes his life to a craft be said to be less in love with it than a man to whom it is merely an alternative to tennis on summer evenings? Edith Evans was an exception. When she was sixteen she joined a dramatic class near Victoria, where, due to a shortage of male students, one of her early parts was Mark Antony. In 1910 her teacher moved to Streatham and formed a band of Shakespeare Players, for whom the little milliner duly performed.

Two years later William Poel, the Shakespearean revivalist and worshipper of Elizabethan stagecraft, saw her playing Beatrice in *Much Ado About Nothing*. At once he launched her on a larger sea. Aged twenty-four, she was Cressida in Poel's production of *Troilus and Cressida* at the King's Hall, Covent Garden. Her Troilus was Esmé Percy, and, by a masterstroke of casting, the role of Cassandra, the prophetic witch, was entrusted to a gawky, plum-voiced young woman named Hermione Gingold. Shortly afterwards Edith Evans left the millinery establishment in Cheapside where she was working, and set up shop as an actress.

George Moore, who had seen and relished her Cressida, gave her a small part in a comedy of his which the Stage Society presented, but her professional voyaging really began in 1914, when she appeared in four plays at an average wage of fifty shillings a week. She performed for the troops in France, and in 1917 she attracted the attention of a legend. This was the sixty-nine-year-old Ellen Terry, with whom she toured the provincial music halls as Mrs. Ford in an excerpt from *The Merry Wives of Windsor* and as Nerissa in the trial scene from *The Merchant of Venice*.

But by 1921 she was still unknown to the public at large, a dismaying plight for an actress in her thirty-fourth year. The critics then started to prick up their ears; she played Lady Utterword in the first production of Shaw's *Heartbreak House*, and followed it with Cleopatra in Dryden's *All for Love*. Pens were now flowing purple in her praise, and of her next performance, in a forgotten drama called *I Serve*, James Agate said that it was 'the most finished piece of acting on the London stage today.' In 1922 she crossed the frontier into public acclaim and theatrical history with her flaunting portrait of Mrs. Millamant in *The Way of the World* at the Lyric, Hammersmith. This miracle of raillery, poise and wit has stayed in the minds of all who saw it. 'Edith Evans,' confided Arnold Bennett to his journal, 'gave the finest comedy performance I have ever seen on the stage.'

She now felt ready for Shakespeare on the grand scale, and tentatively wrote to Lilian Baylis at the Old Vic: 'Can I be of any use . . . ?' She could indeed. In her first season she played a dozen parts, lost seventeen pounds in weight and had one day free from rehearsal, which she put to good use by marrying a petroleum engineer named George Booth. That was in 1925: 'I can't tell you much about him,' she informed the press, 'because I don't know a great deal myself.' (Her husband, whose work kept him overseas for long periods, died ten years later.) That early Vic adventure broke down all her inhibitions and established her as a glittering classical performer, most memorably as the lovesick Rosalind of *As You Like It*. One of her colleagues, after a rehearsal, expressed his amazement that she never seemed to mind making a fool of herself. Exultantly, she replied: 'I haven't got time to mind.'

Since then her life has been an endless gallery of portraits in oil, interrupted only by two brief and disastrous excursions into actress-management. In 1929 she was Florence Nightingale in *The Lady with a Lamp*; next came the Malvern Festival, as Cedric Hardwicke's romping mistress in Shaw's *The Apple Cart*, a role she especially adored. 'On some nights,' she said, 'I feel that I could speak for ever. It comes like water from a fountain.' She visited Broadway, and revisited the Vic. As the declining *prima donna* in *Evensong* she had a clamorous commercial success, and her performance as Gwenny in *The Late Christopher Bean* was so profoundly Welsh that thousands of her admirers argued (and some argue still) that she must have been born west of the border. The mid-thirties were the time of her ripening; one recalls her wheezing, lumbering Nurse in *Romeo and Juliet*, and her macabre gipsy villainess in *The Old Ladies*. In 1938, aged fifty, she happily posed in the nude for the Russian sculptress Dora Gordine. The result, a statuette two feet high, enchanted her; posing, she declared, 'was far better than being psychoanalysed.' Her work, meanwhile, was always subject to rigid discipline: voice training every day, a long siesta every afternoon, and every weekend spent in peace at her farm in Kent.

Just before the war she found the role with which, perhaps, she is most closely associated: Lady Bracknell in *The Importance of Being Earnest*. She played this drawing-room dragon in a voice which had lorgnettes implicit in every dragged and devastating syllable.

War set her to some odd jobs. She tried her hand at intimate revue, helped to run the Garrison Theatre at Salisbury, and toured for the troops as far as India. In 1946 she took another crack at Shakespeare's Cleopatra, which she had first attempted twenty years before. It was not one of her triumphs. A comedienne of eagle eye, a mistress of pathos, she could not conquer the hard tragic heights. Disdain was as close as she could get to regality; she ruled the play as if it were a garden-party, not an Alexandrian orgy. She returned to her best form as the alarming, semi-alcoholic Lady Pitts in Bridie's *Daphne Laureola*, and kept it up in *Waters of the Moon*, where her every sentence shone like a string of giant emeralds. Most recently, as the compassionate countess in Christopher Fry's *The Dark Is Light Enough*, she used her genius to sweeten what many critics thought a pill of a part.

Three universities have honoured her with doctorates, and she has been created a Dame Commander of the British Empire. Her only other reward for a lifetime spent playing everything from *The Cherry Orchard* to *Bulldog Drummond* came last summer in the form of a physical breakdown, from which she has happily recovered.

Anecdotes about her are few and apocryphal, but it may not be impertinent to quote one which shows her in her best *grande dame* vein. When, with Dame Sybil Thorndike and Wendy Hiller also in the cast, *Waters of the Moon* had been running for a year, Dame Edith was at a celebration luncheon with her impresario, 'Binkie' Beaumont, who said that, by way of expressing his gratitude, he proposed to send her to Paris to be fitted for a completely new wardrobe by Pierre Balmain. Dame Edith glowed with pleasure, but had one stipulation to make. 'If I go to Paris,' she said, 'Sybil must have a new cardigan.'

'When I come on to the stage as Millamant,' she once declared, 'I assume without question that I am the most beautiful woman in town, and on the assumption of that consciousness I base all my behaviour.' This is the way of all great actresses. Few of them have been, by classical or any other standards, great beauties. Bernhardt looked piquant but ravaged, Rachel looked — it has been said — 'like a house on fire,' and Edwige Feuillère, in our own time, is frankly puddingy at close quarters. Dame Edith's face, if beauty is measured by symmetry, is tilted and slightly askew. Yet by her trick of total self-confidence she creates beauty in the eye of every beholder. It is a beauty before which many have knelt, among them Marlene Dietrich, who was so overcome by her performance in *The Dark Is Light Enough* that she confessed herself scared to enter Dame Edith's dressing-room. 'I was — overawed,' she said afterwards, and it takes a good deal to overawe Miss Dietrich.

Few actresses have power like this; and because of it a whole era of English acting is likely, in the histories of the theatre, to bear Dame Edith's name. She used to be a keen sailor, and once said that if she had her life to live over again there would be 'much more sea in it.' There could hardly be much more sea in her acting. It is a succession of tremendous waves, with white-caps of pure fun bursting above them. . . . But there I go again, making silly similes and proving, not for the first time, how impossible it is to capture in words the essence of a great actress.

Woman's Journal: January 1956

TENNESSEE WILLIAMS

In Spain, where I saw him last, he looked profoundly Spanish. He might have passed for one of those confidential street dealers who earn their living selling spurious Parker pens in the cafés of Málaga or Valencia. Like them, he wore a faded chalk-striped shirt, a coat slung over his shoulders, a trim, dark moustache and a sleazy, fat-cat smile. His walk, like theirs, was a raffish saunter, and everything about him seemed slept in, especially his hair, a nest of small, wet serpents. Had we been in Seville and his clothes been more formal, he could have been mistaken for a pampered elder son idling away a legacy in dribs and on drabs, the sort you see sitting in windows along the Sierpes, apparently stuffed. In Italy he looks Italian; in Greece, Greek; wherever he travels on the Mediterranean coast, Tennessee Williams takes on a protective colouring which melts him into his background, like a lizard on a rock. In New York or London he seems out of place, and is best explained away as a retired bandit. Or a beachcomber: shave the beard off any of the self-portraits Gaugin painted in Tahiti, soften the features a little, and you have a sleepy outcast face that might well be Tennessee's.

It is unmistakably the face of a nomad. Wherever Williams goes he is a stranger, one who lives out of suitcases and has a trick of making any home he acquires resemble, within ten minutes, a hotel apartment. Like most hypochondriacs, he is an uneasy guest on earth. When he sold the film rights of his play *Cat on a Hot Tin Roof* for half a million dollars, he asked that payment should be spread over ten years, partly out of prudence but mostly out of a mantic suspicion, buzzing in his ears, that in ten years' time he might be dead. He says justly of himself that he is 'a driven person.' The condemned tend always to be lonely, and one of Williams' favourite quotations is a line from a play which runs: 'We're all of us sentenced to solitary confinement inside our own skins.' He says such things quite blandly, with a thick chuckle which is as far from cynicism as it is from self-pity.

To be alone at forty is to be really alone, and Williams has passed forty. In a sense, of course, solitude is a condition of his trade. All writing is an anti-social act, since the writer is a man who can speak freely only when alone; to be himself he must lock himself up, to communicate he must cut himself off from all communication; and in this there is something always a little mad. Many writers loathe above all sounds the closing of the door which seals them up in their privacy. Williams, by contrast, welcomes it: it dispels the haze of uncertainty through which he normally converses, and releases for his pleasure the creatures who people his imaginings — desperate women, men nursing troublesome secrets, untouchables whom he touches with frankness and mercy, society's derelict rag dolls. The theatre, he once said, is a place where one has time for the problems of people to whom one would show the door if they came to one's office for a job. His best-loved characters are people like this, and they are all, in some way, trapped — Blanche DuBois, of *Streetcar*, beating her wings in a slum; Alma of *Summer and Smoke*, stricken with elephantiasis of the soul; Brick in *Cat*, sodden with remorse.

As we shall see, much of what has happened to them has also happened to him. He is the most personal of playwrights. Incomplete people obsess him — above all, those who, like himself, have ideals too large for life to accommodate. There is another, opposed kind of incompleteness, that of materialists like the Polack in *Streetcar* and Big Daddy in *Cat*; and in most of Williams' work both kinds are to be found, staring blankly at each other, arguing from different premises and conversing without comprehension. In his mental battlefield the real is perpetually at war with the ideal; what is public wrestles with what is private, with what drags men down fights what draws them up. This struggle is an allegory, by which I mean that it reflects a conflict within Williams himself. He cannot bring himself to believe that the flesh and the spirit can be reconciled, or to admit that the highest emotion can spring from the basest source. As Aldous Huxley has put it: 'Whether it's passion or the desire of the moth for the star, whether it's tenderness or adoration or romantic yearning — love is always accompanied by events in the nerve endings, the skin, the mucous membranes, the glandular and erectile tissue. . . . What we need is another set of words. Words that can express the natural togetherness of things.' For Williams they remain stubbornly apart, and it is this that gives his writing its odd urgency, its note of unfinished exploration. Alone behind the door, sustained by what one critic called the 'comradeship of his introspection,' he seeks to bridge the gap between his two selves. His work is a pilgrimage in search of a truce. His typewriter stands on the glass top of a hotel table, and most likely neither he nor it will be there tomorrow.

Though he does not need company, he does not shun it. Leaning back on a bar stool, one of a crowd, he can simulate ease with a barely perceptible effort. Mostly he is silent, sucking on a hygienic cigarette holder full of absorbent crystals, with a vague smile painted on his face, while his mind swats flies in outer space. He says nothing that is not candid and little that is not trite. A mental deafness seems to permeate him, so that he will laugh spasmodically in the wrong places, tell you the time if you ask him the date, or suddenly reopen conversations left for dead three days before. Late at night, part of him may come to life: in shreds of old slang ('We're in like Flynn') or bursts of old songs, remembered from St. Louis in the twenties and unexpectedly proceeding, in a voice at once true and blue, from his slumped figure, which you had thought slumbering, in the back seat of somebody else's car. This is Williams on holiday, and you may be sure that his mind is not far from a blank.

He longs for intimacy, but shrinks from its responsibilities. Somewhere in the past, before he became famous, lies the one perfect passion; its object parted from him and afterwards died of cancer. Since then, too cautious to spoil perfection by trying to repeat it, he has kept all emotional relationships deliberately casual. He will incur no more emotional debts, nor extend any more emotional credit. His friendships are many and generous, ranging from Mediterranean remittance men to Carson McCullers; but love is a sickness which he will do anything to avoid. If his deeper instincts crave release, you may find him at a bullfight — or even writing a play.

He was born forty-four years ago in Columbus, Mississippi, the son of an itinerant shoe salesman known throughout the territory as a fiery and accomplished poker player. As a child he lived in Columbus with his mother, his elder sister, and his younger brother at the home of his maternal grandfather, a highly respected Episcopal rector. Here an image took root which has haunted much of his work: the South as a fading mansion of gentility. The first great wrench of his life occurred when he was still very young. His father took a desk job in St. Louis and the family left Columbus to join him. 'We suddenly discovered,' Williams says, 'that there were two kinds of people, the rich and the poor, and that we belonged more to the latter.' It was here, in a stuffy, back-street apartment, that his world split, amoeba-like, into two irreconcilable halves — the soft, feminine world of the room that he and his sister filled with little glass animals, and the cruel, male world of the alley outside, where cats fought and coupled to a persistent screaming. He entered the University of Missouri and at the age of sixteen got a story into *Weird Tales*, but the depression sent him to work for three memorably detested years in a shoe factory. The result was a heart attack, followed by a complete physical breakdown. He returned to his studies and in 1938 took a BA at the University of Iowa. By now his imagination was alive with human voices, and two of his plays had been performed by the St. Louis Mummers. The future offered by his father meant going back to the shoe factory. Subjecting his life to its second great wrench, he left home.

'And it don't look like I'm ever gonna cease my wanderin'. . . He waited on table in New Orleans and worked on a pigeon ranch in California; then a one-act play won him a prize of a hundred dollars and attracted the attention of a Broadway agent, Audrey Wood. He sent her the script of *Battle of Angels*, an ambitious survey of 'the sometimes conflicting desires of the flesh and the spirit.' To his amazement, the Theatre Guild bought it. It opened in Boston in December 1940 and closed without reaching New York. On top of that, and perhaps because of it, Williams developed a cataract in his left eye. The next two years found him a vulnerable and myopic vagabond in Bohemia, always the victim of a hectic nervous system, which alarmed him by expressing its disquiet as often in illness as in imaginative visions. Back to New Orleans, living from pawnshop to mouth; then to Greenwich Village, where he worked as a waiter, wearing a black eye patch which someone adorned with a surrealistic white eyeball.

In 1943 Audrey Wood got him a six-month contract in Hollywood. He spent most of it writing *The Glass Menagerie*, in which his twin worlds of fact and dream came out for the first time distinct and dovetailed. Its Broadway success a year later gave him security: but 'security,' he was soon writing, 'is a kind of death. . . .' To escape it he returned to New Orleans, to cheap hotels and rented apartments. On a trip to Taos, New Mexico, he came down with what proved to be a ruptured appendix; but he heard a nun whisper that it might be cancer, and, spurred by the death sentence, he fled from the hospital. Feverishly he composed what was meant to be his last message to the world.

A new friendship helped him to obey Hemingway's dictum and 'get it out whole.' This was with Carson McCullers. In his own words: 'Carson came to me in the summer of 1946 at the height of my imaginary dying, she came to Nantucket Island, which I had chosen to die on, and the moment she came down the gangplank of the ship from the mainland, in her baseball cap, with that enchantingly radiant crooked-toothed grin of hers, something very light happened in me. I dropped my preoccupation with the thought that I was doomed, and from then on there was a process of adjustment to the new situation, and by the late fall of 1947 I was able to release all the emotional content of the long crisis in *Streetcar*.' The play was produced in the same year and fully deserves Williams' description of it: 'saturated with death.'

More studies in desperation followed: *Summer and Smoke* and *The Rose Tattoo*, perhaps the fullest expression of Williams' special kind of romanticism, which is not pale or scented but earthy and robust, the product of a mind vitally infected with the rhythms of human speech. When overheated, however, it can give off lurid fumes, some of which clouded the air in his next play, *Camino Real*. This was Williams' gaudiest rebellion against materialism, conceived in terms of symbols and carried out mainly in italics. Directed by Elia Kazan in the spring of 1953, the play flopped. There ensued one of those low-energy spells from which Williams frequently suffers. Work became a depressant instead of a stimulant; he kept losing sight of the impulse that sent him to the typewriter and felt that his ideas were being smirched and dog-eared by the well-meaning interference of agents, producers and directors. *Cat on a Hot Tin Roof* was eighteen months in the writing. I now think it his best work, but when I first saw it, it struck me as an edifice somehow tilted, like a giant architectural folly. It was august, all right, and turbulent, but there were moments of unaccountable wrongness, as if a kazoo had intruded into a string quartet. When I saw the published text and read, side by side, the original third act and the version that was presented on Broadway, I guessed at once what had happened. The kazoo was Kazan.

Cat is a birthday party about death. The birthday is that of Big Daddy, a southern millionaire dying of cancer. His son Brick is a quiet, defeated drinker; and the cat of the title is Maggie, Brick's wife, whose frayed vivacity derives from the fact that she is sexually ignored by her husband. The play deals with the emotional lies that are shockingly exposed as people try to 'reach' each other, to penetrate the inviolable cell in which the soul lives. Williams' trade-marks are all there: the spectre of disease, the imminence of death, the cheating implicit in all emotion, the guilt bound up with sex — plus the technical ability to make tragic characters immeasurably funny. But a play might have all these things and still be bad; what distinguishes *Cat* is the texture of its writing. This is dialogue dead to the eyes alone. It begs for speech so shrilly that you find yourself reading it aloud. 'When you are gone from here,' says Big Daddy, 'you are long gone and no where!' — the words fall from the tongue like 'snow from a bamboo leaf,' the image by which Zen Buddhists teach their pupils that 'artless art' which is the goal of contemplation.

But Kazan was not satisfied. He felt that Brick should undergo a change of heart after the showdown with his father; and into Brick's lines a certain hollowness began to creep. In a stage direction Williams had spoken of 'the thundercloud of a common crisis'; with stupefying literalness, Kazan introduced a full-tilt symbolic thunderstorm. Maggie's big lie, uttered to win Big Daddy's inheritance, originally ran: 'Brick and I are going to have a child.' Inflated by Kazan, the line became: 'A child is coming, sired by Brick and out of Maggie the Cat!' The bitterness of the final tableau, when Brick prepares to sleep with Maggie to sustain her lie, was sweetened until the scene seemed to betoken a lasting reconciliation. Williams in no way resents these adjustments, which, he says, 'did not violate the essential truth of the play.' For him Kazan is 'a very big man, the biggest artist in the theatre of our time.' He is at present working on a film script, which Kazan will direct; but some of his admirers feel that a less creative collaborator might, in the long run, be more helpful.

Discussing the incidence of genius, Somerset Maugham once remarked: 'The lesson of anatomy applies: there is nothing so rare as the normal.' Williams' view of life is always abnormal, heightened and spotlighted and slashed with bogy shadows. The marvel is that he makes it touch ours, thereby achieving the miracle of communication between human beings which he has always held to be impossible.

Yet he looks anonymous. One ends, as one began, with the enigma. Arthur Miller, after all, looks Lincolnesque, and Anouilh looks hypersensitive, and Sartre looks crazy. Williams, alone of the big playwrights, seems miscast. From that round, rubbery face, those dazed eyes which nothing, no excess or enormity, can surprise — from here the message comes, the latest bulletin from the civil war between purity and squalour. It will always, however long or well I know him, seem wonderfully strange.

Mademoiselle: February 1956; *Curtains*, 1961

BERNARD SHAW

He is six years dead, and the old saw holds truer than ever: nobody who did not know Shaw personally ever loved him. The Memorial Fund in his honour aimed at £250,000: it received £407. One doubts if Shaw would have cared. He was the Bradman of letters: he scored all round the wicket off all kinds of ideological bowling; he hit centuries off all causes and men that were idle or unrealistic; but though he took great pains to command respect, he took none at all to inspire affection.

In most writers, style is a welcome, an invitation, a letting down of the drawbridge between the artist and the world. Shaw had no time for such ruses. Unlike most of his countrymen, he abominated charm, which he regarded as evidence of chronic temperamental weakness. (Much the same is true of Swift, who likewise despised emotional cheating: and both men, by coincidence, found an outlet for their repressed feelings by using baby-talk in letters to women named Stella.) We may admire Shaw, but, in public at least, he will not allow us to embrace him.

He praises little except at something else's expense. What spurred him was his capacity for being outraged. Righteous indignation at the follies of mankind infallibly roused his adrenal glands: the more indignant he became, the more he rejoiced; and the more he rejoiced, the more brilliant he became. But human folly was always the key to his treasures. 'Fifty million Frenchmen,' he once said, 'can't be right.'

Whatever the majority believed, Shaw derided; whatever it rejected, he applauded. At a time when most people assumed that arms manufacturers were cynical profiteers, Shaw gave them Undershaft, an arms manufacturer who was also a radical philosopher; and revolutionaries, in Shavian plays, usually turn out to be capitalist at heart. Whenever he found that he had fifty million people behind him, he would abruptly change sides and denounce his supporters as servile dupes. He did this more and more in his later years, when many of the causes he championed had been won. Hating to be one of a crowd, he would deliberately isolate himself by defending dictatorship and condoning, in the preface to *Geneva*, the extermination of minorities.

The only lyrical thing about Shaw is his fury: his attacks on Irving and Shakespeare are prose poems of Olympian invective. His style on such occasions flashes like a scythe. It is when he goes in for affirmations that he makes us qualmish. His vision of the future, in *Back to Methuselah*, is frankly repellent: creative evolution, he enthusiastically predicts, will produce a race of oviparous Struldbruggs who live for ever and whose only joy is pure cerebration.

As a private citizen, he loved the arts, but as a public playwright, he could not create an artist. Dubedat is a parasite, and Marchbanks a hollow fraud — Shaw could not conceal his impatience with them. His puritan, muscular, moor-tramping soul (superbly mirrored in Higgins's hymn to the intellect in *Pygmalion*) bred in him a loathing of all things, whether poems or gadgets, that were designed to comfort the human condition without actively trying to improve it. 'Think and work' was his only positive advice. It is a doctrine often heard from the mouths of those who are scared to feel.

Yet he was without doubt a great writer, greater than many whose emotional range was far wider and deeper than his. In the years of his maturity — between 1895, when he wrote his first piece of drama criticism for *The Saturday Review*, and 1919, when *Heartbreak House* was published — he attempted, and almost pulled off, two mountainous tasks: he cleared the English stage of humbug, and the English mind of cant. (They both returned later, but as guests, not as residents.) As a demolition expert he has no rivals, and we are being grossly irrelevant if we ask a demolition expert, when his work is done: 'But what have you created?' It is like expecting a bulldozer to build the Tower of Pisa, or condemning a bayonet for not being a plough. Shaw's genius was for intellectual slum-clearance, not for town planning. As far as modern society is concerned, he came to scoff, and remained to scoff.

We sit through his plays unshocked by most of what he meant to be shocking, embarrassed by his efforts to make us exclaim 'Whatever next!' but continuously diverted by the sheer mad Irishness of the man: by his crazy irrelevancies, his sudden interpolations of surrealism — as when, in *Misalliance*, a young assassin hides in a portable Turkish bath from which he emerges to declare: 'I am the son of Lucinda Titmus.' Shaw's sanity nowadays tends to be tiresome. His lunacy will always be irresistible.

But does he ever move us? Only once, I think: with the speech in which St. Joan reminds herself that 'God is alone.' That came from Shaw's heart, and goes straight to ours. Otherwise, if Chaucer is the father of English literature, Shaw is the spinster aunt. By this I do not mean to imply that he was sexless: St. John Ervine's new biography, if it does nothing else, should squash that myth for ever. It is only in his writing that the aunt in him rises up, full of warnings, wagged fingers and brandished umbrellas. How many of his letters contain phrases like: 'It is no good your trying to excuse your infamous conduct . . .'!

This is the true auntly note, and the psychiatrists may not be wrong when they describe it as filial revenge. Shaw's mother, a cold woman, ignored and neglected him; and he was bent on outdoing her in indifference to the common code of human sympathy; on proving that his heartlessness could exceed even hers. As a man, he was often generous and compassionate. As a writer, the chill sets in. You thought *that* was cruel and clinical? he seems to be saying; just wait till you hear *this* — it will show you that I love you all even less than you ever suspected.

Shaw was unique. An Irish aunt so gorgeously drunk with wit is something English literature will never see again. But there is fruit for the symbolist in the fact that, prolific as he was, he left no children.

Observer: 22nd July 1956; *Curtains*, 1961

GORDON CRAIG

I went to see Gordon Craig partly because he is among the last of the great Edwardians and partly because a blue-haired and brilliant American authoress had spent several hours exhorting me with considerable violence to meet the ageing giants of art while yet they lived. 'Don't just read their books,' she had said. 'That's like just eating the meat of the lobster. Be a gourmet; go to the head and suck the brains. There's tasty chewing there!' Spurred by this daunting advice, I drove up from Nice one Sunday this midsummer to talk to a man who was born in the same year as Aubrey Beardsley.

Although he is eighty-four years old and has published little for a quarter of a century, Gordon Craig is still several lengths ahead of the theatrical avant-garde. Ideas that he expounded fifty years ago, in his breathless prophetic prose, are nowadays bearing fruit all over Europe. He anticipated Bert Brecht when he said of actors: 'Today they *impersonate* and interpret; to-morrow they must *represent* and interpret. . . .' His notion that true drama was a one-man responsibility, in which words, direction, decor, lighting and music should all proceed from the same organising brain, once seemed a fatuous vanity; yet last year Peter Brook, directing *Titus Andronicus*, undertook all these tasks save that of writing the play. Nor would Craig hold this omission against him, since he regards the hegemony of the writer as the supreme tragedy of theatrical history: literary men, he says, are intruders, despoilers of the purity of theatre as a separate art. Dismissed as a crank, he none the less brought modern staging to birth with his productions, a memorable few which include *Hamlet* at the Moscow Art Theatre and Eleanora Duse in *Rosmersholm*. If today we call 'stage-managers' directors and 'scene-painters' designers, it is largely Craig's doing.

He last saw England in 1929, when C. B. Cochran invited him to take on a new production of his own choice. There was a dispute over expenditure, after which Craig left the country in a permanent huff. He lived in France until the Nazis arrived and shut him up in an internment camp. A few months later a German intelligence officer, asking for one of his books at a Paris store, learned from the assistant that its author was imprisoned; shocked, he contrived to have Craig released. For the rest of the war the old theorist worked unmolested in his Paris studio. He now occupies a single cluttered room in a modest *pension de famille* at Vence, high in the hills that overlook Nice. Here, last spring, he learned that a tardily grateful nation had created him a Companion of Honour. He was flattered, but at the same time embarrassed, because he could not afford to come to London and be royally congratulated. His only regular income derives from investments made by his mother, Ellen Terry. It amounts to just over £6 a week.

I arrived in fear of finding a testy sage steeped in pathos and embittered by neglect. As soon as the car drew up in front of the *pension* I knew my error. The figure that greeted me was surely bowed, and slightly crumpled; but what it exuded was neither pathos nor rancour, but mischief. You might have taken him for the oldest truant schoolboy alive — or, more extravagantly, for an indomitable old lady who had just, by some constitutional fantasy, been elected President of the French Republic. He wore a snuff tweed suit with six pens clipped to the breast pocket, a neat cream stock around his neck, a shawl-like garment draped across his shoulders, and a broad-brimmed hat on top of wild white curls.

He clambered into the car, crowing with conspiratorial glee, and told the driver to take us down to a nearby inn for lunch. *'Prenez garde!'* he cried as we moved off, 'Bad corner! Hoot, hoot!' Grinning wickedly and waving his mottled, curry-coloured hands, he began to talk in a voice of such vagrant music that I found myself listening as much to its cadences as to its meaning. He peeped at me from time to time across a nose as sharp as a quill. I was already reassured. There was no bitterness here: only resilience, magnanimity and a great appetite for joy.

'You have the right face for a critic,' he said as we disembarked. 'You have the look of a blooming martyr.' Having ordered the meal in genial and execrable French, he opened the briefcase he was carrying: it contained two razor-edged knives, in case the management had been slack in sharpening its cutlery. We were talking vaguely about Edward Lear when Craig whisked me back eighty years in a single sentence 'One day,' he said, 'when I was very small, that man Charles Dodgson came to tea. Tried to divert me with a puzzle about ferrying six cows across a river on a raft. Very tiresome . . .'

Trowelling sauce-drenched food ('I hate a dry plate') into his mouth, the almost toothless lion avidly reminisced. Irving was the greatest director he had ever known, and as an actor: 'We've had no one so *dangerously* good.' The Terrys, he said, were always a slapdash sort of family: the Irvings were precision instruments. Granville-Barker was 'a small man among giants' — this in a whisper, with a finger wagged for secrecy, as if Barker himself might spectrally be eavesdropping on the conversation. 'Rather an affected man,' said Craig, securely merry and patriarchal.

Far from being pent up in the past, Craig keeps in touch with every new development in theatre, cinema and even television. He was soon urging me to see the new French underwater documentary, *Le Monde du Silence*: 'It's like nothing you've ever dreamed of. Or, rather, it's like *everything* you've ever dreamed of.' He showed a keen interest in 'this fellow Orson Well-ess,' of whose films he had heard much. 'I'll tell you a thing about Well-ess,' he said. 'A Paris paper published an interview with him in which he said that one day he was standing in the American Express in Paris when the door *flew* open to reveal a cloaked figure in a funny hat. *Me!* He threw himself to the ground in veneration. I gathered him up and took him to my studio and spent six months teaching him the art of the theatre.' Craig was now shaking with glee. 'Magnificent, isn't it? *Because I've never met the fellow in my life!*' He nudged me and we rocked.

After lunch he conducted me on foot round the baked medieval village of Tourrette, leading the way in his rangy shuffle and talking of his memoirs, extracts from which are to be published in the autumn under the title *Index to the Story of My Days*. He spoke glowingly of Picasso ('Those eyes!' he said, stabbing two fingers at me like prongs), and gaily of his own poverty: 'I'm as poor as a fish!'

He has a collection of theatrical souvenirs — books, prints, letters and designs — which is worth around £20,000. So far he has rejected all offers for it, mostly because he suspects the buyers of planning to break up the collection and resell it piecemeal. 'A few years ago,' he confided, 'an American made a handsome bid. But I knew as soon as we started to talk business that he wasn't quite the man. He said to me: "Please sit down, Mr. Craig." And I said: "It's *my* room — *you* sit down!" Not quite the fellow, you see. . . .' I reflected that it would be a generous thing if the Arts Council were to purchase his treasures; and the sooner the better. 'I count my life in days now, not in years or months or even weeks.'

Back in the *pension*, he led me up to the dark little room where he sleeps and works. Masks of his own carving hung on the walls (there is more than a touch in him of William Morris); day-books and journals were piled on the floor; implements for painting and writing littered the tables. On a shelf beside the brass bedstead stood a cork into which was stuck a photograph of a composed and glowing beauty: 'My mother,' said Craig. He talked, as he pottered, of his plans for the future. He is making a collection of English farces of the last century; 'and,' he said, 'I'm beginning to solve the problem of staging the cauldron scene in *Macbeth*. I'm not certain yet, mind you, but it's getting clearer every day. . . .' Suddenly: 'Did you ever think that Shakespeare had a cat? Look at the sonnets. Most of them aren't written to a woman or a boy. They're addressed to a *cat*.'

But there was one thing he especially wanted to show me, and he flipped through his scrapbooks to find it. He raced past priceless letters from Irving and Stanislavsky until: 'There!' he said. Following his finger, I stared at an advertisement, cut out of an American magazine, for stainless steel. 'Stainless steel!' he cried. 'There's something serious there!' I pictured towering settings of steel taking shape in that restless, hungry mind. From one of his journals, volume after volume of fastidious, spidery script, there floated to the floor a newspaper cutting. I picked it up. Its headline ran: '£105m. for New Schools.' In the margin was an annotation in Craig's hand: 'Why not educate by the stage?' Seeing that I had read it, he laughed joyously. 'We only need five millions for our theatre,' he said, 'but they'll never let us have it. Never.'

I took my leave exhausted, though he was not. He explained that he had much to do: there were some new ideas about *The Tempest* that needed his attention. As I drove away, he waved, winked and loped back to his den. The theatre is not yet ripe for Gordon Craig. Perhaps, indeed, it will never be. But meanwhile, at Vence, work is still in progress. When the theatrical millennium arrives, he will be its first harbinger and surest witness.

Observer: 29th July 1956; *Curtains*, 1961

BEATRICE LILLIE

Debrett's Peerage, a thick, comely, and infallible volume, correctly refers to Beatrice Gladys Lillie by her married name, Lady Peel. *Who's Who in the Theatre* is also thick and comely, but it is not quite infallible, and one of the most fallible things about it is its habit, in edition after edition, of describing Miss Lillie as an 'actress.' Technically, I suppose the blunder might be defended, since she has been known to impinge on the legitimate stage; in 1921 she appeared in *Up in Mabel's Room* and eleven years later played the Nurse in Shaw's *Too True to Be Good*. But these were transient whims. To call her an actress first and foremost is rather like calling Winston Churchill a bricklayer who has dabbled in politics. If acting means sinking your own personality into somebody else's, Beatrice Lillie has never acted in her life. There may be some mechanical means of disguising that true and tinny voice, or of suppressing that cockeyed nonchalance; but the means might very well involve the use of masks and gags, and the end would not be worth it. She would never be much good at impersonation. One of her recurrent delusions is that she is a mistress of dialects, but in fact the only one she has really mastered is her own brand of Berkeley Square Canadian; and she can hardly open a door on stage without squaring up to the operation as if she were about to burgle a safe.

To some extent, an actress can be judged by measuring her performance against the character she is meant to be playing; but there is nothing against which to measure Miss Lillie. She is *sui generis*. She resembles nothing that ever was, and to see her is to experience, every time, the simple joy of discovery that might come to an astronomer who observed, one maddened night, a new and disorderly comet shooting backward across the firmament. But if she is not an actress, no more is she a parodist, as some of her fans insist; she parodies nothing and no one except herself. Nor does she belong in the main stream of North American female comics. Almost without exception, American comediennes get their laughs by pretending to be pop-eyed, man-hunting spinsters. Miss Lillie is as far removed from these as a butterfly is from a guided missile. The miracle is that this non-acting non-satirist has managed to become the most achingly funny woman on earth.

Twentieth-century show business has a small and incomparable élite: the streamlined international entertainers of the twenties and thirties. Noël

Coward, Gertrude Lawrence, Maurice Chevalier, Alfred Lunt and Lynn Fontanne were among the founder-members of this shining and exclusive gang. Miss Lillie is the Commonwealth representative. She was born fifty-eight years ago in Toronto, the second daughter of John Lillie, a volatile Irish schoolmaster who had served in the British Army under Kitchener. The first recorded event in her life was her summary ejection, at the age of eight, from the choir of the local Presbyterian church. It seems she upset the congregation by pulling faces during the hymns. Both her father, who died in 1933, and her mother, who lives in a Thames-side house near London, achieved an early and lasting tolerance of their child's eccentricities. Sensing that she had something to express, but not knowing exactly what it was, they sent her to a man named Harry Rich — of whom nothing else is known — for lessons in gesture. She loathed the lessons, but they stuck, and many of the odder poses in which she nowadays finds herself are directly attributable to Mr. Rich.

At fifteen she left school and embarked with her mother and sister for England, with the idea of becoming a child soprano. Her official repertoire included such ballads as 'I Hear You Calling Me' and 'Until,' but secretly she and her sister Muriel were rehearsing something a little wilder, entitled 'The Next Horse I Ride On I'm Going to Be Tied On.' This clandestine seed was later to bear lunatic fruit; for the moment, however, it got nowhere.

Her career as a straight singer languished until the summer of 1914, when she was engaged for a week at the Chatham Music Hall on the outskirts of London. Here she sang Irving Berlin's 'When I Lost You,' and the audience reaction indicated that she had lost them for good. Without much hope, she attended an audition held by the Anglo-French impresario André Charlot. Idly, she guyed a serious romantic number, smiled wanly, and was about to leave the theatre when Charlot, in a state verging on apoplexy, seized her arm and offered her forty-two dollars a week to appear in his next revue, *Not Likely!* She accepted, and soon the panic was on. Charlot adored and fostered the madness of her method, constantly giving her bigger spots, and it was under his banner that she made her triumphant Broadway debut in *Charlot's Revue of 1924*.

Around this time she had her hair cut off, for reasons that may give some hint of the devious way her mind works. With Michael Arlen, H. G. Wells, Frederick Lonsdale, and Lonsdale's two daughters, she was cruising on Lord Beaverbrook's yacht. The Lonsdale girls were close-cropped, and Miss Lillie, who favoured plaits, was powerfully impressed by the advantages of short hair for swimming. Back in London she ordered her coiffeur to give her what would now be known as a brush cut. Only when he had finished did it occur to her that there was more to life than swimming. For a while she wore false plaits attached to her ears by rubber bands. One day the elastic snapped, and she has remained, ever since, cropped for immersion. Nowadays she hides her hair beneath a bright pink fez. There is no good reason for this either. It is just one *idée fixe* on top of another.

Meanwhile, she had fallen in love. In 1920 Robert Peel, a young and toweringly handsome great-grandson of Sir Robert Peel, resigned his commission in the Guards and married Charlot's zany soubrette. They spent a raffish honeymoon at Monte Carlo, winning $25,000 at the tables a few hours after arriving and losing $30,000 a few hours before departing. In 1925 Robert's father, the fourth baronet, died, and Miss Lillie became Lady Peel. Her husband, a man of devouring energies, was at various times a sheep farmer in Australia and a race-horse owner in England. During the slump he generously formed an orchestra of unemployed miners and toured the country with it, often losing as much as £500 a week. He died in 1934, leaving one son. Eight years later the young Sir Robert, who had just passed his twenty-first birthday, was killed when the British destroyer *Hermes* was sunk by Japanese dive bombers n the Indian Ocean. His mother received the news in a Manchester dressing room, where she was putting on make-up to appear in a new Cochran revue. It is one of the paradoxes of the theatre that though every actor's ambition is to stop the show, his instructions are that it must go on. The revue went on that night with Miss Lillie clowning on schedule and wishing herself ten thousand miles away. Thereafter an inner withdrawal took place; since her son's death she has entered into no binding personal relationships with anyone.

In forty years on the stage she has been seen in nearly forty shows, many of them bearing prankish, exclamatory titles like *Cheep!* and *Oh! Joy!* and most of them remembered chiefly for her part in them. Apart from the war years, when she sang for the troops in the Mediterranean area, she has seldom been far away from the big money. The movies have intermittently attracted her, but, like Coward and the Lunts, she has never thought of depending on them for a living. Pre-war residents of Hollywood remember her vividly, swinging an enormous handbag within which there rattled a motley haul of jewellery known as 'The Peel Poils.' For a talent so deeply spontaneous, the stage was always the best place. In New York, just before the war, she was paid $8,000 for a week at the Palace, and today one imagines even Las Vegas baulking at her cabaret fee.

Her title sits drolly on her, like a tiara on an emu. and for a certain kind of audience there is an irresistible savour in the spectacle of a baronet's wife shuffling off to Buffalo. There have, however, been moments of embarrassment. In 1936, billed as Lady Peel, Miss Lillie appeared in an Ohio city and rashly chose as her opening number a travesty of a suburban snob. 'Ladies and gentlemen,' she began, 'I'm sure you will appreciate what a comedown this is for me — me that's always 'ad me own 'orses. . . .' Few acts can have fallen flatter. Many women in the house began to sniff audibly, and at the end of the monologue, according to Miss Lillie, some attempt was made to take a collection to sustain her in her fight against poverty.

Offstage she leads a fairly intense social life, and has arguably slept through more hours of daylight than of dark. Her conversation is an unpunctuated flow of irrelevancies which only acute ears can render into sense. As a maker of epigrams her rating is low. It is rumoured that she once said of a tactless friend that 'he doesn't know the difference between tongue-in-cheek and foot-in-mouth,' but remarks like that need a degree of premeditation to which she is a stranger. She excels as the casual impromptu, as when a pigeon flew in at the window of her apartment and she, looking up, briskly enquired: 'Any messages?' To surprise her friends, she will go to considerable lengths. Her last Christmas present to Noël Coward was a baby alligator, to whose neck she attached a label reading: 'So what else is new?' Last year she stood for several hours on a draughty street corner in Liverpool in order to wave maniacally at the Duke of Edinburgh as he drove by with the Queen. She received from the carriage a royal double-take, which she regarded as ample compensation. At parties, with a little pressing, she will try out her newest hallucinations, nursery rhymes villainously revamped or bizarre attempts at mimicry; I once saw her spread-eagled on top of an upright piano, pretending to be Marilyn Monroe.

Some of her leisure time is spent painting, a difficult art for which she has evolved impossible working habits. 'I do children's heads out of my nut,' she told an interviewer. 'I paint on the floor and show my work on the piano in the dark. I call myself Beatrice Van Gone.' She habitually uses as canvasses the cardboard lids of laundry boxes. One of her sitters was the child actor Brandon de Wilde. He is also one of her closest confidants. Whenever Miss Lillie is in New York, she calls up Brandon and the two journey to Coney Island, where they frequently end up in the Tunnel of Love. A radio commentator once asked Brandon what Miss Lillie did in the tunnel. 'It's very dark in there,' the child explained, as to a child, 'so naturally she doesn't do anything.' De Wilde's ingenuous imagination appeals strongly to Miss Lillie, who has a great deal of urchin in her and very little *grande dame*. She also has the kind of knockdown spontaneity that one associates with Zen masters, together with something much more mysterious — that ambiguous, asexual look that so often recurs among the greatest performers.

Her last show, *An Evening with Beatrice Lillie*, took three quarters of a million dollars at the Broadway box office three seasons ago, and then ran for eight successful months in Britain. It enshrined her art in what seems likely to be its final form. The rebuke to Maud for her rottenness, the lament about wind round my heart — they were all there, presented with a relaxed finesse that astonished even her oldest eulogists. She looked like

Peter Pan as Saul Steinberg might sketch him, and the only phrase for her face was one that a French critic used many years ago to describe Réjane — *'une petite frimousse éveillée,'* which means, in James Agate's rough translation, 'a wide-awake little mug.' A supreme economy distinguished all she did. By twirling four Oriental fingers, she could imply a whole handspring, and instead of underlining her gags in red pencil she could bring down the house with a marginal tick. For any line that struck her as touching on the sentimental she would provide a withering facial comment, as if to say (the expression is one of her pets): 'Get *me!*' She would survey the audience with wintry amazement, until it began to wonder why it had come; she would then overwhelm it with some monstrous act of madness, such as wearing an osprey feather fan as a hat, banging her head against the proscenium arch, or impersonating Pavlova and a roller-skating bear, one after the other, in a sketch bearing no relation either to ballet or zoology.

Once, in an effort at self-analysis, she said: 'I guess it's my nose that makes them laugh,' but the explanation is as perfunctory as the nose. One thing is certain: she wrecks the old theory that all great clowns have a breaking heart. Miss Lillie has no more pathos than Ohrbach's basement. Nothing on stage seems to her tragic, though many things arouse in her a sort of cool curiosity. If a ton of scenery were to fall at her feet, she would regard the débris with interest, but not with dismay; after a light shrug and a piercing little smile, she would go on with whatever she was doing. (In wartime this insouciance was a rare asset. Quentin Reynolds, who was often her companion during the blitz, testifies that in the midst of the bombing her demeanour was positively sunny.) She reminds one of a bony, tomboyish little girl attending what, if her behaviour does not improve, will surely be her last party. Her attitude toward events, if she has one, might be summed up in the comment: 'Hmmmm . . .'

I have two theories about her: one about what she does, and another about the way she does it. What she has been doing for the last forty years is conducting guerrilla warfare against words as a means of communication. Having no message to convey, she has no need of language as most of us understand it, so she either abandons words altogether or presents them in combinations aberrant enough to crack a ouija board. Faced with the drab possibility of consecutive thought, she draws herself up to her full lunacy. She will do anything to avoid making sense — lapse into a clog dance, trap her foot under an armchair, or wordlessly subside beneath the weight of a mink coat.

Mime attracts her as an alternative to words. This imperial urchin can let winsome candour, beady-eyed tartness, and appalled confusion chase each other across her face in a matter seconds. Consider the frosty, appraising regard she bestows on the waistcoat of the huge baritone who suddenly interrupts her act to sing 'Come into the Garden, Maud' straight down her throat. Though she takes an early opportunity to seize a chair in self-defence, she betrays none of her apprehension in words.

The traditional comic formula is: Tell them what you're going to do; do it; then tell them you've done it. Miss Lillie's is: tell them what you might do; do something else; then deny having done it. Even the famous purchase of the double-damask dinner napkins embodies her basic theme: the utter futility of the English language. Nobody is a more devout anthologist of the whimpers, sighs, and twitters than the human race emits in its historic struggle against intelligibility. It is not surprising that she turns to French when delivering her demented salute to the home life of cats: '*Bonjour*, all the little kittens all over the world!' When someone in another number fails to understand a question, she tries German, brusquely demanding: '*Sprechen Sie Deutsch?*' And once, into a Cockney sketch already obscured by her inability to speak Cockney, she inserted a sudden moan of Italian. If ever a monument is erected to her, it should be modelled on the Tower of Babel. She is like Eliza Doolittle at Mrs. Higgins' tea party in *Pygmalion*, using what seems to her perfectly acceptable verbal coinage but to everyone else counterfeit gibberish. In certain moods she becomes quite convinced that she is an authority on bird talk. Coward once wrote for her a comic folk song that contained the line: 'And the robin sings ho! on the bough.' Every time she reached it she would pause. 'The robin,' she would firmly declare, 'does *not* say ho.'

In 1954, on a trip to Japan, she visited the Kabuki Theatre and was fascinated by what she saw: the colour, the weirdness, and the elaborate stylization. The idea of using Kabuki technique in a sketch at once took hold of her mind, and she was not in the least perturbed when someone pointed out that British audiences (for whom the sketch was intended) might be slightly befuddled by a parody of something they had never seen. Following instinct, she devised a number called 'Kabuki Lil.' When it was still in the formative stage, by which I mean a condition of nightmarish inconsequence, she described it to me:

'These Kabuki plays, you see, they go on for six months with only one intermission. All the women are men, *of course*, and they're simply furious most of the time, waving swords round their heads and *hissing* at each other. They take off their boots when they come on, and kneel down on cushions. There's a lot of work done with cushions, so I shall have cushions too. And they play some kind of musical instrument that goes right round the back of my neck, only one string, but I expect I shall manage. I don't think I shall say a word of English — after all, *they* don't — but I wish I could get hold of one of those terrific rostrums they have in Tokyo that sail right down the aisle and out of the theatre. I think they have rollers underneath them, or perhaps it's men? Anyway, I think I've got the spirit of the thing. . . .'

Something was dimly taking shape in the chaos of her mind, but what emerged on stage was beyond all imagining. It varied notably from night to night, but the general layout remained the same. Miss Lillie shuffled on attired as a geisha, with a knitting needle through her wig and a papoose strapped to her back. After performing some cryptic act of obeisance, she sat cross-legged on a pile of cushions. Thereafter, for about ten minutes, she mewed like an asthmatic sea gull: the sketch contained not one recognizable word. Tea was served at one point, and the star produced from her sleeve a tiny bottle of Gordon's gin with which to spike it. From time to time she would grasp a hammer and savagely bang a gong, whereupon music would sound, jittery and Oriental. This seemed to placate her; until the sixth bang, which evoked from the wings a sudden, deafening amplified blast of 'Three Coins in the Fountain,' sung by Frank Sinatra.

It was while watching this sketch, so pointless, yet so hysterical, that I hit on the clue to her method. I reveal it without hesitation, because I do not believe that anyone could copy it. The key to Beatrice Lillie's success is that she ignores her audience. This is an act of daring that amounts to revolution. Maurice Chevalier was speaking for most of his profession when he said in his autobiography: 'An artist carries on throughout his life a mysterious, uninterrupted conversation with his public.' To get into contact with the dark blur of faces out front is the Holy Grail of every personality performer except Miss Lillie, who converses not with her public but with herself. Belly laughter, for which most comedians sweat out their life's blood, only disconcerts her; it is an intrusion from another world. She is uniquely alone. Her gift is to reproduce on stage the grievous idiocy with which people behave when they are on their own: humming and mumbling, grimacing at the looking glass, perhaps even singing into it, hopping, skipping, fiddling with their dress, starting and stopping a hundred trivial tasks — looking, in fact, definably batty. At these strange pursuits we, the customers, peep and marvel, but we are always eavesdroppers; we never 'get into the act.'

The theatre is Miss Lillie's hermitage. It is an empty room in which she has two hours to kill, and the audience, like Alice, is 'just a thing in her dream.' She is like a child dressing up in front of the mirror, amusing herself while the grownups are out. The fact that we are amused as well proves that she has conquered the rarest of all theatrical arts, the art of public solitude, which Stanislavsky said was the key to all great acting. To carry it off, as she does, requires a vast amount of sheer nerve and more than a whiff of genius, which is really another word for creative self-sufficiency. One might add that it probably helps to have had experience, at an early age, of pulling faces in church.

Her future, like her act, seldom looks the same from one day to the next. She would like to take her solo show to South America and Asia, with a split week in Tibet, where she feels she has many fans. A musical has been written for her, based on the life of Madame Tussaud. Its title, which she finds hauntingly seductive, is *The Works*. But wherever her choice falls, the queues will form. There is no substitute for this magnetic sprite. She alone can reassure us that from a theatre increasingly enslaved to logic the spirit of unreason, of anarchy and caprice, has not quite vanished.

Holiday: September 1956; *Curtains*, 1961

ARTHUR MILLER

So many American writers who visit Europe fall into the bars and bullfights category, living high, drinking deep and turning out hungover fragments of film scripts. Arthur Miller belongs to a rarer but more representative kind. He is a tall, ascetic folk-hero who might have stepped out of one of John Ford's better films: Lincoln, one might say, in horn-rims, making dry jokes in gnarled, relaxed language.

When Miller talks seriously, he sometimes gets woolly; but the wool is home-spun and durable; it is meant to last. Knotting his eyebrows, he carefully smokes his pipe, biting the stem with strong and grinning teeth; even when pipeless, he bites his cigarettes, and swivels them like guns from tooth to tooth.

What drives him to write is that old-fashioned thing, a sleepless social conscience; and his splay-footed, seven-leagued stride is in this sense a symbol. He seems to have crossed from the thirties to the fifties, while skipping the awkward forties. 'For Miller,' one observer remarked, 'an ivory tower is an uninhabitable slum.' He wants art to reflect society. He is, in short, what we in England used to mean by an intellectual.

His determination, decorous but inflexible, not to compromise his liberal principles has lately led him into grave danger of being indicted for contempt of Congress. Summoned last June to appear before the House Un-American Activities Committee, he did not deny that as late as 1947 he had protested against the outlawing of the Communist Party and opposed the Smith Act, which makes it an offence to advocate the overthrow of the United States government by force.

To clinch its case, the committee confronted him with a revue scene on which he had collaborated in 1939: it presented the committee as a mad Star Chamber where witnesses were gagged, bound and tortured. Having read the scene, the committee's attorney triumphantly asked: 'Well, Mr. Miller?' Ruminant over his pipe, Miller replied: 'But — that was *meant* to be a farce. . . .' (Investigations into Un-American activities began, as we tend to forget, under Roosevelt. Shirley Temple was accused of communist sympathies, and an attempt was made to subpoena Christopher Marlowe.) The threat of indictment arose from Miller's refusal to name people he had seen at communist writers' meetings seventeen years ago. Like the hero of his own play, *The Crucible*, he declined to turn informer.

A stern, Ibsenite heritage permeates all of Miller's work, a lucid maleness that expresses itself most powerfully in masculine roles such as that of Willie Loman, the dying salesman to whom 'attention, attention must finally be paid. . . .' And just as Ibsen needed Chekhov, so Miller needed Tennessee Williams, his great opposite and contemporary, whose chosen vein is a sensuous romanticism and who specialises in enormous parts for women. 'I'm his father, and he's my son,' says Joe Keller in Miller's *All My Sons*, 'and if there's something bigger than that I'll put a bullet in my head.'

The theme of this play, as of its predecessor, *The Man Who Had All the Luck*, and its successor, *Death of a Salesman*, is the uneasy relationship of a father with his two sons. Miller, who is himself the younger of two sons, was born on the East Side of Manhattan forty-one years ago. His brother, now a businessman, began life as a poet; his father, Isidor Miller, was a rich clothing manufacturer whose casual activities included salesmanship; but neither, Miller insists, appears in any of his plays. The grand event that shaped his life was impersonal and economic. It began when he was fourteen. Within a few years it had reduced his family to poverty. Later, he learned to call it the depression.

'America,' Miller believes, 'has undergone only two really national experiences: the civil war and the depression.' Poverty hustled him out to work driving trucks, unloading cargoes and waiting at table in hotels. He could not have embarked on higher education in 1934 if the fees at Michigan University had not been among the lowest in the country. In the four years before graduation, he won three drama prizes. One of them, the Theatre Guild National Award of 1937, he shared with a southern aspirant, one year his senior: Tennessee Williams. His playgoing was cut down to essentials: Ibsen, Strindberg and Odets. Immediately after leaving Michigan, he joined the money-starved Federal Theatre Project, that far-sighted but short-lived monument to the wonders that state aid might have achieved in American drama. For it Miller wrote a tragedy about the conquest of Mexico which remains, like many of his plays, unpublished and unperformed.

In 1939 he began to write expensive radio scripts, and marriage followed, a year later, to Mary Slattery, a Michigan *alumna* by whom he has a son and a daughter. Rejected by the army because of unsteady knees, he spent a year as a fitter in the Brooklyn Navy Yard, whence he was whisked to write the script for a film about Army training. He visited many camps, gathering material that he later published in a book called *Situation Normal*; but a month in Hollywood depressed him, and he left the final script to other hands. It was about this time — 1944 — that he wrote his only novel, a study of anti-semitism called *Focus*.

His first Broadway play, *The Man Who Had All The Luck*, was designed to prove that luck was a man-made, man-willed thing; inconsiderately, it closed after five days. Fame followed in 1947, when *All My Sons* won the Drama Critics' Award; and veneration arrived two years later with *Death of a Salesman*, which won the Critics' Award, the Pulitzer Prize and the transfixed attention of everyone in the audience whose livelihood depended on selling things they could not make. Only one man is on record as having emerged unmoved, and he was a commercial traveller: 'That damned New England territory,' he said, 'never was any good.' Miller's subsequent plays have been *The Crucible* (1953), which looked back in anger on the Salem witch-trials, and *A View from the Bridge* (1955), which began its London run last week at the Comedy Theatre.

Miller wants us, it is clear, to re-examine the premises by which we live. He writes nothing in a vacuum. Each new work is intended to hasten the day when the present equation, man versus society, will give place to the ideal equation, man equals society. 'Mood plays' especially dismay him: 'The pretence,' he says, 'is that nobody wrote them — they were just there.' He has no patience with the present schism between psychology and politics: his ultimate purpose is to weld them together as the Greeks and the Elizabethans did. Shakespeare and Sophocles, he feels, had one thing in common: they tried 'to draw a whole world into one man, to bring a national experience to bear on an individual subject.'

Miller may not be the greatest playwright of his century, but the man who fills the role will have to own a large number of his attributes and ambitions. British drama perturbs him, because: 'No one seems to be asking: Why do we survive? What human impulses hold us together?' Miller's theatre has one aim, strict, firm and simple: to present, in his own words, 'man as the creature of society, and at the same time as its creator.'

When, last summer, he married Marilyn Monroe, many English faces fell at the match. Intellectual weds glamour-puss, they smirked: how transient, how bizarre! Which only proved the narrowness of English taste, compared to American. Manhattan has standards less congealed by class. People in New York who are acquainted with both partners unite in acclaiming Miller's physical attractiveness and his wife's instinctive intelligence. 'How wonderful it would be,' cried one of their friends (reversing Shaw's famous reply to Isadora Duncan's proposal) 'if their first child had his looks, and her brains!'

Observer: 14th October 1956

ANTONIO ORDÓÑEZ

At the heart of the bullfighting world, and at the height of every bull-fighter's aspiration, there is a sort of pantheon, an inner sanctum reserved for the few who have earned the title of *torero de epoca* — matadors, that is to say, with whose names a whole epoch will be associated.

Within living memory, not more than five new names have crept on to this golden list: Joselito and Belmonte, in the great days of their rivalry; Domingo Ortega, the master of the 1930s; Carlos Arruza, the Mexican all-rounder; and, of course, Manolete, who died in 1947 on the right horn of a Miura bull. The tally is short, and you cannot buy your way on to it. Several matadors in the past decade have commanded prices as high as Manolete's: but it takes more than that to satisfy the inner circle of *aficiónados,* those obsessed taurine purists who follow the bulls all summer long, often to the despair of their families, sometimes to the ruin of their businesses. Nor is valour, however insensate, enough; nor, by themselves, are grace, technique and dominating power. The *torero de epoca* must have all these, working consonantly together. He must also endure. A couple of dazzling seasons, followed by prudent retirement, are not enough for an epoch-maker. Finally, at least definably, his style must be personal; inimitable without being eccentric.

In the years immediately after Manolete's death there were many who thought that Luis Miguel Dominguín might qualify; and, certainly, no one alive knows more about the handling of fighting bulls than this tall, contemptuously handsome Castilian. But with his knowledge there went an academic coldness and a style that was a rubber stamp rather than a signature. Something was missing: and Luis Miguel, the self-proclaimed Número Uno, did not help matters by taking a long holiday when it was officially decided to enforce the old taurine code which barred chipping and blunting bulls' horns, a repulsive modern safety measure that had become prevalent. Last summer, gambling a fortune on publicity, he made a full-fledged comeback. And very impressive it was: there were afternoons of textbook classicism. It was also too late. For last summer the word had gone round. The drums of the *afición,* not only in Spain but wherever bull fever rages, were all beating in unison for the first time in eleven years. They were beating not for Luis Miguel but for the young Andalusian named Antonio Ordóñez, who revealed himself, during the Spanish season of 1958, as the first undisputed *torero de epoca* since the death of Manolete.

The revelation was no overnight affair. Ordóñez was then twenty-six and had been fighting bulls in public for a decade. Ever since his début as a *novillero* he had been recognised as a suave and infinitely dexterous performer; but among the critics there had been qualms. Antonio was prone to fits of apathy; his killing was more often feeble and erratic than solid and four-square. In 1953, to top everything, he got married, and wives, who like their husbands whole, are notoriously bad partners for bullfighters. Yet last year he summoned up all his powers, the skills we thought he had forgotten, as well as those he seemed never to have learned, and became the best. Apathy was banished: he fought every bull that faced him as intently as if he were proving himself for the first time before an omniscient audience. 'I wanted this season', he said to me last October, 'to be something special.' In 1958 he confirmed the opinion of Ernest Hemingway, his friend and admirer, who thinks him the greatest bullfighter he has ever seen.

His links with Hemingway go deeper than this. In 1926 Hemingway wrote *The Sun Also Rises*, a central character of which is a seductive matador called Pedro Romero. The name was lifted from a great seminal figure of tauromachy, born in Ronda two centuries ago, but the character was based on Cayetano Ordóñez, nicknamed Nino de la Palma, a popular bullfighter of the 1920s whom Hemingway knew well. He, too, was born in Ronda, and he is the father of Antonio. Between father and son there are differences and similarities which we must study if we are to comprehend them. Both, of course, were fearless, but that in itself means nothing. It simply implies a lack of imagination, an inability to envisage the consequences of a slashed femoral artery or a punctured lung. In this sense all good bullfighters are fearless: their minds do not form images of the possible and terrible future. Conventionally, they all say they feel fear, but what they mean by the word is not what I mean. I once heard a girl tell Antonio that she had seen him receive a goring that put him in hospital for a month. Quite conversationally, he replied: 'Didn't it seem to you a pretty thing?' *Una cosa bonita*: yet if the wound had been a few centimetres deeper he might have died.

It is not courage that makes Antonio unique, but gentleness. This may seem a paradox, applied to a man who last year stabbed about a hundred and fifty bulls to death. Yet he kills with kindness; and he plays his bulls with a generosity that makes them colleagues, not enemies. Alone among star *toreros*, he eschews public arrogance. He never barnstorms, squabbles with the crowd or resorts to phoney melodrama. His fighting is calm and contained, its rhythm as casual as that of a bop drummer dusting his cymbals. He is the opposite of what a non-Spanish audience expects a *torero* to be. Involved as he is in a career which kills men, horses and bulls, he pursues it temperately, with a modest smile. He is of middle height, with elegant shoulders tapering down to light, poised feet; one notices a slight stoop and knees that tend just perceptibly to knock. The face is boyish and considerate, with amused, caressing eyes. Any woman would expect him to invite her to dance. No bull would. Yet he invites both, and both accept the invitation.

Outside the ring he has no hobbies. He owns a Rolls-Royce and a Mercedes and enjoys driving them, sometimes very dangerously indeed; but he is bored by the usual matador's pastimes — riding, shooting and cock-fighting. Disillusioningly, his pet spectator sport is soccer, and one of his ambitions is to see the Bilbao Athletic play in Britain. By Spanish standards he is very rich: he has a nine-room apartment in a smart quarter of Madrid and a thousand-acre ranch in Andalusia. Meeting him, in fact, for the first time, you would not guess that he had ever had to earn money in his life — you would take him for the slightly pampered son of rich parents. Yet he has been earning since adolescence, and in the hardest possible way. The effort has left plenty of scars on his body, but none on his mind, which is a simple book readily opened.

His father once had the same charm and sweetness, though to see him today you would hardly guess it. Surviving on a small pension paid by Antonio, he is a ravaged and depleted veteran who looks much older than his fifty-five years. He first fought in 1921, and a year later the great critic Corrochano consecrated him with the phrase: '*Es de Ronda y se llama Cayetano*' ('He comes from Ronda and his name is Cayetano'). Both place and name have a special resonance in the world of bulls. Ronda, a hilltop city built astride a gorge five hundred feet deep, was the birthplace of the Romero dynasty of bullfighters which flourished two centuries ago and changed the *corrida* from an aristocratic, equestrian sport into a popular art practised on foot. The name Cayetano has equally imposing overtones: it recalls Cayetano Sanz, perhaps the greatest bullfighter of the middle nineteenth century.

For a while the young Cayetano lived up to Corrochano's tribute. In 1925 he was the rage of the peninsula, a prodigy of grace and freshness; nobody could resist him, women and critics alike, and many good judges predicted that he would revitalise the *fiesta brava*. But before long he was brutally gored, and a decline set in. It became precipitate, by what is probably no coincidence, soon after his marriage, in the summer of 1927, to a handsome Andalusian gypsy — the women, as the taurine proverb says, inflict more gorings than the bulls. For whatever reason, his courage dwindled, though he went on fighting until the civil war. The less he earned, the more he spent. He went to the Americas, where he fought himself still further into debt and erotic adventure. By 1932 he had two sons, Cayetano and Juan, and very little money. That was his worst year; he fought only a dozen times. It was also the year in which Antonio was born.

For some curious genetic reason a matador's third son often grows up to outshine his father. Luis Miguel and Antonio Bienvenida are other examples of this. Antonio Ordóñez, with a globe-trotting spendthrift for a father, had strict and obvious reasons for wishing to improve on the paternal example. Both his elder brothers became *toreros,* neither with much success. Of his younger brothers, Pepe made a showy Madrid début but has since, as Antonio says, 'lost heart for the bulls'; and Alfonso, a bulky red-faced boy, embarked last year on an exceptionally unpromising career as *novillero.* None of them is in Antonio's class. He himself would blithely admit this, but he would probably attribute it to the fact that he, alone of the five sons of Cayetano, was born in Ronda. Not that he thinks himself a product of the so-called Ronda school. A famous critic once said of Antonio that his cape came from Seville and his muleta from Ronda. I asked him last year if he agreed. He shrugged and smiled. 'My cape is my own,' he said, 'and my muleta is my own. They come from myself.'

He left school at fourteen to prepare himself for a career as a *torero,* and in his first two seasons displayed a serene, instinctive classicism that at once entranced the purists, though he was overshadowed in publicity by Aparicio and Litri, who had the luck to be handled by Manolete's former manager, the wily and immensely powerful Camara. If anything, top agents control bullfighting even more effectively than they control Hollywood, and Camara saw to it that Antonio was discreetly kept out of the limelight. In Madrid, on May 21st, 1951, he fought what he now remembers as the most crucial fight of his life. He had doubted his ability to graduate to the bigger bulls a full matador must fight, but that day he triumphed, before the harshest eyes in Spain, and two months later he took the *alternativa.*

For three years thereafter he sped across the high plateau of success. For Antonio, as for all *toreros,* there were interludes of disaster: and Spanish crowds enjoy magnifying them, since a bull ring is about the only place in Spain where people can assemble in public and scream with rage without being arrested. Antonio's worst afternoon was in 1952 at Manizales in Colombia, where he heard not just three warning trumpets (after which the bull must by regulation be taken out of the ring alive) but five, a disgrace probably unique in taurine history. 'It was my bull,' he says, 'and I wanted to kill it.' Eventually, he did.

I saw him often in those early years — fluent in Pamplona, commanding in Madrid and managing, during an electric storm at Valencia, to fill the plaza with the creative pleasure he felt while handling a good bull. Lightness of heart and seriousness of purpose went hand in hand. He was, above all, copious; nobody had a longer repertoire, and nobody used it with greater freedom. For Antonio the bullfight was not a tragic conflict, it was a lyrical partnership. There were days, of course, when he seemed lazy and disaffected, but these are inevitable when you are fighting seventy times or more in an eight-month season, and I ascribed them at the time to his gypsy parentage. It was not until the end of 1953 that I began to suspect analogies between Antonio and his ruined father.

He married Maria del Carmen, the pretty dark-haired sister of Luis Miguel, and then, like his father, went into temporary retirement. On his return he looked listless and discomfited. His afternoons of glory were few, and at too many *corridas* he would exert himself only on one bull and, as actors say, 'walk through' the others. Before he could recover himself, military service kept him out of the ring for most of 1955. And no sooner did he come back to the bulls, in the spring of 1956, than he received a near-mortal goring. That summer almost everyone gave him up, except his blindest fans, who couldn't bear to, and his relations, who couldn't afford to. True, he was earning something like £2,500 a fight; but out of that he was supporting his parents, four brothers, a sister, a wife and two baby daughters, Carmen and Ana. Not to mention a cut to his manager, a cut to his squadron of *peónes* and a cut to the critics. One of Antonio's closest friends has estimated that it costs him around £300 in free seats and critical insurance every time he appears. He had, moreover, started the 1956 season flat broke, after his long absence, and several old friends had suddenly turned obstinate about repaying debts.

Just when the new — or perhaps the real — Antonio emerged is hard to say. Late in 1956 he went to Mexico to earn some dollars ('*mi Washingtones*' he calls them), and in December word came of a triumph at Mexico City with a bull named Cascabel, one of the half dozen finest displays, it was said, ever seen in the capital. Back in Spain next season, he grew in stature as the months passed. He had learned to kill and to care about killing and even adopted the ancient, perilous custom of killing *recibiendo*. At the end of the year all the parts fitted. Antonio was a complete *torero*. He had survived the sad time, the period of dusk and disillusion that spurs nine out of ten young matadors into retirement. But the end of 1957, for Antonio, proved to be no more than a foretaste of the splendours of 1958.

It was during the spring that the first rumours filtered through to me: unheard-of things were happening in Spain. My instinct told me to be wary, having been caught that way before; but the English *afición*, a devout and relentless handful, kept nagging at me to check on their ecstasies; and I went last August, to the bull fair at Malaga. Antonio fought on five days and cut from his ten bulls trophies amounting to twelve ears, three tails and a hoof. It was a sustained demonstration of the values that distinguish bullfighting from butchery. Moreover, I saw to my amazement that Antonio was taking pains over difficult, hesitant, conceivably mad bulls which in the past he would have lined up and killed without caring. Now he was the patient instructor, teaching them to charge at his will and to make around him the whorl-like patterns that he wanted. His five fights at Malaga came toward the end of a twenty-day period during which he was contracted for twenty *corridas* across the length and breadth of Spain. His best day at Malaga, and the best bullfight I have ever seen, was the last.

The bulls were of Pablo Romero, an old Sevillian breed renowned for their size and nobility. Antonio was fighting alongside Gregorio Sanchez, a rugged, graceless executioner of notable valour, and Curro Girón, the cocky young gymnast from Venezuela. Angelically poised in fighting his first bull, Antonio cut the expected two ears. Sanchez tried hard, exposing himself in the self-castrating style that nowadays passes for bullfighting, and cut one ear. Little Girón, unable to adapt his frisky athletics to the serious demands of a Pablo Romero, cut nothing. It was the fourth bull, and Antonio's collaboration with it, that belonged to the anthologies.

A newcomer, seeing this as his first bullfight, might well have been bewildered and even disappointed. Where were the frills and the flourishes he had been led to expect? Where were the gestures of arrogance, the tragically haunted eyes, the crowd screaming with fright? For Antonio gave nothing of these. Earlier in the week, with less ponderous, high-speed bulls, he had shown us the full spectacular repertoire, more than once falling to his knees and taking the first charge with a cape brandished over his head. But with this bull, older and soberer than most, older and soberer methods were required: bedrock bullfighting, in fact. Our newcomer would have seen nothing more melodramatic than a pleasant-looking young man walking lightly and firmly toward a bull, regarding it not with fury but with attentive sympathy, and then — of all dull things — making it pass him in what appeared to be slow motion. But this, I am afraid, is the very core of bullfighting, and it is not at all hair-raising to watch. The object is not to make you cry out, clutch your neighbour, avert your eyes. The object is not you at all, but the bull; and the method is to stand still, provoke its charge and control, with your wrist, both its route and its velocity; and thereafter, still motionless, to arrange and vary these passes in series, some high, others low, some with the right hand, others with the left, until the bull's full quality has been revealed, and it is time for the kill.

All this Antonio unassertively did. Even his detractors concede him peerless with the cape; and the eight *verónicas* with which he greeted the Pablo Romero were the finest I remember. Poised with his legs slightly apart, leaning pensively over the bull as he ushered it past him, he seemed almost abstracted, yet when he had finished, the animal was hypnotised. His repose was majestic. When the horses had gone and the *banderillas* were in, he went out with the red cloth and the sword, wearing the breathless half-smile that with him always presages a triumph. A few slow, testing passes, with one knee on the ground; then upright, with sword and cloth extended, while the bull charged and recharged beneath. Then cycles of low, flowing passes with the right hand, the horns slicing close yet conveying, such was Antonio's security, no sense of panic. And then the slow advance with the left hand creeping forward, inciting those profound and lethargic *naturales* of his, each linked with the next, no gaps in the sequence, no flaws in the rhythm, the whole pattern mature and punctuated, now and then, with swooping chest passes to release the tension. He did nothing that was not strictly traditional, and nothing that was not flavoured with his own gentleness.

At last, in the centre of the ring, he sighted along his sword and went in smoothly and squarely above the horns. Stepping back, he raised his hand in the gesture bullfighters use when they know their thrust is mortal. The bull, completing the tableau, rolled over at his feet and died. The ring was a snowstorm of waved handkerchiefs: ears, tail and hoof must be cut for Antonio and the bull dragged round the circle to be cheered. As it passed him, hauled by the horses, he stretched out a hand toward it, indicating that the credit belonged there and not with him. Signalling for the team to stop, he knelt and gave the bull back its ears, which he tried to place in its mouth. As he acknowledged the applause and the tears, I glanced at Sanchez and Girón, who had watched the performance transfixed. Both knew, as we all did, that they had seen the thing itself, the pure and perfect bullfight. And both had to prove to us that they, too, were maestros. The last two bulls were tricky, and neither matador shone, whereupon it was announced that each had decided to buy an extra bull, at a personal cost of about £300 apiece. I have never known this to happen twice in the same *corrida,* and it took Antonio to provoke it. His emulous colleagues both sweated over their encores and cut ears and tails, but the awards were in the nature of consolation prizes. 'Very brave,' said the man next to me, applauding, 'but there is a difference. Antonio is the difference.'

Next day he was at the other end of Spain, fighting at San Sebastian in the the north and cutting ears in both his bulls. Writing of his performance with the second, a perilous hooker, one critic went so far beyond giving value for money that I suspect he must have been sincere: 'On Tuesday, Antonio Ordóñez taught us at length how bulls should be fought, and demonstrated once more that he is one of the greatest artists the bullfight has given us across the centuries. Mastery and art, temperament and perfect outline, authenticity of spirit plus an exquisite sense of form: the truth, in fact.' During this display an eerie, unwonted silence settled on the crowd, as if an experience so rarefied would have been shattered by a rude explosion of *olés*. After one series of passes a man stood up on the shady side and made a simple statement which echoed, such was the hush, around the ring. 'What *torero* was ever better?' he said. 'You are the best.' The next day, in the same plaza, Antonio cut three more ears. His third fight in San Sebastian began with a problematical, wandering bull which he handled correctly but without appealing to the non-expert majority. He dedicated his second bull to ex-Queen Soraya and gave it a regal *faena*, which was approaching its end when, turning prematurely after a series of left-hand passes, he took a great stab with the horn in his left thigh. The impact punted him yards across the sand. Fighting off the *peónes* who scurried in to carry him out of the ring, he returned to the bull, with blood streaming down to his ankle, and gave it four more imperturbable passes, followed by the sword. He waited for the death and even then refused to surrender to his injury. A ceremony had to be completed. The ear was cut: he took it, bowed to Soraya, and fainted. He was carried, as an observer wrote next day, 'not just to the infirmary, but a few metres closer to the pinnacle of bullfighting'.

Juanito Quintana, a wrinkled little man who resembles a shelled tortoise, is a close friend of Ernest Hemingway and one of the most respected *aficiónados* alive. In 1958 he came to the conclusion that Ordóñez was the best *torero* since Joselito, who was killed in the ring thirty-nine years ago. Being a perfectionist, he naturally has reservations. Sometimes, he says, he finds in Antonio *una falta de genio*, which means literally 'a lack of temper' and by extension a tendency to relax the bullfight too much and deprive it of its sense of struggle. This, as Juanito admits, is the price we have to pay for Antonio's encyclopaedic knowledge of bulls. There are other shortcomings. Like most star matadors, Antonio avoids the huge and alarming Miura bulls like the plague. Four years ago one of the breed narrowly failed to kill him, and since that day he has faced them only once — in Seville, where he was so bad that bottles were hurled through the windows of his car as he left the bullring. There is still room for improvement. There is also plenty of time, for Antonio has no intention of retiring until he has convinced every dissenter. 'Is Luis Miguel still Número Uno?' I asked him last year. 'He says so,' said Antonio, speaking without irony but also without very much conviction. He knows the true order of precedence.

Most children, at least in Europe, are brought up on stories of individual valour. In most of them the hero, a knight or warrior, has a sword; often it is a sword of magical properties, and it may have a name, such as Excalibur. It is part of the appeal of the bullring that it is the only place on earth today where you can pay to see a sword being used for the purpose for which it was invented. Yet, oddly enough, the fight with which Ordóñez crowned his career was one in which he used no sword at all. Every year in September, to celebrate the wine harvest, six breeders send six hand-picked bulls to the traditional *corrida* held in Jerez de la Frontera, in the heart of the bull country. Antonio's, last year, was a black beast bred by Benitez Cubero and named Compuesto. Already, when his capework was done, he suspected that this was a *toro de bandera*, a bull for which flags should be waved; and its tremendous assault on the horses convinced him. After one pair of *banderillas* he asked for the punishment to cease. By now the public, too, had realised Compuesto's quality and begun to beseech the president of the ring to pardon his life.

With sword and muleta, Antonio began the last act of the fight. The crowd was in uproar, and at length the president acquiesced. Three blasts of the trumpet declared that the indomitable, innocent bull had been granted a pardon. Smiling, Antonio threw away his sword and continued the fight undefended save by a stick and a yard of serge. Bull and man, both at the height of their power, rose to each other. The *faena* was superb; 'the most monumental,' said one critic, 'seen in Jerez since time immemorial'. At the end of it, Ordóñez lined up the bull as if to kill *recibiendo*. The charge came and Antonio awaited it, leaning over the horns with uncalled-for-courage and placing the palm of his hand on the spot, just behind the mound of neck muscle, where the sword would normally have entered. Compuesto then left the ring alive, to spend his remaining years in the luxurious harem that is the lot of the seed bull. The papers the next day erupted in eulogy, for the bull as much as his partner. I found it somehow appropriate that Ordóñez, the good-tempered bullfighter, should have made history with a bull he did not have to kill.

Sports Illustrated: 26th January 1959; *Bull Fever*, 1966

BERTOLT BRECHT

Wherever you go in Germany, Brecht is inescapable. Frankfurt, which has staged five Brecht plays since 1952, added a sixth last spring, to critical applause so tumultuous that it made half a column in the *New York Times*. The occasion was the West German *première* of *Schweik in the Second World War*, Brecht's version of the adventures that might have befallen Jaroslav Hasek's Good Soldier had he been conscripted by the Nazis to fight against Russia. Schweik, the beaming innocent who makes authority look most foolish when most he seems to embrace it, had an abiding appeal for Brecht, who once said that Hasek's book was one of the three literary works of this century most likely to become classics. In Brecht's play, as Schweik blunders into the Army and toward Stalingrad, the action is constantly interrupted by Hitler and his lieutenants, on a platform high above the stage; the Führer persistently, and pathetically, inquires whether Schweik, the little man, still loves him, because without the love of the little man he cannot go on. Finally, Schweik rejects his advances with unctuous obscenity. Although it is embellished with some of the loveliest lyrics Brecht ever wrote, the text is rough, acid, and brutally contemptuous of Nazi sympathizers. The night I was there, the Frankfurt audience cheered it.

The ubiquity and the influence of Brecht have been growing ever since his death, three years ago, at the age of fifty-eight. In the 1957–8 season he set a record; for the first time in the history of the German theatre a contemporary native playwright was among the four dramatists whose works were most often performed in the German-speaking countries. Shakespeare, as always, came first, with 2,674 performances, and he was followed by Schiller, with 2,000; Goethe, with 1,200; and Brecht, with 1,120. (Molière, Shaw, and Hauptmann, in that order, were the runners–up.) It is doubtful whether any dramatist in history has made a greater impact on his own country in his own era than this stubby, ribald Marxist, who spent his mature creative years — from 1933 to 1948 — away from home, exiled and almost penniless, first in Scandinavia and then in the United States.

I have paid many visits to Brecht's Berliner Ensemble in the five years since it took up residence at the Theater am Schiffbauerdamm, but whenever I approach the place, I still feel a *frisson* of expectation, an anticipatory lift, that no other theatre evokes. Western taxis charge double to go East, since they are unlikely to pick up a returning fare, but the trip is worth it: the arrow-straight drive up to the grandiose, bullet-chipped pillars of the Brandenburg Gate, the perfunctory salutes of the guards on both sides of the frontier; the short sally past the skinny trees and bland neo-classical façades of Unter den Linden (surely the emptiest of the world's great streets), and the left turn that leads you across the meagre, oily stream of the Spree and into the square-*cum*-parking-lot where the theatre stands, with a circular neon sigh — 'BERLINER ENSEMBLE' — revolving on its roof like a sluggish weather vane. You enter an unimposing foyer, present your ticket, buy a superbly designed programme, and take your seat in an auditorium that is encrusted with gilt cupids and cushioned in plush. When the curtain, adorned with its Picasso dove, goes up, one is usually shocked, so abrupt is the contrast between the baroque prettiness of the house and the chaste, stripped beauty of what one sees on the expanses, relatively enormous, of the stage. No attempt is made at realistic illusion. Instead of being absorbed by a slice of life, we are sitting in a theatre while a group of actors tell us a story that happened some time ago. By means of songs, and captions projected on to a screen, Brecht explains what conclusions he draws from the tale, but he wants us to quarrel with him — to argue that this scene need not have ended as it did, or that this character might have behaved otherwise. He detested the reverence of most theatre audiences, much preferring the detached, critical expertise that he noted in spectators at sporting events. Theatrical trickery, such as lighting and scene changes, should not, he felt, be concealed from the customer. In his own words,

. . . don't show him too much
But show something. And let him observe
That this is not magic but
Work, my friends.

Always, as a director, he told his actors that the mere fact of passing through a stage door did not make them separate, sanctified creatures cut off from the mass of humanity — hence his practice, which is still followed to some extent by the Ensemble, of allowing outsiders to wander into rehearsals, as long as they kept quiet. He abhorred the idea that the production of plays is a secret, holy business, like the nurture of some rare hothouse plant. If actors can spend their spare time watching ditchdiggers, he said, why shouldn't ditchdiggers watch actors? Initially, the Ensemble actors were embarrassed by this open-door policy; later, however, they realized how much it had helped them to shed inhibitions. A cast that has rehearsed for weeks before strangers is unlikely to dread an opening night.

I arrived at the theatre this year during a rehearsal, and one that was loaded with nostalgia. *The Threepenny Opera*, Brecht's first decisive success, was being prepared for revival on the same stage that had seen its

première thirty-one years earlier, with the same director in charge — Erich
Engel, now looking gaunt and unwell, despite the jaunty cocksureness of
his beret. As I entered, somebody was singing 'Mack the Knife' with the
tinny, nasal vibrato that one remembers from the old Telefunken records.
Engel and two young assistants interrupted from time to time, talking with
the easy, probing frankness that comes of no haste, no pressure, no need to
worry about publicity, deadlines, or out-of-town reviews. I noticed that
Mr. Peachum, a part usually given to a rubicund butterball, was being
played by Norbert Christian, a slim soft-eyed actor in his thirties. Brecht, I
reflected, would have liked that; he always detested physical type-casting.
In Brecht's theatre it is what people do, not what they feel or how they
look, that counts. Action takes precedence over emotion, fact over fantasy.
'Die Wahrheit ist konkret' ('Truth is concrete') was Brecht's favourite
maxim; for him there could be no such thing as abstract truth. Somebody
once asked him what the purpose of a good play ought to be. He answered
by describing a photograph he had seen in a magazine, a double-page
spread of Tokyo after the earthquake. Amid the devastation, one building
remained upright. The caption consisted of two words: 'Steel Stood.' That,
said Brecht, was the purpose of drama — to teach us how to survive.

The rehearsal continued, the patient denuding process that would
ultimately achieve the naked simplicity and directness on which the
Ensemble prides itself. To encourage the players to look at themselves
objectively, a large mirror had been placed in the footlights, and throughout
the session photographers were taking pictures of everything that happened,
providing a visual record that would afterward be used to point out to the
actors just where, and how, they had gone wrong. One of the most
impressive women alive had meanwhile come to sit beside me — Helene
Weigel, Brecht's widow, who has directed the Ensemble since its inception
ten years ago and plays several of the leading roles. At sixty, she has a lean,
nut-brown face that suggests, with its high cheekbones, shrewdly hooded
eyes, and total absence of make-up, a certain kind of Spanish peasant
matriarch; her whole manner implies a long life of commanding and
comforting, of which she clearly regrets not an instant. Her warmth is
adventurous, her honesty contagious, and her sophistication extreme, and
that is the best I can do to sum up a woman who would, I think, be proud to
be called worldly, since a scolding, tenacious affection for the world is the
main article of her faith. The Weigel — to adopt the German manner of
referring to an actress — has no real counterpart in the American theatre; in
appearance, and in dedication, she resembles Martha Graham, but a Martha
Graham altogether earthier and more mischievous than the one Americans
know. At the end of the rehearsal we exchanged gifts and greetings. I got a
scarf, designed by Picasso in the company's honour; a book about the
Ensemble's seminal production, *Mother Courage*; a photographic dossier
comparing the performances of Charles Laughton and Ernst Busch in

the title role of Brecht's *The Life of Galileo*; and — unexpectedly — a complicated game of the do-it-yourself variety, invented by Mozart to teach children how to compose country dances by throwing dice. The Weigel, alas, got only a cigarette lighter. Talking about the state of the company, she said, 'When Brecht died, I was afraid this place might become a museum.' Her fears have turned out to be unjustified. It is true that the Ensemble mostly performs Brecht plays, but the plays are acted and directed by people steeped in the Brecht spirit. Throughout the theatre his ghost is alive and muscular.

Or, rather, his ghosts, because there were many different Brechts, as I discovered while reading John Willett's invaluable book *The Theatre of Bertolt Brecht* and Martin Esslin's biographical study, *Brecht: A Choice of Evils*. The early Brecht was a touchy child, with a Bavarian accent, whose father ran a paper mill in Augsburg. After serving as a medical orderly in the First World War — an experience that inspired his lifelong hatred of militarism — Brecht plunged into the German *avant-garde* of the twenties, making a name for himself as an outspoken, nihilistic poet-play-wright with a gift for turning gutter idiom into poetry. In Germany, where literature had always spoken a high-flying language unknown to human tongues, this was something new; as Ernest Borneman lately remarked in the *Kenyon Review*, 'There was no precedent (a) for colloquial poetry; (b) for plain storytelling. There was no German equivalent to writers like Kipling, Mark Twain, or Hemingway.' Brecht was impressed by, and freely borrowed from, the work of writers as disparate as Villon, Rimbaud, Büchner, Wedekind, Shakespeare, Kipling, and Luther, and he positively welcomed the charge of plagiarism, retorting that in literature, as in life, he rejected the idea of private property. Through the mouth of Herr Keuner, an imaginary character on whom he fathered many anecdotes and aphorisms, he scoffed at authors whose egotism compelled them to exclude from their work all notions and phrases that were not of their own invention: 'They know no larger buildings than those a man can build by himself.' (In this respect, as in several others, Brecht resembles Picasso, who once remarked, 'To copy others is necessary, but to copy oneself is pathetic.' In the early Montmartre days, according to Roland Penrose's recent biography, Picasso's reading matter included Verlaine, Rimbaud, Diderot, and the adventures of Sherlock Holmes, Nick Carter, and Buffalo Bill; the same list, or one very similar, would serve for the young Brecht. In addition, both men embraced Communism, yet expressed themselves in styles that were utterly antipathetic to Socialist Realism; both revolutionized the arts of their choice; and both, despite shortness of stature and slovenliness of dress, were immoderately attractive to women.)

Brecht's early manner was summed up in 1922 by the German critic Herbert Ihering:

This language can be felt on the tongue, on the palate, in one's ears, in one's spine. . . . It is brutally sensuous and melancholically tender. It contains malice and bottomless sadness, grim wit, and plaintive lyricism.

A little later there was the Brecht who, in collaboration with Kurt Weill, revolutionized the popular musical stage with *The Threepenny Opera* and *The Rise and Fall of the City of Mahagonny*, using the rhythms and slang of a depressed urban society to lacerate Western decadence, and bringing into the 'serious' theatre the sardonic street-corner poetry of post-war Berlin. Already he was moving toward the vantage point that he was to make his own — 'that interesting and largely neglected area,' as Mr. Willett describes it, 'where ethics, politics, and economics meet.' In 1926 Brecht read *Das Kapital* for the first time. Marxism supplied a corrective to his anarchic tendencies, a remedy for his disgust with the world around him, and a mental discipline that delighted his love of logic and paradox. Hence, after 1928 we get Brecht the Communist didact, writing instructional plays in a new, sparse, bony style:

When I address you
Cold and broadly
In the driest terms
Without looking at you
(I apparently fail to recognize you,
Your particular manner and difficulties),

I address you merely
Like reality itself
(Sober, incorruptible, thanks to your manner,
Tired of your difficulties),
Which you seem to me to be disregarding.

From this period come *Die Massnahme*, an austere analysis of revolutionary self-abnegation that is, intellectually, the masterpiece of Communist drama, and *Die Mutter*, Brecht's stage adaptation of the famous Gorky novel. Both plays were savagely attacked in the Marxist press — the latter for being out of touch with working-class reality, the former because it denied the thesis that a good Communist is never torn between the claims of reason and emotion. (Brecht's failure to reconcile these rival claims accounts, in Mr. Esslin's view, for the fascinating ambiguity that runs through his work. The bald statement he wants to make and the poetry with which he makes it often pull in different directions; matter and manner are exquisitely at odds.) Like many of his Leftist contemporaries, Brecht was seeking a method whereby economic processes could be effectively dramatized; he hoped to see money and food some day displace power and sex as the drama's major themes. With most bourgeois writers, he said, 'the fact that moneymaking is never the subject of their work makes one suspect that . . . it may be the object instead.'

The next Brecht was the director who practised, and the theorist who preached, 'Epic Theatre' — a phrase he borrowed from Erwin Piscator in the twenties and went on defining until the end of his life. This, perhaps, is the Brecht who is best known in America, thanks to the energetic prosely-tizing of Eric Bentley. For every American who has seen a Brecht production, there are probably a thousand who are arm-chair experts on the 'alienation effect,' the abolition of suspense, the prefacing of scenes with projected captions, the use of music not to intensify emotion but to neutralize it, the rejection of 'atmospheric' lighting in favour of general illumination, and the outright ban on costumes and props that do not look worn or handled.

> Of all works, my favourite
> Are those which show usage.
> The copper vessels with bumps and dented edges,
> The knives and forks whose wooden handles are
> Worn down by many hands: such forms
> To me are the noblest.

Brecht's opposition to naturalistic acting was really, as he often insisted, a return to the older forms of popular theatre, including (the list is Mr. Esslin's) 'the Elizabethan, the Chinese, Japanese, and Indian theatre, the use of the chorus in Greek tragedy, the techniques of clowns and fairground entertainers, the Austrian and Bavarian folk play, and many others.' His refusal to permit actors to 'identify' with their roles, and thus to create strongly individualized characters, sprang from his conviction that human identity is not fixed but infinitely mutable, dependent on particular social and economic circumstances; this is the left-wing equivalent of Pirandello's theories, at once frivolous and despondent, about the many-faceted impermanence of the human ego. What Pirandello fatalistically accepted, Brecht sought to explain. His loathing of stage emotionalism is more easily accounted for. It was a violent reaction against the bombast of the conventional German theatre. Life in a Brecht production is laid out before you as comprehensively as in a Brueghel painting, and with many of the same colours — browns, greys, and off-whites. It does not seize you by the lapel and yell secrets into your ear; humanity itself, not the romantic individualist, is what it is seeking to explore. In 1936 Brecht stated his attitude:

> The spectator of the *dramatic* theatre says: 'Yes, I have felt the same. I am just like this. This is only natural. It will always be like this. This

human being's suffering moves me because there is no way out for him. This is great art; it bears the mark of the inevitable. I am weeping with those who weep on the stage, laughing with those who laugh.'

The spectator of the *epic* theatre says: 'I should never have thought so. That is not the way to do it. This is most surprising, hardly credible. This will have to stop. This human being's suffering moves me because there would have been a way out for him. This is great art; nothing here seems inevitable. I am laughing about those who weep on the stage, weeping about those who laugh.'

Nobody of any critical intelligence who is familiar with what passes for 'great art' in London or New York could fail to applaud this succinct, startling, and unforgettable distinction between the audience that is all heart and nerves and the audience that tempers feeling with knowledge and observation.

Two more Brechts, and the outline is complete. One was the mellow playwright who reached the peak of his creativity in exile. Between 1937 and 1945 Brecht wrote eleven plays, among them *The Life of Galileo, Mother Courage, The Good Woman of Setzuan, Puntila* and *The Caucasian Chalk Circle*. By that time the ideological element was assumed or implied more often than it was stated. The five works I have named all deal with the tension between instinct, love, and emotion, on the one hand, and, on the other, a society that perverts or exploits all three. The church defeats Galileo by playing on his weakness for the good, sensual life. Mother Courage tries to protect her family by making money out of the Thirty Years' War, but the war, in the end, destroys her children. Shen Te, of Setzuan, finds that you cannot help those you love without injuring your neighbours. The landowner Puntila, all charity and generosity when drunk, is an efficient businessman during bouts of cold-blooded sobriety, from which, unavailingly, he begs to be delivered. In the last of the great plays, *The Caucasian Chalk Circle*, good-heartedness defeats the system. Grusha, the maid, is brought to trial for having kidnapped a high-born baby, but the judge decrees that the child belongs to her, since everything should belong to those who serve it best.

The last Brecht was the sage of East Berlin, at once the pride and embarrassment of the Communist regime, which saw him laurelled in the West (especially at the Paris International Theatre Festivals of 1954 and 1955) and accused in Russia of being a 'formalist' opponent of Socialist realism. Mr. Esslin's book goes deeply into Brecht's ambivalent relationship with the Party when he returned to Germany in 1948 after an inconclusive velitation with the Un-American Activities Committee. Before moving to East Berlin, he not only contrived, with characteristic guile, to obtain an Austrian passport, which would allow him easy access to the West, but gave the copyrights of his works to a West German publisher, who still owns them. When someone asked him, toward the end of his life, why he had elected to stay in the East, he is said to have likened himself to a doctor with a limited supply of drugs who is forced to choose between two patients — a syphilitic old roué and a diseased prostitute who is, however, pregnant. It seems clear, too, that Brecht's acquaintance with Hitlerism had left him with very little faith in the possibility of turning Germany into a true democracy overnight; hence he felt able to support an authoritarian government that, whatever its faults, was at least anti-Nazi and anti-capitalist. (I suddenly remember the occasion when I took Helene Weigel to the West Berlin *première*, three years ago, of *The Diary of Anne Frank*. At the final curtain the audience sat shocked and motionless; Frau Weigel's face was rigid and masklike. Shortly afterward, in the restaurant next door to the theatre, she wept; and I should think she weeps seldom. Wiping her eyes, she shook her head and said firmly, 'I know my dear Germans. They would do this again. Tomorrow.')

Early in 1949, in collaboration with his old friend Erich Engel, Brecht staged *Mother Courage* at the Deutsches Theater in East Berlin. The style — light, relaxed, and ascetically spare — set the pattern for all his subsequent productions. As the tireless old protagonist, dragging her canteen wagon across the battlefields of the Thirty Years' War, Helene Weigel played in a manner that shrank utterly from flamboyance; her performance was graphic yet casual, like a shrug. At two carefully selected moments she was piercingly and unforgettably moving — first in the soundless cry that doubles her up when her son is executed, and again when, to avoid incriminating herself, she must pretend not to recognize his body. She walks over to the stretcher, wearing a feigned, frozen smile that does not budge from her lips until she has surveyed the corpse, shaken her head, and returned to her seat on the other side of the stage. Then she turns to the audience, and we see for an instant the drained, stone face of absolute grief. These moments apart, the production achieved a new kind of theatrical beauty, cool and meaningful, by deliberately avoiding climaxes of individual emotion; with *Mother Courage* the broad canvas and the eagle's-eye view of humanity were restored to European drama after too long an absence.

That autumn the company formally adopted the name Berliner Ensemble, and for the next five years it spent most of its time on tour. In 1952 a detailed, illustrated account of its first six presentations, complete with an analysis of the acting techniques and methods of stagecraft, was published in a huge volume of well over four hundred pages, laconically entitled *Theaterarbeit* (*Theatre Work*). In the spring of 1954 the Ensemble moved into the Theater am Schiffbauerdamm, and Brecht celebrated his homecoming with an extraordinary production of *The Caucasian Chalk Circle*, which opened in June and later astonished Paris and London. A concave white curtain covered the back of the stage, a convex white curtain swept to and fro across the front; between them, the vast revolve whirled around, bearing fragmentary settings for the journeying heroine to encounter, and long silken sheets adorned with Oriental landscapes came billowing down to indicate place and climate. Lee Strasberg, the artistic director of the Actors' Studio and a passionate upholder of Stanislavsky's quest for emotional truth in acting, as opposed to the social truth sought by Brecht, saw the play while the Ensemble was in London. He concluded that what Brecht practised was by no means incompatible with what Stanislavsky preached, and declared that the production was one of the best half-dozen he had ever witnessed.

I met Brecht, for the first and only time, in Paris during the summer of 1955, the year before his death. Ovally built, and blinking behind iron-rimmed glasses, he sported a grey tunic of vaguely Russian cut and conversed in wry, smiling obliquities, puffing on a damp little cigar. To judge by Ernest Borneman's description of him in the twenties, exile had changed his appearance hardly at all: 'He was an eccentric in behaviour, speech, and dress, as well as in politics. He wore clothes that kept a neat balance between those of a soldier, a workman, and a hobo. . . . The hair was sliced off abruptly after two or three inches' growth, all around the head, and hung down . . . like the coiffure you see on busts of Roman emperors.' Max Frisch, the Swiss playwright and novelist, has set down perhaps the best portrait of Brecht in his later years, and I am indebted to Mr. Esslin for introducing me to it. Brecht met Frisch in Zurich in 1947 and would often, when the latter was embarking on a train journey, go to the station to see him off:

Avoiding the crowd, he leaves the platform with rapid, short, rather light steps, his arms hardly swinging, his head held slightly sideways, his cap drawn on to the forehead as if to conceal his face, half conspiratorially, half bashfully. . . . He gives the impression of a workman, a metalworker; yet he is too slight, too graceful for a workman, too much awake for a peasant . . . reserved, yet observant, a refugee who has left innumerable stations, too shy for a man of the world, too experienced for a scholar, too knowing not to be anxious, a stateless person . . . a passer-by of our time, a man called Brecht, a scientist, a poet without incense.

After the Master's death many people in the company, as well as outside it, wondered whether it could survive without his fiery presence. An interim answer was supplied by the Ensemble's triumphant East Berlin presentation, in January 1957, of *The Life of Galileo* — a production begun by Brecht and finished by Engel. I saw it again this summer, and the play still seems to me, as it did at the first night, an incomparable theatrical statement of the social responsibilities of the intellectual. At the outset it looks as if we were in for a straight fight between religious obscurantism and scientific discovery. The only progressive art, says Galileo, is 'the art of doubt,' a remark that echoes Brecht's own dictum: 'Scepticism moves mountains.' But before long we arrive at the author's real purpose, which is to condemn Galileo for cowardice. Intimidated by the threat of torture, cajoled by the promise of a cossetted life, he abjectly recants, and emerges from the Inquisition chamber to be shunned by his pupils, one of whom shouts at him, 'Unhappy is the land that lacks a hero!' Wanly, Galileo responds, 'Unhappy is the land that needs a hero.' Brecht goes on to show how one such concession brings a hundred in its train; within months Galileo is backing the Church in social and political, as well as scientific and theological, affairs. The final tableau epitomizes the argument: in the foreground a choir polyphonously hymns the power of science, while in the background Galileo wolfs a fat roast goose. The play contains two scenes that exemplify, as sharply as anything Brecht ever wrote, his ability to make an intellectual position visible and tangible. In the first of them a provincial ballad singer hails Galileo's challenge to Rome. As he does so, a riotous procession, reminiscent of a painting by Hieronymus Bosch, streams across the stage. Some of the marchers are clad in obscene masks, and coax a jangling music out of saucepans and brass bedsteads; others toss a straw effigy of a cardinal in a blanket; one, a child, is attired as the earth, with water squirting from its eyes at the loss of its position at the centre of the universe; another clumps in horrendously on twenty-foot stilts, surmounted by a gigantic facsimile, acclaimed on all sides, of Galileo's head. The second scene that sticks in my mind is the one in which the liberal Cardinal Barberini, newly installed as Pope, turns against Galileo. At first, skinny in his underwear, waiting to be robed, Barberini refuses to countenance the Inquisitor's demand that the scientist be brought to trial, but as the robing proceeds and he is draped, encased, and almost buried in the ceremonial vestments of his office, the Pope grows more and more receptive to the Inquisitor's plea, to which, at last, he consents. It is instructive, by the way, to contrast Brecht's attitude toward Galileo with Arthur Koestler's in *The Sleepwalkers* — bearing in mind, of course, that Mr. Koestler's Marxism was once as deeply ingrained as Brecht's. According to the Koestler version, Galileo's pride brought about a disastrous and unnecessary breach between science and religion. Brecht, on the other hand, accuses Galileo of not having had enough pride (or self-respect) to make a breach that was healthy and necessary. Koestler wants to reconcile the physical with the metaphysical; Brecht strives to keep them apart. But, whatever one thinks of the argument, it is impossible to deny the unassertive loveliness of Caspar Neher's décor for *The Life of Galileo* — three towering panelled walls of darkly glowing copper, enclosing an area into which informatively beautiful objects, such as Roman bas-reliefs and silver models of the Aristotelian universe, are occasionally lowered. The production proved that the spheres of the Ensemble would continue to revolve without the animating zeal of their great mover. Brecht thus demonstrated, posthumously, the truth of his own apothegm that no man is indispensable, or, if he is, he is up to no good.

The Ensemble today consists of sixty-two actors, plus a staff of administrators, office workers, stagehands, musicians, designers, dressmakers, scene builders, electricians, ushers, waitresses, and cooks that brings the grand total of employees up to nearly three hundred. Its yearly subsidy, paid by the Ministry of Culture, amounts to more than three million marks. Rehearsals, in this happy set-up, may go on for anything between two and six months; when I was there in June, the cast of *The Threepenny Opera* was already wearing full costume and make-up, although the opening was not scheduled until October. It sometimes worries Helene Weigel that in all its ten years of operation the Ensemble has presented no more than twenty-five plays. She need not disturb herself unduly, because the main reason for the company's low output is, quite simply, its fame. Its productions are being reverently filmed for the East Berlin archives, it is constantly being invited to foreign countries (Hungary and Rumania this summer, Scandinavia in the fall, England and China next year), and it spends a lot of time polishing and recasting its existing repertoire.

This summer I attended two productions I had not seen before. One was *Die Mutter*, Brecht's expansion of the Gorky novel about an illiterate Russian mother who begins by urging her son to abandon his revolutionary activities and ends up, after he has been shot, a convinced supporter of the cause. The play is outright *agitprop*, a mosaic of Marxist exhortations, and the last scene shows the whole cast singing in praise of Communism while a film projector fills the backcloth with newsreel shots of Lenin, Khrushchev, Mao Tse-tung, and even — fleetingly — Stalin. It all sounds crudely hysterical until one sees the stealth and subtlety of the performance. There are no exaggerated Czarist villains, no exuberantly heroic proletarians; everyone acts with a detached calm that, if anything, reinforces the message. Weigel plays the mother as a quiet but relentless nagger. ('I picked out the nagging and decided to use it all through,' she told me later. 'I wanted to show that nagging could be constructive as well as nasty.') Looking like Nefertiti lined by years of labour over a hot stove, she permits herself one moment of pure lyricism. Her son, who has escaped from Siberia, appears without warning at a house where his mother is employed as housekeeper. Entering from the kitchen, she sees him and instinctively registers chiding disapproval; then, uncontrollably, she flies to his arms, as weightlessly as Ulanova's Juliet flies to Romeo, letting both legs swing round the boy's waist as he catches her. Throughout the evening one feels Brecht's passion for objects that have been durably used — a sofa, a soup tureen, a hand-operated printing press. Once, in a poem, he said that his wife chose her props with the same loving precision as that with which a poet chooses his words. Weigel's props, he declared, were selected

> ... for age, purpose, and beauty
> By the eyes of the knowing,
> The hands of the bread-baking, net-weaving,
> Soup-cooking comprehender
> Of reality.

After this, one of the company's oldest productions, I went to see the newest — *The Resistible Rise of Arturo Ui*, described in the program as *'ein Gangster-Spektakel von Bertolt Brecht.'* Written in 1941, it is a jagged, raucous parody of Hitler's rise to power, told in terms of Chicago in the twenties, composed mostly in blank verse, and including several malicious revampings of scenes from Shakespeare and Goethe. Hitler-Ui is a small-time thug who, taking advantage of a falling market, blackmails the mayor of the city (Hindenburg) into allowing him to organize a really prosperous protection racket. When the mayor dies, Ui succeeds him. His plans to take over the suburb of Cicero (Austria) are disputed by some of the mob; he slaughters the dissidents with as merry a lack of compunction as Hitler showed in disposing of Ernst Roehm and his friends on the Night of the Long Knives. In the final scene Ui is the boss, high on a rostrum spiky with microphones, through which he shrieks an oration that is cacophonously reproduced, at intervals of roughly half a second, by loudspeakers all over the theatre. The whole play is performed in a style that is somewhere between Erich von Stroheim and the Keystone Cops. The Roehm murders are staged like the St. Valentine's Day massacre; a truck drives into a garage, its headlights blazing straight at the audience, and silhouetted gunmen mow down the victims. The entire cast wears the sort of distorted make-up that one associates with puppets; the revolve whizzes around; and squalling Dixieland jazz interlards the scenes. Macabre farce on this level of inventiveness was something I had never struck before in any theatre. Its quality was condensed in the performance of Ekkehard Schall as Ui — one of the most transfixing human experiments I have ever seen on a stage, and a perfect image of Brechtian acting. Schall, who is under thirty, plays Ui with a ginger moustache, a ginger forelock, a trench coat, and a hat with the brim completely turned down. He invests the part with all the deadpan gymnastic agility of the young Chaplin: clambering on to the back of a hotel armchair and toppling abruptly out of sight; biting his knuckles, and almost his whole fist, when momentarily frustrated; indulging, when left alone with women, in displays of ghastly skittishness; and learning, from a hired ham actor, that the golden rule of public speaking is to preserve one's chastity by shielding — as Hitler always did — the lower part of one's belly. Yet Schall can change gears without warning, swerving from pure knockabout to sudden glooms of fearful intensity; from Chaplin, one might say, to Brando; for the virtue of Brechtian training, as of Brechtian thinking, is that it teaches the infinite flexibility of mankind. The play itself is rowdy and Chaplinesque. What the production — and Schall, above all — has added to it is a fever, a venom, and a fury that make laughter freeze, like cold sweat, on one's lips.

> In me are contending
> Delight at the apple trees in blossom
> And horror at the house-painter's speeches.
> But only the second
> Drives me to my desk.

Thus Brecht; and this production makes one glad that he was so driven. Its directors — Peter Palitzsch and Manfred Wekwerth — are both, like Schall, young men who were shaped by his tuition. The tradition, I would hazard, is safe.

The New Yorker: 12th September 1959; *Curtains*, 1961

George Cukor

What films, over the last thirty years, epitomize Hollywood at its most stylish? I do not mean the greatest films, or the most powerful; I mean, rather, the wittiest, the most sumptuously romantic, the most opulently sophisticated. Put this question to a moviegoer with a long memory, and it is likely that his list will include such pictures as *The Philadelphia Story*, *Camille*, *Born Yesterday*, *The Women*, *Dinner at Eight* and the Judy Garland version of *A Star Is Born* — to which his wife might add *A Bill of Divorcement*, *Gaslight* and the Katharine Hepburn version of *Little Women*. Both of them, I imagine, would be surprised to learn that all these films were directed by the same man — a sixty-one-year-old New Yorker named George Dewey Cukor, who left the Broadway theatre for Beverly Hills just over thirty years ago.

At that time the movies were in dire need of people who could teach them to talk as well as move. Seeking a coach, they summoned Cukor; and he succeeded in imposing on Hollywood high comedy and Hollywood high romance, an acting style that combined cinematic intimacy with theatrical polish and precision. For this achievement he has neither demanded nor received much credit. Ingrid Bergman, Judy Holliday, Shelley Winters, James Stewart and Ronald Colman all won Academy Awards in films of his making; but no Oscar gleams in Cukor's home, although he has four times been nominated for the prize. Outside the industry, he is almost unknown. Even within it, he is often overlooked. Some months ago I asked a reputable screen writer to name the leading Hollywood directors. 'Billy Wilder, William Wyler, George Stevens,' he began. 'Then Ford, Huston, Zinnemann and maybe Kazan.' And what about Cukor? 'Oh, Cukor doesn't make movies,' he continued, 'Cukor just makes actors.'

This relative neglect does not bother him; whatever spurs him, it is not fame. He delights in the company of beautiful things and intelligent people, and he prefers to enjoy it behind the high walls of the rambling, miniature palace in which he lives — a bachelor pleasure-dome, scented with sandalwood, hidden in the hills above the raffish squalor of Sunset Strip. The terrace garden is peopled with Italian statues that are picked out, when the occasion is festive, by tinted rays from concealed spotlights. Inside, the rooms glow with pictures — half a dozen Picassos and as many Toulouse-Lautrecs, together with works by Braque, Rouault, Matisse, Renoir, Buffet, Sutherland and Henry Moore, not to mention a superb Rodin bronze and a gracious Sargent drawing of Ethel Barrymore, bequeathed to Cukor by the sitter. He loves baubles and bibelots. 'George is galvanised by objects,' says one of his friends. 'They perpetually astonish him. He adores possessing them, and if he catches you looking covetously at something he owns, he'll grasp it almost vengefully. Then, as like as not, he'll give it to you for Christmas.'

Three servants maintain the household, which consists, apart from Cukor himself, of two sleek dachshunds and a myopic, venerable poodle named Sasha. Socially, he is outranked by nobody in the Hollywood hierarchy. At dinner, which is candlelit and invariably Lucullan, the guests are likely to include Aldous Huxley, Somerset Maugham, or at least one Sitwell; it pleases Cukor to bring literary and cinematic celebrities together. (It was at a Cukor party that a famous English writer was introduced to Joan Crawford, of whom he afterwards said: 'She reminds me of an unnamed Du Pont product.') The host himself eats sparingly, to his considerable discomfort. He relishes good food, but some time ago he became dangerously portly, whereafter he put himself on a Spartan regime, and would turn up to dinner *chez* somebody else with a meal of his own, dietetically approved and neatly packed in a basket.

He practices moderation in everything but reading and rising: he consumes books omnivorously and — even when not working — habitually gets up at dawn. Physically, he is now in enviable trim, dapper in build, and full of bristling energy that flows out through his voluble finger tips, his blazing eyes and his eager, piscine mouth, which has been compared to that of a big-game fish snapping at a hook. A tribute to his fitness hangs outside his private gymnasium — a diploma in which his physical instructor, a Frenchman, congratulates him on 'sa plastique impeccable'. It is symptomatic of Cukor's modesty that very few people see the document. The photographs in his house are of the stars — most of them female — with whom he has most happily worked; there are none of Cukor alone. Conversationally, he dwells always on the people he admires; it is a rare evening with Cukor that does not include an anecdote or two about Nazimova, Yvette Guilbert, Isadora Duncan, Mrs. Patrick Campbell, or Sarah Bernhardt — the outrageous, beplumed goddesses before whom he eternally goggles.

The writer Lesley Blanch, whose husband, Romain Gary, is the author of Cukor's latest film, *Lady L . . .*, once described him, in a letter to me, as 'a voluptuary in the true classical sense — able to enjoy the greatest luxuries and the smallest toys; finds exquisite pleasures in many ways; which is probably the secret of living. I think he has this. And I think he has not, or has passed, *ambition*, in the destructive sense. This makes him utterly free. And being perfectly sure of who he is, what he is, he does not envy — is not eaten up by competition.'

Mention a performer he knows or worships, and instantly the anecdotes start to pour out. His voice whirrs and buzzes, like an engine that, once revved up, cannot be switched off until it reaches its destination. Two deep lines of concentration bisect his forehead like a highway; and his conductor's fingers begin their dance, sometimes caressing the air or stabbing it for emphasis, and sometimes upheld, with thumb and index joined, to retain one's attention while their owner scans the ceiling in search of the right word. Meanwhile, as Cukor warms to his story, his lower jaw comes swooping forward, revealing seven sharp teeth that gnaw, between phrases, at his upper lip. 'Whenever George gets excited,' somebody once remarked, 'he suddenly acquires four sets of teeth.'

Of Marilyn Monroe, with whom he worked on *Let's Make Love*, he says: 'Her face *moves* — it catches the light — it's genuinely photogenic. And she *thinks boldly*. She thinks as a dog thinks. *Au fond*, her mind is wonderfully unclouded — she doesn't censor her thoughts. She's like Elvis Presley, like all the great performers — whenever she enters, it's an occasion. Maybe I sound like an old hambola, but I love Presley — I think he has *enormous* taste and *enormous* distinction.' (While unquestionably sincere, Cukor's admiration for Miss Monroe does not prevent him from being playful at her expense. Once, in a party game, he was asked what food she most reminded him of. He immediately replied: 'A three-day-old Van de Kamp Bakery angel cake.')

Cukor's background, like that of many people prominent in movies, is Hungarian; it is surprising how much of the history of film-making in the West could be written under the title: *Strictly From Hungary*. Though his parents met in New York, they both belonged to immigrant households and had come to America as adolescents. George's father, Victor, carved a modest niche for himself in American real estate, but the dominant voice in the family counsels was that of Uncle Morris, a prosperous Manhattan lawyer. Almost as soon as George was born, in 1899, it was assumed that he would follow in his uncle's professional footsteps. In his early teens, however, he took to attending the theatre at least twice a week, and the idols he cherished then he cherishes still — Mrs. Fiske, Emily Stevens, Ethel Barrymore, Nazimova and the rest.

In 1918, on the verge of entering law school, he momentously decided to accept a job as assistant stage manager in Chicago. His relations were appalled: 'They acted,' he recalls, 'as if I'd said I was going to become a bookie.' Undeterred, he pushed on; by 1920 he was directing a summer-stock company in Rochester, where he engaged young players like Miriam Hopkins, Bette Davis and Robert Montgomery, endearing himself to all of them except Miss Davis, with whom he never could get on. He also employed a pretty Broadway ingénue named Frances Howard, on whom he exerted so marked an influence that she consulted him before accepting a proposal of marriage from a fledgling movie producer called Samuel Goldwyn.

Mrs. Goldwyn remembers Cukor as 'this great big fat wonderful man. He loved to make actors comfortable. He would bother them, but he would bother them quietly. Whenever he was worried about a show, he would eat — fill himself with cakes and go to sleep. Years later, when Selznick fired him from *Gone With the Wind*, he didn't yell or scream, but he ate a great many cakes.'

Cukor began his Broadway career in 1926 by staging *The Great Gatsby*, one of the stars of which was Florence Eldridge. 'We became fast, fast, fast, *fast* friends,' Cukor told me à propos Miss Eldridge, thereby corroborating the theory of Charles Brackett, the eminent screen writer and producer, who holds that you can never be sure that Cukor means what he says until he has repeated it four times. 'He would look at a page of dialogue,' says Mr. Brackett, 'and tell us it was phony, phony, phony, *phony*. We used to count the phonies. When he got to the fourth, we knew he was serious.' By 1929 Cukor had directed people like Dorothy Gish, Laurette Taylor and Louis Calhern. His reputation, though small, was solid, and he went into films as an authority on spoken dialogue, in which capacity he was assigned to *All Quiet on the Western Front*. Since 1930, his name has appeared on the directorial credits of forty-two movies — a vast output that represents a vast expenditure, for Cukor is not a cheap director. He demands a peerless cast and a cast-iron script; and these are costly items.

'There are lots of creative directors,' he says, 'who can *seize* a script and make it part of their world — like Lubitsch, or Ford, or Hitchcock. And there are others who try to become part of the script's world. Like me.' Cukor's pictures are always obsequious to their subjects; he never obtrudes himself. There are, naturally, limits to the kind of script he will accept. Temperamentally, he shuns violence, and is probably the only Hollywood director whose celluloid record is completely free of gang warfare. He prefers movies that depend on personal relationships and permit him to evoke what he calls 'the climate of comedy'. This may be why actors revere him. 'The understatement of great screen acting,' Charles Brackett declares, 'was mostly George Cukor's invention. He was one of the first to understand the difference between acting for the theatre and acting for the camera.'

Early in his Hollywood career, Cukor tested a New York actress for an important part. She had 'an odd, barking way with her', but he hired her because he liked her gawky self-confidence, and gave her the female lead in *A Bill of Divorcement*. Even today, one cannot watch Katharine Hepburn's performance in the film without marvelling at the assurance with which she takes command, easily outplaying the seasoned professionals — among them John Barrymore — who surround her. Cukor and Hepburn have made eight pictures together, and become the closest of friends and neighbours. 'He makes you trust yourself,' she said to me. 'He maintains your illusion of yourself — out of the ebullience of his energy and the immense generosity of his spirit.'

Miss Hepburn reminded me that in 1936 she had appeared in a Cukor movie called *Sylvia Scarlett*, opposite a young actor of stodgy reputation who had been christened Archie Leach, though his Hollywood pseudonym was Cary Grant. He played a Cockney confidence trickster, and the film changed the course of his career. 'George taught him how to be funny,' said Miss Hepburn. 'He brought out the Archie Leach in Cary Grant.'

Of all his pictures, Cukor's favourite is *Little Women*, in which Miss Hepburn played Jo. Tallulah Bankhead saw it and sobbed uncontrollably, but it cannot be said that Cukor was overwhelmed by this demonstration of empathy. 'She wasn't moved by the picture,' he commented. 'She was weeping for her lost innocence.'

Judy Holliday shares the Hepburn passion for Cukor, though she phrases it differently: 'He didn't *maintain* my illusion of myself — he *gave* me an illusion of myself. Before I met him, I never thought of myself as an actress. Boy, he sidetracked me in a giant way!' And why did he impress her so much? 'Because he doesn't compete. He'll take suggestions from anybody — the actors, the cameraman, even the prop man — and he never resents it. He has a really healthy ego. And another thing I like. After every take he says, "Wonderful, wonderful, wonderful,wonderful — do it again!" ' (For the results, see *Adam's Rib*, *Born Yesterday*, *The Marrying Kind* and *It Should Happen to You*.)

Shelley Winters, who made her screen debut in a Cukor picture and won an Academy Award, is equally agog with gratitude: 'When I met him for the first time, I was hiding myself. I'd assumed the personality of an idiot girl, with pink hair and false eyelashes and a sexy girdle. He took one look at me and said, "Damn it, girl, take off those eyelashes and that girdle." He told me I had a perfectly good intelligence, and why insult my mind that way? It never occurred to me until then that acting meant exposing yourself, not hiding yourself. I never knew anything about the intellectual side of being an actor before. While we were working on the picture I followed him around like he was my daddy.'

The voice of Marilyn Monroe is worth adding to the chorus. 'He cherishes the actor,' she said to me, her pink, vulnerable face reflecting hard thought. 'He and John Huston are directors who honestly respect actors. The first day on the set, he told me not to be nervous. I said I was born nervous. He told me, "If I don't sleep tonight, it'll be because I'm worrying about *you* not sleeping." '

Because of Cukor's success with Hepburn, Garbo, Shearer, Crawford, Garland, Gardner, Magnani, and so on, a legend has grown up to the effect that he is exclusively a 'woman's director'. Jack Lemmon, who gave his first screen performance in Cukor's *It Should Happen to You*, emphatically disagrees. 'Cukor,' he says, 'is the greatest actor's director I've ever worked with.' It was Cukor who taught Lemmon to scale down his flamboyant acting style to screen dimensions. About a week after shooting began, Lemmon played an important scene somewhat listlessly, as he thought, and was horrified to hear Cukor say: 'Print it.' Lemmon protested: 'But I didn't feel as if I was acting.' 'Unfortunately,' replied Cukor, 'you were.' Lemmon brooded over this for a couple of days, and then said: 'You mean — you don't want me to act at all?' Cukor beamed. 'You're beginning to get it,' he said.

Another sequence required Lemmon to fly into a rage with Judy Holliday. It went well enough, but Cukor felt something was missing. He pondered, his internal motor whirring, and suddenly fired a question at Lemmon: 'How do you feel when you're really mad at somebody?' 'I get a stomach ache,' said Lemmon truthfully. 'Play it that way,' said Cukor, and the result was one of the picture's pleasantest moments; halfway through his row with Miss Holliday, Lemmon clutched his belly and collapsed doubled up with colic.

Cukor rejoices in such tiny pieces of inspiration — 'things you pick out of the air'. When he was directing Garbo in *Camille*, he kept remembering details of his mother's death, which was then fresh in his mind — how she had whimpered towards the end, and turned her face resolutely towards the wall. He used these memories in Marguérite's death scene, a small miracle of acting, and the crown of Garbo's finest performance. 'In Cukor's movies,' according to Lemmon, 'each separate scene is beautifully polished, like a pearl. The only trouble is that sometimes the string holding the pearls together is a little weak.' Cukor himself confirms this. 'I'm not desperately interested in story-telling,' he says, contrasting himself with someone like Cecil B. DeMille, whose pictures he describes as 'preposterous, illiterate, ludicrous, *but* — what a master storyteller!'

Another star who confesses a large debt to Cukor is Rosalind Russell, whose career as a comedienne was launched when he cast her in the film version of Clare Boothe's *The Women*. It featured Norma Shearer, Joan Crawford, Joan Fontaine, Paulette Goddard and a flock of white telephones; Miss Russell, then comparatively unknown, had the role of Sylvia, the professional bitch. 'Don't play Sylvia high-comedy,' he instructed her. 'Play her like a freak.' They were rehearsing a scene set in a hotel powder room; Cukor told Miss Russell to behave with exaggerated prissiness while the other girls were present — 'but as soon as they leave, *pick your teeth.*'

The atmosphere on the set of *The Women* was electric with competition; to ease the tension, Cukor would begin each morning's work by giving his own impartially mischievous impressions of the ladies' demeanour on the previous day. He refused to allow Norma Shearer (whom he had directed in MGM's leadenly ornate production of *Romeo and Juliet*) to queen it over her colleagues. One of the key sequences took place at a couturier's, with Miss Russell subjecting Miss Shearer to a barrage of gossip while the latter was being fitted for a dress. 'Norma just had to stand there doing the Jack

Benny bit,' as Miss Russell puts it, 'while I yakked away.' Cukor wanted
her in close-up, hissing her malice directly into Miss Shearer's ear; but
when the time came, Miss Russell found it impossible to get near the lady,
who had thoughtfully changed into a voluminous black crinoline. Cukor
accepted the challenge. After a moment's deliberation, he arranged a three-
faced mirror in front of Miss Shearer, altered the camera angle and peered
through the lens. 'That's much better, Norma dear,' he crooned villainously. 'Now there are *four* Rosalind Russells.' Miss Russell became a
Cukor addict on the spot.

He calls her 'that society girl from Connecticut', in allusion to her
patrician background, which he never tires of mocking. She once turned up
wearing jodhpurs at one of his formal Sunday luncheons. He said nothing,
but that evening he telephoned her. 'Next week,' he said, 'don't come in
costume. Except maybe as a maid — we need some extra help, because I've
got some pretty classy people coming. But don't use any bad language, and
for God's sake don't push yourself into the pictures, because they're
photographing the lunch for *Harper's Bazaar*.'

Here and there one meets mild dissenters from the Cukor cult — Gene
Kelly, for example, who tolerates his 'endless chatter' and enjoyed col-
laborating with him on *Les Girls*, but feels that basically Cukor is a
theatre man who neither cares about nor understands the camera. This view
is warmly contested by Cukor's old friend and *éminence grise*, the
photographer George Huehne, whose pictorial expertise made a notable
contribution to the success of *A Star Is Born* — Cukor's first colour movie,
and the first on which he and Huehne worked together. Nowadays,
according to Huehne, Cukor is vitally interested in the cinema *per se*, in
composition and design, and not merely in photographing plays. Cukor
shot *A Star Is Born* in a semi-impressionist style, boldly splashing his
colours about, and taking what for him were fantastic visual risks. The film
broke few box-office records, but it triumphantly rebuilt the career of Judy
Garland, who regards Cukor as 'the most underrated, underappreciated
director alive'.

It was at Miss Garland's home, quite a while ago, that an informal
weekly dining club used to meet, consisting of the hostess, Fanny Brice,
Katharine Hepburn, Ethel Barrymore and Cukor. One evening Miss
Garland surveyed her guests and wondered, aloud: 'What on earth do you
suppose we all have in common?' 'That's easy, my dear,' said Miss
Barrymore. 'We've all been on the brink of disaster all our lives!' In
Cukor's case, at least, the exaggeration concealed more than a grain of
truth. For much of his early Hollywood career, he followed David Selznick
from studio to studio, turning out a glittering procession of pictures such as
A Bill of Divorcement, *Dinner at Eight*, *Little Women*, *David Copperfield*
and *Camille*. Disaster struck in 1939, when Selznick formed his own
company to produce *Gone with the Wind* with Cukor directing. 'Basically,'

says Selznick, 'George was a transplanted stage director. He didn't know about cutting. I knew he wouldn't want to be bothered with the spectacular side of the picture, the military stuff.' So Selznick himself undertook to supervise the sets, the lighting and the camera work, excusably determined to keep finger-tip control over what was, after all, the supreme gamble of his life — the most expensive and deafeningly publicised movie ever made. The late Clark Gable, as Rhett Butler, found Cukor's delicacy and fastidiousness a trifle disconcerting, but he made no overt complaint; and the ladies adored Cukor's methods — especially Olivia de Havilland and Vivien Leigh.

After a month's shooting, friction grew intense between director and producer. Cukor objected to Selznick's interference; there was a showdown; and Cukor was removed from the picture, which was finished by Victor Fleming. The Misses Leigh and De Havilland threatened to walk out in sympathy, but the gesture was bootless. Cukor was vanquished, and the blow to his pride was thunderous.

Yet he survived; and one understands why he sometimes gets impatient with actors who bring him stories about summary dismissals that wrecked their careers. 'Oh Ga-aa-ahd, will you sta-aaa-rp about being fired?' he cried on one such occasion. 'We've all been fired, for Ga-aaa-ahd's sake!' Since Gone with the Wind, however, he has fought shy of head-on conflicts with the front office; that shocking plunge into insecurity taught him caution. When executives seek to tamper with his work, he will argue and cajole, but he evades the violence of a showdown. A case in point is Bhowani Junction, the most politically conscious of his films, which was brutally cut, but not over Cukor's dead body. He stayed alive. There are those who reprove him for playing safe; for remaining a studio employee — picking up $4,000 a week when he was with Metro, and now earning around $150,000 a picture — instead of braving the hazards of independent production. 'George ought to have got away,' says Selznick. 'He stayed in Hollywood too long, sitting up there in his castle behind that big wall.' Happily immured in his fancy fortress, Cukor had no intention of being dislodged. And anyway, he hated travelling.

He spent 1942 and most of 1943 as a private in the Signal Corps, working on training films; released by the Army when he reached its age ceiling, he went home to Metro and made Gaslight, in which Ingrid Bergman, as the wife, was driven almost insane by Charles Boyer, and won for her pains an Academy Award.

Since then, his prestige has remained steadily high, with several ups and very few downs. In 1955 the name of Selznick cropped up once more to plague him; Irene Selznick, David's ex-wife, invited Cukor to return to Broadway and direct her production of Enid Bagnold's The Chalk Garden. He accepted, but extricated himself from the show before it arrived in New York (where, by the way, it was a notable hit). Hollywood had accustomed him to delegating authority, and he found his patience unequal to the task of supervising all the minutiae of a stage production. 'I got quite discombobulated,' he says (he has a passion for dated slang). 'In the movies I just had to say the word, and seven thousand people would rush in and burn down Lahore. And here were these two dames — Irene and Enid — arguing with me for days on end about a seventy-five dollar table.'

This transient mishap had no effect on his spirits, or on his appetite for work, which for him is a form of play therapy. Pictures like *Adam's Rib*, *Born Yesterday* and *It Should Happen to You* reflect his inimitable ear for the patterns of everyday speech. He treats actors like eccentric children, alternately to be pampered and chided, and propounds theories to account for their behaviour: 'They get more uppish the farther away they are from Hollywood. In England, for example, they're pretty arrogant — but that may be because English studios are kind of inefficient. Everybody's over-employed. I probably sound like a terrible Fascist but believe me, when you're working in England it's happy days in Dixie, with everyone sitting around all day eating Tootsie Rolls. Actors are bad enough when they get to England, but in India they're *unbearable*.' Yet he always forgives them, and discreetly concerns himself with looking after them if they fall on bad times. It was Lesley Blanch, not Cukor, who told me about his generosity to long-forgotten small-part players, 'ghosts who linger on in obscure hospitals.'

I am not sure what kind of artist he is; in fact, I am not sure he would like to be regarded as an artist at all. If art has to do with the expression of a heartfelt and consistent attitude toward life, then Cukor scarcely qualifies. He has no profound emotional commitments; and as an ideologue he hardly exists. Politically, he is an instinctive Democrat. Once, in the course of a presidential campaign, the studio dispatched an emissary to remind him that it was his duty to do all he could to help the Republican cause. 'You're barking up the wrong tree,' said Cukor, and sent the man away. But one cannot say that his political convictions, or indeed any of his convictions, have found embodiment in his work; and for this reason history will probably exclude him from the ranks of the very greatest directors. He has always been interested less in the statement he is making than in the actors through whom he is making it. He is the trainer who sends the players in fighting; he is not fighting for anything himself.

From the great issues of the day, the vast determining factors of our lives, Cukor has generally remained aloof — 'up there in his castle behind that big wall'. Yet he is still in demand; his tiptoe enthusiasm has not waned, and his methods have not grown dated. By cutting himself off from his time, he may well have rendered himself timeless.

Holiday: February 1961; *Tynan Right and Left*, 1967

ORSON WELLES

Some eighteen years ago, in the pages of an English school magazine, there
appeared a brief and sickeningly lush essay, entitled 'The New Playboy of
the Western World.' It read, in part:

There is a man flourishing now and being mighty on the other side of the
Atlantic. He has a lovely wife and twenty-odd years of flamboyant
youth, but his accomplishments do not end here. He has burst on the
American scene with a heavy gesture of ineffable superiority; he is the
artistic saviour of a broad land, and he knows it. For Orson Welles is a
self-made man, and how he loves his maker. . . . He moulds art out of
radio, the scourge of art; he is a wit as only Americans can be wits; and
he is a dandy among impromptu speakers. He is a director of plays in
kingly fashion, independent as a signpost in all he does; and he has
carved out of a face of massy granite the subtle lineaments of a great
actor. He is a gross and glorious director of motion pictures, the like of
which we have not seen since the great days of the German cinema; he
reproduces life as it is sometimes seen in winged dreams.
   He is all these things, vastly exaggerated and blown up into a balloon
of bold promise and brash achievement. Yet with all his many-sidedness
he has no dignity. 'I have,' he once said, 'the dignity of a nude at high
noon on Fifth Avenue.' One requisite of greatness he lacks: artistic
integrity. Perhaps he has burgeoned too soon and too wildly; but it will
come with praise and age, and then we shall behold a gorgeous,
patriarchal figure, worthy of the Old Testament. Until then, watch him,
watch him well, for he is a major prophet, with the hopes of a generation
clinging to his heels.

I was sixteen when I wrote that. I wince today at its alliterations, its
borrowed sonorities, and its tone of midget exhortation. Even more, I wince
at the calmness of my assertion that Welles was deficient in 'artistic
integrity', since that is one kind of integrity he has seldom been accused of
wanting; perhaps I meant 'integration', which would make a little more
sense.
   I quote from the piece not out of vainglory but merely to establish my
credentials. In 1943 I was committed to Welles as to nobody else then
active in the performing arts; and I am sure there were thousands like me,

young people in their teens and twenties for whom Welles was Renaissance man reborn. He seemed to have shortened, almost to vanishing point, the distance between ambition and achievement; no sooner did he approach an art than it surrendered to him. Theatre was the first to fall. We had read of the Negro *Macbeth* he directed in Harlem, and of his two audacious seasons at the helm of the Mercury Theatre. In his spare time he had conquered radio, unhinging America in 1938 with his adaptation of H. G. Wells' *The War of the Worlds*. Then he had gone to Hollywood and subjected the film industry to its first major upheaval since the advent of sound.

Nobody who saw *Citizen Kane* at an impressionable age will ever forget the experience; overnight, the American cinema had acquired an adult vocabulary, a dictionary instead of a phrase book for semi-literates. I first saw it on a Monday afternoon in the English provinces, and was lastingly dazzled by its narrative virtuosity, its shocking but always relevant cuts (do you remember that screeching cockatoo?), its brilliantly orchestrated dialogue, and its use of deep focus in sound as well as in vision. About a dozen other people, scattered throughout the theatre, shared the revelation with me. By the end of the week I had seen the film five times, once with my eyes shut in order to prove to myself that the sound track was expressive enough to be listened to in its own right. That was in 1941; and when *The Magnificent Ambersons* came along, a year or so later, my capitulation was complete. Sceptics had told me that Welles was a technical maestro, incapable of feeling; to confound them, I had only to point to his handling of Booth Tarkington's family saga, in which there were scenes of a naked emotional intimacy rarely matched in the history of Hollywood. Agnes Moorehead's portrait of Aunt Fanny, eaten up with frustrated love for her nephew, seemed to me then (and seems to me still) the best performance of its kind in the English-speaking cinema. At the end of the film came the credit titles, after which a microphone suspended from a boom swung into view. 'I wrote the picture and directed it,' said a serene bass voice. 'My name is Orson Welles.' If my prayer at that moment had been answered, Welles would have written and directed the whole subsequent output of the American film industry. Thus infatuated, I sat down and penned my eulogy.

Time, I am told by many of my friends, has proved me mistaken; if the 'hopes of a generation' ever clung to Welles' heels, they have long since been trampled underfoot. What, I am asked, has the man accomplished in the past eighteen years? A handful of stylish thrillers, a couple of bombastic Shakespeare films, a few hit-or-miss stage productions, a number of self-exploiting television appearances, and several tongue-in-cheek performances in other people's bad epics — what, beyond these, has Welles to show for himself? For one thing, I sometimes reply, he has scars, inflicted by a society which demands that the making of art and the making of money should be yokefellows. For another, he shares with people like

Chaplin, Cocteau, Picasso, Ellington and Hemingway a fixed international reputation that can never wholly be tarnished. Even in eclipse, he remains among the elite, to be judged on their level; the quickest ears prick up and the keenest eyes brighten at the advent of a new Orson Welles production — or rather, manifestation, since one can never predict the form in which his talent will choose to reveal itself. Apart from writing and directing films and plays, and apart from acting in both, he has tried his hand as a novelist, a painter, a ballet scenarist, a public orator, a magician, a columnist and a bullfighter.

To understand why he carries with him this permanent aura of expectation, it is perhaps necessary to know him. In the spring of 1960, I spent a week in Spain at his elbow, listening while he talked about his life and times. In Welles' company, on this occasion as on all previous ones, I automatically assumed the role of stooge. What follow are my memories of what he said, and my comments thereon, which I hope may provide some explanation of why, whenever I find myself bored and wondering whom I would most like to see coming in at the door, the answer is always Orson.

First, a sketch of his physical presence, which is overwhelming. He has the sauntering bulk of a fastidious yet insatiable glutton. Welles is perilously fat, having taken none but the slightest exercise since the time, thirty years ago, when he leapt in to challenge the bulls at every village *corrida* within striking distance of Seville. Jean Cocteau rightly called him 'a giant with the face of a child', adding that he was also 'an active loafer, a wise madman, a solitude surrounded by humanity'. Watch him in repose at a bullfight, lonely in the crowd, his brow contracted above the vast tanned jowls and his eyes bulging with reproach; into such a frame, one feels, the soul of the last American bison might easily migrate. From the pursed lips a tremendous cigar protrudes, and the chin is grimly out-thrust; yet in all this dignity there is somehow an element of dimpled mischief. Beneath the swelling forehead a schoolboy winks, and can readily be coaxed into chuckling. Orson amused is an engulfing spectacle, as irresistible as Niagara. The remark (frequently his) is made; a moment of silence ensues, during which his forehead retracts, causing his eyes to pop and his cheeks to sag, turning his face into a tragic mask. For an instant he looks appalled; and then there breaks through the thunderous cachinnation of his laughter. 'A wonderful laugh,' said Tennessee Williams, having listened to it, 'forced and defensive, like mine.' But I think he was wrong: Orson laughs to goad others out of awe into participation. 'I like people to talk to me,' he says, 'What I can't stand is when they talk to Orson Welles.'

Lunch in the garden of the Ritz in Madrid: Orson, surging across the terrace in white shirt and white tie, arouses thoughts of Moby Dick. Spanish decorum has overcome his habitual tielessness. He is in Spain for three reasons: to shoot a documentary for Italian television, to finish off his movie adaptation of *Don Quixote* (with Akim Tamiroff as Sancho Panza

and an unknown Mexican as the Don), and to go to the bullfights. The first
two projects are tending to overlap, as Orson intended they should. Last
year, dwindling funds forced him to abandon his own picture, with two
weeks' shooting still to be done, and when an Italian TV network invited
him to direct a series of documentaries, he agreed on condition that the first
should deal with Spain. As a title, he suggested *The Land of Don Quixote.*
Thus he manages to work for himself while working for somebody else;
Orson has spent much of his life in this kind of double harness. As for the
bulls, they are his passion; he is one of the very few Anglo-Saxons whose
opinions are valued by the Spanish taurine initiates. Among contemporary
matadors his favourite is Antonio Ordóñez, the graceful young maestro
from Ronda, who achieves with the bulls he fights an intimacy so profound,
so devoid of arrogance, that it once moved Orson to observe: 'With
Antonio, each pass asserts not "how great *I am!*" but "how great *we are!*" '
The remark may stand as a definition of good bullfighting. Though addicted
to the bulls, Orson is bored by all other competitive sports; he has no
interest in skills he has never practised.

As we eat, he talks about his childhood, and Madrid society pretends not
to listen — an effort that must be made by all those who find themselves in
public places where Orson is conducting a private conversation. It is not
that he shouts, merely that he cannot help resounding. Except in solitude, a
state rare with him, Orson has no private personality; everything about him
is public, and he is open daily. This has been true as long as he can
remember. 'Orson at twenty-six,' it was wickedly said at the height of his
Hollywood success 'is still overshadowed by the glorious memory of Orson
at six.' He was born in Kenosha, Wisconsin, forty-six years ago last May,
and claims to be more English than the English, springing as he does from
generations of unmixed colonial stock. 'You can find eighteenth-century
Englishmen in the Middle West,' he says, 'just as you can find sixteenth-
century Spaniards in Peru.' I begin to see in him an extravagant Whig on
the model of Charles James Fox, tinged with more than a hint of Byron, the
first of the great romantic expatriates. But I remember that Orson hates to
be called an expatriate; since the term applies only to people who exile
themselves from the country in which they were raised, how can it apply to
him, who was not brought up in America? And he has a point: until he was
eighteen years old, Orson spent most of his time abroad.

Both his parents were travellers. His father, Richard Welles, was a
Virginian who moved to Wisconsin because he owned two factories there.
He was an accomplished gambler, a sedulous globe-trotter, and an unpredictable inventor. One of his inventions was a carbide bicycle lamp that
made him a great deal of money; others turned out less encouragingly. 'He
tried very hard to invent the airplane,' Orson says. 'He thought the Wright
brothers were working on the wrong principles, so he designed a steam-
driven car with a kind of glider attached to it. He put a Negro servant into

the glider and started out, but the steam got into the Negro's eyes and he crashed into a tree. He and my father were photographed afterward, smiling across the wreckage.' Orson's mother was Beatrice Ives of Springfield, Illinois, a gifted pianist, radical in her view of politics and art, and ravishing in her beauty. To this union of playboy and aesthete, at a time when both partners were approaching middle age, George Orson Welles was born, owing his first name to George Ade, the humorist, and his second to a Chicago business man called Orson Wells. He says he had two remote cousins who later became politically eminent: Sumner Welles and Adlai Stevenson. He also had a brother, Richard, Jr., some ten years his senior, of whose subsequent history little is known; a dreamer and roamer, he was last heard of in Seattle, upholding the family tradition of intelligent dilettantism.

One dwells on Orson's parents because so much about them helped to shape him. He got on splendidly with them both, rather better than they did with each other; where mother had her salon, father favoured the saloon. The child's precociousness was Mozartean. At the age of two he spoke fluent and considered English, and was familiar with the plays of Shakespeare from his mother's readings. The first great wrench came when he was six. His parents separated, and Orson went to live with his mother for two halcyon years, during which he adoringly absorbed her passion for music, poetry, and painting. He hated, however, to practise scales on the piano, and once, at the age of seven, stationed himself on a high window ledge of the Ritz Hotel in Paris, threatening to jump unless his mother told his music teacher to stop badgering him. As always, she complied. The idyll ended when he was eight. Beatrice Welles died, and Orson, already an adult in feeling, was whisked off to share his father's way of life, which revolved round late nights, stage doors, and constant changes of country. 'He was a wandering *bon viveur*,' Orson says, 'and he revelled in theatre people. Before my mother died, painting and music were what interested me most. I'd never thought seriously about the theatre.'

Through his mother he had met Ravel and Stravinsky; through his father he met John Barrymore, together with innumerable circus performers and magicians. He acquired a showman's eye (which later enabled him to act as an unpaid scout for John Ringling North) and an illusionist's dexterity. 'My father loved magic,' he says. 'That's what bound us together.' Such masters as Harry Houdini and Long Tack Sam, the Chinese conjurer who revolutionised card manipulation, were called in to teach him their mysteries. If anything, he improved on what he learned; today Orson is one of the best paid magicians alive. In 1960, at a London hotel, he received more than $1,500 for one performance of a single trick: seizing an axe, he splintered a block of ice within which there was frozen a strongbox, inside which there was locked a scrap of paper, upon which there was inscribed the official registration number of a taxi-driver whom an unbribed guest had brought in from the street just before the axe was lifted. Some years ago Orson agreed to lend his arcane skills to a Hollywood celebration in honour of Louis B. Mayer. So many stars preceded him that by the time his turn came the rabbit concealed in the lining of his suit had urinated 'roughly twenty-seven times'. He has been wary of unpaid performances ever since.

Above all, Orson learned from his father the art of travelling. Who else of his age can declare nowadays, with eyewitness authority, that 'the two great artistic centres of the twenties were Budapest and Peking'? He explored Europe in the care of various tutors, one of whom took him when he was nine to an uncommonly noisy dinner party at Innsbruck, of which he remembers little except the name of the man at the head of the table, one Adolf Hitler. Life with father was more restless and uncertain than it had been with mother. 'How is it,' I suddenly ask Orson, 'that the heroes of your films have no fathers?' I am thinking not so much of Macbeth and Othello as of George in *The Magnificent Ambersons*, who ruins the life of his widowed mother; and especially of Charles Foster Kane, whose father never appears and who is taken away from his mother as a child and transported into an alien world of men and money, rather like George Orson Welles. In answer to my question, Orson says that there is no reason, that he adored his father; and no doubt he did. All the same, the parallel with Kane is curiously haunting. One recalls the sled named Rosebud, Kane's symbol of maternal affection, the loss of which deprives him irrecoverably of the power to love or be loved. (Mr. Bernstein, Kane's loyal business manager, is admittedly based on Dr. Maurice Bernstein, the family physician who acted as Welles's unofficial guardian after his father died in 1928.) It is not inconceivable, as a perceptive American director once suggested to me, that Orson reached a state of perfect self-fulfilment just before his mother's death, and that he has been trying ever since to recapture it.

At ten, under heavy persuasion from his father and Dr. Bernstein, Orson joined the progressive Todd School for Boys in Woodstock, Illinois, where he flourished for five years, admiringly encouraged by the school director, Roger Hill, with whom, while still in his teens, he wrote a fledgling play and edited a popular textbook called *Everybody's Shakespeare*. On principle, however, he disapproves of conventional education in any form, and will have none of it for Beatrice, his five-year-old daughter: 'What does it teach you except to show up at the same hour every morning — and still learn nothing?' In his fourteenth year the death of his father cast him upon a world from which security, as his parents had known it, was about to be banished by the Wall Street crash. An orphaned prodigy, he grew up hoarding nostalgia; in particular, a nostalgia for old-fashioned melodrama, for stock companies, for turn-of-the-century Americana, which he had imbibed from his father. It persisted into later life, as many of his stage productions bear witness: *The Drunkard*, William Gillette's *Too Much Johnson*, *The Green Goddess*, *Around the World in Eighty Days*, and

Moby Dick, which Orson directed in London as it might have been presented by a touring company in the nineties. Again and again he has gone back to the flamboyant era of the actor-manager in the astrakhan collar, the era of Tarkington's Ambersons and Citizen Kane's infancy. Orson has always secretly thought of himself as a vagabond rogue.

Just before he graduated from Todd, at the age of fifteen, an ad appeared in *The Billboard*. It read, in part:

ORSON WELLES—Stock, Characters, Heavies, Juveniles or as cast . . . Lots of pep, experience and ability. Close in Chicago early in June and want place in good stock company for remainder of season.

He was on his own. It is not fanciful to see Orson's life as an unfinished picaresque novel, each chapter of which is a bizarre adventure strung like a bead on the thread of the hero's personality; the raw material, in fact, for a new *Citizen Kane*, different from the old in that the central character would be a maker of art, not merely a collector.

The lunch is over. Orson insists on paying, and summons his Italian henchman, a minor but authentic prince, to look after the bill. The prince sportively doubts whether he has enough cash. 'Very well,' says the ventripotent Orson, beaming broadly. 'My signature against the world!'

I never cease to be fascinated by the spectacle of a talent so huge yet so homeless, so vast yet so vagrant. Other people sink roots; but Orson perpetually wanders, a citizen of no fixed territory save that of art. I had already heard him on the subject of his upbringing; I wanted now to discuss his adult life, during which he had spanned the globe in an effort to recapture the creative security of his childhood.

The next day I lunched with him again, this time at Horcher's, his favourite among the city's great restaurants. Spain has always been one of his chosen countries. Although he is no believer in formal education, he is having his daughter, Beatrice, taught to dance flamenco; when I asked her what she thought about while stamping her feet and flashing her eyes in such precocious frenzy, she pondered and replied, 'I think that I *hate* the *floor*'.

Talking to Orson can be a disquieting experience; one feels one is boring him, wasting his time, especially if the purpose of the meeting is professional. He has so often suffered at the hands of journalists. 'The French are the worst,' he says. 'They ask long questions that *are* the answers. I nod, and the question is printed without the question mark, as my idea.' Having ordered caviare, blintzes and venison, he tells me that his greatest burden has always been his grandiose physical appearance. 'My trouble is that I exude affluence,' he says. 'I look successful. Whenever the critics see me, they say to themselves: "It's time he was knocked — he's had it too good for too long." But I *haven't* had it so good; I just look that

way. I need jobs like anyone else.' He splutters with baritone laughter.
'Every time I bring out a new movie,' he goes on, 'nobody bothers to
review it — at least, not until the last paragraph. Instead, they write a long
essay on "the Welles Phenomenon and what has become of it". They don't
review my work; they review me!'

He left school in 1930, an orphan aged fifteen, and at once set about the
task, which proved to be lifelong, of inventing himself. His first parentless
years were favoured ones. Thanks to his father's legacy, he never felt the
pinch of the depression. Intended for Harvard, he embarked instead on a
painting trip to Ireland, where he gate-crashed the Dublin Gate Theatre and
became a professional actor. 'You handle your voice like a singer,' said the
director, Hilton Edwards, 'and there isn't a note of sincerity in it.' He was
then sixteen. We next hear of him sketching in Morocco, fighting bulls
around Seville, and returning unsung to the States in 1933, when Thornton
Wilder gave him a letter to Alexander Woollcott, who in turn introduced
him to Katharine Cornell. The last lady of the American theatre (as I
sometimes think of her) hired him to join her company in a tour of *Romeo
and Juliet* and *Candida*. Already, at seventeen, he thought of himself as
past the age when he could convincingly play juveniles, and he turned up at
the first rehearsal of the Shaw comedy assuming that he had been cast as
Morell, Candida's husband. He was surprised to see that Basil Rathbone
was also present: 'I took Miss Cornell to one side and told her that I didn't
want to interfere, but didn't she think Rathbone was a little elderly to be
playing Marchbanks, the adolescent poet?' It had to be carefully explained
to him that that was *his* role; Mr. Rathbone had been engaged as Morell.

One of the dates the company played was Atlantic City, where Orson
dabbled for the first time in professional magic. He practised palmistry in a
booth on the boardwalk, so successfully that he almost unnerved himself.
To begin with, he confined himself to simple exercises in applied
psychology: 'I would look into the crystal ball and then say to the customer:
"You have a scar on your knee" — because in fact most people have. If that
didn't work, I would say; "You had a profound emotional experience
between the ages of eleven and thirteen." I don't think I ever failed with
that one.' But he soon discovered that he was less of a charlatan than he had
imagined; too many of his intuitions turned out to be correct. 'I began,' he
says, 'to think of myself as Ming the Merciless.' That Orson is capable of
insights amounting to prophecy is borne out by a number of stories, the best
known of which concerns the occasion when he escorted Eugene O'Neill's
daughter Oona to a Hollywood night club and offered, on the strength of
two hours' acquaintance, to read her hand. 'Within a very short time,' he
declared, 'you will meet and marry Charles Chaplin.' Like so many of her
father's heroines, Miss O'Neill obeyed the voice of destiny.

Orson made his Broadway debut in December 1934, playing the Chorus
and Tybalt in *Romeo and Juliet*. There ensues the first familiar period of his

legend — the four-year battle with the American theatre. 'Paris is the playwright's city,' he says, 'London is the actor's city, and New York is the director's city.' Or if New York wasn't, Orson did much to make it so. In the late thirties, more than at any other time in American history, the development of the theatre seemed intimately bound up with the development of the country as a whole; a radical adventure was under way, and the nation's culture was among the spearheads of the nations's hopes. In 1935 the New Deal sired the Federal Theatre Project, devised not only to alleviate unemployment in the theatre but to bring good drama within the reach of the unemployed audiences. By subsidising the Project, Washington accepted the principle that the fostering of culture was a matter for public as well as private concern. Progressive artists, in a period when nearly all artists were progressives, embraced the scheme; and no one who hopes to understand Orson should forget that his career as a director was launched under its liberal auspices.

The Project set up a Negro branch at the old Lafayette Theatre in Harlem, and it was here, in the spring of 1936, that Orson and John Houseman staged their shattering Negro production of *Macbeth*. 'On opening night,' Orson recalls, 'the curtain never fell. The audience swarmed up onto the stage, cheering.' He afterwards went on tour with the show: 'We had a temperamental Macbeth, and in Indianapolis we lost him. I blacked myself up about three shades darker than anyone else in the cast and played the part for two weeks. Nobody in the audience noticed anything unusual.' Back at the Lafayette, he directed a fiercely anti-segregationist piece called *Turpentine*, and remembers his horror when Noble Sissle's pit orchestra played the first-night audience out to the reactionary strains of 'Is It True What They Say about Dixie?'

On Broadway, still for the Federal Theatre, he staged and starred in Marlowe's *Doctor Faustus*, which ran for six months; but the cultural euphoria in Washington was being blown away by hot winds from the right, whose breath Orson felt in the summer of 1937, when government sponsorship was abruptly withdrawn from his production of Marc Blitzstein's leftist opera *The Cradle Will Rock* on the eve of its première. Locked out of the Maxine Elliot Theatre, he found another (the Venice, later renamed the Century) and led the first-nighters thither on a triumphal march up Sixth Avenue. Confronted by an Actors' Equity ruling that forbade the actors to appear on the stage, he seated them among the audience and had them sing their parts from there. It was a great crusading night. Tom Paine would have enjoyed it; and there is no one in American history (I have his word for this) Orson would rather have been than Tom Paine.

In 1939 the Federal Theatre Project was voted out of existence. By then Orson and John Houseman had spent two seasons in private enterprise, running the Mercury Theatre on Forty-First Street, getting simultaneously into debt and the history books with a string of productions that included *Danton's Death, Heartbreak House,* and the startling modern-dress version of *Julius Caesar.* They regarded the Mercury Theatre's broadcasts simply as money-making adjuncts to its theatrical activities; nobody was more astonished than Orson when, taking a stroll during a break in the dress rehearsal of *Danton's Death,* he saw his name travelling in lights around the Times Building, followed by an announcement that he had panicked America with his radio adaptation of H. G. Wells' *War of the Worlds.* He had intended the programme as a Halloween joke; not for the first time, and certainly not the last, he had over-estimated the intelligence of his audience. Such errors are healthy: what kills art is the assumption that people are stupid. 'About three years after the Martian broadcast,' Orson says, 'I was reading a Whitman poem on a patriotic Sunday programme, when someone ran into the studio and shouted into the mike that Pearl Harbour had been attacked. Nobody paid any attention. They just shrugged and said, "There he goes again." ' The Mercury Theatre survived on Broadway until the spring of 1939, having demonstrated that a repertory company needs more than critical applause and intermittently filled houses to keep it alive; it needs the continuity and security that only steady subsidies can provide.

Lunch, the long Spanish lunch, has come to an end. It is time for the bullfight; and I ask Orson what would have happened if, twenty years ago, he had been given a theatre of his own and enough money to hold a permanent company together. 'No question about it,' he says at once; 'I'd be running it today.' Orson's kind of theatre belongs in a tradition that looks beyond the next flop or the next season's deficit; its affinities are with the great non-commercial institutions — the Comédie Française, the Moscow Art Theatre, the Berliner Ensemble. Even as I say that, I shush myself, realising how much harm it may do to Orson's Broadway reputation.

His relationship with money requires a brief rubric. The legend insists that Orson overspends; the truth is that he is a delayed earner. *Citizen Kane* was a flop in 1941, but over the years it has returned its investment many times over, and the same applies to *The Magnificent Ambersons.* Orson's pictures are long-distance runners in a system dedicated to sprinters. True, *The Lady from Shanghai* was disproportionately expensive, but against that one must balance *The Stranger* and *Macbeth,* both of which he brought in on schedule and under budget. Orson's first large debt was to the United States government, which refused to allow him tax deductions on personal losses (amounting to $350,000) that were incurred by his 1946 Broadway production of *Around the World in Eighty Days.* He moved to Europe, leaving the argument to his lawyers; and since then his financial problems have affected none but his own productions. They have sometimes lost money and left behind them a trail of unpaid bills; but this, in our society, is precisely what one would expect of a man who rates his responsibility to the cause of art above his responsibility to private investment. More subsidy from the state, not less extravagance on Orson's part, is the answer to the perennial Welles predicament. He regards art as a social right, not as an accidental privilege; as a matter for public endowment, not as incentive to private speculation. That his work should occasionally lose money is not only inevitable but honourable.

We meet in the bar of the Palace Hotel after the bullfight; it has been a bad one, but Orson is not depressed, for to the true *aficiónado* there are no dull bullfights. He watches them with the analytical scrutiny of an initiate, which means that he is never bored and rarely transported. He watches films in the same way: 'I'm like a vivisectionist. I dissect them shot by shot. I'd give half my kingdom to be able to see a movie and forget what I know about movie technique.' He responds politely to the group that gathers around him in the bar; perhaps too politely, making me wish he would squander less of his energy in a form as perishable as talk. Tennessee Williams, one of the circle, extracts from his mouth a cigarette holder full of cancer-repelling crystals and murmurs to me that no one should ever attack Orson — 'a man so vulnerable and of such magnitude'. Everyone is vulnerable who is at once gifted and gregarious. Orson is fully aware that for him, as for all great talkers, conversation is what Cyril Connolly once called it, 'a ceremony of self-wastage'. I record a few overheard snatches. Of Antonioni, the director of the wildly praised Italian film *L'Avventura*, he says: 'The critics tell me he's a stylist of the cinema. But how can you be a stylist if you don't understand grammar?' Of a famous American actor, generally renowned for his modesty off-screen: 'There is nothing more frightening than quiet vanity.' Of Oscar Wilde's comedies: 'Why don't people realise that they were written to be acted by tweedy, red-faced Victorian squires, not by attractive faggots?' He flies these conversational kites because they are expected of him, and then subsides into heavy, abstracted brooding. The circle disperses, and he generously wastes himself on me.

We talk about his Hollywood epoch, which lasted on and off for roughly seven years. Leaving Broadway in 1939, he brought the Mercury actors — among them Joseph Cotten and Agnes Moorehead — out to work with him for RKO. The trip produced *Citizen Kane*, which stands in no need of eulogy from me. It revolutionised Hollywood rather as the aeroplane revolutionised warfare; it drove William Randolph Hearst, on whom Kane was putatively modelled, to declare war on Orson in his newspapers; and it cost less than $750,000, which seems a reasonable price to pay for a landmark in cinema history. In 1941 Orson started to shoot *The Magnificent Ambersons*, based on Booth Tarkington's story about the decline of a prosperous southern family. 'I'd finished the rough cut,' Orson says, 'and I needed about two weeks more work to get the picture ready, when Jock Whitney and Nelson Rockefeller, who were both RKO shareholders, asked me to go down to South America and make a film about Latin-American solidarity.' By then the United States had entered the war, and Orson patriotically agreed. The course of shooting was not uneventful; headlines were made in Rio de Janeiro when Orson and the Mexican Ambassador to Brazil protested against an exorbitant hotel bill by carefully throwing a great deal of furniture out of a window of His Excellency's suite.

Meanwhile, in Orson's words: 'RKO had shown *The Ambersons* at a sneak preview, probably in Pomona. The audience laughed at it, so they cut it to pieces, shot a new ending, and released it before I could do anything about it. They called me in Brazil to say they'd broken my contract.' Among the cuts were Agnes Moorehead's finest moments, many of them improvised during the six-week rehearsal period on which Orson had insisted; and the whole epilogue was lopped off, in which Joseph Cotten visited Miss Moorehead in a shabby rooming house and learned from her how and why the magnificence of the Ambersons had faded. 'Nowadays,' Orson says, 'everybody makes pictures three hours long — it's almost obligatory. There are times when I feel a little bit jealous.' He likes the efficiency of Hollywood studios ('where there's no difference between you and the workers except that they're earning more') and admits that his veneration for the cinema derives from his period at RKO. 'The cinema has no boundaries,' he says. 'It's a ribbon of dream.' He sounds genuinely awed.

His later Hollywood pictures, such as *Journey into Fear, The Stranger,* and *The Lady from Shanghai,* are as different from *Kane* and *The Ambersons* as Graham Greene's 'entertainments' are different from his serious novels; in fact, it may even be that Welles influenced Greene's thrillers by his use of shock cutting, bizarre settings, and eccentric characterisation. The last shot of *The Lady from Shanghai,* completed in 1946, symbolises the end of a phase in Orson's life. The film is socially quite outspoken; Orson plays an ingenuous Irish sailor, once a fighter for the Spanish Republic, who gets involved in what he describes as the 'bright, guilty world' of the rich. He falls for, and is cold-bloodedly deceived by, the wife of a millionaire lawyer. After a horrendous showdown in a deserted fun-fair, she is shot by her husband, and appeals to Orson for help. Her injury is mortal; but his decision is moral. He rejects her plea; he has compromised too often, and leaves her, walking out of the fun-fair into the grey dawn of a new morning. (The riddled victim was played by his second wife, Rita Hayworth; they were divorced in 1947 after four years together. His first marriage, to a Chicago actress named Virginia Nicholson, had broken up in 1939.)

One tends to forget that his Hollywood days coincide with the Second World War. Orson himself has not forgotten. Flat feet kept him out of the armed forces: 'I'm still suffering,' he says, 'from the traumatic effect of being forbidden to do what all my friends were doing.' He who had addressed innumerable anti-Nazi rallies, who had rabidly supported the fight against Fascism in Spain, now found himself condemned to inactivity when the crucial battle was joined. He pulled what political strings he could, and from time to time he was bundled out of the country under a false name to examine captured Nazi newsreels and other filmic trivia. But his missions were few, and seldom very secret: 'I was flown into Lisbon as Harrison Carstairs, the ball-bearings manufacturer, and there were twenty people waiting at the airport for my autograph.' (On one such errand he met and briefly beguiled himself with an Argentinian radio actress name Eva, who later emerged from obscurity as the wife of Juan Peron.) Meanwhile, the Hearst press regularly printed snide items inquiring why the playboy Welles was lounging around swimming pools when democracy was in danger; and after each new gibe, Orson usually received a draft notice. One of his periodic medical examinations took place when he had just returned from a mission to Latin America, for the purposes of which he had been created a temporary brigadier general. 'Any of you men ever hold rank above a private?' asked the sergeant at the recruiting depot. Orson shuffled forward. 'State the rank you held.' Orson told him. 'OK, Brigadier General,' said the sergeant enticingly, 'get down on your hands and knees and clean up those cigarette butts.'

Orson has always had a passion for politics. At one time he thought seriously of running for the Senate on the Democratic ticket; had he done so, it would have made a provocative contest, because the Republican candidate in the state of Wisconsin was the late Joseph McCarthy. 'Basically,' Orson says, 'I'm a public orator (as was Charles Foster Kane) and that isn't the same as a television orator, which is what a lot of TV producers keep asking me to be. Television is talking to two or three people through a box, instead of talking to two thousand people and making them *feel* like two or three people.' If Orson were ever to join a party, he would be its first member, and its label would be Liberal Hedonist, or Collective Individualist. Its sympathies would be leftish but it would remain, like its founder, an unaffiliated maverick.

The streets of Madrid have darkened, and drinks have faded into dinner. Orson continues, unfading. After Broadway and Hollywood came his wandering period, which is not yet, and may never be, over. His career since 1946 is a kaleidoscope that baffles chronology. He bids farewell to Broadway with *Around the World in Eighty Days*, the most opulent of his many tributes to the free-wheeling actor-managing days of the late Victorian era. He departs for Europe, leaving a wake of tax problems behind him, but not before filming a sombre truncation of *Macbeth* — around the bard in twenty-one shooting days. Later, after numerous halts and hazards due to inadequate finances, he directs and stars in a massively picturesque film of *Othello*, to be described in some quarters as the movie version of Ruskin's *Stones of Venice*. The echoing voices and footsteps, and the sudden cuts from long-shot silence to close-up animation, stamp it as unmistakably Wellesian; so, alas, does the scrambled text, not to mention Orson's own resonantly impassive performance. 'He never acts,' says Eric Bentley; 'he is photographed.' With peerless skill, he plays the mischievously corrupt Harry Lime in *The Third Man*, and improvises a memorable exchange with its producer, the late Alexander Korda.

ORSON: I wish the Pope would make you a cardinal, Alex.
KORDA: Why a cardinal?
ORSON: Because then we'd only have to kiss your ring.

He is also alleged to have improvised Harry Lime's famous observation that after centuries of democracy the Swiss have produced nothing more inspiring than the cuckoo clock; falsely attributed to Orson, the line was actually written by Graham Greene.

In Paris, Orson presents a double bill of his own composition, consisting of a play about Hollywood called *The Unthinking Lobster* and a modern revamping of the Faust legend, with music by Duke Ellington. Between whiles he plays fiends and frauds in other people's films. He flies to New York to appear, outrageously bewhiskered, in Peter Brook's TV production of *King Lear*. For a day's work as Father Mapple in John Huston's film of *Moby Dick* he is paid $20,000, whereafter he makes his own dramatisation of the novel and stages it in London, transforming the gilded Duke of York's Theatre into a storm-tossed whaling ship, without benefit of scenery. By now he has remarried, his new wife being Paola Mori, a shrewd, lissome Italian actress of noble birth. In 1956 he returns to Broadway in a production of *Lear*. It flops. During the previews, Orson sprains one ankle and breaks the other, and plays the opening performance from a wheelchair, thereby supplying further fuel for those who think him congenitally self-destructive. His acting ability comes up for reappraisal; Walter Kerr contributes a damaging analysis: 'As an emotional actor, Welles is without insight, accuracy, power, or grace. In short, without talent. The only parts he could ever play were parts that were cold, intellectual, emotionally dead.'

In 1958 Orson is summoned back to Hollywood to play a venal cop in a thriller called *Touch of Evil*. While he is considering the offer in the producer's office, the telephone rings; it is Charlton Heston, who has been approached to play the lead but wants to know who else has been signed. 'Well, we've got Orson Welles —' the producer begins. 'Great!' says Heston, cutting in. 'I'll appear in anything he directs.' 'Hold on a minute,' says the producer, feeling that events are slipping out of his hands. Hastily he asks Orson whether he will direct, to which Orson agrees, on condition that he have full control of script and casting. After a pause: 'Sure,' the producer tells Heston, 'sure Welles is directing.' The result is a picture of enormous virtuosity. Orson demands two weeks of private rehearsal before shooting begins, and gets from his actors performances of fantastic, unguarded intimacy. They are shamelessly themselves, and seem imbued with his own conviction that in show business being inhibited gets you nowhere. Meanwhile, the camera swoops and hovers like a kingfisher, inscribing Orson's autograph on every sequence. Charlton Heston, as a Mexican lawyer, gives the best performance of his life. The film wins prizes in Europe, but is shunned in America. Soon afterwards we find Orson directing Olivier in the London production of *Rhinoceros*.

No one is more fertile than Orson in ideas that, for one reason or another, never get carried out. There was *Monsieur Verdoux*, for which he supplied the original script; and which he was to direct, until Chaplin decided to direct it himself. There was the satire, drawn from the love affair of D'Annunzio and Duse, which he planned for Chaplin and Garbo. There was Homer's *Odyssey*, for which he hired a writer whom he was tardy in paying, and to whose repeated pleas for advice about how to make ends meet he finally replied with a single cable: DEAR ——, LIVE SIMPLY, AFFECTIONATE REGARDS, ORSON WELLES. There were also projects involving Conrad, Dickens, Dostoevski, Rostand, and Tolstoy, of which nothing tangible came.

At dinner we are joined by the Earl of Harewood, who runs the Edinburgh Festival and wonders whether Orson would like to bring a production to it in 1962. In principle, Orson would be delighted. In the course of conversation, Harewood remarks that he was lately in Japan, where he saw the Kabuki Theatre and didn't tremendously like it. Orson rounds on him, mountainously glowering, and observes that anyone who doesn't appreciate Kabuki must be an ignoramus. Harewood nods, adding that he must have seen them on a bad night. Even on a bad night, Orson insists, they are far superior to anything the western theatre can produce. A firework display, marking the end of the Madrid *feria*, explodes in the park outside the restaurant. Hoping to pacify Orson, Harewood explains that he immensely enjoyed the Kabuki performers Sol Hurok brought to New York. He hopes wrong. 'That,' Orson thunders, 'was a contemptible travesty. If you liked that, you don't like Kabuki.' Yet within minutes he has charmed us out of embarrassment into laughter; and next day I hear from Harewood that the Edinburgh offer still stands, and that Orson and Maria Callas are the only genuine *monstres sacrés* he has ever met.

At times Orson is prey to depressions, onslaughts of gloom, spleen, and sulks that the Middle Ages would probably have ascribed to the cardinal sin of accidie, which induces a sense of futility and a temporary paralysis of the will. 'From *accidie*,' Aldous Huxley once wrote, 'comes dread to begin to work any good deeds, and finally *wanhope*, or despair. On its way to ultimate *wanhope*, *accidie* produces a whole crop of minor sins, such as idleness, tardiness, *lâchesse*. . . .' It also means *ennui*, the French brand of philosophic boredom. When *accidie* grips him, you feel that Orson has given up people; that he has already seen everything on earth he will ever want to see, and met everyone he will ever want to meet. Faced with that suggestion, however, he will suddenly revive and deny it; Isak Dinesen, Chou En-Lai and Robert Graves are three people he venerates and would adore to meet, if only he felt less intimidated by the prospect. Soon his spirits are soaring, and he is telling you that the only hope for American drama lies (as well it may) in theatres outside New York, municipally supported so that every year they can present their best productions for a short season on Broadway. You feel kindled by his presence, by his mastery of rhetoric, by his uncalculating generosity. 'A superb bravura director,' I once called him, 'a fair bravura actor, and a limited bravura writer; but an incomparable bravura personality.' Orson is a genius without portfolio. When he leaves a room, something irreplaceable and life-enhancing goes with him; something that may eventually install him, given luck and our help, in the special pantheon whose other occupants are Stanislavsky, Gordon Craig, Max Reinhardt, Jacques Copeau and Bertolt Brecht.

Show: October/November 1961; *Tynan Right and Left*, 1967

MILES DAVIS

Now, when the talk is all of free-form jazz and 'action blowing' and 'after third-stream music, what?', may not be a bad time to pay tribute to Miles Davis, who discovered in the arduous course of the 1950s how to make a unique sound with a trumpet. He based a style on that sound; rose to the height of his profession with that style; and is already in danger — such are the quicksands on which jazz reputations are built — of being written off as a reactionary. Miles found himself as a musician some seven or eight years ago; and those who find themselves are seldom objects of affection to those who are still seeking.

'Talent,' said Delacroix, 'does whatever it wants to do. Genius does only what it can.' Miles can make his sound; 'deathly,' as one critic said, 'in its purity'; piercing and orphaned, and so devoid of vibrato that it recalls to one's inner ear the virginal clarity of a Sistine choirboy. With this sound he composes spare, discreet, elliptical solos, avoiding fast *tempi* — which are inimical alike to his temperament and technique — as strictly as he avoids flamboyant emotionalism. To borrow a phrase applied by George Jean Nathan to the ideal critic, he is like a Thermos bottle, suggesting the presence of heat without radiating it.

The modern movement in jazz has many mansions, but only four architects: the late Charlie Parker, Thelonious Monk, Dizzy Gillespie and Miles, the junior partner. These were the four horsemen of the jazz apocalypse that began in the 1940s and ended by transforming the music; new complexities replaced old naïvetés, and in the process jazz grew up.

Yet despite the sophistication of his style, Miles still speaks in a musical idiom to which children can respond; and English children, at that. A few months ago my nine-year-old daughter came in to be kissed while I was playing his most haunting LP, *Kind of Blue*. She listened for a moment and then said: 'That's Miles Davis.' I asked her how she could tell. 'Because,' she replied 'it sounds like a little boy who's been locked out and wants to get in.'

Miles in the flesh is not always as dependably superb as he is on records. In public, he sometimes displays the kind of diffidence that conceals (and often protects) enormous private egotism. I first saw him perform in the mid-fifties, at the opening of a short-lived jazz club in Greenwich Village; he turned up more than an hour late, and backed on to the stand with his horn under his jacket. Apprehensively, he unveiled it, heavily muted, and blew about eight notes into the mike, after which he withdrew, shaking his head; it was if Einstein had been asked to lecture on the quantum theory to a class of backward teenagers.

In 1960 he toured Britain for the first time with his quintet and I followed him from date to date. Musically he gave his audiences full measure, but he irked them, too, by his obstinate reluctance to fraternise. In public, Miles is always alone. He never announces numbers, introduces himself or makes jokes; nor, for that matter, do Oistrakh or Menuhin. Less defensibly, he never takes bows, arguing that his responsibility to the audience ends as soon as the last note has been played. The argument is specious. The truth is that Miles loathes being beholden to anyone, even to the extent of acknowledging applause. He leads a life of rigidly limited obligations. Outside his work, his family and a few close friends, he is committed to nothing. A few years ago he turned down an invitation to pose for the camera of Richard Avedon, not because he disapproved of Avedon but because the record company to which he was under contract had specifically asked him to accept. 'When people *ask* you to do something,' he explained to me, 'all you can say is no.' He spoke as if it were self-evident.

In Britain Miles was at his most isolated, performing in provincial concert halls and metropolitan movie-houses to vast assemblies of ethnic strangers. A dapper, tapering figure in evening dress of black Italian silk, he would take the stage like a fawn in a fairground, or a hermit poet thrust against his will into a populous market place. He had always jibbed at visiting England, because, he once told me, 'I can't stand to hear English spoken that way'; only high financial rewards persuaded him to change his mind. Unidentified, and with no preliminary foot-tapping, the first number would start; Miles and the tenor player stating the theme, with the rhythm section working behind them, then Miles alone leaning back with his trumpet aimed at the footlights, composing bleak, illuminating footnotes to what the ensemble had stated, each note hanging in the air like ripe fruit — plump Moselle grapes when his horn was open, and bottled plums when it was muted.

One thought, as with the best performers one often thinks, of a matador raptly and serenely defying the audience (which in show business is always the bull), and ending up by hypnotising it. Miles has other affinities with Spain, though he has never been there. The Moors fascinate him: were they not the only coloured people to have left a durable mark on European civilisation? He loves the music they bequeathed — *cante flamenco*, *cante hondo* — and has tried, in albums like *Sketches of Spain*, to make his trumpet reproduce the flexible wailing of Spanish song. 'That music has enough space in it,' he says. 'You can go on for hours. And you don't just *attack* a note. You can change the whole sound of it.' For medical reasons, matadors eat sparingly on workdays; for psychological reasons, Miles does the same. 'Food,' he declares, 'makes my mind sluggish.'

His solo completed, his meditations made audible, Miles wanders into the wings, leaving the limelight to the man on the tenor sax. This habit of casual departure tended to worry the British, although, as Miles would remark with mock bewilderment: 'What do they want me to do? Stand around and bug the guy?' Later, he would make spectral re-entrances from unexpected corners of the stage, just in time for the last chorus of each number. Then the curtains would swing together, cutting off the applause in its prime.

Offstage, he would bustle past the assembled admirers, murmuring vaguely in the hoarse, gurgling undertone that is all that remains of his voice; a botched operation nine years ago not only sliced nodes from his vocal cords but the cords themselves. (In fairness to the surgeon, I should add that some people blame Miles's croak on a shouting match in which he indulged too soon after the operation.)

In London he rarely emerged from his hotel room except to be driven to a concert date. 'I don't need to see places I've read about,' he said to me, explaining his lack of curiosity. Conversations with strangers would resolve themselves, when the stranger had run out of small talk, into lengthy silences, broken only by abrupt, staccato irrelevancies from Miles. One night, driven to apology by a particularly sustained bout of taciturnity, I said that by his standards English people must seem very dull. He coughed and chuckled. 'You don't mind people being dull,' he said, 'if you aren't dull yourself.'

He hates to be touched, physically as well as emotionally. Four years ago he had his skull cracked by a cop who saw him outside Birdland, taking the air, and told him to move on. It was not so much the order that Miles resented as the fact that the cop grabbed him in the course of enforcing it. When that happened, Miles lashed out; and headlines blazed.

Similarly, he resents any encroachment on his artistic privacy. Apart from Ralph Gleason and Nat Hentoff, he has no time for critics. An English reviewer of some repute came up to him after a concert and remarked, politely if a trifle uppishly: 'I've just been listening to that first LP you made, back in 1948, and I'd like to tell you that I think you've improved out of all recognition since then.' Miles stared at him gnomishly and said: 'When did you first hear that LP?' 'About a year ago,' said the critic. 'Man,' said Miles, with a broad, emphatic grin, *you should have heard it in 1948!*

The remark was unanswerable, and it sent the critic into a fit of explanation and apology. When he had left, Miles suavely observed: 'That guy's so nervous, *he* fixes *my* tie.' After witnessing a number of similar encounters, I realised that Miles had an innate grasp of the basic English art of one-upmanship. As Lena Horne said to me a year or two ago: 'Miles is a potentate. He's also a puritan, and the combination can be pretty sadistic.'

The potentate was born in Alton, Illinois, in the late spring of 1926. Miles is that new and still relatively rare phenomenon in jazz, a Negro musician who has never known poverty. His father was a prosperous bourgeois dentist, and his mother was a prominent and respected figure in East St. Louis, to which the family moved when Miles was a baby. He liked jazz as soon as he heard it, and when he was thirteen his father gave him a trumpet, to what he now suspects was his mother's deep disapproval. It was only at her urgent request that he refrained from leaving high school to go on the road with Tiny Bradshaw's orchestra; but he drew the line when she tried to send him to Fisk University. The Billy Eckstine band was in St. Louis, starring Charlie Parker and Dizzy Gillespie, and providentially lacking a third trumpet player. The ensuing tableau is one that recurs throughout jazz history: the band in rehearsal, the empty chair, the shy neophyte nursing his instrument case, the invitation to sit in, and finally the offer of a temporary job. Overnight, the seventeen-year-old gained admittance to the heartland of modern jazz.

In 1945, with his father's support, he went to New York and studied at Juilliard. Befriended and overawed by Charlie Parker — the sweet Bird who came, not many years later, to a sour end, destroyed by narcotics and alcohol — he was rushed into the front line of modernism, then fighting its crucial battles with traditional jazz, and he can be heard on many Parker recordings of the period, straining the limits of his technique to keep pace with the master's baffling flights of invention. From Parker and Thelonious Monk he learned new chord progressions; from the late Freddie Webster he learned a sound — the pure, vibratoless tone that was to become his hallmark. At the same time he taught himself not to imitate the high-register coruscations of Dizzy Gillespie. Once, according to Nat Hentoff, he asked Dizzy:

'Why can't I play high like you?' 'Because you don't hear up there,' Gillespie told him. 'You hear in the middle register.'

In the late forties, Miles met the arranger Gil Evans, a diffident, aquiline man more than ten years his senior, and a restless experimenter with new tonal colourings in jazz. Of these experiments Miles became the centrepiece; the jewel had found its appropriate setting. The first fruits of their collaboration are to be heard in a celebrated series of recordings made in 1949-50 and since reissued under the collective title of *The Birth of the Cool*; led by Miles and guided by Evans, the nine-piece group assembled for these sessions included Gerry Mulligan and John Lewis as player-composers, and its instrumental line-up featured a French horn and a tuba. The results, lightly and elegantly swinging, set a new standard of sophisticated lyricism in modern jazz. Since then Miles and Gil Evans have frequently worked together: some of the finest LPs of recent years — among them *Miles Ahead*, *Porgy and Bess* and *Sketches of Spain* — are those on which Miles swoops and soars like a kingfisher above the swirling, kaleidoscopic eddies of an Evans orchestration. Their recording dates are concentrated orgies of perfectionism. Evans tends to be the calmer of the two; Miles gets ulcerously edgy. During *Porgy*, he told me, 'I felt like I'd been eating nails.' Few of Miles' close friends are white, and of these Evans is by far the most intimate. 'Gil,' he says, 'is like my thumb.'

For a jazz musician, Miles is nowadays comparatively affluent. He receives between $3,500 and $4,500 a week in clubs, but will only play in clubs of which he approves (i.e. whose owners are untouched by the Jim Crow tarbrush, and respect his refusal to play requests or chat with the clients). He has not always been able to dictate his terms so securely. In 1949 — perhaps the high point of drug addiction in jazz history — he took desperately to heroin, that last refuge of the outsider in an over-competitive world; and four years of failing income and increasing unreliability went by before pride drove him to kick the habit. By 1955, he had recovered his balance and more than restored his reputation, coming back with the stripped simplicity of utterance that has marked all his subsequent work.

In this simplicity some critics have found only meagreness. 'He just uses fewer notes,' one of them said to me. 'Since he made his comeback, he doesn't play better, he just plays safer. Except when he's following a Gil Evans score, he sticks to the melody. All he does is play it slowly, with a few unexpected notes thrown in to prove that he's modern.' It is true that Miles seldom takes one by storm or surprise; and it is also true that he sometimes under-exerts himself; but as I listen to the marvellous spate of recorded sound that poured out of the Miles Davis Quintet in the late 1950s, I cannot help recalling a definition that Jean Cocteau once made of art. For some people, he said, art was a complicated way of saying very simple things: 'for us,' he continued, 'it is a simple way of saying very complicated things.' So with Miles Davis in his best period. I need hardly add that the simplicity is only apparent.

Miles lives in a noisy, rambling duplex apartment on West 77th Street in New York. With its marble-tile floors, leopard-skin rugs, abstract paintings, white brick walls and proliferating electronic gadgets, it might be the hunting lodge of some preternaturally hip Swedish grandee. An Italian greyhound named Milo prances around the place, and upstairs there are turtles. There are also children, four in number. Three of them derive from Miles' first marriage, an early error committed in Illinois and since erased by divorce. Cherry Anne, at eighteen the eldest, enjoys singing, and Gregory, a year younger, used to play the drums; otherwise the family is resolutely unmusical. After Miles Junior, aged thirteen, we come to a seven-year-old named Jean-Pierre who belongs to his second wife, Frances, from a former marriage. Sly, petite and sparkling, Frances moves with the physical elation of a pedigree pony, as befits a one-time member of the Katherine Dunham company; it was for her that Miles composed the skipping little melody called *Fran-Dance*.

When not working, driving his smart grey Ferrari or keeping his body in trim at a local gymnasium, Miles spends most of his time at home, relaxing in a desultory chaos of family small talk behind which, from some hidden loudspeaker, one can usually hear the faint, appealing cry of the paternal trumpet. Talking to semi-strangers like myself, he is willing to discuss music, but always at a distance, with beady eyes and a disenchanted smile. 'A melody is enough,' he may say; 'I can live on a melody for the next three months. I don't know about third-stream music; it's interesting, but that's all. It's like a woman I don't like, walking naked in front of me.' As he speaks, he is dialling his stockbroker's number: Miles is a dedicated investor. 'Music is like an affair with a woman. If you like her, you like her. But always — no violins. . . . Look, this is Miles. When that other stock goes up to twenty, sell it. Fine. Good-bye. . . . My favourite composers? Debussy, Khachaturian, Bloch and Ravel — *he* was born in the right place, between Spain and France.

Portentously, I asked him to name the five most important people alive. 'Me and Harold,' he promptly began, meaning Harold Lovette, his lawyer and confidant. 'And Gil, and Fran. And any American Negro over fifty years old. I think every Negro over fifty should get a medal for putting up with all that crap.' He rose and gave me a farewell grip, coupled with a husky salutation. The amplifier played pure Spain, the plangent sound of an Andalusian *saeta*; a woman's lament, reproduced by Miles's horn in all its pain and glottal sobbing.

Bullfighting and jazz are two minor arts with much in common. At the beginning of the century they were national and special; and both depended on collective improvisation. In New Orleans, the trumpet, trombone and clarinet improvised on a given melody; in Spain, the picador, banderillero and matador improvised on the theme of a given fighting bull. Suddenly, in the twenties, there arose in both countries a revolutionary performer who not only changed the course of the art he was practising but made it for the first time internationally renowned. In Spain, Juan Belmonte, and in America, Louis Armstrong. Outside their countries of origin, both were predictably reviled as harbingers of fiendish moral depravity.

In the thirties commercialism takes over. We hear on one side that bullfighting has been ruined by the mechanical, crowd-pleasing efficiency of Domingo Ortega; and on the other that jazz has been killed by the popular triumphs of Benny Goodman. The first hints of resurrection appear in 1939; at Minton's, in Harlem, a nucleus of venturesome musicians inaugurates the modern movement in jazz; and in Spain, a lean young rebel named Manolete takes the *alternativa* and becomes a full matador. There follows, in both countries, a ferocious struggle between the supporters of modernism and the adherents to tradition. The arrival of the LP permits a favoured soloist to improvise for fifteen minutes without interruption; at the same time, bullfighters develop the habit of prolonging the *faena* — the series of passes that precedes the kill — until it becomes the focal point of the spectacle. Traditionalists love teamwork; modernists love soloists; and the battle in both countries remains unresolved for more than a decade. An armistice is ultimately achieved. In jazz as in bullfighting, there arises a modern classicist, one who combines the best of both worlds. In Spain, his name is Antonio Ordóñez, the *Número Uno* of living matadors. In America it is Miles Davis.

The Spanish have a word, *duende*. It has no exact English equivalent, but it denotes the quality without which no flamenco singer or bullfighter can conquer the summit of his art. The ability to transmit a profoundly felt emotion to an audience of strangers with the minimum of fuss and the maximum of restraint: that is as near as our language can get to the full meaning of *duende*. Laurence Olivier has it; Maurice Evans does not. Billie Holiday had it, and so did Bessie Smith; but Ella Fitzgerald never reached it. It is the quality that differentiates Laurette Taylor from Lynn Fontanne, Ernest Hemingway from John O'Hara, Tennessee Williams from William Inge. Whatever else he may lack, Miles Davis has *duende*.

Holiday: February 1963; *Tynan Right And Left*, 1967

MARTHA GRAHAM

You do not have to love ballet to admire Martha Graham; all that is necessary is to love the human body and its capacity for expressive movement.

For the merely beautiful, the merely graceful or gymnastic, she has little use. In her dances content struggles to find its appropriate form, and often the struggle is visible in the finished work. Deliberately so; her disciple Agnes de Mille has remarked that where traditional ballet tries to conceal effort, Graham emphasises it, and: 'because effort starts with the nerve centres, it follows that a technique developed from percussive impulses that flow through the body . . . as motion is sent through a whip, would have enormous nervous vitality.'

Graham's dance-language is compressed and angular, as far removed from Fokine's as oriental ideographs are from Victorian copperplate, and when she began to speak it, more than thirty years ago, the cult that grew up around her confused and baffled the bourgeois balletomanes. The late Stark Young, doyen of American drama critics, was an early fan; but even he used to chide her for being 'ethnic' (which she wasn't), and recalls how he said of her: 'I'm always afraid that Martha's going to give birth to a cube on stage.'

Today there are many who would echo Agnes de Mille's eulogy: 'the most startling inventor, and by all odds the greatest performer that trod our native stage. . . . Technically speaking, hers is the single largest contribution in the history of western dancing.' And technique is only the beginning. 'I can see technique at Radio City,' she once told Miss de Mille. 'From you I ask something greater than that. From you I ask what cannot be learned in any class. Reaffirmation.' The tone is evangelical and entirely characteristic. Although I have heard her say: 'I am not a high priestess of *anything*,' she has managed to recruit an army of acolytes. They swarm about her, so many moths around her hard, gem-like flame.

In 1954 she played to thin but ecstatic houses at the Saville Theatre. Seeing her then, I was oppressed at first by her iron solemnity, but as her repertoire unfolded, one rapt female archetype succeeding another, I realised that Eric Bentley was right when he said: 'The diagnostic of the dancer Martha Graham is that she is an actress' — and a great one, at that, in the line of Duse. She dwarfed her company, erasing them, even in repose, by the serene authority of her presence; one thought of the late Ruth Draper, another great performer condemned by the uniqueness of her talent to appear only in works of her own creation.

I met Graham briefly in her dressing-room, but awe confined me to monosyllables. I had read too many daunting things about her: that 'in more than one way she resembles Nefertiti' (de Mille), that her beauty was 'of a formidable sort, enigmatic, ambiguous' and her face 'an unnaturally motionless mask' (Bentley). My own first impression was of a woman who looked forty and might be four hundred, and who combined the salient physical qualities of Helene Weigel as Mother Courage and Beatrice Lillie as Kabuki Lil.

With these images colliding in my mind, it is perhaps no wonder that I kept my trap virtually shut. She did the same: what little she said was slowly and precisely articulated, eked out with large, comprehensive gestures that employed the whole arm, from collarbone to finger-tip. I felt that speech, for her, was essentially a foreign language, a Pyrrhic victory over silence.

We did not meet again until last spring, when I spent an afternoon in her New York apartment. It might be the home of a geisha turned puritan. The floor is wall-to-wall wood, polished like ice; on a low coffee-table marigolds float in a shallow bowl; Chinese scrolls speckle the walls; and the centrepiece is an ornately carved Chinese couch, ideal for meditation though not, I should think, for sleep. Small ornaments abound: talismans in jade and ebony, painted sea-shells from Japan, and a tiny bronze ram from Persia, poised for three thousand years on the brink of attempting a skyward leap.

Her hair stretched back in a high bun, Graham greeted me with both hands. Pensively, and at moments gnomically, she talked about her life and work, sipping brandy between paragraphs, using her whole body to italicise important points, and looking, whenever she paused, as if she were about to disclose some gigantic private sorrow.

She was born in Pittsburgh of Scotch Presbyterian parents, with whom she migrated in childhood to California. Her mother's family were tenth-generation Americans, and there was plenty of Sunday school in her upbringing: 'My great-grandfather would spin in his grave if he knew I was dancing.' Although she is no longer a churchgoer, she thinks of herself as religious and keeps a Bible in her dressing room.

'I feel the twenty-third Psalm in everything I do. And the nineteenth Psalm, too — "The heavens declare the glory of God, and the firmament showeth his handiwork." And later it says: "There is neither speech nor language." I often hear that when I'm on stage. To my mind there are three sorts of language. First of all, there is the cosmic language, which is movement. Next, there is the language of sound. And finally, the language of particular words. As my father used to tell me: "Movement never lies."'

She was introduced to the pleasures of theatre by an illiterate Irish nurse named Lizzie, who took her to Punch and Judy shows. Her father was opposed to dancing as a career, but he died when she was in her teens, and she promptly joined the Denishawn School in Los Angeles, where she was duly enthralled by the preaching and practice of the great dancer-teacher, Ruth St. Denis. Her training completed, she moved to New York and taught for a while, but soon decided that she could not meet the demands of her talent without forming a company of her own. By 1931 she had achieved coterie fame on the East Coast, and the coterie has been spreading ever since.

The torments and anxieties of women — Biblical, mythological, Victorian and contemporary — stand at the centre of her work. 'All I have ever wanted to do,' she said to me, her lower jaw projecting as she paused in thought, 'was to create a vocabulary that would be adequate to the past and to the twentieth century. Not one or the other, but both. I am a thief. I'll steal from anyone, and any period. But I'm not interested in television or anything two-dimensional. The stage is my area. Theatre used to be a *verb*; it used to be an *act*. But nowadays it is just a noun. It is a place.'

Oriental drama and philosophy have always attracted her: 'I had a Zen master when I was in California. He affected me tremendously, and I've studied Zen on and off ever since. But I don't like what they call in San Francisco "Beat Zen". That's just *talking* about aesthetics, and anyway I hate the word "aesthetic". Real Zen has to do with physical behaviour. I've always been fascinated by oriental theatre, although I didn't go to Japan until 1956. I met one of their great, ancient female impersonators, and I went down on my knees.' Swinging off her chair, Graham folded the hinges of her body in an illustrative genuflection, so that her forehead brushed the shining floor. Righting herself with equal suddenness, she continued: 'I saw Mei Lan-fang when he came to America. He was the greatest Chinese actor of his time, and he always played female parts. He was that curious creature — a complete man and a complete woman.'

According to rumour, Graham's sense of vocation excludes private emotional allegiances; in the words of de Mille, 'one does not domesticate a prophetess'. I asked her whether rumour was right, and she smiled forgivingly. 'I do not believe in the cloister for the artist,' she said. 'An artist can live a full domestic life. I was married once, but it broke up. I wanted children, but I was told I couldn't have them without a difficult and dangerous operation. The choice I made had nothing to do with art.'

She runs a school of dance in a building owned by her most faithful patron, Bethsabbé de Rothschild, and there she has a family of nearly two hundred, drawn from nineteen countries. Stringently and devotedly, she moulds her pupils in her own durable image: 'Out of this wonderful thing that is man, you make a world. "We did it — you and I": that's what a great artist says to the audience. Look at Fonteyn in *The Sleeping Beauty* — such triumphant exaltation! — and Helene Weigel in *Mother Courage*, and Gielgud in *Hamlet*.' I reminded her that many of her ballets were concerned with untriumphant, even self-destructive, women. 'Yes, but tragedy is a sort of triumph. Did you ever see Ulanova? She's self-destructive, and that's how she achieves — what is the word? — *illumination*.'

Graham is unimpressed by her reputation as a living legend. 'The works themselves don't matter,' she said as we parted, 'and the legend only matters if it makes other people work. I have no opinion of myself except that I'm glad to be my own master. And if you want to know my philosophy — well, I once knew a man who told his maid that it was her sacred, bounden duty to go on scrubbing his floors. "Mister," she said, "I don't have to do *anything*, except to die."'

Observer: 18th August 1963; *Tynan Right and Left*, 1967

JOAN LITTLEWOOD

The most original and unpredictable director in the British theatre today is a stocky middle-aged woman who attended the International Drama Conference at last year's Edinburgh Festival and announced to an audience of two thousand people: 'I'm not a professional director. I don't know what professional directors are.'

She spoke casually but with passion, her perky crumpled face looking, as always, as if tears had lately dried on it. 'I'm an impostor here,' she went on, gesturing toward her fellow-delegates, who included Judith Anderson, Lillian Hellman, Laurence Olivier, Harold Pinter and dozens more. 'I haven't sat through a play in my life since I was fifteen. I spend my time watching the accidents and the courtesies and the hates and the loves and the acting of people in the streets — because that's where I live.' The audience was beginning to be ignited. She held them like an evangelist, but with no oratorical tricks. Her eyes, heavily lidded like those of an ornamental carp, were as noncommittal as her tone of voice, their twinkle almost hidden. A few centuries ago, I reflected, such a woman might easily have been burned as a witch.

She continued, this wily holy innocent, in language that bypassed logic, making only emotional sense: 'People ask why I came into the theatre. I didn't come into it. We're all part of it, because theatre is the soul of the people. It's the joy they feel in life. It's the way they express the art of living. Let's set the clowns free, the villains and the nut-cases — and what they make will be theatre.' The Conference had been discussing the relative importance of playwright, actor and director: she waived these formal distinctions. 'When artists or scientists set out, they don't know what the end product will be. It changes. It changes in collaboration, each man trusting and mistrusting the people he works with. That happened in Shakespeare's Globe Theatre, it happened in Greece, it happened in all those times and at all those places under God's sky where men and women have joined together for delight. We must have places where we can eat, drink, make love, be lonely, be together, and share in the theatre of living. That is my theatre.' She wanted a theatre born of spontaneous contact between people, living on the lips and through the limbs of those who created it, not a theatre which practised artificial respiration on printed texts. 'I say to hell with geniuses in the theatre. Let's have the authors by all means, the Lorcas and the Brendan Behans, but let's get them together with their equals, the actors, with all their wit and stupidity and insight. And this clash, this collaboration, this *anti*-collaboration will create an explosion more important than any bomb. Let the bomb be dead, not named. That's all I have to say.'

And with that Joan Littlewood sat down, to wild applause, having made a speech that from any other mouth would have sounded crazily presumptuous. But Joan (I cannot call her Miss Littlewood) is the woman who made Brendan Behan's name with her productions of *The Quare Fellow* and *The Hostage*; who plucked a teenage playwright called Shelagh Delaney from obscurity by directing *A Taste of Honey*; who staged *Fings Ain't Wot They Used t'Be*, the long-running London musical which someone described as '*Guys and Dolls* with its fly open'; and whose greatest success, *Oh What a Lovely War* (a musical version, do you mind, of World War One), has just opened on Broadway after eighteen months in the West End.

Joan is given to talking in visionary riddles, like some latterday William Blake let loose on show business; but she differs from most street-corner prophets in a couple of vital respects. Firstly, with Joan it is always the beginning of the world that is at hand, not the end. Secondly, although much of what she says sounds like nonsense in theory, it has a way of working in practice. In 1945 she formed her own company of actors, Theatre Workshop, in pursuit of a dream of theatre as a place of communal celebration, a Left-wing shrine of Dionysus dedicated to wiping the puritan frown off the popular image of Socialist art. After two decades of toil, the dream is coming to pass. It now seems quite likely that when the annals of the British theatre in the middle years of the twentieth century come to be written, Joan's name will lead all the rest. Others write plays, direct them or act in them: she alone 'makes theatre'.

She also makes friends and enemies, both of equal intensity. The former concede what the latter complain: that she is a walking paradox, a ragbag of contradictions. She is quiet-spoken, yet outspoken; warm, even gentle, in manner, but in matter abrasive and sometimes obscene. A believer in theatre as a collective art (according to the programme, *Oh What a Lovely War* was 'written by Charles Chilton and the Members of the Cast'), she is a dominating director whose rehearsal methods consist — in the words of one of her playwrights — of 'bellowing instructions through a megaphone in terms that would shame a Fascist traffic cop'. A lifelong Leftist, she has been kicked out of the Communist Party several times for incorrigible independence, and now calls herself 'a Red, which means a Socialist verging toward anarchy'; yet her last permanent address was a sumptuously decorated house in Blackheath, and she often relaxes aboard a yacht owned by her close friend and business manager, Gerry Raffles. She is also a notable gourmet. Shelagh Delaney, her protégée and daughter-figure, regards her as a supreme authority on caviare; and once, in a moment of wry self-scrutiny, Joan summed herself up as 'the synthetic prole'.

Like any good liberal, she admires Negro artists, and three years ago she went to Nigeria to study them at the source. She returned still admiring, but not for reasons that conventional liberals would necessarily endorse: 'They're all thieves and drunks and villains. I used to wonder what people meant when they talked about "the black Irish". Now I know: they meant Nigerians. I'd love to get them into a Shakespeare play, and I know where I'd stage it — in the courtyard of a brothel I went to. It was called "Independence". They'd be marvellous bloody actors because they've never seen European theatre. They've never heard of good taste. They'd have nothing to unlearn. They could start from scratch and be Shakespearean without knowing it.' In Africa as in Britain, Joan is a missionary whose aim is the total destruction of complacent, well-behaved middle-class theatre.

She is coeval with modern warfare. Stockwell, a glum London suburb south of the Thames, was her birthplace in October 1914. When she was born, her mother (who still lives in Stockwell) was sixteen years old and unmarried. Joan has never met her father, though she acquired a stepfather at the age of five, when her mother married a Cockney worker. Joan was a bridesmaid at the wedding. She learned early on to cherish the people she calls 'nuts, clowns and villains' — in other words, outsiders, among whom she has always counted herself. The Socialist habit of idealising 'the simple man' repels her; being a complex proletarian herself, she knows that poverty does not always engender simplicity. She agrees with Ernst Fischer, the venerable Austrian poet and critic, who declares that under socialism 'the "simple" man gradually turns into a subtle and highly differentiated man'. He is not levelled down; he is levelled up and outward. Joan's greatest pleasure is to tour the East End pubs, relishing the company of 'my villains' and marvelling at their corrupt, outrageous variety. 'When I was sixteen,' she says, 'I lived in half a bathroom at five shillings a week, and talked mostly to whores. Like everybody else.' She really believes that that is what everybody else does.

Her London resembles the London that Jean Genet — another perceptive outsider — saw and recorded in 1963: a city of people concealing robustly antisocial desires beneath a mask of formality. In Genet's words:

> One might well think you were a nation of neuters, but only at a surface glance. Because everywhere there is the steady beat of the battened-down impulses, the throbbing of the choked unhappy sexual life force oozing into the streets.
>
> Nobody touches anyone else. If, by chance, I am introduced to an Englishman, I feel my right hand instantly anxious. I never saw a movement made in your streets just for its own sake, for the sheer pleasure of movement. When you see the English walking, you know they are going somewhere. . . .

But how can you not want to touch? Touching for me is every-thing. . . . I find it so strange that you seem not to like to touch; stranger still, that while you you will not touch, yet you will brush each other, make no effort to avoid brushing each other, because in that there is no caress. . . .

God save the Queen, her golden carriage and her horses, her nephews and her navy, though I can't think from what. . . . Delicious ruffians, I must tell you that England has never bored me. Despite your dubious moral sense, your flaccid minds, your uncertain friendliness, the vagaries of your relationships, dressed as your bodies are, overdressed even, to the point of indecency — I was never bored among you, because I had to watch too carefully lest I be robbed or twisted. . . .

That is Joan's London, a city whose dormant anarchic instincts she has spent much of her life trying to awaken. Like Genet, she 'wants to touch'. And her motive (though she would deride the idea) is partly patriotic: she would like to revive the Elizabethan London of bear-pits and bordellos thronged with 'delicious ruffians'. She has a huge, affectionate knowledge of English local history, and her current obsession is to erect on the banks of the Thames a 'Fun Palace' which would do for the twentieth century what the pleasure gardens of Vauxhall and Ranelagh did for the seventeenth and eighteenth.

Joan's palace would feature and foster all the aspects of life that qualify as 'play'. There would be areas devoted to dancing, eating, electronic games, music-making, love-making, do-it-yourself film-making and do-it-yourself drama; and each activity would be separated from the others not by solid walls but by penetrable barriers of light. (I quote from the prophet herself.) To construct her gigantic, free-form monument to the pleasure principle, Joan hopes to enlist the aid of architects like Buckminster Fuller — 'good dome men', as she crisply describes them. There is in her dream a whiff of nostalgia: the Fun Palace may turn out to be nothing more than a flood-lit, jazz-oriented version of a medieval village green. But even that would be a magical achievement in a country where pleasure for its own sake is still a slightly disreputable concept. To live in a Socialist society entirely peopled by individualists: that is the ideal toward which Joan has always steered, and of which the Fun Palace would be a microcosm.

She was educated at a convent school near her home; it was chosen because of proximity, not piety. Neither her mother nor her stepfather is a Catholic, and of her convent upbringing nothing is nowadays discernible, except perhaps her habit of signing letters and telegrams 'Hell'. (This baffled me too, until I realised that 'Hell' is how cockneys pronounce the initial letter of her name.) Joan the child was a painter and writer. At the age of eleven she directed *Hamlet*, playing all the parts herself. In her teens she saw dozens of classical productions from the gallery of the Old Vic and detested nearly all of them: one of the exceptions was John Gielgud's

Hamlet in 1930. When she was sixteen she won a working-class scholarship to the Royal Academy of Dramatic Art, and left both school and home for good. She had a chance, a year later, to study theatre in Moscow, with all expenses paid by the Soviet government; she turned it down at the last moment, because 'the other people who were going looked such bloody bores'.

Then began a long spell of wandering. She drifted to Paris, came back to England and migrated to the industrial centres of the north, which she found more congenial than the softer, less militant south. A sharp-eyed nomad, she absorbed on the wing the lessons of the depression and the hunger marches, flitting from one borrowed bed to another. Even today, she refuses to settle down, and is apt, after spending a week in an East End basement, to move into a penthouse at the Hilton Hotel.

The 1930s (which were her teens and twenties) defined her loyalties. She hated those who made profits and befriended those from whose labour profit was made. She wrote film treatments, 'Agitprop' journalism and BBC documentaries. Late in that ominous decade she met and married a folk-singer called Ewan MacColl, who managed a theatre group in Manchester and from whom she is now divorced.

'He didn't like the classics,' she says, 'but that didn't matter, because we were always in touch with the *modern* classics — the contemporary, international plays that the commercial blokes ignored. We knew all about Bertolt Brecht in the thirties. On Broadway and Shaftesbury Avenue he's still a novelty in the sixties. Ewan and I must have founded about fifty revolutionary theatre groups in the north before the war. The feeling was always international. You'd go to a mining village in Yorkshire, and there would be three Poles in top hats performing for the workers.'

When Stalin signed his pact with Hitler in 1939, Joan was frozen out of the BBC, and was not readmitted until the Nazis invaded Russia two years later. Throughout the war she was gathering around herself a nucleus of like-thinking actors, and in 1945 she gave them a name: Theatre Workshop.

Their immediate aim was to be a Leftist living newspaper presenting instant dramatisations of contemporary history. Ewan MacColl wrote many of the scripts, and the troupe's finances were supervised by Gerry Raffles, whom Joan had met in the late 1930s, when he was a burly schoolboy at Manchester Grammar School. The company was run on a completely egalitarian basis: actors, directors, designers and stage staff all got an equal share of the takings. The classics began to seep into the repertoire, especially those which could be tilted to the Left without undue strain — plays like Lope de Vega's *Fuenteovejuna*, Marlowe's *Edward II* and Jonson's *Volpone*. Theatre Workshop spent eight penniless years on the road, touring Germany, Norway, Sweden and Czechoslovakia as well as Britain, before coming to rest in 1953 at the Theatre Royal, Stratford-atte-Bowe, a shapely Victorian playhouse deep in East London. Here Joan's actors toiled and fasted, many of them so poor that they slept in hammocks slung across the boxes and dressing rooms.

And Joan's beloved Cockney audience failed her. Grudging reviews and thin attendances were her reward until, in 1955, the company appeared at the Paris International Theatre Festival and scored a thunderous success. Suddenly the London critics discovered them, and Joan became *chic* overnight. Legends started to cluster around her, most of them true. There was the story, for instance, of how she interrupted an actor who was auditioning for her and said: 'Let's drop all that and improvise. You want X pounds a week. Argue with me and prove that you need it. Lie as much as you like. If you convince me, you get the job.' (He did.) She enmeshed her actors in tight bonds of family loyalty. Renegades who 'went commercial' (i.e., appeared on television or defected to the West End) had to apologise to the assembled company before being reinstated; but there was justice in her possessiveness, because nearly all of Joan's actors were people whom she had personally recruited, trained and moulded. Her brisk, ribald, overwhelmingly candid approach either intimidated you (in which case you fled), or enslaved you (in which case you rapidly learned that the *sine qua non* of good acting was never to be afraid of making a fool of yourself). Inhibitions crumpled beneath Joan's hammer-blows, with results that are joyfully evident in *Sparrers Can't Sing*, the ebullient East End movie she directed two years ago. ('A primitive thing,' she now calls it.) Always she urged her actors to improvise, even when a show had been running for weeks or months. 'As soon as a production's fixed,' she would say, 'it's dead'; anything, she felt, was preferable to the petrified monotony of a commercial run. At Edinburgh last year I chided her for arguing thus. 'Isn't it true,' I demanded, 'that you flew back to London the other day because you'd heard that your latest production was getting out of hand?' 'Oh, no,' she said, gently rebuking. 'It was getting *in* hand.'

In the late 1950s, somewhat against her conscience, she began to transfer her productions to the West End. *The Quare Fellow*, Brendan Behan's savage comedy about the effect of capital punishment on prison inmates, was the first of a flood of Littlewood successes that included *Fings Ain't Wot They Used t'Be* (with lyrics by Lionel Bart), *A Taste of Honey* and *The Hostage*. With the last-named, in 1960, she made her debut as a Broadway director. She became a celebrity and scorned herself for it, because whenever one of her shows moved into the commercial theatre, it hastened the destruction of everything she had fought for. Having coaxed a play to birth, she would see it praised by the critics and whisked off to the West End or Broadway, there to make money for landlords and *entrepreneurs*. It would also make money for Theatre Workshop, of course; but every such transfer meant the loss of a group of actors she had picked, coached and welded into unity.

Each triumph eroded her ideal — a permanent repertory group whose members were all equal contributors. The more her achievements travelled, the more her company dwindled. Lacking a state subsidy, her art was divided and conquered by commerce.

Joan discovered that she had devoted her life to creating a training-ground for other people to poach on. Hence, in 1961, she resigned from Theatre Workshop and announced that she was embarking on a two-year sabbatical. 'I blew my top,' she says, 'and took off for anywhere.'

She went to Africa, returning to make *Sparrers Can't Sing*, and gave innumerable interviews knocking the theatrical set-up; but at last, in the spring of 1963, she succumbed to her old addiction, and came back to the East End playhouse where she had made her name. The bare boards of her home ground were filled once more with the passion of Joan's home team. A radio programme of soldiers' songs from World War One was what fired her: why not, she asked herself, tell the whole story of that repulsive massacre in a single evening of musical theatre? She summoned her actors — by now dispersed in movies, TV series and West End plays — and gave them a reading list of books on the 1914-18 disaster. When they had absorbed the basic facts, she guided them through a maze of improvised scenes designed to explain why the war happened and how it felt to be involved it it. Her method, as always, was what she calls 'the composite mind bit' — whereby everyone in the cast feels responsible for everyone else.

The result was *Oh What a Lovely War*. The programme defined it as 'a group production under the direction of Joan Littlewood', but it was essentially a one-woman show. The big, purposeful heart that beat throughout the evening belonged only to Joan. You felt that her actors had a common attitude toward something larger than acting, a shared vision that extended to life in general; for it is thus, and not by means of rehearsal techniques or new approaches to stagecraft, that true theatrical style is born. After the opening night, I wrote:

The plot is history: nothing less than the First World War. The cast is decked out in the ruffs and white satin suits of a seaside Pierrot show. We are to witness (the MC brightly confides) that famous extravaganza, 'the War Game', enacted by the entire company, with musical interludes drawn from songs of the period. The proscenium sparkles with fairy lights; and a terrible counterpoint is soon set up between the romanticism of the lyrics — all gaiety and patriotic gusto — and the facts of carnage in France, illustrated by stills of the trenches and news reports flickering across an electrified ribbon screen.

Between songs, the cast performs a montage of brisk, laconic sketches. . . . We glimpse a bayonet practice, conducted in lightning gibberish; a military ball, rippling with intrigue; a shooting party of international tycoons, blazing away at wildfowl while debating the relative merits of various neutral trade routes for exporting arms to the enemy; and the Christmas truce on the Western front, which Miss Littlewood handles with utter disdain for sentimentality — the Tommies recoil with nausea from a gift of German cheese, and respond by lobbing an inedible Christmas pudding into the opposite trenches.

Meanwhile the songs grow more bitter. The lunatic Haig has taken command, and the dead are rotting in mountains, monuments to his unswerving conceit. And still, indestructibly if not always suddenly, everyone bursts out singing.

In the second half the show tends to repeat itself, as the war so tragically did; but by then Miss Littlewood's passion has invaded one's bloodstream, and after the final scene, in which a line of reluctant heroes advances on the audience, bleating like sheep entering a slaughterhouse, one is ready to storm Buckingham Palace and burn down Knightsbridge Barracks.'

Joan is strong meat, and her work is aimed at strong stomachs. 'Emotion is the word,' she once said to me. 'I like emotion in the theatre. Look at its derivation. It means something that moves outward. Towards people. Everything else is dead.'

Holiday: November 1964; *Tynan Right and Left*, 1967

DUKE ELLINGTON

In our teens we make hero-lists of those we worship and intend one day to meet. Mine when I was thirteen, included a cricketer, a stripper, a painter, a drama critic, several actors, a film director and a jazz musician. I crossed them off as I met them, either socially or professionally, but until recently one name remained unblotted — that of the remote and lordly musician who brought the sound of Harlem chugging and wailing into my Birmingham suburb late in the thirties. On records only, of course; he had visited England with the band in 1933, before I had outgrown hymns and the national anthem; but by 1940 I knew the precise, poignant noise of the Ellington reed section as well as I knew Henry Hall's signature tune, and when a growling trumpet cut across the lyrical brushwork of the saxophones, I could tell you whether it was Bubber Miley or Cootie Williams. I struck the band in what is still regarded by many good listeners as Ellington's most brilliant period (jazz, like bullfighting — another art then held to be immoral and disreputable outside the racial group that invented it — went through a convulsion of creative replenishment between 1939 and 1942). *Ko-Ko, Jack the Bear, Dusk, Across the Track Blues, Take the A Train, Bojangles* and *Cotton Tail* are among the many three-minute marvels I bought as they were issued. A band of individualists — the throaty lamentations of Joe Nanton's muted trombone, the slippery nostalgia of Johnny Hodges' alto, the bedrock grumbles of Harry Carney on baritone sax — spoke with a general voice, which was Ellington's. I felt a special though spurious kinship with them because the year of their first fame (1927, when they moved into the Cotton Club in Harlem) was also the year of my birth.

When I last saw them — a couple of months ago, playing to a full house in London that ranged in age and ethnic background from infant Trinidadians to sixtyish American professors on sabbaticals — the sixteen-piece band still featured three Cotton Club survivors: Cootie Williams in the rollicking back row of trumpets, and Hodges and Carney in the apparently slumbering front row of reeds. And swaying gently before them, his long back loosely swathed in Italian silk, his lacquered hair and immaculate bandit's smile suggesting a Negro Cesar Romero: the perennial duke himself, a black prince who should have ruled Haiti in the days of Toussaint l'Ouverture. He conducted us and the band through a retrospective audition of his work from the late twenties to last autumn, pausing between numbers to soothe us with his catch-phrase ('We want you to know that we love you *madly*', delivered in tones of the blandest mockery), and taking several opportunities to demonstrate that those who question his skill as a solo pianist are out of their minds.

Next morning the band flew back to New York. Ellington stayed on at the Dorchester, whither he invited me to talk. We both knew, though neither of us said so, that this might well be his last professional visit to Europe; four decades on the road is enough for anyone, and I offer this account of our meeting as a birthday salute to a diehard nomad who will be sixty-six years old next Thursday.

He greeted me in sweater, slacks and socks, attended by Ferdinanda, a blonde Frenchwoman of Algerian *colon* origins who acts as his travelling major-domo. Almost the first thing he said was: 'I've been captain of the ship for forty years. I'm like an old Negro conductor who gets fired by the railroad. When a train whistle blows in the middle of the night, that old man's heart is going to break.' He gave a deep, easy chuckle and put his feet up. I asked whether his standards of band discipline had slackened over the years. Not at all, he said; occasionally he had to reprimand a musician who felt 'a spirit of reluctance' and was unable to play, but there was no more to it than that. As for his own weaknesses: 'When I was around forty I gave up the juice. Ten years later I went back, and then gave it up again. But even when I was on it, I could never get drunk. One time in Cleveland I acted as referee at a drinking contest between two cats in the band. I took drink for drink with them, and at nine a.m. I wound up carrying them both home. Nowadays I take a glass of wine now and then — Beaujolais or champagne — but ice-cream is the danger. After a concert I order it by the gallon. And caviare: I picked up the caviare habit on tour in Iran.' Ellington dresses sleekly, but without dandyism; during his London stay he astonished Lobb's, the St. James' Street bootmakers, by commissioning them to duplicate a favourite pair of shoes he bought thirty years ago in a New York department store for $12.95.

He talked expansively and unpretentiously about his music: 'I used to listen a lot to people like Debussy and Delius, and I admire Britten — especially *The Rape of Lucretia* — but basically I'm a sort of primitive musician. For me the art of writing music is the art of hearing it before you write it. You have to hear it first — cool, fresh, bang, right out of the air. I once played a concert hall in Stockholm, and outside it there was this statue of a girl blowing on pan-pipes in the middle of a field. I said to myself: "That's me in drag." I take the music seriously, but I hope I don't take myself seriously.' He was the first great jazz musician whose inspiration was urban rather than grass-roots; the first to orchestrate the sound of the big city — a powerhouse pierced from within by the cry of a Negro jungle. When he composed *Sophisticated Lady* in 1933, some critics complained that it wasn't Negro music, by which they meant that it wasn't crude and

ingenuous enough to fit their stereotype of the Negro: 'It's the Negro I
know,' Ellington told them, 'even if *you* don't.' He has often (though
always quietly) been ahead of his time in the field of racial relationships. In
1941 he wrote the score for a revue called *Jump for Joy*: 'a big social-
significance show,' he told me. 'Orson Welles saw it, and hired me to work
with him on a movie about the history of jazz. I'd written just twenty-eight
bars of trumpet solo when RKO cancelled Orson's contract. But I
automatically go on accumulating material, and that solo ended up as a
forty-minute composition called *A Drum is a Woman*.'

In 1947, with lyricist John LaTouche, he wrote *Beggar's Holiday*, a
Broadway musical distantly based on *The Beggars' Opera*, in which the
white hero (Alfred Drake) fell in love with the daughter of a Negro police
chief: 'That was really far-out, but nobody seemed to notice.' He has
composed incidental music for Le Sage's classic comedy *Turcaret* at the
TNP, and for *Timon of Athens* at Stratford, Ontario. Yet despite the weight
and variety of his work, he keeps very few files of band parts and often
finds it impossible to revive a number once it has been recorded.
Sometimes it slips his memory altogether: when I played him the original
recording of *Across the Track Blues*, he couldn't remember the title, which
is as if Schönberg were to forget *Pierrot Lunaire*. I had to remind myself
that Ellington lives in a hard-pressed commercial world of night-club dates,
dances, parties and receptions, where fun (for the band as much as the
customers) is the main attraction. 'In other words,' as Humphrey Lyttelton
has written, 'what is bizarre and "out of place" in an Ellington band show is
not the trumpet pyrotechnics, the comic dancing or the leader's flash
clothes, but the surpassing virtue of the music itself.' I asked Ellington what
kind of criticism annoyed him most. 'Critics,' he said, 'who expect you to
play what they want you to play.' Critics, in fact, who expect art instead of
high jinks. I understand how he feels, though I doubt whether devotion to
art would deplete his audiences as much as he fears. Meanwhile he lives
smiling behind the walls of his reputation, securely hemmed in by
achievement.

His hobby (he stunned me by saying) is writing plays which nobody is
allowed to read. One of them is called *A Man with Four Sides* — in other
words, a square — and deals with a jazz musician who, oppressed by the
primness of his wife, invents an imaginary girl-friend whom he addresses in
fantasy. 'You have the authority of a thoroughbred,' he tells her, 'Walk for
me, baby'; at which point his wife pops her head round the door and says:
'Otho, time for bed — it's Tuesday, you know.' The strain of lush romantic
dreaming that runs through Ellington's music positively stampedes through
his dramaturgy. His latest unread play, entitled *Queenie-Pie*, concerns a
prosperous lady beautician whose looks are fading. 'An old cat who works
for her warns her that the young chicks are catching up on her. He comes
from an island of sunshine, where you get two summers back to back. On

this island there's a man-eating tree which contains a serum that is the secret of eternal domination of men. Get that product, he says, and you'll be safe. So she takes a yacht and goes to the island. The old cat tells her that the tree must be approached at midnight, because at that time its limbs open to embrace the sky. But when she's made the grab and got the serum that will make her the *permanent* Queenie-Pie, the tree gets mad and causes an eruption. The yacht sinks, she loses the serum in the sea, there's a great multi-coloured foam, and she gets washed up on another island. The natives want to worship her, but all she wants is to be loved. The king is an old way-back swinger. She teaches his people how to make alcohol and dress well and get civilised, and they elect her queen. Then a rescue boat arrives. "We have to get spears and put on skins and be fierce," says Queenie. The cats on the boat recognise her and want to take her back to New York. But when she decides to go with them, the king tells her that royal women are forbidden to leave the island. So she has to stay. Queenie-Pie has become a *real* queen, and she hates it.' It would be fascinating to see this curious fable staged, especially with Ella Fitzgerald, for whom Ellington wrote the leading part.

A Christian and a Bible reader, he told me with pride that he had just been invited to compose a choral number for a religious concert at a High Episcopalian cathedral in San Francisco. His personal creed is confined to no particular church: 'I have a private religion — a direct line that embraces all faiths. It's a matter of love, unconditional love.' He thinks Britain 'the most civilised country I know, because you make allowances for human weakness. After all, who's going to decide whether it's more damaging and degenerate to be a liar, an adulteress or a dope-fiend? All I know about morality is that too much passion about *anything* is destructive to people.' He dislikes extremists, however just their cause. On tour in India, he met an American lady who insisted that birth control ought to be compulsory in over-populated countries. Offended by her dogmatism and 'feeling plain shitty', he said he thought birth control was a bad idea; rather than spend money on teaching contraception, why not spend it on feeding and healing the children? 'Suppose you've had seventeen children,' he went on, 'and you prohibit the eighteenth, and he happens to be the world's greatest poet? Suppose he flies round the world in limbo for a hundred years? When he finally comes out of someone else's womb, he may find that poetry's gone out of style.'

Some Negroes feel that Ellington regards the struggle for racial equality as a form of extremism; and certainly he has never taken a public stand on the subject. 'Duke doesn't like to be bugged by political things,' says his impresario, Norman Granz, 'they keep him from working.' He even shuts himself off from the fact of poverty: when I mentioned that it was fairly widespread even in the United States, he seemed puzzled and incredulous. His work, of course, reflects the Negro condition — witness the fifty-minute suite *Black, Brown and Beige* (1943), his first attempt at extended composition. ('The title doesn't mean the colour of a Negro's skin, but the colour of his attitudes towards the enemy. Black means he wants to eat them. Brown means he just resents them. Beige means he's happy to integrate.') But neither this nor the show called *My People* which he wrote, composed, directed and part-choreographed in Chicago two years ago evokes much response in the modern, militant Negro. He is a gradualist in a time of lightning change, a black Kerensky overtaken by revolution. When Ellington plays the blues, with whatever sophisticated use of impressionist harmonies, he does so in a spirit of acceptance, as if pain and Negro life were permanently inseparable; whereas the blues that James Baldwin sings are for Mister Charlie, the white oppressor who is soon to be overthrown. When I asked Ellington about the racial situation, he said: 'This is the great playground of international chess. You have to generalise, and I can't do that. I don't know anyone who knows all the Negroes in the United States. I know a lot of them myself, but they're all different. One may have a bend in his nose that makes him different from all the others.' But, as any Jew can testify, there comes a time in the history of a race when one has to generalise or surrender.

Perhaps the truest image of Ellington is that of a blinkered, dedicated musical genius who has spent his life tinkering with a magnificently flexible toy: his orchestra. 'Retire?' he said when I put the final question 'What could I retire to? What else am I going to play with?'

Tynan Right and Left, 1967

LENNY BRUCE

Constant, abrasive irritation produces the pearl: it is a disease of the oyster. Similarly — according to Gustave Flaubert — the artist is a disease of society. By the same token, Lenny Bruce is a disease of America. The very existence of comedy like his is evidence of unease in the body politic. Class chafes against class, ignorance against intelligence, puritanism against pleasure, majority against minority, easy hypocrisy against hard sincerity, white against black, jingoism against internationalism, price against value, sale against service, suspicion against trust, death against life — and out of all these collisions and contradictions there emerges the troubled voice of Lenny Bruce, a night-club Cassandra bringing news of impending chaos, a tightrope walker between morality and nihilism, a pearl miscast before swine. The message he bears is simple and basic: whatever releases people and brings them together is good, and whatever confines and separates them is bad. The worst drag of all is war; in didactic moments Bruce likes to remind his audience that ' "Thou shalt not kill" *means just that*'. Although he occasionally invokes Christ as source material, I think he would applaud a statement recently made by Wayland Young, an English writer and agnostic, in a book called *Eros Denied*:

> Christian and post-Christian and Communist culture is a eunuch; pornography is his severed balls; thermonuclear weapons are his staff of office. If there is anything sadder than a eunuch it is his balls; if there is anything more deadly than impotence it is murder.

If it is sick to agree with that, then God preserve us from health.

This may be the time to point out the primary fact about Bruce, which is that he is extremely funny. It is easy to leave that out when writing about him — to pass over the skill with which he plays his audience as an angler plays a big-game fish, and the magical timing, born of burlesque origins and jazz upbringing, that triggers off the sudden, startled yell of laughter. But he is seldom funny without an ulterior motive. You squirm as you smile. With Bruce a smile is not an end in itself, it is invariably a means. What begins as pure hilarity may end in self-accusation. When, for example, he tells the story of the unhappily married couple who achieve togetherness in the evening of their lives by discovering that they both have gonorrhoea, your first reaction is laughter; but when you go on to consider your own far-from-perfect marriage, held together (it may be) by loveless habit or financial necessity or fear of social disapproval — all of which are motives less concrete and intimate than venereal disease — your laughter may cool off into a puzzled frown of self-scrutiny. You begin to reflect that there are worse fates than the clap; that a curable physical sickness may even be preferable, as a source of togetherness, to a social or spiritual sickness for which no cure is available. And thus another taboo is dented.

Bruce is the sharpest denter of taboos at present active in show business. Alone among those who work the clubs, he is a true iconoclast. Others josh, snipe and rib; only Bruce demolishes. He breaks through the barrier of laughter to the horizon beyond, where the truth has its sanctuary. People say he is shocking and they are quite correct. Part of his purpose is to force us to redefine what we mean by 'being shocked'. We all feel impersonally outraged by racialism; but when Bruce mimics a white liberal who meeting a Negro at a party, instantly assumes that he must know a lot of people in show business, we feel a twinge of recognition and personal implication. Poverty and starvation, which afflict more than half of the human race, enrage us — if at all — only in a distant, generalized way; yet we are roused to a state of vengeful fury when Bruce makes public use of harmless, fruitful syllables like 'come' (in the sense of orgasm) and 'fuck'. Where righteous indignation is concerned, we have clearly got our priorities mixed up. The point about Bruce is that he wants us to be shocked, *but by the right things*; not by four-letter words, which violate only convention, but by want and deprivation, which violate human dignity. This is not to deny that he has a disenchanted view of mankind as a whole. Even his least Swiftian bit, the monologue about a brash and incompetent American comic who tries to conquer the London Palladium, ends with the hero winning the cheers of the audience by urging them, in a burst of sadistic inspiration, to 'screw the Irish'. But the cynicism is just a façade. Bruce has the heart of an unfrocked evangelist.

I first saw him six years ago in a cellar room under the Duane Hotel in New York. Lean and pallid, with close-cropped black hair, he talked about Religions, Inc., a soft-selling ecumenical group on Madison Avenue whose main purpose was to render the image of Billy Graham indistinguishable from that of Pope John. ('Listen, Johnny, when you come out to the Coast, *wear the big ring.*') Clutching a hand mike, he slouched around a tiny dais, free-associating like mad; grinning as he improvised, caring as he grinned, seldom repeating in the second show what he said in the first, and often conducting what amounted to a rush job of psychoanalysis on the audience he was addressing. He used words as a jazz musician uses notes, going off into fantastic private cadenzas and digressions, and returning to his theme just when you thought he had lost track of it for ever. I saw him at the Duane four times, with four separate groups of friends. Some found him offensive — a reaction they smartly concealed by calling him boring.

Others thought him self-indulgent, because he felt his way into the audience's confidence by means of exploratory improvisation, instead of plunging straight into rehearsed routines. Among my guests he was not universally liked. 'Where's Lenny Bruce?' 'Down the Duane,' so ran a popular riposte. During the Duane engagement I met him for the first time — an archetypal night person, hypersensitive, laconic and withdrawn. Terry Southern once said that a hipster was someone who had deliberately decided to kill a part of himself in order to make life bearable. He knows that by doing this he is cutting himself off from many positive emotions as well as the negative, destructive ones he seeks to avoid; but on balance he feels that the sacrifice is worth while. By this definition Bruce was (and is) authentically, indelibly hip.

In the years that followed, it was not Bruce but my friends who improved. One by one they began to discover that they had always admired him. I recalled a saying of Gertrude Stein's: 'A creator is not in advance of his generation but he is the first of his contemporaries to be conscious of what is happening to his generation.' Bruce was fully, quiveringly conscious, and audiences in Chicago and San Francisco started to respond to his manner and his message. So did the police of these and other great cities, rightly detecting in this uncompromising outsider a threat to conventional mores. Arrests began, on narcotics and obscenity charges, but Bruce pressed on, a long-distance runner whose loneliness was now applauded by liberals everywhere, including those tardy converts, my chums in Manhattan. Mort Sahl, brilliant but essentially non-subversive, had long been their pet satirist; but the election of John F. Kennedy robbed Sahl of most of his animus, which had been directed toward Eisenhower from the lame left wing of the Democratic Party. It became clear that Bruce was tapping a vein of satire that went much deeper than the puppet warfare of the two-party system. Whichever group was in power, his criticisms remained valid. Myself, I wished he had broadened his viewpoint by a little selective reading of Marx as well as Freud; but that, I suppose, is too much to expect of any comic operating west of Eastport, Maine.

In the spring of 1962, he paid his first and (thus far) only visit to London, where he appeared for a few explosive weeks at The Establishment, a Soho night club devoted to satire and run by Peter Cook of *Beyond the Fringe*. Clad in a black tunic sans lapels, as worn by the late Pandit Nehru, he roamed out on stage in his usual mood of tormented derision; ninety minutes later there was little room for doubt that he was the most original, free-speaking, wild-thinking gymnast of language our inhibited island had ever hired to beguile its citizens. I made notes of the ideas he toyed with on opening night, and herewith reproduce them:

The smoking of marijuana should be encouraged because it does not induce lung cancer. Children ought to watch pornographic movies: it's

healthier than learning about sex from Hollywood. Venereal disease is
news only when poor people catch it. Publicity is stronger than sanity;
given the right PR, armpit hair on female singers could become a
national fetish. Fascism in America is kept solvent by the left-wing
hunger for persecution: Liberals will buy anything any bigot writes. If
Norman Thomas, the senior American socialist, were to be elected
president, he would have to find a minority to hate. It might conceivably
be midgets — in which case his campaign slogan would run: 'Smack a
midget for Norm.'

He went on to talk about the nuances of race relations, with special
emphasis on whites who cherish the Negro cause but somehow never have
Negroes to dinner; about a prison movie to end them all (starring Ann
Dvorak, Charles Bickford and Nat Pendleton) in which the riot is quelled
by a chaplain named Father Flotsky; about the difficulties of guiltless
masturbation, and the psychological duplicity ('It's a horny hoax') involved
in sleeping enjoyably with a prostitute; about pain of many kinds, and
laughter, and dying. At times he drawled and mumbled too privately,
lapsing into a lexicon of Yiddish phrases borrowed from the showbiz world
that reared him. But by the end of the evening he had crashed through
frontiers of language and feeling that I had hitherto thought impregnable.
The British comedian Jonathan Miller, who watched the performance in
something like awe, agreed with me afterwards that Bruce was a bloodbath
where *Beyond the Fringe* had been a pinprick. We were dealing with
something formerly unknown in Britain: an impromptu prose poet who
trusted his audience so completely that he could talk in public no less
outspokenly than he would talk in private.

His trust was misplaced. Scarcely a night passed during his brief sojourn
at The Establishment without vocal protests from offended customers,
sometimes backed up by clenched fists; and this, at a members-only club, is
rare in London. The actress Siobhan McKenna came with a party and
noisily rose to leave in the middle of Bruce's act; it seems she was outraged
by his attitude towards the Roman Church. On her way out Peter Cook
sought to remonstrate with her, whereupon she seized his tie while one of
her escorts belted him squarely on the nose. 'These are Irish hands,' cried
Miss McKenna dramatically, 'and they're clean!' 'This is an English face,'
replied Mr. Cook curtly, 'and it's bleeding.' A few days later a brisk, pink-
faced sextet of young affluents from London's stockbroker belt booked a
ringside table. They sat, half-heartedly sniggering, through jokes about
money-making, sexual contact with Negroes, onanism as an alternative to
VD, and genetic hazards proceeding from fall-out. Suddenly Bruce ven-
tured on to the subject of cigarettes and lung cancer. At once, as if in obedience to some tribal summons, the brisk, pink, stockbroker host sprang to his
feet. 'All right,' he said tersely, 'Susan, Charles, Sonia! Cancer! Come on!

Cancer! All out!' And meekly, in single file, they marched out through the door. Bruce kept tape recordings of both the McKenna and the cancer demonstrations, and made unsparing use of them on subsequent evenings.

At the end of his engagement he was rushed out of the country with the conservative press baying at his heels. The following year, Peter Cook applied for permission to bring him back to London. The Home Secretary brusquely turned down the application; Bruce, it seemed, was classified as an undesirable alien. (Off stage, he appears to have behaved quite desirably, apart from a rumoured occasion when the manager of a London hotel, awakened by complaining guests, strode into Bruce's room at four a.m. to find him conducting a trio of blondes whom he had taught to sing 'Please fuck me, Lenny' in three-part harmony.) In 1963 the Earl of Harewood invited him to take part in an International Drama Conference at the Edinburgh Festival. Despite the august source of the invitation, the Home Office once again said no. Lenny Bruce is too wild an import for British officialdom to stomach.

We miss him, and the nerve-fraying, jazz-digging, pain-hating, sex-loving, lie-shunning, bomb-loathing life he represents. There are times when I wish he would settle in Europe, for long enough at least to realise that capitalism — from which so many of his targets derive — is not necessarily a permanent and unchangeable fact of human existence. But even if he died tomorrow, he would deserve more than a footnote in any history of modern western culture. I have heard him described, somewhat portentously, as 'the man on America's conscience'. Hyperbole like that would not appeal to Lenny Bruce. 'No,' I can hear him dissenting, 'let's say the man who went down on America's conscience. . .'

How To Talk Dirty And Influence People, 1965;
The Sound Of Two Hands Clapping, 1975

HUMPHREY BOGART

First, the confession. unlike most journalists, I never got drunk with Humphrey Bogart. I met him only once, at a Mayfair club in 1952, when I had just described his face in print as 'a triumph of plastic surgery'. He called me over to his table, where he was studiously noisy and three parts crocked. We did not love each other at sight, though I happily submitted to what John Crosby once described to me as 'that basilisk authority of his'. He overawed me because he was rich and raucous and because he ate nothing. He looked like 'a great famished wolf', which is how Ellen Terry summed up Irving's performance as Macbeth. I decided later that I preferred the lines his scriptwriters gave him to the ones he ad-libbed that night.

I have now read about eighty-three accounts of him, in magazines or books, and I still cannot find it in me to be mesmerised by Bogart the Man. Successful hard-drinking iconoclasts who can't act frequently express the same opinions as successful hard-drinking iconoclasts who can (such as Bogart). To hate phonies and prize loyalty is a fairly common attribute, even among the untalented. And on every other page of the Bogart dossiers there are tributes from colleagues that bring me out in a sweat of incredulous embarrassment. My favourite comes from Joseph L. Mankiewicz, according to whom: 'He had a kind of eighteenth century, Alexander Pope nature.' Alexander Pope was a cripple who wrote heroic couplets. There's an eighteenth-century novel called *Humphrey Clinker*: possibly Mankiewicz had got his Humphreys confused.

Perhaps the most irritating thing about Bogart's hagiographers is their failure to agree on basic items of information, beginning with the date of his birth. Ezra (*Bogey: The Good-Bad Guy*) Goodman says it was Christmas Day, 1899. Clifford (*Bogey: The Films of Humphrey Bogart*) McCarty loftily dismisses this as a studio myth, and plumps instead for 23 January, 1899; while in *Bogey: The Man, The Actor, the Legend*, Jonah Ruddy and Jonathan Hill put their money on 25 December, 1900. Similarly, no one seems quite sure how Bogart acquired the scar on his upper lip. One account explains that during his naval service in World War One he was bashed in the face by the handcuffs of a bad-tempered prisoner he was escorting. Another, rather more heroically, insists that the injury came from a splinter of wood, dislodged by an exploding shell.

Writing about his apprenticeship on Broadway in the twenties, Ruddy

and Hill claim that he was 'the originator of that famous theatrical line —
"Tennis anyone?" ' In the Goodman version, Bogart denies that he ever
uttered it. From Alistair Cooke in *The Atlantic Monthly*, we learn that he
popularised the phrase: 'Drop the gun, Louie'. Goodman's Bogart is quite
categorical: 'I never said "Drop the gun, Louie." ' Of all the biographers,
Ezra Goodman the Man comes across least adorably in print. He got much
of his background material while interviewing Bogart in what is shallowly
known as depth for a *Time* magazine cover story in the 1950s. His approach
to his subject, alternately sneering and cringing, recalls a famous remark of
Max Beerbohm's. A tailor had written to the great essayist, demanding
immediate payment in tones that reeked of servility. 'My dear sir,'
Beerbohm replied, 'kindly cease from crawling on your knees and shaking
your fist.'

Most of the Bogart buffs are content to contradict one another: Goodman
breaks new ground by contradicting himself. On page 61 he quotes Bogart
as follows:

> In John Huston's house, years ago, a group of us played touch football in
> the living room with a grapefruit. It was high spirits. There were Collier
> Young, Charley Grayson, John Huston and myself. After the first
> scrimmage in the second game, I got on the side of the big guy whom I
> had been opposed to. He played real football. It was exercise, shall we
> say.

On page 170, the same incident reappears in a less innocent light, shall we
say. It is now an outdoor event, with a cast augmented by the director
Richard Brooks. This is Brooks' story:

> There was a fine actress . . . whose husband nobody could stand. John
> Huston said: 'Let's jump him.' Instead, we decided to get a football game
> rolling. . . . We got a grapefruit off a tree. Bogey goes on the husband's
> side with Collier Young (a producer). John and I are on the other side.
> It's two against three. Together John and I tackled the husband with the
> grapefruit. Bogey switches sides to join us. Now it's the three of us
> against Collier Young and the husband. Then Collier Young switches
> sides and the four of us hit him. We were all wearing tuxedos and we
> were playing in the mud.

John Crosby, formerly of the *New York Herald Tribune* and now with the
London *Observer,* is one of the few journalists who knew Bogart well. He
was and remains an unswerving admirer of Bogart the Man. 'Off screen,'
he told me, 'Bogart didn't diminish, which is more than you can say of
most movie stars. He was a drinker, but never a wencher. And although he
loathed gossip columnists, he liked real newspapermen. Some of us used to

meet at a place called Bleeck's on West 40th Street. The sign outside read: BLEECK'S WRITERS AND ARTIST'S TAVERN AND FORMERLY CLUB. We called ourselves the Formerly Club, and Bogart was an honorary member whenever he was in New York. If he was buying me a drink, he wouldn't just pass it across — he'd take me by the wrist and screw the glass into my hand as if it was a lamp socket. He'd seen Osgood Perkins — Tony's father — do that in some Broadway comedy in the twenties. Another thing about Bogey: he never went around with hoods and bums. That's pure legend. He was an upper-class boy, and if Jock Whitney or Vincent Astor were giving a party, he'd be there.'

On one point all the biographies agree: that Bogart's physical courage, in the long months of wasting and waiting before cancer finally took his life in January 1957, was tremendous and exemplary. But there are more kinds of courage than one, and it could be argued that Bogart, ten years earlier, had laid himself open to the charge of moral cowardice. In a chartered plane full of movie notables, he flew to Washington to protest against the House Un-American Activities Committee, which had subpoenaed many Hollywood writers, actors and directors to testify to their political affiliations. In the early hearings, several of the witnesses took the Fifth Amendment when asked whether they were (or had ever been) members of the Communist Party. Ten of them — the so-called Hollywood Ten — were subsequently held in contempt of Congress and imprisoned. Bogart promptly issued a statement in which he said that his trip to Washington had been 'ill-advised, foolish and impetuous'. No doubt he was upset to find that some of his fellow travellers were in fact fellow travellers, or at any rate holders of views pinker than his own. Whether he should have withdrawn his support quite so publicly and abjectly is another matter. 'Never rat on a rat' was the slogan of the Holmby Hills Rat Pack. For once in his life, Bogart exposed himself to the taunt of being a fink.

If I seem to knock the cult of Bogart the Man, it is because I invented the cult of Bogart the Actor. Not the glib Broadway juvenile who went to Hollywood in 1930 and made nine pictures impressing no one, but the sardonic, close-cropped bandit who flew back to the Coast in 1936 to play Duke Mantee in *The Petrified Forest*. Aged ten, I saw the film when it opened in Britain, and immediately wrote a letter to a movie magazine, begging Warner's to give us more of this untamed man with the warning eyes and the rasping voice. It was my debut in print. Between 1936 and 1941 Warner's heeded my plea in spades; Bogart made twenty-eight films, of which I missed very few.

Already the critics were getting him wrong, as they have ever since. They all said he lisped, whereas I, who could mimic him perfectly, knew that he did nothing of the sort. What he did was to fork his tongue and hiss like a snake. This was new, and so was the sheer bravura of his decision to use his own name. Like all good fans, my schoolmates and I had long been aware that Robert Taylor was Spangler Arlington Brugh, and we wouldn't have been surprised to learn that John Wayne was the pseudonym of Adrian Mumchance III. But Bogart had actually been christened Humphrey DeForest Bogart: which impressed, because — in Britain, at least — Humphrey was a name with strong associations of pompousness and/or faggotry. We respected Bogart for having the guts to live with it. To us, a heavy named Humphrey was about as bizarre as a flautist named Bugsy.

At that time, the king thug on the Warner lot was Edward G. Robinson, wearing vast lapels like the swept-back wings of a jet. Bogart, lean and hungry, was Cassius to his Caesar. We rooted for Bogart because, although he got second billing, he never said 'Yes, boss' as if he meant it. He was nobody's man but his own. And this extended to his relationship with the audience. You had to take him on his own terms. He never stooped to ingratiation, and though his bullying was silken, it was also icy. In latterday terminology, he was 'inner-directed', steering by a private compass that paid no attention to storm signals from outside. Moreover, if the needle led him (as it usually did) into a hail of bullets, he would die with a shrug: no complaints, no apologies, no hard feelings. Indeed, he rarely displayed strong feelings of any kind. And this, in an age when stars were supposed to emote and be vibrant, was something else we admired. It reflected, in part, the emotional tact of a man who seemed genuinely repelled by sentimentality; and, in part, the professional assurance of an actor who knew damned well that he could get along without it. Either way, it was revolutionary, and we relished it.

The year 1937 was full of vintage Bogart: Turkey Morgan in *Kid Galahad* and — supreme misnomer — Baby Face Martin in William Wyler's *Dead End*, the first of the mother-fixated gangsters, who announced his presence (if memory serves) by flipping a knife into the tree trunk around which Leo Gorcey and his chums were huddled. That was the year we all started wincing, as Bogart did when engaged in any mild form of physical exertion, like loading a gun. To wince correctly, you had to imagine that your upper lip was split, and then try to smile. (We used to wince while filling our fountain pens.) I've sometimes wondered how much of Bogart's appeal in England was due to the fact that he was the first movie hero who literally had a stiff upper lip.

Less propitiously, 1937 was the year of *Marked Woman*, starring Bette Davis, in which Bogart appeared as David Graham, the crusading district attorney. The opinion in my set was unanimous. The film proved not only that Bogart was a rotten DA (he gave an equally flat rendering of a similar role in *The Enforcer*, fourteen years later), but that he could never, in any circumstances, play a character named David Graham. Another blotch on *Marked Woman* was that it gave us our first glimpse of Mayo Methot, soon to become Bogart's third wife. (She was the brawling one, subsequently renowned as a zealous fan of General MacArthur and a dead shot with a highball glass across a crowded room.) We disliked her on sight and sent her anonymous letters, pointing out that she was something of a pig and that Bogart deserved better. We all knew — or hindsight tells me we did — that the better girl would be a lean, nonchalant baritone, like himself. But she didn't turn up until 1945, when he made *To Have and Have Not* and whistled for her.

The great Bogart-Cagney confrontation was held in 1938-39. It spanned three movies. I missed the second, a western called *The Oklahoma Kid*, but the key encounters — the eyeball-to-eyeball stuff — took place in the other two: Michael Curtiz's *Angels with Dirty Faces* and Raoul Walsh's *The Roaring Twenties*. James Cagney was the spruce, ebullient urchin who killed with Irish charm and died in dogged, tenacious spasms of life-loving energy. Ever since *Public Enemy*, in 1931, he had been Hollywood's most dynamic and disarming hood. Murder, as he committed it, seemed like a high-spirited exercise, performed out of pure exuberance. He made vice look spunky and debonair, even funny. No one who saw him in the late 1930s will ever forget the grace of his spring-heeled walk and the rich, elated derision of his voice. Bogart was five years older than Cagney when Warner's sent him into the ring with their most triumphant romantic outlaw. It's easy, when surveying Bogart's career, to overlook the basic fact of his age. He didn't become a star until his late thirties, by which time most aspirants have given up and settled for character parts.

Bogart countered Cagney's agile footwork with unruffled expertise. He was like a laconic Hemingway hero up against Studs Lonigan. Often he out-stared Cagney, so shrewdly and mockingly that he looked like a walking ad for that essential Hemingway prop, the built-in shit detector. The contrast of styles was beautiful to watch. It was Bogart the wily debunker versus Cagney the exultant cavalier. With every punch Cagney threw, Bogart lazily rode. Long afterward I wrote: 'Each had perfected his own version of the fanged killer's smile, and a good deal of *The Roaring Twenties* developed into a sort of grinning contest.' The verdict, on points, went to Bogart's sewage snarl.

Thus far, Bogart's main achievement was to have played George Raft parts better than George Raft had ever played them, and better than Alan Ladd was ever going to play them. There was a significant change in 1941, a subtle modulation that led his career out of what might have been a blind alley. Between 1929 and 1932, in a sudden and strenuous burst of creativity, Dashiell Hammett had written five novels. He never wrote another, nor did he need to: the existing quintet was enough to ensure him a modest but durable niche in American literature. One of them, *The Thin Man*, had been filmed, and so sweetened in the filming that it spawned a series, starring William Powell, Myrna Loy and a lovable dog.

Another, *The Maltese Falcon*, had been waiting on the shelf for the advent of someone like Bogart, who could show the world what Hammett was really about. The Hammett private eye was the first anti-hero. No Batman he: operating in a corrupt society, he was not above using corrupt means. He was a cynic to whom nothing human, however squalid, was alien; a man soured but still amused by the intricate depravity of his fellow creatures; and he could, on occasion, be extremely brutal. In short, he was virtually indistinguishable from the Bogart gangster in every respect but one: he was on the side of the law. From now on Bogart could be ruthless — he could even kill — with no loss of glamour and every appearance of moral rectitude. He could engage in mayhem and emerge untarnished. Still as fascinating as ever, he was no longer reprehensible. This farewell to overt criminality was what enabled Bogart to become a world star and a household god.

Bogart's Sam Spade in *The Maltese Falcon* set the pattern for his maturity, and for my adolescence. With the same director (John Huston) and the same supporting team (including Mary Astor and Sydney Greenstreet), he played a similar role in *Across the Pacific*, this time working for the government as an undercover agent. Later, in 1946, we saw him as Philip Marlowe, Raymond Chandler's savagely disenchanted outlaw-within-the-law, in *The Big Sleep*. But it was Hammett who fixed and defined the Bogart figure: it all began with Sam.

He looked battered before anything had happened, as if survival at an honourable wage was all he hoped for. There was a dimple on each cheekbone, but you would be unwise to call him cute. He wore his hangover like a long-service medal, and his voice, metallic and nasal, was that of a martyr to drinker's catarrh. You could imagine him demanding a pre-breakfast vodka to cut the phlegm. He was always unsurprised. Wherever he went, you felt that he had been there before and learned nothing he did not already know. Greeting an attractive female customer, he would eye her frankly from shoes to chignon, like the lawyer in Thurber's cartoon who murmurs: 'You're not my client, you're my meat, Mrs. Fisk.' And if he took her to bed, that would be that. You could count on the Bogart figure never to utter either of the lines on which romantic melodrama depends: 'I love you' and 'I hate you.' He resisted commitment of this or any other kind. One of his most characteristic moments occurred in *Passage to Marseille* (1944). Playing a Free French journalist, he is asked to declare his nationality. 'Eskimo,' he replies, not batting an eyelid.

The wartime Bogart was mostly a soldier of fortune, typified by Rick in *Casablanca* (1943), the erstwhile idealist who fought against Franco in the Spanish Civil War but now refuses to stick his neck out. Since civilisation is crumbling, he finally abandons his detachment and takes sides. After Bogart's death, Alistair Cooke said that he was 'the romantic democratic answer to Hitler's New Order. . . . He is the first romantic hero who used the gangster's means to achieve our ends.' According to this thesis, we trusted Bogart because he looked deadly enough to face the Nazis and come out on top. But I wonder. Bogart's great money-making years were the late forties and early fifties, and it wasn't until 1954 that Nunnally Johnson singled him out as the only star whose name could go unaided over the title of a movie.

I suspect that the Bogart cult in its present form — classless and international — dates from the Cold War. We trusted him because he was a wary loner who belonged to nobody, had personal honour (that virtue which, as Bernard Shaw once said, is nowhere mentioned in the Bible), and would therefore survive. Compared with many of his Hollywood colleagues, he seemed an island of integrity, not perhaps very lovable but at least unbought. His film *persona* was that of a man for whom patriotism was something, but not nearly enough. He was a neutralist at large in Beverly Hills.

In these later years his face, with its slanting planes and wry indentations, had become as complex as a Cubist portrait. As he approached the last of 75 feature films, the highbrows adopted him, most possessively in France. (Jean-Luc Godard's *Breathless*, made in 1960, is a tribute to the Bogart way of life.) I admired him in *The Treasure of the Sierra Madre* and *The African Queen*, but the former was Walter Huston's picture and the latter Katharine Hepburn's; and anyway, I always preferred Bogart indoors. His habitat was the city, not the plain. I don't think we can say he was a great actor, but he remained, to the end, a great *behaver*. Without effort, and with classic economy, he could transfer the essence of himself to a camera and be sure that it could be eloquent on a screen.

And what was that essence? I trace it back to Seneca, of whom Bogart might very well never have heard. He flourished in the first century AD and wrote violent tragedies that had an enormous influence on Shakespeare and many other Elizabethan dramatists. (T. S. Eliot composed a celebrated essay about his effect on English literature.) What he preached and put into his plays was the philosophy known as Stoicism. It meant: accept the fact of transience, don't panic in the face of mortality, learn to live with death.

This sums up the Bogart stance. Soon after he died, I reread the letters that Seneca wrote to his friend Lucilius. Certain passages in them seemed to echo and epitomise what I had thought about Bogart during his lifetime. The poet-philosopher might have been writing additional dialogue for the actor's *persona*. 'What is freedom, say you? To be the slave of nothing, of no necessity, of no accident, and to make fortune face you on the level.' Therefore, live close to trouble and care nothing. Live outrageously, if you can carry it off. I remember Richard Burton's story of how he and Bogart were among the guests at a top-level Bel Air party in honour of a visiting foreign diplomat. Bogart, who had been warned in advance to watch his language, sat black-tied and tongue-tied until dinner was over, when he turned to the visitor and said: 'You speak very good English.' 'Thank you,' said the diplomat, 'I had an English governess.' Bogart nodded. Then, with no change of expression: 'Did you fuck her?' he asked civilly, in tones of polite interest.

'Life's like a play,' Seneca tells his friend, 'it's not the length but the excellence of the acting that counts. Where you stop isn't important. . . . To die soon or die late matters nothing: to die badly or die well is the important point.' Bogart was always dying. It was the thing he knew most about. 'In my first thirty-four pictures,' runs a famous quote, 'I was shot in twelve, and electrocuted or hanged in eight. . . .' 'If a man dies an unconcernedly as he is born,' Seneca continues, 'he has learned wisdom.' People came to see him die, because he did it with such model nonchalance. Raoul Walsh (who directed Bogart in *High Sierra*) knew what was happening when he said: 'You can't kill Jimmy Stewart, Gary Cooper or Gregory Peck in a picture. But you can kill off Bogart. The audience doesn't resent it.'

Back to Seneca: 'This is the moment on which you've been cast. You may perhaps prolong it, but how far? . . . Death's one of the obligations of life.' Yet how stunned we were when Bogart finally fulfilled it. We had watched him die so often, had seen him so regularly sacrificed on the altar of the motion-picture code, that we had come to think of him as indestructible. There would always, surely, be another Bogart movie, in which he would be killed again.

'We're wrong in looking *forward* to death,' says Seneca, 'in great measure, it's past already. Death is master of all the years that are behind us.' And Bogart's voice told us as much. Even in the most flippant context, it carried with it a bass note of mortality. The voice was his key attribute, the feature by which we recognized him: and it was cruelly appropriate that when cancer singled him out, it went for his throat.

'Everything's in other hands, Lucilius; time alone is ours.' That would have made a nice encore for Sam. Let it stand as an epitaph for Bogart.

Playboy: June 1966; *Tynan Right and Left*, 1967

LAURENCE OLIVIER

My theme is the growth of a performance, first mooted early in 1963 and brought to birth at the Old Vic Theatre on 23 April 1964, in honour of William Shakespeare's four hundredth birthday. Let me begin by discussing the performer.

Laurence Olivier at his best is what everyone has always meant by the phrase 'a great actor.' He holds all the cards; and in acting the court cards consist of (a) complete physical relaxation, (b) powerful physical magnetism, (c) commanding eyes that are visible at the back of the gallery, (d) a commanding voice that is audible *without effort* at the back of the gallery, (e) superb timing, which includes the capacity to make verse swing, (f) *chutzpah* — the untranslatable Jewish word that means cool nerve and outrageous effrontery combined, and (g) the ability to communicate a sense of danger.

These are all vital attributes, though you can list them in many orders of importance (Olivier himself regards his eyes as the ace of trumps); but the last is surely the rarest. Watching Olivier, you feel that at any moment he may do something utterly unpredictable; something explosive, possibly apocalyptic, anyway unnerving in its emotional nakedness; the lion's paw may lash out. There is nothing bland in this man. He is complex, moody and turbulent; deep in his temperament there runs a vein of rage that his affable public mask cannot wholly conceal. I once asked Ralph Richardson how he differed, as an actor, from Olivier. He replied: 'I haven't got Laurence's splendid fury.'

Fame, which isolates men from all but their closest colleagues and servitors, has enabled Olivier to preserve in his late fifties the hair-triggered emotional reactions of adolescence. He has never developed the thick social skin of conformity beneath which most of us hide our more violent or embarrassing impulses. With him they are still close to the surface, unashamed and readily accessible. The volcano remains active, the eruption for ever imminent. This is an actor ruled by instinct, not a rational being or a patient arguer or a paragon of consecutive thought; and when you ally this intuitive fire with exceptional technical equipment and a long knowledge of audience responses, you have something like the theatrical equivalent of the internal combustion engine.

Out of a sense of duty, he has occasionally tried to play what is insultingly known as 'the common man' — the seedy schoolmaster, for instance, in the film *Term of Trial*. He seldom succeeds. That outsize emotional candour cannot help breaking through, the actor impatiently bursts the seams of the role, and the common man becomes extraordinary. That is why he has spent the greater part of his professional life with his trousers off — playing bare-legged or in tights the great exceptional characters around whom the playwrights of the past built their tallest tragedies and highest comedies. He has acted in many good movies, but seldom at the height of his talent: partly because the reticence of movie acting is awkward for him, but mostly because his performances need to be seen as flowing, consecutive wholes, not chopped up into long-shots and close-ups and spread over months of shooting. You cannot make love by instalments, and Olivier's relationship with his audience is that of a skilled but dominating lover. He is one of that select group of performers (great athletes, bullfighters, singers, politicians, ballet dancers and vaudeville comedians are some of the others) whose special gift is to be able to exercise fingertip control over the emotions of a large number of people gathered in one place to witness a single unique event. He can do other things, of course; but that is what he does peerlessly and irreplaceably. His absorption in the hows and ifs and whys of his craft is total. How does he vote? What is his religion? What is his philosophy of life? The questions simply do not arise. Although I have worked quite closely with him in the last few years, I have no idea what his convictions are on any other subject than acting. This separation of work from private beliefs is not necessarily a virtue in him; but I suspect that it contributes to his acting its curious amoral strength. He approaches each new character quite unencumbered by preconceived value judgments.

The best British actors often come in pairs. A century and a half ago we had John Philip Kemble, all dignity and word-music, and the galvanic rule-breaker Edmund Kean, all earth and fire. People accused Kean of mangling blank verse, but Coleridge said that when he acted it was like reading Shakespeare by flashes of lightning; and Hazlitt's comment on his death-scene in *Richard III* is a set-piece of unforgettably dramatic criticism:

He fought like one drunk with wounds: and the attitude in which he stands with his hands stretched out, after his sword is taken from him, had a preternatural and terrific grandeur, as if his will could not be disarmed, and the very phantoms of his despair had a withering power.

In modern terms John Gielgud is Kemble to Olivier's Kean — the aesthete, as opposed to the animal. 'John is claret,' as Alan Dent once put it, 'and Larry is burgundy.' The difference between them reminds me more of Edmund Burke's famous essay on the Sublime and the Beautiful. According to Burke's definition, the Beautiful (i.e. Gielgud) comprises that which is shapely, harmonious and pleasing; while the Sublime (i.e. Olivier) is irregular, jagged and awe-inspiring, like thunder over the Matterhorn. A dozen or so years ago it looked as if a similar conflict might be stirring between Paul Scofield the poet and Richard Burton the peasant; but Burton went film-wards, and battle was never joined. Incidentally, one of Olivier's most cherished possessions is the sword that Kean used in *Richard III*. It was a gift from Gielgud, inscribed with a characteristically generous tribute to his performance.

Young actors trust and venerate Gielgud, but the man they tend to copy is Olivier. What, after all, could be more seductive than performances like his Richard, his Macbeth, his Henry V, his Oedipus, his Coriolanus — acting explosions that opened up new horizons for each of these parts, so that we felt we had never truly seen them before? His mimics are countless, but they always miss his essence. One half of Olivier loves ceremony, hierarchy and ritual — the full panoply of the *status quo* — and I even suspect that he would not mind being the first theatrical peer. The other half loves eccentricity: he relishes the abnormal, the antisocial, the offbeat, the bizarre. You could see this split in his direction of *Hamlet*, the inaugural production of the National Theatre at the Old Vic in October, 1963. It combined, not always too happily, an atmosphere of fanfare and glamour with sharp, gleeful insights into unglamorous quirks of character. Ophelia, for example, behaved in the mad scenes like a suicidal nymphomaniac. In 1944, the two sides of Olivier's nature met and married in one supreme coalition: he played a raging psychotic who adored pomp and circumstance — Richard of Gloucester, multiple murderer and anointed king.

It was not easy to persuade him to play Othello. At least, he made it seem difficult; perhaps, deep in his personal labyrinth, where the minotaur of his talent lurks, he had already decided, and merely wanted to be coaxed. Elia Kazan once told me that the adjective he would choose to sum up Olivier was 'girlish'. When I looked baffled, he elaborated: 'I don't mean that he's effeminate — just that he's coy, he's vain, he has tantrums, he needs to be wooed.' It took careful wooing to talk him into Othello, the only major role in Shakespearean tragedy that he had not played. He pointed out that no English actor in this century had succeeded in the part. The play, he said, belonged to Iago, who could always make the Moor look a credulous idiot — and he spoke with authority, since he had played Iago to Ralph Richardson's Othello in 1938. 'If I take it on,' he said, 'I don't want a witty, Machiavellian Iago. I want a solid, honest-to-God NCO.' The director, John Dexter, fully agreed with this approach. He and Olivier went through the play in depth and detail, at the end of which process the National Theatre had cast its Othello.

Soon afterwards I passed the news on to Orson Welles, himself a former Othello. He voiced an instant doubt. 'Larry's a natural tenor,' he rumbled, 'and Othello's a natural baritone.' When I mentioned this to Olivier, he gave me what Peter O'Toole has expressively called 'that grey-eyed myopic stare that can turn you to stone'. There followed weeks of daily voice lessons that throbbed through the plywood walls of the National Theatre's temporary offices near Waterloo Bridge. When the cast assembled to read the play on February 3rd, 1964, Olivier's voice was an octave lower than any of us had ever heard it.

Dexter, dapper and downright, made a bold preliminary speech. After two or three days of 'blocking' (i.e. working out the moves), there would be a first run-through with books. Of the text as a whole, he said that 'this is the most headlong of the plays'; for the purposes of this production, it would be assumed that the action took place within roughly forty-eight hours — a night in Venice, a night in Cyprus, and a final night during which Desdemona is killed. The settings (by Jocelyn Herbert) would be sparse and simple, with no elaborate scene-changes and almost nothing in the way of furniture except the indispensable nuptial couch. Pride, he said, was the key to all the characters, especially to that of Othello; already he was touching on the theme that was to be the concealed mainspring of the production — the idea of Othello as a man essentially narcissistic and self-dramatising. The germ of this came from a famous essay by Dr. F. R. Leavis, which Dexter and I had already studied with Olivier. 'Othello', Dexter told the cast, 'is a pompous, word-spinning, arrogant black general. At any rate, that's how you ought to see him. The important thing is not to accept him at his own valuation. Try to look at him objectively. He isn't just a righteous man who's been wronged. He's a man too proud to think he could ever be capable of anything as base as jealousy. When he learns that he *can* be jealous, his character changes. The knowledge destroys him, and he goes berserk. Now let's have a good loud reading this afternoon.'

That first read-through was a shattering experience. Normally on these occasions the actors do not exert themselves. They sit in a circle and mumble, more concerned with getting to know one another than with giving a performance. Into this polite gathering Olivier tossed a hand-grenade. He delivered the works — a fantastic, full-volume display that scorched one's ears, serving final notice on everyone present that the hero, storm-centre and focal point of the tragedy was the man named in the title. Seated, bespectacled and lounge-suited, he fell on the text like a tiger. This was not a noble, 'civilised' Othello but a triumphant black despot, aflame with unadmitted self-regard. So far from letting Iago manipulate him, he seemed to manipulate Iago, treating him as a kind of court jester. Such contumely cried out for deflation. There are moral flaws in every other Shakespearean hero, but Othello is traditionally held to be exempt. Olivier's reading made us realise that tradition might be wrong; that Othello was flawed indeed with the sin of pride. At the power of his voice, the windows shook and my scalp tingled. A natural force had entered the room, stark and harsh, with vowel-sounds as subtly alien as Kwame Nkrumah's; and the cast listened pole-axed. I wondered at the risks he was taking. Mightn't the knockdown arrogance of this interpretation verge too closely for comfort on comedy? Wasn't he doing to Othello precisely what he deplored in the Peter Brook–Paul Scofield *King Lear* (or '*Mr Lear*', as he called it) — i.e. cutting the hero down to size and slicing away his majesty? Then he came to 'Farewell the plumed troop,' and again the hair rose on my neck. It was like the dying moan of a fighting bull.

Like the cast, I was awed. We were learning what it meant to be faced with a great classical actor in full spate — one whose vocal range was so immense that by a single new inflexion he could point the way to a whole new interpretation. Every speech, for Olivier, is like a mass of marble at which the sculptor chips away until its essential form and meaning are revealed. No matter how ignoble the character he plays, the result is always noble as a work of art. I realised how vital, for an actor, is the use to which he puts the time available to him before his bodily resources begin to flag. In the last fifteen years Olivier has played more than twenty stage parts, ancient and modern. During the same period Marlon Brando — once, potentially, an American Olivier — has not appeared on stage at all. He had the quality; but quantity is the practice that makes quality perfect.

Othello was rehearsed for nine weeks before it opened on tour at the Alexandra Theatre, Birmingham, on April 6th. For three of the nine weeks Olivier was absent, suffering from a virus infection which (as he put it) 'shook me like a dog shakes a rat'. Rather than follow his performance as it evolved day by day, I propose to deal with it scene by scene, using the notes I kept during rehearsals of what was intended and what was achieved.

Act I Scene ii. His first entrance: an easy, rolling gait, enormous sly eyes, and a tender-tigerish smile. It is clear from the start that whatever else this performance may be, it is going to be a closely studied piece of physical impersonation. (Odd how rare this element is in contemporary theatre: modern actors in general — as Max Beerbohm said of Duse — 'never stoop to impersonation', wrongly holding it to be a facile and suspect skill.) In the opening exchanges with Iago, Olivier displays the public mask of Othello: a Negro sophisticated enough to conform to the white myth about Negroes, pretending to be simple and not above rolling his eyes, but in fact concealing (like any other aristocrat) a highly developed sense of racial superiority. This will not be a sentimental reading of the part, nor one that white liberals will necessarily applaud.

Note on props: during the early part of the scene he sniffs at and toys with a long-stemmed pink rose. Is this a foreshadowing of the lines in v. ii.

> '. . . When I have pluckt the rose,
> I cannot give it vital growth again,
> It needs must wither . . .'?

'Keep up your bright swords, for the dew will rust them' is delivered almost affably, with a trace of sarcastic condescension in the second half of the line. Othello's mere presence is enough to silence a brawl. This is a man who does not need to raise his voice to be obeyed.

Act I Scene iii. The Senate scene: a midnight meeting, convened in panic at the impending Turkish threat. Dexter tells the senators to chatter among themselves about what really concerns them — namely, the effect on their own pockets if the Turks seize a trading centre as important as Cyprus: 'Look at the economics of the scene. It's not about religion, it's not about politics, it's about money.'

Othello, a fully 'assimilated' Moor, wears a crucifix round his neck and crosses himself when Brabantio accuses him of having won Desdemona's love with witchcraft. For the great account of the wooing, he is still and central. 'Her father — loved me' is directed straight at Brabantio, in tones of wondering rebuke. There is lofty pride in the re-telling of his magical adventures; and when he reaches the line about 'the Cannibals, that each other eat, The Anthropophagi,' he utters the Greek word by way of kindly parenthetical explanation, as if to say, 'That, in case you didn't know, is the scholarly term for these creatures.' He also manages to convey his sardonic awareness that this is just the kind of story that Europeans would expect Africans to tell. (All this in a single phrase? Yes, such is the power of inflexion when practised by a master.) 'She wisht she had not heard it: yet she wisht/ That heaven had made her such a man' modulates from gentle, amused reminiscence to proud, erotic self-congratulation. 'Upon this hint I spake' is preceded by a smiling shrug, the actor dwelling on 'hint' as a jocular understatement, and forcing the senators to share his pleasure. On 'This only is the witchcraft I have used,' Olivier isolates the word 'witchcraft' so that you can almost hear the inverted commas, deliberately making the second vowel harsh and African, and pointedly eyeing Brabantio as he delivers it. Throughout the speech, he is at once the Duke's servant and the white man's master. Every time we rehearse it, the room is pin-still. For some of us, this is the high point of the performance.

Act II Scene i. The arrival at Cyprus, after a hot, wild hurricane that signals our entry into a world quite different from that of super-civilised Venice. Embracing Desdemona, Othello is beside himself with deep, internal joy, wreathed in smiles and barely able to speak. He greets the Cypriots as old friends; they are closer to him in blood than the Venetians.

Act II Scene iii. Contrary to custom, Iago's first song ('And let me the canakin clink') is a homesick soldier's lament instead of the usual rousing chorus: a perceptive idea of John Dexter's. The Cassio–Montano squabble develops (as Stanislavsky suggested in his notes on the play) into a popular riot, with the mutinous Cypriots rising against their Venetian overlords; thus Othello has something more to quell than a private quarrel. He enters nursing a scimitar; Iago lines the Venetian soldiers up before him, as if on parade.

Act III Scene iii. The great jealousy scene, the fulcrum that thrusts the energy of the play towards tragedy. To Desdemona's pleas for the reinstatement of Cassio, Othello reacts with paternal chuckles, a man besotted by the toy white trophy he has conquered. For the duologue with Iago, Dexter deliberately makes things technically hard for both actors. Othello usually sits at a desk, riffling through military documents while Iago begins his needling; Dexter forbids the desk, thereby compelling the actors to make the scene work without recourse to props. He is swiftly proved right. With no official tasks to perform, Othello ceases to be a sitting target, and Iago must struggle to hold his attention: both actors must find reasons deeper than accidents of duty to keep them together long enough for the deadly duologue to be irrevocably launched. Stroke of genius by Olivier: no sooner has Iago mentioned Cassio than *he* takes the initiative. Iago seems to be hiding something, so Othello determines to quiz *him*, in order to get a full report on Cassio's character; after all, Desdemona wants the lieutenant reinstated, and the general owes it to his wife to find out all the facts. 'What dost thou *think*?' he asks with avuncular persistence, like a headmaster ordering one prefect to tell tales on another. On 'By heaven, he echoes me,' he is mock-severe, rebuking Iago for talking in riddles. He whole attitude is one of supreme self-confidence. (Query: will the public and critics realise that this is an egocentric Othello, not an egocentric performance?) What he expects is that Iago will disclose a story about a mess bill that Cassio left unpaid, or some similar peccadillo. At this point Othello is cat to Iago's mouse.

As Othello's interrogation progresses, Iago retreats and hedges, refusing to reveal his thoughts. A showdown is the last thing he wants to precipitate; he is unprepared for anything so drastic. Driven into a corner, he suddenly says, 'O, beware, my lord, of *jealousy*.' This is pure improvisation, a shot in the dark. The notion has never before crossed Othello's mind: he thought they were discussing matters of military discipline, and his immediate response is angry incomprehension. When Iago continues, 'But, O, what damned minutes tells he o'er/Who dotes, yet doubts, suspects, yet strongly loves!' — he replies 'O misery!' with a bewildered emphasis that implies: 'Yes, it must be miserable to feel like that, but what has it to do with me?'

Next development: Othello explodes in outrage, and Iago is almost frightened by the ferocity he has inadvertently unleashed. But having gone so far, he must now go further, stressing that a girl unnatural enough to deceive her father and marry a black is capable of anything. Such is

Olivier's shame that he cannot face Iago while delivering the treacherous order: 'Set on thy wife to observe.' Once Iago has departed, his ego reasserts itself: 'Why did I marry?' is uttered with the first person singular heavily italicised, as if to say: 'I — of all people.'

The entry of Desdemona: when Othello complains of 'a pain upon my forehead,' he presses two fingers above his eyebrows, indicating to us (though not to her) the cuckold's horns. At 'Come, I'll go in with you,' he leads her off in a close, enfolding embrace that will end in bed. During his absence, we have Iago's seizure of the handkerchief dropped by Desdemona. Note: in Frank Finlay's interpretation, endorsed by Dexter, Iago has been impotent for years — hence his loathing of Othello's sexuality and his alienation from Emilia.

When Othello returns ('Ha! ha! false to *me*?'), he has been unable to make love to Desdemona; he sniffs his fingers as if they were tainted by contact with her body. He ranges back and forth across the stage for 'Farewell the tranquil mind!'; the speech becomes an animal moan of desolation, the long vowels throbbing and extended, and the 'ear-piercing fife' rising to an ecstasy of agonised onomatopoeia.

On 'Villain, be sure thou prove my love a whore,' Olivier locks Finlay by the throat and hurls him to the ground, threatening him with a trick knife-blade concealed in a bracelet. (He will later — in v. ii — use the same weapon to cut his own jugular vein.) This assault leaves Iago hoarse and breathless. From now on Othello is a boundlessly destructive force, needing only to be steered to its target.

Dexter risks a textual emendation to hammer home the hero's egoism. Instead of: '. . . her name, that was as fresh/As Dian's visage, is now begrimed and black/As mine own face.' — he reads: '. . . *my* name, that was as fresh' etc.

The danger with all Iagos is that they make Othello seem too credulous. Unless we find their lies plausible, the play becomes a tale of an oaf gulled by a con man. Dexter asks Finlay to play the whole scene as if he really believed that Cassio was sleeping with Desdemona. Only thus can he create provocation enough to trigger off Olivier's gigantic passion. Approaching the scene in this way (as of course he should; Iago's hypocrisy must be perfect and impenetrable), Finlay almost bursts into tears while recounting Cassio's dream — 'In sleep I heard him say, "Sweet Desdemona,/Let us be wary, let us hide our loves" ' — as if he could not bear to think of the general being so vilely deceived. This is a long step towards the true Iago, the one who could fool *us*. As I had expected, Olivier gets through 'Like to the Pontic sea . . .' — eight lines of blank verse — with only one pause for breath. His cadenzas hereabouts are hypnotic. After 'Now, by yon ma-a-a-arble heaven' — a surging atavistic roar — he tears the crucifix from his neck and flings it into the air. Othello's a Moor again.

Act III Scene iv. The handkerchief scene. As Othello tells the story of this talismanic heirloom ('there's magic in the web of it'), we get a glimpse of the narrative spell-binder who conquered Desdemona with his tales. She sits at his feet to listen, drawn back once again into the exotic world of the Anthropophagi. These will be their last peaceful moments together. Her rueful comment on the missing handkerchief ('Then would to God that I had never seen't!') produces a sudden, terrific spasm of fury: '*Ha! wherefore?*' — the words detonate like thunder-claps. Before his exit, Othello repeats 'The handkerchief!' three times. Olivier reaches a climax of pointblank intimidation in the first two, but for the third and last he finds a moving new inflexion, uttering the line like a desperate suppliant, whimpering for reassurance, his hands clasped before him in prayer.

Act IV Scene i. Othello is now Iago's creature. The new lieutenant is merely a passenger aboard the great plunging ship of Othello's wrath. 'All you have to do,' says Olivier to Finlay, 'is toss him a bit of meat from time to time, and he gobbles it whole.' Dexter to Finlay: 'At this point you're like Lady Macbeth after Macbeth's killed Duncan — there's really nothing left to do except go mad.' Iago and the Moor enter together and drift slowly downstage; the sinister responses and repetitions are murmurously chanted, like a satanic litany spoken in a trance:

> 'Or to be naked with her friend in bed
> An hour or more, not meaning any harm?'
> 'Naked in bed, Iago, and not mean harm . . .'

The two men even begin to sway gently from side to side, locked together in the rhythm of Othello's pain. In the epileptic fit Olivier pulls out all the stops; but, as always, there is science in his bravura. The symptoms of epilepsy (the long, shuddering breaths; the head flung back; the jaw thrust out) are painstakingly reproduced; and when he falls thrashing to the ground like a landed barracuda, Iago shoves the haft of a dagger between his teeth to keep him from biting off his tongue.

Othello's re-entry after eavesdropping on the Cassio-Iago scene and Bianca's intervention with the handkerchief: he circles the stage, a caged jungle king *in extremis*, with Iago immobile at the centre. Dexter to Finlay: 'Think of yourself as a ring-master. Just give him an occasional flick of the whip — like "Nay, that's not your way" — to keep him in order.'

The arrival of Lodovico from Venice: as Dexter points out, this changes the whole situation. Iago's moment of triumph is over, his peak is passed. From 'O, beware, my lord, of jealousy' right up to this instant, he is in complete control; from now on he is at the mercy of events. The news of Othello's recall to Venice and of Cassio's appointment as governor of Cyprus throws all his plans into confusion; he is forced to improvise, this time with disastrous results — viz. the bungled attempt on Cassio's life.

Othello strikes Desdemona across the face with the rolled-up proclamation he has received from Lodovico. Her reaction (as played by Maggie
Smith) is not the usual collapse into sobs; it is one of deep shame and
embarrassment, for Othello's sake as well as her own. She is outraged, but
tries out of loyalty not to show it. After the blow, she holds herself rigidly
upright and expressionless, fighting back her tears. 'I have not deserved
this' is not an appeal for sympathy, but a protest quietly and firmly lodged
by an extremely spunky girl.

'Cassio shall have my place': Olivier turns this line into an ironic
double entente — hasn't Cassio already usurped his place in bed?

Act IV Scene ii. The interrogation of Emilia (Joyce Redman) and the
confrontation with Desdemona, whom Othello now openly treats as a
prostitute. The scene is a nightmare of cruelty, and Olivier plays it to the
hilt: the superman runs amok, the bull wrecks the china-shop. On lines like:

> '. . . turn thy complexion there,
> Patience, thou young and rose-lipt cherubin, —
> I there look grim as hell . . .'

Olivier resorts to shrill and wailing headnotes that savour slightly of self-
indulgence. Answer: it is Othello, not Olivier, who is indulging himself
emotionally. Question: yes, but will the audience know the difference?

At 'O thou weed, /Who art so lovely fair, and smell'st so sweet,' he
crawls across the stage and lies on top of Desdemona: for a moment, desire
almost overcomes disgust: or rather, both emotions co-exist. Othello comes
close to committing the crime of which Brabantio accused his daughter: he
very nearly 'falls in love with what he fears to look on'.

Act V Scene i. The street scene, including the abortive stabbing of Cassio by
Roderigo, and the latter's murder by Iago. Othello's brief and dramatically
pointless appearance is cut, in accordance with sound theatrical custom.

Act V Scene ii. The killing of Desdemona in the bedroom. Entrance of
Othello: white-robed and dark-limbed, picked out by a shaft of moonlight
through a grille over the chamber door. On 'Who's there?', Desdemona
wakes up in a convulsion of fear, as if from a nightmare; then says with a
sigh of relief, 'Othello!' The 'murder, which I thought a sacrifice' is
accomplished with relentless, implacable precision; honour having been
offended, the prescribed penalty must be enforced.

Turning-point of the case against Iago: Emilia can prove that her
husband is a dirty-minded gossipmonger, but not until Othello reveals that
he has seen Cassio with the handkerchief ('I saw it in his hand') can she

prove that Iago is guilty of conspiracy to murder. It takes her a second or two to react to the implication of what Othello has said; but then she bursts out with 'O God! O heavenly God!' — and after this clinching double-take it is all up with Iago, since she now reveals that she gave him the handkerchief. The end of Iago: he offers himself masochistically to Othello's sword. 'I bleed, sir; but not kill'd' is spoken with quiet satisfaction. The end of Othello: kneeling on the bed, hugging the limp corpse of Desdemona, he slashes his throat with the hidden stiletto we saw in III. iii. And slumps like a falling tower.

About six months after the production opened, the Italian director Franco Zeffirelli saw it for the first time. Of Olivier's performance he said: 'I was told that this was the last flourish of the romantic tradition of acting. It's nothing of the sort. It's an anthology of everything that has been discovered about acting in the last three centuries. It's grand and majestic, but it's also modern and realistic. I would call it a lesson for us all.'

Othello: The National Theatre Production, 1966;
The Sound Of Two Hands Clapping, 1975

MARLENE DIETRICH

There are aspects of Dietrich as they surface in my memory, coloured no doubt by fifteen years of knowing her and some thirty years of quietly lustful admiration.

First, there is my friend the nurse — the sender of appropriate pills, the source of uncanny medical tips, the magic panacea. For this Marlene, healer of the world's wounded, I have often been thankful. Her songs are healing, too. Her voice tells you that whatever hell you inhabit, she has been there before, and survived. Some trace of ancient Teutonic folk-wisdom — many would call it witchcraft — still adheres to her. For example, she can predict a child's sex before its birth. This must, of course, be inspired guesswork or shrewdly applied psychology. She calls it science, as any witch would.

Then there is the self-punishing worker, daughter of an exacting German father, brought up to take pleasure as a prize and a privilege, not as a birthright. This is the Marlene who worships excellence — a high-definition performer who daily polishes her unrusting skills. A small eater, sticking to steaks and greenery, but a great devourer of applause. For some people (said Jean Cocteau), style is a very complicated way of saying very simple things; for others, it is a very simple way of saying very complicated things. Marlene is one of the others. Her style looks absurdly simple — an effortless act of projection, a serpentine lasso whereby her voice casually winds itself around our most vulnerable fantasies. But it is not easy. It is what remains when ingratiation, sentimentality and the manifold devices of heart-warming crap have been ruthlessly pared away. Steel and silk are left, shining and durable.

And a tireless self-chronicler. For the first half-hour of every meeting with this Marlene, you will be told how she wowed them in Warsaw, mowed them down in Moscow, savaged them in Sydney, was pelted with poppies in Isfahan. It is all true and, if anything, understated. She is merely keeping you up to date. Then she moves in — critical, probing and self-abnegating — on your own life and its problems. For the time being, you transfer your burdens to the willing shoulders of this gallant Kraut.

From the flat screen she stormed the senses, looking always tangible but at the same time untouchable. Her eyes were a pair of mournful rebukes, twin appeals to us not to lose our heads by becoming 'emotionally involved': but the milk-soft skin (which still shows no signs of curdling) gave the lie to them. And how cynically witty were her lips! This was not the fatal woman panting for fulfilment, like Theda Bara and the rest: it was the fatal woman fulfilled, gorged and sleek with triumph. The aftermath (*vide* Ovid) is sadness, and it was sadness that Dietrich communicated, even in her first youth. 'There is a gloom in deep love,' said Landor, 'as in deep waters.' But Dietrich had not alone the earth-melancholy of Lilith: she could awake and sing, brandishing her hips like Eve defying the Fall. 'Beware the *amazing* blonde women!' she cried in one of her early songs: and there was in her voice that note of quasi-military harshness you find in so many Germanic heroines. The order rings out riotously, and men come cringing to heel: the rule is instant obedience, the sheep must beg to be slaughtered. That, anyway, was the Dietrich myth, and it has its echoes in fictional women as disparate as Wedekind's Lulu and La Mort in Cocteau's *Orphée*. Many women, according to an old joke, have gender but no sex. With Dietrich the opposite is true. She has sex, but no particular gender. Her ways are mannish: the characters she played loved power and wore slacks, and they never had headaches or hysterics. They were also quite undomesticated. Dietrich's masculinity appeals to women, and her sexuality to men. They say (or, at least, *I* say) that she was the only woman who was allowed to attend the annual ball for male transvestites in pre-Hitler Berlin. She habitually turned up in top hat, white tie and tails. Seeing two exquisite creatures descending the grand staircases, clad in form-hugging sequins and cascading blonde wigs, she wondered wide-eyed: 'Are you two in love?' '*Fräulein*,' said one of them frostily, 'we are not Lesbians.' This Marlene lives in a sexual no man's land — and no woman's, either. She dedicates herself to looking, rather than to being, sexy. The art is in the seeming. The semblance is the image, and the image is the message. She is every man's mistress and mother, every woman's lover and aunt, and nobody's husband except Rudi's — and he *is* her husband, far off on his ranch in California.

She believes in the stars but makes her own luck. Impresarios unnerve her. She has no agent or business manager except herself. Where once, in the high noon of the thirties, she depended on Joseph von Sternberg, she now looks to Burt Bacharach, her arranger and conductor. In his absence, she frets; at his excuses, she expressively shrugs. Burt is her generalissimo, the musical overlord on whom, quite asexually, she dotes.

She laughs a lot, making a honking sound that is not without melancholy. A special note of mournful bitchery invades her voice when the conversation turns to jumped-up starlets who need to be put down. ('What *about* that picture? She has to be out of her mind. Honey, it's to *die!*') This professional Marlene is not what anyone would call a woman's woman. I was not surprised to learn that she had never met Greta Garbo, her major rival in the World Eroticism Stakes of the pre-war era. She venerates many kinds of men — great strenuous helpers of our species like Sir Alexander Fleming; great life-enhancing performers like Jean Gabin and Orson Welles; great self-revealing writers like Ernest Hemingway and

Konstantin Paustovsky; great masters of timing and nuance like Noël Coward; and men of great power like General Patton, John Fitzgerald Kennedy and — the latest recruit to the clan — Moishe Dayan. Marlene relishes the breath of power. She is rabidly anti-war, but just as rabidly pro-Israeli. This paradox in her nature sometimes worries me.

Aloof, imperious, unfeeling, icy and calculating: these are some of the things she is not. Proud, involved, challenging, ironic and outgoing: these are apter epithets. On stage, in the solo act to which she has devoted the last decade or so, she stands as if astonished to be there, like a statue unveiled every night to its own inexhaustible amazement. She shows herself to the audience like the Host to the congregation. And delivers the sacred goods. She *knows* where all the flowers went — buried in the mud of Passchendaele, blasted to ash at Hiroshima, napalmed to a crisp in Vietnam — and she carries the knowledge in her voice. She once assured me that she could play Bertolt Brecht's *Mother Courage*, and I expect she was right. I can picture her pulling a wagon across the battlefields, chanting those dark and stoical Brechtian songs, and setting up shop wherever the action erupts, as she did in France during the Ardennes offensive — this queen of camp followers, the Empress Lili Marlene.

What we have here, by way of summary, is a defiant and regal lady with no hobbies except perfectionism, no vices except self-exploitation, and no dangerous habits except an infallible gift for eliciting prose as monumentally lush as this from otherwise rational men. Marlene makes blurb-writers of us all. She is advice to the love-lorn, influence in high places, a word to the wise, and the territorial imperative. She is also Whispering Jack Schmidt, Wilhelmina the Moocher, the deep purple falling, the smoke in your eyes, how to live alone and like it, the survival of the fittest, the age of anxiety, the liberal imagination, nobody's fool and every dead soldier's widow. On top of which, she has limitations and knows them.

She is now on public show in person for the first time in New York. Roll up in reverence.

Playbill: October 1967; *The Sound of Two Hands Clapping*, 1975

Harry Kurnitz

When I was writing last week about the ubiquitous influence of Hollywood on American culture, I did not know that Harry Kurnitz had died a few days earlier. If the news had reached me in time, I would have written instead about the ubiquitous influence of Harry Kurnitz on Hollywood.

He first came to Beverly Hills in 1938, at the height of the cinema's myth-making era, and during the next three decades he wrote more than forty movies. Among them were *The Thin Man Goes Home*, *Melba*, *Land of the Pharaohs*, Carol Reed's *The Man Between* and Hitchcock's *Witness for the Prosecution*. Between scripts, he turned out what he called a 'a thin but unimpressive collection of novels' (pseudonymous detective stories that sold in paperback millions), a couple of prosperous Broadway comedies, and a musical version of Rattigan's *The Sleeping Prince*, on which he collaborated with Noël Coward. Not a masterpiece on the list: merely a succession of streamlined, professional artefacts.

What gave Kurnitz his unique reputation in the Upper Bohemia of the performing arts was not so much his writing as his life-style, and the conversation that expressed it. For something like twenty years, busily commuting between America and Europe, he patiently lived with the knowledge that he had been elected Hollywood's court jester, and was well on the way to becoming a 'legendary wit.'

He was a troubled, stooping man, with lantern jaws, a fuzz of hair and watery eyes, rueful behind their spectacles. Once married, he looked much divorced. It was obvious that he had several first-class tailors. (When a starlet accidentally poured champagne over his sleeve, he said, lying gallantly: 'Think nothing of it. This suit has had so much wine spilled on it that I never have it cleaned — I just send it out to be trampled by peasants.') His laugh was a dry, infectious cackle. I first heard it when I asked him what it was like to live in Hollywood. 'It's marvellous,' he said. 'The general sensation is like sinking slowly into a giant hopper of warm farina.'

Though never a Communist, he was a pinkish liberal; and it dismayed him when, unlike so many of his friends, he was not commanded to give evidence before the Un-American Activities Committee. 'I am suffering,' he complained, 'from a bad case of subpoena envy.'

At least two of Kurnitz's *impromptus* have entered into the permanent Western gag-book. While staying at St. Moritz, he declined an invitation to go skiing on religious grounds. 'What's your religion?' asked his host. 'Orthodox coward,' said Kurnitz. He was later involved in a feud with Lynn Loesser, whose husband Frank wrote the music and lyrics of *Guys and Dolls*. In Kurnitz's unforgettable phrase: 'Lynn is the evil of two Loessers.'

He was also a practised and exquisite raconteur. In 1955, for instance, he was hired to collaborate with William Faulkner on the script of *Land of the Pharaohs*. With what awe (he told me) he awaited the advent of the Nobel Prize-winner at Cairo airport. A full week after the advertised time, the Prize-winner touched down. He emerged from the aircraft on a stretcher in an alcoholic trance, and was instantly whisked off to a nearby hospital. Several days later Kurnitz received a card summoning him to start work in Faulkner's suite the following morning at 10 a.m. He turned up to find the Prize-winner pouring himself a full tumbler of Bourbon. Would Kurnitz like a shot? No, it was a touch too early. At which point the Prize-winner raised his glass to his lips in quivering fingers, and mumbled, by way of explanation: 'Can't seem to shake this cold.'

Kurnitz was not a violent man, but he was profoundly Jewish and could not help mistrusting the Germans. In 1953 he went to Berlin to write *The Man Between* and detested the city on sight. He even constructed a fantasy about it. According to this mock-epic, Kurnitz would arrive in Berlin mounted on a parapet ('a special kind of horse') and carrying a Vassar 36 ('a light sporting rifle with compact and mirror attached'). He would then put into action a plan to poison the city's water supply by means of lethal pellets concealed in the mouth of Schmierkäse, the Submarine Wonder Dog.

Kurnitz bought good paintings and listened to good concerts wherever his planes touched down. He was a civilised man with a plenitude of wit and charity. 'What did Harry think?' we used to ask, always knowing that there was only one Harry whose opinion counted in the higher reaches of show business. There won't come such another.

Observer: 31st March 1968

NOËL COWARD

One night in the spring of 1959 I sat down to dine at Sardi's, the New York theatrical restaurant. Crowded before the Broadway curtains rise and after they fall, it is usually empty in between, and was on this occasion. Suddenly I looked up from the menu and froze. Noël Coward, also alone, had come in; and that very morning the *New Yorker* had printed a demolishing review by me of his latest show, an adaptation of Feydeau called *Look After Lulu*.

I knew him too well to ignore his presence, and not well enough to pass the whole thing off with a genial quip. No sooner had he taken his seat than he spotted me. He rose at once and came padding across the room to the table behind which I was cringing. With eyebrows quizzically arched and upper lip raised to unveil his teeth, he leaned towards me. 'Mr. T.,' he said crisply, 'you are a cunt. Come and have dinner with me.'

Limp with relief, I joined him, and for over an hour this generous man talked with vivacious concern about the perils of modishness ('There's nothing more old-fashioned than being up to date'), the nature of the writer's ego ('I am bursting with pride, which is why I have absolutely no vanity'), the state of the theatre in general and of my career in particular. Not once did he mention my notice or the play. It would have been easy to cut or to crush me. It was typical of Coward that he chose, with an almost certain flop on his hands, to amuse and advise me instead.

As a writer, this was one of his bad times, and there had been many since the war — since, indeed, the high period from 1925 to 1941, which produced the five plays by which he will be remembered: *Hay Fever, Private Lives, Design for Living, Blithe Spirit* and *Present Laughter. Sigh No More*, the revue he wrote in 1945 to celebrate the return to peace, was an especially low point, although it contained some marvellous things: the title song, for example, at once joyful and elegiac, and 'Nina from Argentina', a model of intricate rhyming on which Cole Porter at his best could hardly have improved. Lowest of all was *Pacific 1860*, Coward's Drury Lane musical of 1946, of which I remember little except Graham Payn singing about his awestruck affection for a South Sea volcano by the name of Fum-Fum-Bolo. But even if we agree that Coward the post-war writer was past his prime, it's impossible to accept the judgment laid down by Cyril Connolly in 1937:

One can't read any of Noël Coward's plays now . . . they are written in the most topical and perishable way imaginable, the cream in them turns sour overnight.

In fact his best work has not dated, by which I mean his most devotedly ephemeral. One feels the same about many movies of the 1930s: with the passage of time, the profundities peel away and only the basic trivialities remain to enchant us. They have certainly enchanted John Osborne, who learned from Coward the disparaging use of 'little' (as in 'nasty little', 'repulsive little', 'disgusting little', etc.), and Harold Pinter, whose spare, allusive dialogue owes a great deal to Coward's sense of verbal tact. Consider *Shadow Play*, a haunting one-act piece that Coward wrote in 1935. A couple whose marriage has gone sour attempt to reconstruct their halcyon days, correcting each other as they misremember. The parts were originally played by Coward and Gertrude Lawrence. 'Small talk,' Miss Lawrence says at one point, 'a lot of small talk, with other thoughts going on behind.' What could be more Pinterish, or for that matter more Chekhovian? And what more subtly sexy than the four brief declarative sentences that Miss Lawrence addresses to Coward at their first meeting:

You're nice and thin. Your eyes are funny. You move easily. I'm afraid you're terribly attractive.

An exquisite bone-dry lyric precedes the marital flashbacks:

Here in the light
Of this unkind, familiar now,
Every gesture is clear and cold for us,
Even yesterday's growing old for us.
Everything's changed somehow . . .

Coward took the fat off English comic dialogue: he was the Turkish bath in which it slimmed. Nothing could be more elliptical than the country-house conversation in which Coward and Miss Lawrence (Simon and Victoria) discover between the lines that they are mad about each other:

VICTORIA: Are you good at gardens?
SIMON: Not very, but I'm persevering . . . I can tell a Dorothy Perkins a mile off.
VICTORIA: That hedge over there is called *cupressus macrocarpa*.
SIMON: Do you swear it?
VICTORIA: It grows terribly quickly, but they do say it gets a little thin underneath in about twenty years.
SIMON: How beastly of them to say that. It's slander . . .

I first met Coward in the early 1950s, during his cabaret seasons at the Café de Paris, and heard him exploding with mock-outrage when he found

in 1954 that the place had been completely redecorated in honour of
Marlene Dietrich's impending début. 'For Marlene,' he said, 'it's cloth of
gold on the walls and purple marmosets swinging from the chandeliers. But
for me — sweet fuck all!' To describe his own cabaret appearances, I went
back to his boyhood and wrote: 'In 1913 he was Slightly in *Peter Pan*, and
you might say that he has been wholly in *Peter Pan* ever since.' The young
blade of the 1920s had matured into an old rip, but he was as brisk and
energetic as ever; and if his face suggested an old boot, it was
unquestionably hand-made. The qualities that stood out were precision of
timing and economy of gesture — in a phrase, high definition performance.
After a lifetime of concentration, he gave us relaxed, fastidious ease.

I once said of an uxorious writer that he had put his talent into his work,
and his genius into his wife. Coward did not make that mistake. The style
he embodied — as writer and performer alike — was the essence of high
camp. He was one of the brightest stars in the homosexual constellation that
did so much to enliven the theatre between the wars. Coward invented the
concept of cool, and may have had emotional reasons for doing so. At all
events, he made camp elegant, and wore a mask of amused indifference —
'Grin and rise above it' — to disguise any emotions he preferred not to
reveal. From the beginning of his career he was a shrugger-off of passion
and a master of understatement — queerdom's answer (you might say) to
Gerald du Maurier, the matinée idol of his day. It was du Maurier who led
the attack on Coward's first hit, *The Vortex*, on the grounds that it was a
dustbin drama.

In later years Coward himself was not above knocking his juniors,
especially if they wrote plays of ideas. 'Political and social propaganda in
the theatre,' he wrote, 'as a general rule, is a cracking bore.' Many of his
own post-war works (presumably the exceptions) show him to be a
convinced reactionary. In *Peace in Our Time*, which deals with London if
Germany had won the war, the first Englishman to collaborate with the
Nazis is a left-wing intellectual. And *Relative Values* (1951) ends with a
toast to 'the final inglorious disintegration of the most unlikely dream that
ever troubled the foolish heart of man — Social Equality.' But more often
his objection to contemporary drama was simply that it was drab. After he
saw David Storey's *The Changing Room*, his companion said that the rugby
players, when stripped in the bath scene, were not physically very
impressive. 'No,' said Coward, 'fifteen acorns are hardly worth the price of
admission.'

In 1964 we decided to put *Hay Fever* into the repertoire of the National
Theatre and to ask Coward to direct it. Nobody alive knew more about
sophisticated comedy, and I remembered Coward's remark to Rex
Harrison: 'If you weren't the finest light-comedy actor in the world next to
me, you'd be good for only one thing — selling cars in Great Portland
Street.' Coward himself was astonished by the invitation. Soon after it was

issued, I was walking along a Mayfair street when a Rolls pulled up at the kerb. The electric window zoomed down and Coward peered out. 'Bless you,' he said, 'for admitting that I'm a classic. I thought you were going to do nothing but Brecht, Brecht, Brecht.' When he arrived to start rehearsals with a company led by Edith Evans and Maggie Smith, he made a little speech that began, 'I'm thrilled and flattered and frankly a little flabbergasted that the National Theatre should have had the curious perceptiveness to choose a very early play of mine and to give it a cast that could play the Albanian telephone directory.'

The rehearsals yielded a classic *mot.* Dame Edith persisted in upsetting Coward's rhythm by saying 'On a very clear day you can see Marlow,' instead of 'On a clear day you can see Marlow.' After weeks of patience Coward interrupted. 'Edith,' he said, 'the line is "On a clear day you can see Marlow." On a *very* clear day you can see Marlowe *and* Beaumont *and* Fletcher.' The production was a huge success, and spawned a still-continuing vogue of Coward revivals.

Was he ever (and will he ever be) as highly regarded outside the English-speaking countries? I doubt it. He was above all a virtuoso of linguistic nuance. I cannot think that it will ever be possible to explain to a Belgian or Italian audience exactly why Budleigh Salterton is funny and Henley-in-Arden is not. One of the last and best stories I heard about Coward depends for its full effect on the choice and timing of an English proper noun. He was staying in Brighton with the Oliviers when their five-year-old daughter Tamsin saw in the street a male dog sniffing a female dog. She asked Uncle Noël what the animals were doing. 'The doggie in front,' he replied, 'has suddenly gone blind, and the other one has very kindly offered to push him all the way to St. Dunstan's.'

Incidentally, it is Olivier's theory that the authentic Noël Coward note in English literature was first struck by Sir John Falstaff, who says, when Mistress Quickly suggests putting an egg into his cup of sack: 'I'll no pullet sperm in my brewage.'

Not long before his death, Coward appeared in a Gillette advertisement. It required him to give a list of things that in his view had style. His reply was a brilliant, if oblique, self-portrait: 'A candy-striped Jeep; Jane Austen; Cassius Clay; *The Times* before it changed; Danny La Rue; Charleston in South Carolina; 'Monsieur' de Givenchy; a zebra (but *not* a zebra crossing); evading boredom; Gertrude Lawrence; the Paris Opera House; white; a seagull; a Brixham trawler; Margot Fonteyn; any Cole Porter song; English pageantry; Marlene's voice . . . and . . . Lingfield has a tiny bit.'

About a year ago my wife and I dined at the Savoy Grill. At the next table sat Noël and his hard-core court, consisting of Graham Payn, the designer Gladys Calthrop and the actress Joyce Carey. When they had finished I felt a tap on my shoulder. It was Noël, standing beside me and explaining that he had just returned from a winter in Jamaica. The spring weather in London was warm, and my wife said he had picked a good time to come. 'Do you swear it?' said Noël gravely, unconsciously quoting from *Shadow Play*. He went on to tell us that he had recently met a very famous dwarf who had turned out to be enormously tedious. 'There's only one thing worse than being a dwarf,' he said, 'and that's being a boring dwarf.'

We were still laughing when he turned to go and we saw with a shock that he could hardly hobble. It took him more than two minutes to leave the room, with Graham Payn supporting one arm and Joyce Carey the other. His rubicund face and ebullient manner had fooled us. Noël had suffered a *coup de vieux*, and I felt sadly sure that I would not — nor did I — see him again.

Observer: 1st April 1973; *The Sound Of Two Hands Clapping*, 1975

ERIC MORECAMBE

Early in 1973, Eric Morecambe and Ernie Wise, who are both in their mid-forties, celebrated their thirtieth anniversary as a double act. Before they were in their teens, they had appeared separately in northern working-men's clubs. They teamed up during the war and have since worked together in music-hall, radio, movies and television. They have been getting better all the time. There comes a point at which sheer professional skill, raised to the highest degree by the refining drudgery of constant practice, evolves into something different in kind, conferring on its possessors an assurance that enables them to take off, to ignite, to achieve outrageous feats of timing and audience control that would, even a few years before, have been beyond them. Morecambe and Wise have now reached that point. In their last TV series, written by the intuitive Eddie Braben, they came on as masters, fit to head any list of the most accomplished performing artists at present active in this country. What has happened to star quality in Britain? Morecambe and Wise have; or, to be invidiously precise, Eric Morecambe has, with unselfish, ebullient and indispensable help from Ernie Wise.

Every year, when their last TV show is safely in the can, they dart around the provinces carrying out what they call 'bank raids'. Twice nightly, on Fridays and Saturdays, they appear at a selected few of the biggest theatres outside London, making from these brief jaunts more money (their PR man half-boasts, half-complains) than thirteen BBC shows would bring in. The first half of the programme is a straight variety bill; they occupy the second, which can last up to ninety minutes and consists of the legendary routines they use to warm up studio audiences and have prudently declined to squander on the tube. Last spring I saw them at the New Theatre in Oxford, an echoing barn which they packed to the roof. 'We still get the dry lip,' Eric had told me beforehand. 'A lot of our comedy's based on fear.' But he was talking about television tension, the surge of adrenalin that can lead to berserk ad libs and sudden jumps in the script. On stage their confidence is total. But apart from certain TV trademarks — gags about Ernie's alleged wig and 'little short legs'; the affectionate pats, just crisp enough to sting, that Eric bestows on Ernie's cheek; and catch-phrases like the mysterious cry of 'Arsenal!', which was used in one BBC programme and now gets a round of applause whenever Eric utters it — apart from these, their style and material at Oxford reached back to their music-hall days.

The act, so to speak, was Morecambe and Wise Mark I — the original model, fitted with automatic gearshift and power steering. In other words, a traditional male duo, but performed at a pace, with a delicacy, and above all *in clothes* (matching suits from Savile Row) that would have amazed such earlier couples as Murray and Mooney or Clapham and Dwyer. Male double acts, once numerous, are today fairly thin on the ground; thinner still are male-female teams, such as Caryll and Mundy or Kenway and Young; and the vogue for girl twosomes, like Revnell and West, Gert and Daisy and the Houston Sisters, appears to have vanished. Morecambe and Wise inspire reflections like these, so firmly is their stage work rooted in pre-war vaudeville. You can also trace the influence of Abbott and Costello and Wheeler and Woolsey, who ranked among the top movie teams during their adolescence. In M and W Mk. I, Ernie is the classic stooge, dapper and aggressive, like a sawn-off Lew Hoad: Eric is the comic off whose foolishness Ernie scores. Huge black horn-rims are a vital part of his persona. They highlight the ocular reactions that are among his specialities — the look of suddenly dawning enlightenment, the blank stare aimed straight at the camera, the smug *oeillade* that accompanies asides like: 'This boy is a *fool*.' Behind the spectacles the face is boyish and vulnerable, with the long upper lip that all great comics seem to have. Wise is boyish, too. Indeed, the characters they present in their act are both fixed at a mental and emotional age of approximately fifteen. They ape the manners and vocabulary of adults, but are always falling back on the idioms, habits and local references of a North-country childhood. Hence they cannot deal with adult sex, except indirectly, through innuendo, as in their famous TV encounter with Frank ('Casanova') Finlay:

FINLAY (*furtively*): I have a *long felt want*.
MORECAMBE (*after subliminal pause*): There's no answer to that.

Nor would they wish to go further. As Ernie says: 'We never touch anything blue.' Such is their sexual innocence that, although they frequently share a bed in TV sketches, no whiff of queerness ever intrudes. They once did a routine in which it was hinted that Ernie might have been responsible for an illegitimate pregnancy: thirty letters of protest arrived, and they worried about it for weeks. They shun politics, too; in fact, I have no doubt that Lenny Bruce would have appalled them. Cynicism, the moral stock-in-trade of most American comics, is utterly alien to them. If, as we are always being told, comedy must have an attitude towards life, they are not comedians at all. Their laughs — and this is something very British, observable in talents as disparate as Pinter and the Goons — depend on nuance and inflexion, minute details of vocal and verbal eccentricity:

WISE: I'm going to make you the greatest singer in the world.

MORECAMBE: You're only saying that.
WISE: No, I'm not.
MORECAMBE: Somebody just did.

Morecambe's reflexes — the effortless speed and timing with which he changes expressions and tones of voice — are among the wonders of the profession. He can modulate through a series like Alarm/Aggression/Collapse/Recovery/Snide Insinuation in about four seconds, each phase being distinct in itself and leading logically to the next. My notes on the stage act include the following sequence, accomplished in roughly the same time: 'Apology/nervous cough/challenging glare/business with brown paper bag/false smile/business of adjusting glasses/voice suddenly strident and serious.' For theatrical purposes the speed may even be excessive: after years of TV, Morecambe's style often needs the close-up camera to do justice to its intimacy and understatement.

'In the early days,' Morecambe told me, 'people kept saying to us: "You'll never be a success till you find something to hang your hat on" ' — i.e. a durable routine like Sid Field's golfing sketch, or a stock trait like Jack Benny's meanness. They never found one, unless you count (as I would) the ventriloquist bit that is the high point of their variety act. Morecambe, equipped with doll, seats himself and says to the audience: 'Good evening, little man, and how are you? I'm very well, thank you. And what are you going to do for the ladies and gentlemen? I'll sing a song.' He pronounces every word at dictation speed with elaborate lip movements. The dummy's lips do not move at all. At length Wise, who has been watching incredulously, interrupts:

WISE: But I can see your lips moving!
MORECAMBE: (*impatiently, as to a halfwit*): Of *course* you can see
   my lips moving!

Wise carefully explains that the whole point of ventriloquism is that the ventriloquist's lips should not move. This, when at last it gets through to Morecambe, strikes him as self-evidently absurd, and he confides to the audience that Wise is a crazy fantasist: 'He lives in a dream world.'

WISE (*shouting*): Don't you understand?
MORECAMBE (*shouting back*): No, but does it matter at this late
   stage?

Finally, under pressure from Wise, he tries to make the dummy's lips work, and in the attempt detaches the head from the body. Brandishing it by the neck, he hopefully crows: 'A throat with knuckles — they've never seen that before!' Any other comic would ventriloquize *badly*; only a

Morecambe would take the wild imaginative step of not ventriloquizing *at all*. Another stage routine that might qualify, if extended, for hat-hanging status is the one in which Morecambe enters in full evening dress as a star magician. He stoops beneath the weight of an outsize tail-coat, from the bulging shoulders of which feathers are escaping.

WISE: What have you got in there?
MORECAMBE: Five chickens, three parrots, two vultures, four turkeys
 and a tom tit.
WISE: What does the tom tit do?
MORECAMBE: Not a lot.

They seldom address the audience directly — once at the beginning of their act, when Morecambe peers into the darkness and genially remarks: 'What a fat woman you are, madam. You. Are. Fat. Did you come on a lorry?'; and again at the end, when they invite questions from the house. They have a wide range of prepared answers and have only once been baffled. That was when a passionate voice rang out from the gallery: 'Should mopeds be allowed on the motorway?' Even Eric dried.

Their curtain calls are numerous. 'We never used to be able to do a good warm-up,' Ernie had said to me. 'Now the only thing we can't do is take a good bow.' But it really isn't true. Eric, as we know from TV, is a superb user of curtains, whether to burst through, peer round, lurk behind, or feign strangling himself with one hand in the folds of. It was he who told me the advice an old pro had given him on the art of taking bows: 'Rattle the corner of the curtain to show you're still there.' In any case, they have no need to milk applause. They are unmistakably loved — so much so that even the money they earn is not resented. 'When I'm driving through towns in the North,' Ernie says, 'people hate the Rolls until they see who's in it. Somehow they forgive us.'

Over supper after their Oxford appearance, Eric talks about comedy. Like Ernie (who had driven home to Harrow) he is a mobile repository of vaudeville lore, an encyclopedia of English-speaking gags, their genealogy, past effectiveness and current ownership. Give him a paper cup and within seconds it will have become a false nose and he'll be into a Durante impersonation. His favourite variety house is the Birmingham Hippodrome, on which I was brought up, so I quiz him about about some of the lesser-known names of the '40s. Does he remember Freddie Bamberger and Pam? 'Very good act. A bit ahead of its time, maybe a bit too sophisticated. Freddie always smoked a cigar, and in the provinces a cigar means it's Christmas.' For Eric, as for most British comedians, the comics' comic is Tommy Cooper. (The American equivalent is George Burns.) 'My dressing-room', Eric says, 'is the Cooper shrine. You can tell how good he is because everyone does impressions of him. If Tom's in the same room with a lot of other comedians, they're all waiting to see what he says next. He always surprises you.' A typical Cooper story: a man walks up to a shabby house and knocks on the door. It is opened by an anguished woman in black. 'Can I speak to Harry Jones?' asks the man. The woman bursts into tears. Another man wearing a black tie and a black arm-band appears behind the woman and asks the visitor what he wants. 'Can I speak to Harry Jones?' the first man asks. 'Harry Jones died two hours ago,' says the other man sombrely. 'I am his brother and this is his wife.' 'Oh,' says the first man, after a short pause. 'Did he say anything about a pot of paint?' If you find that unfunny, you are probably not a comedian.

Eric, who is married with two grown-up children, was born in Morecambe and christened Eric Bartholomew, an only child with no show-business background. His father was a corporation workman; his mother — 'a very intelligent woman' — taught him music. He can still, at a pinch, play accordion, trumpet, clarinet, trombone and euphonium. Ernie Wise, a native of Leeds, was one of five children and came from a lower social level than Eric. His father worked on the railways and as a semi-pro entertainer in working-men's clubs. Ernie joined the act at the age of seven; Eric, urged on by his mother, was working the clubs at eleven; and they met in Swansea at the beginning of the war. In 1943, aged sixteen, they made their West End début in *Strike a New Note*, the hit revue that brought Sid Field to London after years in the provinces. Because Ernie was a friend of George Black, the producer, they were billed as 'Morecambe and Wise', although they didn't appear together in the show (except on a couple of occasions when somebody's illness left a hole in the programme). Their act, Eric says, was: 'Terrible. With the full American accent. God knows why.' Towards the end of the war, Ernie went into the merchant navy and Eric was sent down the mines, an experience that left him with a weakened heart. They were reunited in 1947. In the 1950s came *Running Wild*, a disastrous TV series for the BBC ('We were *pummelled*'); in the 1960s they triumphed on both channels and plunged into a frenzied period of overwork, including pantomimes, summer shows, films, and fourteen trips to the States to appear on the Ed Sullivan show. They also played the northern clubs, where they prospered in an atmosphere they did not always relish: too much drink in an audience isn't good for the finer points of comedy. Eric does a definitive impression of a club comic mumbling a hoarse stream of racist gags into a pencil mike: 'There was this Pakistani went into this synagogue . . .'

In 1968 Eric had a heart attack. John Ammonds, an affable, hirsute little man who has produced all their BBC shows for the past four years, believes that this setback, which seemed so shattering at the time, has had beneficial results. 'It forced the boys to give up all their outside activities and focus their attention on thirteen television shows a year. It allowed them to rehearse longer, and it made them concentrate.' Ammonds was the man who taught Eric to work to a specific camera (on asides like: 'A cunning little barb!') instead of to the studio audience. And it was from Ammonds, who copied it from Groucho Marx, that they picked up the curious skipping exit, like a sort of camp hornpipe, which they use to end their shows. (As many dance routines have disclosed, Eric is probably the most graceful bespectacled man on television.) Like Tony Hancock, and unlike almost all other British comedians, they actually improved on the way from the variety stage to the small screen. Already, in the mid-sixties, Morecambe and Wise Mark II had evolved. They were no longer comic and stooge, but two egotists in more or less equal competition. 'In old-fashioned double acts,' Eric says, 'the straight man would do something right and the comic would get it wrong. With us, Ernie would probably get it wrong as well. You get the same kind of thing with Laurel and Hardy.' Until Eric's heart attack, their scripts were written by Sid Green and Dick Hills, who also took part in the shows. Since 1969, and the advent of Eddie Braben, a Liverpudlian recluse who dispatches his scripts from Merseyside and hates coming to London, Morecambe and Wise Mark III have emerged, and Eric in particular has burgeoned into one of the most richly quirkish and hypnotic performers in the history of the box.

It is doubtful whether much that is memorable will be left in print about him. He may well be a literary casualty, because he lacks the easily identifiable characteristics by which other comics impress themselves on the memory. He is not a tramp, like Chaplin. He is not a lecher, like Groucho. He is not a boozy misanthrope, like W. C. Fields. Nor does he fall down or get kicked in the pants, like Norman Wisdom and Cast of Thousands. Some of the time he is simply a pro comic making pro-comic jokes, e.g.:

QUEEN VICTORIA (*Glenda Jackson*): This audience is finished.
DISRAELI (*Eric*): Rubbish. They're good for another ten minutes yet.

But if you study the team's recent work closely, you will find that the primitive, Mark I relationship has been radically changed. Nowadays Ernie is usually the idiot — writing his terrible plays, composing his vacuous doggerel, giving his atrocious impersonations of James Cagney, etc. If someone must appear in drag, it is Ernie, not Eric. The new Ernie is like a rubber beach toy, slapped, shoved and prodded by his partner. Eric, meanwhile, has moved into the power vacuum. 'Eddie Braben', he says, 'has made me tougher, less gormless, *harder* towards Ern.' He is brisk, verbose, officious; always the imposer, always (however inefficiently) in command, whether quietly dropping *verb. -sap.* hints (as when, seeing his little pal with Frank Finlay, he intrudes with elaborate unconcern to mutter into Ernie's ear: 'A drunk from the audience. On your left. *A drunk.*') or suddenly hectoring Ernie in measured cadences of fruity, high-pitched intensity. There is a remarkable passage in the Finlay show where Eric has a long speech explaining to Ern, who has dressed up as a woman to save his sister's honour from Casanova, that if he goes thus clad to the great lover's bedroom, 'it could be a touch of the Hello-folks-and-how-about-the-workers.' Faced with incomprehension from Ernie, Eric repeats the entire speech three times, syllable for syllable. Another comedian would have made it louder every time, with diminishing comic returns; Eric uses the same even, rational tones throughout, and brings down the house.

The new Eric is a quasi-managerial type, jumped-up perhaps, but inspiring confidence with his balding dome and look of beady-eyed myopia; radiating a sense of leave-it-to-me and watch-it-buster; never quite humiliated, always quick to strike back, capable of accelerating from discomfiture to triumph in 0.7 seconds; and betraying vestigial signs of insecurity only by fleeting adjustments of the spectacles or momentary saggings of the jaw. He can even bully André Previn and the London Philharmonic. What other soloist, rebuked from the podium for not playing the right notes in the Grieg Piano Concerto, would seize the conductor by the lapels, lifting him well off the ground, and snarl into his face: 'Listen, sunshine — I'm playing all the right notes, but not necessarily in the right order.' Not long ago the boys tried out a sketch in which Eric was maltreated by Ernie, who played a temperamental movie director. It didn't work: because the new Eric would have rebelled and slapped Ernie down. What has happened is more complex than a simple reversal of roles. Ernie today is the comic *who is not funny*. And Eric — the dominating character who patronises the comic — is the straight man *who is funny*. The combination is brilliant, wholly original, and irresistible. How much of it is due to Braben, and how much to the performers, is hard to determine; but we know that the scripts are heavily modified in rehearsal, and that most of the changes come from Eric.

I am not sure what will become of him. Towards the end of the last BBC series Braben was making the team stretch itself by writing longer and longer sketches: there was one about the British Empire and the North-West Frontier that went on for over thirty minutes and never flagged for a second. The three films they've made so far have been as leadenly infantile as films starring British comedians traditionally are: Eric thinks they need a script plotted by somebody else, with Braben to write in additional gags. He is utterly uninterested in what, for every British comic before him, would represent the summit of ambition: starring in his own West End show. 'It would have no appeal for me,' he says politely. Why, after all, try something that might hurt the act, could not possibly help it, and might tie them down for a long time in a town that, being 'Northern comics' (a phrase dinned into their ears from childhood), they cannot think of as home? They have decided to avoid TV next winter, for fear of being over-exposed; but they must clearly do something. Eric views the future with pragmatic apprehension. When I asked him why so many comedians voted Tory, he replied, 'Because of tax.' Money is important to him. The history of comedy, especially in the TV era, is a graveyard of suddenly eclipsed reputations. (Rowan and Martin, where are you now?) 'For Ernie and I to play one minute without a laugh is murder,' Eric told me. '*It is fear.*'

Whatever happens, there will be no more where he came from. Because they started so young, he and Ernie form a unique link between pre-war vaudeville and contemporary television. The halls are closing; the clubs cannot develop comics with Eric's range and finesse; the British cinema has never created a great comedian (except possibly Peter Sellers); and you cannot learn from films or TV the ability to control a thousand people by your physical presence. I asked Eric what he thought of American comedy today. 'There's one thing I miss,' he said. '*There are no funny men.* There are funny lines, but no funny men.' The night before I met him, I dreamed about a surrealist show in which Eric kept stalking on stage in a burnous, bellowing: 'Where are my shock troops? I knew I should never have sold that wicker table.' Even with lines like that, I would trust Eric Morecambe to convince any English-speaking audience on earth that he was an incomparably funny man.

Q. Is there not, faintly detectable beneath the mask of the clown, an undertow of pathos, a strain of that inconsolable melancholy that haunts all sublunary things?

A. No. There is not.

Observer Magazine: 9th September 1973;
The Sound Of Two Hands Clapping, 1975

NICOL WILLIAMSON

On February 24, 1969, Richard Nixon arrived in London at the end of a European tour. he dined that evening at Chequers, the Buckinghamshire mansion that is the official country home of Britain's Prime Ministers. After dinner, his host, Harold Wilson, drew him over to a sofa, where (as Nixon tells it) 'he engaged me in a very extended and animated conversation'. The other guests assumed that some international problem had grabbed the two men's attention, and wondered busily what it was. In reality, they were talking about an actor. An infrequent and normally unenthusiastic playgoer, Wilson had recently attended the first night of a new production of *Hamlet*, staged at the Roundhouse — a converted Victorian railway shed in north London — by Tony Richardson, and what he was now so urgently saying was that the President must make a point of seeing Nicol Williamson, whose performance in the title role had been highly praised by the London critics. Williamson, said Wilson grandly, was the best Hamlet of his generation, perhaps of the century. Nixon explained that he had no free evenings, and this seemed to be the end of the matter. But the name clearly stuck in his mind, because later in the year items began to appear in the American press about the President's interest in Williamson's work.

These clippings reached the desk of Abe Schneider, the chairman of Columbia Pictures, which is the company responsible for distributing the movie version of Williamson's *Hamlet*. Schneider called Raymond Bell, his man in Washington, and instructed him to find out from the White House whether the President would like to see the film. It seemed that he didn't have time. Too bad, said Bell. In that case, how would it be if Williamson came out to Washington and gave the President an hour or so of *Hamlet* in person? It was now late in January, 1970. Red Skelton had just inaugurated a series of so-called Evenings at the White House, which would subsequently include the Broadway cast of *1776* and a *tour de chant* by Peggy Lee. A fair, square sampling of popular culture — but a touch of *Hamlet* in the night could do the Nixons' intellectual status nothing but good, and the Columbia proposal was referred to the President for a decision.

At about this time, a London newspaperman telephoned Oscar Beuselinck, a stocky, outspoken London solicitor, who acts as Williamson's agent in England, and asked him to confirm or deny reports that his client was going to Washington to entertain the President. Beuselinck replied, with that bluntness of manner and delicacy of grammar which characterise him, 'Who's kidding whom?' He scented a hoax and, knowing Williamson to be of a mischievous nature, suspected that he might have started the rumours himself. A few days later, Columbia got the answer it was hoping for: Nixon wholeheartedly approved of its suggestion and would be happy to devote an Evening to Nicol Williamson, who thus became, at the age of thirty-two, the only legitimate actor ever to be invited to give a solo performance at the White House.

I first met Williamson about seven years ago — fleetingly, at theatrical parties in London. Not that he relished parties as such: he was rightly reputed to be a solitary, and lived alone in a cramped ground-floor flat in Notting Hill Gate. From time to time, there were girl friends (or so one heard), intensely cherished until some long-ticking emotional time bomb exploded, after which all would be over, but what he mainly needed was 'mates to stay up with' (as one mate put it) — companions to see him through the dark hours when extreme dismay might strike. Among people he trusted, he could be excellent party value. I think of him at John Osborne's house, one night in 1965, singing jazz standards of the twenties and thirties and accompanying himself on an eighteenth-century keyboard in a style you might describe as stride spinet. Already he was a figure of some mystery and consequence, his work admired by his fellow-actors as well as by the critics and the public, his general demeanour a boon to the show-biz columns, where epithets like 'wild man' and 'hell-raiser' were ritually dusted off in his honour. He was known to have talked back to noisy late-comers, to have walked offstage in more than one fit of self-hating rage, and even to have slugged David Merrick backstage in Philadelphia. (Oscar Beuselinck, a stickler for the proprieties, had repeatedly warned him, 'You're in the public eye, cock, and you've bloody well got to learn how to behave.') He had made his first London success in 1962, at the age of twenty-four, when he joined the Royal Shakespeare Company and appeared — within a single season — as a thieving aircraft man in Henry Livings' *Nil Carborundum*, a penniless Russian gambler in Gorky's *The Lower Depths*, and a seedy Jacobean cuckold in Middleton's *Women Beware Women*. At the Royal Court Theatre, he had gone on to play the inordinate hero of J. P. Donleavy's *The Ginger Man* and (quite indelibly) Bill Maitland, the cynical, defeated lawyer in John Osborne's *Inadmissible Evidence*.

From a few encounters in the mid-1960s I learned that he was savagely observant. He had a disconcerting ear and eye for one's weaknesses, for the tricks of gesture, accent and inflexion that expose and define one too vividly for comfort. Even today, I cannot think of Tony Richardson or John Osborne without recalling Nicol's rendering of their voices: the impersonation has usurped the original. His physical presence was immediately potent — the tall, stooping, tapering silhouette, the receding ginger hair, the worn forehead, the bemused blue eyes, and the smile that was all tired commiseration, suggesting an ex-champ making a dubious comeback rather than a young contender for the title of best actor in the world. The lower lip protruded Hapsburg-fashion, as in a Velázquez portrait of Philip IV. Now and then, there would be a winning flash of a grin, crooked and raffish, accompanied by an upward flick of the eyebrows, which he shrugs as others shrug their shoulders — a grin of wicked complicity. At the same time, his eyes would roll, making him look slightly desperate. I remember talking to him about *Inadmissible Evidence*. He said he used to sit onstage 'with the stench of death in my nostrils'. He acted best, he told me, when he was contemplating death — 'not the character's death but my own'. He added, 'You must go to the edge; you must look over the brink into the abyss.' He did not sound in the least pretentious.

He has a sly but well-organised urge to dominate whatever group he finds himself in. When listening to a substandard anecdote, I normally manage to stay poker-faced, no matter how eminent the raconteur, but if it is Nicol, my lips automatically crease into a smile. He makes you feel that not to respond, not to complete the emotional circuit, would be an act of betrayal. By seeming to be always vulnerable, he succeeds in being always one up. He is fond of quoting a phrase that was brayed at him by a young Birmingham intellectual when he was in his teens: 'Dear Nick — *yet* so hesitant, *yet* so sure!' He is at once hypersensitive and supremely self-confident, and it can be difficult to tell, from one moment to the next, which is the kernel and which the shell. A girl named Pauline Peters, who recently interviewed him for the magazine *Nova*, has shrewdly remarked, 'You feel that whatever you say you're putting the boot in.'

I tentatively reached the same conclusion some four years ago, when he came to dinner with me for the first time. He behaved like a king stag transported to an alien domain and exercising the territorial imperative as if it were a divine right. To begin with, he turned up an hour early — a masterly ploy that caught my wife and me unwashed and unchanged. Full of apologies, he volunteered to pass the time by Hoovering the living-room, on the mildly annoying tacit assumption that the carpet was dirty. Before we could dissuade him, he had dragged the machine down from an upstairs closet and was passionately mowing away. 'Who else is coming?' he asked when I returned in a clean shirt to prise the Hoover from his grasp. I told him that one of the guests was Jonathan Miller, the director, writer and former comedian. 'Biggest phony in London,' Nicol said crisply. 'Who else?' I said that, apart from the Millers, there would be a pretty girl named Yvonne Stacpoole, who had been having a lengthy affair with the celebrated Italian director Piero Ghiberti. (Both Stacpoole and Ghiberti are pseudonyms.) Nicol stored up this information for later use. No sooner had the other guests arrived than he strangled conversation almost at birth by producing an LP of the Mamas and the Papas and playing it at full volume on the stereo. It takes a lot to silence Dr. Miller, who had already launched into a vivacious chat about Byzantine art, but even he had no answer to tactics so blatantly anti-social. When we moved downstairs to the dining-room, Nicol munched for several minutes in silence before addressing his first remark to Miss Stacpoole. 'So you're the girl', he said engagingly, 'who was being fucked by Ghiberti?' He reinforced the remark by placing his left hand on his right bicep and making a swift upward jab with his clenched right fist. For the second time in the evening, everybody stopped talking. Miss Stacpoole, who had never met Nicol before, was exquisitely unfazed. 'I'm afraid you've got it wrong, Mr. Williamson,' she said simply. 'I *am* being fucked by Ghiberti.' Nicol grinned and nodded, but he was obviously affronted by her cool, and a few minutes later he got up and left the room. We soon heard a deafening five-minute blast of the Mamas and the Papas, followed by a clatter of footsteps on the stairs and a slammed front door. 'I enjoy sacred monsters,' said Jonathan Miller, 'but preferably in zoos.' That night was Nicol at his worst, trapped among intellectuals, uncertain of the rules and therefore opting out of the game. Penelope Gilliatt, one of his closest friends, said to me on another occasion, 'Nick likes jousting with people, but he jousts to win. And, of course, he's a congenital no-sayer. He regards a lot of quite considerable men as vermin.'

For some time after that aborted dinner, my only contacts with him were professional. In the winter of 1967, I did a long filmed interview with him for an American TV programme on the art of acting. Leaning against his own mantelpiece, sipping his own champagne, he was fluent and secure. Among other things, we discussed the conventional wisdom that urges young actors to play as many parts as they can in order (so the cliché goes) 'to keep the instrument in tune'. I asked him why, since his success three years earlier in *Inadmissible Evidence*, he had played only three new parts, each for a strictly limited run.

His reply was an adroitly modulated tirade: 'Every man knows his own instrument, and I know mine. I know what it is capable of, and there are certain things I want to play. But I don't want to stand up there every night and do all the parts in the book. People say "Keep the instrument tuned," but there are a lot of hairy parts that you just have no time for, that it would bore the anus off you to play. So what — so you can do it, so you're the most technically accomplished actor in the world — but why? It's like that camera filming us. If you keep that machine running and running and running and running, it is going to have to be serviced, it is going to break down. Now, I've talked to actors who have played the same parts I have, and when I tell them I'm tired or I'm shattered or I'll go nuts if I do this any longer, they say, "Oh, but I played it for *x* number of performances and I didn't find it tiring at all." The simple answer to that is "No, because you don't work the way I do." Because I am playing it totally and absolutely, which means that I sink everything in it to make it the most marvellous, compelling, total thing you can see. And nobody will do that better than I will. They will do it differently, but they won't do it better. Now, you can't go on working like that all the time. I am going to die quite young anyway and move into the ashes department, but before I do I am going to *choose* what I do, and it's going to be the most exciting departments of drama and comedy that I can think of, and you can't do that indefinitely or you are going to thrash yourself into the grave, and for what? For "I did six hundred and thirty-two performances of *The Bells*"? *But how well did you do them, Henry Irving?* Or "I played *Othello* three hundred times"? *But how do we know, Edmund Kean, that you were really all that good?* If you are going to be the best at your job — if you feel that, which I do feel — then you have got to take it easy. Most audiences don't want to go under the skin, they don't want to get into the heart and bones of things, because it frightens them and they don't like it. But they have *got* to be frightened. They may not like what I do, but they won't fault me on it — at least, not much. I am going to do certain pieces of work in certain areas that actually mean my life, that are going to keep me alive by their value and excitement. And that is all. There is nothing else in my life. I've lost about three women that I was deeply in love with because I didn't pay enough attention to them. Look at all this, for Jesus' sake.' He indicated the little room. 'Not that it's all that much, but it *is* comfortable and it *is* happy, and we can smash out the odd bottle of Bollinger and it's lovely. *But . . . But* my whole life is circled and centred round the next piece of work, and I've got to take time over it because it's going to have you on the edge of your seat, and I want you to like it and be destroyed by it.'

I asked him what he would like to have engraved on his tombstone. He gave me the slanting grin and said,' "Life isn't all you want, but it's all you've got, so stick a geranium in your hat and be happy." '

In January, 1970, I took him to lunch at his favourite London restaurant — the Etoile, in Soho — to find out whether he would like to work with Laurence Olivier's National Theatre Company, where I was employed as literary adviser and general ideas man. I wasn't particularly sanguine: a notorious non-joiner, he had turned down many such invitations since quitting the Royal Shakespeare in 1962. All the same, the offer that Olivier had authorised me to make him was certainly better — as the Australians quaintly say — than a poke in the eye with a burnt stick. For his first season with the troupe, he could pick any three of the following roles: Rogozhin in an adaptation of Dostoevsky's *The Idiot*, Judge Brack in *Hedda Gabler* (directed by Ingmar Bergman), Danton in *Danton's Death*, Hildy Johnson in *The Front Page*, the elder son in *Long Day's Journey Into Night*, and the title part in *Macbeth*. If he chose the O'Neill, I added, I could promise him Olivier as his father and Mike Nichols to direct. Royal flushes like that are rarely dealt to young actors. Nicol gave me a sympathetic hearing, generously praised the bouquet of the La Tache '61 that we were drinking, and took just twenty hours to consider and reject the whole glittering package.

Nicol regards it as a weakness to answer the telephone. Moreover, when he is using it to call others, he never identifies himself; you have to guess who it is, and if you hesitate your uncertainty instantly puts him one up. On February 11th, 1970 his phone rang all morning, but he was in a non-answering mood, to the high annoyance of Oscar Beuselinck, who was fuming at the other end of the line. 'I might have been offering him a million dollars, but he still wouldn't have given a damn,' Beuselinck said later. 'If that client of mine doesn't take care, he's going to end up in the gutter. You can cry wolf just so often, and then the offers stop coming. He isn't really an actor at all. He's a bloody busker.' (Buskers are kerbside entertainers who perform for theatre queues, passing the hat round afterwards; when Nicol heard of Beuselinck's remark, he said that, if anything, he felt flattered.) He went out to lunch and came back to find a message from his charwoman: 'Ring Oscar B. He sounds very excited.' He dialled the number and learned that Columbia had confirmed the rumour: Nixon wanted him to give a Shakespeare recital at the White House on Thursday, March 19th, just over five weeks away. Columbia would pay all expenses. Almost for the first time in his professional life, Nicol said yes without hesitation.

I heard about the project (and formed the idea of joining him on it) a few days later, when he called me up to discuss it. Already it was clear that his plans for the Evening were rather more ambitious than anyone in Washington imagined. 'I don't want to just read bits of Shakespeare, or even just read bits of other books, or even just read,' he said. 'I want to give them something breathtaking, something not many people can do.' He told me he had decided to sing as well as act. Knowing his taste in music, which was nurtured at Jimmy Ryan's under the tutelage of people like J. C. Higginbotham and the De Paris brothers, I wasn't surprised to hear that his accompanists would be a nine-man group called the World's Greatest Jazz Band, led by Yank Lawson and Bob Haggart, and dedicated to basic Dixieland. (The seven other members of the ensemble included such survivors from the pre-microgroove era as Billy Butterfield, Lou McGarity, Kai Winding and Bud Freeman.) I asked him whether, as a presumed liberal, he had any qualms about serving as court jester to Nixon. 'I wouldn't act in South Africa,' he replied after a pause, 'but otherwise anything goes.' This was the first entrance of a theme that was to be heard with several variations during the next few weeks.

While the Evening took shape in odd corners of his mind, he busied himself professionally by recording an LP for Columbia Records. (Entitled simply 'Nicol Williamson', it was released in the summer of 1971.) I turned up at the studio to watch the first session. It was 8 p.m., but work had only just begun: Nicol is a night creature. A large orchestra, twenty strings strong, was playing a ballad; the star murmured soulfully into a mike, his forehead a map of undulating furrows, his face resembling one of those sad but resilient saints you see carved on the portals of Romanesque churches. He was wearing a blue shirt with a silk scarf knotted inside it, and looked hairier (except on the thinning scalp) than I remembered him. Near-Dundrearies now flourished on his jowls, and the moustache drooped down to the chin in a thin reddish line. When he smiled, he put me in mind of Randle Patrick McMurphy, the obstreperous hero of Ken Kesey's *One Flew Over the Cuckoo's Nest*: 'This guy is red-headed with long red sideburns and a tangle of curls out from under his cap . . . broad across the jaw and shoulders and chest, a broad white devilish grin, and he's hard . . . kind of the way a baseball is hard under the scuffed leather.'

As the song built to a climax, he let rip with an amazingly rich and pungent tenor voice. It was obvious from his timing and breath control that he had not studied Sinatra for nothing. 'They can say what they like,' said a young sound-mixer in the control room, 'he's the best pop singer who ever played Hamlet.' The number ended, and Nicol came in to hear the playback. When it was over, he said, 'I'm a quarter-tone flat in the middle section, and I bet nobody noticed it.' Nobody had.

'Were you nervous at all?' asked the producer.

'What you think is nervousness is in fact my tremolo,' Nicol said. 'That's not what's wrong. Let's do another take.'

'Can you bear to?'

'Six times a week and twice on Sundays. But first, where's the thunderbox?'

While he was gone (thunderbox is archaic military slang for toilet), an engineer said incredulously, 'Is he really making his first LP.?'

I gathered that from the beginning of the session Nicol had been commanding retakes, suggesting changes in instrumental entries, and generally running the show. He loves to be a pro among pros: to talk football to footballers, music to musicians; to be accepted by the inner circles of professions other than his own. When he got back, he had somehow acquired three bottles of champagne (Taittinger Blanc de Blancs), which he distributed in teacups to the crew. Someone asked him about the film of *Inadmissible Evidence*, which was the first he had ever made. 'I didn't see it,' Nicol said. 'But when it was finished I said to the cameraman, "Am I any good? Am I as good as Spencer Tracy at his best?" Because those are the boys who really know. And he said I was. So that was enough for me.'

'Shall we go on, Nick?' said the producer tentatively.

Nicol clapped him on the shoulder. 'You know us actors,' he said. 'A glass of champagne, a pat on the arse, and we'll eat fucking grass.'

In all, the session lasted three hours and yielded one fine track — a version of Jim Webb's 'Didn't We, Girl?' — of which I later obtained a test pressing. Guests at my house have confidently identified the performer as (among others) Perry Como, Dean Martin and Andy Williams. The trouble with Nicol's singing voice may well be that it makes you think of everyone but Nicol.

On February 24th, he phoned me to say that word of his Washington gig had appeared in the *New York Times*, in an article about Mrs. Connie Stuart, director of Mrs. Nixon's staff, and 'producer-in-residence' (the *Times* said) of all White House entertainment. Mrs. Stuart was described as 'a tall, peppy redhead' who liked moose-hunting and had taken a degree in speech and drama at the University of Maryland. 'When you come to the White House, it's a real cultural experience,' she said, adding that future Evenings would 'run the whole gamut'. (To illustrate where that might lead, she revealed that the President 'would like to have good college choruses from the Midwest'.) Nicol, she announced, would be doing scenes from Shakespeare. Either the *Times* man wasn't listening very closely or Mrs. Stuart's speech was slurred (unlikely, in view of that Maryland degree), because the piece went on to say that Nicol's name had been proposed by 'Earl Wilson, the night-club columnist'. 'So it's all fixed now,' Nicol said to me gloomily. 'That's when you start to panic.'

Another recording session took place on March 6th, with more Taittinger out of teacups. This time, there were no violins; the supporting group was a Chicago-style septet, bursting with middle-aged pep, and featuring the veteran Max Kaminsky, who had been flown in from New York at Nicol's request to play lead trumpet. The star rehearsed and recorded 'I Ain't Gonna Give Nobody None of My Jelly Roll', then paused to pass out champagne to a bunch of theatre people who had dropped in to listen. 'You look a bit wild tonight, Dad,' said a dapper little actor, accepting a cup. 'You've been pulling at your hair again.' Nicol was absorbed in argument about the liquor intake of a celebrated jazzman: 'I tell you, before every set he used to sink *two half-pint tumblers* of neat Courvoisier.'

Finishing his drink, he went off to run through 'I Wish I Could Shimmy like My Sister Kate', and I chatted with John McGrath, a handsome Scots playwright in his thirties, who had written two of the films — *The Bofors Gun* and *The Reckoning* — in which Nicol had starred. McGrath's version of *The Seagull*, modernised and set in the Scottish Highlands, had been directed by Anthony Page for the Dundee repertory company in 1960; Nicol had played Duncan, which was how McGrath renamed Chekhov's suicidal hero, Constantin. 'After the performance one night, Nick and I were drinking in a pub with some of the cast,' McGrath told me. 'Suddenly he said that, like Constantin, he was going to kill himself. He leaped up and ran out of the bar towards the Tay estuary. On the way, he stopped to take off his shoes and socks, which seemed a rather eccentric touch. Maybe he was just giving us a chance to catch up with him. Anyway, he actually did jump into the river, and we actually had to pull him out. Nick has some great spiritual discomfort. I mean, you can't go *on* chucking yourself off things.' On at least two other occasions, it seemed, Nicol had convinced McGrath that he was about to die. 'Once, in the pub next door to the Royal Court Theatre, he said he'd had an electro-cardiogram and his heart was going to pack up at any moment. I think he really believed it by the time he'd finished telling me. I certainly did. Another time, he conned me into driving him to Harley Street by saying he'd had some tests and the doctor was going to tell him that afternoon whether or not he had terminal cancer. Of course, there were no tests and no doctor. But he gave a great performance.'

We talked about Nicol's acting. 'In Dundee, he wasn't a star,' McGrath said. 'He was an actor the way other people are coal miners. Nowadays he's become something you might call the Actor as Existential Hero. You know the story of how he walked offstage halfway through *Hamlet*, saying he didn't feel good enough to act that night? That was a kind of Existential bravado. He had to show that you could do it and survive. Really he deserves a four-hundred-page preface by Sartre. As a matter of fact, there's a bit about acting in Camus's *Myth of Sisyphus* that comes pretty close to Nick.' (Consulting the Camus book later, I found the following passage, in which the author explains why the Catholic Church used to condemn actors: 'She repudiated in that art the heretical multiplication of souls, the emotional debauch, the scandalous presumption of a mind that objects to living but one life and hurls itself into all forms of excess.')

McGrath's first stage play, *Events While Guarding the Bofors Gun*, was filmed in 1968, with Nicol as the central character, a self-destructive psychopath: both play and part were written 'for and in some minute measure about Nick', McGrath told me. 'What I like about him as an actor is his ambiguity,' McGrath said. 'He's capable of thinking — and expressing — two different things at the same time. And what I like about him as a person is that he has no ultimate goal, no overriding ambition. You remember he appeared with Wilfrid Lawson in *The Lower Depths*?' Lawson, who died in 1966, at the age of sixty-six, was a performer of wayward genius — sometimes galvanic, never predictable, given to bouts of alcoholism, and venerated by many of his juniors in the profession. 'Nick reminds me of Lawson. He gives off the same sense of danger, and he doesn't give a damn. More than anything, I'd like to see him play Macbeth.' It seemed to me, I told McGrath, that Nicol the actor was dazzling in wild attacking vein ('Who the hell do they think they are?') and in moods of abject vulnerability ('They'll louse me up the way they always do'), but that he was sometimes less persuasive in more temperate emotional zones, such as tenderness and charity. 'Ah,' McGrath said, 'he can do *them* to music. Next to Macbeth, I'd like to see him in a musical.' As if to prove his point, Nicol's voice floated gently over the mike:

> Leave them laughing when you go —
> And if you care, don't let them know.

I should have recalled that Nicol had in fact appeared in a musical, though only for one night. He played the title role in T. S. Eliot's *Sweeney Agonistes*, set to music by John Dankworth and performed in London as part of a tribute to the poet shortly after his death. He had been hair-raisingly good, especially in a song beginning with Eliot's lines:

> I knew a man once did a girl in
> Any man might do a girl in
> Any man has to, needs to, wants to
> Once in a lifetime, do a girl in.

McGrath's most recent collaboration with Nicol had been on the film called *The Reckoning*. The role, again written with Nicol in mind, was that of a ruthless, thuggish company director from the slums of Liverpool. 'Nick's commitment to the character was total. He identified with it so much that he nearly overbalanced the picture. The thing about Nick is that he really likes the jungle. That's where he lives.'

On March 8th, the Variety Club of Great Britain held its annual luncheon, at which Nicol was presented with its award as the best film actor of 1969 for his performances in *Inadmissible Evidence*, *The Bofors Gun* and *The Reckoning*. He made a one-sentence speech of thanks and sat down. 'I didn't even feel patronizing,' he told me. 'I just felt nausea and self-disgust. But at least I resisted the temptation to just say "Bollocks".'

Despite the acclaim his film appearances have received, I haven't always found them convincing. In *The Bofors Gun*, directed by Jack Gold, he played a baleful Irish private, serving with the British Army in postwar Germany, who spends a long and increasingly drunken night on guard duty trying to provoke a saintly young bombardier (David Warner) into having him arrested. The bombardier is a decent liberal who believes in trusting people. Expecting the best of mankind, he meets the worst in Nicol, a symbolic Lucifer to his Christ. The rest of the cast assembles in true theatrical style, a cross-section of British society fully aware that it is taking part in a play and that a moral crisis must therefore be precipitated and duly resolved. The satanic Irishman is so bombastically overwritten, his madness and death wish are so heavily signalled ('I should not be at large,' 'I hate all goodness,' 'I am not long for this world'), that the part can hardly be played without being overplayed. Nicol did his best, and it was far more than enough.

Laughter in the Dark (1969), one of the numerous cinematic progeny of *The Blue Angel*, was directed by Tony Richardson and concerned a rich middle-aged art connoisseur who falls for a sexy little usherette (Anna Karina) and is destroyed by her. After losing his sight in a car crash, he retires to a Mediterranean villa, into which the girl smuggles her new boyfriend; together they mock the blind man by making love almost under his nose. Nicol seemed ill at ease playing a member of the ruling class, and in several early scenes he looked like a sheepish butler in his own house. The authority that should have gone with the character's wealth and rank just wasn't there: he was too easily flustered, too perceptibly dismayed, so that one began to suspect that Nicol's face might be too expressive for the movies. Moreover, he lacked the effortless confidence we associate with the thirties superstars (where did they get it, with the Depression at home and Hitler prowling abroad?), and it was only in his blindness that he showed his real class. Defenceless and humiliated, he came into his own: it isn't easy to forget the scene in which he weeps, his fingers fumbling for a cigarette, as Karina describes the view of mountains and ocean that he cannot see.

The film that Tony Richardson made of Nicol's *Hamlet* was shot in the Roundhouse, where the production had been staged, but it was mostly big heads spotlit in the dark and seemed to be taking place in a sunless nowhere. Nicol was a sedulously anti-romantic prince, a Hamlet out of Grünewald or Dürer, superlative in moments of rancour, contempt and needling resentment, worrying the lines like a terrier worrying a bone. But he made some curious verbal slips, one of which killed outright the only surefire laugh in the play. This occurs when Polonius takes his leave and Hamlet comments, 'You cannot, sir, take from me any thing that I will more willingly part withal.' Nicol said, ' . . . I would *not* more willingly part withal,' which is meaningless. The performance, for all its power in negation and its genuine pain, seemed unwilling or unable to convey any objective passion, by which I mean a passion for such things as ideas, ideals and causes. Something in the actor's temperament appeared to inhibit — even to exclude — strong feelings about anything outside himself. Quite often this was Hamlet at Hamlet's own lowest valuation ('a dull and muddy-mettled rascal . . . a-cursing like a very drab, a scullion'); he could never have been as Ophelia describes him — 'the courtier's, soldier's, scholar's eye, tongue, sword'. It is relevant to note that Roman Polanski at one time considered inviting Nicol to play the lead in his movie of *Macbeth* but finally decided against it. When I asked him why, he said, 'Nicol Williamson should not play geniuses or kings or princes. He should play ordinary men who are extraordinary.'

Sometimes, as *Variety* might put it, crix nix Nick's pix. 'I could go on for ever about how people have put the knife into me,' he once told me. 'It doesn't matter. Pull it out, turn round, move on.' While it's in, however, it hurts. Some of the worst perforations were inflicted in January, 1970, by Pauline Kael, who wrote in the *New Yorker*:

> Nicol Williamson is a violently self-conscious actor whose effect on the camera is like that of the singers who used to shatter crystal . . . He goes from being gracelessly virile to being repulsively masochistic, and, whichever it is, he's too much . . . Williamson is always 'brilliant' and 'dazzling'. He *is* brilliant, he *is* dazzling — yet he's awful . . . probably the worst major (and greatly gifted) actor on the English-speaking screen today.

'That review', Nicol said to me, 'was like POW!' He has buddies among the critics, but only after they have gone on record in his favour; he would never try to charm a good notice out of a stranger. Alan Brien, in the *Sunday Times*, called him 'this most versatile of our young actors', and said that his West End début in *Inadmissible Evidence* had 'probably not been matched since the first appearance of the youthful Charles Laughton'. Having listed a few of his physical characteristics — 'eyes like poached eggs, hair like treacle toffee, a truculent lower lip like a pink front step protruding from the long, pale doorway of his face' (Nicol breeds similes in critics like a god kissing carrion) — Brien summed him up thus:

> However small the part or the theatre, however short the run or sparse the house, he plays for honesty and truth, callously unsympathetic towards the prejudices and sentimentalities of his audience.

Although Brien is *persona grata* to Nicol, his favourite critic is unquestionably Ted Kalem, of *Time*. When the stage production of *Hamlet* reached New York, Kalem jumped in off the deep end:

> His Hamlet is a seismograph of a soul in shock. Here is a Hamlet of spleen and sorrow, of fire and ice, of bantering sensuality, withering sarcasm, and soaring intelligence. He cuts through the music of the Shakespearian line to the marrow of its meaning . . . Take him, all in all, for a great, mad, doomed, spine-shivering Hamlet, and anyone who fails to see Nicol Williamson during this limited engagement will not look upon his like again.

Later, drawing on his most incantatory prose, Kalem installed Nicol in his private pantheon of living great ones:

> Some actors occupy the stage; a few rule it. Some actors hold an audience; a few possess it. Some actors light up a scene; a few ignite the

play. These combustible few blaze with the x factors of acting — intensity, intelligence, and authority. There is a royalty apart from role, and when an Olivier, Gielgud, Nicol Williamson, or Irene Papas treads the stage, their fellow actors are as rapt as the audience.

If Kalem is Nicol's trusty pilot fish, there is no doubt about the identity of the Creature from the Black Lagoon. This role belongs, by right of devastation, to Walter Kerr. The *Time* eulogy of *Hamlet*, published on May 16th, 1969 was by way of being a counterblast to a scorching piece by Kerr that had appeared a few days earlier in the Sunday drama section of the *New York Times*. Kerr's general point was that Nicol played *Hamlet* in exactly the same manner that he had played *Inadmissible Evidence*. He granted the actor's intelligence. What he missed was, first of all, 'physical tension':

Mr. Williamson's arms hang idly from shoulders already idle. His is a pale, flattened face, with kinky uncut hair billowing out so far behind him that it becomes his head, robbing his features of dimension. It is also a face that seems to have severed association with the listless members that might have been expected to carry it anywhere . . . His coming or going makes no emotional difference.

No ignition here, no shivered spine. Kerr's second, and major objection was to 'the particular noise Mr. Williamson makes':

The voice is a quick twang, the sort of sound a man might make if he spoke rapidly while carefully pinching the bridge of his nose . . . The performance, as a whole, seems one given by a museum guide who obviously knows what he is talking about but is severely crippled by a blocked sinus.

The notice was headed 'Oliver Twist as Hamlet', and Nicol deeply resented it. 'He reviewed my voice, not my interpretation,' he said. 'Jesus Christ, I was trying to make an *interesting* noise, not a beautiful one. The trouble with people like Kerr is that they can't forgive me for making Hamlet someone who is *insufferably alive*.'

The name of Kerr recurred to haunt the next development in the White House project. On March 11th, Nicol and I were to fly from London to New York, where he planned to rehearse for a week before the big night. At two o'clock that morning, I was awakened by the phone. 'It's all off,' said Nicol, sounding insufferably alive. 'The whole thing is off. Forget it.' His New York agent, an expatriate Englishman named Lionel Larner, had just received a copy of the guest list for his Evening, and had called to tell Nicol that they had invited Walter Kerr. The star was in a state of near-paranoid fury: 'Why should I spend all this time and energy just to go and be savaged? It's diabolically immoral. I've told Lionel that either they cancel Kerr's invitation or they can forget the whole thing.' He hung up. Hoping to persuade Kerr to have a diplomatic illness, I called the *Times*, and learned that he was attending an opening at the Ethel Barrymore Theatre. By 3 a.m., I was through to the box office, leaving a message for Kerr to call me collect during the intermission. Soon Nicol was on the line again, with a short bulletin: 'Lionel has talked to the White House people. They said they couldn't withdraw an invitation. So the hell with them.' Around 4 a.m., a bewildered Walter Kerr spoke to me from the theatre lobby; he said he couldn't get to Washington anyway, because of a prior engagement, and had just mailed a letter expressing his regrets. I dialled Nicol's number, only to find out from the operator that, with characteristic elusiveness, he had changed it the day before (for the third time in a month), and that, in any case, it was ex-directory. I then went back to bed for roughly thirty minutes, after which the phone rang again. 'Listen to this,' said Nicol, chuckling richly. 'The White House has just called Lionel back. They finally got mad and said to him, "Who's running this show — Mr. Williamson or Mr. Nixon?" And Lionel said very coolly, "Mr. Williamson is running the *show*. The President is running the *country*." ' I told him the news from the Ethel Barrymore, which appeared to mollify him: the trip was on again. In its uneasy blend of confusion, hysteria and exhaustion, this nocturnal episode encapsulated much that was to come.

Later that morning, on the plane to New York, Nicol orders champagne and tells me the story of his life. He was born on September 14th, 1938, in Hamilton, Scotland, a mining town eleven miles from Glasgow. His parents were poor. 'When they got married, they came out of the registry office with half a crown in their pockets. That was in the morning. Dad went back to work in the afternoon.' When he was eighteen months old, the family moved to Birmingham, where his father worked as a labourer in a foundry. 'I had the usual boring suburban childhood. I kept saying to myself, "I've got to get out of here or I'll *die*." I read a lot at first. By the time I was five, I knew all about the Macedonian phalanx and things like that. But when I was twelve or thirteen I stopped reading — or, at least, I stopped amassing useless knowledge.' Nicol's father (whom John McGrath had described to me as 'an imposing man, strong and gentle, very Scottish') looms up in his conversation as a powerfully reassuring figure. 'He came to London to see me in *Inadmissible* and afterwards I introduced him to George Devine, the director of the Royal Court. George said to him, "Your son's doing very well, isn't he?" 'Yes," he said, without a flicker. "That's what he's there for." ' In 1957, Williamson senior returned to Scotland; now in his late fifties, he owns a small factory that makes aluminium ingots. 'Typically, he hates the unions, but he pays his workers more than union rates.'

From 1947 to 1953, Nicol went to the Central Grammar School in Birmingham, where a man named Tom Reader taught him English and prophesied success for him as a classical actor. 'I still see Tom. One rainy day in 1963, when I was feeling miserable because of a bird, I got on a train and went to see him at his home in Staffordshire. We went out to a pub, but he insisted on buying the drinks, which meant beer when I was dying for vodka. I asked his advice about getting married, and he was all against it. "He that hath wife and children", he said, "hath given hostages to fortune." Peter Hall had just offered me a long-term contract with the Royal Shakespeare and Tom said I should accept. He told me I should learn to "use the system". I said that wasn't possible for me — I wasn't patient enough. I went home and turned Peter Hall down.'

In 1953, he enrolled in the Birmingham School of Speech Training and Dramatic Art. He was there for three years, during the last of which he was lent to the celebrated Birmingham Repertory Theatre to play unpaid walk-ons. (One of the paid members of the company was the young Albert Finney, then half-way through his first season as a professional.) Under the false impression that Easter Monday was a holiday for actors, Nicol missed a performance and was fired. The management gave him the option of playing one more night if he would make a public apology to the cast, but he preferred to leave on the spot. 'I told myself, "I'm after that mountain. This little hill is nothing to trip over." ' After drama school, he spent two years at Aldershot, doing compulsory military service as a gunner in an air-borne division. He made fourteen parachute jumps, but he never gained promotion. He discovered, however, that he could impose himself on people and become their leader by force of temperament. 'Somebody told me I was very good at what he called "personality blackmail".' The phrase means: Play ball with me or I shall exude such a dislike of you that you will feel simply dreadful. Out of the army, he went to Scotland and worked for a while with his father. Growing restless, he wrote to the management of Dundee Repertory Theatre, which hired him to play a pirate in *Sinbad the Sailor*. Three months of unemployment followed, and, in desperation, he was about to audition for a job as a crooner when a telegram arrived inviting him to return to Dundee. 'There were actors there,' he says, 'who were definitely U.F.P.' (under false pretences), and it wasn't difficult for him to distinguish himself. During the next seventeen months, he appeared in thirty-three productions, most of them staged by Anthony Page, the company's resident director. Word of Page's discovery filtered south, and in 1961 Nicol made his London début at the Royal Court Theatre in *That's Us*, a colourless piece of social realism by Henry Chapman. It was at the Court that he met (and soon afterward worked with) Tony Richardson, who was then George Devine's second-in-command.

Nicol demands and obtains extra caviare to augment our BOAC lunch.

He then launches into a dissertation on loyalty, declaring that although he has been scrupulously loyal to Richardson and Page, they have both betrayed him in their time. 'When Tony Page wanted to cast me in *Inadmissible* in 1964, Tony Richardson sent him a cable saying "Nicol Williamson very bad idea stop nothing more than good rep actor."' Page none the less stuck to his guns. When the play reached America after its London run, David Merrick wanted to fire Page during the Philadelphia try-out. Nicol defended his director, and a noisy argument broke out backstage. 'As a rule, I detest people who get into fights. They are *thunderously* boring, and that kind of behaviour is *fantastically undesirable*. But Merrick had to be insulted, and insults must be delivered with style. I was holding a glass of Budweiser. Suddenly, I remember how José Ferrer had thrown champagne over Fred MacMurray at the end of *The Caine Mutiny*. He didn't chuck it at him, he flicked it forward like this.' Gesture as of a man throwing a dart. 'So I said, "I won't stoop to spit in your eye," and let him have it with the beer. Then he sort of rushed at me, and I stuck out my fist and he was on the floor. The funny thing was that nobody in his entourage tried to attack *me* or help *him*.' Page stayed. It was shortly after the Broadway opening that his alleged act of treachery occurred. Merrick had asked Nicol to take a salary cut until the weekly gross improved. 'I refused. So he talked to Tony Page, and Tony Page came to see me and absolutely *begged* me to accept the cut. It was pathetic. I haven't forgiven him for that and I never will.' His relationship with Tony Richardson declined to a nadir of comparable bitterness. Just before the *Hamlet* production was due to go to America, Richardson returned from a Riviera holiday to see the last London performance. Not liking what he saw, he called a company meeting at which he singled out Nicol for particular blame. Describing the incident, Nicol leans towards me and speaks with venomous distaste: 'I said to him, "I'm not going to *ask* you not to talk to me like that again. *You. Will. Never. Talk. To. Me. Like. That. Again.*"'

Signalling for more BOAC champagne, he says, 'I'm not what they call a good company man.' Togetherness in any form has invariably been a hazard for him; it is a room that he enters warily and, more often than not, wrecks before quitting. Outraged by the faithlessness of women, he has been known to stub cigarettes out on the palm of his hand. 'He wounds and is wounded easily,' one of his female mates had told me, 'and he's always very courteous to other walking wounded. He gives them bottles of Dom Pérignon.' During the Broadway run of *Inadmissible Evidence*, he fell in love with a young actress who was appearing in the show; when it closed, she got a TV job in Hollywood. He followed her there, and she deserted him for a stunt man. 'I almost destroyed myself. I got extremely drunk and drove a car at top speed down a hill full of hairpin bends.' He crashed off the road into someone's patio; the accident cost him a week in hospital. On his next trip to Hollywood, he dined at Chasen's restaurant with Lionel

Larner and Jenny Beuselinck, a pretty, dark-haired young woman who is the wife of his London agent. The bill, which included a selection of his favourite wines ('*great* Moselles, Burgundies like La Tache and Grands Echezeaux, and the very *best* champagne'), came to more than three hundred dollars. After dinner, Nicol, who was driving, insisted on re-enacting the zigzag jaunt he had so narrowly survived a few years earlier. With his two agonised passengers clutching each other and sobbing with fright in the back seat, he carried out his threat, and finally swung safely into the driveway of the Beverly Hills Hotel. Mrs. Beuselinck retired, trembling, to bed; Nicol and Larner unwound by consuming more champagne, to the value of two hundred dollars. 'I have the Jonah hangup,' Nicol says serenely. 'I seem to bring bad luck on myself and my friends.' (On July 17th, 1971, he married Jill Townsend, the actress whose defection had provoked that first hell-bent excursion.)

We land at Kennedy Airport, with slight loss of focus on my part. The alcoholic pace is beginning to tell, so I resolve to rely on a journal, rather than my memory, for a record (or fever chart) of the next eight days, which are now all that stand between us and Nixon.

Wednesday, March 11th. Our flight is met by Lionel Larner, brisk, dapper, soft-voiced, dark-haired, fur-collared, somewhere in his thirties. Manner: expatriate showbiz British, or camp on the verge of being struck. Has some trouble with his R's. In addition to Nicol, he represents the music-hall singer Tessie O'Shea. He has organised a limo to take us to New York. On the way, Nicol shows us the official White House invitation, an ornately printed card announcing the appearance of 'Nichol Williamson in Five Hundred Years of Entertainment in Poetry, Drama and Song.' Sounds like a longish evening. Nicol finds the misspelling inoffensive but ominous.

Installed in the Cecil Beaton Suite at the St. Regis, he rings for cocktails and outlines what he intends to give the Pres. From *Hamlet*: the speech to the players, the 'O what a rogue and peasant slave' soliloquy, and possibly 'To be or not to be'. Elsewhere in Shakespeare: Macbeth seeing the dagger, Malvolio finding the letter, Hotspur confronting Henry IV, and mainstream-jazz settings of 'Sigh No More', 'Blow, Blow, Thou Winter Wind', and 'When Icicles Hang by the Wall'. From the modern repertoire: Willy Loman's protest against the callousness of superannuation ('A man is not a piece of fruit'), from *Death of a Salesman*; Bill Maitland's attack on the uncaring coolness of the young, from *Inadmissible Evidence*; an extract from Eliot's 'Little Gidding'; an erotic poem by e.e. cummings, and the final pages of Samuel Beckett's novel *How It Is*. In addition, Nicol will sing 'Baby, Won't You Please Come Home?', 'Darktown Strutters' Ball', and a song by John Dankworth about Macbeth, called 'Dunsinane Blues'. To give the star pause for breath, the World's Greatest Jazz Band will play 'South Rampart Street Parade' and Kid Ory's 'Savoy Blues'.

We are silenced. The proposed range is enormous, even for Nicol. My mind races, wondering what the Nixons will make of the Beckett, which I recall as a prolonged nihilistic shriek of despair. Lionel coughs, and says the White House isn't expecting more than a 45-minute act. Penelope Gilliatt, who has shown up to greet her old pal, is worried by the anti-youth content of the *Inadmissible Evidence* bit; she feels that Nicol must avoid giving aid and comfort to Presidential prejudices. She therefore makes a few discreet cuts to soften the tone of conservative crustiness already audible in John Osborne as early as 1964, and much amplified since. I suggest adding a comic set piece — Robert Benchley's 'The Treasurer's Report' — and Nicol agrees. Muttering in a corner, Lionel and I debate the major problems. First, can Nicol prepare and learn all this material in a week? Second, even if he can, will he, with no director to keep him on schedule? The White House engagement is important for Lionel. After ten years with one of the big agencies, he struck out on his own only eighteen months ago, and Nicol is his most prominent client.

Evening: With Nicol to the Grill in the basement of the Roosevelt Hotel, where his backing group, the World's Greatest Jazz Band, is appearing. Champagne in bulk. The nine veterans on the stand (led by Yank Lawson on trumpet and Bob Haggart on bass) are tearing into 'Up, Up and Away' as if it were a Dixieland standard (though Kai Winding's trombone strikes a more modern note — early 1950s, say). You would think they were a board of jolly school trustees living out a childhood fantasy. They resemble those volatile silver-haired gentlemen who in old Hollywood musicals used to waggle their index fingers and start trucking on down when taught to jitterbug by Gloria de Haven or Madcap Michael Rooney. At the end of the set, members of the band swarm up to embrace Nicol: Bud Freeman (tenor), mistakable for a bank president or prosperous dentist; Yank Lawson, beefy and beaming; and the more studious-looking Bob Haggart, perhaps an early James Stewart part. They are as flattered by Nicol's respect as he is by theirs. He has known them for years; jazz clubs offer the only kind of nightlife he enjoys. During the next set, he joins them on the stand to sing 'Baby, Won't You Please come Home?' He grows exuberant in their company — this shambling cultural missionary, with his long pink face hanging out.

In the taxi home, he is reminded that this trip is an expedition into anxious territory. Three midtown offices have been bombed today.

THE CABDRIVER: Know what they should do with any guy that plants a bomb? The '*lec*tric chair. Rapists and muggers? The '*lec*tric chair. Guys who kill cops? The '*lec*tric chair. Guys who beat up prison guards? The '*lec*tric chair. They killed six cabdrivers in the last three months. Show no mercy.They'll take your life, you take theirs.

NICOL: How fantastically undesirable.

I propose — and Nicol accepts the idea — that it would help to relate his programme to local reality if he were to add a few admonitory lines from Yeats' 'The Second Coming', beginning with 'Things fall apart. The centre cannot hold.'

I am staying at the Algonquin, and he drops me there at about 1 a.m. There is a wakeful light in his eyes.

Thursday, March 12th. By early-morning limo to LaGuardia with Nicol and Lionel: we are going to Washington to examine the White House — to check technical facilities, and, in general, to decide whether it rates as what the trade would call a class room. The star, swathed in overcoat and muffler, slumps in his seat, racked by bronchial paroxysms. He was out (whispers Lionel, rolling his eyes upward) until 4 a.m., no one knows where.

LIONEL: If they don't like the look of us in Washington, they may cancel the whole thing. We have nothing in writing.

At the airport, the star sips a beer, obviously (in Dashiell Hammett's precise but repulsive phrase) to cut the phlegm. En route for the boarding gate, he treads with extreme wariness. Noticing that I have noticed this, he explains carefully, 'I walk on my heels, leaning backwards and slightly to the right. If I tilt two inches too far' — he indicates the concrete floor — 'it's a cracked skull.'

Mrs. Penny Adams, spruce and wholesomely pretty in her mid-twenties, who is a member of Mrs. Nixon's eight-woman staff, meets the plane, and we drive to the White House. Here Mrs. Adams introduces us to Mrs. Connie Stuart, thirty-one, the First Lady's staff director and press secretary, also wholesomely pretty, and very gay with it. Over her desk there is a framed motto at which Nicol raises a startled, Alastair Sim eyebrow. It reads 'WHATEVER TURNS YOU ON'. Penny says that Connie is a magnificent actress, or was at college. The star responds by telling a long, obscure and totally irrelevant story about a misdemeanour he committed in the army, involving the burning of some boxes containing kippers. Smiling a little dutifully, Connie suggests that we take a quick tour round the building.

LIONEL *(chirpily, as Connie shows us the State Banqueting Chamber)*: It may not be much to look at, but it's home.

Faced with a portrait of Jefferson, Lionel observes that it doesn't look a bit like Howard da Silva. With something of a flourish, Connie escorts us into the East Room, long and rectangular, with windows at either end, where the Evening is to take place. The star at once reacts to the cavernous echo.

NICOL: The band will have a *hernia*.

LIONEL: Oh, Nicol, it could easily be —

NICOL: *(flatly)*: Dreadful.

After some debate with White House technicians, it's decided that a stage (for the band and Nicol) will be erected halfway down one of the long walls, with the audience in a shallow arc around it. Nicol and I are discussing lighting angles, with illustrative gestures, when we see two unintroduced men regarding us with heavy-lidded interest.

NICOL (*jerking his head towards them*): Secret Service. They think we're discussing angles of fire.

Back in her office, Connie invites us out to eat. As we leave, Nicol unnerves her secretary (who wasn't present during his telling of the anecdote) by laying a hand on her shoulder and murmuring in her ear, 'Don't light any fires with kipper boxes.'

Lunch at the Sans Souci (at the taxpayers' expense, except for two bottles of Echezeaux '62, contributed by Nicol):

PENNY: How do you feel before you go onstage?

NICOL: Elated. There's always the chance of getting that extra ingredient, that jab of adrenalin. When that happens, you do things that can scare you stiff.

PENNY: Are you good at taking direction?

NICOL: I'm the ideal subject for a director. I work from subjective to objective. I start from here (*he indents a small circle on the tablecloth with a fork*) and move outwards to here (*he draws a large concentric circle round the first*). That's the object of the exercise — not my ego.

CONNIE: Do you find that diet affects your work?

NICOL: I never booze before acting. I tried it ten years ago in rep and said never again. Also, I can't eat food cooked in butter or with garlic. If I do, I'm likely to vomit all over the stage.

The girls are giggly by now and propose taking us back to the office, for some sherry. (*Sherry?*) Demurring, with thanks, we depart for the airport.

Cocktails at the St. Regis: P. Gilliatt feels there should be something in Nicol's programme to dissociate him from Nixon. For an hour or so, he will have the ear of the most powerful man on earth. He should choose at least one item to indicate to the Pres why 'people like us' do not support him. Hamlet caused the players to enact 'something like the murder of my father' in front of Claudius while Horatio observed the King's looks. Similarly, Nicol should perform something referring to (though not directly about) Vietnam, police brutality or the Black Panther shootings before the President, presumably with me standing in for Horatio. But what is the something to be? Being the man's guest, Nicol cannot actually spit in his face: what is needed is something oblique, analogical, but none the less crystal clear to all present. I come up with an idea: Creon has a speech in Sophocles' *Antigone* extolling the merits of absolute subservience to authority. But the danger (and the likelihood) is that the President would miss the intended irony and take the speech straight.

Dinner at the Russian Tea Room: Several New York friends of Nicol's come up to our table and give him their reactions — in varying tones of shock and reproach — to the news that he is going to entertain Nixon. One of them calls him 'a collaborator'. Nicol is uneasy and starts to brood: 'I should never have accepted the invitation.' He is discovering the difference between being a hell-raiser and being a rebel. Because he knocks critics, uses rude words on TV talk shows, and generally goes his own way, he is regarded as an anti-system man. In reality, he is simply an anarchic individualist. But he projects individuality with such intensity that he has become, however inadvertently and in however peripheral a way, something of a symbol. It is this symbol that he is now being called on to live up to, and it upsets him.

LEONARD LYONS (*greeting Nicol, who looks distraught and barely registers his presence*): The only good thing I can say about this Administration is that they've invited you to Washington.

MYSELF: Do you think he should have accepted?

LYONS: Why not? He's honouring the office, not the man.

Troubled by all this, Nicol suddenly rises and plunges out of the restaurant without a word. The experience of this evening is forcing him to make commitments, to declare himself, to *join*. Which he hates.

An hour later, guesswork leads me to seek him at Jimmy Ryan's. He is singing 'Sister Kate' with a band headed by Max Kaminsky. The number over, he walks through the middle-aged audience to join me at the bar, where he introduces me to two preposterously obese men called The Bookends, for whom he buys drinks. He tells me equably that he sees no good reason to go on living, since he isn't interested in praise or acceptance or public love: 'I know myself, but I don't understand myself.' The proprietor of the club approaches and shakes his hand. Nicol grips my arm.

NICOL: Listen. There will be a statement. I shall make a statement at the White House.

PROPRIETOR: You're going to meet a beautiful man in Mr. Nixon. A really beautiful man.

NICOL (*paying the bill and staring at a wild-eyed, martyred-looking photo of himself by Lord Snowdon that hangs behind the bar*): Christ never looked so *hopefully* sorrowful.

A Bookend, performing a grotesque solo dance, pauses to wave us goodbye.

Friday, March 13th. The star informs me by phone that, although he was in bed by 2 a.m., he has awakened with a throbbing pain in the liver and a strong feeling of terror: 'There's so much to learn, I'm paralysed.' He will spend the morning studying the script and try a run-through in the afternoon. The significance of the day and date has not escaped him.

After lunch, pacing up and down his living-room, 'like a great famished wolf' (Ellen Terry's description of Henry Irving as Macbeth), he rehearses the non-musical parts of the Evening. Accusation and complaint, disgust and self-disgust are the dominant moods. The *Hamlet* bits are unmelodious harangues, but they ache with real distress. He is as fine as I remember him in the Osborne, and there is genuine pathos in his straw-clutching Willy Loman. Best of all are the cummings poem, delicately wry, very nearly charming, and the Beckett, a staccato tirade of negation, taken at tracer-bullet speed. This latter, and the Benchley, he cannot possibly learn and will have to read. But even in the excerpts from plays he is appallingly shaky on words: unless he masters them, he will be lectern-bound and thus denied all mobility. Already, it's clear that the programme, including music, may top seventy minutes. More than the President bargains for, but, as Lionel says, 'what are they going to do — throw him off the rostrum?'

Working out a running order, Nicol discovers that he has no finale. He wants to make 'O what a rogue and peasant slave' his climax. Hereabouts, I suggest, a hint of self-deprecation wouldn't come amiss, so we add a few lines from Eliot's 'J. Alfred Prufrock':

No! I am not Prince Hamlet, nor was meant to be;
Am an attendant lord, one that will do
To swell a progress, start a scene or two,
Advise the prince; no doubt, an easy tool,
Deferential, glad to be of use,
Politic, cautious, and meticulous;
Full of high sentence, but a bit obtuse;
At times, indeed, almost ridiculous —
Almost, at times, the Fool

An ending is found by not shunning the obvious. Nicol settles for a bushel of evergreen corn. From the Eliot he will go straight into Prospero's 'Our revels now are ended . . .'

Last night's conscience pangs seem to have abated. The individualist speaks only *for* himself; the egotist speaks only *of* himself. In Nicol there are elements of both, and they combine to precipitate a deep resistance to the idea of speaking for others.

Work is interrupted by an urgent phone call from Oscar Beuselinck, in London. A lucrative film offer has come up, requiring an immediate yes or no. His face contorted with boredom and impatience, Nicol turns it down. Somewhat wanly, Lionel remarks that his client is truly uninterested in money; if he were not, why would he come so far to do so much for nothing? He adds that Nicol recently rejected a bid of four hundred thousand dollars to play Enobarbus in Charlton Heston's film of *Antony and Cleopatra*. Possessions do not attract him. As long as his food, drink, shelter and transportation are paid for, he has no financial ambitions.

It is 4.30 p.m. Vodka sours begin to arrive; we have thus far been nipping at minor Burgundies and Valpolicella. Rehearsals are over for the day.

NICOL (*sunk in an armchair*): Actually, I've got about two years left to live.

(*Pause*) I think I'm the most boring man in the world. I really do. People say I'm lucky because I'm free, because I can do what I like. But they don't understand. And why should they? Who can analyse anguish?

This is said ruminatively, without rhetoric, though in full awareness of the effect it is producing. Nicol, I reflect, would be a superb Dostoevski actor. And I remember how good he was as the hero of Gogol's *Diary of a Madman*.

NICOL (*saturnine smile*): I believe I know how I shall end the show. (*He rises and declaims.*) '. . . and our little life — is rounded — with a sleep.' (*He mimes unscrewing a bottle cap and swallowing handful after handful of pills. Rolling his eyes, he clutches at his throat and collapses on the carpet.*)

He is never exultant or euphoric. His relaxed moods are respites — temporary, you feel — from an unassuageable melancholy.

Saturday, March 14th. The star has lost a morning. He was singing at Ryan's until 4.30 a.m. Telephoned at lunchtime, he claims to be learning lines: 'They'll get their money's worth.'

We meet for drinks at 5 p.m., and again the question comes up of the 'statement' he promised to make at the White House. He says he thought of a solution last night but has since forgotten the process by which he reached it. From here he steers the conversation towards safety.

NICOL: Some people can remember rational processes of argument. I can't. What I do remember, after ten or fifteen years, is exactly how a man fiddled with a match box while he was talking. Nervously. Tensely. I slot it away with lots of other details I pick up about him. Then later I take them out and mix in some of myself, and then I've got something separate that I've made.

6 p.m. First band rehearsal at the Roosevelt Grill. The star, who has a curiously stately wardrobe, arrives in a well-cut, sober check suit and a crisply laundered shirt by Turnbull & Asser of St. James's. Lawson and Haggart (of 'St. James's Infirmary') have written some gay and bouncy arrangements of the Shakespearean settings, and it's nice to hear the sound made by their ripping, rasping four-man front line of brass. Nicol is much intimidated by their expertise and preparedness.

He takes me to a dowdy bar on Third Avenue for whisky sours. A large elderly Irishman in a Homburg hat gravely embraces him — an ex-barman, it turns out, recently retired from another of the star's pet haunts. Nicol's best friends seem to be permanently dispersed on some kind of rota system in unfashionable bars throughout the major cities in Britain and the United States, patiently awaiting the off-chance of his arrival. I have entered many such places with him, seldom without running into an unsurprised lifelong chum. It is always a man, and the man is never an actor.

We dine at Lionel's bijou bachelor pad in the East Fifties. Nicol's frame of mind as he contemplates next Thursday veers abruptly between groundless optimism and extremely rational pessimism. Immediately after eating, he departs alone on some unspecified mission. Lionel shrugs helplessly and shakes his head.

Later. Johnny Carson's special TV guest (with tinted glasses and deep décolletage) is Richard Harris, whose career and personality in many ways parallel Nicol's. Both played the title role in productions of *The Ginger Man* (Harris in Dublin, Nicol in London); both starred in (different) adaptations of *The Diary of a Madman*; both have reputations for tumultuous living and warlike imprudence; and both fancy themselves as pop singers. Following the traditional practice of such maniacs on talk shows, Harris says that seriously, Johnny, all kidding aside, he is a devout believer in discipline and professionalism. Tremulously, he sings a new Jim Webb song, looking almost as vulnerable as, and undeniably lovelier than, Nicol. He then announces that he's about to direct and star in *Hamlet*, but, Johnny, he says, although that's a hell of a big responsibility, he puts just as much of the old discipline and professionalism into singing one song on the 'Tonight' show. Applause. I can *just* imagine Nicol saying that, but (to his credit) it would not sound so sincere.

Sunday, March 15th. Lionel opens the door as I arrive at his apartment for lunch. He says nothing but looks alarmed. I walk past him and halt, seeing why. Standing before us is his client, regarding me with a bemused and rueful smile. On his forehead is an egg-sized bump surrounded by contusions. The injury proves to have been self-inflicted.

NICOL: I got back to the hotel at 5 a.m., pissed out of my mind. While I was taking off my trousers in the bathroom, I fell and knocked myself out. The moral is: If you are pissed out of your mind, keep your trousers on.

Over lunch:

NICOL: If I ever write an autobiography, it will be called *Waif and Astray*.

LIONEL: That sounds very sweet.

NICOL: (*dangerously*): When I sound sweet, that's the time to avoid me.

In the afternoon, we drink Puligny-Montrachet while Lionel plays records for Nicol — camp collectors' items, nostalgic tracks from pre-war England featuring people like Evelyn Laye, Dorothy Dickson, and the crooner Al Bowlly. Nicol requests a novelty number called 'My Canary Has Circles Underneath Its Eyes' and says he hopes to record it with Yoko Ono and John Lennon. 'John was going to come to Washington with us, but he couldn't get an American visa.' The ban on Lennon is due to his criminal record: he was found guilty in London of possessing pot. Lionel puts on a series of Noël Coward records. All thought of rehearsing evaporates. Nicol venerates Coward.

NICOL: That's the right way to sock it to them.

By 'them' he means guarded people, prudent people, anti-impulse people, those whom he sometimes calls simply 'the foe'. He listens raptly to the famous duologue between Coward and Gertrude Lawrence in *Private Lives* and then lets slip a remarkable pronouncement on his craft.

NICOL: Acting is nothing but reminding people. That's all it is. It's reminding people of things. (*Pause*) Sometimes, if it's very good, it can even remind them of themselves. (*Pause. More Puligny-Montrachet*) I don't think I shall ever act on stage again.

LIONEL: How about next Thursday?

NICOL; I mean after that. (*Pause. Then, portentously, as if imparting great news in strict confidence*) It's going to go over *very big*.

LIONEL: Of course it —

NICOL: Like the *biggest lead balloon ever.*

My impressions of Monday and Tuesday, March 16th and 17th, are blurred. The handwriting in which I kept my notes begins to lurch about, and sentences of glaring banality are inscribed in a large, childish hand and doubly underlined — an infallible sign of powerful alcoholic sedation. The reason is that during this period of our association I tried to 'drink for' Nicol, as I phrased it to myself. When he ordered wine, I would consume as much of it myself as I discreetly could, in order to keep his energies fresh for rehearsal. I do not know whether this unselfishness was of any real use to him. It nearly crippled me.

From these two days, then, I retain only fragments — a few meals *in toto*, certain courses of others, moments of elation and apprehension during rehearsals, self-questioning about what constitutes a fatal dose of Alka-Seltzer — the one constant factor being a steady drain on Manhattan's reserve supplies of wines imported from the communes of Vosne-Romanée and Flagey-Echezeaux. One clear memory is of part of a lunch at the St. Regis, with Nicol, in the grip of a 'massive depression', telling me that more than anything else he needs a woman in his life, but 'I'm too destructive, I make too many demands'. He says he is sexually obsessed and states that throughout the run of one London production in which he appeared he made love to the leading lady twice every night in the dressing room *during the performance*. (His italics.) To alleviate gloom, he either gets smashed or takes tranquillizers (Valium for preference) to make him feel nonchalant and uncaring, so that the obligatory question — 'What's it all for?' — temporarily recedes.

Other flashes from the lost days: Nicol repeating, with unconvincing assurance, 'Don't worry, I'm going to wing it'; Nicol aware that he is terribly unready for Thursday, yet remaining stubbornly inert in the face of crisis, daring the lightning to strike; Nicol briefly coming to life, baring his teeth, and galvanising everyone, even the band, with his delivery of the Osborne, the Miller and the Beckett. 'He really is a fabulously talented man,' breathes Lionel, and, after the Beckett, Bud Freeman walks up to shake his hand, saying, 'You're one hell of a tenor-sax player.' (I see what he means; it's like listening to the worrying, burrowing frenzy of Paul Gonsalves playing 'Crescendo and Diminuendo in Blue' on a good night several years ago.) Freeman continues, 'I thought I knew you pretty well, Nicol, but *man* — as the jazz people say — that was *something else.*'

Now, on D Day minus 2, it's discovered that Nicol has no technical staff, no one to light the act or cue the musicians. A dumbstruck Bob Haggart is told that he must compose and arrange a short overture and half a dozen mock-Elizabethan music bridges. Midnight phone calls produce a young stage manager, Warren Crane ('He's worked the White House before,' Lionel says. 'He was there with Helen Hayes during the Johnson Administration'); and Rosaleen (Ro) Diamond, Lionel's pretty 25-year-old secretary, who has bought her first mink coat for the Washington trip, is roped in to prompt and give music cues. In the early hours of Wednesday morning, the makeshift crew has its first conference with Nicol, at the St. Regis. The Echezeaux intake becomes particularly onerous during this session. Voices emerge from the general clamour: 'I shall snarl Willy Loman right in the President's face.' 'Will Tricia be there? We have "balls" in the Beckett and "come" in the cummings.' And, summing it all up (Nicol): 'If this thing works, it will be like a Heath Robinson machine giving birth to a baby.'

Footnote. William Heath Robinson (1872-1944): English cartoonist who, like Rube Goldberg, designed elaborate mechanical devices for carrying out useless tasks.

Wednesday, March 18th. I awake at noon like a dwarf refreshed. To the Roosevelt Grill for a full rehearsal before an invited audience of band members' wives and friends. Nicol fluffs repeatedly, misses laughs, and sends line after line winging out into the dark only to fall (as Noël Coward said, in a comparable plight) wetly, like pennies into mud. Perversely, the star regards this disaster as propitious.

NICOL: Tomorrow night will be something disquieting, disturbing, *weird.*

I dine with him at the Ground Floor, on Sixth Avenue (all glass and black leather, the kind of place you'd expect to find in the Michelin guide to Alphaville), and bring along a guest: the beautiful black actress and writer Ellen Holly. During the meal (about half a crate of Echezeaux '61), Nicol proposes marriage to her, not wholly unseriously, and is gently turned down. Richard III's 'Now is the winter of our discontent' goes into the act, replacing Malvolio's letter scene, which had died an especially grisly death at the Roosevelt. A Columbia Pictures limo, with an elderly, battered-looking P.R. man in attendance, rushes the star and me to LaGuardia. On the way, a car rams into our rear fender ('My Jonah hangup again,' says Nicol breezily), and time is squandered on the rituals of recrimination and name-taking. We just make the last flight to Washington, passing through the departure lounge at a brisk trot.

Another P.R. man, physically indistinguishable from the first, awaits us at Washington with an identical limo. Nowadays, Nicol's life is upholstered throughout with such aids and easements, shock-absorbent cushions against the brute impact of reality. There will always be a limo, and someone will always pick up the hotel and restaurant bills. If America does this for an actor whose screen credits include no American movies and no box-office smashes, what on earth does it do for Jack Nicholson? It's approaching 2 a.m. when we pull up at the Mayflower Hotel. I blench to hear Nicol talking about night-caps and asking (in the words of B. Brecht) the way to the next whisky bar. The P.R. man tells him that Washington goes to bed early and that the bars are all closed, and the star seems to have reconciled himself to sleep when suddenly, in pursuit of a hunch, he crosses the street, walks a few blocks, and finds the only bar in town that is still open. The P.R. man fades, leaving the night to Nicol and to me.

Inside the bar (which is underlit to the point of inducing disorientation), I begin to hallucinate. Brain damage of some rare kind appears to have set in. Not without panic, I point out to Nicol that the walls are covered with close-up colour transparencies of the female pudenda. From the middle of the room, where we are sitting, Nicol squints through the darkness, but to no purpose: he says there is nothing there. I hesitate to go over to the wall and check, in case he is right. I recall Laurence Olivier's warning to me before I left London: 'Be careful, or that man will magic you.' I had better believe it. He is looking straight at me, smiling curiously and nodding. At my urgent request, we finish our drinks and go. I am aware, as we do so, of all those flamboyant mirages shimmering obscenely away in the gloom, and I half-close my eyes. (On a subsequent trip to Washington, I retraced my steps and shyly revisited the bar. It is marvellous what tricks exhaustion and an overheated imagination can play with travel posters of the Canadian Rockies.)

Over at the hotel, Nicol sends out for hamburgers. We go up to his suite, where the food arrives thirty minutes later. There is Dom Pérignon on ice in his sitting-room, but I manage to restrict consumption to one bottle. At 3 a.m., I drag myself away. Outside in the corridor I see a little sign-post pointing to Nicol's door. It reads 'The Puerto Rican Hospitality Suite'. I hope to God it is there tomorrow.

Thursday, March 19th. Donne may have got it wrong. Perhaps some men are islands. Fuelled from within himself, responsible to nothing and no one outside himself, impervious to all social, moral and professional pressures that seek to influence or modify his behaviour, Nicol is at least a formidably isolated peninsula, a sort of human Mont Saint-Michel. Today will see him wind-swept and wave-battered.

I return to the Puerto Rican Hospitality Suite (sign still there) at 11 a.m. Stripped to the waist, the star is pacing up and down, villainously hung over. Inexplicably, Lionel and Ro have failed to turn up. This does not lighten his mood.

NICOL: Today I can be a monster. No more of this lovable crap.

A newspaper is delivered. Nicol peers at the front page, freezes, and passes it to me in silence. I read that the Cambodian government has collapsed; Sihanouk has been deposed while away in Peking. So Nixon has a crisis on his hands. There's nothing a man needs more than a cultural soirée when his South-East Asian policy is falling apart. I notice that I am cowering in a corner. Nicol broaches a bottle of champagne. I point out that I am disintegrating fast, but he cajoles me into taking a glass. I emerge a little way from my corner.

NICOL (*seriously*): Do you think I drink a lot?

MYSELF (*ever the plain speaker*): On the whole, yes.

NICOL (*struck by this new idea*): Funny, I always thought I drank less than most people. (*Pause. He muses.*) You see, I have low blood pressure and a low blood-sugar count. Sometimes I get terribly dizzy. I drink to prevent myself from collapsing. (*The thought entertains him.*) Listen, if you ever see me staggering about on the verge of collapse, just *rush* the alcohol to me. Preferably champagne — it has a high sugar content. I have to have it to avoid passing out.

The phone rings. Lionel and Ro have arrived, and I go down to join them in a coffee shop. They missed the early flight because (Jonah strikes again) the car in front of theirs crashed on the way to the airport, holding up traffic. Lionel is in a state of petulant fatalism, bitching about everything to cover up specific forebodings about the hours ahead.

LIONEL: The rooms here are *too crucial*. You ought to see mine. I walked in so quickly I nearly fell out of the window. The only way to enter that room is blindfold, with a sleeping pill in one hand.

He reminisces about Nicol, dwelling morbidly on examples of erratic behaviour.

LIONEL: I was there when he walked offstage in the middle of the first night of *Hamlet* in Boston. It was incredible. He flung a goblet clear across the stage and marched off. The management argued with him for twenty minutes, and then he came back and told the audience he didn't feel at his best and he thought they were being cheated. He said they could have their money back if they wanted. As it happened, they didn't, so he went on with the show.

In the minds of both of us, I can see, there is a fear that something of the sort may happen tonight. Accompanied by Ro and the star — all four of us thickly wrapped against the bitter spring weather — we limo off to the White House for a final rehearsal.

LIONEL (*airily, glancing out of the window*): Wonderful to be back in Philadelphia.

A White House guard stops us as we enter.

GUARD: Are you the entertainment?

NICOL: I beg your pardon?

GUARD: I said, are you the entertainment?

NICOL (*utterly dulcet*): Yes. To be exact, *I* am the entertainment. In just one moment, a dove will escape from my hip pocket and I shall pull the flags of all nations out of my mouth.

We are admitted to the building, which today suggests a large Swiss hotel in the off season — all uniformed flunkeys and no guests. Another guard takes us to the East Room, where the band and the stage manager (whom we greet thankfully) have just arrived. Security men are searching their instrument cases. One of Connie Stuart's assistants brightly points out to Nicol that the East Room was where Lincoln's body lay in state. He thanks her for the information. After one look at the stage, he says it must be enlarged. While this is being done, we move into the adjoining (and aptly named) Green Room for a word rehearsal.

LIONEL: Take your coat off, Nicol.

NICOL: No, thanks, I'm not staying.

He wanders over to the wall and stares at it for a moment, hands deep in pockets.

NICOL: Lend me a pen, will you?

LIONEL: What for?

NICOL: I want to write up here, 'For a good time call TE 8-4622.'

I sit in for the President. Nicol makes a sweeping entrance, bows, mimes pulling a pin from a hand grenade with his teeth, and blithely tosses it into my lap. Soon his flipness fades and the rehearsal stops. He says he wishes he were with his parents in Scotland — 'anywhere but here'. There is a great lack of yeast in his spirit; sadness weighs him down. (What is he mourning?) Lionel chatters on, wondering what Nicol is going to wear tonight. The answer is grey slacks, a blue sweater and a silk scarf. By now, it is 3 p.m.; he goes on at eight, and still the stage and the lighting aren't ready. A further nerve-scraping half hour passes before the run-through can begin.

It goes smoothly enough and lasts sixty-four minutes. The star, rightly, performs at no more than half pressure. He is unsmiling but as relaxed as only the profoundly hung over can be. The first quarter hour is filmed for television.

'And now', says Lionel, 'for the female Mafia.' Nicol, who has not eaten all day, has agreed to be interviewed for the social columns by lady members of the Washington press corps.

The first question is so outlandish that it stuns him into silence. 'Would you say', asks a grey-haired woman, 'that Shakespeare was the James Bond of his day?' Lionel bustles over to help him out.

GREY-HAIRED WOMAN: What was that first song that Mr. Williamson sang?

LIONEL: 'Sigh No More.'

GREY-HAIRED WOMAN: What show is it from?

LIONEL: *Much Ado About Nothing.*

GREY-HAIRED WOMAN: Is that a musical?

SECOND GREY-HAIRED WOMAN: I'm going to London next week, Mr. Williamson. Is it possible to get Chinese food in London?

NICOL: Oh, yes. Quite good Chinese food.

SECOND GREY-HAIRED WOMAN: Where would you recommend me to go?

NICOL: Well, my favourite place is the Wan King.

SECOND GREY-HAIRED WOMAN: Have you the address?

NICOL: Oh, you won't need an address. Just go up to anyone in the street and say, 'Can you direct me to the Wan King?' or 'Where is the Wan King?'

Nicol's face is glowing with sincerity. To understand why Lionel is compelled to move away, his lips compressed and his shoulders shaking, it is necessary to know that the verb 'to wank' is British demotic usage for the act of self-abuse.

Five-thirty. We rush back to the hotel to change. Lionel and Ro cravenly disappear to their rooms, leaving me to keep watch over Nicol. Up in Little Puerto Rico, the phone rings. It is Lionel, hissing, 'Force him to eat something.' I call room service. While I am ordering deep-fried butterfly shrimps, a cork pops and Nicol offers me champagne. Taking a selfless decision, I bring up the name of Tony Richardson, which I count on to provoke a monologue and/or an impersonation. It provokes both ('Tony Richardson', he begins, 'symbolizes power without love'), thereby diverting the star's attention from what he is drinking to what he is saying, and enabling me to dispose of all but one glass of the bottle. Room service is not at its most appetising, and when we depart for the White House at seven-forty (Ro in her mink, Lionel and I in dinner jackets), Nicol's stomach is vacant apart from a glass of champagne and two bites of shrimp encased in congealed fat.

This time, the man on the door recognises us.

GUARD (*beaming*): Good to see you again, Mr. Nicholson.

Lionel winces. Nicol's eyes are beady, but his smile does not flicker. We deposit him backstage, with much patting on the back and gripping of the upper arm. Braided guards escort us into the East Room, where most of the audience — two hundred and seventy in all — has already arrived. The band sits red-faced and black-tied on the rostrum. Lionel turns to me with a fixed grin and says, 'I am petrified.' We slump in the second row and consult his guest list. Many of the names are those of campaign contributors, here to receive their social reward. John Chapman, the damson-complexioned drama critic of the *Daily News*, is among the journalists present; so, exuding loyalty, is Ted Kalem, of *Time*. John Freeman, the British ambassador (and former editor of the *New Statesman*), has a ringside seat. Top Columbia Pictures brass is represented by Leo

Jaffe, the president, and Abe Schneider, the chairman of the board. Other notabilities include the daughter of the Australian Prime Minister, a granddaughter of President Cleveland, Vice-Admiral Rickover, Henry Cabot Lodge, David Eisenhower, and, of course, Henry Kissinger, bleeper no doubt in pocket. Also Dick Cavett, the actor Lee Bowman, and Harold Smith, of Harold's Club, Reno.

To prolonged applause, Mr. and Mrs. Nixon (he in tuxedo, she in something long and pink) enter and seat themselves front centre. The President rises and tells the story of how he heard about Nicol from Harold Wilson more than a year ago.

NIXON (*hands clasped before him*): . . . So because I couldn't stay to see that star in London, that star is here tonight — the man the Prime Minister says is the greatest Hamlet!

The President returns to his chair. Nicol ambles on, takes a bow, and launches into the address to the players.

NICOL: Speak the speech, I pray you, as I pronounced it to you . . .

Silence. He has dried. Five long seconds pass before he completes the sentence, with a phrase that could hardly be less appropriate.

NICOL: . . . trippingly on the tongue.

He covers up well, making it look as if it were Hamlet, and not he, who was groping for the right words, and he finishes the piece without further problems. The band now contributes to the tension by wrecking the first musical bridge. Two howling clinkers are blown, and I can see Bob Haggart's face, bug-eyed with shock. The first song ('Blow, Blow, Thou Winter Wind') finds Nicol still uneasy. But in the Osborne and the cummings he starts to hit his stride. Command enters his voice. There is still, in his stance vis-à-vis the audience, a nonchalance that seems to border on contempt, but it is electric, corrosive contempt, a passion not to be tamed or ignored. (Nobody can complain that he doesn't follow Hamlet's instruction to 'show scorn her own image'.) 'To be or not to be' is first-rate: the morose, familiar lines bite into the mind like acid into metal. The songs — especially 'Dunsinane Blues' and the 'Winter' lyric from *Love's Labour's Lost* — are warming the audience up. The President is seen to smile, and rounds of applause are coming, still faintly, but frequently. Lionel and I are going with the flow, even enjoying ourselves.

Then we both jerk forward, hearing Nicol say, 'Things fall apart.' They certainly do. He has jumped straight from *Love's Labour's* to Yeats, omitting the Miller, the Benchley, and two whole songs. The band is baffled. We are sweating, realising that at this rate he will end twenty-five minutes early. The champagne churns within me. When he gets to the end of the Yeats, there is a frozen pause, after which he says, 'Howard, all I need to set my table is fifty dollars a week.' — and we relax. He has spotted his error, gone into *Death of a Salesman*, and put the derailed Evening back on its tracks. From here, everything builds superbly. The Miller extract —

Willy's lament for the heroic days of salesmanship and his old pal Dave Singleman ('And by the way he died the death of a salesman, in his green velvet carpet slippers in the smoker of the New York, New Haven & Hartford, going into Boston'), and his bewildered rage at a business ethic that discards spent human beings like garbage — comes fervently across. I'm surprised what a punch Miller still packs for an audience like this, especially when the part is played, as now, entirely without sentimentality.

Nicol finds the right note of insanely jovial pedantry for Benchley's bumbling Treasurer. 'O what a rogue and peasant slave' is given in a splendid tempest of self-laceration. But it's with the Beckett that he and his material really fuse. The sound we hear is that of a man (or at least a being) in his last extremity, living on the very margin of existence:

. . . alone in the mud yes the dark yes sure yes panting yes someone hears me no no one hears me no murmuring sometimes yes when the panting stops yes not at other times no in the mud yes to the mud yes my voice yes mine yes not another's no mine alone yes sure yes when the panting stops yes on and off yes a few words yes a few scraps yes that no one hears no but less and less no answer LESS AND LESS yes

so things may change no answer end no answer I may choke no answer sink no answer sully the mud no more no answer the dark no answer trouble the peace no more no answer the silence no answer DIE screams I MAY DIE screams I SHALL DIE screams good . . .

The way Nicol punctuates this into lucidity is a technical *tour de force*. I have never heard his voice more hypnotic: as it rises from a wintry monotone to a high, urgent, terrified whinny, you would think he was a medium, possessed and shaken by an unquiet demon. Nixon's face is rigid and expressionless, but he is staring straight into Nicol's eyes. I don't think he has ever heard anything quite like this before.

Finally, the star gives us his dying fall — 'Alfred Prufrock', followed by Prospero's farewell to the revels — and bows. Applause crashes over him, wave upon wave. He withdraws, returns to cheers and bravos, shares them with the band, withdraws again. Lionel stops clapping for a second to give me the thumbs-up sign. Against all the auguries, his wayward client has pulled it off. He is the Entertainment.

The audience moves into the next room, where there is a hot buffet. Dick Cavett sniffs as we enter.

CAVETT: Something's burning.

MYSELF: Someone's let Agnew into the library again.

A big Williamson fan, Cavett enjoyed the show immensely; so did Kissinger. Like many others, John Freeman was particularly knocked out by the Beckett. Outside in the hall, the guests are shuffling along in line to shake the Nixons and Nicol by the hand. I receive an exceptionally slow and searching wink from the Entertainment. The President — his face like a leather brief-case that has seen long service: you expect to find a pocket for ballpoint refills behind one ear — says he thought the Miller and Osborne outstandingly memorable:

NIXON (*with the admiration of one pro for another*): It's so wonderful the way he changes so quickly. One thing ends, something completely different begins. And to think that your Prime Minister started it all.

Passing on, I hear Mrs. Nixon whisper to Nicol, 'Stand on the carpet, not the stone floor. It's easier on the feet.' In the State Banqueting Chamber, the Marine Corps Band is playing the score of *Hair* in strict ballroom tempo. Careless of tomorrow, Lionel, Ro and I drink champagne while the fiscal caryatids of the Republican Party swing and sway. After a few minutes, the marines quit the stand, to be replaced (at Nicol's request, we learn) by the W.G.J.B. The Chamber livens up; some portly jitter-bugging is observed. The Nixons smile briefly in at the door, then retire. No slight intended — they are notoriously quick off the mark to Blanket Bay. And tonight, no doubt, the President will be anxious to know who is minding the store in Phnom Penh. Nicol, looking ten years younger, grabs the microphone.

NICOL: This should be an evening that swings. We should all have fun and get boozed. And I hope to God we don't wake the people upstairs.

He dances fancifully with Ro, Mrs. Ted Kalem and others, sings 'Darktown Strutters' and 'I Can't Give You Anything but Love, Baby', and even borrows Yank Lawson's trumpet to blow a stammering but heartfelt chorus of 'Tin Roof Blues'. The whole place begins to vibrate like a Hamburg dance palace on Saturday night. An astonishing amount of affectionate goosing is going on. It is half past midnight before Nicol is ready to move. His departing gait is regal.

NICOL: We leave with dignity. With our own dignity. (*He stands on the steps of the White House and contemplates the sky.*) Tonight this is our town, Thornton Wilder! Do you hear? Our town!

A private bus takes us and the musicians to a jazz club called Blues Alley, where Charlie Shavers is playing. The W.G.J.B. sit in, and for two hours Nicol blows, sings, drinks, and spreads himself. Chewing a cigar, sardonically grinning, rolling his rheumy eyes, he looks like a Mississippi gambler on a winning streak. I reflect: How limited is the range of things he wants to do with these moments of riot. All he asks of triumph, all he means by relaxation and release, is the opportunity to drink a few great wines from the Champagne district and the Côte de Nuits, and to go to places where small-group mainstream jazz is played late at night.

At 3.30 a.m., Nicol, Lionel, Ro and I bring hamburgers back to the Puerto Rican Hospitality Suite and eat them with more champagne. Nicol's hair clings to his skull like damp ginger worms.

NICOL (*holding up a half-eaten hamburger*): So this is what it was all for.

RO (*ecstatically phoning a friend in California*): Listen, I just spilled Dom

Pérignon over my mink coat!

NICOL: Nixon said he could take the programme twice over. 'You must come and do it again,' he said.

LIONEL: Why did you do it in the first place?

NICOL (*with mock-heroic shrug*): A challenge.

He has come three thousand miles to please and impress a man who was not, perhaps, all that interested in what he was doing, or all that capable of being pleased and impressed in those regions of human response where Nicol's talent is best equipped to strike. All one can say is that by his unpaid exertions Nicol has enabled Nixon to keep a diplomatic promise.

A fortnight later, the following letter arrived in Nicol's mail:

Dear Mr. Williamson,

Your magnificent performance in the White House on March 19th surpassed even the exceptionally favorable advance notice which I had received, and I want to express my thanks to you once more for your generous gift of your time and talent. Your presence made a spectacularly successful evening deeply memorable as well.

> With best wishes,
> RICHARD M. NIXON

Friday, March 20th. Press reactions are good. The *New York Times* says that Nicol 'shifted mood, pace and tone with seeming ease', and Richard Coe, of the *Washington Post*, reviews the act in the style of *Variety*:

Known for mod treatment of classics as well as savvy way with smart stuff (T. S. Eliot and Samuel Beckett, Nobel '69), thesp cooked up novel touch . . . Williamson, using characteristic North Country nasal twang, feels for and finds total meaning of excerpts from *Hamlet, Richard III* and modern material . . . Construction of act is ingenious, nicely fitting counterparts of today with classic stuff . . . Sock hits, finding star wholly at home as singer, include *Macbeth* follow-piece, 'Dunsinane Blues', and encored 'Blow, Blow, Thou Winter Wind' . . .

Nicol celebrates by giving lunch at the Jockey Club to Lionel, Ro, me, and a couple of Washington friends of mine. The occasion is pleasantly hysterical (Taittinger Blanc de Blancs, Château Margaux '61), with the Entertainment at his most ebullient. Just before going on last night, he tells us, he contemplated chickening out by pretending to be under the impression that the invitation was to entertain the Nixons *and nobody else.* Most of the restaurant is watching as he mimes what he planned to do: stride in beaming at the President; come to an affronted halt as his eyes register the presence of *other people*; sniff querulously; raise eyebrows; turn on heel;

march straight off stage and out of the building. He meditates on what he actually did.

NICOL: I don't know why it happened, but it happened, and I stand by it. Why they asked for it, Christ only knows. Why they got it, Christ only knows. But they got it.

Together with Ro and Lionel, he has to leave for the airport. They are returning to New York; I am booked on a later flight direct to London. As he gets into the limo, one of my friends, a young woman who has never met him before, shakes his hand and says, 'You're a very extraordinary man, Mr. Williamson.'

NICOL: Lady, the mome rath isn't born that could outgrabe me.

That evening, I sit with a beer at Dulles Airport, trying to exorcise Nicol from my consciousness. I have been too close for too long. But there is no escape. In a corner of the bar, on a TV set badly in need of adjustment, he comes looming through a snowstorm of video tape to sing 'Dunsinane Blues':

> Now's the time for you to be —
> A wary 'un:
> I wasn't really born, it was a —
> Caesarean . . .

No, the barman says, he isn't allowed to switch off the set, which now adds a slow rolling-frame effect to its repertoire. Dozens of Nicols float before my eyes: Will the line stretch out to the crack of doom? He looks supremely buoyant in his blizzard; I, on the other hand, feel drained and enfeebled, a mere husk of a man. How much (I wonder) of Nicol's neurosis is a deliberate, expertly adopted pose? On the whole, actors are not the compulsive neurotics we take them for. Many of them come from idyllic and unbroken homes, where they were idolized by their parents. They seek (and will go to any lengths to obtain) the same central position, the same applause, the same devout attention in adult life. These things, to use behaviourist language, are their reinforcers. No, actors are not crazy, nor are they compensating for emotional neglect. They are simply re-enacting golden childhoods. Remove the reinforcers, however, even temporarily, and what one gets is that other Nicol, sunk in accidie, of whom I've had so many glimpses this past week.

I buy a paperback by Simon Raven (*Friends in Low Places*) to read on the plane. Just as I am settling down, with my usual sense of pleasurable loathing, into Captain Raven's archaically structured world, a sentence brings Nicol vividly back to my mind: 'Mark had an acute sense of self-preservation (an attribute which is often very strong in second-rate performers and does much to explain their mediocrity) . . .'

Whatever else he is, Nicol is not a second-rater.

The last time I saw him was in May, 1971, when we had another of our lunches at the Étoile in London. On this occasion, the part I had to offer him was King Lear. The answer was no, as it had been when I approached him with an assortment of other roles sixteen months earlier. He said he was no longer interested in being 'the greatest actor of my generation, and all that jazz'. Although he had made a film, he had not appeared before a live audience since the White House date, more than a year before.

'The individualist', says B. F. Skinner, in *Beyond Freedom and Dignity*, 'can find no solace in reflecting upon any contribution which will survive him. He has refused to act for the good of others and is therefore not reinforced by the fact that others whom he has helped will outlive him. He has refused to be concerned for the survival of his culture and is not reinforced by the fact that the culture will long survive him. In the defence of his own freedom and dignity, he has denied the contributions of the past and must therefore relinquish all claim upon the future.'

The New Yorker: 15th January 1972
The Sound Of Two Hands Clapping, 1975

RALPH RICHARDSON

Sir Ralph Richardson celebrated his seventy-fourth birthday on December 19, 1976, the day after Harold Pinter's *No Man's Land*, in which he co-starred with his old friend Sir John Gielgud, ended its Broadway run at the Longacre. Sir Ralph played Hirst, a wealthy Englishman with an awe-inspiring thirst, incessantly slaked, for vodka and Scotch. Hirst is also a famous writer, although we do not discover this until page 67 of the published text (which ends on page 95) — a little late in the day, some may think, for such an important disclosure. Some, indeed, would get downright shirty if another playwright were thus to withhold essential infor-mation that could easily have been revealed in the first ten minutes; but when Mr. Pinter does it, audiences marvel at what they have been taught to recognise as his skill in creating an atmosphere of poetic suspense. At all events, Hirst, protected by a pair of sinister servants called Foster and Briggs, lives in a palatial Hampstead house, where he is bearded by Spooner, a threadbare poetaster (played by Sir John) whom he may or may not have cuckolded — Mr. Pinter leaves us in poetic doubt — on the eve of the Second World War. Spooner, who seeks employment as Hirst's secretary, is under pressure throughout the play to quit the household. I don't propose to offer an interpretation of *No Man's Land*, but it may not be irrelevant to point out that all of its four characters are named after English cricketers who flourished around the turn of the century. Mr. Pinter is known to be a fanatical lover of cricket — a game in which a batsman (e.g., Spooner) invades the territory of the opposing team (e.g., Hirst, Foster, and Briggs), which then attempts, by a variety of ploys that include bluff, deceit, and physical intimidation, to dismiss him from the field. The dialogue, garlanded with bizarre non sequiturs, is often hilarious. Whether the play is more than a cerebral game is a decision that will have to wait until we see it performed by second-rate actors. Fortunately for Mr. Pinter, the English theatre is well equipped with senior players who can bestow on whatever material comes their way a patina of seignorial magic.

Sir Ralph is one such. Devotees of the Richardson cult — who had last seen their idol on Broadway in 1970, when he appeared (also with Sir John) as a benevolent lunatic in David Storey's *Home* — observed with relief that immersion in Pinterdom had left his professional trade-marks unchanged. There was the unique physical presence, at once rakish and stately, as of a pirate turned prelate. There was the balsawood lightness of movement, which enabled him to fall flat on his face three times in the course of a single act — a rare feat for septuagenarians. There was the peculiar method of locomotion, whereby he would spring to his feet and, resembling a more aloof and ceremonious Jacques Tati, propel himself forward with the palms of his hands turned out, as if wading through waist-deep water. There was the pop-eyed, poleaxed look, with one eyebrow balefully cocked, whenever he was faced with a remark that was baffling or potentially hostile. Above all, there was the voice, which I once described as 'something between bland and grandiose: blandiose, perhaps.' Or, as I wrote in another context, when he played *Cyrano de Bergerac* in 1946:

> His voice is most delicate; breath-light of texture; more buoyant even than that of M. Charles Trenet. . . . It is a yeasty, agile voice. Where Olivier would pounce upon a line and rip its heart out, Richardson skips and lilts and bounces along it, shaving off pathos in great flakes.

A personal note: The noise that Sir Ralph makes has sometimes struck me as the vocal equivalent of onionskin writing paper — suave, crackling, and resonant. This curious association is no doubt strengthened by my memories of his definitive performance as Peer Gynt, in 1944 — specifically, of the scene in which Peer tries to find his true identity by symbolically peeling an onion, only to discover that beneath the last layer of skin there is no core of selfhood but, simply and literally, nothing. Sir Ralph has often been at his best when playing men in whose lives, gamely though they keep up appearances, there is a spiritual emptiness, a certain terror of the void. One of his greatest regrets is having turned down Samuel Beckett's *Waiting for Godot* in the early nineteen-fifties, when he and Alec Guinness were invited to play the two Godot-forsaken tramps. They were dissuaded in part by Gielgud, who decried the play — in a phrase of which he is now thoroughly ashamed — as 'a load of old rubbish.' Sir Ralph, then appearing at the Haymarket Theatre in London, asked Beckett to come and discuss the script with him. 'I'd drawn up a sort of laundry list of things I didn't quite understand,' Sir Ralph recalls. 'And Beckett came into my dressing room — wearing a knapsack, which was very mysterious — and I started to read through my list. You see, I like to know what I'm being asked to do. March up the hill and charge that blockhouse! Fine — but I wasn't sure which was the hill and where the blockhouse was. I needed to have a few things clear in my mind. But Beckett just looked at me and said, "I'm awfully sorry, but I can't answer any of your questions." He wouldn't explain. Didn't lend me a hand. And then another job came up, and I turned down the greatest play of my lifetime.'

Richardson became an indisputably great actor in the latter half of 1944.

Since then, despite some wildly misguided choices of roles, he has continued to ripen. Today, both as a man and as a performer, he is more expansive in his uniqueness and his eccentricity than ever before. He is the eldest of a formidable trio of English actors — the others being Gielgud and Laurence Olivier, his juniors by, respectively, two and five years — who were born early in the century, and whose careers, which have frequently crisscrossed, form a map that covers most of the high points of English theatre in the past five decades. (Richardson and Olivier were knighted in 1947; Gielgud had to wait for his accolade until 1953.) Gielgud and Olivier, from their earliest days in the profession, were that godsend to critics, a pair of perfect opposites. You could list their qualities in parallel columns:

GIELGUD	OLIVIER
Air	Earth
Poet	Peasant
Mind	Heart
Spiritual	Animal
Feminine	Masculine
John Philip Kemble	Edmund Kean
Introvert	Extrovert
Jewel	Metal
Claret	Burgundy

Concerning the great Shakespearean parts that both actors have played, the critical consensus is that Gielgud has defeated Olivier as Hamlet and Romeo, while Olivier has knocked out Gielgud as Othello, Antony, and Macbeth. King Lear has outpointed both of them. But where does this all leave Sir Ralph? Very much the odd man out. Many of his greatest Shakespearean successes have been in parts like Falstaff, Caliban, Bottom, and Enobarbus, which the other members of the triumvirate have never attempted. In 1960, he contributed a series of autobiographical pieces to the London *Sunday Times*, in one of which he wrote, 'Hamlet, Lear, Macbeth and Othello are the four glorious peaks of dramatic literature.' Of Macbeth, a role he played in 1952, he said, 'I couldn't do it for nuts — not for a second did I believe in the air-drawn dagger, and if I couldn't, no wonder no one else did.' In 1938, he failed as Othello, though he cannot have been much helped by his Iago: Olivier, who elected to play the part along Freudian lines, as a man consumed by a smoldering homosexual passion for the Moor, but who neglected to inform Sir Ralph that he intended, in the course of the performance, to kiss him full on the lips. James Agate, the leading London critic of the time, headed his review 'Othello Without the Moor.' In it he sombrely concluded:

The truth is that Nature, which has showered upon this actor the kindly gifts of the comedian, has unkindly refused him any tragic facilities whatever. His voice has not a tragic note in its whole gamut, all the accents being those of sweetest reasonableness. He cannot blaze.

As for Hamlet and Lear, Sir Ralph has avoided them both — wrongly, I think, as far as the latter role is concerned, but this is a point to which I'll return. 'Clearly,' he wrote in 1960, 'I don't belong to the first division. It could be that my place is in doomed second.' Alternatively, it could be just that he lacks the traditional (but now surely outdated) attributes of the tragic hero — the rumbling voice, the aquiline nose, the high cheekbones, the profile of ruined beauty. Critics have written of his 'round, sober cheese-face,' his 'broad moony countenance,' which has also been likened to a 'sanctified potato.' Interviewed on British TV in 1975, he said, 'I don't like my face at all. it's always been a great drawback to me.' He is utterly sincere about this, the proof being that although he has been working in the cinema since 1933, he has never seen any of the rushes. 'It discourages me,' he says of his physical appearance. 'I lose confidence in myself.' Yet despite this alleged handicap, and despite his failure to conquer the tragic Big Four, he has remained, both in and out of the classics, a star with an assured place in the Big Three — a wine to be judged on the same level as burgundy and claret, even if nobody can quite manage to locate the vineyard.

To explain his continued presence in the top trio, a special category had to be invented for him. Ralph Richardson, it was said, represented not the Tragic Hero or the Poetic Hero but the Common Man. I once asked him how he differed as a performer from Olivier. He ruminated for a moment and then replied, 'I've not his size or range. I'm a more rotund kind of actor. Laurence is more the spiky sort. I haven't got his splendid fury.' Fury, of course, takes many forms that are not explicit, and hearty bluffness can veil many kinds of desolation and misanthropy. To this matter, too, I shall return. During the thirties and early forties, it became an article of theatrical faith that Richardson was Everyman, the chap you cast when you wanted an embodiment of common-place decency, of sterling (if slightly tongue-tied) honesty — in short, a sort of human dobbin. Not everyone was deceived. Barbara Jefford, a handsome classical actress with whom he has worked at the Old Vic, once said to me, 'People called him the epitome of the ordinary man, I suppose because of his round face. They were absolutely wrong. I can imagine him as a kind of Thomas Hardy hero — a plebeian type transmogrified and exalted. But he could never be your average worker.' In 1963, she went on, she appeared with Sir Ralph in Pirandello's *Six Characters in Search of an Author*. He played the father, a fictitious creature permanently condemned to a twilit half existence, since the play-within-a-play of which he is the protagonist is never completed. 'And, of course, he was superb,' Miss Jefford said, '*because he was playing a ghost.* That's the point about Ralph. There's always something spectral about him. He really is a man from Mars.' In 1957, he scored a great hit in *Flowering Cherry*, Robert Bolt's first stage success, as a dowdy suburban husband with delusions of grandeur. His performance gave the lie to the theory that he was Everyman reborn in Surbiton. 'To any role that gives him half a chance,' I wrote at the time, 'he brings outsize attributes, outsize euphoria, outsize dismay. Those critics who hold that he excels in portraying the Average man cannot, I feel, have met many Average Men. . . . He gives us fantasy, not normality.'

If Sir Ralph was not Everyman, what was he? Two quotations may be helpful. One is from George Jean Nathan: 'Drama is a two-souled art: half divine, half clownish.' The other is from Sir Ralph himself: 'The ability to convey a sense of mystery is one of the most powerful assets possessed by the theatre.' If Sir Ralph was the odd man out, the operative word was 'odd.' Mystery, clownishness, oddity: all of them forms of protective carapace — smokescreens, layers of the onion.

First Interlude: 5 P.M. on June 14, 1976. Interview between Sir Ralph and me at his London house, which is extremely grand — designed by Nash and overlooking Regent's Park. The meeting has been easy to fix: strangely, for a man so deeply private in other respects, he does not bother to have an unlisted telephone number. I have known him slightly for twenty-odd years: Will he remember that I described him in *Macbeth* as 'a sad facsimile of the Cowardly Lion in *The Wizard of Oz*' and as 'the glass eye in the forehead of English acting'? I ascend by lift (still a great rarity in London houses) to wait in a resplendent L-shaped living room with floor-to-ceiling windows. My qualms are allayed when he bursts in beaming and asks if I'd care to join him in one of his special cocktails. I accept with thanks. He pads across to a well-stocked drinks table, selects two half-pint tumblers, and pours into each of them three fat fingers of Gordon's gin, followed by a huge slug of French vermouth. I reach out for my drink. He shakes his head and adds a lavish shot of Italian vermouth. I repeat business; he repeats headshake. Into each glass he now pours three *thumbs* of vodka. 'That,' he says gravely, 'is what makes the difference.' I can well believe him. Three things are known about Sir Ralph's relationship with alcohol. One: He enjoys it. Two: On working days he restricts himself, until the curtain falls, to a couple of glasses of wine, taken with luncheon. Three: He is never visibly drunk. I recall a story told me by a former director of a famous classical repertory theatre, who wanted Sir Ralph to join the company and went to his home to discuss what parts he might play. 'There was this long mahogany table,' my informant said, 'Ralph sat at one end and put a full bottle of gin in front of me. "That," he said, "is for you." Then he got another full bottle and placed it at his end of the table. "And that," he said, "is for me." Then he sat down. "Now, my dear fellow," he said, "what do we want to talk about?" '

I stealthily consult some notes I have made about his career, but before I have framed my first question he says, 'I've no idea what we're going to say to each other. After all, where did we come from? Did you ever have a vision of the place we came from before we were born? I did, when I was about three years old. I used to dream about it a good deal. I even drew pictures of it.' He leans forward confidentially. '*It looked rather like Mexico*,' he says with quiet emphasis. Wind utterly removed from sails, I am silenced: Who else would start a conversation like this? I sip his lethal cocktail, which he leaps up to replenish as soon as the level falls more than half an inch below the rim of the glass. From life before birth it is a short step to life after death. 'I've been very close to death,' he muses. 'It's like dropping into an abyss — very drowsy, rather nice.' Is he referring to wartime experiences in the Fleet Air Arm or to the motorbike on which, pipe in mouth, he habitually zooms around London? In a conversation recently recorded in the London *Observer*, Gielgud said to Sir Ralph, 'The last time you took me on the pillion, I practically had a fit. I was a stretcher case.' Sir Ralph nodded and esoterically replied, 'I have been killed several times myself.' Meanwhile, he pursues his metaphysical speculations: 'God is very economical, don't you think? Wastes nothing. Yet also the opposite. All those galaxies, stars rolling on forever . . .'

By a mighty effort, I turn the conversation to contemporary realities. What does he think, after all these years, of his old partner Olivier? He springs from his seat, arms outstretched above his head. 'I *hate* Larry. Until I see him. Then he has more magnetism than anyone I've ever met. Except Alexander Korda. I had a film contract with Korda from 1935 until he died, in 1956. I would go to see him with a furious speech about what I wanted, and what I'd do if I didn't get it. And all the time he'd be staring at my feet. When I'd finished, he'd say, "Where did you get those marvellous shoes? I'd give anything to have shoes like those." And I would be defeated.' He subsides into a chair. 'I admire anyone who has a talent that makes me tingle. Like Chopin, or Conrad, or Pinter, or Beckett. Though not the later Beckett. I am sadly literal-minded, and in Beckett's recent work I find obscurity instead of mystery. And, of course, I worship Ethel Merman.'

We talk about Peter Hall, who succeeded Olivier as artistic director of Britain's National Theatre, and for whom Sir Ralph has lately worked in Ibsen's *John Gabriel Borkman* as well as in *No Man's Land*. A few months earlier, Hall confided to his associates that Sir Ralph was 'the greatest poetic actor alive, with perhaps two or three good years left in him,' adding that it was their duty to make sure that he spent these precious days at the National. Accordingly, Hall acquired the rights to *The Kingfisher*, a new play written for Sir Ralph by the popular boulevard dramatist William

Douglas Home and originally intended for presentation in the commercial theatre. Hall's ingenious plan was that after a token run of a few weeks at the National the play should be moved to the West End. The director (Hall) and any stars in his cast would then be remunerated at West End levels, which are considerably higher than those at the National, since they include percentages of the box-office gross. A profitable operation for all concerned — though there were purists who doubted whether the true function of a national theatre was to stage commercial productions for quick moneymaking transfers to the West End. Sir Ralph makes no claims for the play as a work of art: '*The Kingfisher* is two bits of cobweb stuck together with stamp edging and sticking plaster. It's about two elderly people — Celia Johnson plays the woman — who very nearly had an affair when they were much younger but didn't quite. He's now an old novelist, and her husband has just died. They try to begin again where they left off all those years ago. Things like that happen all the time. When I was, oh, about twelve, I met a girl named Francesca. I never kissed her, never even touched her, doubt if I saw her more than a couple of times, but as long as I live I shan't forget her.' Topping up our drinks, he lowers his voice. 'Don't you think Peter Hall has something *Germanic* about him? I do hope he doesn't get Germanic with the Willie Douglas Home play, because if he does we shall all go down with the Titanic. Pause. Then a broad, beatific smile: 'Or the Teutonic.' (Since this conversation took place, Hall has had a change of heart. Influenced, perhaps, by the increasingly vocal doubts of the purists, the National has relinquished the play to the commercial theatre, where it will be staged by another director, with Sir Ralph still in the lead, but without the aid of public subsidy.)

Before we part, he reminisces about his pet ferret. He really used to have a pet ferret. He washed it every week in Lux soap flakes. (There were rabbits, too, and hamsters. 'Whether it's a ferret or a motorbike or a firework,' said Barbara Jefford, 'he concentrates entirely on his extraordinary enthusiasms. It's a boy we're talking about, a great boy.') 'Goodbye, my dear chap,' he says, waving me into the lift. I leave feeling (a) that I have known this man all my life, and (b) that I have never met anyone who more adroitly buttonholed me while keeping me firmly at arm's length.

Sir Ralph once said, 'I've never given a good performance, that has satisfied me, in any play.' Is this false modesty or genuine diffidence? A young actor I know appeared with Sir Ralph in a recent production. One evening, as they stood in the wings awaiting their entrance, Sir Ralph turned to my friend and murmured, 'I had a little talent once. A very little talent. If you should ever come across a tiny talent labelled R. R., please let me know.' Then the cue came, and he surged imperiously into the spotlight.

Ralph Richardson was born in 1902 in the intensely respectable West country town of Cheltenham. His mother was a devout Catholic and his father a Quaker — according to Sir Ralph, 'a shortish man with a beard and cold blue eyes,' who wore bright-coloured waistcoats and taught art at the local Ladies' College. Ralph had two elder brothers, of whom — as of Cheltenham and, indeed, of his father — he remembers very little, since when he was four his mother ran away from home, taking him with her. When he is asked why she bolted, he maintains a silence that may betoken either tact or ignorance. On a minute allowance of two pounds and ten shillings a week, provided by his father, they lived at Shoreham-by-Sea, in Sussex, in a pair of disused railway carriages standing side by side on the beach and joined together by a tin roof. This meant that they had, in Sir Ralph's words, 'a front door and a back door, as well as about twenty side doors.' Their neighbours were few. 'I had one friend for a time,' Sir Ralph has written, 'until I was accused of murder.' It seems that when he was idly twirling an iron hoop on a stick it flew off and accidentally struck his friend, a small girl, on the head. Unfortunately, her mother was an explosive pioneer feminist on a very short fuse, who came storming out of her nearby bungalow and howled, 'You brute! You have killed my daughter!' He had in fact merely grazed her scalp. Since his mother had hopes of grooming him for the priesthood, he was sent to several Catholic schools; one of them was a seminary, from which, to her great disappointment, he ran away. Academic subjects bored him: 'I was not passionate enough and had not the character to be rebellious. I think I was just a big oaf.'

He recalls from his school days only one moment of fulfillment, when a teacher called on him to get up and recite a passage from Macaulay's *Lays of Ancient Rome*. He accepted the challenge and astounded himself. 'It frightened the life out of the class, and it frightened the life out of me. They were horrified, they were electrified. It was really very good, I never read again. No one ever asked me to.' Around 1910, he and his mother moved to South London, and thence to Brighton, living in a succession of cheap flats, hotels, and boarding houses. 'I had no education at all, really,' he later told a TV interviewer. 'I was sort of professionally ill when I was a little boy.' He was forever catching things — mumps, scarlet fever, diphtheria — and his mother, a lonely and possessive woman, as well as an expert hypochondriac in her own right, saw to it that he stayed at home as much as possible. There was money on the Richardson side of the family, which included prosperous leather manufacturers in Newcastle-upon-Tyne, but Ralph's father had forfeited his share of the fortune by abjuring commerce and taking to the arts. Even so, the boy remembered his paternal grandfather, controller of the dynastic loot, with fondness:

He came to take me out in London one day when he was about eighty. Wonderful white beard and very ironic, like a pirate in a good mood. It was my day, he said, and we'd do exactly what I liked. I took him to the Crystal Palace and we spent hours on the switchbacks; he never turned a whisker. I was told afterwards I might have killed him.

What follows could easily be a novel by H. G. Wells modulating into a novel by J. B. Priestley. In 1919, young Richardson is employed as an office boy in a Brighton insurance company. Being a sprightly lad with a taste for heights and none for his job, he amuses himself one day by shuffling his way around the office building on a narrow outside ledge, vertiginously overlooking Brighton High Street. Crowds gather on the sidewalk, watching him in horror. (He later admitted that he was partly motivated by exhibitionism; after all, 'the alpine climber's audience is sparse.') He has timed his exploit to coincide with a period when the boss will be out of the building. His timing is off. The boss re-enters his office to find Richardson passing slowly by outside his window, and freezes in the act of removing his hat. Richardson smiles and waves in a friendly manner. Receiving no response, he puts his head in over the top of the window and affably explains, 'I was chasing a pigeon.' His employer, too nonplussed to take disciplinary action, nods vaguely and makes a mental note: 'Richardson is not reliable.'

Soon afterward, Richardson's Newcastle grandmother died — a wealthy woman he had hardly met. When he was six, she summoned him to visit her. He took with him a pet mouse named Kim. The servant who met him at the station shook her head and said, 'You'll never be allowed to take that creature up to the big house.' 'Why not?' said Ralph. 'I've been invited to see my grandmother, and I never travel without Kim.' 'She won't let it in the house,' said the servant. 'In that case,' said Ralph, 'when's the next train back to Brighton?' He stood his ground, and the matriarch was forced to capitulate; but she was so impressed by his stubbornness that she remembered him in her will. In fact, she left him five hundred pounds — a sum large enough to change the course of his life. 'Kim cost me sixpence,' he reflected later. 'It was the happiest buy I ever made.'

He gave up insurance and enrolled in the Brighton School of Art. But not for long. A few months afterward, Sir Frank Benson and his renowned Shakespearean company appeared at the Theatre Royal, and Richardson went to see them in *Hamlet*. This was 'the decisive moment that moved my compass,' he wrote later. 'I suddenly realised what acting was and I thought: By Jove, that's the job for me.' He abandoned painting and applied for work with a semiprofessional troupe run in Brighton by a stubby, hooknosed actor-manager named Frank R. Growcott. He chose as his audition piece a speech by Falstaff. Growcott was appalled. 'That is quite awful,' he said. 'It is shapeless, senseless, badly spoken. . . . You could never, never be any good as Falstaff.' (This diatribe burned itself into

Richardson's mind. When Olivier, a quarter of a century later, asked him to play Falstaff, his first reaction was to say that he couldn't possibly do it.) Nonetheless, Growcott agreed to hire him for six months. During the first half of the engagement he would pay Growcott ten shillings a week, after which Growcott would pay him the same sum. In the following year, 1921, he achieved full professional status. He joined a touring repertory company led by a now forgotten Irish actor called Charles Doran. The Doran productions were rehearsed in London, so Richardson — who until then had never seen a play on the West End stage — was able to study the work of people like Charles Hawtrey ('I think the best actor I've ever seen') and Mrs. Patrick Campbell ('who knocked me flat'). For three years, he toured with Doran, building a solid Shakespearean technique on the basis of parts like Orlando, Macduff, and Bottom. A fellow member of the troupe was Muriel Hewitt, whom he married in 1924, and later summed up as 'the perfect example of the natural actress.' They went on to work together at the Birmingham Repertory Theatre, which was then the most adventurous regional ensemble in Britain, and in 1926 Richardson made his West End debut, in *Yellow Sands*, a Birmingham success by Eden and Adelaide Phillpotts that moved to London and ran for over six hundred performances, with Cedric Hardwicke in the leading role. Richardson's wife was also in the cast. In his own words:

> Her career on the stage was brilliant but brief, and her courage was terribly tested, for after a few years of work she fell under some rare nervous attack, perhaps akin to polio, and some years later she died.

'Ralph's first wife contracted some kind of sleeping sickness in Croydon,' John Gielgud told me recently. 'Her death was long and painful.' It finally took place in 1942. 'They were devoted to each other,' Gielgud added.

Richardson's first real blossoming began in 1930 at the Old Vic, where, over a period of two years, he played a full range of classical roles, among them Prince Hal in *Henry IV*, part I, Caliban, Bolingbroke, Iago, Toby Belch, the Bastard in *King John*, Petruchio, Kent in *King Lear*, Enobarbus, and Henry V. Gielgud remembers 'his marvellous performances of shaggy-dog faithfulness — the kind of part Shakespeare wrote so well,' and says, 'He was unforgettable as the Bastard and Enobarbus and Kent. And he always gave them a touch of fantasy. But he couldn't bear fights. When I played Hotspur to his Hal, and he had to kill me, he used to count the strokes out loud. "Come on, cockie," he'd say. "One, and two, and three, and four . . ." I never really felt his heart was in it.'

By the midthirties, he was an established star in modern plays (*For Services Rendered* and *Sheppey*, both by Somerset Maugham, and J. B. Priestley's *Eden End*) as well as the classics. In 1935, Broadway saw him for the first time, playing the Chorus and Mercutio in *Romeo and Juliet*, with Katharine Cornell as the Capulet heiress. A year later, back in London, he plunged into the title role of *The Amazing Dr. Clitterhouse*, a long-running thriller, in which he was supported by Meriel Forbes, who subsequently became — as she still is — his wife. Thus far, he was a thoroughly respected actor, versatile and dependable, yet somehow earthbound. Agate had written of 'his stolid, inexpressive mien, altogether admirable . . . in all delineations of the downright,' and the phrase epitomised what up to that point most playgoers felt about him. His stage persona, however, did not reflect the combustible *bizarrerie* of the man within.

Second Interlude: November 5, 1937 or 1938. (None of the surviving participants is quite sure of the year.) It is Guy Fawkes Day, on which the British let off fireworks to celebrate the discovery (and frustration) of a Catholic plot to blow up the Houses of Parliament. It is also Vivien Leigh's birthday. She and Olivier — as yet unmarried, because Olivier's divorce from his first wife, Jill Esmond, is not final — have moved into a tiny house in Chelsea. Miss Leigh has spent months and a great deal of money turning it into (Olivier's phrase) 'a perfect little bandbox,' full of costly trinkets, with a minuscule garden behind. Instead of giving a large house-warming party, they decide to invite only two old friends — Ralph Richardson and Meriel Forbes, the later known by the nickname of Mu. What follows is Sir Ralph's account of the festivity, as he recalled it for me last year: 'I took great trouble and care. I arrived at the house with Mu and a huge box of fireworks that I had bought with loving joy. I took the biggest rocket out into the garden — it was one of the kind you use to attract attention if your ship is sinking — and there I set it off. It came straight back into the dining room and burned up the curtains and set the pelmet on fire.' According to Olivier, it also wrecked a lot of priceless antique crockery and left him and Vivien, who were cowering behind the sofa, blackened about the face like Al Jolson. 'I knew that Vivien had taken great trouble with her decorations and that her pelmet was unpleasantly burned. But it was my *benevolence* that had caused it all. "Let's get out of here," I said to Mu. "These people don't understand us." I grabbed the doorknob, and through no fault of mine it came off in my hand. I have to admit that I was very hurt, next day, when nobody rang me up to say, "How kind of you, Ralph, to have thought of bringing those fireworks." '

Some years later, Sir Ralph mentioned to Olivier that he had given birth to a splendid idea for the National Theatre, should it ever come into being. Every night (he said), as the curtain went up, a synchronized rocket should rise from the roof of the theatre, to inform the populace that an event of national significance was about to take place. It would be known as Ralph's Rocket. This suggestion was adopted, and in March, 1976, when the

National Theatre finally moved into its new home, on the south bank of the Thames, the first rocket was duly launched. Sir Ralph himself lit the fuse.

It was not until 1944, after five wartime years spent as a pilot in the Fleet Air Arm, that Ralph Richardson's great period began. He outgrew his humility, burst the bounds of sobriety that had theretofore constrained him, and started to allow his fantasy free flight. 'He had always wanted to be a matinee idol,' Gielgud says, 'and felt inadequate because he couldn't be.' Or, as Barbara Jefford puts it, 'he was always a wonderfully flexible film performer — better in many ways than Gielgud or Olivier — but he never had the obvious good looks you expect of The Great Actor.' Now that he had entered his forties, this lack of physical glamour began to seem less important. He joined the revived Old Vic company, which was to be temporarily housed at the New Theatre, in the West End, since its original (and much humbler) home, south of the Thames, had been gutted by German bombs. Richardson shared the artistic directorship with Olivier and a promising newcomer named John Burrell, and launched the inaugural season, on August 31, 1944, by playing the title role in *Peer Gynt*. Tyrone Guthrie directed, with the assistance 'in grouping and movement' from Robert Helpmann, then at the height of his powers as dancer and choreographer. Sybil Thorndike, Margaret Leighton, and Olivier (in the small but spine-chilling part of the Button-Molder) were in the supporting cast; and Richardson, as the peasant who circumnavigates the globe in fruitless search of self-fulfillment, gave the most poetic performance of his life — volatile, obsessed, constantly surprising. (He has said that Peer Gynt, who is 'a little mad,' is his favourite part.) In the same season he played Bluntschli, the pragmatic soldier in Shaw's *Arms and the Man*; Richmond to Olivier's overwhelming Richard III; and Uncle Vanya in the tender, unsparing play of that name. In the autumn of 1945, he opened as Falstaff in both parts of Shakespeare's *Henry IV*. These were the productions that — coupled with those left over from the previous season, and augmented by the flabbergasting double bill in which Olivier played Sophocles' Oedipus and (after the intermission) Mr. Puff in Sheridan's *The Critic* — established the highwater mark of English acting in the twentieth century.

'Falstaff,' Sir Ralph wrote in 1960, 'proceeds through the plays at his own chosen pace, like a gorgeous ceremonial Indian elephant.' As an undergraduate at Oxford, I said of his performance, 'Here was a Falstaff whose principal attribute was not his fatness but his knighthood. He was Sir John first and Falstaff second.' I continued:

> The spirit behind all the rotund nobility was spry and elastic. . . .
> There was also, when the situation called for it, great wisdom and
> melancholy. ('Peace, good Doll! do not speak like a death's head: do
> not bid me remember mine end' was done with most moving

authority.') Each word emerged with immensely careful articulation, the lips forming it lovingly and then spitting it forth. In moments of passion, the wild white halo of hair stood angrily up and the eyes rolled majestically; and in rage one noticed a slow, meditative relish taking command . . . it was not a sweaty fat man, but a dry and dignified one. . . . He had good manners and also that respect for human dignity which prevented him from openly showing his boredom at the inanities of Shallow and Silence. . . . He was not often jovial, laughed seldom, belched never. . . . After the key-cold rebuke [from Prince Hal, once his fellow-boozer, now his monarch], the old man turned, his face red and working in furious *tics* to hide his tears. . . . 'I shall be sent for soon at night.'

But we know, of course, that he will not. Of the preceding scenes, lyrically comic, set in a twilit Gloucestershire orchard, where Falstaff basks in the sycophantic adulation of Justice Shallow (Olivier), a shrivelled drinking crony of his youth, I see no reason to revise what I wrote thirty years ago: 'If I had only half an hour more to spend in theatres, and could choose at large, no question but I would have these.' In the 1946-47 season, Sir Ralph's exuberant, opportunistic performances as Cyrano de Bergerac and Face, the scheming servant in Jonson's *The Alchemist*, set the seal on his new reputation. Always excepting Olivier, no actor in England was riding higher.

Third Interlude: The summer of 1946. Ralph and Meriel Richardson are motoring down to spend the weekend at Notley Abbey, in Buckinghamshire. The Oliviers have recently acquired the fifteenth-century abbot's lodge, and converted it, at ridiculous expense, into a stately home. Stopping his car on the brow of a hill that overlooks the abbey and its domain, Richardson turns to Mu and says (they both recall the exact words), 'I hope to God I don't put my foot in it this time.' Since the Chelsea holocaust, purely social contacts between the two couples have been limited — mainly because the war has kept them apart but also because of a lingering sense (on Mrs. Olivier's part) that there is something inherently hazardous, almost poltergeistic, about Richardson's presence.

The day passes sweetly. The guests are shown over the estate. Across a candlelit dinner table, good stories are told and plans made for the future of the Old Vic. Richardson conducts himself with extreme caution, a man walking on eggshells. Olivier talks of the abbey's history, and of some remarkably preserved frescoes painted by the monks on beams in the attic. Wouldn't the Richardsons (he suggests after dinner) like to come up and see them? Mu declines the invitation; her husband, the model guest, accepts. The men having left, the wives chat over their coffee. Mrs. Olivier feels obscurely uneasy, but after five, ten, fifteen minutes have passed without incident, she is ready to scoff at her qualms. At this moment, there is a prolonged splintering noise from above, followed by a colossal crash that makes the whole house shake. The women dash upstairs, where, in the main guest room, lovingly decorated under Mrs. Olivier's personal supervision, they find Richardson flat on his back and covered in plaster, on a bed that has collapsed under his weight. Above it there is a gaping hole in the ceiling, through which he has evidently fallen. It emerges that the attic has no floor and can be traversed only on narrow rafters. Olivier had brought a flashlight, with which he directed Richardson's attention to the paintings on the beams above their heads. Two versions exist of what happened next. According to Sir Ralph, 'Larry said to me, "Why don't you take a step back to see the pictures better?" ' Olivier denies this, saying, 'Ralph just whirled round in pure wonderment and toppled off.' At all events, Mrs. Olivier was seen to be foaming with rage, like a Cassandra whose prophecies of doom have gone unheeded.

'I felt pretty dogsbody, I can tell you,' Sir Ralph remarked to me later. At the time, he thought himself slightly more sinned against than sinning, but now he admits that his hostess had some cause to be upset. 'There was a rational basis to Vivien's fury, which we must salute,' he said to me the other day. 'If you prod a tigress twice in her lair, you must not expect her to purr.'

Knighted (along with Olivier) in 1947, his film career thriving, Sir Ralph was at his perihelion when, in a fit of collective paranoia, the governors of the Old Vic did an extraordinary thing. Fearing that the company had lost its identity as a people's theatre offering high art at low prices, and was in danger of becoming a gilded playground for West End stars, they fired the entire directorship at a stroke, without warning, in the middle of the 1948-49 season. 'We felt rather badly treated,' Sir Ralph told me years afterward, with the stoicism of hindsight, 'but a fired butler doesn't complain of his master.'

Burrell, Olivier, and Richardson were jobless overnight. It did not, of course, take them long to find other employment; but the three men, despite differences of temperament, had formed a spectacularly successful and cohesive team, like a jazz trio in which contrasting styles coalesce into a whole that is greater than the sum of its parts. The decision to axe them changed the course of theatrical history in England, and during the years that followed, Sir Ralph, bereft of the stimulation that group leadership can provide in the theatre (for the leaders no less than the led), sometimes looked a little lost. Something he said of his colleagues in the Fleet Air Arm may also apply to his co-directors at the Vic: 'They brought the best out of you by being so absolutely certain you'd got the best in you.' He continued, of course, to have his triumphs — as Peggy Ashcroft's glacially possessive Papa in *The Heiress* (adapted from Henry James's *Washington Square* and directed by Gielgud) and as Vershinin, the philosopher-philanderer in

Chekhov's *The Three Sisters*. But the creative interplay, the artistic checks and balances, the argumentative crosscurrents of the Old Vic days had gone forever. Thenceforward, Sir Ralph was on his own.

His plague year was 1952, in which he went to Stratford-upon-Avon to play Prospero, Macbeth, and Volpone, and failed in all three. He said himself, 'I don't know which was the worst.' The night I saw his Volpone, many of the lines eluded him, and replacements were smuggled in from other plays. At one point, he stunned his fellow actors by addressing them as 'Ye elves of hills, brooks, standing lakes, and groves,' and went on (since there was clearly no going back) to favour us with the rest of the famous speech from *The Tempest* which begins with that phrase. In 1953, having seen him in *The White Carnation*, a puny play by R. C. Sherriff, I wrote:

> He has taken to ambling across our stages in a spectral, shell-shocked manner, choosing odd moments to jump and frisk, like a man through whom an electric current is being intermittently passed.

The year 1956 brought us a most erratic *Timon of Athens*, containing 'gestures so eccentric that their true significance could be revealed only by extensive trepanning.' But even at his most aberrant he remained supremely watchable. Once the curtain had risen, you could never be sure (nor, it seemed at times, could he) what he would do next. A moment of pure dottiness might be followed by a flash of revelation. More and more, he was bringing the aura of his own private world onto the stage with him, like a glass bell with which to protect himself from the audience — for whom, in any case, he had never felt any overpowering fondness. 'I'm rather inclined,' he told a man from *The Guardian* last year, 'to think of them as a cage of bloody tigers that will bite you, and will put you out of the stage door if they can. . . . You must never let them command.' (Even the theatregoers of Brighton, to whose applause he had so often bowed during his apprenticeship, he described in 1975 as 'very dangerous.') A master of all the stratagems of self-protection, he has always been extremely wily if he suspects that an attempt is being made, in Hamlet's phrase, to pluck out the heart of his mystery. Not long ago, he and Gielgud were photographed by Jane Bown, of the London *Observer*. She had hardly arrived when Sir Ralph began to profess amnesia about his identity. 'The trouble is I can never remember who I am whenever I'm photographed. Who *am* I? I find I'm no one in particular.'

'However close you get to him, he's still distant,' Barbara Jefford says. 'In life and onstage, he has a kind of remote intimacy. When you're acting with him there's no eye contact. He never looks at you. and he never touches people onstage. I played his stepdaughter in *Six Characters in Search of an Author*, and there's a big scene where he's supposed to grope me. He never even touched me. And yet I'm told the audience got a very sensual impression from the whole scene.' The play was staged by the American director William Ball. Miss Jefford recalls, 'The most typical thing that Ralph did happened during rehearsals. One morning, Bill called the company together and said, "Today, I want us all to throw away our scripts and improvise our way through the play." Ralph didn't say a word. He was perfectly polite. He just quietly rose and left the room. Oh, he was *about*, he didn't leave the building, but he didn't come back to that room. He couldn't bear the thought of *exposing* himself like that.'

In 1964, as part of the festivities in honour of the quater-centenary of Shakespeare's birth, the British Council sent Sir Ralph on a tour of Mexico (his prenatal homeland), South America, and Europe, playing Shylock in *The Merchant of Venice* and Bottom in *A Midsummer Night's Dream*. Miss Jefford went along as Portia and Helena. Lady Richardson, although she had never before appeared in Shakespeare, decided at the last moment to volunteer her services as Titania. I saw *The Merchant* before it left England. It had a lot of very old-fashioned sets, with equally old-fashioned blackouts between scenes, and was memorable chiefly for Sir Ralph's physical appearance. He wore a bright yellow skullcap, set off by lurid green makeup, and he brandished what I took to be a shepherd's crook. 'He looks like the Demon King in a pantomime,' a junior member of the cast told me, with awe in his voice, before the performance. I paid a brief visit to Sir Ralph's dressing room afterward. When I asked about the shepherd's crook, he explained although he based his interpretation on the assumption that Shylock was 'a gent,' it was vital not to forget that 'the Jews were a race of nomadic shepherds.' He added, 'Shylock knows all about breeding sheep. Look at his speech abut Jacob and Laban and the ewes and the rams — typical piece of Shakespearean illumination.' The notion of a pastoral Shylock was something I was not quite ready for, and, as I remember, our conversation ended there. During the months that followed, however, I often thought of this strange, glaucous, eerily imposing apparition, and what the citizens of Lima or Buenos Aires must have made of it as it came looming at them over the Andes. Miss Jefford has vivid memories of Sir Ralph off duty during the three-month tour. 'In Latin America, he became intensely English, very much the squire, with a yellow waistcoat and a panama hat at a jaunty angle.' In another vignette, he is standing beside her in the wings, watching his wife — an excellent actress in modern roles — tackling Titania. 'She tries very hard,' he muses. 'But' — and here he mimes the gestures of a violinist — 'she hasn't got the *bowing*.'

He and Miss Jefford met in 1956 when they were at the Old Vic together, though not in the same plays. 'He was only in *Timon*, so I didn't know him at all, but one night he came to see me as Imogen in *Cymbeline*.

Next day, I got one of his beautiful little notes, written in exquisite script, so delicately arranged on the page, with wide, wide margins all covered with little sketches. He said that in the bedroom, when Iachimo creeps out of the trunk to examine me, he thought my *sleep* was especially convincing. Rather an odd tribute, considering that I didn't move a muscle throughout the scene. But I appreciated it.' A great Richardson fan, Miss Jefford concedes that he was below his best as Shylock. She says shrewdly, 'He's not good at portraying *mundane* sins and desires. There isn't enough poetry in Shylock for Ralph.' She agrees with me that he ought to have a crack at King Lear. There's no doubt that he would be heartbreaking in the final exchanges with Cordelia:

> We too alone will sing like birds i' the cage:
> When thou dost ask me blessing, I'll kneel down,
> And ask of thee forgiveness.

In these passages, Lear has fought his way through to a simplicity and an emotional sanity that lie on the far side of complexity and madness. (It is the early Lear, the capricious and egocentric despot of the opening scene, who is truly mad.) I have heard it objected that Sir Ralph lacks the vocal firepower for the 'Blow, winds, and crack your cheeks' aria on the storm-blasted heath; but the point, nearly always forgotten, about this speech is that Lear is not attacking the storm or trying to shout it down. Its fury confirms his misanthropy: *he is on its side.* Played thus (as I have yet to see it played), the speech would be well within Sir Ralph's compass.

At 5 p.m. on January 11, 1976, I visit Sir John Gielgud in his suite at the Drake Hotel in New York. My host is spruce, poker-backed, voluble, eyes wickedly gleaming — a lighthouse spraying words instead of candlepower. 'It's true that Ralph is wary about the audience,' Sir John says. 'He watches it like a hawk. Quite often he'll say to me, "Did you notice that man in the fifth row groping that girl during the second act?" ' We talk about *No Man's Land*: 'I always think that Hirst, the character Ralph plays, is very much like Hamm, the hero of Beckett's *Endgame* — a sort of tyrant who's dominated by his domestic staff. Did you know, by the way, that Larry wanted to play the part? I think Ralph is so marvellous in the second act, when he's doing his bland-clubman stuff. In some ways, he's the great successor to A. E. Matthews.' (Not, perhaps, the most overwhelming of tributes: Matthews, a brilliantly accomplished light comedian who went on acting into his eighties, was never regarded as a player of the first rank.) Since the two knights co-starred in *Home* seven years ago, they have been endlessly interviewed and photographed together, and are frequently mistaken for one another on the street. 'We're like the Broker's Men in *Cinderella*,' Gielgud says, referring to a pair of slapstick clowns in traditional English pantomime. For interview purposes, he and Sir Ralph have evolved what amounts to a double act, in which certain routines and catch phrases (including the one about the Broker's Men) ritually recur. There's usually a formal exordium, such as the following taken from the London *Observer* in October, 1975, during the West End run of *No Man's Land*:

> SIR RALPH: You're looking very well, by the way.
> SIR JOHN: Thank you.
> SIR RALPH: I haven't seen much of you lately.
> SIR JOHN: We meet in costume.
> SIR RALPH: We meet as other people.

These encounters, normally held in restaurants at lunchtime, seldom pass without providing opportunities for Sir Ralph, a fervent and mercurial gourmet, to leap into action. Here are three examples:

> I love bread so much; I want it to be taken out of my temptation. I have made a vow. I am going to give up my beautiful rolls. (*The Guardian*, November, 1976.)

> It has been my experience, in the past, that most of the wine served in American restaurants is cat's urine, disguised in French labels. (Luncheon with present writer, though without Gielgud, November, 1976.)

> SIR RALPH (*suddenly jumps, points to his plate dramatically. Waiters surround him*): What is THAT?
> SIR JOHN: I think it's a bit of liver, Ralph.
> SIR RALPH: Never touch it. Take the liver away. . . . Bear the offending liver away. (*The Observer*, October, 1975.)

This confirms what Gielgud now tells me — that Sir Ralph, though a superb host, is not a good guest. 'I eat out of tins, but Ralph always insists on the best.' From the same *Observer* interview, Gielgud recalls Sir Ralph's response when Peter Brook was mentioned as a director of world renown:

> SIR RALPH: What was that *terrible* production Brook did? . . . That *ghastly* thing. You were in it.

He was referring to Seneca's *Oedipus*, directed by Brook for the National Theatre, in which Gielgud played the protagonist. It was far from ghastly, at least in my opinion; I was working for the National at the time

and selected the play for its repertoire. I don't deny, however, that there
were unusual elements in Brook's staging, notably in his handling of the
chorus. Let Sir Ralph continue:

SIR RALPH: When I went to see the production, somehow I hadn't
got a programme. So I said to Mu, 'Leave it to me.' And I went
down the aisle to a chap, but he was lashed to a pillar. I didn't know
what was going on. It turned out that he was in the show. I think he
was one of the chorus. But the show hadn't started yet. Mu said, 'Did
you get a programme?' And I had to say it wasn't possible because
all the programme-sellers were lashed to the dress circle. Very
strange.

SIR JOHN: But what did the poor actor who was lashed to the pillar
say to you?

SIR RALPH: Well, of course, when I asked him for a programme all
I got were these strangled sounds. He was gagged, you see. The
whole experience upset me very much. I'm a very *square* man.

Gielgud first appeared with Sir Ralph in 1930, and has enormous respect
for his old confrere. 'He loves the craftsmanship of his art. He prepares his
work and exhibits it with the utmost finesse. It's like Edith Evans — she
used to open a window to her heart and then slam it shut, so that you'd
come back the next night to see more. My own tendency, on the other hand,
is always to show too much. Ralph says he never thinks anything he does is
a success. He doesn't even want to repeat his Falstaff. I wish he would; it's
his greatest performance. And he was wonderful as John Gabriel Borkman
at the National last year. I shall never forget the noise he made when
Borkman died. As if a bird had flown out of his heart.'

We sip white wine while Gielgud recalls Sir Ralph as he first knew him:
'He had a very unhappy early life as an actor. He used to walk with his
behind stuck out, and thought he was terribly unattractive to women. He
was very poor, and then there was his first wife's dreadful illness. But now
he's acquired such control of movement, such majesty. Of course, he does
have a violent side to his nature — a powerful sadistic streak, sudden
outbursts of temper. But you have to remember that he went through a
really wretched time before he was able to marry Mu.' Gielgud smiles.'He
used to expect her to be the perfect hostess during dinner, and then, after
coffee was served, to kick up her legs like a chorus girl. It must have been
difficult, at times, to reconcile those two demands.'

Fourth Interlude: 1:45 P.M. on November 11, 1976. Luncheon with Sir
Ralph at the Algonquin Hotel. He arrives late, bustling through the crowded
restaurant, moustache bristling, eyes moist with apology. We talk first about
the honorary D. Litt. he received from Oxford University in 1969. It was

bestowed by Harold Macmillan, the Chancellor of the University and former Prime Minister, who delivered a Latin oration. 'What he said, in essence, was that the gods have been graceful and lucky for you, and that we of this university wish to add to their smiling,' Sir Ralph says. When we have ordered, I ask Sir Ralph whom he would invite to an ideal dinner party, given free choice from the living and the dead. His list, like a good deal more about him, is highly idiosyncratic. 'Samuel Butler, demolisher of Victorian fathers. Robert Louis Stevenson. Joseph Conrad, provided that he admired Shakespeare. Scott of the Antarctic. And another explorer, Shackleton, to whom I'm distantly related. Einstein, definitely. And, above all, David Lloyd George, that rascally fellow-actor, that bandit, that saviour of our country, without whom Kaiser Bill might even now be walking through Buckingham Palace waxing his moustache.' Sir Ralph eats for a while in silence, apparently — and to my great relief — with pleasure. 'I've just been reading some of Freud's lectures. Amazing how these tiny little childhood things can have repercussions like the atomic bomb. I wouldn't mind having him at our dinner table. He had such a great sense of humour.' Another pause for for eating. 'I've always been intrigued by his picture of life — the sex down there, the caretaker up here. But I wouldn't put sex ace high, No. 1, the thing that winds up the whole clock. I think murder is more basic. Before you get the woman, you must kill the man who possesses her. Hunger is the first impulse of all. But then I must *possess* something. And then I must *enjoy* something. And that may involve destroying somebody else. For reasons of policy and politeness, of course, we put the brakes on.'

It is getting late, and the room has emptied. The waiters are laying tables for dinner. For a moment, Sir Ralph watches them. Then he says, 'I wouldn't mind running through this restaurant and smashing all those glasses. I see them glittering there.' A pause. 'One is putting the brakes on all the time.' While we wait for the check, his mind reverts to *No Man's Land*: 'Hirst is capable of murder, you know. I believe he was responsible for the drowning of a girl in a lake, although Mr. Pinter might not necessarily agree. He is certainly capable of killing Spooner. We all have original sin. Hirst has it. *I* have it.' Sir Ralph's eyes are blazing. As I escort the former altar boy (for such he was in his papist youth) to his limousine, he says, 'I would much rather be able to terrify than to charm. I like malevolence. What an enjoyable lunch.'

In September, 1975, Sir Ralph went on London Weekend Television and gave a sixty-minute interview by which (his finest stage performances apart) I would not mind remembering him. He was freewheeling and free-associating, seeming artless in his candour, yet laying artful diversionary smokescreens whenever anything central to his privacy appeared to be threatened. We were watching a master mesmerist. No great lover of publicity for its own sake, he had undertaken this chore at the behest of the

National Theatre, by whom he was currently employed. His interlocutor was Russell Harty, a dapper North Countryman, who runs the most popular chat show on the British commercial channel. The setting was the usual studio mockup — in this case, a semi-circular arrangement of window draperies with nothing behind it, and a low window seat and a pair of tulip-shaped chairs (one of them occupied by Harty) in front of it. A packed house applauded as Harty urged it to welcome 'one of the most distinguished actors in the British theatre.'

Sir Ralph enters around one side of the draperies, wearing a tweed suit, a pink satin tie, and bright-yellow socks. Instead of taking his expected place in the empty chair, he walks straight past it (and Harty) toward the audience, before whom he halts, bounteously beaming. He seems in a genial frame of mind. Cameras whirl round to keep him in shot, none too successfully.

> SIR RALPH (*to Harty, over his shoulder*): You've got a very nice place here, haven't you? It's a great deal bigger than my place, where you came to see me the other day.
> HARTY (*left high and dry, but keeping his cool*): Yes, but it's not as posh as yours.
> SIR RALPH: No, but you've got a lot more friends than I have.

In his voice we note a false bonhomie, as of a Dr. Watson — played, of course, by Nigel Bruce — behind whose slightly fatuous façade a canny, Holmeslike intelligence is at work.

> SIR RALPH: Are they friends of yours? Or are they enemies?
> HARTY: Well, we don't know.
> SIR RALPH: Shall I address them? Ladies and gentlemen of the jury, I assure you that this man Harty is innocent.

Who said he was guilty? Already Sir Ralph has taken control.

> SIR RALPH: You've got a lot more cameras in your place than I've got in mine. Cameras always make me rather nervous. They sort of prowl in on you. Of course, you know them. You probably feed them. What do they eat? Celluloid and chips?

Thus far, he has been strolling around inspecting the technology. He now wanders past Harty, still glued to his tulip, toward the window seat. On this he sits, and he peeps gently through the draperies at what we know perfectly well is the wall of the studio.

> SIR RALPH: I say, what a wonderful view you've got here! I mean,

you could see anything from here, couldn't you — the Tower of London, Buckingham Palace, the Post Office Tower? I'll bet you could.

Consenting at last to occupy a chair, Sir Ralph immediately begins to interview Harty, asking him about his past career and whether his parents have secure and pensionable jobs. Some times passes before Harty manages to sneak in a question about the Pinter play.

> SIR RALPH: There isn't any plot. But that never bothers an actor. And the characters are never really rounded off. They don't quite know who they are. But that's rather natural in a way. We don't know exactly who we are, do we? We hardly know anybody else, really completely. We none of us know when we're going to die. . . . We're a mystery to ourselves, and to other people.

He goes on to say that acting is never boring, because the audiences are always different.

> SIR RALPH: In music, the punctuation is absolutely strict, the bars and the rests are absolutely defined. But our punctuation cannot be quite strict, because we have to relate it to the audience. In other words, we are continually changing the score. . . . For me, what gives our work its special fascination is the challenge that has to do with time. If you're a writer or a painter, you write or paint whenever you want to. But we have to do this task at a precise moment. At three minutes past eight, the curtain goes up, and you've got to pretend to believe, because no one else will believe you unless you believe it yourself. A great deal of our work is simply making ourselves dream. That is the task. At three minutes past eight you must dream.
>
> HARTY: Do you dream when you go to bed?
>
> SIR RALPH: Yes, I dream a lot. I lead a fairly sheltered life. Things are fairly peaceful, and nobody tries to murder me much. . . . Fortunately, I am able to remember my nightmares. They help me in my work. When I'm asleep, I'm earning my living if I have a nightmare. I get murdered a good deal. I get stabbed quite a bit.

Harty suggests that Sir Ralph doesn't much like his own body. Conceding the point, Sir Ralph proposes that they might swap. Perhaps feeling cornered, he fires a sudden question at Harty: 'Do you hate your face?' Commendably unfazed, Harty replies that he hates not only his face but his name and his body from the waist down. 'Oh, really?' says Sir Ralph. 'I can't see anything the matter with it.' Harty now tries yet again to seize the initiative.

HARTY: I wondered whether you'd gone into acting because you weren't satisfied with your face or your body.

SIR RALPH (*not to be drawn*): There are lots of reasons why people become actors. Some to hide themselves, and some to show themselves. As for my face, I've seen better-looking hot cross buns.

Before long, Sir Ralph, back in the driver's seat, is asking Harty what kind of people he finds the easiest to talk to. Having given a long and honest answer, Harty reverses the question.

SIR RALPH: I like talking to engineers best. They build bridges, they're very precise, they're very disciplined, yet I find they have roving minds. They can talk about anything. My other favourite people are explorers and potholers. To *choose* to be brave is a great sign of character, I think. They have great accuracy, and also great fantasy.

Harty shows a clip from Sir Ralph's latest film, *Rollerball*, and afterward points out to the viewers that throughout the excerpt Sir Ralph busied himself with lighting his pipe and carefully averted his eyes from the screen. Emitting clouds of smoke, Sir Ralph resumes the questioning. Does Russell Harty like his own name? Harty says that he doesn't. Sir Ralph hastens to reassure him.

SIR RALPH: I think Russell Harty is a jolly decent name. . . . I'm very fond of Russell because half my family are Russells. My mother was a Russell, so I'm very used to the name. And I don't mind Richardson. I think it suits me, because it's rather plain.

Here he drifts off into free association, before the eyes of approximately twelve million viewers.

SIR RALPH: How weird it is, the way people's names seem to suit them — how they get a name and grow up to be like it. . . . Shakespeare, for instance — it's an arresting, an aggressive word. You can see the man. . . . And Velazquez — how the name suits the painter! It's a delicious sound; you can feel him laying on the paint, you could almost eat the paint itself. And Rembrandt — he's an old ruminative man, drawing old things with long memories. . . . But I tell you, I like the name Richardson, and I like the name Russell. . . .

HARTY: Are you viewing the prospect of old age with regret or happiness?

SIR RALPH: I'm amazed that I'm as old as I am. I always had the idea that when I was old I'd get frightfully clever. I'd get awfully learned, I'd get jolly sage. People would come to me for advice. But nobody every comes to me for anything, and I don't know a thing.

Later, as if it were a matter of trifling consequence, he remarks that he has 'never been particularly afraid of dying.' Finally, at Harty's gentle instigation, he goes to a lectern and brings their conversation to an end by reading Keats's 'To Autumn,' that being the season of the year.

As I watched, I remembered him, thirty years ago, as the dying Cyrano, sitting in a convent garden, with autumn leaves twirling and floating around him. Sir Ralph looked, even then, very odd, and absent minded, and solitary, and absurd, and noble, and desolate. When he spoke, he sounded at once defiant and merciful. There has always been in his voice a mixture of challenge and benison.

Like Gielgud, I wanted to see him again as Falstaff, a role of which W. H. Auden once wrote:

Falstaff never really does anything, but . . . the impression he makes on the audience is not of idleness but of infinite energy. He is never tired, never bored, and until he is rejected he radiates happiness as Hal radiates power, and this happiness without apparent cause, this untiring devotion to making others laugh becomes a comic image for a love which is absolutely self-giving.

Very delicately, Auden goes on to suggest nothing less than that Falstaff is a comic symbol of Jesus Christ. When the Christian God presents himself on earth, 'the consequence is inevitable,' as Auden points out. 'The highest religious and temporal authorities condemn Him as a blasphemer and a Lord of Misrule, as a Bad Companion for mankind.' Which, of course, is what happened to Falstaff. Quite apart from its fun and its lunatic grandeur, there was a charity about Sir Ralph's performance, a magnanimity and a grief, that made you wonder whether Auden's audacious hint might not be the simple truth, after all.

In fact, to take a step further, if a playwright were to revive the anthropomorphic conception of the deity and write a play about God himself, and if he were then to ask my help in picking an actor for the central role, I know exactly in which direction I would point him. I would find it entirely credible that the creator of the universe as we know it was someone very like Sir Ralph. This does not mean either that I accept the Christian hypothesis or that I approve of the current state of the world; but if we imagine its maker as a whimsical, enigmatic magician, capable of fearful blunders, sometimes inexplicably ferocious, at other times dazzling in his innocence and benignity, we are going to need an actor who can imply metaphysical attributes while remaining — to quote C. S. Lewis on God — 'a positive, concrete, and highly articulated character.' Someone, in short, who is at once unapproachable and instantly accessible. Sir Ralph's number, as I have said, is in the book.

The New Yorker: 21st February 1977;
Show People, 1980

TOM STOPPARD

In *Jumpers*, a play by Tom Stoppard, whose other works include *Rosencrantz and Guildenstern Are Dead*, *Travesties*, and *Dirty Linen*, a man carrying a tortoise in one hand and a bow and arrow in the other, his face covered with shaving cream, opens the door of his apartment. Standing outside is a police inspector bearing a bouquet of flowers. There is a perfectly rational explanation for this.

In *After Magritte*, a much shorter play by the same author, we learn that a one-legged blind man with a white beard, who may in fact have been a handicapped football player with shaving cream on his face, has been seen hopping, or perhaps playing hopscotch, along an English street, wearing striped pyjamas, convict garb, or possibly a West Bromwich Albion football jersey, waving with one arm a white stick, a crutch, or a furled parasol while carrying under the other what may have been a football, a wineskin, an alligator handbag, or a tortoise. (One of the characters, discounting the hypothesis that the man was blind, scornfully inquires whether it was a seeing-eye tortoise.) There is also a perfectly rational, though much longer, explanation for this.

In 'The Language of Theatre,' an address delivered by the same author in January, 1977, at the University of California at Santa Barbara, the lecturer began by stating that he was not going to talk about the language of theatre. ('That was just a device to attract a better class of audience,' he said, eying the spectators. 'I see it failed.') Instead — and among other things — he told a story about a man he knew who bought a peacock on impulse and, shortly afterward, while shaving in his pyjamas, observed the bird escaping from his country garden. Dropping his razor, he set off in pursuit and managed to catch the feathered fugitive just as it reached a main road adjoining his property. At that moment, a car flashed by, middle-aged husband at the wheel, wife at his side. For perhaps five seconds — *vrrooommm* — they caught sight of this perplexing apparition. Wife: 'What was that, dear?' Husband: 'Fellow in his pyjamas, with shaving cream all over his face and a peacock under his arm.' There was, as we know, a perfectly rational explanation. (Stoppard went on to say that several of his plays had grown out of images such as this. He added that when he tried the peacock anecdote out on the members of a literary society at Eton College, it was received in bewildered silence. He soon realised why: 'They all *had* peacocks.')

In none of the same author's plays will you find any reference to (or echo of, or scene derived from) the following singular, and partly equivocal, story. During the nineteen-thirties, there lived in Zlin — a town in Czechoslovakia that is now known as Gottwaldov — a middle-class physician named Eugene Straussler, who worked for a famous shoe company. Either he or his wife (nobody seems quite sure which) had at least one parent of Jewish descent. In any case, Dr. Straussler sired two sons, of whom the younger, Thomas, was born on July 3, 1937. Two years later, on the eve of the Nazi invasion of their homeland, the Strausslers left for Singapore, where they settled until 1942. The boys and their mother then moved to India. Dr. Straussler stayed behind to face the Japanese occupation. He died in a Japanese air raid, or in a prisoner-of-war camp, or on a Japanese prison ship torpedoed by the British (nobody seems quite sure which). In 1946, his widow married a major in the British Army, who brought the family back with him to England. The two Straussler scions assumed their stepfather's surname, which was Stoppard. Thomas, who claims to have spoken only Czech until the age of three, or possibly five and a half (he does not seem quite sure which), grew up to become, by the early 1970s, one of the two or three most prosperous and ubiquitously adulated playwrights at present bearing a British passport. (The other contenders are Harold Pinter, who probably has the edge in adulation, and Peter Shaffer, the author of *Equus*, whose strong point is prosperity.) There is no perfectly rational explanation for any of this. It is simply true.

Preliminary notes from my journal, dated July 24, 1976:
Essential to remember that Stoppard is an émigré. A director who has staged several of his plays told me the other day, 'You have to be foreign to write English with that kind of hypnotised brilliance.' An obvious comparison is with Vladimir Nabokov, whom Stoppard extravagantly admires. Stoppard said to me not long ago that his favourite parenthesis in world literature was this, from *Lolita*: 'My very photogenic mother died in a freak accident (picnic, lightning) when I was three.' He is at present adapting Nabokov's novel *Despair* for the screen; Rainer Werner Fassbinder, who commissioned the script, will direct. Stoppard loves all forms of wordplay, especially puns, and frequently describes himself as 'a bounced Czech.' Like many immigrants, he has immersed himself beyond the call of baptism in the habits and rituals of his adopted country. Nowadays, he is *plus anglais que les anglais* — a phrase that would please him, as a student of linguistic caprice, since it implies that his Englishness can best be defined in French. His style in dress is the costly-casual dandyism of London in the nineteen-sixties. According to his friend Derek Marlowe, who wrote the best-selling novel *A Dandy in Aspic*, 'Tom goes to some very posh places for his clothes, but he finds it hard to orchestrate all his gear into a sartorial unity. The effect is like an expensive medley.' (Told

of this comment, Stoppard protests to me that Marlowe is exaggerating. 'Derek,' he says, 'is a fantasist enclosed by more mirror than glass.') Because Stoppard has a loose, lanky build, a loose thatch of curly dark hair, liver tinted lips, dark, flashing eyes, and long, flashing teeth, you might mistake him for an older brother of Mick Jagger, more intellectually inclined than his frenetic sibling.

Stoppard often puts me in mind of a number in *Beyond the Fringe*, the classic English revue of the sixties, in which Alan Bennett, as an unctuous clergyman, preached a sermon on the text 'Behold, Esau my brother is an hairy man, and I am a *smooth* man.' The line accurately reflects the split in English drama which took place during (and has persisted since) this period. On one side were the hairy men — heated, embattled, socially committed playwrights, like John Osborne, John Arden, and Arnold Wesker, who had come out fighting in the late fifties. On the other side were the smooth men — cool, apolitical stylists, like Harold Pinter, the late Joe Orton, Christopher Hampton (*The Philanthropist*), Alan Ayckbourn (*The Norman Conquests*), Simon Gray (*Otherwise Engaged*), and Stoppard. Earlier this year, Stoppard told an interviewer from the London weekly *Time Out*, 'I used to feel out on a limb, because when I started to write you were a shit if you weren't writing about Vietnam or housing. Now I have no compunction about that. . . . *The Importance of Being Earnest* is important, but it says nothing about anything.' He once said that his favourite line in modern English drama came from *The Philanthropist*: 'I'm a man of no convictions — at least, I *think* I am.' In *Lord Malquist and Mr. Moon* (1966), Stoppard's only novel to date, Mr. Moon seems to speak for his author when he says, 'I distrust attitudes because they claim to have appropriated the whole truth and pose as absolutes. And I distrust the opposite attitude for the same reason.' Lord Malquist, who conducts his life on the principle that the eighteenth century has not yet ended, asserts that all battles are discredited. 'I stand aloof,' he declares, 'contributing nothing except my example.' In an article for the London *Sunday Times* in 1968, Stoppard said, 'Some writers write because they burn with a cause which they further by writing about it. I burn with no causes. I cannot say that I write with any social objective. One writes because one loves writing, really.' On another occasion, he defined the quality that distinguished him from many of his contemporaries as 'an absolute lack of certainty about almost anything.'

Seeking artistic precedents for this moral detachment, this commitment to neutrality, I come up with four quotations. The first is from Oscar Wilde:

A Truth in art is that whose contradictory is also true.

The second is from Evelyn Waugh's diary:

I . . . don't want to influence opinions or events, or expose humbug or anything of that kind. I don't want to be of service to anyone or anything. I simply want to do my work as an artist.

Then these, from John Keats's letters:

It struck me what quality went to form a Man of Achievement, especially in Literature, and which Shakespeare possessed so enormously — I mean *Negative Capability*, that is, when a man is capable of being in uncertainties, mysteries, doubts, without any irritable reaching after fact and reason. . . .

The only means of strengthening one's intellect is to make up one's mind about nothing — to let the mind be a thoroughfare for all thoughts, not a select party.

In Stoppard's case, 'negative capability' has been a profitable thoroughfare. When I asked him, not long ago, how much he thought he had earned from *Rosencrantz and Guildenstern Are Dead*, his answer was honestly vague: 'About — a hundred and fifty thousand pounds?' To the same question, his agent, Kenneth Ewing, gave me the following reply: '*Rosencrantz* opened in London in 1967. Huge overnight success — it stayed in the National Theatre repertory for about four years. The Broadway production ran for a year. Metro bought the screen rights for two hundred and fifty thousand dollars and paid Tom a hundred thousand to write the script, though the movie was never made. The play had a short run in Paris, with Delphine Seyrig as Gertrude, but it was quite a hit in Italy, where Rosencrantz was played by a girl. It did enormous business in Germany and Scandinavia and — oddly enough — Japan. On top of that, the book sold more than six hundred thousand copies in the English language alone. Up to now, out of *Rosencrantz* I would guess that Tom had grossed well over three hundred thousand pounds.'

And now, on this sunny Saturday afternoon, to Gunnersbury Park, in West London, where a cricket match is to be played. Cricket, to which I am addicted, is a pastime of great complexity and elegance. Shapeless and desultory to the outsider, it has an underlying structure that only the initiate perceives. At the international level, a match may last five days, end in a draw, and still be exciting. Cricket may seem to dawdle, to meander, to ramble off into amorphous perversity; but for all its vagaries and lapses into seeming incoherence there is, as in a Stoppard play, a perfectly rational explanation. Not surprisingly, Stoppard is a passionate fan of the game — an enslavement he shares with many British writers of the cool school. Generalisation: Cricket attracts artists who are either conservative or nonpolitical; e.g., P.G. Wodehouse, Terence Rattigan, Samuel Beckett,

Kingsley Amis, Harold Pinter, and Stoppard, all of them buffs who could probably tell you how many wickets Tich Freeman, the wily Kent spin bowler, took in his record-breaking season of 1928. Leftists, on the whole, favour soccer, the sport of the urban proletariat. It's hard to imagine Wesker, Arden, Trevor Griffiths, or the young Osborne (the middle-aged Osborne has swung toward right-wing anarchism and may well, for all I know, have taken up the quarterstaff) standing in line outside Lord's Cricket Ground. As a cricket-loving radical, I am an anomaly, regarded by both sides with cordial mistrust.

Today's game is an annual fixture: Mr. Harold Pinter's XI versus the *Guardian* newspaper's. The field, rented for the occasion, is impressively large, with a well-equipped pavilion, inside which at 2.30 P.M., the advertised starting time, both teams are avidly watching another match — England versus the West Indies — on television. Eight spectators, including two children and me, have turned up. The *Guardian* XI looks formidably healthy, featuring several muscular typesetters and the paper's industrial correspondent. The Pinter squad seems altogether less businesslike. To begin with, only nine of the players are present, the principal batsman having discovered on his arrival that he had left his contact lenses at home. Since he lives in an outlying northern suburb, the game may easily be over by the time he returns. Moreover, Skipper Pinter, inscrutable as always, discovers that he is unable to play at the last moment, thereby leaving his lads leaderless. Among the nine remaining are a somewhat bald fortyish publisher, a retired Chelsea football player, Pinter's teenage son Daniel (already a published poet, who has lately won a scholarship to Magdalen College, Oxford), and — by far the most resplendent, in gauntlets of scarlet leather and kneepads as blindingly white as Pitz Palu — Tom Stoppard, the team's wicketkeeper, who swears to me that he has not played cricket for over a year.

He asks me to take the place of the myopic batsman. I refuse, on the ground that I have no white flannels. Characteristically, Dandy Tom has brought a spare pair. I counter by pleading lack of practice, not having put bat to ball for roughly twenty years, and am grudgingly excused.

Many amateur cricket teams have specially designed ties; I learn from Stoppard that the Pinter outfit does not. 'But if it had,' he adds, alluding to the pauses for which Pinter's plays are famous, 'the club insignia would probably be three dots.' The *Guardian* XI, having torn itself away from TV and won the toss, has elected to bat first; it is time for the Pinter XI (reduced to IX) to take the field. Stoppard goes out, managing as he does so to drop a smoldering cigarette butt between kneepad and trousers. 'There may be a story here,' he calls back to me. ' "Playwright Bursts Into Flames at Wicket." '

Having no fast bowlers, who are the match-winning thunderbolts of cricket, the Pinter team is forced to rely on slow spinners of the ball, oblique and devious in their approach. To hazard an analogy: Pinter onstage is a masterly spinner, but his surrogates on the field, lacking his precision, are mercilessly bashed about by their opponents. The tough and purposeful *Guardian* team scores eighty-three runs, and the figure would be much higher if it were not for the elastic leaps and hair-trigger reflexes of Stoppard behind the stumps, where (in the role that approximates the catcher's in baseball) he dismisses no fewer than four of the enemy side. This leaves room for hope — though not for all that much, as we realise when the Pinter IX starts to bat. Its acting captain, the somewhat bald publisher, holds his own, scoring with occasional suave deflections, the picture of public-school unconcern; but the *Guardian* bowlers have muscle and pace, and wicket after wicket falls to their intimidating speed. The game is all but lost when Stoppard ambles in to bat, with the score at sixty and only two men to follow him. Within ten minutes, in classic style, he has driven three balls to the boundary ropes for four runs apiece. Six more graceful swipes bring his personal total to twenty, thereby making him the top scorer and winning the game for his side. He is welcomed back to the pavilion with cheers.

We repair to the riverside pub, where Skipper Pinter has just heard the news. Bursting with pride, he embraces Stoppard and buys expensive drinks for the whole team. He has been informed of certain crass errors made in the course of play, and sharply chides those responsible. It is like listening to Wellington if an attack of gout had kept him away from Waterloo. (Pinter's record commands respect: turning out every Saturday afternoon, he has a batting average that has seldom dipped below seventy, which is very high indeed.) In T-shirt and slacks, this sun-drenched evening, he looks dapper and superbly organised behind his thick horn-rimmed spectacles. Pinter has two basic facial expressions, which alternate with alarming rapidity. One of them, his serious mask, suggests a surgeon or a dentist on the brink of making a brilliant diagnosis. The head tilts to one side, the eyes narrow shrewdly, the brain seems to whirr like a computer. His stare drills into your mind. His face, topped by shiny black hair, is sombre, intent, profoundly concerned. When he smiles, however, it is suddenly and totally transformed. 'Smile' is really the wrong word: what comes over his face is unmistakably a *leer*. It reveals gleaming, voracious teeth, with a good deal of air between them, and their owner resembles a stand-up comic who has just uttered a none too subtle sexual innuendo. At the same time, the eyes pop and lasciviously swivel. There seems to be no halfway house between these two extremes, and this, as Pinter is doubtless aware, can be very disconcerting.

Pinter's absence from the field, which might have spelled disaster, has in fact made no difference at all, thanks to Stoppard's dashing performance. Where a lesser man might have been nettled, Pinter is genuinely delighted. Team spirit has triumphed: the leer is positively euphoric. Stoppard makes his farewells and departs leaving the skipper surrounded by disciples. One might, I suppose, discern a kind of metaphorical significance in the fact that while the top-ranking English playwright's back was turned the runner-up nipped in and seized the victor's crown. But, as Noël Coward said in *The Scoundrel*, I hate stooping to symbolism.

Back home after the match, I decided that for Stoppard art is a game within a game — the larger game being life itself, an absurd mosaic of incidents and accidents in which (as Beckett, whom he venerates, says in the aptly entitled *Endgame*) 'something is taking its course.' We cannot know what the something is, or whither it is leading us; and it is therefore impermissible for art, a mere derivative of life, to claim anything as presumptuous as a moral purpose or a social function. Since 1963, when the first professional performance of a script by Stoppard was given, he has written one novel, four full-length plays, one miniplay (*Dirty Linen*) that was cheekily passed off as a full-length entertainment, five one-acters for the stage, and ten pieces for radio or television. Thus far, only one of his performed works (*Jumpers*, to my mind his masterpiece, which was first produced in 1972) could be safely accused of having a moral or political message; but the critics are always sniffing for ulterior motives — so diligently that Stoppard felt it necessary to announce in 1974, 'I think that in future I must stop compromising my plays with this whiff of social application. They must be entirely untouched by any suspicion of usefulness. I should have the courage of my lack of convictions.' In another interview, he said he saw no reason that art should not concern itself with contemporary social and political history, but added that he found it 'deeply embarrassing ... when, because art takes notice of something important, it's claimed that the art is important. It's not.' Hating to be pinned down, politely declining to be associated with the opinions expressed by his characters, he has often remarked, 'I write plays because dialogue is the most respectable way of contradicting myself.' (Many of his apparent impromptus are worked out beforehand. Himself a onetime journalist, he makes a habit of anticipating questions and prefabricating effective replies. Indeed, such was his assurance of eventual success that he was doing this long before any-one ever interviewed him. When he read the printed result of his first con-versation with the press, he said he found it 'very déjà vu.' Clive James, the Australian critic and satirist, now working in London, has rightly described him as 'a dream interviewee, talking in eerily quotable sentences whose English has the faintly extraterritorial perfection of a Conrad or a Nabokov.')

Philosophically, you can see the early Stoppard at his purest in *Lord Malquist and Mr. Moon*, which sold only four hundred and eighty-one copies in 1966, when it was published. Malquist says:

> Nothing is the history of the world viewed from a suitable distance. Revolution is a trivial shift in the emphasis of suffering; the

capacity for self-indulgence changes hands. But the world does not alter its shape or its course. The seasons are inexorable, the elements constant. Against such vast immutability the human struggle takes place on the same scale as the insect movements in the grass, and carnage in the streets is no more than the spider-sucked husk of a fly on a dusty window-sill.

Later, he adds, 'Since we cannot hope for order, let us withdraw with style from the chaos.'

When Moon, his biographer and a professed anarchist, attacks Malquist's antihumanism on the ground that whatever he may say, the world is made up of 'all *people*, isn't it?' Malquist scoffs:

> What an extraordinary idea. People are not the world, they are merely a recent and transitory product of it. The world is ten million years old. If you think of that period condensed into one year beginning on the first of January, then people do not make their appearance in it until the thirty-first of December; or to be more precise, in the last forty seconds of that day.

Such trivial latecomers sound barely worth saving.

Though Stoppard would doubtless deny it, these pronouncements of Malquist's have a ring of authority which suggests the author speaking. They reflect a world view of extreme pessimism, and therefore conservatism. The pessimist is necessarily conservative. Maintaining, as he does, that mankind is inherently and immutably flawed, he must always be indifferent or hostile to proposals for improving human life by means of social or political change. The radical, by contrast, is fundamentally an optimist, embracing change because he holds that human nature is perfectible. The Malquist attitude, whatever its virtues, is hardly conducive to idealism. I recall a conversation with Derek Marlowe about Stoppard's private beliefs. 'I don't think,' Marlowe said, 'that there's anything he would go to the guillotine for.' I found the choice of instrument revealing. We associate the guillotine with the decapitation of aristocrats. Marlowe instinctively identified Stoppard with the nobility rather than the mob — with reaction rather than revolution.

• •

There are signs, however, that history has lately been forcing Stoppard into the arena of commitment. Shortly after I wrote the above entry in my journal, he sent me a typescript of his most recent work. Commissioned by André Previn, who conducts the London Symphony Orchestra, it is called *Every Good Boy Deserves Favour* — a mnemonic phrase familiar to students of music, since the initial letters of the words represent, in ascending order, the notes signified by the black lines of the treble clef. Involving six actors (their dialogue interspersed with musical contributions from Mr. Previn's big band), it had its world première in July, 1977, at the Royal Festival Hall, in London. It started out in Stoppard's mind as a play about a Florida grapefruit millionaire, but his works have a way of changing their themes as soon as he sits down at his typewriter. The present setting is a Russian mental home for political dissidents, where the main job of the staff is to persuade the inmates that they are in fact insane. What follows is a characteristic exchange between a recalcitrant prisoner named Alexander and the therapist who is assigned to him:

> PSYCHIATRIST: The idea that all the people locked up in mental hos-
> pitals are sane while the people walking about outside are all mad is
> merely a literary cliché, put about by the people who should be locked
> up. I assure you there's not much in it. Taken as a whole, the sane are
> out there and the sick are in here. For example, *you* are here because
> you have delusions that sane people are put in mental hospitals.
> ALEXANDER: But I *am* in a mental hospital.
> PSYCHIATRIST: That's what I said.

Alexander, of course, refuses to curry Favour by being a Good Boy. Beneath its layers of Stoppardian irony, the play (oratorio? melodrama?) is a point-blank attack on the way in which Soviet law is perverted to stifle dissent. In the script I read, Alexander declares, at a moment of crisis, 'There are truths to be shown, and our only strength is personal example.' Stoppard, however, had crossed this line out, perhaps being reluctant to put his name to a platitude, no matter how true or relevant it might be. Simplicity of thought — in this piece, as elsewhere in his work — quite often underlies complexity of style. *E.G.B.D.F.* rests on the assumption that the difference between good and evil is obvious to any reasonable human being. What else does Stoppard believe in? For one thing, I would guess, the intrinsic merits of individualism; for another, a universe in which everything is relative, yet in which moral absolutes exist; for a third, the probability that this paradox can be resolved only if we accept the postulate of a presiding deity. In 1973, during a public discussion of his plays at the Church of St. Mary Le Bow, in London, he told his interlocutor, the Reverend Joseph McCulloch:

> The whole of science can be said, by a theologian, to be operating
> within a larger framework. In other words, the higher we penetrate
> into space and the deeper we penetrate into the atom, all it shows to a
> theologian is that God has been gravely underestimated.

Nietzsche once said that convictions were prisons — a remark that the younger Stoppard would surely have applauded. Later, I shall try to chart the route that has led Stoppard, the quondam apostle of detachment, to the convictions he now proclaims, and to his loathing for the strictly unmetaphorical prisons in which so many people he respects are at present confined.

Stoppard's childhood was full of enforced globe-trotting. Much of it was spent on the run from totalitarianism, of both the European and the Oriental variety. By the time he was five years old, he had moved from his Czechoslovakian birthplace to Singapore and thence — with his mother and elder brother — to India. His father, as we have seen, stayed in Singapore, where he died in circumstances that remain obscure. (Not long ago, I asked Stoppard why this question, like that of the family's Jewish background, could not be cleared up by his mother, who, together with his stepfather, nowadays lives in the Lake District. 'Rightly or wrongly, we've always felt that she might want to keep the past under a protective covering so we've never delved into it,' he said. 'My father died in enemy hands, and that's that.') Stoppard attended a multiracial, English-speaking school in Darjeeling. There his mother managed a shoe store and met Major Kenneth Stoppard, of the British Army in India, whom she married in 1946. By the end of the year, Major Stoppard had brought his new family back to England. Demobilised, he prospered as a salesman of machine tools, and Tom went through the initial hoops of a traditional middle-class education. From a preparatory boarding school in Nottinghamshire he moved on to 'a sort of minor public school' in Yorkshire. He summed up his extracurricular activities for me in a recent letter:

> I wrote a play about Charles I when I was twelve. It was surprisingly conventional: he died in the end. I edited no magazines but I did debate. I remember being completely indifferent as to which side of any proposition I should debate on.

In 1954, aged seventeen, he left school to live with his family in the West Country port of Bristol, where they had settled a few years earlier. He bypassed higher education and plunged into local journalism, first at the *Western Daily Press* and later at the Bristol *Evening World*, in a variety of posts, including those of news reporter, humorous columnist, feature writer, and reviewer of plays and films. For a while, although he was unable to drive, he held down the job of motoring correspondent on the *Daily Press*. ('I used to review the upholstery,' he says.) He rejoiced in the life of a newspaperman, relished 'the glamour of flashing a press card at flower shows,' and had no higher ambition than to make a gaudy mark in Fleet Street. He did not contemplate becoming a playwright until the late nineteen-fifties, when a new breed of English authors, led by John Osborne, began to assert themselves at the Royal Court Theatre, in London. Simultaneously, a new breed of actors emerged, to interpret their work. One

of the latter, the then unknown Peter O'Toole, joined the Bristol Old Vic —
probably the best of Britain's regional repertory companies — and in the
course of the 1957-58 season he played a series of leading parts, among
them the title role in *Hamlet* and Jimmy Porter in Osborne's *Look Back in
Anger*. (This was the unique and original O'Toole, before he submitted his
profile to surgical revision, which left him with a nose retroussé and anonymous enough to satisfy the producer of *Lawrence of Arabia*.) Years later, at
a seminar in California, a student asked Stoppard, 'Did you get into the
theatre by accident?' 'Of course,' he said innocently. 'One day, I tripped
and fell against a typewriter, and the result was *Rosencrantz and Guildenstern*.' In reality, it was O'Toole's blazing performances — and the plays
they adorned in Bristol — that turned Stoppard on to theatre. By the end of
the season, he was incubating a new vocation.

Meanwhile, he stuck to journalism, writing two columns (both
pseudonymous) in every issue of the *Daily Press*. 'They became a bit tiring
to read, because they were a little too anxious to be funny,' he says nowadays. 'At the time, I was desperate to be printed in *Punch*. I was over-
extended.' During this period, Bristol was a seedbed of theatrical talent.
Geoffrey Reeves, who directed the first performance of *After Magritte* and
collaborated with Peter Brook on several of the latter's productions, was
then a research student in Bristol University's Drama Department. He
recalls Stoppard as 'a cynical wit in a mackintosh, one of the very few
sophisticated journalists in town — though I would never have thought of
him as a potential playwright.' Peter Nichols (the author of *A Day in the
Death of Joe Egg*) and Charles Wood (who wrote the screenplays of *The
Knack*, *How I Won the War*, and *The Charge of the Light Brigade*) were
both growing up in Bristol when Stoppard was there. Wood remembers
Stoppard as 'a sort of Mick Jaggerish character, who wrote some rather
unfunny newspaper columns,' and adds, 'He wasn't a part of our world.'
Nichols's recollections are similarly tinged with waspishness: 'Tom was a
great figure in Bristol, to be mentioned with bated breath. His comings and
goings were reported as if he were Orson Welles.' When Nichols told me
this, he had just returned from Minneapolis, where one of Stoppard's works
was being performed. With a glint of malice in his voice, he continued,
'Tom is very big in Minneapolis. Unlike a lot of modern British drama, his
stuff travels well. No rough edges on Tom. None of those awkward local
references. There never were.' During the nineteen-sixties, Stoppard's
Rosencrantz and Guildenstern, Wood's *H* (a chronicle of the Indian Mutiny
of 1857), and Nichols's *The National Health* were all to be presented at the
National Theatre, thereby provoking rumours of a Bristolian conspiracy to
dominate British drama. *H*, stunningly written but structurally a mess, was a
box-office failure; the Nichols play, in which a hospital ward symbolised
the invalid state of the nation, had a great success with British audiences;
but Stoppard's was the runaway smash, at home and abroad, with critics

and the public alike.

His career as a playwright began in 1960, when he wrote a one-act piece called *The Gamblers*, which he described to me in a recent letter as '*Waiting for Godot* in the death cell — prisoner and jailer — I'm sure you can imagine the rest.' (It was staged in 1962 by Bristol University undergraduates, and has never been revived.) Later in 1960, he spent three months writing his first full-length play, *A Walk on the Water*. It was so weightily influenced by Arthur Miller and by Robert Bolt's *Flowering Cherry* that he has come to refer to it as 'Flowering Death of a Salesman.' He said in 1974 that, although it worked pretty well onstage, 'it's actually phony because it's a play written about other people's characters — they're only real because I've seen them in other people's plays.' A few years afterward, indulging in his hobby of self-contradiction, he told a group of drama students, 'What I like to do is take a stereotype and betray it, rather than create an original character. I never try to invent characters. All my best characters are clichés.' This is Stoppard at his most typical, laying a smoke screen designed to confuse and ambush his critics. Run the above statements together and you get something like this: 'It's wrong to borrow other writers' characters, but it's all right as long as they're clichés.' *A Walk on the Water* is about George Riley, a congenital self-deceiver who declares roughly once a week that he is going to achieve independence by leaving home and making his fortune as an inventor. Never having won more bread than can be measured in crumbs, he is entirely dependent — for food, shelter, and pocket money — on his wife and their teenage daughter, both of whom are wearily aware that, however bravely he trumpets his fantasies of self-sufficiency in the local pub, he is sure to be back for dinner. For all his dottiness (among his inventions are a pipe that will stay perpetually lit provided it is smoked upside down and a revolutionary bottle opener for which, unfortunately, no matching bottle top exists), Riley has what Stoppard describes as 'a tattered dignity.' This attribute will recur in many Stoppard heroes, who have nothing to pit against the hostility of society and the indifference of the cosmos except their obstinate conviction that individuality is sacrosanct. C. W. E. Bigsby says in a perceptive booklet he wrote on Stoppard for the British Council:

> While it is clear that none of his characters control their own destiny . . . it is equally obvious that their unsinkable quality, their irrepressible vitality and eccentric persistence, constitute what Stoppard feels to be an authentic response to existence.

The first performance of *A Walk on the Water* (and the first professional production of any Stoppard play) was given on British commercial television in 1963. Considerably rewritten, and retitled *Enter a Free Man*, it was staged in the West End five years later, when *Rosencrantz and*

Guildenstern had established Stoppard's reputation. Both versions of the text are indebted not only to Miller and Bolt but to N. F. Simpson (the whimsical author of *One Way Pendulum*, a gravely surreal farce that contains a character whose ambition is to train a team of speak-your-weight machines to sing the 'Hallelujah Chorus'), and both pay respectful homage to P. G. Wodehouse and to British music-hall comedy, especially in exchanges between Riley and saloon-bar companion named Brown. In one of these, Riley insists that Thomas Edison was the inventor of the light-house. Brown, anxious to avoid a row, hints at the probably source of his friend's misapprehension by gently singing the opening lines of the well-known folk song: 'My father was the keeper of the Eddystone light and he met a mermaid one fine night.' This causes 'a terrible silence,' after which:

> RILEY: Your father was what?
> BROWN: Not my father.
> RILEY: Whose father? . . . Whose father was a mermaid?
> BROWN: He wasn't a mermaid. He *met* a mermaid.
> RILEY: Who did?
> BROWN: This man's father.
> RILEY: Which man's father?
> BROWN (*testily*): I don't know.
> RILEY: I don't believe you, Jones.
> BROWN: Brown.
> RILEY: This is just sailors' talk, the mythology of the seas. There are no such things as mermaids. I'm surprised at a grown man like you believing all that superstitious rubbish. What your father saw was a sea lion.
> Brown: My father didn't see a sea lion!
> Riley (*topping him*): So it *was* your father!

Both scripts are flawed by a running gag that the passage of time has tripped up. The invention that is supposed to demonstrate Riley's invincible stupidity beyond all doubt — viz., an envelope with gum inside and out, so that it can be used twice — has since been widely adopted as an efficient method of sending out bills. (Hazards of this kind are endemic to humorists who mistrust the march of science. Cf. the English wit J. B. Morton, who convulsed his readers in the nineteen-thirties by predicting the advent of an electric toothbrush.) Wherever the 1968 text differs from the original, the changes are for the better, as witness the addition of Riley's crowning fancy — a device that supplies indoor rain for indoor plants. From Stoppard's deletions, however, we learn something crucial about the nature and the limitations of his talent.

'Tom cares more about the details of writing than anyone else I know,' Derek Marlowe told me. 'He's startled by the smallest minutiae of life.

He'll rush out of a room to make a note of a phrase he's just heard or a line that's just occurred to him. But the grand events, the highs and lows of human behaviour, he sees with a sort of aloof, omniscient amusement. The world doesn't impinge on his work, and you'd think after reading his plays that no emotional experience had ever impinged on his world. For one thing, he can't create convincing women. His female characters are somewhere between playmates and amanuenses. He simply doesn't understand them. He has a dual personality, like the author of *Alice in Wonderland*. His public self is Charles Dodgson — he loves dons, philosophers, theorists of all kinds, and he's fascinated by the language they use. But his private self is Lewis Carroll — reclusive, intimidated by women, unnerved by emotion.'

Geoffrey Reeves agrees with this analysis: 'However abstract Beckett may seem, he always gives you a gut reaction. But Tom hasn't yet made a real emotional statement.'

This is not to say that he hasn't tried. In the telecast of *A Walk on the Water*, as in the stage version, Riley's daughter is horrified to discover that her lover, whom she thought to be unmarried, has a wife. Before the play reached the theatre, however, Stoppard excised the following outburst, addressed by the girl to her mother:

> He said he loved me. Loved me enough to have me on the side, didn't he? For his day off. . . . I asked him if he'd meant it, about loving me, really, and he said, he liked me a lot. It's murder. . . . If I was king, I'd hang people for that. Everybody saying they love each other when they only like each other a lot — they'll all be *hung* and there'll be no one left except hangmen, and all of them will say how they love each other when they only like each other a lot, until there's only one left, and he'll say — That's everybody, king, except me, your only true and loving hangman. And I'll say, you don't love me, you only like me a lot, and I'll *hang* him, and I'll be king, and I'll like myself a lot.

There was more in that vein, which playgoers were luckily spared. Not long ago, I asked Stoppard what he thought of Marlowe's charge that his plays failed to convey genuine emotion. He reflected for a while and then replied, 'That criticism is always being presented to me as if it were a membrane that I must somehow break through in order to grow up. Well, I don't see any special virtue in making my private emotions the quarry for the statue I'm carving. I can do that kind of writing, but it tends to go off, like fruit. I don't like it very much even when it works. I think that sort of truth-telling writing is as big a lie as the deliberate fantasies I construct. It's based on the fallacy of naturalism. There's a direct line of descent from the naturalistic theatre which leads you straight down to the dregs of bad

theatre, bad thinking, and bad feeling. At the other end of the scale, I dislike
Abstract Expressionism even more than I dislike naturalism. But you asked
me about expressing emotion. Let me put the best possible light on my
inhibitions and say that I'm waiting until I can do it well.' And what of
Marlowe's comment that he didn't understand women? 'If Derek had said
that I don't understand *people*, it would have made more sense.'

(A word on Stoppard and women. It is felt by some of his friends that his
sexual ambitions, compared with his professional ambitions, have always
been modest. He has been twice married. He met his first wife, a nurse
called Jose Ingle, in London in 1962; Derek Marlowe remembers her as
being 'svelte and sun-tanned.' Their marriage produced two sons, who bear
the Dickensian names of Oliver and Barnaby. But the dramatic change in
Stoppard's way of life that followed the triumph of *Rosencrantz and
Guildenstern* in 1967 was more than Jose could cope with, and that familiar
show-business phenomenon — severance from the pre-success partner —
took its sad accustomed course. According to one observer, 'Jose was a
feminist before her time, and she got bloody-minded about being overshadowed by Tom.' Divorce proceedings began when Stoppard left home,
in 1970. Shortly afterward, he set up house with Miriam Moore-Robinson, a
dark-haired pouter pigeon of a girl, buxom and exuberantly pretty, whom
he had known, on and off, for about four years, and whose marriage to a
veterinary surgeon was already at the breaking point. Miriam was the same
age as Stoppard, and her ancestry included a Jewish grandparent who was
born in Czechoslovakia. A qualified doctor, she worked for a
pharmaceutical company that specialised in birth-control research, and has
gone on to become its managing director. She has also made vivacious
appearances on popular-science programmes on British TV, answering
questions on biology, zoology, and sex. Since 1972, when she and Stoppard
were married, she has given him two more sons, William and Edmund. In
matters of emotion, Stoppard is one of nature's Horatios; you could never
call him passion's slave, or imagine him blown off course by a romantic
obsession. He thrives in the atmosphere of a family nest. 'I can't work away
from domestic stability,' he once told me.)

To revert to chronology: In 1960, the text of *A Walk on the Water* landed
on the desk of Kenneth Ewing, the managing director of a newly formed
script agency, which now represents such writers as Michael Frayn, Charles
Wood, Adrian Mitchell, and Anthony (*Sleuth*) Shaffer. Ewing sent Stoppard
an encomiastic letter; the two men lunched in London; and Ewing has ever
since been Stoppard's agent. 'When I first met him, he had just given up his
regular work as a journalist in Bristol, and he was broke,' Ewing says. 'But
I noticed that even then he always travelled by taxi, never by bus. It was as
if he knew that his time would come.' In 1962, Stoppard heard that a new
magazine called *Scene* was about to be launched in London; he applied for
a job on the staff and was offered, to his amazement, the post of drama

critic, which he instantly accepted. He then left Bristol for good and took an apartment in Notting Hill Gate, a dingy West London suburb. Derek Marlowe lived in the same dilapidated house. 'Tom wrote short stories, and smoked to excess, and always worked at night,' Marlowe recalls. 'Every evening, he would lay out a row of matches and say, "Tonight I shall write twelve matches" — meaning as much as he could churn out on twelve cigarettes.' *Scene* made its debut early in 1963. Virulently trendy in tone and signally lacking in funds, it set out to cover the whole of show business. In seven months (after which the money ran out and *Scene* was no longer heard from), Stoppard reviewed a hundred and thirty-two shows. Years later, in a sentence that combines verbal and moral fastidiousness in a peculiarly Stoppardian way, he explained why he thought himself a bad critic: 'I never had the moral character to pan a friend — or, rather, I had the moral character never to pan a friend.'

Since the magazine was ludicrously understaffed, he filled its pages with dozens of pseudonymous pieces, most of which he signed 'William Boot.' The name derives from Evelyn Waugh's novel *Scoop*, in which William Boot is the nature columnist of a national newspaper who, owing to a spectacular misunderstanding, finds himself shipped off to cover a civil war in Africa. (As things turn out, he handles the assignment rather well.) Boot took root in Stoppard's imagination, and soon began to crop up in his plays, often allied to or contrasted with a complementary character called Moon. As a double act, they bring to mind Lenin's famous division of the world into 'Who' and 'Whom' — those who do and those to whom it is done. In Stoppard's words, 'Moon is a person to whom things happen. Boot is rather more aggressive.' Early in 1964, BBC radio presented two short Stoppard plays entitled *The Dissolution of Dominic Boot* and *M Is for Moon Among Other Things*. The leading characters in *The Real Inspector Hound* (1968) are named Birdboot and Moon. Apropos of the eponymous heroes of *Rosencrantz and Guildenstern*, the English critic Robert Cushman has rightly said:

> Rosencrantz, being eager, well-meaning, and consistently oppressed or embarrassed by every situation in which he finds himself, is clearly a Moon; Guildenstern, equally oppressed though less embarrassed and taking refuge in displays of intellectual superiority, is as obviously a Boot.

Cushman once asked Stoppard why so many of his characters were called Moon or Boot. Stoppard crisply replied that he couldn't help it if that was what their names turned out to be. 'I'm a Moon, myself,' he went on. 'Confusingly, I used the name Boot, from Evelyn Waugh, as a pseudonym in journalism, but that was because Waugh's Boot is really a Moon, too.' Having thus befogged his interviewer, he added a wry etymological touch.

'This is beginning to sound lunatic,' he said.

In 1964, a cobbler sticking to his last, Stoppard wrote a ninety-minute TV play called *This Way Out with Samuel Boot*, which he equipped with a *pair* of Boots, who represent diametrically opposed attitudes toward material possessions. Samuel Boot, a fortyish man of evangelical fervour, preaches the total rejection of property. Jonathan, his younger brother, is a compulsive hoarder of objects, unable to resist mail-order catalogues, who fills his home with items bought on credit which are constantly being repossessed, since he never keeps up the payments. ('It's like Christmas in a thieves' kitchen,' Samuel cries, surveying a room stacked with vacuum cleaners, goggles, filing cabinets, miners' helmets, boomerangs, knitting machines, miniature Japanese trees, and other oddments.) At one point, a salesman comes to deliver a hearing aid for a week's free trial. Having fitted the device into Jonathan's ear, he shouts into the box, 'There! That's better, isn't it?' 'You don't have to shout,' says Jonathan sharply. 'I'm not deaf.' He demands to know who told the salesman that he suffered from this infirmity.

> SALESMAN: It was an assumption.
> JONATHAN: If I told you I'd got a wooden leg, would you assume I was one-legged?
> SALESMAN: Yes.
> JONATHAN: Well, I have. And you may have noticed I'm wearing skis. You seem to be making a lot of nasty assumptions here. You think I'm a deaf cripple.

This *reductio ad absurdum* is pure Stoppard. An unreasonable man uses rational arguments to convince a reasonable man that he (the latter) is irrational. The salesman flees in panic, but Jonathan still has the hearing aid. Though both brothers are Boots by name, Samuel turns out to be a Moon by nature. He ends up defeated by his own innocence. When he claims to have found an exit from the commercial rat race, Jonathan brutally demolishes his dream:

> There's no out. You're in it, so you might as well fit. It's the way it is. Economics. All this stuff I've got . . . people have been paid to make it, drive it to the warehouse, advertise it, sell it to me, write to me about it, and take it away again. They get paid, and some of them buy a carpet with the money. [He has just had a carpet repossessed.] That's the way of it and you're in it. There's no way out with Samuel Boot.

Jonathan has a vast collection of trading stamps. Samuel steals them and holds a public meeting at which he proposes to give them away. He is mobbed and killed by a crowd of rapacious housewives. 'He died of people,' says one of his disciples, a young deserter from the army. 'They trod on him.' To this, Jonathan replies, 'That's what it is about people. Turn round and they'll tread on you. Or steal your property.' The deserter delivers Samuel's epitaph:

> He was a silly old man, and being dead doesn't change that. But for a minute . . . his daft old crusade, like he said, it had a kind of dignity.

Whereupon he picks up, as a souvenir of Jonathan's acquisitive way of life, a newly delivered vacuum cleaner. Rising to the defence of property, Jonathan shoots him dead with a mail-order harpoon gun.

Samuel Boot is patchily brilliant, an uneasy blend of absurdist comedy and radical melodrama. I have dwelt on it because (a) it is the last Stoppard play with a message (i.e., property is theft) that could be described as leftist, and (b) it is one of the few Stoppard scripts that have never been performed in any medium. Kenneth Ewing offered it to a London commercial-TV company and took Stoppard with him to hear the verdict. It was negative. 'Stick to theatre,' he advised his dejected client on the way back. 'Your work can't be contained on television.' Then Ewing's thoughts moved to Shakespeare, and for no reason that he can now recall, he brought up a notion he had long cherished about *Hamlet*. Quoting the speech in which Claudius sends Hamlet to England with a sealed message (borne by Rosencrantz and Guildenstern) enjoining the ruler of that country to cut off Hamlet's head, Ewing said that in his opinion the King of England at the time of their arrival might well have been King Lear. And, if so, did they find him raving mad at Dover? Stoppard's spirits rose, and by the time Ewing dropped him off at his home he had come up with a tentative title: *Rosencrantz and Guildenstern at the Court of King Lear*. A seed had clearly been planted. It pleases Ewing to reflect that agents are not necessarily uncreative.

In the spring of 1964, the Ford Foundation awarded grants to four British playwrights (or would-be playwrights) enabling them to spend six months in West Berlin. The senior member of the chosen quartet was James Saunders, then thirty-nine years old and very much in vogue as the author of *Next Time I'll Sing to You*, a lyrical-whimsical play that seemed to some critics anaemic and to others a near-masterpiece. The remaining grants went to Derek Marlowe, Piers Paul Read (son of Sir Herbert, the illustrious poet and critic), and Stoppard, an avowed admirer of Saunders, by whose penchant for fantasy and wordplay his own work had been visibly affected. The four authors were installed, courtesy of Ford, in a mansion on the shore of the Wannsee. 'We were there as cultural window dressing,' Saunders says, 'to show the generosity of American support for European art.' They were all eager to see Brecht's Berliner Ensemble, in East Berlin, and three of them immediately did so. Stoppard alone hung back, and did not make the trip until his stay in Berlin was nearly over. He had never set foot in Communist territory, and the prospect of crossing the border repelled him. Although his passport was British, it stated that he was born in Czechoslovakia, and this had planted in him a superstitious fear that, once in East Berlin, he might never be allowed to return.

In the house by the Wannsee, he wrote a one-act comedy in verse, *Rosencrantz and Guildenstern Meet King Lear*. His work, like that of his colleagues, was performed by English amateur actors in one-night stands at a theatre on the Kurfürstendamm, with no decor apart from a large photograph of the author. Saunders, having seen Stoppard's *jeu d'esprit*, urged him to expand it into a full-length play. In his spare time, Stoppard was recruited by a young Dutch director to appear in a low-budget film based on a short story by Borges. He played a cowboy, and Marlowe has vivid memories of a sequence that showed Stoppard belligerently twirling a pair of six-shooters in front of the Brandenburg Gate. While Stoppard was in Germany, a Hamburg theatre presented the first stage production of *A Walk on the Water*, and he flew from Berlin for the premiere. The performance passed off in silence but without incident; and when the curtain fell Stoppard's German agent rashly urged him to go onstage and take a bow. He did so, with a cigarette between his lips — perhaps in emulation of Oscar Wilde, who had once used the same method of showing his indifference to audience reaction. He was greeted, for the first time in his life, by a storm of booing. It was directed, as he readily admits, at the text, not the tobacco.

Summing up his impressions of Stoppard, in Berlin and afterward, James Saunders says, 'Diffident on the surface, utterly unworried underneath. He's extremely cautious about being thought too serious. I've heard him quote Auden's famous remark to the effect that no poet's work ever saved anyone from a concentration camp. Well, that may be true, but it's terrible to *admit* that it's true. After all, the writer's job is constantly to redefine the role of the individual: What can he do? What *should* he do? And also to redefine the role of society: How can it be changed? How *should* it be changed? As a playwright, I live between these two responsibilities. But Tom — Tom just plays safe. He enjoys being nice, and he likes to be liked. He resists commitment of any kind, he hides the ultimate expression of his deepest concerns. He's basically a displaced person. Therefore, he doesn't want to stick his neck out. He feels grateful to Britain, because he sees himself as a guest here, and that makes it hard for him to criticise Britain. Probably the most damaging thing you could say about him is that he's made no enemies.' Since Berlin, Stoppard's star has risen while Saunders's has tended to decline. I asked Saunders how this had affected their relationship. He smiled, and quoted a well-known British dramatist who had once told him, 'Whenever I read a rave review of a young playwright in the Sunday papers, it spoils my whole day.' He continued, 'When Tom first became famous, he gave a series of expensive lunches at the Café Royal to keep in touch with his old pals. I thought that was pretty ostentatious behaviour. Meeting him nowadays I do feel a sort of cutoff.' He made a gesture like a portcullis descending. 'I don't think that he's overrated, as much as that many other writers are underrated. He has distracted attention from people who have an equal right to it.'

(A word on Stoppard and friendship. Most of those who know him well regard him as an exemplary friend. 'He actually drops in unannounced, which hardly anyone does in London,' says a close female chum, 'and he usually brings an unexpected but absolutely appropriate present. And he mails huge batches of postcards, which are not only funny but informative and helpful. He really works on his friendships.' When Derek Marlowe wrote a novel entitled *Nightshade*, Stoppard, who knew that Marlowe venerated Raymond Chandler, sought out an antique pulp magazine containing a Chandler story called 'Nightshade,' and arranged for it to reach Marlowe on publication day.)

After Stoppard returned from Berlin, he shared a flat in Westminster with Marlowe and Piers Paul Read. 'At this period, his idol was Mick Jagger,' Marlowe says. 'He looked like him, he dressed like him, and he was thrilled when he found out that Jagger loved cricket as much as he did.' Stoppard transmuted *Rosencrantz and Guildenstern* from verse into prose, and turned out a couple of short plays for television; but for the greater part of 1965 'he lived on the Arabs,' as Kenneth Ewing puts it. 'For some unfathomable reason, the BBC hired him to write the diary of an imaginary Arab student in London, which was then translated into Arabic and broadcast on the Overseas Service. He alternated with another author, and every other week he was paid forty pounds for five episodes. As far as I know, he had never met an Arab in his life. But the job kept him going for about nine months.' Eager to scan the results of this bizarre assignment, I approached the BBC for permission to consult its files. I was told that no copies of the scripts were in existence — a body blow to theatrical history but conceivably good news to Stoppard.

Early in 1965, the Royal Shakespeare Company took a twelve-month option on a play that was by then called *Rosencrantz and Guildenstern Are Dead*. The company failed to fit the play into its repertoire, and after the option expired the script went to several other managements, all of which rejected it. In the summer of 1966, the president of the Oxford Theatre Group walked into Kenneth Ewing's office and asked for permission to present an amateur production of the play on the Fringe of the forthcoming Edinburgh Festival. (The Fringe is Edinburgh's Off and Off-Off Broadway.) At first reluctant, Ewing eventually consented. He did not regret his decision. The opening night got a handful of bad notices, but over the weekend the momentous, life-changing review appeared. Ronald Bryden, writing in *The Observer*, described the play as an 'erudite comedy, punning, far-fetched, leaping from depth to dizziness,' and continued, 'it's the most brilliant debut by a young playwright since John Arden's.' At the time, I was working for Laurence Olivier as literary manager of the National Theatre, whose company was housed at the Old Vic. Minutes after reading Bryden's piece, I cabled Stoppard, requesting a script. Olivier liked it as much as I did, and within a week we had bought it. Directed by Derek Goldby, it opened at the Vic in April 1967. Very seldom has a play by a new dramatist been hailed with such rapturous unanimity. Harold Hobson, of the *Sunday Times*, called it 'the most important event in the British professional theatre of the last nine years'; that is, since the opening of Harold Pinter's *The Birthday Party*. Stoppard, who had subtly smoothed and improved the text throughout rehearsals, found himself overnight with his feet on the upper rungs of Britain's theatrical ladder, where several hobnailed talents were already stamping for primacy.

When *Rosencrantz and Guildenstern* had its London triumph, Vaclav Havel was thirty years of age, just nine months older than Stoppard. He wore smart but conservative clothes, being a dandy in the classic rather than the romantic mode. Of less than average height, he had the incipient portliness of the gourmet. His hair was trimmed short, and this gave him a somewhat bullet-shaped silhouette. He both walked and talked with purposeful briskness and elegance. He drove around Prague (where he was born on 5 October 1936) in a dashing little Renault, bought with the royalties from his plays — for in 1967 Havel was the leading Czechoslovakian playwright, and the only one to have achieved an international reputation since Karel Capek wrote *R. U. R.* and (with his brother Josef) *The Insect Play*, between the wars. Havel's family connections were far grander than Stoppard's. Vera Blackwell, a Czech émigré who lives in London and translates Havel's work into English, has said that 'if Czechoslovakia had remained primarily a capitalist society Vaclav Havel would be today just about the richest young man in the country.' One of his uncles was a millionaire who owned, apart from vast amounts of real estate and a number of hotels, the Barrandov studios, in Prague, which are the headquarters of the Czech film industry. All this was lost in the Communist takeover of 1948, and during the dark period of Stalinist rigour that followed, Havel's upper-class background prevented him from receiving any full-time education above grade-school level. Instead, he took a menial job in a chemical laboratory, spending most of his off-duty hours at evening classes, where he studied science. In 1954, he began two years of military service, after which he made repeated attempts to enter Prague University. All his applications were turned down. His next move was to offer himself for any theatrical work that was going. He found what he was looking for in the mid-sixties, when he was appointed *Dramaturg* (i.e., literary manager, a post that in Europe quite often means not only play selector and script editor but house playwright as well) at the Balustrade Theatre, which was Prague's principal showcase for avant-garde drama.

We nowadays tend to assume that the great thaw in Czech socialism began and ended with the libertarian reforms carried out by Alexander Dubcek's regime in the so-called Prague Spring of 1968. By that time, artistic freedom had in fact been blooming for several ebullient years: a period that saw the emergence of filmmakers like Milos Forman, Ivan Passer, Jan Nemec, and Jan Kadar; of theatrical directors like Otomar Krejca and Jan Grossman (who ran the Balustrade); and of a whole school of young dramatists, at whose head Vaclav Havel swiftly established himself. In one sense, he was a traditional Czech writer. Using a technique that derived from Kafka, Capek, and countless Central European authors before them, he expressed his view of the world in nonrealistic parables. His plays were distorting mirrors in which one recognised the truth. Stoppard belongs in precisely the same tradition, of which there is no Anglo-Saxon equivalent. Moreover, Havel shares Stoppard's passion for fantastic word juggling. Some critics have glibly assigned both writers to the grab bag marked Theatre of the Absurd. But here the analogy falters, for Havel's Absurdism is very different from Stoppard's. Vera Blackwell says:

> Havel does not protest against the absurdity of man's life *vis-à-vis* a meaningless universe, but against the absurdity of the modern Frankenstein's monster: bureaucracy. . . . The ultimate aim of Havel's plays . . . is the improvement of man's lot through the improvement of man's institutions. These, in their turn, can become more 'human' only insofar as the individual men and women who invent and people these institutions are prepared to be fully human — i.e., fully responsible for their actions, fully aware of their responsibility.

If Dubcek's policies represented what Western journalists called 'Socialism with a human face,' Havel's work gave Absurdism a human face, together with a socially critical purpose.

Like Stoppard, he had his first play performed in 1963. Entitled *The Garden Party*, it was staged by Grossman at the Balustrade. The hero, Hugo Pludek, is a student whose consuming interest is playing chess against himself. 'Such a player,' says his mother sagely, 'will always stay in the game.' His parents, a solid bourgeois couple, base their values on a storehouse of demented proverbs that they never tire of repeating; e.g., 'Not even a hag carries hemp heed to the attic alone,' 'He who fusses about a mosquito net can never hope to dance with a goat,' 'Not even the Hussars of Cologne would go to the woods without a clamp,' and — perhaps the

most incontrovertible of all — 'Stone walls do not an iron bar.' They worry
about Hugo, since he shows no inclination to apply for work in the ruling
bureaucracy. Under their pressure, he attends a garden party thrown by the
Liquidation Office, where he poses as a bureaucrat so successfully that
before long he is put in charge of liquidating the Liquidation Office. From a
high-ranking member of the Inauguration Service — the opposite end of the
scale from the Liquidation Office — he learns the Party line on intellectual
dissent: 'We mustn't be afraid of contrary opinions. Everybody who's
honestly interested in our common cause ought to have from one to three
contrary opinions.' Eventually, the authorities decide to liquidate the
Inauguration Service, and the question arises: Who should inaugurate the
process of liquidation — an inaugurator or a liquidator? Surely, not the
former, since how can anyone inaugurate his own liquidation? But, equally,
it can't be the latter, because liquidators have not been trained to
inaugurate. Either liquidators must be trained to inaugurate or vice versa.
But this poses a new question: Who is to do the training? At the end of the
play, driven mad by living in a society in which all truths are relative and
subject to overnight cancellation, Hugo feels his identity crumbling. He
knows what is happening to him, but, good bureaucrat that he now is, he
cannot resist it. In the course of a hysterical tirade, he declares:

> Truth is just as complicated and multiform as everything else in
> the world — the magnet, the telephone, Impressionism, the magnet
> — and we are all a little bit what we were yesterday and a little bit
> what we are today; and also a little bit we're not these things.
> Anyway . . . some of us are more and some of us are more not; some
> only are, some are only, and some only are not; so that none of us
> entirely is, and at the same time each one of us is not entirely.

This was Absurdism with deep roots in contemporary anxieties. The play
was an immediate hit in Prague, and went on to be performed in Austria,
Switzerland, Sweden, Finland, Hungary, Yugoslavia, and West Germany.
Meanwhile, Havel composed a series of 'typographical poems' to amuse
his compatriots. One of them, labelled 'Philosophy,' went

Another, wryly political, was printed thus:

```
                         FORWARD
          FORWARD                  FORWARD
          FORWARD                  FORWARD
          FORWARD                  FORWARD
          FORWARD                    FORWARD
          FORWARD                      FORWARD
          FORWARD                      FORWARD
           FORWARD                     FORWARD
            FORWARD                  FORWARD
             FORWARD               FORWARD
                         FORWARD
```

And the following is Havel's succinct comment on the role of humour under Stalinism:

100%	100%	100%	100%	100%	100%	100%
100%	100%	100%	100%	100%	100%	100%
100%	100%	100%	100%	100%	100%	100%
100%	100%	100%	100%	100%	100%	100%
100%	100%	100%	100%	100%	100%	100%
100%	100%	100%	100%	100%	100%	100%
100%	100%	100%	100%	100%	100%	100%
100%	100%	100%	100%	100%	100%	100%
100%	100%	100%	100%	100%	100%	100%
100%	100%	100%	100%	100%	99%	100%
100%	100%	100%	100%	100%	100%	100%
100%	100%	100%	100%	100%	100%	100%

It is captioned 'Constructive Satire.'

Authentic satire operates on the principle of the thermos flask: it contains heat without radiating it. Havel's second play, *The Memorandum* (1965), was a splendid example: burning convictions were implicit in a structure of ice-cold logic and glittering linguistic virtuosity. His target was the use of language to subvert individualism and enforce conformity. Josef Gross, the managing director of a huge but undefined state enterprise, grows unsettled when he discovers that, on orders from above, the existing vernacular is being replaced by a synthetic language called Ptydepe, uncontaminated by the ambiguities, imprecisions, and emotional vagaries of ordinary speech. Its aim is to abolish similarities between words by using the least probable combination of letters, so that no word can conceivably be mistaken for any other. We learn from the Ptydepe instructor who has been assigned to Gross's organisation, 'The natural languages originated . . . spontaneously, uncontrollably, and their structure is thus, in a certain sense, dilettantish.' For purposes of official communication, they are utterly unreliable. In Ptydepe, 'the more common the meaning, the shorter the word.' The longest entry in the new dictionary has three hundred and nineteen letters and means 'wombat.' The shortest is 'f' and at present has no meaning, since science has not yet determined which word or expression is in commonest use. The instructor lists several variations of the interjection 'Boo' as it might be employed in a large company when one worker seeks to 'sham-ambush' another. If the victim is in full view, unprepared for the impending ambush and threatened by a hidden colleague, 'Boo' is rendered by 'Gedynrelom.' If, however, the victim is *aware* of the danger, the correct cry is 'Osonfterte' — for which 'Eg gynd y trojadus' must be substituted if *both* parties are in full view and the encounter is meant only as a joke. If the sham-ambush is seriously intended, the appropriate expression is 'Eg jeht kuz.' Jan Ballas, Gross's ambitious deputy, points out to his baffled boss that normal language is fraught with undesirable emotional overtones: 'Now, tell me sincerely, has the word "mutarex" any such overtones for you? It hasn't, has it! You see! It is a paradox, but it is precisely the surface inhumanity of an artificial language that guarantees its truly human function!' Gross's problems are compounded by the fact that he has received an official memorandum in Ptydepe, but in order to get a Ptydepe text translated one must make an application in Ptydepe, which Gross does not speak. 'In other words,' he laments, 'the only way to know what is in one's memo is to know it already.' Ever willing to compromise (and this is Havel's underlying message), he does not complain when he loses his job to Ballas; and it is through no effort of his own that he regains it at the end. The authorities have observed that, as one of their spokesmen resentfully puts it, wherever Ptydepe has passed into common use, 'it has automatically begun to assume some of the characteristics of a natural language: various emotional overtones, imprecisions, ambiguities.' Therefore, Ptydepe is to be replaced by a new language, Chorukor, based on the principle not of abolishing but of intensifying the similarities between words. Gross, reinstated to spearhead the introduction of Chorukor, remains what he has never ceased to be: a time-serving organisation man.

This small masterpiece of sustained irony was staged throughout Europe and at the Public Theatre, in New York, where it won the 1968 *Village Voice* award for the best foreign play of the Off Broadway season. In April of that year, Havel's next work, *The Increased Difficulty of Concentration*, opened in Prague. If the logical games and verbal pyrotechnics of *The Memorandum* suggested analogies with Stoppard, there were aspects of the new piece which anticipated a play that Stoppard had not yet written; namely, *Jumpers*. Havel's central character is Dr. Huml, a social scientist engaged (like Professor Moore in *Jumpers*) in dictating a bumbling lecture on moral values which goes against the intellectual grain of his society. He is interrupted from time to time by a couple of technicians bearing an extremely disturbed and unreliable computer with which they propose to study his behaviour patterns. Here are some telescoped samples of Huml at work, with Blanka, his secretary:

HUML: Where did we stop?
BLANKA(*reads*): 'Various people have at various times and in various circumstances various needs —'
HUML: Ah yes! (*Begins to pace thoughtfully to and fro while dictating to Blanka, who takes it down in shorthand*) — and thus attach to various things various values — full stop. Therefore, it would be mistaken to set up a fixed scale of values — valid for all people in all circumstances and at all times — full stop. This does not mean, however, that in all of history there exist no values common to the whole of mankind — full stop. If those values did not exist, mankind would not form a unified whole — full stop. . . . Would you mind reading me the last sentence? . . . There exist situations — for example, in some advanced Western countries — in which all the basic human needs have been satisfied, and still people are not happy. They experience feelings of depression, boredom, frustration, etc. — full stop. In these situations man begins to desire that which in fact he perhaps does not need at all — he simply persuades himself he has certain needs which he does not have — or he vaguely desires something which he cannot specify and thus cannot strive for — full stop. Hence, as soon as man has satisfied one need — i.e., achieved happiness — another so far unsatisfied need is born in him, so that every happiness is always, simultaneously, a negation of happiness.

Can science help man to solve his problems? Not entirely, says Huml, because science can illuminate only that which is finite, whereas man 'contains the dimensions of infinity.' He continues:

I'm afraid the key to a real comprehension of the individual does not lie in a greater or lesser understanding of the complexity of man as an object of scientific knowledge. . . . The unique relationship that arises between two individuals is thus far the only thing that can — at least to some extent — mutually unveil their secrets. Values like love, friendship, compassion, sympathy, even mutual conflict — which is as unique and irreplaceable as mutual understanding — are the only tools we have at our disposal. By other means we may perhaps be able to explain man, but never to understand him. . . . The fundamental key does not lie in his brain, but in his heart.

Meanwhile, the computer has broken down, and emits a shrill bombardment of imbecile questions, endlessly repeated:

> Which is your favourite tunnel? Are you fond of musical instruments? How many times a year do you air the square? Where did you bury the dog? Why didn't you pass it on? When did you lose the claim? Wherein lies the nucleus? Do you know where you're going, and do you know who's going with you? Do you urinate in public, or just now and then?

On August 21, 1968, the Soviet Union, alarmed by the experiment in free socialism that was flowering in Czechoslovakia, invaded the country and imposed on it a neo-Stalinist regime. One of the first acts of the new government was to forbid all performances of Havel's plays.

By the summer of 1968, Stoppard had had his third London premiere within fourteen months. *Enter a Free Man* which I've already discussed, had opened to mixed notices at the St. Martin's Theatre in March, and *The Real Inspector Hound*, to which I'll return later, had been more happily received (*The Observer* compared it to a Fabergé Easter egg) when it arrived at the Criterion Theatre, in June, just two months before the Russian tanks rolled into Prague. *Rosencrantz and Guildenstern* remained a great drawing card in the repertory — a hand already stacked with aces — of the National Theatre. A couple of weeks before its first night, in 1967, I had written a piece on the performing arts in Prague. In it I said that the new Czech theatre was 'focusing its attention not only on man vs. authority but on man vs. mortality,' and that 'the hero is forced to come to terms not merely with the transient compulsions of society but with the permanent fact of death.' Under liberal governments, I added, authors tend to concern themselves with 'the ultimate problem of dying as well as the immediate problems of living.' With the benefit of hindsight, I realise that every word of this might have been written about *Rosencrantz and Guildenstern*: it fitted perfectly into my group portrait of Czech drama. (Perhaps the most memorable speech in the play occurs when the former and dumber principal character asks, 'Whatever became of the moment when one first knew about death?' — that shattering instant, surely inscribed on everyone's memory, which for some reason no one can remember.) Of course, one can also spot Western influences. The sight of two bewildered men playing pointless games in a theatrical void while the real action unfolds offstage inevitably recalls Beckett. Stoppard has said, 'When *Godot* was first done, it liberated something for anybody writing plays. It redefined the minima of theatrical validity. It was as simple as that. He got away. He won by twenty-eight lengths, and he'd done it with so little — and I mean that as an enormous compliment.' When Guildenstern says, 'Wheels have been set in motion, and they have their own pace, to which we are . . . condemned,' we think once more of Beckett's doom-laden slogan, 'Something is taking its course.' The debt to Eliot's 'Love Song of J. Alfred Prufrock' is equally transparent:

> No! I am not Prince Hamlet, nor was meant to be;
> Am an attendant lord, one that will do
> To swell a progress, start a scene or two . . .
> Full of high sentence, but a bit obtuse;
> At times, indeed, almost ridiculous —
> Almost, at times, the Fool.

'Prufrock and Beckett,' Stoppard has said, 'are the two syringes of my diet, my arterial system.' But has anyone noticed another mainline injection? Consider: Rosencrantz and Guildenstern are unaccountably summoned to a mysterious castle where, between long periods of waiting, they receive cryptic instructions that eventually lead to their deaths. They die uncertain whether they are the victims of chance or of fate. It seems to me undeniable that the world they inhabit owes its atmosphere and architecture to the master builder of such enigmatic fables — Franz Kafka, whose birthplace was Prague, and who wrote of just such a castle.

Stoppard is nothing if not eclectic. His play even bears traces of Wittgenstein, according to whose *Philosophical Investigations* (1953) it is conceivable that:

> . . . two people belonging to a tribe unacquainted with chess should sit at a chessboard and go through the moves of a game of chess. . . . And if we were to see it, we would say they were playing chess. But now imagine a game of chess translated, according to certain rules, into a series of actions which we do not ordinarily associate with a *game* — say, into yells and stamping of feet. And now suppose these two people to yell and stamp instead of playing the form of chess that we are used to. . . . Should we still be inclined to say they were playing a game? What *right* would one have to say so?

Stoppard's twin heroes are clearly involved in 'a series of actions which we do not ordinarily associate with a game.' They are caught up in a strict and ferocious plot — both onstage and off, people are being killed — but the total experience, however unplayful it looks, may still be a kind of game, as formal in its rules as chess.

Again, Oscar Wilde (a good fairy, in the elfin sense of the word, who has more than once waved an influential wand over the *accouchement* of a Stoppard work) supplies an apt quotation, from *De Profundis*:

I know of nothing in all Drama more incomparable from the point of view of Art, or more suggestive in its subtlety of observation, than Shakespeare's drawing of Rosencrantz and Guildenstern. They are Hamlet's college friends. They have been his companions. . . . At the moment when they come across him in the play he is staggering under the weight of a burden intolerable to one of his temperament. . . . Of all this, Guildenstern and Rosencrantz realise nothing.

Which they prove in the funniest speech of Stoppard's play, when, having been told to 'glean what afflicts' Hamlet, the two spies quiz each other about his state of mind and come up with the following conclusion:

ROSENCRANTZ: To sum up: your father, whom you love, dies, you are his heir, you come back to find that hardly was the corpse cold before his young brother popped on to his throne and into his sheets, thereby offending both legal and natural practice. Now why exactly are you behaving in this extraordinary manner?

Wilde goes on:

They are close to his secret and know nothing of it. Nor would there be any use in telling them. They are little cups that can hold so much and no more. . . . They are types fixed for all time. To censure them would show a lack of appreciation. They are merely out of their sphere: that is all.

Despite its multiple sources, *Rosencrantz and Guildenstern* is a genuine original, one of a kind. As far as I know, it is the first play to use another play as its decor. The English critic C. E. Montague described *Hamlet* as 'a monstrous Gothic castle of a poem, full of baffled half-lights and glooms.' This is precisely the setting of *Rosencrantz and Guildenstern*: it takes place in the wings of Shakespeare's imagination. The actor-manager who meets the two travellers on the road to Elsinore says that in life every exit is 'an entrance somewhere else.' In Stoppard's play, every exit is an entrance somewhere else in *Hamlet*. Sometimes he writes like a poet:

We cross our bridges when we come to them and burn them behind us, with nothing to show for our progress except a memory of the smell of smoke, and a presumption that once our eyes watered.

And at other times with fortune-cookie glibness:

Eternity is a terrible thought. I mean, where's it going to end?

But we are finally moved by the snuffing out of the brief candles he has lit. Tinged perhaps with sentimentality, an emotional commitment has nonetheless been made. To quote Clive James:

> The mainspring of *Rosencrantz and Guildenstern Are Dead* is the perception — surely a compassionate one — that the fact of their deaths mattering so little to Hamlet was something that ought to have mattered to Shakespeare.

The Real Inspector Hound, which joined *Rosencrantz and Guildenstern* on the London playbills in June, 1968, need not detain us long. It is a facetious puzzle that, like several of Stoppard's minor pieces, presents an apparently crazy series of events for which in the closing moments a rational explanation is provided. Two drama critics, Birdboot and Moon, are covering the premiere of a thriller, written in a broad parody of the style of Agatha Christie. At curtain rise, there is a male corpse onstage. Stoppard unconvincingly maintains that when the play was half finished he still didn't know the dead man's name or the murderer's identity. (How did he find out? 'There is a God,' Stoppard says when he is asked this question, 'and he looks after English playwrights.') Toward the end, the two critics implausibly leave their seats and join in the action. In the dénouement, Moon, who is the second-string critic for his paper, is killed onstage by the envious third-string critic, who, posing as an actor in the play within a play, has previously slain the first-string critic (the curtain-rise corpse) and rigged the evidence to frame Moon. (A general rule about Stoppard may be stated thus: The shorter the play, the harder it is to summarise the plot without sounding unhinged.) People sometimes say that Stoppard, for all his brilliance, is fundamentally a leech, drawing the lifeblood of his work from the inventions of others. In *Rosencrantz and Guildenstern*, he battens on Shakespeare, in *Inspector Hound* on Christie, in *Jumpers* on the logical positivists, in *Travesties* on Wilde, James Joyce, and Lenin. The same charge, of course, has been levelled against other and greater writers; in 1592, for example, the playwright and pamphleteer Robert Greene accused Shakespeare of artistic thievery, calling him an 'upstart crow, beautified with our feathers.'

Allegations of this kind do not ruffle Stoppard's feathers. 'I can't invent plots,' he admitted in a public discussion of his work which was held in Los Angeles earlier this year. 'I've formed the habit of hanging my plays on other people's plots. It's a habit I'm trying to kick.' Apropos of borrowings, I may as well reveal my suspicion that a hitherto undetected influence on *Inspector Hound* is that of Robert Benchley. At one point, when the stage is empty, a phone rings, and the critic Moon gets up to answer it. Surely this calls to mind the legendary moment during a Broadway premiere when a phone rang on an empty stage and the critic Benchley, remarking, 'I think that's for me,' rose and left the theatre. Nor is Stoppard's play the first in which a drama critic has been seen dead onstage. Back in 1917, seeking material for a newspaper article, a writer lately employed as the drama critic of *Vanity Fair* played the role of a corpse in *The Thirteenth Chair*. His name, guessably, was Robert Benchley.

Jumpers, produced in 1972, was the next milestone in Stoppard's career; but something should first be said of his work for radio, a medium he has used more resourcefully than any other contemporary English playwright. In *Albert's Bridge* (1967) and *Artist Descending a Staircase* (1972), both written for the BBC, he explores two of his favourite themes. the first is the relativity of absolutely everything. (It all depends on where you're sitting.) The second is the definition of art. (Is it a skill or a gift? Is it socially useful? Or does that, too, depend on where you're sitting?) Albert, in the earlier play, is painting a lofty railway bridge that will have to be repainted as soon as he has finished painting it. Despite the repetitious and mechanical nature of his job, he loves it, because it has a symmetry and coherence that are lacking in his life on the ground. He is joined by Fraser, a would-be suicide, who has climbed the bridge in order to jump off. The world below, Fraser explains, is doomed:

> Motor-cars nose each other down every street, and they are beginning to breed, spread, they press the people to the walls by their knees, and there's no end to it, because if you stopped making them, thousands of people would be thrown out of work, and they'd have no money to spend, the shopkeepers would get caught up in it, and the farms and factories, and all the people dependent on them, with their children and all. There's too much of everything, but the space for it is constant. So the shell of human existence is filling out, expanding, and it's going to go bang.

After a while, however, he changes his mind. Seeing it all from above, at a distance, he finds order in the chaos. 'Yes,' he says, 'from a vantage point like this, the idea of society is just about tenable.' So he descends; but shortly afterward he returns, convinced that he was right the first time. The bridge finally collapses, with both men on it, when a massed phalanx of assistant painters marches across it without breaking step. It is a fine catastrophe, but also a neat escape hatch for Stoppard, who is thus absolved from the responsibility of telling us which view of life we should espouse — the long shot or the closeup.

Artist Descending a Staircase has a plot that starts out backward and then goes forward. I shall not take up the challenge to summarise it, except to say that it concerns the careers and beliefs of three artists, one of whom is dead and may have been murdered by either of the others, or by both working in cahoots. The title derives from Marcel Duchamp's painting

'Nude Descending a Staircase,' and the play contains plenty of evidence that self-cannibalism is not alien to Stoppard. For example:

> The artist is a lucky dog. . . . In any community of a thousand souls there will be nine hundred doing the work, ninety doing well, nine doing good, and one lucky dog painting or writing about the other nine hundred and ninety-nine.

Slightly compressed, this superb speech reappears in *Travesties*; and there are references to Lenin and Tristan Tzara (and their joint sojourn in Zurich during the First World War) which look forward to the same play. Stoppard leaves us in no doubt about his attitude toward twentieth-century art in its more extreme manifestations, which he calls 'that child's garden of easy victories known as the avant-garde.' Again:

> Skill without imagination is craftsmanship and gives us many useful objects such as wickerwork picnic baskets. Imagination without skill gives us modern art.

He also takes a sharp sideswipe at an artist who, having gone through a period of making ceramic food, realises that this will not help to fill empty bellies. The artist decides instead to sculpture edible art out of sugar. One of his colleagues says, 'It will give Cubism a new lease of life.' I think we can take it that Stoppard is expressing his own feelings in the following definition, which recurs unchanged in *Travesties*:

> An artist is someone who is gifted in some way that enables him to do something more or less well which can only be done badly or not at all by someone who is not thus gifted.

I once told Stoppard that, impressive though his dictum sounded, it could equally well be applied to a jockey. He wandered out of the room for a full minute, presumably to ponder, and then wandered back. 'That's exactly what I meant,' he said. 'In other words, a chap who claims to be a jockey and wears a jockey's cap *but sits facing the horse's tail* is not a jockey.'

During the four years that separate *Inspector Hound* from *Jumpers*, the total of new work by Stoppard consisted of three one-acters and a short play for television. This apparent unproductiveness was due partly to distracting upheavals in his private life (the collapse of his first marriage, the cementing of his new relationship with Miriam) and partly to an ingrained habit of preparing for his major enterprises with the assiduity of an athlete training for the Olympics. Or, to use Derek Marlowe's simile: 'For Tom, writing a play is like sitting for an examination. He spends ages on research, does all the necessary cramming, reads all the relevant books, and

then gestates the results. Once he's passed the exam — with the public and
the critics — he forgets all about it and moves on to the next subject.'
Moreover, the second play is always a high hurdle. Although *Inspector
Hound* came after *Rosencrantz and Guildenstern*, it didn't really count,
being a lightweight diversion, staged in a commercial theatre. The real test,
as Stoppard knew, would be his second play *at the National*.

Early in 1970, he told me, over lunch, that he had been reading the
logical positivists with fascinated revulsion. He was unable to accept their
view that because value judgments could not be empirically verified they
were meaningless. Accordingly, he said, he was toying with the idea of a
play whose entire first act would be a lecture in support of moral
philosophy. This led us into a long debate on morality — specifically, on
the difference between the Judaeo-Christian tradition (in which the creator
of the universe also lays down its moral laws, so that the man who breaks
them is committing an offence against God) and the Oriental tradition
represented by Zen Buddhism (in which morality is seen as a man-made
convention, quite distinct from God or cosmogony). Only with Stoppard or
Vaclav Havel can I imagine having such a conversation about a play that
was intended to be funny. A few days later, Stoppard sent me a letter in
which he said that our chat had 'forced me to articulate certain ideas, to
their immense hazard, which I suppose is useful,' and went on, 'All that
skating around makes the ice look thin, but a sense of renewed endeavour
prevails — more concerned with the dramatic possibilities than with the
ideas, for it is a mistake to assume that plays are the end-products of ideas
(which would be limiting): the ideas are the end-products of the plays.'

The theatrical image that triggered *Jumpers* came from an exchange in
Rosencrantz and Guildenstern, when Rosencrantz says, 'Shouldn't we be
doing something — constructive?' and Guildenstern replies, 'What did you
have in mind? A short, blunt human pyramid?' Stoppard subsequently told
an interviewer:

> I thought, How marvellous to have a pyramid of people on a stage,
> and a rifle shot, and one member of the pyramid just being blown out
> of it, and the others imploding on the hole as he leaves. . . . Because
> of the success of 'Rosencrantz' it was on the cards that the National
> Theatre would do whatever I wrote, if I didn't completely screw it
> up. . . . It's perfectly true that having shot this man out of the
> pyramid, and having him lying on the floor, I didn't know who he
> was or who had shot him or why or what to do with the body.
> Absolutely not a clue.

Cf. Stoppard's virtually identical and identically unpersuasive statement
about a similar situation in *Inspector Hound*. However, play it again, Tom:

> At the same time, there's more than one point of origin for a play, and the only useful metaphor I can think of for the way I think I write my plays is convergences of different threads. . . . One of the threads was the entirely visual image of the pyramid of acrobats, but while thinking of that pyramid I knew I wanted to write a play about a professor of moral philosophy. . . . There was a metaphor at work in the play already between acrobatics and mental acrobatics, and so on.

In December, 1970, I got a note from Stoppard saying that the new piece would not be ready until the following autumn. In the late summer of 1971, I called him and begged him to give us some idea of its substance, since within a couple of weeks we had to fix our plans for the forthcoming season. He replied that, although he had nearly finished the first draft, he could not possibly get it typed so soon. Might he therefore read it to us himself? Acting on this suggestion, I arranged a singular audition at my house in Kensington. The audience consisted of Laurence Olivier, John Dexter (then associate director of the National Theatre), and me. The time was late afternoon, and Olivier had come straight from an exhausting rehearsal. Stoppard arrived with the text and a sheaf of large white cards, each bearing the name of one of the characters. We had a few glasses of wine, after which Stoppard announced that he would read the play standing at a table, holding up the appropriate card to indicate who was speaking. What ensued was a gradual descent into chaos. *Jumpers* (which was then called *And Now the Incredible Jasmin Jumpers*) is a complex work with a big cast, and before long Stoppard had got his cards hopelessly mixed up. Within an hour, Olivier had fallen asleep. Stoppard gallantly pressed on, and I have a vivid memory of him, desperate in the gathering dusk, frantically shuffling his precious pages and brandishing his cards, like a panicky magician whose tricks are blowing up in his face. After two hours, he had got no farther than the end of Act I. At that point, Olivier suddenly woke up. For about thirty seconds, he stared at the ceiling, where some spotlights I had recently installed were dimly gleaming. Stoppard looked expectantly in his direction: clearly, Olivier was choosing his words with care. At length, he uttered them. 'Ken,' he said to me ruminatively, 'where did you buy those lights?' Stoppard then gave up and left. Next day, it took all the backslapping of which Dexter and I were capable to persuade him that the play was worth saving.

Jumpers turned out to be something unique in theatre: a farce whose main purpose is to affirm the existence of God. Or, to put it less starkly, a farcical defence of transcendent moral values. At the same time, it is an attack on pragmatic materialism as this is practised by a political party called the Radical Liberals, who embody Stoppard's satiric vision of socialism in action. They have just won an election (the time, unspecified, seems to be the near future), and no sooner are the votes counted than they take over the broadcasting services, arrest the newspaper proprietors, and appoint a veterinary surgeon Archbishop of Canterbury. A prominent Rad-Lib — and the villain of Stoppard's piece — is Sir Archie Jumper, vice-chancellor of an English university and an all-round bounder, who holds degrees in medicine, philosophy, literature, and law, and diplomas in psychiatry and gymnastics. Archie encourages the philosophers of his staff (mostly logical positivists) to be part-time athletes, and it is they who form the human pyramid, perforated by a bullet, with which the action begins.

The killing takes place during a party thrown at the home of George Moore, professor of moral philosophy — a middle-aged word-spinner and resolute nonacrobat, who is implacably opposed to Archie's values, or lack of them. This is Stoppard's hero, and it is not the least of his problems that he bears the same name as the world-famous English philosopher (d. 1958) who wrote *Principia Ethica*. However, being one of Stoppard's unsinkable eccentrics, he does not let this mischievous coincidence get him down. On hearing that the veterinarian Clegthorpe is the new Primate, he ironically observes, 'Sheer disbelief hardly registers on the face before the head is nodding with all the wisdom of instant hindsight. "Archbishop Clegthorpe? Of course! The inevitable capstone to a career in veterinary medicine!" ' (The use of a rare word like 'capstone' instead of the more obvious 'keystone' or 'climax' is typical of Stoppard. Nabokov, another exile with a taste for verbal surprises, might have made the same choice.) George's role, one of the longest in the English comic repertoire, is devoted mainly to the composition of a hilarious, interminable, outrageously convoluted lecture designed to prove that moral absolutes exist — and closely analogous, as I've said, to the address dictated by Dr. Huml in Havel's *The Increased Difficulty of Concentration*. Theatrically, it disproves the philistine maxim that intellectual comedy can never produce belly laughs.

Seeking to demonstrate that purely rational arguments do not always make sense, George cites the Greek philosopher Zeno, who concluded that 'since an arrow shot towards a target first had to cover half the distance, and then half the remainder, and then half the remainder after that, and so on *ad infinitum*, the result was . . . that though an arrow is always approaching its target, it never quite gets there, and Saint Sebastian died of fright.' To underline his point, George actually uses a bow and arrow, just as he employs a trained tortoise and a trained hare (both of which escape) to refute another of Zeno's famous paradoxes, 'which showed in every way but experience . . . that a tortoise given a head start in a race with, say, a hare, could never be overtaken.' Hare, tortoise, arrow, and bow come together at the play's climax, which is one of the supreme — tragicomic is not quite the word, let us say tragi-farcical — moments in modern theatre.

George sums up his beliefs in a discussion with Archie:

When I push *my* convictions to absurdity, *I* arrive at God. . . . All I know is that I think that I know that I know that nothing can be created out of nothing, that my moral conscience is different from the rules of my tribe, and that there is more in me than meets the microscope — and because of *that* I'm lumbered with this incredible, indescribable and definitely shifty *God*, the trump card of atheism.

He dismisses Archie's supporters as 'simplistic score-settlers.' George versus Archie is Stoppard's dazzling dramatisation of one of the classic battles of our time. Cyril Connolly gives a more dispassionate account of the same conflict in *The Unquiet Grave*, his semiautobiographical book of confessions and aphorisms:

The two errors: We can either have a spiritual or a materialist view of life. If we believe in the spirit then we make an assumption which permits a whole chain of them, down to a belief in fairies, witches, astrology, black magic, ghosts and treasure-divining. . . . On the other hand, a completely materialistic view leads to its own excesses, such as a belief in Behaviourism, in the economic basis of art, in the social foundation of ethics, and the biological nature of psychology, in fact to the justification of expediency and therefore ultimately to the Ends-Means fallacy of which our civilisation is perishing. If we believe in a supernatural or superhuman intelligence creating the universe, then we end by stocking our library with the prophecies of Nostradamus, and the calculations on the Great Pyramid. If instead we choose to travel via Montaigne and Voltaire, then we choke amid the brimstone aridities of the Left Book Club.

In that great debate there is no question where Stoppard stands. He votes for the spirit — although he did not state his position in the first person until June of this year, when, in the course of a book review, he defined himself as a supporter of 'Western liberal democracy, favouring an intellectual elite and a progressive middle class and based on a moral order derived from Christian absolutes.'

The female principle in the George-Archie struggle is represented by George's wife, Dotty. Some ten years his junior, she is a star of musical comedy who has suffered a nervous breakdown (and gone into premature retirement) because the landing of men on the moon has destroyed her romantic ideals. She says:

Not only are we no longer the still centre of God's universe, we're not even uniquely graced by his footprint in man's image. . . . Man is on the moon, his feet on solid ground, and he has seen us whole . . . and all our absolutes, the thou-shalts; and the thou-shalt-nots that seemed to be the very condition of our existence, how did *they* look to two moonmen with a single neck to save between them?

We already know the answer. Captain Scott, the first Englishman to reach the moon, has a damaged spaceship that may not make it back to earth. To reduce the weight load, he has kicked Astronaut Oates off the ladder to the command module, thereby condemning him to death. What is moral has been sacrificed in favour of what is practical. Remember that we are still dealing with a high — a very high — comedy. In this context, Geoffrey Reeves's opinion is worth quoting:

> 'Rosencrantz' is a beautiful piece of theatre, but 'Jumpers' is *the* play, without any doubt. The ironic tone perfectly matches the absurd vision. It's far more than an exercise in wit; it ends up making a fierce statement. Not necessarily one that I would agree with — politically and philosophically. Tom and I have very little in common. But it's a measure of his brilliance that in the theatre I suspend rational judgment. He simply takes my breath away. People sometimes say he has a purely literary mind. That's not true of 'Jumpers.' It uses the stage *as* a stage, not as an extension of TV or the novel.

Jumpers went into rehearsal at the Old Vic in November, 1971. Diana Rigg played Dotty, and Michael Hordern, as George, had the part of his life: quivering with affronted dignity, patrolling the stage like a neurotic sentry, his face infested with tics, his fists plunging furiously into his cardigan pockets, he was matchlessly silly and serious at the same time. Ten days before the premiere, however, the play was still running close to four hours. I begged Olivier for permission to make cuts. He told me to approach the director, Peter Wood, who said he was powerless without the author's approval. Stoppard felt that alterations at this stage would upset the actors. Faced with this impasse, I took unilateral action. The next afternoon, just after the lunch break, I nipped into the rehearsal room ahead of the director and dictated to the cast a series of cuts and transpositions which reduced the text to what I considered manageable length. They were accepted without demur, and the matter, to my astonished relief, was never raised again. *Jumpers* opened in February, 1972, to resounding acclaim. B. A. Young, of the *Financial Times*, spoke for most of his colleagues when he wrote, 'I can't hope to do justice to the richness and sparkle of the evening's proceedings, as gay and original a farce as we have seen for years.'

Two months later, the London *Sunday Times*, whose regular critic had given a rhapsodic account of the first night, unexpectedly published a second review of the play — written by Sir Alfred Ayer, Wykeham

Professor of Logic at Oxford and, by general consent, the foremost living
English philosopher. He had made his name (which was then plain A. J.
Ayer) in the nineteen-thirties as the precocious author of *Language, Truth
and Logic*, probably the most masterly exposition in English of the
principles of logical positivism. Thus, Ayer represented, in its most
Establishment form, the philosophical tradition that Stoppard had set out to
undermine. George tells us in the play that his next book will be entitled
Language, Truth and God, and Dotty summarises the archfiend Archie's
views on morality in a speech that might have been borrowed from Ayer:

> Things and actions, you understand, can have any number of real
> and verifiable properties. But good and bad, better and worse, these
> are not real properties of things, they are just expressions of our
> feelings about them.

It seemed on the cards that Ayer-Archie would resent being cast as
Stoppard's villain. But nothing of the sort: he 'enormously enjoyed' the
evening, and 'came away feeling the greatest admiration for its author and
for the actor Michael Hordern, who takes the leading part.' If he identified
himself with any of the characters, it was not Archie but George, in whom
'I thought, perhaps conceitedly, that I occasionally caught echoes of my
own intonations' — though not, needless to say, of his ideas. He analysed
the play's philosophical content with detached but devastating aplomb:

> The argument is between those who believe in absolute values, for
> which they seek a religious sanction, and those, more frequently to be
> found among contemporary philosophers, who are subjectivists or
> relativists in morals, utilitarians in politics, and atheists or at least
> agnostics. . . .
> George needs not one but two Gods, one to create the world and
> another to support his moral values, and is unsuccessful in obtaining
> either of them. For the creator he relies on the first-cause argument,
> which is notoriously fallacious, since it starts from the assumption
> that everything must have a cause and ends with something that lacks
> one. As for the view that morals can be founded on divine authority,
> the decisive objection was beautifully put by Bertrand Russell: 'The-
> ologians have always taught that God's decrees are good, and that
> this is not a mere tautology; it follows that goodness is logically inde-
> pendent of God's decrees.' This argument also shows that even if
> George had been able to discover his second God it would not have
> been of any service to him, It would provide a utilitarian motive for
> good behaviour, but that was not what he wanted. It could, more
> respectably, provide an object for emulation, but for that imaginary or
> even actual human beings could serve as well. . . .

The moral of the play, in so far as it has one, seemed to be that George was humane, and therefore human, in a way the others were not. This could have been due to his beliefs, but it did not have to be. Whatever Kant may have said, morality is very largely founded on sympathy and affection, and for these one does not require religious sanctions. Even logical positivists are capable of love.

After reading Ayer's review, Stoppard invited him to lunch, and the two men became close friends.

We now flash forward to an entry in my journal for October 19, 1976, when Stoppard and I motored to New College, Oxford, to be Ayer's guests for dinner at High Table. An English drama critic once said, 'Stoppard, who never went to a university, writes more like a University Wit than any graduate dramatist now practising.' The trip to New College would be Stoppard's initiation into Oxford life, and he would be going in off the top board, since, of all the dons currently teaching at the university, Ayer is the reigning superstar.

En route to Oxford, Tom and I lunch at the Waterside Inn, plush French restaurant forty minutes west of London by car. The Thames idles past our table, visible through plate glass and weeping willows. Tom talks of how, earlier this year, he lunched with the Queen at Buckingham Palace: 'Everything you touch is beautiful, and the food is superb. The other guests were writers, athletes, accountants — all kinds of people. Don't expect me to knock occasions like that. I'm very conservative. As a foreigner, I'm more patriotic than anyone else in England except William Davis.' (Davis is the German-born editor of *Punch*.) I ask whether there's any living person he especially longs to meet. Three names cross his mind: Marlon Brando, Alexander Solzhenitsyn, and Sugar Ray Robinson. We discuss his view of politics in general and British politics in particular: 'I don't lose any sleep if a policeman in Durham beats somebody up, because I know it's an exceptional case. It's a sheer perversion of speech to describe the society I live in as one that inflicts violence on the underprivileged. What worries me is not the bourgeois exception but the totalitarian norm. Of all the systems that are on offer, the one I don't want is the one that denies freedom of expression — no matter what its allegedly redeeming virtues may be. The only thing that would make me leave England would be control over free speech.' Of his plays he says, 'My characters are all mouthpieces for points of view rather than explorations of individual psychology. They aren't realistic in any sense. I write plays of ideas uneasily married to comedy or farce.' Has he got any manuscripts hidden away in a bottom drawer? He grins and answers, 'No — with me everything is top drawer.' We talk about James Joyce's exuberantly erotic letters to his wife, which have recently been published for the first time. If

Tom had read them before writing *Travesties*, in which Joyce is a leading character, would he have made use of them? 'I wouldn't have dreamed of it. I'm interested in Joyce the author of *Ulysses*, not Joyce the husband. Nor, by the way, do I think of him as a biochemical parcel consumed by worms. I believe there is something of him that is still around, still capable of suffering because of the revelations made public by Faber & Faber.'

After lunch, coffee at the large nondescript Victorian house that Tom bought four years ago in the nearby village of Iver, in Buckinghamshire. The garden, though spacious, is a bit too close for comfort to a traffic roundabout. In his book-upholstered study, he shows me his most prized possessions, among them a first edition of Hemingway's *In Our Time* and a framed letter, written in January, 1895, at the Albemarle Hotel, London, in response to an insolent request for an interview, a photograph, and a job as the addressee's literary agent:

Sir, — I have read your letter and I see that to the brazen everything is brass.

Your obedient servant,
OSCAR WILDE

What would Tom do if he found a gold mine under his garden and never needed to work again? 'Nothing spectacular. I love books — nonfiction for preference. If I had a gigantic windfall of bullion, I'd take a six-month sabbatical, pluck out of my shelves the two or three hundred books I haven't opened, and just read. The secret of happiness is inconspicuous consumption.' For such a wealthy writer, he leads a comparatively simple life. He employed his first secretary only a year ago ('I got the idea from Harold Pinter') and knows little about his financial affairs, which are handled by his brother, a professional accountant.

Thence to Oxford, an hour's drive away, and the back quad of New College, where Freddie Ayer, scholastically gowned, gives us sherry in his rooms. A busy, bright-eyed man, short of stature and formidably alert, he tells me that C. S. Lewis, the great critic, novelist, and Christian apologist, described him after their first meeting as 'a cross between a rodent and a firefly.' He shares Tom's passion for cricket. 'I used to captain the New College Senior Common Room XI,' he says proudly. 'The first time I played for the team, I was fifty-three years old and I scored seventy-five' — a highly respectable total. We then pass through the ritual stages of an Oxford banquet.

Phase I: We meet the Warden of the College at his lodgings, where the other dons and their guests are assembled, making about forty in all. More sherry is consumed, with champagne as the alternative option. 'My taste in theatre is mainly classical,' Freddie says, adding that the twentieth-century playwrights he most admires are Pirandello, Coward, Maugham, and Sartre. 'I vastly prefer Sartre's plays to his philosophy. Existentialism works much better in the theatre than in theory.'

Phase II: We march in procession to take our place at High Table, set on a dais overlooking hundreds of already seated undergraduates. Tom and I sit on either side of Freddie. Food forgettable; wines exceptional (hock, Burgundy, Sauternes). 'Tom is the only living dramatist whose work I would go to see just because he wrote it,' Freddie says. 'There was a time when I would have said the same about John Osborne, but now — well, let's say I would wait to be taken by other people. With John, the rhetoric runs away with the context. Tom plays with words and makes them dance. John uses them as a sledgehammer.'

Phase III: We move on to a panelled, candlelit chamber and are seated at tables where port, Madeira, and Moselle are circulated. Tom tells me a story of how he attended a performance of *Travesties*, at the Aldwych Theatre, in London, in order to be introduced to the proposed French translator of the play. In the intermission, he presented himself at the manager's office, where a group of people were sipping drinks. Before long, they were joined by a foreign-looking stranger with flaring nostrils. Taking the newcomer into a corner, Tom embarked on a detailed explanation of the major linguistic problems posed by the text. The man seemed a little perplexed, but he nodded politely, and Tom pushed ahead for fully five minutes. Suddenly, a thought shot through his mind: What an odd coincidence that I should have a French translator who looks exactly like Rudolf Nureyev. At that moment, there was knock on the door, and in came a little man in a beret, smoking a Gauloise. . . .

Phase IV: We end up in a common room for coffee and/or brandy. Here Tom amazes me. Either he has put himself through a refresher course (which is by no means impossible) or he is even cleverer than I suspected. He shows himself splendidly equipped to hold his own with Freddie and his colleagues in philosophical debate. With scintillating skill, he defends such theses as the following: (a) that Wagner's music is not as good as it sounds, and (b) that there are *fewer* things in heaven and earth than are dreamed of in philosophy. I am also impressed by his ability, under whatever pressure, to quote Bertrand Russell verbatim, especially after five hours of steady alcoholic intake. At one point, I interject a tentative reference to Eastern philosophies, but Freddie pooh-poohs them with Hegelian vehemence, dismissing Taoism, Confucianism, Hinduism, and Buddhism in a single barking laugh. 'They have some psychological interest, but nothing more than that,' he adds. 'For the most part, they're devices for reconciling people to a perfectly dreadful earthly life. I believe there were one or two seventh-century Indians who contributed a few ideas to mathematics. But that's about all.' I expect Tom would agree.

By 1972, the year of *Jumpers*, the voice of Vaclav Havel had been efficiently stifled. The ban on Czech productions of his work had remained in operation since 1969. Censorship had returned to the press and the broadcasting stations as well as to the theatre and the cinema; and in January, 1969, Gustav Husak (Dubcek's successor as Communist Party Secretary) made an ominous speech in which he said that the time had come to 'strengthen internal discipline.' He issued a strong warning to those who held 'private meetings in their apartments for inventing campaigns' against the regime. Havel and Jan Nemec, the film director, at once sent a courageous telegram to President Ludvik Svoboda, protesting against Husak's threats and predicting (with melancholy accuracy) that the next step would be police interrogations and arrests. Later in 1969, Havel received an American foundation grant that would enable him to spend a year in the United States. The Czech government responded by confiscating his passport. Productions of his plays outside Czechoslovakia had been effectively forbidden, because the state literary agency, through which all foreign contracts had to be negotiated, refused to handle Havel's work, on the ground that it gave a distorted picture of Czechoslovakian life. This meant that thenceforward there was no officially sanctioned way for anything by Havel to be performed anywhere in the world. The authorities, however, were far from satisfied. What irked them was that they could drum up no evidence on which to bring him to court. He had engaged in no antistate activities, and nothing in his plays could be construed as seditious. They recognised in him a stubborn naysayer, a noncollaborator; but dumb insolence was not a criminal offence. One of the archetypes of Czech literature is the hero of Jaroslav Hasek's novel *The Good Soldier Schweik*, who drives his superior officers to distraction by practising passive resistance beneath a mask of pious conformity. Like many Czech dissidents before him, Havel had learned from Schweik's example.

He continued to write. In 1971, the first draft of his latest play, *Conspirators*, translated by Vera Blackwell, reached my desk at the National Theatre. It is set in an unnamed country, conceivably South American, where a corrupt dictatorship has just been overthrown and replaced by a cautious and indecisive democratic government. A group of five staunch patriots (including the chief of police and the head of the general staff) hear rumours of a conspiracy to reinstate the deposed tyrant, now living in exile. Fearful that the new regime will be too weak to prevent a coup, they plan a countercoup of their own. One of them says, 'In order to preserve democracy, we shall have to seize power ourselves.' Their plot necessitates the use of violence, but whenever they meet they learn that their opponents are preparing to commit acts of comparable, if not greater, ferocity. This compels them to devise even more bloodthirsty countermeasures. The process of escalation continues until we suddenly realise what is actually happening. The rumours they hear about the exiled conspirators are in fact

quite accurate accounts of their own conspiracy — reported by a
government spy in their midst and then fed back to them by one of their
own agents in the Secret Service. In other words, as Havel put it in a letter
to me, 'they have been plotting to save the country from themselves.' He
warned me not to suppose that because the play dealt with politics it was a
political play:

> I am not trying either to condemn or to defend this or that political
> doctrine. . . . What I am concerned with is the general problem of
> human behaviour in contemporary society. Politics merely provided
> me with a convenient platform. . . . All the political arguments in the
> play have a certain plausibility, and in some circumstances they might
> even be valid. . . . The point is that one cannot be sure. For truth is not
> only what is said: it depends on who says it, and why. Truth is
> guaranteed only by the full weight of humanity behind it. Modern
> rationalism has led people to believe that what they call 'objective
> truth' is a freely transferable commodity that can be appropriated by
> anyone. The results of this divorce between truth and human beings
> can be most graphically observed in politics.

I was ready to recommend the play for inclusion in the National
Theatre's repertoire as a pirated, unauthorised production (thereby keeping
Havel legally in the clear), but the script needed extensive revision, and the
author, trapped in his homeland, could not come to London to work on it.
For this reason, we decided regretfully to shelve the project. Around this
time, his German publishers (coincidentally, the same as Stoppard's)
decided to thwart the Czech veto by acting as his agents in the Western
world. The state literary agency retaliated by intercepting and withholding
all royalties sent to Havel by Western producers of his work. As far as I
know, *Conspirators* remains unrevised and unperformed.

In 1974, Havel's savings began to run out, and he took the only employment he could find — a post in a brewery in Trutnov, about eighty miles
from Prague. Apart from the income it provided, he welcomed the opportunity of meeting Czech citizens who were not members of the secret
police. Havel's job consisted of stacking empty beer barrels. This period of
his life yielded two short plays, both of them patently autobiographical. In
Audience, thinly disguised under the name of Frederick Vanek, he is summoned to an interview with the head maltster of the brewery, a chain
drinker and experienced compromiser, who jovially offers him a chance to
better himself. Wouldn't it be more seemly for an intellectual like him to
have a post in the stock-checking department, where no manual labour
would be involved? All that Vanek has to do to be thus upgraded is to
submit a weekly report on his thoughts and activities, and to bring a certain
actress (much admired by the maltster) to an office party. Vanek is quite

happy to invite the actress, but he politely explains that he cannot see his way to informing on himself. This provokes the maltster into a self-pitying alcoholic tirade against intellectuals and their so-called principles: 'The thing is, you can live on your flipping principles! But what about me? All I can expect is a kick in the pants if I so much as *mention* a principle.' And so on. Vanek gravely lets the storm pass over his head. The maltster then falls into a stupor, from which, a few moments later, he briskly recovers. Having erased the confessional outburst from his memory, he starts the interview over again as if nothing had happened.

Audience is Havel's vignette of life among the workers. *Private View*, its companion piece, takes a similarly ironic look at life among the intelligentsia. Vanek/Havel is invited to dinner by a sophisticated middle-class couple who are eager to show off their newly redecorated apartment, with its stereo deck, its costly clutter of modern and antique furniture, and its crates of bourbon, picked up on a trip to the States. All this *douceur de vivre*, they point out, could be his. Why does he insist on burying himself in a brewery? If only he would stop associating with people who criticise the regime ('Communists,' his hostess disdainfully calls them), he could easily get a well-paid job in a publishing house. Like the maltster, the couple feel personally affronted (and accused) by his perverse reluctance to make the few small adjustments that could gain him such shining privileges. 'You're an egoist!' his hostess shrieks. 'Disgusting, unfeeling, inhuman egoist! Ungrateful, stupid, bloody traitor!' But her diatribe, like the maltster's, ends as abruptly as it began, and when the curtain falls she and her husband are entertaining their guest with the very latest pop single from New York. (The two plays were broadcast on BBC radio in April, 1977. The role of Vanek was played by Harold Pinter.)

In 1974, the year Havel started stacking beer barrels, Stoppard's third major work, *Travesties*, opened at the Aldwych Theatre, presented by the Royal Shakespeare Company and directed (as *Jumpers* had been) by Peter Wood. The play had its origin in Stoppard's discovery that James Joyce, Lenin, and Tristan Tzara, the founder of Dadaism, had all lived in Zurich during the First World War — a conjunction of expatriates that made instant comic connections in his mind. In addition, he had long wanted to write a leading role for his friend John Wood, a tall aquiline actor who had a matchless capacity for delivering enormous speeches at breakneck speed with crystalline articulation. From Richard Ellmann's biography of Joyce, Stoppard learned that during his stay in Zurich Joyce had been the business manager of a semi-professional troupe of English actors, whose inaugural production was *The Importance of Being Earnest*. The part of Algernon Moncrieff was played by a young man named Henry Carr, who held a minor post at the British consulate. Carr bought a new pair of trousers to embellish his performance, and later sued Joyce for reimbursement. Joyce counterclaimed that Carr owed him the price of five tickets for the show, and, for good measure, accused him of slander. Stoppard sought to link this story, true but implausible, with the hypothesis, plausible but untrue, that Joyce, Tzara, and Lenin had known one another in Zurich. He hit on the idea of filtering the action through the faulty memory of Henry Carr in old age, a querulous eccentric in whose mind fact and fantasy were indissolubly blended. With Henry myopically at the wheel, Stoppard was off to the races. Clive James said of the play in *Encounter*:

> Before John Wood was halfway through his opening speech I already knew that in Stoppard I had encountered a writer of my generation whom I could admire without reserve. It is a common reaction to *Travesties* to say that seeing it is like drinking champagne. But not only did I find that the play tasted like champagne — I found that in drinking it I felt like a jockey. Jockeys drink champagne as an everyday tipple, since it goes to the head without thickening the waist. *Travesties* to me seemed not an exotic indulgence, but the stuff of life. Its high speed was not a challenge but a courtesy; its structural intricacy not a dazzling pattern but a perspicuous design; its fleeting touch not of a feather but of a fine needle.

There were many such panegyrics, not only in London but on Broadway, where the play won Stoppard his second Tony award. (The first had been for *Rosencrantz and Guildenstern*.) I gladly concede that the grotesque rhetorical ramblings of Henry Carr, whether in soliloquy or in his long first-act confrontation with Tzara, are sublimely funny; but at the heart of the enterprise something is sterile and arbitrary. As Ronald Hayman, a devout Stoppard fan, put it, 'there is no internal dynamic.' Stoppard imposes the plot of Wilde's play, itself thoroughly baroque, upon his own burlesque vision of life in wartime Zurich, which is like crossbreeding the bizarre with the bogus. Following Wilde's blueprint, he gives Carr (Algernon) and Tzara (Jack Worthing) a Cecily and a Gwendolen with whom, respectively, to fall in love; while James Joyce stands unconvincingly in for Lady Bracknell. In an interview with Hayman, Stoppard said he was particularly proud of the scene in the first act between Joyce and Tzara:

> It exists almost on three levels. On one it's Lady Bracknell quizzing Jack. Secondly, the whole thing is actually structured on [the eighth] chapter in *Ulysses*, and thirdly, it's telling the audience what Dada is, and where it comes from.

All of which is undeniable, and the well-read playgoer will happily consume such a layer cake of pastiche. But cake, as Marie Antoinette discovered too late, is no substitute for bread. To change the metaphor, the scene resembles a triple-decker bus that isn't going anywhere. What it lacks, in common with the play as a whole, is the sine qua non of theatre; namely, a narrative thrust that impels the characters, whether farcically or tragically or in any intermediate mode, toward a credible state of crisis, anxiety, or desperation. (Even the two derelicts in *Waiting for Godot*, so beloved of Stoppard, are in a plight that most people would consider desperate.) In *Rosencrantz and Guildenstern, Inspector Hound,* and *Jumpers,* acts of homicide are committed — acts insuring that a certain amount of pressure, however factitious, is exerted on the characters. They are obviously in trouble; they may be killed, or, at least, be accused of killing. Trying, as Stoppard does in *Travesties,* to make a play without the magic ingredient of pressure toward desperation is — to lift a phrase from *Jumpers* — 'tantamount to constructing a Gothic arch out of junket.'

The opening speech, for instance, is made up of words that Tristan Tzara has silently cut out of an unidentified newspaper and drawn from a hat. He arranges them at random, and recites them in the form of a limerick. It concludes:

> Ill raced alas whispers kill later nut east.
> Noon avuncular ill day Clara.

To French-speaking members of the audience, the lines sound roughly the same as:

> *Il reste à la Suisse parce qu'il est un artiste.*
> *'Nous n'avons que l'art,'* il déclara.

Which means, roughly Englished:

> He lives in Switzerland because he is an artist.
> 'We have only art,' he declared.

No translation or explanation, however, is offered in the text. Nonspeakers of French are thus left in outer darkness, while French-speakers who have not read the published version are unaware that what they have just heard is a linguistic joke. The result is that nobody laughs. This seems to me unadulterated junket.

As for the arbitrary element in the play, I once asked Stoppard what he would have done if Joyce's company of actors had chosen to present Maxim Gorky's *The Lower Depths* instead of Wilde's comedy. He breezily replied that he would probably have based his plot on Gorky. I have since fed into his mind what I regard as a perfectly corking scenario. During the Second World War, Arnold Schönberg, Swami Prabhavananda, and W. C. Fields were simultaneously working in Hollywood. Cast that trio in

The Lower Depths, and who knows what monument of junket you might come up with?

The hard polemic purpose of *Travesties* is to argue that art must be independent of the world of politics. Carr says to Tzara, 'My dear Tristan, to be an artist *at all* is like living in Switzerland during a world war.' Tzara is the target for Stoppard's loathing of the avant-garde. He is made to describe himself as 'the natural enemy of bourgeois art' (which Stoppard cherishes) and as 'the natural ally of the political left' (which Stoppard abhors). By lending his support to the antibourgeois forces, Tzara has pledged himself to the destruction of art. At one point, he rounds on Joyce and says:

> Your art has failed. You've turned literature into a religion and it's as dead as all the rest, it's an overripe corpse and you're cutting fancy figures at the wake. It's too late for geniuses!

What's needed, the zealous Dadaist goes on, is vandalism and desecration. Having set up Tzara in the bowling alley, Stoppard proceeds to knock him down with a speech by Joyce, which was not in the original script (it was suggested by the director) but which Stoppard now regards as 'the most important . . . in the play.' Joyce begins by dismissing Tzara as 'an overexcited little man, with a need for self-expression far beyond the scope of your natural gifts.' This, he says, is not discreditable, but it does not make him an artist: 'An artist is the magician put among men to gratify — capriciously — their urge for immortality.' If the Trojan War had gone unrecorded in poetry, it would be forgotten by history. It is the artists who have enriched us with its legends — above all, with the tale of 'Ulysses, the wanderer, the most human, the most complete of all heroes.' He continues, 'It is a theme so overwhelming that I am almost afraid to treat it. And yet I with my Dublin Odyssey will double that immortality, yes by God *there's* a corpse that will dance for some time yet and *leave the world precisely as it finds it.*'

So much for any pretensions that art might have to change, challenge, or criticise the world, or to modify, however marginally, our view of it. For that road can lead only to revolution, and revolution will mean the end of free speech, which is defined by Lenin, later in the play, as speech that is *'free from bourgeois anarchist individualism.'* Stoppard's idol — the artist for art's sake, far above the squalid temptations of politics — is, unequivocally, Joyce. The first act ends with Henry Carr recounting a dream in which he asked Joyce what he did in the Great War. ' "I wrote *Ulysses*," he said. "What did you do?" '

The implication of all this — that Joyce was an apolitical dweller in an ivory tower — is, unfortunately, untrue. He was a professed socialist. And this is where Stoppard's annexation of the right to alter history in the cause of art begins to try one's patience. (A minor symptom of the same sin occurs when Carr says that Oscar Wilde was 'indifferent to politics' — a statement that will come as a surprise to readers of Wilde's propagandist handbook *The Soul of Man under Socialism*.) In a recent essay in the *New York Review of Books*, Richard Ellmann has pointed out that Joyce's library in Trieste was full of works by leftist authors; that the culmination of his political hopes was the foundation of the Irish Free State; and that Leopold Bloom, in *Ulysses*, is a left-winger of long standing who annoys his wife by informing her that Christ was the first socialist. Moreover, Ellmann quotes a speech from the quasi-autobiographical first draft of *A Portrait of the Artist* in which Joyce addresses the people of the future with oratorical fervour:

> Man and woman, out of you comes the nation that is to come, the lightening of your masses in travail, the competitive order is arrayed against itself, the aristocracies are supplanted, and amid the general paralysis of an insane society, *the confederate will* issues in action.

The phrase I've italicised can only mean, as Ellmann says, 'the will of like-minded revolutionaries.' It is all very well for Stoppard to claim that he has mingled 'scenes which are self-evidently documentary . . . with others which are just as evidently fantastical.' The trouble with his portrait of Joyce is that it is neither one thing nor the other, neither pure fantasy nor pure documentary, but is simply based on a false premise. When matters of high importance are being debated, it is not pedantic to object that the author has failed to do his homework.

The second act of *Travesties* is dominated by Lenin. Stoppard quotes him fairly and at length but cannot fit him into the stylistic framework of the play. Somerset Maugham once said that sincerity in society was like an iron girder in a house of cards. Lenin is the girder that topples *Travesties*. Stoppard fleetingly considered making him the equivalent of Miss Prism, the governess in *The Importance* — 'but that,' he wisely concluded, 'would have killed the play because of the trivialisation.' On the other hand, he did think it would be funny to start Act II with a pretty girl (Cecily) delivering a lecture on Lenin. 'And indeed it *was* funny,' he told an interviewer, 'except that I was the only person laughing.' (I wonder, incidentally, what he found so comic about the idea of a pretty girl taking Lenin seriously.) At all events, the lecture stayed in, funny or not, together with the ensuing scenes, which deal with Lenin and his plans for revolution. Too frail a bark to bear such weighty cargo, the play slowly capsizes and sinks.

A footnote from Derek Marlowe: 'With Tom, words always precede thoughts. Phrases come first, ideas later. The Stoppard you find in *Travesties* doesn't sound any older than the Stoppard of *Rosencrantz and*

Guildenstern. You'd think that nothing had happened to him in the intervening seven years. But, by God, a great deal has.'

After *Travesties*, a literary circus of a play in which historical figures jumped through hoops at the flick of Stoppard's whim, it was clear that he had spent long enough in the library. The time had come to turn his attention to events in the outside world. Not unexpectedly, the field he chose to explore was the treatment of political dissidents in Eastern Europe and the Soviet Union. First, however, he had to fulfill an obligation to Ed Berman. Berman is an expatriate American, bursting with bearded enthusiasm, who came to London in 1968 and set up a cooperative organization called Inter-Action, which presents plays in schools, remand homes, youth clubs, mental hospitals, community centres, and the streets. Inter-Action also runs a thriving farm in the dingy heart of a London suburb and launched the Almost Free Theatre, in Soho, where the price of admission is whatever you think the show will be worth. Berman produced the world premiere of two one-acters by Stoppard (*After Magritte*, in 1970, and *Dogg's Our Pet*, the following year), and not long afterward Stoppard, learning that Berman had applied for British citizenship, promised to give him a new play if the application was successful. It was, and *Dirty Linen*, Stoppard's deadpan farce about sexual misconduct in the House of Commons, opened at the Almost Free Theatre in April, 1976. It was an instant hit. The Czech émigré had done honour to his American counterpart, welcoming him to membership in the Western European club.

Simple chronology may be the best way to set out the convergence that subsequently developed between the lives, and careers, of Stoppard and Vaclav Havel.

August, 1976: Stoppard addresses a rally in Trafalgar Square sponsored by the Committee Against Psychiatric Abuse, from which he joins a march to the Soviet Embassy. There he attempts to deliver a petition denouncing the use of mental homes as punishment camps for Russian dissidents. 'The chap at the door wouldn't accept it,' he told me afterward, 'so we all went home.'

October 5, 1976: Havel celebrates his fortieth birthday at the converted farmhouse, ninety miles from Prague,where he and his wife live. The next day, he is officially ordered to quit the place, on the ground, patently false, that it is unfit for human habitation.

January 11, 1977: *Dirty Linen* opens on Broadway, to generally favourable reviews. Walter Kerr, in his Sunday column in the *New York Times*, sounds one of the few discordant notes:

Intellectually restless as a hummingbird, and just as incapable of lighting anywhere, the playwright has a gift for making the randomness of his flights funny. . . . Busy as Mr. Stoppard's mind is, it is also lazy; he will settle for the first thing that pops into his head. . . . Wide-ranging as his antic interests are, delightful as his impish mismatches can occasionally be, his management of them is essentially slovenly.

One speech that gets an unfailing ovation, however, is the following tribute to the American people, paid by a senior British civil servant:

> They don't stand on ceremony. . . . They make no distinction about a man's background, his parentage, his education. They say what they mean, and there is a vivid muscularity about the way they say it. . . . They are always the first to put their hands in their pockets. They press you to visit them in their own home the moment they meet you, and are irrepressibly good-humoured, ambitious and brimming with self-confidence in any company. Apart from all that I've got nothing against them.

On the thirteenth of the month, Stoppard flies from New York to the West Coast, where he is to undergo a sort of Southern California apotheosis. At the Mark Taper Forum, which is the fountainhead of theatrical activity in Los Angeles, *Travesties* and *The Importance of Being Earnest* are being staged in repertory for the first time. *Inspector Hound* is about to open at a new theatre in Beverly Hills. And the University of California at Santa Barbara is holding 'a Tom Stoppard Festival, during which I will be carried through the streets and pelted with saffron rice,' Stoppard has told me in a letter, adding, 'That is if I haven't gone out of fashion by then.' I hasten to southern California. Stoppard, whisked from the airport to a press conference at the Mark Taper, where I join him, fields every question with effortless charm. For example, 'I suspect I am getting more serious than I was, though with a redeeming streak of frivolity.' And 'We get our moral sensibility from art. When we have a purely technological society, it will be time for mass suicide.' What American playwrights does he admire? Sam Shepard, for one; and Edward Albee, 'especially for *The Zoo Story* and *A Delicate Balance*. But my favourite American play is *The Front Page* — though I might have to admit, if extremely pressed, that it wasn't *quite* as fine as *Long Day's Journey into Night*.'

January 14, 1977: Vaclav Havel is arrested in Prague and thrown into jail. The real, though unacknowledged, reason for his imprisonment is that he is one of three designated spokesmen for a document called Charter 77, signed by over three hundred leading Czech writers and intellectuals, which urges the government to carry out its promises, made in the Helsinki accords of 1975, to respect human rights, especially those relating to free speech.

On the same day, leaving Los Angeles at dawn, I drive Stoppard to the Santa Barbara campus, which is preposterously pretty, palm-fringed, and moistened by ocean breakers. A silk scarf is knotted round his neck, and he wears flashy cowboy boots. We are met by Dr. Homer Swander, professor of English. A bronzed, gray-haired fan, he proudly informs Stoppard that no fewer than four of his plays will be presented at the university within the next week. In addition, there will be mass excursions to L.A. to see *Inspector Hound*, *The Importance*, and *Travesties*. During the morning, Tom discusses his work with a class of drama students. 'I'm a very conventional artist,' he says when someone quizzes him about Dadaism. 'I have no sympathy at all with Tristan Tzara. The trouble with modern art, from my point of view, is that there's nothing left to parody.'

A girl asks him, 'Which of your plays do you think will be performed in fifty years' time?'

He replies, 'There is no way I can answer that question without sounding arrogant to the point of mania or modest to the point of nausea.'

Lunch with the top brass of the faculty is followed by a tour of the campus. The Mark Taper Forum has paid Tom's round-trip air fare from New York; a thousand dollars is his reward for spending the day at Santa Barbara. His lecture that evening fills a nine-hundred-seat auditorium to overflowing. Dr. Swander introduces him as an author in whom Santa Barbara has long taken a proprietary interest. (This is his second visit to the place in two years.) 'We claim him as our own,' Dr. Swander declares, to applause, 'and I personally acclaim him as the most Shakespearean writer in English drama since Webster.'

Stoppard lopes into sight, detaches the microphone from its stand to gain mobility, and lights a cigarette. 'I've been brought ten thousand miles to talk to you about theatre,' he says, 'which I find only slightly more plausible than coming here on a surfing scholarship.' Solid laughter. 'I should explain that my technique when lecturing is to free-associate within an infinite regression of parentheses. Also, it's only fair to confess that what you are about to hear is in the nature of an ego trip.' To illustrate the problems of dramatic composition, he has brought along two dozen drafts of the blast of invective that Tzara launches against Joyce in *Travesties*. He reads them out, from the first attempt, which begins, 'You blarney-arsed bog-eating Irish pig,' to the final version, which starts, 'By God, you supercilious streak of Irish puke!' What isn't commonly understood, he adds, is that 'all this takes *weeks*.' He paces for a while, and then notices a heavy glass ashtray that has been thoughtfully placed on a table in front of him. 'Writing a play,' he continues, 'is like smashing that ashtray, filming it in slow motion, and then running the film in reverse, so that the fragments of rubble appear to fly together. You start — or at least *I* start — with the rubble.'

Strolling back and forth across the stage, meditatively puffing on his cigarette, he says, 'Whenever I talk to intelligent students about my work, I feel nervous, as if I were going through customs. "Anything to declare, sir?" "Not really, just two chaps sitting in a castle at Elsinore, playing games. That's all." "Then let's have a look in your suitcase, if you don't mind, sir." And, sure enough, under the first layer of shirts there's a pound of hash and fifty watches and all kinds of exotic contraband. "How do you explain this, sir?" "I'm sorry, Officer, I admit it's there, but I honestly can't remember packing it." ' He says he has addressed only one American campus audience apart from the present assembly; that was at Notre Dame, in 1971, and the occasion did not get off to an auspicious start. 'I began my talk by saying that I had not written my plays for purposes of discussion,' he recalls in Santa Barbara. 'At once, I felt a ripple of panic run through the hall. I suddenly realised why. To everyone present, *discussion was the whole point of drama.* That was why the faculty had been endowed — that was why all those buildings had been put up! I had undermined the entire reason for their existence.'

There are questions from the floor.

Q.: May I say, Mr. Stoppard, that I think you are less slick this time than you were two years ago?

STOPPARD: Oh, good. Or — I'm sorry. Depending on your point of view.

Q.: Why don't you try directing your own work? Or acting in it?

STOPPARD: Look, I spend only about three and a half percent of my life writing plays. I'm trying very hard to build it up to four and a half percent. That's all I can handle at the moment.

(Tom's modesty is a form of egoism. It is as if he were saying, 'See how self-deprecating I can be and still be self-assertive.')

His act has a strong finish. For an hour and a half, he says, he has shared his thoughts with us and answered many of our questions. But what is the real dialogue that goes on between the artist and his audience? By way of reply, he holds the microphone close to his mouth and speaks eight lines by the English poet Christopher Logue:

> Come to the edge.
> We might fall.
> Come to the edge.
> It's too high!
> **COME TO THE EDGE!**
> And they came

> and he pushed
> and they flew.

A short silence. Then a surge of applause. In imagination, these young people are all flying.

February 11, 1977: Stoppard has an article in the *New York Times* about the new wave of repression in Prague. It starts:

> Connoisseurs of totalitarian double-think will have noted that Charter 77, the Czechoslovak document which calls attention to the absence in that country of various human rights beginning with the right of free expression, has been refused publication inside Czechoslovakia on the grounds that it is a wicked slander.

Of the three leading spokesmen for Charter 77, two were merely interrogated and released — Jiri Hajek, who had been Foreign Minister under Alexander Dubcek in 1968, and Jan Patocka, an internationally respected philosopher. (Patocka, however, was later rearrested, and, after further questioning, suffered a heart attack and died in hospital.) Havel alone was charged under the subversion laws, which carry a maximum sentence of ten years. 'Clearly,' Stoppard says, 'the regime had decided, finally and after years of persecution and harassment, to put the lid on Vaclav Havel.'

February 27, 1977: Stoppard travels to Moscow with a representative of Amnesty International and meets a number of victimised Soviet nonconformists, in support of whom he writes a piece for the London *Sunday Times*.

May 20, 1977: After four months' imprisonment in a cell seven feet by twelve, which he shared with a burglar, Havel is released. The subversion indictment is dropped, but he must still face trial on a lesser charge, of damaging the name of the state abroad, for which the maximum prison term is three years. He agrees not to make 'any public political statements' while this new case is *sub judice*. The state attempts to make it a condition of his release that he resign his position as spokesman for Charter 77. He rejects the offer. Once outside the prison gates, however, he unilaterally announces that, although he remains an impenitent supporter of Charter 77, he will relinquish the job of spokesman until his case has been settled in court. He returns, together with his wife, to the farmhouse from which they were evicted the previous fall. (In October, when Havel's case came up for trial, he received a fourteen-month suspended sentence.)

June 18, 1977: By now, Stoppard has recognised in Havel his mirror image — a Czech artist who has undergone the pressures that Stoppard escaped when his parents took him into exile. After thirty-eight years' of absence (and two weeks before his fortieth birthday), Stoppard goes back to his native land. He flies to Prague, then drives ninety miles north to Havel's home, where he meets his *Doppelgänger* for the first time. They spend five or six hours together, conversing mainly in English. Stoppard tells me later that some of the Marxist signatories of Charter 77 regard Havel primarily as a martyr with celebrity value, and didn't want him as their spokesman in the first place. 'But they didn't go to jail,' Stoppard adds. 'He did. He is a very brave man.'

Like Stoppard, Havel asks only to be allowed to work freely, without political surveillance. But that in itself is a political demand, and the man who makes it on his own behalf is morally bound to make it for others. Eleven years earlier, Stoppard's hero Lord Malquist said, undoubtedly echoing his author's views, 'Since we cannot hope for order, let us withdraw with style from the chaos.' Stoppard has moved from withdrawal to involvement. Some vestige of liberty may yet be reclaimed from the chaos, and if Stoppard has any hand in the salvage operation we may be sure that it will be carried out with style.

Nothing that he writes, however, is likely to give comfort to those who are not content to delegate the administration of liberty to 'an intellectual elite and a progressive middle class' — the phrase, as I've already noted, that Stoppard has recently used to indicate where his deepest loyalties lie. He is not a standard-bearer for those who seek to create, anywhere in the world, a society like that which permitted the Prague Spring of 1968 to put forth its prodigious, polymorphous flowering. For that was a socialist society, and, of the many artists who flourished in it, Vaclav Havel was almost alone in not being a socialist. I wonder — or, rather, I doubt — whether Stoppard would seriously have relished living in the libertarian socialist Prague whose suppression by the Soviets he now so eloquently deplores.

July 1, 1977: World premiere, at the Festival Hall, in London, of Stoppard's latest piece, *Every Good Boy Deserves Favour*, acted by members of the Royal Shakespeare Company (including John Wood) and accompanied by the London Symphony Orchestra. Its subject: the use of pseudo-psychiatry to brainwash political dissenters in Soviet mental hospitals. With few exceptions, the reviews are eulogistic. Michael Billington writes in the *Guardian*:

> Stoppard brilliantly defies the theatrical law that says you cannot have your hand on your heart and your tongue in your cheek at the same time. . . . An extraordinary work in which iron is met with irony and rigidity with a relaxed, witty defiance.

Bernard Levin, in the London *Sunday Times*, pulls out all the stops:

> Although this is a profoundly moral work, the argument still undergoes the full transmutation of art, and is thereby utterly

changed; as we emerged, it was the fire and glitter of the play that possessed us, while its eternal truth, which is that the gates of hell shall not prevail, was by then inextricably embedded in our hearts. . . . I tell you this man could write a comedy about Auschwitz, at which we would sit laughing helplessly until we cried with inextinguishable anger.

What is Stoppard's picture of happiness? Work and domesticity, of course, enlivened by friendship and the admiration of his artistic peers. But of the thing itself — pure, irresponsible joy — his work gives us only one glimpse. It is an image summoned up from childhood and scarred by the passage of years. In *Where Are They Now?*, a radio play he wrote in 1969, a middle-aged man attends a class reunion at his public school and recalls a single moment of unalloyed delight. He was seven years old at the time:

I remember walking down one of the corridors, trailing my finger along a raised edge along the wall, and I was suddenly totally happy, not elated or particularly pleased, or anything like that — I mean I experienced happiness as a state of being: everywhere I looked, in my mind, *nothing was wrong*. You never get that back when you grow up; it's a condition of maturity that almost *everything* is wrong, *all the time*, and happiness is a borrowed word for something else — a passing change of emphasis.

The New Yorker: 19th December 1977;
Show People, 1980

MEL BROOKS

On a warm night in October, 1959, I was bidden to a party at Mamma Leone's, a restaurant on Forty-eighth Street that was (and is) one of the largest and most popular in Manhattan's theatre district. Random House had taken it over for the evening to celebrate the publication of *Act One*, the first volume of Moss Hart's autobiography, which in no way surprised its publishers by turning out to be a best-seller. A further excuse for festivity was the fact that the author's fifty-fifth birthday was to take place the following day. By any standards, the guest list — some three hundred strong — was fairly eye-catching. In addition to a favoured bunch of critics and columnists, it included a representative selection of the show-business celebrities then active or resident in New York, among them Claudette Colbert, John Gielgud, Jose Ferrer, Margaret Leighton, Ed Sullivan, Alan Jay Lerner, Yves Montand, Simone Signoret, Ethel Merman, Alec Guinness, Truman Capote, Rosalind Russell, and Marlene Dietrich — at which point my memory gives out. A group of Moss Hart's admirers had put together a floor show in his honour, and this was already under way when I arrived. Betty Comden and Adolph Green were just finishing a routine that satirized some of the more disastrous ways in which *Act One* might be adapted for the screen. During the applause, I was burrowing through the resplendent mob, and like many of my fellow guests, I failed to catch the names of the next performers when they were introduced by the master of ceremonies, Phil Silvers.

Peering over the heads of a hundred or so standees, in front of whom the other spectators sat, squatted, or sprawled, I saw two men in business suits. One, tall and lean, was conducting an interview with the other, who was short and compact. Their faces were among the few in the room that were not instantly recognizable. Though I took no notes, I recall much of what they said, and the waves of laughter that broke over it, and the wonder with which I realized that every word of it was improvised. The tall man was suave but relentlessly probing, the stubby one urgent and eager in response, though capable of outrage when faced with questions he regarded as offensive. Here, having been shaken through the sieve of nineteen years, is what my memory retains:

Q.: I gather, sir, that you are a famous psychoanalyst?
A.: That is correct.

Q.: May I ask where you studied psychiatry?

A.: At the Vienna School of Good Luck.

Q.: Who analyzed you?

A.: I was analyzed by No. 1 himself.

Q.: You mean the great Sigmund Freud?

A.: In person. Took me during lunchtime, charged me a nickel.

Q.: What kind of man was he?

A.: Lovely little fellow. I shall never forget the hours we spent together, me lying on the couch, him sitting right there beside me, wearing a nice off-the-shoulder dress.

Q.: Is it true, sir, that Mr. Moss Hart is one of your patients?

A.: That is also correct.

[As everyone present knew, Moss Hart had been in analysis for many years, and made no secret of the benefits he had derived from it.]

Q.: Could you tell us, sir, what Mr. Hart talks about during your analytic sessions?

A.: He talks smut. He talks dirty, he talks filthy, he talks pure, unadulterated smut. It makes me want to puke.

Q.: How do you cope with this?

A.: I give him a good slap on the wrists. I wash his mouth out with soap. I tell him, 'Don't talk dirty, don't say those things.'

Q.: What are Mr. Hart's major problems? Does he have an Oedipus complex?

A.: What is that?

Q.: You're an analyst, sir, and you never heard of an Oedipus complex?

A.: Never in my life.

Q.: Well, sir, it's when a man has a passionate desire to make love to his own mother.

A.: (*after a pause*): That's the dirtiest thing I ever heard. Where do you get that filth?

Q.: It comes from a famous play by Sophocles.

A.: Was he Jewish?

Q.: No, sir, he was Greek.

A.: With a Greek, who knows? But, with a Jew, you don't do a thing like that even to your wife, let alone your mother.

Q.: But, sir, according to Freud, *every* man has this intense sexual attachment to his —

A.: Wait a minute, wait a minute, whoa, hee-haw, just hold your horses right there. Moss Hart is a nice Jewish boy. Maybe on a Saturday night he takes the mother to the movies, maybe on the way home he gives her a little peck in the back of the cab, but going to bed with the mother — get out of here! What kind of smut is that?

Q.: During your sessions with Mr. Hart, does he ever become

emotionally overwrought?

A.: Very frequently, and it's a degrading spectacle.

Q.: How do you handle these situations?

A.: I walk straight out of the room, I climb up a step-ladder, and I toss in aspirins through the transom.

When they stopped, after about a quarter of an hour, the cabaret ended, and that was just as well, for nobody could have followed them. A crowd of professional entertainers erupted in cheers. The idea of a puritanical analyst was a masterstroke of paradox, and the execution had matched the concept in brilliance. Moss Hart was heard to say that the act was the funniest fourteen minutes he could remember. The room buzzed with comment, yet hardly anyone seemed to know who the little maestro was. Diligent quizzing revealed that he was a thirty-three-year old television writer, that he had spent most of the preceding ten years turning out sketches for Sid Caesar, and that his name was Mel Brooks. Facially, he had one attribute that is shared, for reasons I have never been able to fathom, by nearly all top-flight comedians; viz., a long upper lip. I later discovered that his interrogator was Mel Tolkin, another, and a senior, member of the renowned menagerie of authors whose scripts, as interpreted by Caesar, Imogene Coca, and a talented supporting cast, had made 'Your Show of Shows' a golden landmark in the wasteland of television comedy. Tolkin (a harassed-looking man, once compared by Brooks to a 'a stork that dropped a baby and broke it and is coming to explain to the parents') was standing in at the party for Carl Reiner, a gifted performer who had also been part of the Caesarean operation. Ever since they met, in 1950, Brooks and Reiner had been convulsing their friends with impromptu duologues. The Moss Hart jamboree was an important show-business event, and, the press being present in force, it would have marked their semi-public debut. Unfortunately, Reiner had a TV job in Los Angeles and could not make the date; hence his replacement by Tolkin, who had performed with Brooks on several previous occasions, though never in front of such a daunting audience. I knew nothing of this at the time; Tolkin struck me as a first-rate straight man. All I knew as I left Mamma Leone's that night was that his stubby, pseudo Freudian partner was the most original comic improviser I had ever seen.

We move forward to Hollywood in 1977. Carl Reiner, who has just directed a boomingly successful comedy called *Oh, God!*, recalls for me the events that led up to Brooks's appearance at the Hart party. 'During the fifties,' he says, 'we spent our days inventing characters for Caesar, but Mel was really using Caesar as a vehicle. What he secretly wanted to do was to perform himself. So in the evening we'd go to a party and I'd pick a character for him to play. I never told him what it was going to be, but I always tried for something that would force him to go into panic, because a brilliant mind in panic is a wonderful thing to see. For instance, I might say, "We have with us tonight the celebrated sculptor Sir Jacob Epstone," and he'd have to take it from there. Or I'd make him a Jewish pirate, and he'd complain about how he was being pushed out of the business because of the price of sailcloth and the cost of crews nowadays. Another time, I introduced him as Carl Sandburg, and he made up reams of phony Sandburg poetry. There was no end to what he could be — a U–boat commander, a deaf songwriter, an entire convention of antique dealers.

'Once, I started a routine by saying "Sir, you're the Israeli wrestling champion of the world, yet you're extremely small. How do you manage to defeat all those enormous opponents?" "I give them a soul kiss," he said, "and they're so shocked they collapse. Sometimes I hate doing it, like when it's a Greek wrestler, because they have garlic breath." I asked him whether he was homosexual. "No, I have a wife." "But what's the difference between kissing her and kissing a wrestler?" "My wife," he said, "is the only one I know who kisses from the inside out." That was pure Mel — a joke so wild it was almost abstract. I used to enjoy trying to trap him. One night, when he was doing an Israeli heart surgeon, I said, "Tell me, sir, who's that huge man standing in the corner?" "Who knows? Who cares?" "But surely, sir, you don't want a total stranger hanging around your operating theatre, bringing in germs?" "Listen, in a hospital, a few germs more or less, what's the difference?" "Even so," I said, "I'm still curious to know what that very large gentleman does." "Look,"he said. "He's a big man, right? With a lot of muscle? You're small and Jewish, you don't mess around with big guys like that. Let him stand there if he wants to." I still wouldn't let him off the hook. "But what's that strange-looking machine beside him?" "You mean the cyclotron?" "No, the one next to that." "Oh," he said, "that is the Rokeach 14 machine. It makes Jewish soap powder. As you well know, we Jewish doctors are incredibly clean, and we try not to soil our patients during the macabre process of cutting them to pieces. We get through an awful lot of Rokeach 14." Which is in fact a brand of kosher soap used by orthodox Jews.' (Brooks later told me, apropos of Reiner's attempts to outwit him, 'He was absolutely dazzling. I'd be going along pretty good, getting laughs, and he would suddenly people the room with alien characters bearing mysterious devices. What was I supposed to do? I had to come up with an explanation or die.')

'Another time,' Reiner continues, 'we created a family consisting of a Jewish mother, a black father, and a homosexual son. Mel was playing all three parts when I threw him a curve. "Tell me," I said, "why is your son white-haired when you are not?" He answered as the mother. "I told him always to stay inside the building," he said, "because it's full of Jews. One day, he went out and saw a whole bunch of Gentiles on the next block and his hair turned white overnight. It was his own fault. He should have stayed indoors." Sometimes, if a party went on late, Mel would get punchy and forget the name of the character I'd given him. Once, I said, "Here is Irving Schwartz, author of the best-selling novel *Up*." We developed that for ten minutes or so, and then I said, "Your book has a very unusual jacket. It's triangular in shape." "I'm glad you noticed that," he said. "It's a one-breasted seersucker jacket. The name is on the lapel — Irving Feinberg." "I think you've got that wrong, sir. Your name is Irving Schwartz." "Wait," he said. "Wait till I look at my driver's licence." He pulled out his wallet, looked at the licence, and reacted with shock. "Hey!" he said. "My name is Mr. William Faversham." "Well, Mr. Faversham, could you tell us how you came to write a book under the name of Schwartz?" "I think somebody stole my wallet." But if Mel had a speciality, it was psychiatrists. He did dozens of them, maybe because he was in analysis himself between 1951 and 1957. When I made him a Greek psychiatrist, he said he was Dr. Corinne Corfu, the man who analyzed Socrates. And there was one amazing evening when he played eight different psychiatrists simultaneously, without getting any of them mixed up. He was never at a loss.'

'Never' may be an overstatement. Mel Tolkin remembers a party at which Brooks, sans Reiner, delivered a soaringly funny monologue but could not find a satisfactory payoff line. He finally broke off in the middle of a sentence and walked out of the room. After the guests had waited for a while in expectant silence, Tolkin went out to look for him. He had gone home in self-disgust, leaving a scribbled note on a table. It read, 'A Jew cries for help!'

'In the fifties,' Reiner says, 'Mel and I performed just for fun, among friends.' Around 1953, Reiner bought a tape recorder on which to preserve some of their routines. One evening, after dinner at his home in Westchester, inspiration nudged him. He turned on the machine, picked up the microphone, strolled over to where Brooks was sitting, and said, 'Ladies and gentlemen, we are fortunate to have with us tonight a man who was present at the crucifixion of Jesus Christ.' The curve had been thrown. Brooks rose to the challenge and hit it out of the park, with repercussions to which we shall return: enough, for the moment, to note that this occasion marked the birth of a comic figure indestructible in every sense of the word; namely, the Two-Thousand-Year-Old Man. 'The guy who gave us our entrée into the celebrity world was a well-known playwright named Joe Fields,' Reiner goes on. 'He heard us performing somewhere in the late fifties and invited us to eat at his apartment, along with people like Lerner and Loewe, Harold Rome, and Billy Rose. We became a sort of upper-bohemian cult. Then, in 1959, I appeared in a movie called *Happy Anniversary*, and Mel came to the wrap party for the cast and crew at a restaurant in the Village. Moss Hart was dining with his wife on the other side of the room. Mel recognized him. All of a sudden, he got up and walked across to Hart's table and said, very loudly, "Hello. You don't know who I am. My name is Mel Brooks. Do you know who you are? Your name is Moss Hart. Do you know what you've written? You wrote *Once in a Lifetime* with George Kaufman, and *You Can't Take It with You* and *The Man Who Came to Dinner*. You wrote *Lady in the Dark* and you directed *My Fair Lady*." And he ran right through the list of Hart's credits. "You should be more arrogant!" he shouted. "You have earned the right to be supercilious! *Why are you letting me talk to you?*" He went ranting on like that, and Hart looked petrified. it took him quite a time to realize that Mel wasn't just a nut case. But eventually he started laughing, and everything was fine. Later on, Mel and I did one of our bits. Hart couldn't help hearing it and that was how we got the invitation to Mamma Leone's.'

In the autumn of 1959, Reiner's career was prospering, both on TV and in the cinema. As he put it to me, 'I didn't need to sing for my supper anymore.' Brooks's position was very different. Sid Caesar, for whom he had worked at a steeply rising salary for ten years, had been taken off the air, and Brooks was almost broke. 'One day it's five thousand a week, the next day it's zilch,' he said in a magazine interview long afterward, 'I couldn't get a job anywhere! Comedy shows were out of style, and the next five years I averaged eighty-five dollars a week. . . . It was a terrifying nose dive.' Recently, he told me, 'At the time of that Random House party, I was on the brink of disaster.' Even during the high-flying days with Caesar, he had been prone to recurrent fits of depression. 'There were fourteen or fifteen occasions when I seriously thought of killing myself. I even had the pills.' One of his colleagues on 'Your Show of Shows' recalls how Brooks snapped out of a particularly black mood by grabbing a straw hat and cane and ad-libbing a peppy, up-tempo number that ended:

Life may be rotten today, folks,
But I take it all in stride,
'Cause tomorrow I'm on my way, folks —
I'm committing suicide!

Mamma Leone's gave me my first sight of Brooks in performance. My last (to date) took place in the summer of 1977, when he was shooting his Hitchcockian comedy *High Anxiety*. In the intervening eighteen years, and most drastically in the last three of them, his life had changed beyond recognition. A trio of successive hits (*Blazing Saddles, Young Frankenstein,* and *Silent Movie*) had made him a millionaire. In December, 1976, the exhibitors of America had placed him fifth on their annual list of the twenty-five stars who exert the greatest box-office appeal — a fantastic achievement for a middle-aged man whose only starring appearance up to that time had been in a picture, *Silent Movie*, that did not even require him to speak. His friend Burt Reynolds, rated sixth that year, grew accustomed to picking up the phone and hearing a jubilant voice announce, 'Hello, Six, this is Five speaking.' In the 1977 poll, Reynolds rose to fourth position, while Brooks slipped to seventh, but considering that no new film by Brooks had been shown in the preceding year, it was remarkable, as he pointed out to me, that he had retained a place in the top ten. 'And in 1978,' he said, 'I'm sure I'll be No. 5 again.'

I draw on my journal for the following impressions of the Once and Future Five at work (and play) on *High Anxiety*, a quintuple-threat Brooks movie in which he functioned as producer, director, co–author, title-song composer, and star:

July 14, 1977: Arrive in Pasadena for the last day of shooting. By pure but pleasing coincidence, location is named Brookside Park. Temperature ninety degrees, atmosphere smog-laden. Only performers present are Brooks, leaping around in well-cut charcoal-gray suit with vest, and large flock of trained pigeons. As at Mamma Leone's, he is playing a psychiatrist. Sequence in rehearsal is parody of *The Birds*, stressing aspect of avian behaviour primly ignored by Hitchcock: Pigeons pursue fleeing Brooks across park, subjecting him to bombardment of bird droppings. Spattered star seeks refuge in gardener's hut, slams door, sinks exhausted onto upturned garbage can. After momentary respite, lone white plop hits lapel, harbinger of redoubled aerial assault through hole in roof. Brooks's hundred-yard dash is covered by tracking camera, while gray-haired technicians atop motorized crane mounted on truck squirt bird excreta (simulated by mayonnaise and chopped spinach) from height of thirty feet. Barry Levinson, one of four collaborators on screenplay, observes to me, 'We have enough equipment here to put a man on the moon, and it's all being used to put bird droppings on Brooks.' After each of numerous trial runs and takes, pigeons obediently return to their cages, putty in the hands of their trainer — 'the same bird wrangler,' publicity man tells me, 'who was employed by Hitchcock himself.' Find manic energy of Brooks, now fifty-one years old, awesome: by the time shot is satisfactorily in can, he will have sprinted, in this depleting heat, at least a mile, without loss of breath, ebullience, or directorial objectivity, and without taking a moment's break.

Each take is simultaneously recorded on videotape and instantly played back on TV screen — a technique pioneered by Jerry Lewis — to be scrutinized by Brooks, along with his fellow-authors, Levinson, Rudy DeLuca, and Ron Clark, who make comments ranging from condign approval to barbed derision. Dispelling myth that he is megalomaniac, Brooks listens persuadably to their suggestions, many of which he carries out. The writers, receiving extra pay as consultants, have been with him throughout shooting, except for three weeks when they went on strike for more money. Brooks coaxed them back by giving up part of his own share of profits not only of *High Anxiety* but of *Silent Movie*, on which he worked with same three authors. Main purpose of their presence is not to rewrite —

hardly a line has been changed or cut — but to offer pragmatic advice. In addition, they all play supporting roles in picture. Later, as also happened on *Silent Movie*, they will view first assembly of footage and help Brooks with process of reducing it to rough-cut form. 'Having us around keeps Mel on his toes,' Levinson explains to me. 'he likes to have constant feedback, and he knows we won't flatter him.' All of which deals telling blow to already obsolescent *auteur* theory, whereby film is seen as springing fully armed from mind of director. Good to find Brooks, who reveres writers, giving them place in sun: he has often said that he became a director primarily in self-defence, to 'protect my vision' — i.e., the script as written. 'There's been no interference from the front office,' Levinson continues, as Brooks trudges back to his mark for yet another charge through cloudburst of salad dressing. 'Nobody from Fox has even come to see us. Mel has free rein. Jerry Lewis once had that kind of liberty, but who has it now? Only Mel and, I guess, Woody Allen.'

Am reminded of remark made to me by Allen a few days earlier: 'In America, people who do comedy are traditionally left alone. The studios feel we're on a wavelength that's alien to them. They believe we have access to some secret formula that they don't. With drama, it's different. Everybody thinks he's an expert.'

Writers and camera crew gather round tree-shaded monitor to watch replay of latest take. Smothered in synthetic ordure, star bustles over to join them:

BROOKS: I stare at life through fields of mayonnaise. (*Wipes eyes with towel.*) Was it for this that I went into movies? Did I say to my mother, 'I'm going to be a big star, momma, and have birds shit on me'? I knew that in show business *people* shit on you — but *birds*! Some of this stuff is not mayonnaise, you know. Those are real pigeons up there.

The take (last of twenty) is generally approved, and Brooks orders it printed. Welcoming me to location, he expresses pleasure at hearing British accent, adding, 'I love the Old World. I love the courteous sound of the engines of English cabs. I also love France and good wine and good food and good homosexual production designers. I believe all production designers should have a brush stroke, a scintilla, of homosexuality, because they have to hang out with smart people.' (Brooks once declared, in an interview with *Playboy*, that he loved Europe so much that he always carried a photograph of it in his wallet. 'Of course,' he went, 'Europe was a lot younger then. It's really not a very good picture. Europe looks much better in person.' He lamented the fact that his beloved continent was forever fighting: 'I'll be so happy when it finally settles down and gets married.')

Brooks's version of shower scene from *Psycho*, shot several days before, now appears on monitor. An unlikely stand-in for Janet Leigh, Brooks is seen in bathrobe approaching fatal tub. Cut to closeup of feet as he daintily sheds sandals, around which robe falls to floor. Next comes rear view of Brooks, naked from head to hips, stepping into bath. Star watches himself entranced.

BROOKS (*passionately*): When people see this, I want them to say, 'He may be just a small Jew, but I love him. A short little Hebrew man, but I'd follow him to the ends of the earth.' I want every fag in L.A. to see it and say, 'Willya *look* at that *back*?'

Before lunch break, he takes opportunity to deliver speech of thanks to assembled crew, whose reactions show that they have relished working with him.

Recall another apposite quote from Woody Allen, who said to me in tones of stunned unbelief, 'I hear there's a sense of enjoyment on Mel's set. I hear the people on his movies love the experience so much that they wish it could go on forever. On my movies, they're *thrilled* when it's over.'

'As you all know,' Brooks begins, 'you'll never get an Academy Award with me, because I make comedies.' This is a recurrent gripe. Brooks feels that film comedy has never received, either from industry or from audience, respect it deserves, and he is fond of pointing out that Chaplin got his 1971 Academy Award 'just for surviving,' not for *The Gold Rush* or *City Lights*.

BROOKS (*continuing*): I want to say from my heart that you're the best crew I ever found. Of course, I didn't look that hard. But you have been the most fun, and the costliest. I wish to express my sincere hope that the next job you get is — *work*.

Over lunch, consumed at long trestle tables under trees, he recounts — between and sometimes during mouthfuls — how he visited Hitchcock to get his blessings on *High Anxiety*.

BROOKS: He's a very emotional man. I told him that where other people take saunas to relax, I run *The Lady Vanishes*, for the sheer pleasure of it. He had tears in his eyes. I think he understood that I wasn't going to make fun of him. If the picture is a sendup, it's also an act of homage to a great artist. I'm glad I met him, because I love him. I love a lot of people that I want to meet so I can tell them about it before they get too old. Fred Astaire, for instance. And Chaplin. I've got to go to Switzerland and tell him — just a simple 'Thank you,' you know? [Chaplin died five months later, before this pilgrimage could be made.]

More Brooksian table talk, in response to student writing dissertation on his work:

STUDENT: What's the best way to become a director?

BROOKS: The royal road to direction used to be through the editing room. Today my advice would be: write a few successful screenplays. Anybody can direct. There are only eleven good writers. In all of Hollywood. I can name you many, many screenwriters who have gone on to become directors. In any movie, they are the prime movers.

STUDENT: Have you any ambition to make a straight dramatic film?

Brooks (*vehemently*): No! Why should I waste my good time making a straight dramatic film? Sydney Pollack can do that. The people who can't make you laugh can do that. Suppose I became the Jean Renoir of America. What the hell would be left for the other guys to do? I would take all their jobs away. It would be very unfair of me.

Student: In other words, 'Shoemaker, stick to your last'?

Brooks: Yes. And in Hollywood you're only as good as your last last.

Student: But don't you want to surprise your audience?

Brooks: Sure. Every time. I gave them *Blazing Saddles*, a Jewish Western with a black hero, and that was a megahit. Then I gave them a delicate and private film, *Young Frankenstein*, and that was a hit. Then I made *Silent Movie*, which I thought was a brave and experimental departure. It turned out to be another Mel Brooks hit. *High Anxiety* is the ultimate Mel Brooks movie. It has lunatic class.

Student: But what if you had a serious dramatic idea that really appealed to you? Would you —

Brooks: Listen, there are one hundred and thirty-one viable directors of drama in this country. There are only two viable directors of comedy. Because in comedy you have to do everything the people who make drama do — create plot and character and motive and so forth — and *then*, on top of *that*, be funny.

Unidentified bearded man: Have you ever thought of being funny onstage?

Brooks: No, because I might become this white-belted, white-shoed, maroon-mohair-jacketed type who goes to Vegas and sprays Jew-jokes all over the audience. A few years of that and I might end up going to England, like George Raft or Dane Clark, wearing trench coats in B movies.

Debate ensues about differences (in style and personality) between Brooks and the other 'viable director of comedy,' Woody Allen. Both are New York Jewish, both wrote for Sid Caesar, both are hypochondriacs, much influenced by time spent in analysis. There is general agreement at table on obvious distinction — that Brooks is extrovert and Allen introvert.

Barry Levinson: They're total opposites. Mel is a peasant type. His films deal with basic wants and greeds, like power and money. Woody's films are about inadequacies — especially sexual inadequacy — and frailty and vulnerability. Also, like Chaplin, Woody is his own vehicle. His movies are like episodes from an autobiography. You couldn't say that about Mel.

Howard Rothberg (*slim, dark-haired young man who has been Brooks's personal manager since 1975*): The big difference is that Mel's appeal is more universal. *Blazing Saddles* grossed thirty-five million domestically and *Silent Movie* is already up to twenty million. Woody, on the other hand, appeals to a cult. I love his pictures, but they have a box-office ceiling. They don't go through the roof.

BROOKS: (*who has been wolfing cannelloni, followed by ice cream*): No matter how much *High Anxiety* grosses, it won't give me one more iota of freedom. I have the freedom right now to do anything I want. My contract is with the public — to entertain them, not just to make money out of them. I went into show business to make a noise, to *pronounce myself*. I want to go on making the loudest noise to the most people. If I can't do that, I'm not going to make a quiet, exquisite noise for a cabal of cognoscenti.

This is Brooks the blusterer speaking, the unabashed attention-craver who started out as a teenage timpanist and is still metaphorically beating his drum. Can testify that drummer has alter ego, frequently silenced by the din: Brooks the secret connoisseur, worshipper of good writing, and expert on the Russian classics, with special reference to Gogol, Turgenev, Dostoevski, and Tolstoy. Is it possible that — to adapt famous aphorism by Cyril Connolly — inside every Mel Brooks a Woody Allen is wildly signalling to be let out?

STUDENT: I think your films are somehow more benevolent and affirmative than Woody Allen's.

BROOKS: Let's say I'm beneficent. I produce beneficial things. A psychiatrist once told me he thought my psyche was basically very healthy, because it led to *product*. He said I was like a great creature that gave beef or milk. I'm munificent. I definitely feel kingly. Same kind of Jew as Napoleon.

STUDENT: Napoleon was Jewish?

BROOKS: Could have been. He was short enough. Also, he was very nervous and couldn't keep his hands steady. That's why he always kept them under his lapels. I put him in one of my records. [Fans will remember how the Two-Thousand-Year-Old Man took a summer cottage on Elba, where he met the exiled Emperor on the beach — 'a shrimp, used to go down by the water and cry' — without at first realizing who he was: 'The guy was in a bathing suit, how did I know? There was no place to put his hands.'] Anyway, there's something disgustingly egotistical about me. I never truly felt inferior. I never developed small defences. I never ran scared. Even in comedy, you don't want your hero to be a coward. You want him to go forth and give combat, which is what I do in *High Anxiety*. Now, Woody makes Fellini-ish, Truffaut-ish films. He starts out with the idea of making art. He feels that his art is his life. And more power to him. The difference is that if someone wants to call my movies art or crap, I don't mind.

Detect, once more, sound of obsessive drumbeating; last sentence, in particular, seems intended to convince drummer himself as much as anyone else. Conversation breaks off as Brooks returns to work. Hear him in distance inviting youthful assistant to take over direction of brief scene in gardener's hut, already rehearsed, where star is deluged anew with bird droppings — 'a job,' he graciously declares to the grinning apprentice, 'fully commensurate with your latent talents.'

Finishing my coffee, I mull over recent conversation with Gene Wilder, who has been directed thrice by Brooks (in *The Producers*, *Blazing Saddles*, and *Young Frankenstein*) and once by Allen (in *Everything You Always Wanted to Know about Sex but Were Afraid to Ask*). According to Wilder: 'Working with Woody is what it must be like to work with Ingmar Bergman. It's all very hushed. You and I were talking quietly now, but if we were on Woody's set someone would already have told us to keep our voices down. He said three things to me while we were shooting — "You know where to get tea and coffee?" and "You know where to get lunch?" and "Shall I see you tomorrow?" Oh, and there was one other thing: "If you don't like any of these lines, change them." Mel would never say that. The way Woody makes a movie, it's as if he was lighting ten thousand safety matches to illuminate a city. Each one of them is a little epiphany, topical, ethnic, or political. What Mel wants to do is set off atom bombs of laughter. Woody will take a bow and arrow or a hunting rifle and aim it at small, precise targets. Mel grabs a shotgun, loads it with fifty pellets, and points it in the general direction of one enormous target. Out of fifty, he'll score at least six or seven huge bull's-eyes, and those are what people always remember about his films. He can synthesize what audiences all over the world are feeling, and suddenly, at the right moment, blurt it out. He'll take a universal and crystallize it. Sometimes he's vulgar and unbalanced, but when those seven shots hit that target, I know that little maniac is a genius. A loud kind of Jewish genius — maybe that's as close as you can get to defining him.'

This reminds me of something written in 1974 by the critic Andrew Sarris:

> Allen's filmmaking is more cerebral, and Brooks's more intuitive. In a strange way, Brooks is more likable than Allen. Thus, even when Allen tries to do the right thing, he seems very narrowly self-centred, whereas even when Mel Brooks surrenders to the most cynical calculations — as he does so often in *Blazing Saddles* — he still spills over with emotional generosity. . . . What Allen lacks is the reckless abandon and careless rapture of Brooks.

Reflect that this positive judgment is not necessarily incompatible with negative opinion I have lately heard from former colleague of Brooks; viz., 'Woody has become a professional, whereas Mel is still a brilliant amateur. Amateurs are people putting on parties with multimillion-dollar budgets.'

Return to set, where, after nearly twelve weeks' shooting, current party is over. Brooks has brought in picture — budgeted at four million dollars — four days ahead of schedule. Though in buoyant mood, he expresses horror at rocketing cost of filmmaking: 'One actor and a few birds, but I'll bet you this has been a twenty-thousand-dollar day.' (Studio accounting department afterward confirms that he would have won his bet.) I take my leave. Brooks clicks heels and bows, saying, 'Your obedient Jew.' He misses no opportunity to brandish his Jewishness, which he uses less as a weapon than as a shield. Remember (he seems to be pleading) that I must be liked, because it is nowadays forbidden to dislike a Jew.

Manager Rothberg accompanies me to parking lot, explaining how much success of movie means to Brooks. I suggest that surely he can afford to make a flop. 'Financially, he can,' Rothberg says. 'Psychologically, he can't.'

August 31, 1977: 'My beloved, you are guinea pigs.' It is a balmy evening seven weeks later, and Brooks is introducing first showing of rough-cut to audience of two hundred (including workers on picture, their friends and relations, and minor studio employees such as waiters, cleaners, and parking attendants) who have crowded into private theatre at Fox. He continues, 'There are children present. Some of them may be mine, so I'm not going to do the filthy speech that is customary on these occasions. For the nonce, by which I mean no offence, this movie is called *High Anxiety*, a phrase that I hope will enter common parlance and become part of the argot of Americana. But what you will see tonight has no music, no sound effects, and no titles. You won't even see our swirling artwork. You will, however, see a lot of crayon lines, which I will explain for the benefit of the editor. They indicate something called opticals. This picture has one hundred and six dissolves, of which you will see *not one*. There are some other very fancy opticals that I am having processed in Cairo right now. There is also one crayon mark that should be on a men's room wall, but we couldn't get it out in time. As you know, it's incumbent on us all to be killed in a Hitchcock movie, and you will see several people being very tastefully slaughtered. I regret to tell you that in casting four crucial roles we ran out of money, so the people who *wrote* the picture are *in* it. Finally, let me say that I wish you well, but I wish myself better.'

Screening gets warm response, punctuated by applause. Brooks scampers down front and thanks audience for their attention, their laughter, and their profound awareness that 'there are eighteen million Arabs surrounding two hundred and six Jews, and — no, wait, that's from some other speech, at some hospital somewhere.' He then requests detailed and candid criticism: Where did movie drag? Which gags failed? Was plot clear? He listens raptly to all answers, asks other spectators for corroboration or dissent, makes careful notes of points on which action should be taken. And goes back to three and a half more months of furious work, polishing the film for a December premiere, in order to qualify for the Academy Award, which, as he repeatedly, belligerently, fate-placatingly asserts, no comedy can ever win.

The man we know as Mel Brooks was born in a Brooklyn tenement on June 28, 1926. To the question 'What were you born?' when it was posed by David Susskind on a TV panel show in 1960, he replied, 'George M. Cohan.' (Later in the programme, he admitted that he really had two diametrically opposed selves, that there were two different sides to 'the strange amalgam, the marvellous pastiche that is me.' Under Susskind's remorseless interrogation, he confessed, 'The first side of me is Sir Anthony Eden. . . . And the other is Fred Astaire.') In reality, what he was born was Melvin Kaminsky, the youngest of four boys, whose parents were Eastern European immigrants. His father, Maximilian Kaminsky, came from Danzig, and his mother, née Kate Brookman, from Kiev. According to Brooks, one reason for the success of his collaboration with people like Carl Reiner and Mel Tolkin was that they all shared 'the same background, the second-generation Russian-Ukrainian-Jewish intellectual heritage.' He told Susskind that his mother left Kiev in early childhood, never having learned Russian, and that her English was still fairly impenetrable, mainly because the voice of authority, which she took as her model on arrival in New York, invariably belonged to an Irish cop. The result, Brooks said, was that 'she speaks no known language, and speaks it with an Irish accent.'

His father, a process server, died suddenly of a kidney disease at the age of thirty-four, when Brooks was two and a half years old. The shock left him with a sense of loss that persisted into adult life. For example, he recognizes that his relationship with Sid Caesar was that of a child clamouring for the attention and approval of a father. When Brooks went into analysis, in 1951, his purpose, he recently told me, was 'to learn how to be a father instead of a son.' (His six years on the couch, two to four sessions per week, undoubtedly hastened the emergence of Brooks the father figure, patriarchal ruler of movie sets. 'He's sometimes my mother hen, and sometimes even my brother,' Gene Wilder says, 'but most of the time he's my father.' On a wall of Wilder's office at Fox, there is a photograph of the two men, inscribed 'To my son Gene, with love, Daddy Mel.') Kate Kaminsky, widowed and penniless, with four boys to support, took a job in the garment district, putting in a ten-hour day and bringing home extra work in the evening. A miniature dynamo, less than five feet in height, she also found time and energy to keep her children fed, their clothes washed and mended, and their apartment in spotless trim. The roach or bedbug that entered her domain had signed its own death warrant. She exemplified what Brooks said to Susskind of Jewish mothers in general: 'Until they die themselves, they *clean* and *kill*.' He went on to sum up his feelings about this indomitable woman by declaiming, 'If I could, I would go skinny-dipping with my mother.' (Still vigorous in her eighty-third year, she nowadays lives in Florida.) Irving and Leonard, the eldest two sons, were sent out to work when they were twelve and, on a family income that averaged about thirty-five dollars a week, ends were precariously made to meet. Mrs. Kaminsky was obsessed with the idea of preserving what Brooks describes as a 'certain threshold of dignity,' and for this reason she always refused to go on relief. It must be remembered that her husband died shortly before the Wall Street crash and that Brooks spent his childhood in the roughest years of the Depression. To be Jewish, Brooklyn-born, fatherless, impoverished, and below average stature — no more classic recipe could be imagined for an American comedian. Or, one might suppose, for an American suicide.

Not long ago, discussing Brooks with a prosperous Jewish movie producer, I remarked that he had once been prone to suicidal impulses. 'Nonsense,' the producer said, 'that's self-dramatization. Jews don't kill themselves. Look at their history. They're too busy fighting to survive.'

When I reported this conversation to Brooks, he said, 'You were talking to a rich Jew. Poor people kill themselves, and a lot of poor people are Jews. One evening, when I was a kid, a woman jumped off the top of a building next door to where I lived. She was Jewish. And there were plenty of other Jewish suicides during the Depression.' The image of that death is burned into Brooks's memory. He was playing with friends on a nearby street. Hearing screams and police sirens, he ran to see what had happened. A corpse, covered by a sheet so that only the feet were visible, was being loaded into an ambulance, and he was sure he recognized the shoes as a pair belonging to his mother. His own apartment was empty. Unknown to him, Mrs. Kaminsky was working overtime in Manhattan. The hours that passed before she returned were the worst he ever lived through.

Some revealing sidelights on Brooks's relationship with his parents are thrown by the recorded routine in which he plays a two-hour-old baby, precociously endowed with the faculty of speech. Interviewed by Carl Reiner, he declares that he already knows his mother, though he hasn't yet 'seen the outside.'

REINER: Do you hope she's good-looking?

BROOKS: I don't care what she looks like. I'm not going to date her. I'm her child. But I know she's good. Because you can tell a person by what they are inside. . . . And I was there, I was inside, and I looked around. She's great. . . . I remember when I was a tadpole, a little fetus there, swimming around.

REINER: You remember having a tail?

BROOKS: Sure. Oh, that was the best part. I loved the tail.

REINER: Were you unhappy when it disappeared?

BROOKS: When I lost my tail, I got a nose. . . . The nose is much more important, because — you can't blow your tail, know what I mean?

He has a simple theory to account for the attacks of queasiness that women suffer during the early months of pregnancy:

> BROOKS: I think the moment they realize that there's a living creature in them, they puke.
> REINER: But why?
> BROOKS: Wouldn't you be nauseous if there was somebody running around inside of you? . . . It's a frightening thing.

His knowledge of world celebrities is extremely limited. Reiner reels off a list of names including Queen Elizabeth, Winston Churchill, Fidel Castro, and Pandit Nehru, none of whom means anything to him. Then:

> REINER: Have you heard of Cary Grant?
> BROOKS: Oh, sure. Everybody knows Cary Grant.

Pressed by Reiner, he explains that while he was still in the womb his mother went to a lot of Cary Grant pictures, whereas she never took him to any Pandit Nehru pictures. 'But I'm sure,' he generously adds, 'that he's a *hell* of an actor.'

At one point, he leaps to the conclusion that he is a girl ('That's *adorable!*'), but Reiner gently disabuses him. 'That's all right,' he says, putting a bold face on it. 'I'll play ball and get drunk and things. I'll be fine.' He tentatively asks whether Burt Lancaster is a girl. Reiner gives him a negative answer, which seems to relieve him. 'That's good,' he says, reconciled at last to masculinity. 'I'll be like him.' It has been established earlier that Baby Brooks's linguistic skill is a freakish and short-lived gift, likely to be withdrawn at any moment. As long as the theme is his mother, he is eagerly articulate. Significantly, the withdrawal symptoms begin to appear in the following passage, when Reiner introduces a new subject.

> REINER: I'd like to know what you feel about your father.
> BROOKS: I feel that Dad is the kind of guy that will gah-gah-san.
> REINER: Will what? I didn't get that.
> BROOKS: I feel that my father will always be the kind of a guy that will take me to ballgames, and we'll be buddies, and we'll sy–ny-ny, ny-foy.
> REINER: I don't understand you.
> BROOKS: I think that my father and I will probably get along well together, since we're both boys. We'll probably run around and play ball and *nah-nah-hah, nah–nah–hah.*
> REINER: I do believe he's losing his intelligence.

And the track ends with Brooks regressing into wailing, bawling, frantic inarticulacy. It is quite an unnerving sound. Listening to it, I recall something that an old friend of Brooks, the novelist Joseph Heller, once said to me: 'There's a side of Mel that will never be fulfilled, no matter how hard he drives himself, and it all goes back to his father's death.'

At P.S. 19, Brooks was bright but unstudious — the kind of disruptive, obstreperous child that teachers slap down on principle, wearily aware that he will bounce right back-up. 'I wasn't an avid reader,' he says. 'I was always an avid talker and doer. Reading books seemed too conservative for me to bother with.' He quickly established himself as the clown of the classroom. One of his favourite movies was *Frankenstein* (the 1931, James Whale version), and he discovered at the age of eight that he could reduce his closest chum, a boy called Gene Cogen, to uncontrollable hysterics by singing 'Puttin' On the Ritz' in the manner of Boris Karloff. 'We had *folie à deux*,' Brooks told me. 'It got so bad that Cogen couldn't hear that song near a window, because he might roll out and fall to his death. I would start to sing and he would collapse. He would have to be dragged to the principal's room by his feet, with his head banging on the steps, still laughing.' Thus the infant Brooks achieved what every comic traditionally strives for — a knockdown, drag-out exit. (He stored up this triumph for future use: Peter Boyle performs the same routine in *Young Frankenstein*.) Despite, or perhaps because of, the damage to his head, young Cogen remained a fan of Brooks, and said to him one day, 'You're going to be famous when you grow up. I know that because nobody else uses words like "urchin" in English composition.'

On the streets, where Irish, Italian, and Polish gangs roamed only a few blocks away, Brooks was funny in self-defence. He later said to a *Playboy* interviewer, 'If your enemy is laughing, how can he bludgeon you to death?' Whenever it was possible, he and his pals would travel in the company of a well-built Gentile. Even today, it is an article of faith with Brooks that 'every small Jew should have a tall goy for a friend, to walk with him and protect him against assault.' Much of Brooks's humour, as we shall see, is inspired by fear: fear of injury, illness, sex, and failure; and also of unfriendly Gentiles, especially large ones, and most particularly if they are Germans or Cossacks. Fear, too, of predatory animals, though not, apparently, of sharks. My evidence for this is drawn from the Susskind programme mentioned previously.

SUSSKIND: Now let's talk about Jewish mothers.

DAVID STEINBERG (*another of the panellists*): Forget about Jewish mothers, let's talk about sharks.

BROOKS (*instantly assuming a lecturer's voice, plummy and pedantic*): A shark could never harm you. The shark is a benign creature of the sea. Of course, if you thrash about in the water or if you wear shiny bracelets, the shark will be attracted to you. On occasion, the shark has followed people out of the water and has gone to their blanket and eaten their beach ball. One time, the shark followed my brother Irving home on the Brighton local, and, upon being admitted to the apartment house, the shark entered his apartment — Apartment 4-B — and ate his entire family and a brand-new hat. Apart from that, the shark is a pussycat.

All the apprehensions that surface in Brooks's comedy have the same eventual source: a fear — or, to put it more positively, a hatred — of death. The noise he makes is literally death-defying. I append some Brooksian reflections on mortality, culled from various conversations over the past year.

BROOKS: The whole business of death is too formal nowadays. Bing Crosby just succumbed to the great spectre at the age of seventy-three, but the way it's covered by radio and television and newspapers it is no longer a calamity. It is worded in correct obituary paragraphs and it becomes a normal and ordinary event. The good shock value is taken out of it. The moments of horrible grief over somebody's death are handled for us so that we don't experience them, and then they stay with us too long because we didn't grieve properly. The media formalize the tragedy, put a quick film of Saran Wrap over it, so that we don't feel, 'My God, one of us has suddenly ceased to be,' so that millions of people don't ask, 'Where did Bing Crosby go?' Well, where *did* he go? Don't just tell me he died. I want to know where he went. And I want to grieve a little bit.

MYSELF: Are you scared of dying?

BROOKS: Not right now, not just this moment, because I'm feeling good, I'm not in a lot of pain. But I always intend to be afraid of it. To pay proper respect and homage to it. When I was nine, my friend Arnold said to me that we were both going to die. I said, 'You're obviously not right, you can't be right. We're not going to die, because why were we born? It wouldn't make any sense.' He said, 'What about your grandfather? He died. And what about fish?' I said my grandfather was *very* old, *exceptionally* old, and fish had nothing to do with us. I thought I sounded very clever. All the same, that was the first time I knew I was going to die.

Again:

MYSELF: Do you believe in life after death?

BROOKS: No, I don't. I think that's silly. And there's no Judgment Day, either. There isn't a day when we all kiss the little fishes and shake hands and walk together into God's green heaven. So what are we doing here? My guess is that we are part of an evolving process that has no knowable purpose. What's happened is that we were given too many brains, and our brains have screwed up our biological evolution. If we didn't think so much, we'd know what it was all about. When one leaf on a tree begins to turn yellow, it doesn't turn to the other leaves and say, 'Jesus Christ, all you guys are green and I'm turning yellow! What the hell is this?' They just turn yellow, and then red, and then brown, and then they leave the tree, and it's all proper. But we say, 'Look at this grey hair! Look at this wrinkle! And, my God, I'm so tired after I walk up fourteen steps!' We defer far too much to our brains, our logic, our powers of rational thought. That's why we're so vain, so egotistical, so full of complaining. Leaves never complain.

MYSELF: You're saying that we ought to go along with the processes of nature. But science tells us that we live on a dying planet, where everything — leaves and people alike — is ultimately doomed to extinction. If that's correct, surely the best way to obey the laws of nature would be to kill ourselves now and have done with it?

BROOKS: But we don't have to, because we're going to die anyway. And, because of that, let's have a merry journey, and shout about how light is good and dark is not. What we should do is not *future* ourselves so much. We should *now* ourselves more. '*Now* thyself' is more important than '*Know* thyself.' Reason is what tells us to ignore the present and live in the future. So all we do is make plans. We think that somewhere there are going to be green pastures. It's crazy. Heaven is nothing but a grand, monumental instance of future. Listen, *now* is good. *Now* is wonderful. (*Catching himself on the brink of sounding pretentious, he retreats to the safety of self-mockery, and adopts the tone of a humourless pseudo intellectual.*) By this, of course, I do not mean to intimate that I espouse a totally Sartrean position.

MYSELF: But you're in the movie business. You have to plan ahead.

BROOKS: I only look ahead commercially. I never look ahead spiritually.

On his records with Reiner, there was no advance planning; Brooks lived entirely in the moment, wholly committed to *now*. For this reason (which we'll examine later), they may well represent his most personal comic achievements.

A final exchange with Brooks on eschatology:

MYSELF: When you're playing the Two-Thousand-Year-Old Man, Reiner asks whether you and your fellow cave dwellers believed in a superior being. You answer, 'Yes. A guy Phil.' You used to offer up prayers to him, like 'O Philip, please don't take our eyes out.' Then, one day, he was struck dead by lightning. Reiner asks how you felt about that, and you say, 'We looked up. We said, "There's something bigger than Phil." ' Is there?

BROOKS: Yes. There *is* something bigger than Phil, and I'm afraid of it. That's where my standards of morality come from — fear. And not only fear of God. I know how strong *I* am, how powerful *I* can be, how aggressive *I* can get. And I don't want a world where that kind of force can be turned against me. It frightens me. That's why we've all got to behave. That's the beginning of civil behaviour. Fear of ourselves.

In 1939, the Kaminskys moved to Brighton Beach, where they shared a house a block and a half from the sea. 'It was sort of rustic out there,' Brooks recalls. 'We actually got to see *trees*. I loved it.' One of their neighbours was Buddy Rich, Artie Shaw's new drummer, who befriended Brooks and gave him an occasional free lesson in the art of percussion. The following summer, Brooks took a vacation job as a general helper at a hotel in the Catskills, washing dishes, keeping the tennis courts clean, and yelling things like 'Mrs. Bloom, your time is up!' at people in rented rowboats. The food supplied to the staff still haunts his nightmares. Of one especially feculent pie, he says, 'It lay under my heart for three years. I called it Harold. I used to pat it every morning and ask it how it was — "Remember how you were when I ate you, you little devil?"' He worked out a simple comedy routine, which as a reward for good conduct, he was occasionally allowed to perform. Clad in a black overcoat and derby hat, and toting two suitcases, the fourteen-year-old Brooks would trudge out onto the high diving board. Pausing at the edge, he would suddenly scream 'Business is terrible! I can't go on!' and plunge into the pool.

After two years of seaside life, Mrs. Kaminsky brought her family back to the old neighbourhood; the reason, Brooks says, was that 'she missed the friendships of the ghetto.' He attended Eastern District High School, where he was either an all-talking, all-singing version of Harpo Marx or a major nuisance, depending on whether you were his classmate or his teacher. Through his brother Lenny, he met Don Appell, a Broadway actor who had appeared with Canada Lee in Orson Welles's 1941 production of *Native Son*. Appell introduced him to the social director of a borscht-belt hotel in Ellenville. Brooks made a strong impression and was hired, for the summer season of 1942, as drummer and part-time *tummler*. Two quotations may here be helpful. (1) Brooks to *Playboy*: 'Jews don't do comedy in winter. In summer, all right.' (2) Brooks to me: 'A *tummler* can be defined as a resident offstage entertainer at a Jewish mountain resort, mostly after lunch.' He found it hard to decide on a professional name. Melvin Kaminsky was too overtly Jewish for a comedian. David Daniel Kaminsky, also of Brooklyn but unrelated to Brooks, had faced much the same problem a decade or so earlier, and had solved it by billing himself as Danny Kaye. (Just why Jews in the performing arts were — and, for the most part, still are — expected to Anglicize their names is a question worthy of a separate study. To take three cases at random, is it to simplify pronunciation, to enhance euphony, or to disarm bigotry that Emanuel Goldenberg becomes Edward G. Robinson, Benny Kubelsky becomes Jack Benny, and Isadore Demsky becomes Kirk Douglas? The whole rigmarole discredits the public that demands it.) Brooks's first thought was to borrow his mother's maiden name, but Melvin Brookman turned out to be a nonstarter, because he told me, 'I couldn't get it all on my drum.' Chopping off a syllable, he settled for Melvin Brooks.

That summer, two events occurred that helped to lay down the course of his future career. In the band at the Avon Lodge, a neighbouring Catskill pleasure dome, there was a pretty good saxophone player called Sid Caesar. Brooks met him in off-duty hours, howled at his mimetic gifts, and formed a friendship that was renewed, to the lasting gratitude of TV audiences, after the war. The other significant event took place back in Ellenville. It was a classic demonstration of the First Show-Biz Law of Psychokinetics, according to which major talent, if unfulfilled, acquires the power of temporarily disabling minor talent that comes within its sphere of influence and impedes its development. One morning, in obedience to this law, the regular stand-up comic fell mysteriously sick and had to be shipped back to New York. Brooks, inevitably, was asked to replace him. He went on that night and improvised, using real characters — the manager, staff, and clientele of the lodge — as his points of departure into fantasy. He also found time to prepare a short blackout spot, for which he co-opted a girl assistant. 'It was entitled "S. and M.," thirty years before anyone had heard of S. and M.,' he told me. 'The girl and I walked out from the wings and met in the centre of the stage. I said, "I am a masochist." She said, "I am a sadist." I said, "Hit me," and she hit me, very hard, right in the face. And I said, "Wait a minute, wait a minute, hold it. I think I'm a sadist." Blackout. That was the first sketch I ever wrote.' Within a few days, he had composed his own theme song, the climax of which was a rousing plea for sympathy:

> I'm out of my mind,
> So won't you be kind
> And please love Melvin Brooks?

He was not an overnight smash, but he improved with every performance and held down the job for the rest of the season, in the course of which, incidentally, he celebrated his sixteenth birthday.

• •

One night last winter, Brooks dined with me at my rented house in Santa Monica. Although I was the host, he insisted on providing the wine, which turned out to be Mouton-Rothschild 1961. (He makes the same stipulation wherever he eats. Even at the most expensive restaurants in Beverly Hills, Brooks will arrive with a neat leather case that holds two bottles from his own cellar. He does this partly because few wine lists offer items of comparable quality and partly because he sees no reason to pay exorbitant markups if he can avoid it. Thus he exploits his status while restricting his expenditure, since the restaurateurs would rather slim their profits than lose his patronage.) Over dinner, he told me a little-known story, the saga of Brooks at war, which I here reproduce in his own words:

'I came in at the end. I went overseas with the artillery, and we docked at Le Havre, France, in February, 1945. Then I was transferred into the 1104th

Combat Engineer Group. We travelled in a big truck through the nation of France on our way to Belgium, and every time we passed through a little town, we'd see these signs — "*Boulangerie*," "*Pâtisserie*," and "*Rue*" this, and "*Rue*" that, and rue the day you came here, young man. When we got to our hundred and eightieth French village, I screamed at the top of my lungs, "The joke is over! English, *please*!" I couldn't believe that a whole country couldn't speak English. One-third of a nation, all right, but not a whole country. There was very little actual shooting in Belgium, but there was plenty of mortar and artillery fire, and it was very noisy, and I thought that I would not want to be in the war very long, because of the noise. The earth was very hard when I was there, and I could not dig a V–shaped foxhole, as I wanted to, and stay down in the bottom of the V for the rest of the war. All these hot fragments of shrapnel and stuff were flying around, and I did not want to die, so it was awful. I remember hiding under a desk in a kindergarten while there were air battles going on above us, and bombs rattling.

'I was a PFC. Once, I was out on patrol with seven other men, and we found a case of German rifles near an old railway siding — beautiful sharpshooting rifles with bolt action. Sure enough, there were some cartridges right next to them. So we had a contest. There were these white insulation things up on the telephone poles, and any man who shot one down won a dollar from each of the others. I was pretty good at that, and I'd made about twenty-one dollars when suddenly we got a strange call on our jeep radio. It said that German werewolves — guerrillas operating behind our lines — had cut all communication between the 1104th and the Ninth Army by destroying the telephone wires. Holy shit, I realized it was us, so we barrelled right back to camp, and they said, "Did you see anything?" and we said "Not a thing." Then I became very brave. I said, "Give me some men, sir, and I'll go back. We gotta stop these werewolves." So I was sent out again on patrol to hunt them down. We hung around the railway siding for about four hours and then came back. My colonel offered to make me a corporal on the spot, and I said, "No, no, sir, I'm not worthy of it." Because I knew that noncoms and officers got killed and that somehow privates could survive in This Thing Called War.

'Along the roadside, you'd see bodies wrapped up in mattress covers and stacked in a ditch, and those would be Americans, that could be me. And I sang all the time; I made up funny songs; I never wanted to think about it. Some guy would say, "We're gonna be killed, we'll never get out of this war," and I'd say, "Nobody dies — it's all made up." Because otherwise we'd all get hysterical, and that kind of hysteria — it's not like sinking, it's like slowly taking on water, and that's the panic. Death is the enemy of everyone, and, even though you hate Nazis, death is more of an enemy than a German soldier.

'At the end, it was very sad, because the Germans were sending old men and little boys to fight against us. I was very good about that. I'd say, "No shooting, throw down your guns and talk to them in Yiddish and German." Of course, when we ran into pockets of trained German soldiers, genuine S.S. *Flammenwerfer* Nazis who wanted to die rather than surrender, I'd hide, because they'd kill you as soon as look at you. But these groups of little boys and old men wanted nothing but just to go to their mothers or their toilets. From around April 25 onward was the worst two weeks of my life. Then it was over, and it was V-E Day. And on V-E Day I hid again, because the Americans all got drunk and fired off every round of ammunition they had, and a lot of people were killed in the festivities. I knew if I went on the street I'd get shot to death. I was in a village near Wiesbaden, and the May wine was still green. It can make you very drunk, so I found a wine cellar and opened a hundred bottles of it and poured it all over me. I stayed there for twenty-four hours, until the shooting had stopped.'

'And then you went back to the States?' I asked.

'No,' Brooks said. 'You see, I was the barracks character, and they didn't want to lose me. My major said to me, "Melvin, why not stay with us and travel around providing the boys with entertainment?" I said "Great!" So he made me a corporal and gave me an old Mercedes, a real beauty. Then I told him I'd need a chauffeur, and he said, "I can't let you have a military man." I said, "Could you spare a few pfennigs for a German civilian driver?" He said "Fine," so I found a German fiddle player named Helga, who became my chauffeuse. My official title was Noncom in Charge of Special Services, and I did shows for enlisted men and officers' clubs. Sometimes for a whole division, with tens of thousands of people out front. I told big, lousy jokes. Every time Bob Hope came by, I would write down all his jokes and use them. Nothing frightened me. I sang like Al Jolson. Everybody could do the low Jolson, but I did the high Jolson that nobody else could do — things like "I love you as I loved you when you were *sweeeet sixteeeen*." People said they appreciated that. My chauffeuse played the fiddle for them and together we fiddled in the back seat of the Mercedes.

'I used to go to Frankfurt with my special pass and obtain certain rare cognacs and stick them in my car. I shoved them into every orifice that would take them. There wasn't a nineteen-year-old soldier who got drunker than I did. Helga played Brahms's "Lullaby" beautifully. I'd say, "Pull over to the curb and play Brahms's 'Lullaby.'" That dream world lasted for four months. Then they told me my Occupation duties were over and I could go back to civilian life. And I said, "No, no — let me die in the back of the Mercedes with Helga." But they sent me home anyway.'

Professionally speaking, what he returned to was almost three years of not very much. During his absence, things had been moving fast for his friend Caesar. While serving in the Coast Guard, Caesar had appeared in a recruiting revue called *Tars and Spars*; its director was Max Liebman, a sharp-eyed impresario who already numbered Imogene Coca and Danny (Kaminsky) Kaye among his discoveries. Dominated by Caesar's comedy routines, *Tars and Spars* opened in Florida and then went on a national tour, after which Columbia made a movie version that retained nothing of the original except the title and Caesar. His notices when the film was released, in 1946, launched him on a thriving career in nightclubs and vaudeville houses. Nobody, however, seemed inclined to discover Brooks. To demonstrate the versatility of his face, he hired a photographer to snap him in four contrasting moods — Brooks beaming, Brooks scowling, Brooks pensive, and Brooks aghast — and had the results printed on one page, copies of which he sent to every agent in town. He once arrived without an appointment at the headquarters of the eminent producer Kermit Bloomgarden. 'There were dozens of actors waiting to see him, some of them quite famous,' Brooks told me. 'I walked up to his secretary and said, "Paul Muni is here. I have to go in three minutes." She got on the intercom, and within ten seconds Bloomgarden came running out of his office. He looked at me and said, "This boy is not Paul Muni." I said, "Muni's name is Harold Gottwald. I am the *real* Paul Muni." [Whose *real* real name, incidentally was Muni Weisenfreund.] Then Bloomgarden grabbed me by the collar and said, "You've got a lot of moxie. I'm going to remember you." But he didn't give me an audition.'

Under the pressure of need or fear, Brooks was capable of any audacity. One night during this period, he went out to New Jersey to see the comedian Ronny Graham, who was a friend of his, performing in cabaret. After the show, Graham gave him a lift back to New York. To continue in Brooks's words: 'We stopped off on the way to have a sandwich at a diner. It was about 3 A.M. and the place was full of enormous truck drivers. Ronny was still wearing his stage makeup and some pretty avant-garde clothes, and these big hairy men all swivelled round and started to stare at us. Some of them even stood up. While were were eating, everything went very quiet. I was terrified. Suddenly, I turned on Ronny like a cobra and said, "I want my ring back." he said, "What?" I said, "You *spoke* to that *man*. Back at the club. Don't think I didn't see you speaking to him, because I did. *I want my ring back*. And I'll tell you something else — *you'll never have my tongue again!*" And we both went into this berserk faggot row. Finally, I picked up my cup of coffee and threw it in his face. Then I flounced out to the car with Ronny right behind me, wiping his eyes and screaming. Some of the truck drivers followed us out to the parking lot. They just stood there, dumbstruck, with their hands on their hips, as we drove off, kissing and making up. I waved at them out of the window.'

In the autumn of 1947, Caesar invited Brooks to come and see him at the Roxy, where he was starring in the stage show that accompanied the long-running movie *Forever Amber*. Afterward, in his dressing room, Caesar mentioned that Max Liebman was planning a revue for presentation on television. 'What is that?' Brooks claims to have asked, and to have received the reply 'It's a thing that takes pictures of you and sends them into people's living rooms.'

'Don't do it,' Brooks begged him, straight-faced, 'It's trafficking in graven images, and there are strict Jewish laws against that. You better stay away from that stuff or you'll never get your image back. The very least that can happen is that you'll be sterilized by the cameras.'

A superstitious man, Caesar was thoroughly unnerved by Brooks's little joke. A few months later, however, when Brooks was directing a shoestring production at Red Bank, New Jersey, Caesar called him with the news that he had decided to risk infertility. He had signed with NBC to appear in 'The Admiral Broadway Revue,' a sixty-minute programme, produced by Liebman, that would make its debut in January, 1949. Caesar proposed a deal whereby he personally would pay Brooks a weekly stipend of fifty dollars to supply him with special material. Brooks jumped at the offer.

'The Admiral Broadway Revue,' which ran for nineteen sparkling weeks, was an acorn that soon grew into an oak. With many of the same participants — e.g., Caesar and Imogene Coca as performers, Mel Tolkin and Lucille Kallen as principal writers, and Liebman as producer — it reappeared in February, 1950, now expanded into a full-blown, high-budget, prime-time, ninety-minute Saturday-night event, entitled 'Your Show of Shows.' Brooks refused to renew his private arrangement with Caesar; as he put it, 'I don't want to be your boy.' Instead, Liebman hired him, at a hundred and fifty a week. His first contribution to the new series was the famous sketch in which Caesar played a jungle boy who is discovered, clad in a lion skin, roaming the streets of New York.

INTERVIEWER: Sir, how do you survive in New York City? . . . What do you eat?

CAESAR: Pigeon.

INTERVIEWER: Don't the pigeons object?

CAESAR: Only for a minute.

INTERVIEWER (*bringing up a recurrent Brooksian obsession*): What are you afraid of more than anything?

CAESAR: Buick.

INTERVIEWER: Your're afraid of a Buick?

CAESAR: Yes. Buick can win in death struggle. Must sneak up on parked Buick, punch grille hard. Buick die.

Within a couple of months, Brooks's salary had risen to two hundred dollars, from which it steadily ascended to the peak of five thousand.

Many detailed accounts exist of the writing team that worked on 'Your Show of Shows.' Not since the Algonquin Round Table has a group of

American wits been more extensively chronicled. In addition to Tolkin, Kallen, and Brooks, it eventually included Joseph Stein (who wrote the book of *Fiddler on the Roof*), Larry Gelbart, and Neil Simon, with Michael Stewart (author-to-be of *Hello, Dolly!*) acting as typist, a post in which he was later replaced by 'a little red-headed rat' — to cite Brooks's affectionate phrase — named Woody Allen. Carl Reiner and Howard Morris, from the supporting cast, threw in ideas; and Caesar, with Liebman at his side, presided over the collective delirium, a madhouse of competing egos in which nobody could outshout Brooks. According to Miss Kallen, 'Mel imitated everything from a rabbinical student to Moby Dick thrashing about on the floor with six harpoons sticking in his back.'

Tolkin told me, 'He used to bare his teeth like a rodent if you crossed him. Half of Mel's creativity comes out of fear and anger. He doesn't perform, he screams.' (By the end of 1950, Tolkin and Caesar were already in psychoanalysis, and it is not surprising that in the following year Brooks also took to the couch. His therapist had been analyzed by Theodore Reik, who had been a protégé of Sigmund Freud. Brooks felt that what he learned, though it might not be straight from the horse's mouth, was at least feedbox noise from the same stable.)

Addressing the American Film Institute in 1977, Brooks said, 'We wrote things that made *us* laugh, not what we thought the audience would dig. . . . What really collapsed us, grabbed our bellies, knocked us down on the floor and made us spit and laugh so that we couldn't breathe — *that* was what went into the script. Except for the dirty portions, which we couldn't do on live television.'

A character in which Brooks specialized, and in which his distinctive comic style first began to assert itself, was the German Professor, played by Caesar. He appeared under many names — such as Kurt von Stuffer, the dietitian, or Siegfried von Sedativ, the authority on sleep — always pontificating with the same majestic fraudulence in the same bedraggled and ill–fitting frock coat. His ignorance, exposed by Carl Reiner's questions, was boundless in its scope and variety. How, for instance, do aircraft fly? As Dr. Rudolf von Rudder, aeronautical expert, he spelled out the answer in layman's language: 'It's a simple theory. Matter is lighter than air. You see, the motors, they pull the plane forward and they cause a draft, and then it taxis faster down the field and the motors go faster and the whole plane vibrates, and then, when there's enough of a draft and a vacuum created, the plane rises off the runway into the air. From then on, it's a miracle. I don't know what keeps it up.'

After a complex buildup, the laugh comes not from a witty, climactic payoff but from a sudden plunge into bathos. We hear exactly what we would expect to hear from this obvious half-wit. Cf. the reply of Dr. Heinrich von Heartburn when Reiner asked him for his advice on keeping one's marriage alive: 'Make it interesting. . . . I showed a friend of mine once how to keep his marriage exciting. . . . One day he'd come home from work, his wife would open the door, he's a French soldier. . . . The next day he's a policeman, he comes in, he starts to run around with the handcuffs and the badges, and the next day he don't come through the door, he jumps through the window, he's a clown. He somersaults all over the living room and throws his wife all around the place. [Pause.] She left him. He was a maniac.'

A final glimpse of the Professor (for which, as for the preceding quotes from the original scripts, I draw on the lengthy extracts reprinted in Ted Sennett's book *Your Show of Shows*): in the guise of a mountaineering pundit, he is mourning the loss of a colleague, Hans Goodfellow, who gave his life trying to prove that it was possible to climb mountains on roller skates. What should a climber do, Reiner inquires, if his rope breaks?

CAESAR: Well, as soon as you see the rope breaking, scream and keep screaming all the way down. . . . This way they'll know where to find you.

REINER: But, Professor, isn't there anything else you can do?

CAESAR: Well, there's the other method. As soon as the rope breaks, you spread your arms and begin to fly.

REINER: But humans can't fly.

CAESAR: How do you know? You might be the first one. Anyway, you can always go back to screaming.

REINER: Was Hans Goodfellow a flier or a screamer?

CAESAR: He was a flying screamer, and a crasher, too.

In this exchange, and dozens like it, Brooks was breaking fresh ground, exploring territory that he was eventually to make his own. He was invening the interview as a new form of comic art.

The last edition of 'Your Shows of Shows' went out in 1954, by which time Brooks was married to Florence Baum, a dancer in Broadway musicals. They had three children — in order of appearance, Stefanie, Nicholas, and Edward. The youngest is now studying music in Manhattan, while both of the older ones are taking courses in film at New York University. Brooks refers to them as 'these nice friends I've grown.' Their parents were divorced in 1962. 'We had married too young,' Brooks said, more than a decade later. 'I expected I would marry my mother, and she expected she would marry her father.' Minus Coca, Caesar returned to the small screen in 1954, starring in a show of his own called 'Caesar's Hour.' He was also minus Brooks, who, determined to go his own way, had rejected the offer of a top writing job on the new programme. Before long, however, Brooks regretted his decision to quit the nest. His own way was leading him nowhere but into debt, and after the show's first season, unable to resist the money, he rejoined his old boss, under whose paternal shadow he stayed until 1959. Which brings us back to Mamma Leone's.

Although Brooks left a lasting impression on everyone who saw him at the Moss Hart jamboree, it did nothing to help his career. He was a brilliant party turn, but what had after-dinner improvisation to do with professional comedy? In 1960, with his marriage crumbling and no source of income, he went job-hunting to Hollywood, where Carl Reiner was already working. Hearing that they were both in town, the producer Joe Fields threw a party in their honour, on the tacit understanding that they would provide the entertainment. Before an audience of celebrities that included Steve Allen and George Burns, they got up and did the Two-Thousand-Year-Old Man. When the applause had died down, Burns said, 'Listen, you better put that on a record, because if you don't, I'll steal it.' Allen, who shared Burns's enthusiasm, had highly placed friends in the recording business. He made a call to one of them the following morning.

'A few days later,' Reiner told me, 'Mel and I walked into a studio at World Pacific Records and ad-libbed for over two hours.' The edited result was an LP that came out in the spring of 1961 and sold over a million copies. 'That was a turning point for Mel,' Reiner continued. 'It gave him an identity as a performer for the first time.' Moreover, it gave him a comic persona that at once embodied and exorcised his own deepest anxieties; for the main point about this jaunty survivor — more than twice as old as Methuselah and still going strong — is that he has conquered death. By playing a character who was immortal, Brooks may have staked his principal claim to immortality as a comedian.

Gene Wilder summed up for me his mental image of Brooks: 'I see him standing bare-chested on top of a mountain, shouting "Look at me!" and "Don't let me die!" Those are the two things that rule his life.' They recur throughout his records with Reiner, of which, to date, there are four. Following the runaway success of the original LP, further revelations by the garrulous oldster of his close encounters with 'the great and the near-great' of the past two millennia were issued in the fall of 1961, with sequels in 1962, 1963, and 1973. In these classic interviews, Brooks triumphs not only over death, but over another of his besetting phobias, that of the lifelong seeker after father substitutes who fears he will never make a convincing father himself; for what is the Two-Thousand-Year-Old Man if not the most prolific parent on earth? He tells us that he has been married 'several hundred times' and that when he looks back on his wives 'a thousand violins explode in my mind.'

REINER: How many children do you have?

BROOKS (*with stoical self-pity*): I have over forty-two thousand children, and not one comes to visit me.

But, at least, he misses their company, which is more than can be said for Warren Bland, the Gentile advertising executive who is one of the many other characters Brooks plays on these remarkable discs. Bland lives in the city of Connecticut, Connecticut, 'a very exclusive community,' where they don't allow children. They *have* children, of course, but 'we send them to Hartford . . . to Jewish and Italian families, people who like children.' 'From time to time,' Bland goes on, 'I might just mosey over to Hartford, say "Hi, gang!" you know, then speed right back to Connecticut, Connecticut.'

As Bland, Brooks's accent is quintessential WASP. As the bimillenarian, it is not Jewish but — Brooks is insistent on this — *American*–Jewish. 'Within a couple of decades, there won't be any more accents like that,' he said to me. 'They're being ironed out by history, because there are no more Jewish immigrants. It's the sound I was brought up on, and it's dying.' Beneath the jokes, these recordings are a threnody. Even on the surface, there are odd moments of unexpected melancholy, as when the patriarch reflects, 'We mock the thing we are to be. We make fun of the old, and then we become them.' Although he has foxed the grim reaper, it has often been by inches. He has led a life dominated by peril and hostility, in which practically every human activity springs from one motive.

> BROOKS: Everything we do is based on fear.
> REINER: Even love?
> BROOKS: Mainly love.
> REINER: How can love stem from fear?
> BROOKS: What do you need a woman for? . . . In my time, to see if an animal is behind you. You can't see alone, you don't have eyes in the back of your head. . . . The first marriages were: 'Will you take a look behind me?' 'OK, how long do you want?' 'Forever.' 'We're married.'
> REINER: I see. And you walked back to back for the rest of your life?
> BROOKS: Yes. You looked at her once in a while —
> REINER: When you knew you were safe?
> BROOKS: When you were on high ground.

All of which corroborates the spiritual doctrine that perfect love casteth out fear. (And, I might add, compares very favourably with the behaviour of a well-known English writer who fled London during the wartime blitz, pausing only to explain to his girlfriend, 'Perfect fear casteth out love.') Again, consider the following exchange:

> REINER: What was the means of transportation then?
> BROOKS: Mainly fear. . . . You would see an animal that would growl, you would go two miles in a minute. Fear would be the main propulsion.

As for the origins of human speech.

> BROOKS: We spoke Rock, basic Rock. . . . Two hundred years before Hebrew, there was the Rock language. Or Rock talk.
> REINER: Could you give us an example of that?
> BROOKS: Yes. 'Hey, don't throw that rock at me! What you doing with that rock? Put down that rock!'

In other words — or, rather, in no other words — the need to communicate arose from the threat of imminent assault. Similarly, the custom of shaking hands 'stemmed from fear.' In order to check whether the other fellow was carrying a rock or a dagger, 'you grabbed his hand — "Hi there, Charlie!" "How you doing, Bertram?" — and you held that hand, then you looked and you opened it up and you shook it a little.' The primal art of dance evolved because it was an even more comprehensive means of self-protection. By dancing with your antagonist, you immobilize *both* his hands and 'you keep the feet busy, so he can't kick you.' Song, too, had its roots in terror. If you were in real danger, a high-pitched rhythmical yelling was the only way to make anyone pay attention. The message had to be simple and ear-catching, as witness the opening lines of the first lyric ever sung:

> A lion is eating my foot off,
> Will somebody call a cop?

Shortly afterward came national anthems, with which each group of cave dwellers tried to frighten its neighbours; e.g.:

> Let them all go to hell
> Except Cave Seventy-six.

The old man has immunized himself against death by obeying a number of rules — some pragmatic, some purely superstitious — which he *is* eager to share with us. Every morning, for instance, he sinks to his knees and prays 'fiercely' for twenty-two minutes 'that the ceiling shouldn't fall on me, and my heart should not attack me.' Among his other precepts for longevity: avoid fried food; consume nectarines in bulk ('Even a rotten one is good. . . . I'd rather eat a rotten nectarine than a fine plum'); never run for a bus; and 'stay out of a Ferrari or any small Italian car.' He has also preserved his pep by using drugs derived from 'certain barks of certain trees that made you jump in he air and sing "Sweet Sue." '

His fear of illness, though intense, is more than matched by his fear of hospitals, which are run today, he believes, on principles that have not changed since his troglodytic youth.

REINER: What are these principles?

BROOKS: The principle of people walking past you when you are screaming, and not caring. The same wonderful indifference to the sick and the dying.

Over the centuries, some of this indifference has rubbed off onto his own philosophy. It emerges most vividly when Reiner challenges him to define the difference between comedy and tragedy. His reply, brutally concise, is an aphorism as memorable as any I have heard on this ancient subject: 'Tragedy is if I cut my finger. . . . Comedy is if you walk into an open sewer and die.'

He drops names like a drunken waiter dropping plates: few great reputations pass through his hands unchipped. Robin Hood 'stole from everybody and kept everything'; Shakespeare, though personally 'a pussycat,' was a terrible writer ('He had the worst penmanship I ever saw'); Sigmund Freud was nothing more than a good basketball player; and, as for Michelangelo's painting, 'I thought it stunk,' because it showed naked people flying around, and 'you can't hang a naked in your living room.' Perhaps his most startling disclosure is that he cohabited with Joan of Arc. He volubly describes the ups and downs of their relationship, after which Reiner intervenes.

REINER: How did you feel about her being burned at the stake?
BROOKS (*with instant, understated finality*): Terrible.

For me — and, I have discovered, for Brooks himself — this is the high point of the whole extravagant saga.

Laughter becomes extreme only if it be consecutive. There must be no pauses for recovery. . . . The jester must be able to grapple his theme and hang on to it, twisting it this way and that, and making it yield magically all manner of strange and precious things, one after another, without pause. *He must have invention keeping pace with utterance.* He must be inexhaustible. Only so can he exhaust us.

The words are Max Beerbohm's, the italics mine. The Two-Thousand-Year-Old Man fulfils Beerbohm's demands to the letter. With this verdict Brooks, who is not noted for bashfulness, would probably agree. 'Everybody knows,' he has said of his work on these records, 'that *that* is terrific stuff.' It extracts a unique comic euphoria from a fundamentally pessimistic view of life. I've dwelt on it not only as a milestone in Brooks's past (and in the history of comedy) but as a signpost to which, in the future, he is likely to return for guidance.

Early in the nineteen-sixties, Brooks began to acquire a cult following. To the relatively small number of people who buy nonmusical LPs he became, in his own words, 'a royal personage, an emperor of comedy.' In other respects, he remembers the years between 1959 and 1965 as 'that terrible period when I couldn't get anything off the ground.' In 1961, Jerry Lewis had an idea for a screenplay, *The Ladies' Man*, and hired Brooks to work on it. To' Brooks's furious chagrin, Lewis took the script and had it entirely rewritten, so that few of Brooks's lines survived. (Show business offers few pleasures keener than that of paying tribute to a former foe who happens to be in eclipse. Brooks's present opinion of Lewis is that 'he was an exciting, dynamic creature, and I learned a lot from him.' He cannot, however, resist adding, 'High-key comics like that always burn themselves out. Lewis could do thirty-one different takes [i.e., physical reactions], and when you'd seen them all, that was it. Low-key, laid-back comics like Jack Benny are the ones that last.' Moreover, Lewis stooped to sentimentality — something utterly foreign to Brooks. Gene Wilder told me, 'There's not much white sugar in Mel's veins. He would never ask an audience for sympathy.') For some time, Brooks had been working on a novel; he now revamped it as a play, called *Springtime for Hitler*. No producer would touch it. *All American*, a Broadway musical with a book by Brooks, was among the more resounding flops of 1962. In the same year, during which his divorce became final, he turned out another screenplay, entitled *Marriage Is a Dirty Rotten Fraud*. Nobody bought it. Meanwhile, most of his colleagues on the Caesar shows were prospering — a fact that neither escaped his attention nor soothed his frustration.

After separating from his wife in 1960, Brooks had spent a bleak and insolvent period in an unfurnished fourth-floor walkup on Perry Street, for which he paid seventy-eight dollars a month. He then moved in with a friend called Speed Vogel, who had an apartment on Central Park West and a studio on West Twenty-eighth Street, where he made what Brooks describes as 'direct metal sculpture.' Vogel had left his wife shortly before Brooks arrived. The two men cooked for themselves, carried their clothes to the laundromat, rose at conflicting hours (Brooks late, Vogel early), and bickered over practically every aspect of housekeeping — a setup uncannily prophetic of Neil Simon's *The Odd Couple*.

One Tuesday in the summer of 1962, Vogel gave a party at West Twenty-eighth Street. Among his guests were Zero Mostel, who had a studio in the same building; Joseph Heller, whose first novel, *Catch 22*, had appeared the previous year; and Ngoot Lee, a painter and calligrapher of Chinese parentage. These three, together with Vogel and Brooks, enjoyed one another's company so much that they decided to commemorate the occasion by reassembling every Tuesday for food and talk. Meetings were held at cheap Chinese restaurants selected by Ngoot Lee, who knew where the best chefs worked, and kept track of their movements from job to job. The nucleus, itself a fairly motley crew, grew steadily motleyer as it swelled in numbers. Brooks introduced a diamond dealer named Julie Green, who could do eccentric impersonations of movie stars. Heller contributed a fellow-novelist, George Mandel, who had a steel plate in his head as a result of injuries suffered in the Battle of the Bulge. 'One night,' Heller recalls, 'Mandel told us in detail how he had been wounded. There was a long pause, and then Mel did something typical. He said, very slowly, "I'm sure glad that happened to you, and not to me." He wasn't being cruel, he was being honest. He just blurted out what we were all thinking but didn't dare to say.' Mandel, in turn, brought in Mario Puzo, later to become famous as the author of *The Godfather*. These were the charter members of the fraternity. They called themselves the Group of the Oblong Table or, in more pretentious moments, the Chinese Gourmet Club. What bound them together, apart from revelry in conversation, is best epitomised in a statement volunteered to me by Heller. 'I'd rather have a bad meal out than a good meal at home,' he said. 'When you're out, it's a party. Also, I like a big mediocre meal more than a small good one.'

The membership list has been closed for many years. Approved outsiders, like Carl Reiner and Joseph Stein, are invited to the Oblong Table from time to time, but merely as 'honoured guests.' The club has strict rules, some of which I learned from Reiner: 'You are not allowed to eat two mouthfuls of fish, meat, or chicken without an intermediate mouthful of rice. Otherwise, you would be consuming only the expensive food. The cheque and tip, and the parking fees, if any, are equally divided among the members. It is compulsory, if you are in New York, are not working nights, and are in reasonable health, to be present at every meeting.' He continued, 'The members are very polite. Once, I had a seat facing the kitchen door and I looked through and saw a rat strolling across the floor. They immediately offered me a chair facing the other way.' Anxious to retain his status of 'honoured guest,' Reiner begged me to quote Heller and Brooks on the subject at greater length than I quoted him.

Brooks recently told an interviewer that the talk at the Oblong Table mainly deals with such weighty subjects as 'whether there is a God, what is a Jew, and do homosexuals really do it.' Reiner has other recollections. 'From the sessions I've attended,' he said to me, 'I would put that group up against the Algonquin Round Table and bet that, line for line, they were funnier. The speed of the wit is breathtaking. It just flies back and forth.' Brooks's comment on this: 'I'm sure we're funnier than the Algonquin crowd, but we're not as bright.'

Hershy Kay, the composer and Broadway arranger, had a bitter experience that confirmed what Reiner said about the club's rigorous eating procedure. According to Brooks: 'Hershy Kay came once as a guest and took the nicest bits of the lobster and the choicest parts of the chicken, including the wings, which I like. He did not touch his rice. He had to go, and he went.' There may, however, have been another reason for Kay's rejection. My source here is Heller, who said, 'Bear in mind that I am the only tall member of the group. At the next meeting after the Hershy Kay incident, Mel made a little speech. "Let's face it," he said. "Except for Joe, all of us are quite short. Some of us are very short. *Hershy is too short."* '

Brooks, incidentally, has grave reservations about Heller's own table manners. 'From the very start,' he declares, 'we accepted Joe on Speed Vogel's word that he would behave, and Speed lied to us, because he did not behave. He took the best pieces of everything and laughed in our faces. One Tuesday, we ordered a tureen of special soup full of delicious things, and Joe grabbed it, scooped all the good stuff into his own bowl, and then said, "Here, let me serve this." We each got a spoonful of nothing.'

Far from denying this story, Heller openly confesses, 'I am a greedy man. I'll eat anything. I even use a fork instead of chopsticks, so I can eat faster. I'm known in the club as the plague of locusts.' Presumably, his physical bulk protects him against reprisals.

Puzo, the only non-Jewish member other than Ngoot Lee, is tolerated because of his limited appetite. 'Being Italian, Puzo is no threat to us,' Brooks says. 'He doesn't really like exotic dishes. He prefers noodles and rice — things that remind him of home. He is provincial, and that saves us from the rape of our best food.' A stickler for party discipline as well as a dedicated glutton, Brooks never misses a club meeting when he is in Manhattan. If business suddenly compels him to fly in from the Coast on a Tuesday evening, his first act on arrival at JFK is to ring every eligible restaurant in Chinatown until he finds the chosen venue. Thither he dashes, straight from the airport; and before saying a word, he heaps a plate with whatever is left.

Despite their differences over matters of etiquette, Heller has a high respect for Brooks. He freely admitted to me that he used a lot of Brooks's lines in his second novel, *Something Happened*, and that in his next book, *Good as Gold*, 'the hero is a small Jewish guy, and there's a great deal of Mel in that.' In the early seventies, Heller was teaching writing at City College of New York. He had long been aware that Brooks was vulnerable to practical jokes. One evening, Heller casually lied about his salary, saying that it was sixty-eight thousand dollars a year — more than double the truth. A couple of days later, Heller's accountant, who also worked for Brooks, called him up and said, 'For God's sake, Joe, what the hell have you done? First thing this morning, Mel was up here screaming, "Why am I in the entertainment business? Why aren't I teaching and earning seventy thousand a year like Joe Heller?" He was out of his mind!' Having told me this story, Heller went on, 'Mel has always had plenty of resentment and aggression that he can sublimate into creativity. He's usually at his best when he's envying people more successful than he is. Now that there's hardly anyone more successful, what will he do?'

I cited a mot attributed to Gore Vidal: 'It is not enough to succeed. Others must fail.'

'I thought that was La Rochefoucauld,' Heller said. 'But anyway it doesn't apply to Mel. He likes to see his rivals fail, but not his friends. Provided, of course, that *he's* succeeding.'

I asked whether, in Heller's opinion, fame had changed Brooks.

'Not a bit. He's just as nasty, hostile, acquisitive, and envious today as he ever was. Please be sure to quote me on that,' Heller said warmly. He went on, 'You have to distinguish between Mel the entertainer and Mel the private person. He puts on this manic public performance, but it's an act, it's something sought for and worked on. When he's being himself, he'll talk quietly for hours and then make a remark that's unforgettably funny because it comes out of a real situation. You might say that he's at his funniest when he's being most serious. He has a tremendous reverence for novelists and for literature in general, because it involves something more than gag writing. In his serious moments, I don't think he regards movies as an art. For Mel, the real art is literature.'

Brooks staunchly challenges this view: 'When Joe says things like that, he's just electioneering for the novel, because that's what he writes. I think *La Grande Illusion* is as good as *Anna Karenina*, and *Les Enfants du Paradis* is in the same class as *La Chartreuse de Parme*. If we're talking about art at the most exquisite level, Joe may conceivably have a point. But I'm a populist. I want colour, I want visual images, I want the sound of the human voice.'

In February, 1961, Brooks attended a rehearsal of a Perry Como TV special in which Anne Bancroft, then starring on Broadway in *The Miracle Worker*, was making a guest appearance. Brashly introducing himself, Brooks started to woo her on the spot. They were married in 1964 and are still together, now accompanied by a six-year-old son — 'Mel in miniature,' according to Miss Bancroft — named Maximilian. 'On our second date,' Brooks told me, 'I asked her, "Where do you keep your awards?" She'd already won two Tonys. She said she gave them to her mother. I said, "Funny, so do I" — although the only thing I'd won up to then was a Writers Guild Award for "Your Show of Shows." Then I asked her, "Where does your mother keep them?" She said, "On top of the TV set." My heart stopped, and I said, "So does mine." My mother now has two Oscars and an Emmy. But Annie has something like thirty major awards — Oscars, Emmys, Tonys, Cannes Festival, about everything an actress can win.' Miss Bancroft, whose parents were the children of immigrants, was christened Anna Maria Louisa Italiano, and it took Brooks a long time to reveal to his mother that he intended to marry an Italian girl. If we believe (as we can't) the account he gave David Susskind on TV, his mother's reaction when he finally broke the news and announced that he was bringing his lasagna-loving fiancée over to meet her was simply to say,

'That's fine. I'll be in the kitchen; my head'll be in the oven.'

In the early sixties, Miss Bancroft was continuously working, either on Broadway or in movies. Brooks had many evenings to kill, and she suspects that this may explain why he founded the Chinese Gourmet Club. 'But in any case, Mel really loves men, he has a terrific sense of male camaraderie,' she said to me recently. 'Have you noticed how all his films before *High Anxiety* end up with two men together? His attitude toward women can be very primitive. When we have big rows, he yells, "No more monogamy with women for me! Next time, it'll be with a man!" He actually threatens me with Dom DeLuise! Once — and only once — I managed to find out where the club was meeting, and I crashed the dinner. As soon as I came in the restaurant, it was as if a blanket had descended on the gathering. Dead silence. Faces falling. I turned around and left, without eating.' She smiled and shrugged. 'All the same,' she said, 'whenever he comes home at night the whole place lights up. He's like an incandescent schoolboy. There are no dull moments.'

One evening in the spring of 1962, Brooks was sitting in a Manhattan movie theatre watching a dazzling abstract cartoon by the Canadian animator Norman MacLaren. 'Three rows behind me,' he recalls, 'there was an old immigrant man mumbling to himself. He was very unhappy because he was waiting for a story line and he wasn't getting one.' Brooks listened hard, and the result of his eavesdropping was that, for the first time, a film based on a Brooks idea actually got made. 'I asked my pal Ernie Pintoff to do the visuals for a MacLaren-type cartoon,' he says. 'I told him, "Don't let me see the images in advance. Just give me a mike and let them assault me." And that's what he did. There was no script. I sat in a viewing theatre looking at what Ernie showed me, and I mumbled whatever I felt that old guy would have mumbled, trying to find a plot in this maze of abstractions. We cut it down to three and a half minutes and called it *The Critic*. It opened at the Sutton in New York, later to become renowned as the home of Mel Brooks hits. It was a smash then and has been ever since.' In 1964, it won Academy Awards for both Brooks and Pintoff. A fact to remember: the film's comic impact was entirely dependent on something nonvisual — Brooks's mesmeric power of vocal improvisation.

Alan Schwartz, an urbane, silver-haired native of Brooklyn who has been Brooks's legal adviser and friend since 1962, said to me not long ago, 'By Mel's standards, an improviser isn't class. He wanted to be classy. Writing is classy. A screenplay is classy.' Schwartz's other clients include Peter Shaffer, Tom Stoppard, and Joseph Heller. 'Mel is as intelligent as any of them,' he says. 'He must have a fantastic IQ. But sometimes, if he's with playwrights or novelists, he feels he has to prove that he's a serious literary person. When he met Shaffer, for instance, he kept saying things like "pari passu" and "ipso facto." '

Brooks's return to the affluence of network TV came in 1965, when he collaborated with Buck Henry on 'Get Smart,' a series of half-hour episodes from the career of Maxwell Smart, a dangerously incompetent secret agent. ABC, which financed the pilot script, found the central character too charmless and the satiric twists too bizarre. NBC took over the project (which nowadays looks tame enough), and it became a long-running success, relieving Brooks of such urgent financial worries as alimony and child support. It also left behind it a heritage of bad blood between Brooks and his co–author. Buck Henry, who wrote the screenplay of *The Graduate* a couple of years later, resented the billing he received on 'Get Smart' — 'by Mel Brooks with Buck Henry' — and there were rumours that, once the series was launched, Brooks's main contribution was to arrive at an advanced stage of rehearsals, propose a few radical and impracticable changes, and then disappear. Rebutting the charge of self-aggrandizement, Brooks says that his agent wanted to exclude Henry's name altogether and that it was he who demanded that both names should appear. 'Buck envied me because of the hit I'd made with the Two-Thousand-Year-Old Man,' Brooks asserts. 'I'd galloped like a greedy child, and got ahead and taken off. I had a reputation for being a crazy Jew animal, whereas Buck thought of himself as an intellectual. Well, I was an intellectual, too. I knew that Dante's last name was Alighieri, but I didn't flaunt it. What Buck couldn't bear was the idea of this wacko Jew being billed over him. The truth is that he reads magazines, but he's not an intellectual, he's a pedant.'

Time has not softened Henry's reciprocal animosity toward Brooks. 'I'll bet you,' he said to me in 1977, 'that his name appears five times on the credits of *High Anxiety*.'

Informed of this, Brooks replied, 'Tell him from me he's wrong. The correct number is six.'

The Producers, shot in New York in 1967, was the first Brooks script to reach the movie screen. It also marked his debut as a director — a job he undertook out of no sense of vocation but simply to protect his work against the well-meaning vandalism of rewrite experts. The script had gone through a strangely protracted gestation period. Brooks had originally conceived it, more than ten years earlier, as a novel. He had never thought of himself as a writer until 1950, when he saw his name on the credits of 'Your Show of Shows.' 'I got scared,' he told me, 'and I figured I'd better find out what these bastards do. I went to the library, and read all the books I could carry — Conrad, Fielding, Dostoevski, Gogol, Tolstoy. I decided that Tolstoy was the most gifted writer who ever lived. It's like he stuck a pen in his heart and it didn't even go through his mind on its way to the page. He may not even have been talented. And I said to myself, "My God, I'm not a writer, I'm a *talker*." I wished they'd change my billing on the show so that

it said "Funny Talking by Mel Brooks." Then I wouldn't feel so intimidated.' Before long, however, he stifled his fears and embarked on a novel.
'One little word at a time, but, by God, I was going to do it.'

The title was *Springtime for Hitler*, and the hero was a nervous young
accountant called Leopold Bloom. 'I stole the name from *Ulysses*,' Brooks
said to me. 'I don't know what it meant to James Joyce, but to me Leo
Bloom always meant a vulnerable Jew with curly hair. In the course of any
narrative, the major characters have to metamorphose. They have to go
through an experience that forces them to learn something and change. So
Leo was going to change, he was going to bloom. He would start out as a
little man who salutes whatever society teaches him to salute. Hats are
worn. Yes, sir, I will wear a hat. Ties are worn. Definitely, sir. No dirty
language is spoken in this world. *Absolument, Monsieur*. But in Leo
Bloom's heart there was a much more complicated and protean creature —
the guy he'd never dare to be, because he ain't gonna take them chances.
He was going to play it straight and trudge right to his grave, until he ran
into Max Bialystock, the Zero Mostel character. Bialystock is a Broadway
producer who's so broke he's wearing a cardboard belt. He sleeps with little
old ladies on their way to the cemetery. They stop off to have quick affairs
on the leather couch in his office, which charm them so much that they
write out cheques for any fictitious show he claims to be promoting.
Compared with Bloom, Bialystock is the Id. Bite, kiss, take, grab, lavish,
urinate — whatever you can do that's physical, he will do. When Bloom
first meets him, he's appalled. But then they get embroiled in each other's
lives, and they catalyze each other. Bialystock has a profound effect on
Bloom — so much so that this innocent young guy comes up with the idea
of making a fortune by producing a surefire flop and selling twenty-five
thousand percent of the profits in advance to little old ladies. On the other
hand, Bloom evokes the first sparks of decency and humanity in Bialystock.
It was a nice give-and-take. But after a while all they did was talk to each
other. So I said, "Oh, shit, it's turning into a play," and I rewrote it, with a
big neo-Nazi musical number right in the middle.'

At this point (1963), Anne Bancroft was appearing on Broadway in the
title role of Brecht's *Mother Courage*. Gene Wilder played the Chaplain,
her cynical hanger–on and occasional bedfellow. He is now Brooks's
closest friend and most impassioned fan. 'Whenever Mel says "Let's go," '
he told me recently, 'I drop anything I'm doing and follow him.' They met
backstage during the run of the Brecht play. 'Anne introduced me to this
little borscht-belt comic she was going with,' Wilder recalls. 'I knew his
name from the Caesar shows, which I'd been brought up on. I used to do
Caesar impersonations at junior high, and it turned out that all my favourite
bits had been written by Mel. Now he started to give me advice on
Brechtian acting. The Chaplain has these long ironic speeches and lyrics on
war and injustice, and I didn't know how to handle them, with my Actors

Studio and Uta Hagen training. Mel said to me, "Don't try to work them out in terms of psychology and motivation. He's stopped his play to pamphleteer. Step out of character and treat them like song-and-dance routines." I didn't agree with him then, but I do now. Without knowing it, he was talking pure Brechtian technique. One day, we went out to Fire Island, and he said, "I've written a play with a terrific part for you." He read me the first twenty minutes and I was knocked out. Brooks told me, "You *are* that character, and if it's ever done on stage or screen you're going to play it! But that's an easy promise, because I've never written a play or a screenplay and you've never had a starring role in a movie, so let's just dream together and eat warm pretzels and drink beer and think about reaching the stars." Even so, he made me swear not to take any other job without checking with him. Not long afterward, I was offered a part in the Broadway production of *One Flew Over the Cuckoo's Nest*. I told Mel, and he made me write a month's release clause into my contract, which I did. Then *three years* passed, during which — nothing. He didn't even call me. Finally, I'm back on Broadway, in Murray Schisgal's play *Luv*. After a matinée, there's a knock on my dressing-room door, and it's Mel. "You didn't think I forgot, did you?" he says. Then he explains that *Springtime for Hitler* has become a movie and that I'm going to play Leopold Bloom. I took the script home and read it, and at 3 A.M. I called him and said, "It's magnificent! When do we start?" I didn't ask about my salary, and I don't think I ever did.'

What had happened in the lengthy interim was that Brooks had found the action of his play spreading all over New York, spilling out onto sidewalks and rooftops, leaping from place to place with a spatial flexibility for which film seemed the obvious form. Helped by an inventive secretary with the arresting name of Alfa-Betty Olsen, he refashioned it as a movie. Several agents had 'run with it' — to lapse into Hollywood patois — and got nowhere. It then fell into the hands of Sidney Glazier, a fund-raiser and contact man who had won an Academy Award for producing *The Eleanor Roosevelt Story*. Brooks describes Glazier, whom he met on Fire Island, as 'a crazy man, he drank and he bellowed, he faced the ocean and roared like a sea lion.' Glazier ordered Brooks not to read the script to him but simply to tell him the story. 'About halfway through,' Brooks continues, 'Sidney was drinking coffee and he laughed so much it went up his nose. He collapsed on the floor, spitting and snorting and coughing. As he rolled around, he stuck up his arm, and when I reached out for it he grabbed my hand and said, "We're going to make this movie. it's the funniest thing I ever heard." And he knew what an impossible deal I was demanding: My first condition was that I had to direct the picture.' Glazier budgeted the production at a million dollars, supplied half of it through his own company, and ran with the script around all the major studios. No dice. He eventually appealed to the independent producer Joseph E. Levine, who had just raised what he claimed to be the last cent at his disposal to finance an extremely risky project called *The Graduate*. Like every other moneyman who had seen the script, Levine said that no Jewish exhibitor would put *Springtime for Hitler* on his marquee. Brooks, for his part, rejected the suggestion that it should be retitled *Springtime for Mussolini*. By now, however, he was reluctantly prepared to settle for something as neutral as *The Producers*. There was one major point in Levine's favour: he genuinely liked what Brooks had written. Against this was the fact that he could not see his way to hiring the author as director.

Desperate to resolve these matters, Glazier brought the two men together over lunch. 'I ate very nicely,' Brooks says. 'Nothing dropped out of my mouth. I didn't eat bread and butter, because I didn't know whether you should cut bread or break it. Meanwhile, Joe Levine ate like an animal. Just on top of some trout, he said, "What would you do if I said yes? Could you direct it? What do you say, kid? Tell me from your heart. Don't lie to me; it may be the end for me." He was impressed with me because I was cute and funny. So I said "Yes, I can do it." And he said "OK," and we shook hands.' (Long after the film was made, Levine admitted to Brooks, 'I was wrong. We should have called it *Springtime for Hitler*.' Brooks told me, 'Actually, they did call it *Springtime for Hitler* in Sweden. And when *The Twelve Chairs* came out, they called it *Springtime for the Twelve Chairs*. *Blazing Saddles* was *Springtime for the Black Sheriff*, and *Young Franken-stein* was *Springtime for Frankenstein*. I'm big stuff in Sweden. Everything is springtime there.')

Ten years from conception to handshake, and still not an actor signed: such is the life-devouring pace at which the movie business conducts its affairs. A deal with Gene Wilder was quickly concluded, but Zero Mostel, whom Brooks had always wanted for the role of Bialystock, read the script with mounting horror. 'What is this?' he bellowed to Brooks. 'A Jewish producer going to bed with old women on the brink of the grave? I can't play such a part. I'm a Jewish person.' Enlisting the support of Mostel's wife, Brooks finally managed to change his mind, but their working relationship, once shooting (and shouting) began, was not easy. Between takes, Mostel would be found lying in his dressing room like a beached whale, moaning, 'That man is going to kill me! He keeps saying, "Do it again." '

According to Brooks: 'He was wonderful and he was a great friend, and he was a great pain in the ass. It was like working in the middle of a thunderstorm. Bolts of Zero — blinding flashes of Zero — were all around you. When he wasn't *on*, he was very dear, very pensive, very accessible. We had family feuds. He had a sense of the grandeur of an artist. He had what I like in an actor — power, stature, and enormous bravery. I knew that if I could reach the end of the solar system of his talent, if I could just prod him into some outburst of insane anger, I could wake up the sleeping emotional depths of that extraordinary man. And I did, and, although he protested bitterly, he was fabulous.'

The picture took eight weeks to shoot and eleven months to edit: Brooks was then learning his trade. Nowadays, he gets through the editing period in about four months. *The Producers* was brought in under budget, at nine hundred and forty-one thousand dollars. It opened in 1968 and, despite murderous notices, acquired a cult reputation that enabled it to creep into the black within four years. Brooks has little faith in critics, believing that they always catch up with him one movie too late. 'I never got good reviews in my life and I never will,' he declares. 'They took one look at *The Producers* and said it stank. Then I gave them *The Twelve Chairs* and they said it lacked the great chaotic buoyancy of that majestic triumph *The Producers*. Then came *Blazing Saddles*, and they said that everything I'd learned about films had been forgotten in this disgusting mess.'

Badly wounded by the reception of his maiden effort, Brooks was resoundingly compensated by the members of the Motion Picture Academy, who, showing an unusual disdain for the opinions of both the press and the general public, awarded him the Oscar for Best Original Screenplay of 1968. It was a bold and unexpected choice. In order to enjoy *The Producers*, you have to cultivate a taste for grotesque and deliberate over-statement. In the early scenes, Mostel and Wilder play together like figures out of a Jonsonian comedy of humours. Cupidity (Mostel) seduces Conformity (Wilder): in each, a single trait is exaggerated to the point of plethoric obsession, and beyond. These are cartoon creatures, whose dialogue seems to be written in capital letters, heavily italicized. To say that this makes it too 'theatrical' is irrelevant, for as soon as we agree to abandon the convention of naturalism, anything goes, and the screen can be as unrealistic as the stage. (Who complains, after all, that the Marx Brothers' *Cocoanuts* is merely a photographed stage production?) The film's peak is the sequence, already a modern classic, in which a chorus of Storm Troopers, shot from above à la Busby Berkeley, sings 'Springtime for Hitler' — a lilting melody composed by Brooks — while revolving in swastika formation. Afterward, everything runs downhill. The idea of playing the Führer as a southern red-neck high on flower power and LSD not only mixes up too many incompatible jokes but destroys the bed-rock plausibility of plot without which even the looniest farce collapses. Like most of Brooks's work for the cinema, *The Producers* shows him at his best and at his worst.

Academy Award notwithstanding, there was no stampede in the movie industry for Brooks's services. His fame is now so widespread that we tend to forget (though he does not) how recent its origins are. It was not until 1974, with *Blazing Saddles*, that the days of wine and grosses began. His second picture, *The Twelve Chairs*, opened in 1970, nearly three frustrating years after *The Producers*, and crashed to immediate box-office failure. It was based on a satirical Soviet novel of the nineteen-twenties, by Ilya Ilf and Eugene Petrov. Like *The Producers*, it dealt with greed — the prize in this case being a hoard of diamonds concealed in one of a dozen chairs that are confiscated from a palace during the revolution. Again, the characters are raging obsessives, with the difference that here the model is Gogol rather than Jonson. The atmosphere of rural Russia is lovingly evoked, and Brooks himself, making his movie debut, is superb in the minor role of a masochistic, vodka-sodden caretaker with an insatiable yearning for the good old days of servitude. Yet the film as a whole never comes to life; its jokes seem shod with lead, and one watches glumly as, like the wounded snake in Pope's poem, it drags its slow length along. Perhaps excess of ambition was what betrayed it. Alan Schwartz told me, 'It was meant to be a great statement about man's relationship to man, and how revolutions fail to work because of human frailty. Mel wanted to be serious and literary.'

Two ironic footnotes should be added. (1) In 1945, an updated travesty of the same novel, transplanted to New York and entitled *It's in the Bag*, was shot in Hollywood. Starring Fred Allen, it treats the source material as an excuse for a parade of cameo appearances by well-known names, among them (the roll is worth calling) Victor Moore, Don Ameche, Jerry Colonna, William Bendix, Rudy Valee, Jack Benny, and Robert Benchley. Though rampantly disloyal to the original, it has many more laughs than the Brooks version, mired in reverence. Benchley, who plays a hotel rat-catcher, must surely have written his own best line. Frock-coated at his son's wedding, he draws the lad aside to calm his nerves with a last-minute word of advice. 'In–laws' suits never fit,' he says gravely. 'Remember that, boy.' (2) Nothing in *The Twelve Chairs* is as funny as the account of its making which Brooks gave in an interview with *Playboy*, published in February, 1975. Having explained that shooting took place in Yugoslavia, where he spent nine months, Brooks continued:

> It's a very long flight to Yugoslavia and you land in a field of full-grown corn. They figure it cushions the landing. . . . Now, at night, you can't do anything, because all of Belgrade is lit by a ten-watt bulb, and you can't go anywhere, because Tito has the car. It was a beauty, a green '38 Dodge. And the food in Yugoslavia is either very good or very bad. One day, we arrived on location late and starving and they served us fried chains. When we go to our hotel rooms, mosquitoes as big as George Foreman were waiting for us. They were sitting in armchairs with their legs crossed.

It is tempting to quote more. Brooks's performance throughout the twelve seventy-five-minute sessions he devoted to answering *Playboy's* questions was a marathon display of his gift for chat in full flower. The printed result deserves a place in any anthology of modern American humour. The Master is back on home ground. Brooks is showing off his own invention — the interview as comic art — and doing so with a virtuosity that makes one wonder how any other form could ever put his talents to better use.

Fifty thousand dollars was Brooks's reward for writing, directing, coproducing, and acting in *The Twelve Chairs*. It consumed three years of his life, and this means that, after taxes, he was subsisting on an annual sum of approximately eight thousand dollars. Since then — except on one eccentric and abortive occasion — he has shrunk from writing a film alone, preferring to test his ideas in the crucible of collaboration. In his words, 'I didn't want to go back to the tables and risk another gambling session with my career.' By resorting to teamwork, he has turned out the hits that have established his reputation; in pragmatic terms, he cannot be faulted. Even so, there are those — Alan Schwartz is one of them — who feel that the time may now have come for Brooks to trust his own intuitions and fly solo again. 'Mel surrounds himself with other writers because the screenplay, to him, is the most important part of a movie,' Schwartz told me. 'But I'd like to see him doing his own stuff. He ought to give us pure, vintage Brooks, not Brooks riding on the backs of a lot of other people. There's a strange legal phrase that expresses what I mean. Suppose I'm working as a driver for a guy named Al. If I run someone over in the course of my duties, Al is responsible. But if I take the car to the beach and run someone over, that is called in law a "frolic and detour," and *I'm* responsible. I think Mel should go in for more frolics and detours.'

In 1970, when *The Twelve Chairs* were pulled out from under him by critics and public alike, Brooks was forty-four years old and was still, by his own standards, a failure. ('To be the funniest has always been my aim' — statement to *Newsweek*, 1975.) Unable to resist another fling at the tables, he plunged into his last frolic and detour to date — a flirtation with culture which was so alien to his temperament that it seems, in retrospect, a gesture of self-destructive defiance. He saw and was impressed by an Off Broadway production of Goldsmith's comedy *She Stoops to Conquer*. The play struck him as 'Mozartean,' and he promptly adapted it for the screen. His plan was to shoot it in England, with Albert Finney as Tony Lumpkin. Not long before, Finney had spent several weeks on a remote Pacific island with only one record, 'The Two-Thousand-Year-Old Man,' which he played every night. 'When I met him in New York,' Brooks recalls, 'he was in awe of me, he couldn't believe I lived, he thought I was God.' Finney listened to the divine proposition and reverently turned it down. Brooks took his screenplay on the familiar round of agents, producers, and studios without raising a flicker of interest, and got ready to face the fact that he was finished in show business.

David Begelman, recently fined for financial misdeeds committed while he was head of Columbia Pictures, here enters the story. Despite the cloud of scandal over Begelman's head, Brooks remains his impenitent admirer. 'When he took over Columbia in 1973,' Brooks says, 'David Begelman turned it around and made it, by dint of his aggression and his perspicacity and his acumen, a wonderful, working, winning company. I love it the way I love Fox, where I work, because it is not Gulf & Western, it's not Transamerica, it's Columbia Pictures.' Before Begelman moved to Columbia, he was vice-chairman of Creative Management Associates, perhaps the most powerful talent agency in the entertainment industry. One day in 1972, Brooks was aimlessly trudging the streets of New York. Begelman spotted him and approached him. According to Brooks, the following conversation took place:

BEGELMAN: Where are you going?

BROOKS: Nowhere. I am walking in circles.

BEGELMAN: Why is the most talented man in the world walking in circles?

BROOKS: Because the most talented man in the world is out of a job and is maybe not the most talented man in the world.

BEGELMAN: Can I buy you lunch?

BROOKS: Oh, I would be so happy if you would, because I haven't eaten in days.

(*They have lunch, after which Brooks is whisked off to Begelman's sumptuous office, where 'even the indirect lighting is good.'*)

BEGELMAN: The first thing you should do is sign with me. You're nobody and I'm everybody. It's a good deal.

BROOKS: You're right. (*He signs.*)

Soon afterward, a friend in the script department of Warner Brothers sent him a treatment by Andrew Bergman of a Western comedy called *Tex X*. Would Brooks like to rewrite it? Immobilized by self-mistrust, Brooks passed the script on to Begelman for advice. This led to another exquisitely lit confrontation.

BEGELMAN: I think this could be very funny. Do you want to do it?

BROOKS: No.

BEGELMAN: All right, you don't want to do it. Fine. You'll do it.

BROOKS: Why do I have to do it?

BEGELMAN: Because you owe a fortune in alimony, because you are in debt, and because you have no choice. You have to do it, and with all the talent you possess.

BROOKS: OK. I'll do it. As long as I can have Andrew Bergman to work with.

BEGELMAN: Swell. I'll make that one of the conditions.

BROOKS: And not only Bergman. (*His mind races to recapture the security of the past.*) I want to do it the way we did 'Your Show of

Shows.' We'll get a black writer, maybe Richard Pryor, and a comedy team like Norman Steinberg and Alan Uger, and we'll lock ourselves up and write it together, fancy-free and crazy.

Through Begelman's mediation with Warners, this group was rapidly assembled. He negotiated a contract whereby Brooks received fifty thousand dollars for the screenplay (his fellow authors split a smaller sum four ways) and a hundred thousand more if the studio liked the result and asked Brooks to direct it. Brooks regards *Blazing Saddles* — his new title for *Tex X* — as 'a landmark comedy,' a historic blast of derision at the heroic myths of the Old West. 'I decided that this would be a surrealist epic,' he said to me. 'It was time to take two eyes, the way Picasso had done it, and put them on one side of the nose, because the official movie portrait of the West was simply a lie. For nine months, we worked together like maniacs. We went all the way — especially Richard Pryor, who was very brave and very far-out and very catalytic. I figured my career was finished anyway, so I wrote berserk, heartfelt stuff about white corruption and racism and Bible-thumping bigotry. We used dirty language on the screen for the first time, and to me the whole thing was like a big psychoanalytic session. I just got everything out of me — all my furore, my frenzy, my insanity, my love of life and hatred of death.'

Warners snapped up the completed script and hired Brooks to direct his first Hollywood movie. There was one stipulation: the campfire sequence, in which the bean-fed cowpokes audibly befoul the night air, must be cut. Brooks and his colleagues stood firm: either the scene stayed or they quit. Here, and elsewhere in the screenplay, they saw no reason to disown what is called 'healthy vulgarity' when it occurs in Chaucer, but 'childish smut' when it infiltrates the cinema. Eventually the studio gave in, provided that Brooks would consent, as an executive put it, 'to for God's sake hold the decibels down.' Casting, however, was not without problems. Brooks wanted Richard Pryor to play the black protagonist, whom knavish State Procurer Harvey Korman appoints as sheriff of a white chauvinist community in the hope of destroying its faith in law and order. Warners rejected Pryor, whom they thought too undisciplined. Cleavon Little (a suave performer with no flair for comedy) got the job instead. Dan Dailey was engaged for the role of the Waco Kid, the burnt-out alcoholic gunfighter whom Little enlists to support him. On the Friday before shooting began, Dailey suffered an attack of qualms and cabled that he was pulling out. With forty-eight hours to go, he was replaced by Gig Young, but when Young arrived on the set it was obvious that he was in no shape to act. Personal problems, it seemed, were oppressing him, and at the end of a wasted day he was discreetly fired.

'It's a sign from God!' Brooks suddenly cried. 'Get me Gene Wilder on the phone in New York!' Though Wilder knew the script and was eager to help, he was about to leave for England, where he was due to appear in *The Little Prince*, directed by Stanley Donen. 'Nothing's impossible!' Brooks shouted at him. 'Call Donen in London now and ask him to rearrange his schedule. If he can let you out for three weeks, or even two, it's enough.'

A couple of hours later, Wilder called back with the news that Donen had generously agreed to reshuffle his plans and release Wilder for three and a half weeks. 'I'll fly out tomorrow,' Wilder said. Brooks met him at Los Angeles Airport and drove him straight to the costume department of Warners, where he was transformed within minutes into something out of *Stagecoach*. Next morning, roughly thirty-six hours after the idea had first come up, Gene Wilder, word perfect, was playing the Waco Kid. 'I don't believe in fate,' Wilder said to me recently, 'but I'm tempted to when I think of my relationship with Mel. If I hadn't been miscast in *Mother Courage*, none of this would have happened. And if two actors hadn't dropped out of *Blazing Saddles* at the last moment, I would never have got the part.'

When shooting (ten weeks) and editing (nine months) were over, Brooks and his producer, Michael Hertzberg, held an afternoon showing of their rough-cut for a dozen top executives at Warner Brothers. The occasion was about as festive — to borrow a phrase dear to Laurence Olivier — as a baby's open grave. The jury sat like so many statues on Easter Island and filed out at the end in frozen silence. Brooks was shattered, convinced that he had thrown away his last chance in movies. Hertzberg was more resilient. Grabbing a phone, he instructed his staff that he was going to run the picture again that evening, in a larger viewing theatre, and that he wanted it packed with at least two hundred people: secretaries, janitors, cleaning women, waiters — anyone but studio brass. Let Brooks continue the story: 'So 8 P.M. comes and two hundred and forty people are jammed into this room. Some of them have already heard the film is a stinker because of the afternoon disaster. So they're very quiet and polite. Frankie Laine sings the title song, with the whip cracks. Laughs begin — good laughs. We go to the railroad section. The cruel overseer says to the black workers, "Let's have a good old nigger work song." Everybody gets a little chilled. Then the black guys start to sing "I get no kick from champagne. . . ." And that audience was like a Chagall painting. People left their chairs and floated upside down and the laughter never stopped. It was big from that moment to the last frame of the last reel.'

Blazing Saddles opened in 1974 and went on to become one of the two top-grossing comedies in the history of the cinema, out-earned only by Robert Altman's *M*A*S*H*. It is a farce with the gloves off, a living proof of the adage that a feast can be every bit as good as enough. We are not invited to smile: we either laugh or cringe. The major gags are blatant to the point of outrage, as when a thug on foot, faced with a mounted adversary, fells his opponent's horse with a roundhouse right to the jaw. Brooks's method is the comedy of deliberate overkill. The annoyance of Hedley Lamarr (the Harvey Korman character) at being addressed as Hedy is funny the first time and tedious the third, but by the fifth or sixth it is funnier than ever; in a film full of unexpected twists, the expected twist can pay surprising dividends. Though the jokes run wild, the plot is tightly organised, and parts of the script are remarkably literary — e.g., this far from untypical exchange:

> Q.: Don't you see it's the last act of a desperate man?
> A.: I don't care if it's the first act of *Henry V*.

With *Blazing Saddles*, a low comedy in which many of the custard pies are camouflaged hand grenades, Brooks made his first conquest of Middle America. He told *Playboy* that it was 'designed as an esoteric little picture,' but the statement simply does not ring true; he had always wanted the big audience in addition to the art-house minority, and now he had both.

Young Frankenstein (1974) started life as a phrase doodled by Gene Wilder during an Easter vacation at West Hampton in 1973. He called Brooks and explained what he had in mind: one of Frankenstein's scions revisits the family castle in Transylvania and revives the monster his ancestor created. Brooks had no time to do more than express interest, since *Blazing Saddles* was already in preparation. A deal was set up with Columbia whereby Wilder would write a first draft and then, after *Blazing Saddles* was finished, work with Brooks on a revised version. Their collaboration was speedy and harmonious, Brooks supplying the broad comic emphases and Wilder the grace notes. Wilder restrained Brooks, who, in turn, liberated Wilder. 'Mel has all kinds of faults,' Wilder said to me. 'Like his greed, his megalomania, his need to be the universal father and teacher, even to people far more experienced than he is. Why I'm close to him is not in spite of those faults but because of them. I need a leader, someone to tell me what to do. If he were more humble, modest, and considerate, he would probably have more friends, but I doubt whether he and I would be such good friends. He made me discover the *me* in Mel. He taught me never to be afraid of offending. It's when you worry about offending people that you get in trouble.' (Compare something that Cocteau once said: 'Whatever the public blames you for, cultivate it — it is yourself.')

Brooks and Wilder presented their final draft to Columbia before *Blazing Saddles* appeared. The estimated budget was two million two hundred thousand dollars. The studio wanted it reduced to a million and three-quarters. Happy to compromise, Brooks asked, 'How about two million?' The answer was an unyielding no. 'So we took the script to Fox, and made the picture there for two million eight,' Wilder told me. 'We were

already shooting when *Blazing Saddles* came out and hit the jackpot.'
Wilder thinks — and is not alone in thinking — that this was the biggest
mistake Columbia ever made. Since *Young Frankenstein*, which has so far
grossed over thirty-four million dollars, Brooks has remained unshakably
loyal to Fox. (In his office on the Fox lot, the wall overlooking his desk is
dominated by a large portrait of Tolstoy, hanging alongside a blown–up
label from a bottle of Château Latour 1929 — 'to remind me,' Brooks says,
'that there are more important things than grosses.') 'On the set of *Blazing
Saddles*, there was a lot of love in the air,' Wilder continues. 'But *Young
Frankenstein* was the most pleasurable film I've ever done. I couldn't bear
to leave Transylvania.'

It would be fair to call *Young Frankenstein* the Mel Brooks movie that
appeals to people who don't like Mel Brooks. 'I like *things* in all his films,'
Woody Allen said to me cautiously, 'but they're a little in-and-out for my
taste. *Young Frankenstein* is the most consistent whole.' The parts mesh
instead of clashing. The pace throughout, audaciously stately for comedy, is
modelled on that of James Whale's *Frankenstein*; and Gerald Hirschfeld's
black-and-white photography exactly matches Whale's crepuscular visual
style. The members of the supporting cast play together with a self-denying
temperance unique in Brooks's work: I think particularly of Frau Blücher
(Cloris Leachman), the fright-wigged housekeeper, at every mention of
whose name we hear the distant whinnying of terrified horses; and of the
Transylvanian police chief (Kenneth Mars), with an expatriate accent even
less penetrable than the late Albert Bassermann's, and with a prosthetic arm
that he uses as a battering ram when he leads the pitchfork-brandishing
peasants against the gates of Schloss Frankenstein. In the title role, Gene
Wilder — his eyes burning, his voice an exalted, slow-motion tenor —
gives the finest performance yet seen in a Brooks picture. In the best
sequence, fit to be set beside the 'Springtime for Hitler' routine in *The Producers*, Wilder proudly appears before an assembly of grave Victorian
scientists to introduce his new, improved monster, who clumps onto the
stage and goes into a halting impression of Boris Karloff singing 'Puttin' on
the Ritz.' The spectators instantly subject the zombie and his master to a
bombardment of cabbages and broccoli, the underlying joke being that an
audience of bearded savants should have come laden with vegetable
missiles in the first place. It is not the gags, however, that give the film its
motive force. We have seen that Brooks is driven by a fear, amounting to
hatred, of mortality; and what is *Young Frankenstein* but the story of a man
who succeeds in defeating death?

Brooks now began to savour the delights of power. 'It's an achievement
of a kind,' he told me sometime ago, 'to know that I can walk into any
studio — any one in town — and just say my name, and the president will
fly out from behind his desk and open his door. It's terrific, it's a great
feeling. My worst critic is my wife. She keeps me straight. She says, "Are

you pleasing that mythical public of yours again, or is this really funny and heartfelt?" ' Brooks refers to the byproducts of success under the collective title of the Green Awning Syndrome. He explains what he means in an imaginary anecdote: 'Mike Nichols has just made *The Graduate*, and it's a worldwide smash, and he goes to his producer, Joe Levine, and says, "Now I want to do *The Green Awning*." "The what?" "*The Green Awning*." "What is that?" "It's a movie about a green awning." "Does any famous star walk under the green awning?" "No, all unknowns." "Are there any naked women near the green awning?" "No, no naked women." "Are people talking and eating scrambled eggs under the green awning?" "No. It's just a green awning. Panavision. It doesn't move." "How long would it be?" "Two hours. Nothing but a green awning." Levine sticks out his hand. "All right, what the hell, we'll do it!" That's the Green Awning Syndrome.'

Brooks knew that the syndrome had descended upon him when he proposed *Silent Movie* as his next picture for Fox: given his track record, the studio simply dared not turn it down, though Brooks admits that he helped Fox to be brave by revealing that there would be cameo roles for Liza Minnelli, Anne Bancroft, Paul Newman, James Caan, and Burt Reynolds. The idea for a movie with no spoken words (apart from a resonant 'No!' to be uttered by the mime Marcel Marceau) had come from Ron Clark, a laconic playwright and comedy writer. Clark suggested that he and Brooks should collaborate on the script with Rudy DeLuca and Barry Levinson, widely admired as the writers of 'The Carol Burnett Show'; and so it worked out. For more than twelve months — very much on and off, to fit in with their other assignments — the four men met in a room at Fox and reduced one another to hysteria. Shooting began in January, 1976, and the film had its premiere before the end of the year.

A string of sight gags linked by captions (the verbals in many instances being funnier than the visuals), *Silent Movie* consolidated Brooks's international fame. No dubbing was required to make its more explosive set pieces as accessible in Bora Bora as they were in South Bend. It spoke softly but carried a big slapstick. Moreover, it established Brooks as a movie star: Mel Funn, the ex-alcoholic director who saves his old studio from conglomerate takeover with a silent movie called *Silent Movie*, was the first leading role he had ever played. The picture was his third comedy hit in three years, and up to the beginning of 1978 it had brought in more than twenty million dollars at the box office. Yet there are times when one not only can but must argue with success. Even as I smiled (which was more often than I laughed) at *Silent Movie*, I knew I was watching an act of supreme perversity. Here was a master of the improvised word devoting more than a year of his life to something speechless and meticulously planned in advance. Do not suppose, by the way, that Brooks is a director who works on impulse, prancing around the set in ecstasies of Felliniesque free association. The final script of *Silent Movie* was the film the public saw, except for a brief but expensive sequence that Brooks described to me afterward: 'It was called "Lobsters in New York," and it starts with a restaurant sign that reads "Chez Lobster." Inside, a huge lobster in maître d's tuxedo is greeting two very well-dressed lobsters in evening dress and leading them to a table. Already we thought this was hysterical. Then a waiter lobster in a white jacket shows them a menu that says "Flown in Fresh from New York." They get up and follow the waiter lobster to an enormous tank, where a lot of little human beings in bathing suits are swimming nervously around. The diner lobsters point to a tasty-looking middle-aged man. The waiter's claw reaches into the tank. It picks up the man, who is going bananas, and that was the end of the scene. We loved it; we thought it was sensational. Every time we saw it, there was not enough Kleenex to stuff into our mouths.' Nobody else, however, so much as snickered — not even at the sneak previews — with the result that Brooks decided to jettison the whole sequence. Never before had he faced such a setback, and the memory of it still ruffles him. Seeing *Silent Movie* for the second time, I found myself recalling and endorsing something that Gene Wilder had said to me: 'Mel has no physical skills, like Chaplin or Fields. His skills are vocal. Not verbal but vocal.' And in *Silent Movie*, for all its popularity, rusting unused.

Excerpts from a dinner with Brooks at the Chambord Restaurant in Beverly Hills late in 1977. He is wearing a dark-blue coat, gray slacks, a light-blue shirt, and a striped blue tie; as usual, he has arrived with a leather case containing two bottles of absurdly expensive wine from his own cellar. Neither of them, alas, comes from the case of magnums of Haut Brion, 1961, which Alfred Hitchcock recently sent him as a gesture of gratitude for *High Anxiety*. In reminiscent mood, Brooks speaks: 'Just before *Silent Movie* came out in 1976, I was approached by a staff writer from *Time* who asked me whether I'd like to be on the cover. Well, I expected to be described in *Time* as "Mel Brooks, flinty, chunky Jew," but nevertheless I said yes. I had no idea what an insane Pandora's box of heartache would be opened by this simple exchange. Reporters followed me around night and day for weeks. They tortured my mother and my children, all the time looking for negative things about me. Everyone I ever knew was called and cross-examined. Everyone eagerly cooperated. Then, a couple of weeks before the cover was due, I was told I'd been dumped and replaced by Nadia Comaneci. So I asked, "Isn't the election coming up soon?" "Don't worry," they said. "It's you next week for sure." Next week, Ford gets the cover. I called them up and said, "I'm disgusted with myself. I feel used and humiliated, and I may hang myself in my cell." They said, "Look, if you'll just help us fill in one or two gaps, there's a good chance that next week, perhaps . . ." Even then I hesitated, but I finally said no.'

I asked what seemed the obvious question.

After a pause, Brooks slowly replied, 'If I could get a legal guarantee that they wouldn't bother my immediate family, and if that guarantee was signed by every member of the Supreme Court, then the answer is yes, I *would* do it all again for a *Time* cover.'

High Anxiety, which featured the same star, director, and writing team as *Silent Movie*, made its debut in the closing weeks of 1977. Sniffed at by some of the critics (though not by the public, which has swept it into the black with a box-office take that so far amounts to about twenty million dollars), it borrows elements from a number of Hitchcock films — in particular, *Spellbound*, *Vertigo*, *Psycho*, *The Birds*, and *North by North-West* — and, having given them all a ferociously farcical twist, arranges them in a way that would make narrative sense to an audience entirely ignorant of Hitchcock. Brooks once told me that for him the Marx Brothers were 'the healthiest of all comics,' and it is not fortuitous that the middle initial of Dr. Robert H. Thorndyke, the character he plays in *High Anxiety*, stands for Harpo. The best half-dozen moments in the picture have the antisocial outrageousness that was always the Brothers' trademark — moments when inhibitions evaporate and excesses long dreamed of are allowed free play; e.g., Thorndyke's fulsome impersonation of Frank Sinatra in a hotel nightclub, and his first dinner as the newly appointed head of the Psycho-Neurotic Institute for the Very, V*ery* Nervous. In the latter sequence an establishing shot shows us, by night, a mansion like Manderley in *Rebecca*. The script continues:

> *The lights are on in the elegantly appointed dining room.* CAMERA SLOWLY MOVES *toward the lighted window. It* MOVES *closer and closer, until it actually hits the window and crashes through. We* HEAR *the* SOUND *of the window panes breaking. Everybody at the dining table stops eating their fruit cup, their spoons poised in mid-air.*

When *High Anxiety* failed to receive a single nomination, either from the Academy or from the Writers Guild, Brooks was in despair. 'He was as low as I've ever known him,' his wife said to me.

Despite its virtues, *High Anxiety* fitted into a confining pattern. Brooks had now made four films in succession, all of them based on other kinds of films — the Western, the horror picture, the silent comedy, and the Hitchcock thriller. Nor was he alone in this dependence on incest — or, if you prefer, cannibalism. Barry Levinson remarked to me, '*Rocky* is a remake even though it's never been made before.' In the *Times* on September 25, 1977, Roger Copeland dealt with the whole subject of movies about movies:

> Consider, for example, George Lucas's *Star Wars* — a film that

indignantly wrote to a friend: 'All these attempts to exploit the immediate past show the rapidity of the bankruptcy of the movies as purveyors of popular entertainment.'

Brooks, discussing his future plans, sometimes sounds worryingly unaware of the perils involved in continued addiction to the Self-Regarding Cinema. In the past twelve months, I have heard him frothing with enthusiasm about such projects as (1) 'a World War Two picture to end all World War Two pictures'; (2) a remake of the Lubitsch masterpiece *To Be or Not to Be*, starring Anne Bancroft and himself; and (3) 'a Busby Berkeley-style musical where crazy people sing for no reason,' which would be tantamount to self-plagiarism, since the perfect comment on Berkeley already exists in the 'Springtime for Hitler' sequence from *The Producers*. Not long ago, he called up Gene Wilder and said, 'When we work together again, we're going to have to bring up the big guns, and there are only two — love and death.' Which is all very well except for the fact that *Love and Death* is the title of a film by Woody Allen.

Intermittently, however, Brooks will say something that bolsters one's faith in the curious inner compass that guides him. This, for instance: 'I've tied myself to no end but the joy of observation. And I need to pass that on. I'm a celebrator. That's why I like the Russians. They'll look at a tree and cry out, "Look at that tree!" They're full of original astonishments.' And, still more reassuringly, this — a remark uttered in a context that had nothing to do with Brooks's own career: 'We are all basically antennae. If we let ourselves be bombarded by cultural events based on movies, we won't get a taste of what's happening in the world.'

Springtime, 1978: A sunny lunch in Los Angeles with Anne Bancroft, who is, according to her husband, 'a strange combination of the serf and the intellectual.' They live in a one-storey house (no pool) in Malibu. She tells me that Brooks's newest obsession is to make a film called, *tout court*, *The History of the World, Part One*. She likes the idea, because it means, as she puts it, 'that he can play any period in which he feels happy.' This, of course, was precisely what he did in the footloose days when he was recording 'The Two-Thousand-Year-Old Man.' The story of mankind would be an ideal frolic, a definitive detour; and Miss Bancroft agrees with me that he ought to write on his own. 'One evening, I came back late from a difficult rehearsal,' she says. 'Mel had been working at home all day. I was feeling very sorry for myself, and I wailed, "Acting is so hard." Mel picked up a blank sheet of paper and held it in front of me. "*That's* what's hard," he said. I've never complained about acting again.'

The New Yorker: 30th October 1978;
Show People, 1980

LOUISE BROOKS

None of this would have happened if I had not noticed, while lying late in bed on a hot Sunday morning last year in Santa Monica and flipping through the TV guide for the impending week, that one of the local public-broadcasting channels had decided to show, at 1 P.M. that very January day, a film on which my fantasies had fed ever since I first saw it, a quarter of a century before. Even for Channel 28, it was an eccentric piece of programming. I wondered how many of my Southern Californian neighbours would be tempted to forgo their poolside champagne brunches, their bicycle jaunts along Ocean Front Walk, their health-food picnics in Topanga Canyon, or their surfboard battles with the breakers of Malibu in order to watch a silent picture, shot in Berlin just fifty years earlier, about an artless young hedonist who, meaning no harm, rewards her lovers — and eventually herself — with the prize of violent death. Although the film is a tragedy, it is also a celebration of the pleasure principle. Outside in the midday sunshine, California was celebrating the same principle, with the shadows of mortality left out.

I got to my set in time to catch the credits. The director: G. W. Pabst, reigning maestro of German cinema in the late nineteen-twenties. The script: Adapted by Ladislaus Vajda from *Erdgeist* (Earth Spirit) and *Die Büchse der Pandora* (*Pandora's Box*), two scabrously erotic plays written in the eighteen-nineties by Frank Wedekind. For his movie, Pabst chose the title of the later work, though the screenplay differed markedly from Wedekind's original text: *Pandora's Box* belongs among the few films that have succeeded in improving on theatrical chefs-d'œuvre. For his heroine, Lulu, the dominant figure in both plays, Pabst outraged a whole generation of German actresses by choosing a twenty-one-year-old girl from Kansas whom he had never met, who was currently working for Paramount in Hollywood, and who spoke not a word of any language other than English. This was Louise Brooks. She made only twenty-four films, in a movie career that began in 1925 and ended, with enigmatic suddenness, in 1938. Two of them were masterpieces — *Pandora's Box* and its immediate successor, also directed by Pabst, *The Diary of a Lost Girl*. Most, however, were assembly-line studio products. Yet around her, with a luxuriance that proliferates every year, a literature has grown up. I append a few excerpts:

Her youthful admirers see in her an actress who needed no directing, but could move across the screen causing the work of art to be born by her mere presence. — *Lotte H. Eisner, French critic.*

An actress of brilliance, a luminescent personality, and a beauty unparalleled in film history. — *Kevin Brownlow, British director and movie historian.*

One of the most mysterious and potent figures in the history of the cinema . . . she was one of the first performers to penetrate to the heart of screen acting. — *David Thomson, British critic.*

Louise Brooks is the only woman who had the ability to transfigure no matter what film into a masterpiece. . . . Louise is the perfect apparition, the dream woman, the being without whom the cinema would be a poor thing. She is much more than a myth, she is a magical presence, a real phantom, the magnetism of the cinema. — *Ado Kyrou, French critic.*

Those who have seen her can never forget her. She is the modern actress *par excellence*. . . . As soon as she takes the screen, fiction disappears along with art, and one has the impression of being present at a documentary. The camera seems to have caught her by surprise, without her knowledge. She is the intelligence of the cinematic process, the perfect incarnation of that which is photogenic; she embodies all that the cinema rediscovered in its last years of silence: complete naturalness and complete simplicity. Her art is so pure that it becomes invisible. — *Henri Langlois, director of the Cinémathèque Française.*

On Channel 28, I stayed with the film to its end, which is also Lulu's. Of the climactic sequence, so decorously understated, Louise Brooks once wrote in *Sight & Sound*, 'It is Christmas Eve and she is about to receive the gift which has been her dream since childhood. Death by a sexual maniac.' When it was over, I switched channels and returned to the real world of game shows and pet-food commercials, relieved to find that the spell she cast was still as powerful as ever. Brooks reminds me of the scene in *Citizen Kane* in which Everett Sloane, as Orson Welles's aging business manager, recalls a girl in a white dress whom he saw in his youth when he was crossing over to Jersey on a ferry. They never met or spoke. 'I only saw her for one second,' he says, 'and she didn't see me at all — but I'll bet a month hasn't gone by since then that I haven't thought of that girl.'

I had now, by courtesy of Channel 28, seen *Pandora's Box* for the third time. My second encounter with the film had taken place several years earlier, in France. Consulting my journal, I found the latter experience recorded with the baroque extravagance that seems to overcome all those who pay tribute to Brooks. I unflinchingly quote:

> Infatuation with L. Brooks reinforced by second viewing of 'Pandora.' She has run through my life like a magnetic thread — this shameless urchin tomboy, this unbroken, unbreakable porcelain filly. She is a prairie princess, equally at home in a waterfront bar and in the royal suite at Neuschwanstein; a creature of impulse, a creator of impulses, a temptress with no pretensions, capable of dissolving into a giggling fit at a peak of erotic ecstasy; amoral but totally selfless, with that sleek jet *cloche* of hair that rings such a peal of bells in my subconscious. In short, the only star actress I can imagine either being enslaved by or wanting to enslave; and a dark lady worthy of any poet's devotion:

For I have sworn thee fair and thought thee bright,
Who art as black as hell, as dark as night.

Some basic information about Rochester, New York: With two hundred and sixty-three thousand inhabitants, it is the sixth-largest city in the state, bestriding the Genesee River at its outlet into Lake Ontario. Here, in the eighteen-eighties, George Eastman completed the experiments that enabled him to manufacture the Kodak camera, which, in turn, enabled ordinary people to capture monochrome images, posed or spontaneous, of the world around them. He was in at the birth of movies, too. The flexible strips of film used in Thomas Edison's motion-picture machine were first produced by Eastman, in 1889. Rochester is plentifully dotted with monuments to the creator of the Kodak, among them a palatial Georgian house, with fifty rooms and a lofty neo-classical portico, that he built for himself in 1905. When he died, in 1932, he left his mansion to the University of Rochester, of whose president it became the official home. Shortly after the Second World War, the Eastman house took on a new identity. It opened its doors to the public, and offered, to quote from its brochure, 'the world's most important collection of pictures, films, and apparatus showing the development of the art and technology of photography.' In 1972 it was imposingly renamed the International Museum of Photography. Its library now contains about five thousand movies, many of them unique copies, and seven of them — a larger number than any other archive can boast — featuring Louise Brooks. Hence I decide to pay a visit to the city, where I check in at a motel in the late spring of 1978. Thanks to the generous cooperation of Dr. John B. Kuyper, the director of the museum's film department, I am to see its hoard of Brooks pictures — six of them new to me — within the space of two days. Screenings will be held in the Dryden Theatre, a handsome auditorium that was added to the main building in 1950 as a gift from Eastman's niece and her husband, George Dryden.

On the eve of Day One, I mentally recap what I have learned of Brooks's early years. Born in 1906 in Cherryvale, Kansas, she was the second of four children sired by Leonard Brooks, a hardworking lawyer of kindly disposition and diminutive build, for whom she felt nothing approaching love. She herself was never more than five feet two and a half inches tall, but she raised her stature onscreen by wearing heels as high as six inches. Her mother, née Myra Rude, was the eldest member of a family of nine, and she warned Mr. Brooks before their marriage that she had spent her entire life thus far looking after kid brothers and sisters, that she had no intention of repeating the experience with children of her own, and that any progeny she might bear him would, in effect, have to fend for themselves. The result, because Myra Brooks was a woman of high spirits who took an infectious delight in the arts, was not a cold or neglectful upbringing. Insistent on liberty for herself, she passed on a love of liberty to her offspring. Louise absorbed it greedily. Pirouetting appealed to her; encouraged by her mother, she took dancing lessons, and by the age of ten she was making paid appearances at Kiwanis and Rotary festivities. At fifteen, already a beauty *sui generis*, as surviving photographs show, with her hair, close-cropped at the nape to expose what Christopher Isherwood has called 'that unique imperious neck of hers,' cascading in ebony bangs down the high, intelligent forehead and descending on either side of her eyes in spit curls slicked forward at the cheekbones, like a pair of enamelled parentheses — at fifteen, she left high school and went to New York with her dance teacher. There she successfully auditioned for the Denishawn Dancers, which had been founded in 1915 by Ruth St. Denis and Ted Shawn, and was by far the most adventurous dance company in America. She started out as a student, but soon graduated to full membership of the troupe, with which she toured the country from 1922 to 1924. One of her fellow-dancers, Martha Graham, became a lifelong friend. 'I learned to act while watching Martha Graham dance,' she said later, 'and I learned to move in film from watching Chaplin.'

Suddenly, however, the discipline involved in working for Denishawn grew oppressive. Brooks was fired for lacking a sense of vocation, and the summer of 1924 found her back in New York, dancing in the chorus of George White's *Scandals*. After three months of this, a whim seized her, and she embarked without warning for London, where she performed the Charleston at the Café de Paris, near Piccadilly Circus. By New York standards, she thought Britain's Bright Young Things a moribund bunch, and when Evelyn Waugh wrote *Vile Bodies* about them, she said that only a genius could have made a masterpiece out of such glum material. Early in 1925, with no professional prospects, she sailed for Manhattan on borrowed money, only to be greeted by Florenz Ziegfeld with the offer of a job in a musical comedy called *Louie the 14th*, starring Leon Errol. She accepted, but the pattern of her subsequent behaviour left no doubt that what she meant by liberty and independence was what others defined as irresponsibility and self-indulgence. Of the director of *Louie the 14th*, she afterward wrote, 'He detested all of Ziegfeld's spoiled beauties, but most of all me, because on occasion, when I had other commitments, I would wire my nonappearance to the theatre.' In May, 1925, she made her movie début, at the Paramount Astoria Studio, on Long Island, playing a bit part in *The Street of Forgotten Men*, of which no print is known to exist. She has written a vivid account of filmmaking in its Long Island days:

> The stages were freezing in the winter, steaming hot in the summer. The dressing rooms were windowless cubicles. We rode on the freight elevator, crushed by lights and electricians. But none of that mattered, because the writers, directors, and cast were free from all supervision. Jesse Lasky, Adolph Zukor, and Walter Wanger never left the Paramount office on Fifth Avenue, and the head of production never came on the set. There were writers and directors from Princeton and Yale. Motion pictures did not consume us. When work finished, we dressed in evening clothes, dined at the Colony or '21', and went to the theatre.
>
> The difference in Hollywood was that the studio was run by B. P. Schulberg, a coarse exploiter who propositioned every actress and policed every set. To love books was a big laugh. There was no theatre, no opera, no concerts — just those god-damned movies.

Despite Brooks's erratic conduct in *Louie the 14th*, Ziegfeld hired her to join Will Rogers and W. C. Fields in the 1925 edition of his *Follies*. It proved to be her last Broadway show. One of her many admirers that year was the atrabilious wit Herman Mankiewicz, then employed as second-string drama critic of the *Times*. Blithely playing truant from the *Follies*, she attended the opening of *No, No, Nanette* on Mankiewicz's arm. As the houselights faded, her escort, who was profoundly drunk, announced his intention of falling asleep, and asked Brooks to make notes on the show for use in his review. She obliged, and the *Times* next day echoed her opinion that *No, No, Nanette* was as 'a highly meritorious paradigm of its kind.' (Somewhat cryptically, she added that the score contained 'more familiar quotations from itself . . . than even *Hamlet*.') Escapades like this did nothing to endear her to the other, more dedicated Ziegfeld showgirls, but an abiding intimacy grew up between her and W. C. Fields, in whose dressing room she was always graciously received. Later, in a passage that tells us as much about its author as about her subject, she wrote:

> He was an isolated person. As a young man he stretched out his hand to Beauty and Love and they thrust it away. Gradually he reduced reality to exclude all but his work, filling the gaps with alcohol whose dim eyes

transformed the world into a distant view of harmless shadows. He was also a solitary person. Years of travelling alone around the world with his juggling act taught him the value of solitude and the release it gave his mind. . . . Most of his life will remain unknown. But the history of no life is a jest.

In September, 1925, the *Follies* left town on a national tour. Brooks stayed behind and sauntered through the role of a bathing beauty in a Paramount movie called *The American Venus*. Paramount and MGM were both pressing her to sign five-year contracts, and she looked for advice to Walter Wanger, one of the former company's top executives, with whom she was having an intermittent affair. 'If, at this crucial moment in my career,' she said long afterward, 'Walter had given me some faith in my screen personality and my acting ability, he might have saved me from further mauling by the beasts who prowled Broadway and Hollywood.' Instead, he urged her to take the Metro offer, arguing that if she chose Paramount everyone would assume that she got the job by sharing his bed and that her major attribute was not talent but sexual accessibility. Incensed by his line of reasoning, she defiantly signed with Paramount.

In the course of twelve months — during which Brooks's friend Humphrey Bogart, seven years her senior, was still labouring on Broadway, with four seasons to wait before the dawn of his film career — Brooks made six full-length pictures. The press began to pay court to her. *Photoplay*, whose reporter she received reclining in bed, said of her, 'She is so very Manhattan. Very young. Exquisitely hard-boiled. Her black hair and black eyes are as brilliant as Chinese lacquer. Her skin is white as a camellia. Her legs are lyric.' She worked with several of the bright young directors who gave Paramount its reputation for sophisticated comedy; e.g., Frank Tuttle, Malcolm St. Clair. and Edward Sutherland. Chronologically, the list of her credits ran as follows: *The American Venus* (for Tuttle, who taught her that the way to get laughs was to play perfectly straight; he directed Bebe Daniels in four movies and Clara Bow in six). *A Social Celebrity* (for St. Clair, who cast Brooks opposite the immaculately caddish Adolphe Menjou, of whose style she later remarked, 'He never felt anything. He used to say, "Now I do Lubitsch No. 1," "Now I do Lubitsch No. 2." And that's exactly what he did. You felt nothing, working with him, and yet see him on the screen — he was a great actor'). *It's the Old Army Game* (for Sutherland, who had been Chaplin's directorial assistant on *A Woman of Paris*, and who made five pictures with W. C. Fields, of which this was the first; the third, *International House*, is regarded by many Fieldsian authorities as the Master's crowning achievement. Brooks married Sutherland, a hard-drinking playboy, in 1926 — an error that was rectified inside two years by divorce). *The Show-Off* (for St. Clair, adapted from the Broadway hit by George Kelly). *Just Another Blonde* (on loan to

First National). And, finally, to round off the year's work, *Love 'Em and Leave 'Em* (for Tuttle), the first Brooks film of which the Eastman house has a copy. Here begin my notes on the sustained and solitary Brooks banquet that the museum laid before me.

Day One: Evelyn Brent is the nominal star of *Love 'Em and Leave 'Em*, a slick and graceful comedy about Manhattan shopgirls, but light-fingered Louise, as Brent's jazz-baby younger sister, steals the picture with bewitching insouciance. She is twenty, and her body is still plump, quite husky enough for work in the fields; but the face, framed in its black proscenium arch of hair, is already Lulu's in embryo, especially when she dons a white top hat to go to a costume ball (at which she dances a definitive Charleston). The plot calls for her to seduce her sister's boyfriend, a feckless window dresser, and she does so with that fusion of amorality and innocence which was to become her trademark. (During these scenes, I catch myself humming a tune from *Pins and Needles*: 'I used to be on the daisy chain, but now I'm a chain-story daisy.') Garbo could give us innocence, and Dietrich amorality, on the grandest possible scale; only Brooks could play the simple, unabashed hedonist, whose appetite for pleasure is so radiant that even when it causes suffering to herself and others we cannot find it in ourselves to reproach her. Most actresses tend to pass moral judgments on the characters they play. Their performances issue tacit commands to the audience: 'Love me,' 'Hate me,' 'Laugh at me,' 'Weep with me,' and so forth. We get none of this from Brooks, whose presence before the camera merely declares, 'Here I am. Make what you will of me.' She does not care what we think of her. Indeed, she ignores us. We seem to be spying on unrehearsed reality, glimpsing what the great photographer Henri Cartier-Bresson later called '*le moment qui se sauve.*' In the best of her silent films, Brooks — with no conscious intention of doing so — is reinventing the art of screen acting. I suspect that she was helped rather than hindered by the fact that she never took a formal acting lesson. 'When I acted, I hadn't the slightest idea of what I was doing,' she said once to Richard Leacock, the documentary-film maker. 'I was simply playing myself, which is the hardest thing in the world to do — if you *know* that it's hard. I didn't, so it seemed easy. I had nothing to unlearn. When I first worked with Pabst, he was furious, because he approached people intellectually and you couldn't approach me intellectually, because there was nothing to approach.' To watch Brooks is to recall Oscar Wilde's Lady Bracknell, who observes, 'Ignorance is like a delicate, exotic fruit; touch it, and the bloom is gone.'

Rereading the above paragraph, I pause at the sentence 'She does not care what we think of her.' Query: Was it precisely this quality, which contributed so much to her success on the screen, that enabled her, in later years, to throw that success so lightly away?

To return to Frank Tuttle's film: Tempted by a seedy and lecherous old horseplayer who lives in her rooming house, Brooks goes on a betting spree with funds raised by her fellow-shopgirls in aid of the Women's Welfare League. The aging gambler is played by Osgood Perkins (father of Tony), of whom Brooks said to Kevin Brownlow years afterward, 'The best actor I ever worked with was Osgood Perkins. . . . You know what makes an actor great to work with? Timing. You don't have to feel anything. It's like dancing with a perfect dancing partner. Osgood Perkins would give you a line so that you would react perfectly. It was timing — because *emotion means nothing.*' (Emphasis mine.) This comment reveals what Brooks has learned about acting in the cinema: Emotion *per se*, however deeply felt, is not enough. It is what the actor shows — the contraband that he or she can smuggle past the camera — that matters to the audience. A variation of this dictum cropped up in the mouth of John Striebel's popular comic-strip heroine Dixie Dugan, who was based on Brooks and first appeared in 1926. Bent on getting a job in *The Zigfold Follies*, Dixie reflected, 'All there is to this Follies racket is to *be cool and look hot.*' Incidentally, Brooks's comparison of Perkins with a dancing partner reminds me of a remark she once made about Fatty Arbuckle, who under the assumed name of William Goodrich, apathetically directed her in a 1931 two-reeler called *Windy Riley Goes to Hollywood*: 'He sat in his chair like a dead man. He had been very nice and sweetly dead ever since the scandal that ruined his career. . . . Oh, I thought he was magnificent in films. He was a wonderful dancer — a wonderful ballroom dancer in his heyday. It was like floating in the arms of a huge doughnut.'

What images do I retain of Brooks in *Love 'Em and Leave 'Em*? Many comedic details; e.g., the scene in which she fakes tears of contrition by furtively dabbling her cheeks with water from a handily placed goldfish bowl, and our last view of her, with all her sins unpunished, merrily sweeping off in a Rolls-Royce with the owner of the department store. And, throughout, every closeup of that blameless, unblemished face.

In 1927, Brooks moved with Paramount to Hollywood and starred in four pictures — *Evening Clothes* (with Menjou), *Rolled Stockings*, *The City Gone Wild*, and *Now We're in the Air*, none of which are in the Eastman vaults. To commemorate that year, I have a publicity photo taken at a house she rented in Laurel Canyon: poised on tiptoe with arms outstretched, she stands on the diving board of her pool, wearing a one-piece black bathing suit with a tight white belt, looking like a combination of Odette and Odile in some modern-dress version of *Swan Lake*. Early in 1928, she was lent to Fox for a picture (happily preserved by the museum) that was to change her career — *A Girl in Every Port*, written and directed by Howard Hawks, who had made his first film only two years before. Along with Carole Lombard, Rita Hayworth, Jane Russell, and Lauren

Bacall, Brooks thus claims a place among the actresses on David Thomson's's list (in his *Biographical Dictionary of Film*) of performers who were 'either discovered or brought to new life by Hawks.' As in *Love 'Em and Leave 'Em*, she plays an amoral pleasure-lover, but this time the mood is much darker. Her victim is Victor McLaglen, a seagoing roughneck engaged in perpetual sexual rivalry with his closest friend (Robert Armstrong); the embattled relationship between the two men brings to mind the skirmishing of Flagg and Quirt in *What Price Glory?*, which was filmed with McLaglen in 1926. In *A Girl in Every Port*, McLaglen, on a binge in Marseilles, sees a performance by an open-air circus whose star turn is billed as 'Mam'selle Godiva, Neptune's Bride and the Sweetheart of the Sea.' The submarine coquette is, of course, Brooks, looking svelter than of old, and clad in tights, spangled panties, tiara, and black velvet cloak. Her act consists of diving off the top of a ladder into a shallow tank of water. Instantly besotted, the bully McLaglen becomes the fawning lapdog of this 'dame of class.' He proudly introduces her to Armstrong, who, unwilling to wreck his buddy's illusions, refrains from revealing that the lady's true character, as he knows from a previous encounter with her, is that of a small-time gold-digger. In a scene charged with the subtlest eroticism, Brooks sits beside Armstrong on a sofa and coaxes McLaglen to clean her shoes. He readily obeys. As he does so, she begins softly, reminiscently, but purposefully, to fondle Armstrong's thigh. To these caresses Armstrong does not respond, but neither does he reject them. With one man at her feet and another at her fingertips, she is like a cat idly licking its lips over two bowls of cream. This must surely have been the sequence that convinced Pabst, when the film was shown in Berlin, that he had found the actress he wanted for *Pandora's Box*. By the end of the picture, Brooks has turned the two friends into mortal enemies, reducing McLaglen to a state of murderous rage, mixed with grief, that Emil Jannings could hardly have bettered. There is no melodrama in her exercise of sexual power. No effort, either: she is simply following her nature.

After her fling with Fox, Paramount cast its young star (now aged twenty-one) in another downbeat triangle drama, *Beggars of Life*, to be directed by another young director, William Wellman. Like Hawks, he was thirty-two years old. (The cinema is unique among the arts in that there was a time in its history when almost all of its practitioners were young. This was that time.) At first, the studio had trouble tracing Brook's whereabouts. Having just divorced Edward Sutherland, she had fled to Washington with a new lover — George Marshall, a millionaire laundry magnate, who later became the owner of the Redskins football team. When she was found, she promptly returned to the Coast, though her zest for work was somewhat drained by a strong antipathy to one of her co-stars — Richard Arlen, with whom she had appeared in *Rolled Stockings* — and by overt hostility from Wellman, who regarded her as a dilettante. Despite these malign auguries,

Beggars of Life — available at Eastman house — turned out to be one of her best films. Adapted from a novel by Jim Tully, it foreshadows the Depression movies of the thirties. Brooks plays the adopted daughter of a penniless old farmer who attempts, one sunny morning, to rape her. Seizing a shotgun, she kills him. As she is about to escape, the crime is discovered by a tramp (Arlen) who knocks at the door in search of food. They run away together, with Brooks wearing oversized masculine clothes, topped off by a large peaked cap. (This was her first serious venture into the rich territory of sexual ambiguity, so prosperously cultivated in later years by Garbo, Dietrich, et al.) Soon they fall in with a gang of hoboes, whose leader — a ferocious but teachable thug, beautifully played by Wallace Beery — forms the third point of the triangle. He sees through Brooks's disguise and proposes that since the police already know about her male imposture, it would be safer to dress her as a girl. He goes in search of female attire, but what he brings back is marginally too young: a gingham dress, and a bonnet tied under the chin, in which Brooks looks like a woman masquerading as a child, a sort of adult Lolita. She stares at us in her new gear, at once innocent and gravely perverse. The rivalry for her affection comes to its height when Beery pulls a gun and tells Arlen to hand her over. Brooks jumps between them, protecting Arlen, and explains that she would prefer death to life without him. We believe her; and so, to his own befuddled amazement, does Beery. There is really no need for the caption in which he says that he has often heard about love but never until now known what it was. He puts his gun away and lets them go.

Footnote: During the transvestite scenes, several dangerous feats were performed for Brooks by a stunt man named Harvey. One night, attracted by his flamboyant courage, she slept with him. After breakfast next day, she strolled out onto the porch of the hotel in the California village where the location sequences were being shot. Harvey was there, accompanied by a group of hoboes in the cast. He rose and gripped her by the arm. 'Just a minute, Miss Brooks,' he said loudly. 'I've got something to ask you. I guess you know my job depends on my health.' He then named a Paramount executive whom Brooks had never met, and continued, 'Everybody knows you're his girl and he has syphilis, and what I wanted to know is: Do you have syphilis?' After a long and frozen pause, he added, 'Another reason I want to know is that my girl is coming up at noon to drive me back to Hollywood.' Brooks somehow withdrew to her room without screaming. Events like these may account for the lack of agonized regret with which she prematurely ended her movie career. Several years later, after she had turned down the part that Jean Harlow eventually played in Wellman's *Public Enemy*, she ran into the director in a New York bar. 'You always hated making pictures, Louise,' he said sagely. She did not bother to reply that it was not pictures she hated but Hollywood.

The Canary Murder Case (directed by Malcolm St. Clair from a script based on S. S. Van Dine's detective story, with William Powell as Philo Vance: not in the Eastman collection) was the third, and last, American movie that Brooks made in 1928. By now, her face was beginning to be internationally known, and the rushes of this film indicated that Paramount would soon have a major star on its hands. At the time, the studio was preparing to take the plunge into talkies. As Brooks afterward wrote in *Image* (a journal sponsored by Eastman house), front offices all over Hollywood saw in this radical change 'a splendid opportunity . . . for breaking contracts, cutting salaries, and taming the stars.' In the autumn of 1928, when her own contract called for a financial raise, B. P. Schulberg, the West Coast head of Paramount, summoned her to his office and said that the promised increase could not be granted in the new situation. *The Canary Murder Case* was being shot silent, but who knew whether Brooks could speak? (A fragile argument, since her voice was of bell-like clarity.) He presented her with a straight choice: either to continue at her present figure (seven hundred and fifty dollars a week) or to quit when the current picture was finished. To Schulberg's surprise, she chose to quit. Almost as an afterthought, he revealed when she was rising to leave that he had lately received from G. W. Pabst a bombardment of cabled requests for her services in *Pandora's Box*, all of which he had turned down.

Then forty-three years old, Pabst had shown an extraordinary flair for picking and molding actresses whose careers were upward bound; Asta Nielsen, Brigitte Helm, and Greta Garbo (in her third film, *The Joyless Street*, which was also her first outside Sweden) headed a remarkable list. Unknown to Schulberg, Brooks had already heard about the Pabst offer — and the weekly salary of a thousand dollars that went with it — from her lover, George Marshall, whose source was a gossipy director at MGM. She coolly told Schulberg to inform Pabst that she would soon be available. 'At that very hour in Berlin,' she wrote later in *Sight & Sound*, 'Marlene Dietrich was waiting with Pabst in his office.' This was two years before *The Blue Angel* made Dietrich a star. What she crucially lacked, Pabst felt, was the innocence he wanted for his Lulu. In his own words, 'Dietrich was too old and too obvious — one sexy look and the picture would become a burlesque. But I gave her a deadline, and the contract was about to be signed when Paramount cabled saying I could have Louise Brooks.' The day that shooting ended on *The Canary Murder Case*, Brooks raced out of Hollywood en route for Berlin, there to work for a man who was one of the four or five leading European directors but of whom a few weeks earlier she had never heard.

Pandora's Box, with which I had my fourth encounter at the Eastman house, could easily have emerged as a cautionary tale about a *grande cocotte* whose reward is the wages of sin. That seems to have been the impression left by Wedekind's two Lulu plays, which were made into a film in 1922 (not by Pabst) with Asta Nielsen in the lead. Summing up her predecessor's performance, Brooks said, 'She played in the eye-rolling style of European silent acting. Lulu the man-eater devoured her sex victims . . . and then dropped dead in an acute attack of indigestion.' The character obsessed many artists of the period. In 1928, Alban Berg began work on his twelve-tone opera *Lulu*, the heart of which — beneath the stark and stylized sound patterns — was blatantly theatrical, throbbing with romantic agony. Where the Pabst-Brooks version differs from the others is in its moral coolness. It assumes neither the existence of sin nor the necessity for retribution. It presents a series of events in which all the participants are seeking happiness, and it suggests that Lulu, whose notion of happiness is momentary fulfilment through sex, is not less admirable than those whose quest is for wealth or social advancement.

First sequence: Lulu in the Art Deco apartment in Berlin where she is kept by Peter Schön, a middle-aged newspaper proprietor. (In this role, the great Fritz Kortner, bulky but urbane, effortless in the exercise of power over everyone but his mistress, gives one of the cinema's most accurate and objective portraits of a capitalist potentate.) Dressed in a peignoir, Lulu is casually flirting with a man who has come to read the gas meter when the doorbell rings and Schigolch enters, a squat and shabby old man who was once Lulu's lover but is now down on his luck. She greets him with delight; as the disgruntled gas man departs, she swoops to rest on Schigolch's lap with the grace of a swan. The protective curve of her neck is unforgettable. Producing a mouth organ, Schigolch strikes up a tune, to which she performs a brief, Dionysiac, and authentically improvised little dance. (Until this scene was rehearsed, Pabst had no idea that Brooks was a trained dancer.) Watching her, I recollect something that Schigolch says in the play, though not in the film: 'The animal is the only genuine thing in man. . . . What you have experienced as an animal, no misfortune can ever wrest from you. It remains yours for life.' From the window, he points out a burly young man on the sidewalk: this is a friend of his named Rodrigo, a professional athlete who would like to work with her on an adagio act.

Unheralded, Peter Schön lets himself into the apartment, and Lulu has just time to hide Schigolch on the balcony with a bottle of brandy. Schön has come to end his affair with Lulu, having decided to make a socially advantageous match with the daughter of a Cabinet Minister. In Lulu's reaction to the news there is no fury. She simply sits on a sofa and extends her arms toward him with something like reassurance. Unmoved at first, Schön eventually responds, and they begin to make love. The drunken Schigolch inadvertently rouses Lulu's pet dog to a barking fit, and this disturbance provokes the hasty exit of Schön. On the stairs, he passes the muscle man Rodrigo, whom Schigolch presents to Lulu. Rodrigo flexes his impressive biceps, on which she gleefully swings, like a schoolgirl gymnast.

A scene in Schön's mansion shows us his son Alwa (Francis Lederer in his pre-Hollywood days) busily composing songs for his new musical revue. Alwa is joined by the Countess Geschwitz (Alice Roberts), a tight-lipped lesbian who is designing the costumes. Lulu dashes in to announce her plans for a double act with Rodrigo, and it is immediately clear that both Alwa and the Countess have eyes for her. She strolls on into Peter Schön's study, where she picks up from the desk a photograph of his bride-to-be. Typically, she studies it with genuine interest; there's no narrowing of eyes or curling of lip. Peter Schön, who has entered the room behind her, snatches the picture from her hands and orders her to leave. Before doing so, she mischievously invents a rendezvous next day with Alwa, whom she kisses, to the young man's embarrassed bewilderment, full on the mouth. With a toss of the patent-leather hair and a glance, half-playful, half-purposeful, at Alwa, she departs. Alwa asks his father why he doesn't marry her. Rather too explosively to carry conviction, Peter replies that one doesn't marry women like that. He proposes that Alwa give her a feature role in the revue, and guarantees that his newspapers will make her a star. Alwa is overjoyed; but when his father warns him at all costs to beware of her, he quits the room in tongue-tied confusion.

So much for the exposition; the principal characters and the main thrust of the action have been lucidly established. Note that Lulu, for all her seductiveness, is essentially an exploited creature, not an exploiter; also that we are not (nor shall we ever be) invited to feel sorry for her. I've already referred to her birdlike movements and animal nature: let me add that in the context of the plot as a whole she resembles a glittering tropical fish in a tank full of predators. For the remainder of this synopsis, I'll confine myself to the four great set pieces on which the film's reputation rests.

(1) Intermission at the opening night of Alwa's revue: Pabst catches the backstage panic of scene-shifting and costume-changing with a kaleidoscopic brilliance that looks forward to Orson Welles's handling, twelve years later, of the operatic début of Susan Alexander Kane. Alwa and Geschwitz are there, revelling in what is obviously going to be a hit. Peter Schön escorts Marie, his fiancée, through the pass door to share the frenzy. Lulu, changing in the wings, catches sight of him and smiles. Stricken with embarrassment, he cuts her and leads Marie away. This treatment maddens Lulu, and she refuses to go on with the show: 'I'll dance for the whole world, but not in front of that woman.' She takes refuge in the property room, whither Peter follows her. Leaning against the wall, she sobs, shaking her head mechanically from side to side, and then flings herself onto a pile of cushions, which she kicks and pummels. Despite her tantrum she is watching Schön's every move. When he lights a cigarette to calm himself, she snaps 'Smoking isn't allowed in here,' and gives him a painful hack on the ankle. The mood of the scene swings from high histrionics through sly comedy to voluptuous intimacy. Soon Schön and Lulu are laughing, caressing, wholeheartedly making love. At this point, the

door opens, framing Marie and Alwa. Unperturbed, Lulu rises in triumph, gathers up her costume, and sweeps past them to go onstage. Peter Schön's engagement is obviously over.

(2) The wedding reception: Lulu is in a snow-white bridal gown, suggesting less a victorious *cocotte* than a girl celebrating her first Communion. Peter's wealthy friends flock admiringly round her. She dances cheek to cheek with Geschwitz, who rabidly adores her. (The Belgian actress Alice Roberts, here playing what may be the first explicit lesbian in movie history, refused point-blank to look at Brooks with the requisite degree of lust. To solve the problem, Pabst stood in her line of vision, told her to regard him with passionate intensity, and photographed her in closeups, which he then intercut with shots of Brooks. Scenes like these presented no difficulty to Brooks herself. She used to say of Fritzi LaVerne, one of her best friends in the *Follies*, 'She liked boys when she was sober and girls when she was drunk. I never heard a man or a woman pan her in bed, so she must have been very good.' A shocked Catholic priest once asked her how she felt playing a sinner like Lulu. 'Feel!' she said gaily. 'I felt fine! It all seemed perfectly normal to me.' She explained to him that, although she herself was not a lesbian, she had many chums of that persuasion in Ziegfeld's chorus line, and added, 'I know two millionaire publishers, much like Schön in the film, who backed shows to keep themselves well supplied with Lulus.') The action moves to Peter's bedroom, where Schigolch and Rodrigo are drunkenly scattering roses over the nuptial coverlet. Lulu joins them, and something between a romp and an orgy seems imminent. It is halted by the entrance of the bridegroom. Appalled, he gropes for a gun in a nearby desk and chases the two men out of his house. The other guests, shocked and aghast, rapidly depart. When Peter returns to the bedroom, he finds Alwa with his head in Lulu's lap, urging her to run away with him. The elder Schön orders his son to leave. As soon as Alwa has left, there follows, between Kortner and Brooks, a classic demonstration of screen acting as the art of visual ellipsis. With the minimum of overt violence, a struggle for power is fought out to the death. Schön advances on Lulu, presses the gun into her hand, and begs her to commit suicide. As he grips her fingers in his, swearing to shoot her like a dog if she lacks the courage to do it herself, she seems almost hypnotized by the desperation of his grief. You would think them locked in an embrace until Lulu suddenly stiffens, a puff of smoke rises between them, and Schön slumps to the floor. Alwa bursts in and rushes to his father, from whose lips a fat thread of blood slowly trickles. The father warns Alwa that he will be the next victim. Gun in hand, Lulu stares at the body, wide-eyed and transfixed. Brooks wrote afterward that Pabst always used concrete phrases to trigger the emotional response he wanted. In this case, the key image he gave her was '*das Blut.*' 'Not the murder of my husband,' she said, 'but the sight of the blood determined the expression on my face.' What we see is

not *Vénus toute entière à sa proie attachée* but a petrified child.

(3) Trial and flight: Lulu is sentenced to five years' imprisonment for manslaughter, but as the judge pronounces the sentence, her friends, led by Geschwitz, set off a fire alarm, and in the ensuing courtroom chaos she escapes. With perfect fidelity to her own wilful character, Lulu, in defiance of movie cliché, comes straight back to Schön's house, where she acts like a débutante relaxing after a ball — lighting a cigarette, idly thumbing through a fashion magazine, trying out a few dance steps, opening a wardrobe and stroking a new fur coat, running a bath and immersing herself in it. Only Brooks, perhaps could have carried off this solo sequence — so unlike the behaviour expected of criminals on the run — with such ingrained conviction and such lyrical aplomb. Now Alwa arrives and is astounded to find her at the scene of the crime. The two decide to flee together to Paris. No sooner have they caught the train, however, than they are recognized by a titled pimp, who blackmails them into accompanying him aboard a gambling ship. Geschwitz, Schigolch, and the tediously beefy Rodrigo are also afloat, and for a while the film lurches into melodrama — sub-Dostoevski with a touch of ship's Chandler. Rodrigo threatens to expose Lulu unless she sleeps with him; the Countess, gritting her teeth, distracts his attention by making love to him herself — an unlikely coupling — after which she disdainfully kills him. Meanwhile, the pimp is arranging to sell Lulu to an Egyptian brothelkeeper. Anxious to save her from this fate, Alwa frenetically cheats at cards and is caught with a sleeve full of aces. The police arrive just too late to prevent Alwa, Lulu, and Schigolch from escaping in a rowboat. For the shipboard episode, Pabst cajoled Brooks, much against her will, into changing her coiffure. The spit curls disappeared; the black bangs were parted, waved, and combed back to expose her forehead. These cardinal errors of taste defaced the icon. It was as if an Italian master had painted the Virgin and left out the halo.

(4) London and catastrophe: The East End, icy and fog-bound, on Christmas Eve. The Salvation Army is out in force, playing carols and distributing food to the poor. A sallow, mournfully handsome young man moves aimlessly through the crowds. He gives cash for the needy to an attractive Army girl, and gets in return a candle and a sprig of mistletoe. Posters on the walls warn the women of London against going out unescorted at night: there is a mass murderer at large. In a garret close by, its broken skylight covered by a flapping rag, Lulu lives in squalor with Alwa and Schigolch. The room is unfurnished except for a camp bed, an armchair, and a kitchen table with an oil lamp, a few pieces of chipped crockery, and a bread knife. Lulu's curls and bangs have been restored, but her clothes are threadbare: all three exiles are on the verge of starvation. Reduced by now to prostitution, Lulu ventures down into the street, where she accosts the young wanderer we have already met. He follows her up the stairs but stops halfway, as if reluctant to go farther. We see that he is

holding behind his back a switchblade knife, open. Lulu proffers her hand and leans encouragingly toward him. Her smile is lambent and beckoning. Hesitantly, he explains that he has no money. With transparent candour, she replies that it doesn't matter: she likes him. Unseen by Lulu, he releases his grip on the knife and lets it fall into the stairwell. She leads him into the attic, which Alwa and Schigolch have tactfully vacated. The scene that follows is tender, even buoyant, but unsoftened by sentimentality. The cold climax, when it comes, is necessary and inevitable. Ripper and victim relax like familiar lovers. He leans back in the armchair and stretches out his hand; she leaps onto his lap, landing with both knees bent, as weightless as a chamois. Her beauty has never looked more ripe. While they happily flirt, he allows her to pry into his pockets, from which she extracts the gifts he received from the Salvation Army. She lights the candle and places it ceremonially on the table, with the mistletoe beside it. In a deep and peaceful embrace, they survey the tableau. The Ripper then raises the mistletoe over Lulu's head and requests the traditional kiss. As she shuts her eyes and presents her lips, the candle flares up. Its gleam reflected in the bread knife on the table holds the Ripper's gaze. He can look at nothing but the shining blade. Long seconds pass as he wrestles, motionless, with his obsession. Finally, leaning forward to consummate the kiss, he grasps the handle of the knife. In the culminating shot, he is facing away from the camera. All we see of Lulu is her right hand, open on his shoulder, pressing him toward her. Suddenly, it clenches hard, then falls, limply dangling, behind his back. We fade to darkness. Nowhere in the cinema has the destruction of beauty been conveyed with more eloquent restraint. As with the killing of Peter Schön, extreme violence is implied, not shown. To paraphrase what Freddy Buache, a Swiss critic, wrote many years later, Lulu's death is in no sense God's judgment on a sinner; she has lived her life in accordance with the high moral imperatives of liberty, and stands in no need of redemption.

After the murder, the Ripper emerges from the building and hurries off into the fog. It is here, in my view, that the film should end. Instead, Pabst moves on to the forlorn figure of Alwa, who stares up at the garret before turning away to follow the Salvation Army procession out of sight. A glib anticlimax indeed; but I'm not sure that I prefer the alternative proposed by Brooks, who has said, with characteristic forthrightness, 'The movie should have ended with the knife in my vagina.' It may be worth adding that Gustav Diessl, who played the Ripper, was the only man in the cast whom she found sexually appealing. 'We just adored each other,' she has said in an interview with Richard Leacock, 'and I think the final scene was the happiest in the picture. Here he is with a knife he's going to stick up into my interior, and we'd be singing and laughing and doing the Charleston. You wouldn't have known it was a tragic ending. It was more like a Christmas party.' At Brook's request, Pabst had hired a jazz pianist to play between takes, and during these syncopated interludes Brooks and Diessl would often disappear beneath the table to engage in intimate festivities of their own.

The Berlin critics, expecting Lulu to be portrayed as a monster of active depravity, had mixed feelings about Brooks. One reviewer wrote, 'Louise Brooks cannot act. She does not suffer. *She does nothing.*' Wedekind himself, however, had said of his protagonist, 'Lulu is not a real character but the personification of primitive sexuality, who inspires evil unawares. She plays a purely passive role.' Brooks afterward stated her own opinion of what she had achieved. 'I played *Pabst's* Lulu,' she said, 'and she isn't a destroyer of men, like Wedekind's. She's just the same kind of nitwit that I am. Like me, she'd have been an impossible wife, sitting in bed all day reading and drinking gin.' Modern critics have elected Brooks's Lulu to a secure place in the movie pantheon. David Thomson describes it as 'one of the major female performances in the cinema,' to be measured beside such other pinnacles as 'Dietrich in the von Sternberg films, Bacall with Hawks, Karina in *Pierrot le Fou.*' It is true that in the same list Thomson included Kim Novak in *Vertigo*. It is also true that we are none of us perfect.

Day Two: My first view of the second Pabst-Brooks collaboration — *The Diary of a Lost Girl*, based on *Das Tagebuch einer Verlorenen*, a novel by Margarethe Boehme, and shot in the summer of 1929. After finishing *Pandora*, Brooks had returned to New York and resumed her affair with the millionaire George Marshall. He told her that a new movie company, called RKO and masterminded by Joseph P. Kennedy, was anxious to sign her up for five hundred dollars a week. She replied, 'I hate California and I'm not going back.' Then Paramount called, ordering her to report for duty on the Coast; it was turning *The Canary Murder Case* into a talkie and required her presence for retakes and dubbing. She refused to come. Under the impression that this was a haggling posture, the studio offered ever vaster sums of money. Brooks's determination remained undented. Goaded to fury, Paramount planted in the columns a petty but damaging little story to the effect that it had been compelled to replace Brooks because her voice was unusable in talkies.

At this point — April, 1929 — she received a cable from Pabst. It said that he intended to co–produce a French film entitled *Prix de Beauté*, which René Clair would direct, and that they both wanted her for the lead — would she therefore cross the Atlantic as soon as possible? Such was her faith in Pabst that within two weeks she and Clair ('a very small, demure, rather fragile man' is how she afterward described him) were posing together for publicity shots in Paris. When the photographic session was over, Clair escorted her back to her hotel, where he dampened her enthusiasm by revealing that he proposed to pull out of the picture forthwith. He advised her to do the same; the production money, he said, simply wasn't there, and might never be. A few days later, he officially retired from the project. (Its place in his schedule was taken by *Sous les Toits de Paris*, which, together with its immediate successors — *Le Million* and *À Nous la Liberté* — established his international reputation.) With nothing to do, and a guaranteed salary of a thousand dollars a week to do it on, Brooks entrained for a spree in Antibes, accompanied by a swarm of rich admirers. When she got back to Paris, Pabst called her from Berlin. *Prix de Beauté*, he said, was postponed; instead, she would star under his direction in *Diary of a Lost Girl*, at precisely half her present salary. As submissive as ever to her tutor, she arrived in Berlin aboard the next train.

Lovingly photographed by Sepp Allgeier, Brooks in *Lost Girl* is less flamboyant but not less haunting than in *Pandora's Box*. The traffic in movie actors traditionally moved westward, from Europe to Hollywood, where their national characteristics were sedulously exploited. Brooks, who was among the few to make the eastbound trip, became in her films with Pabst completely Europeanized. To be more exact: in the context that Pabst prepared for her, Brooks's American brashness took on an awareness of transience and mortality. The theme of *Lost Girl* is the corruption of a minor — not by sexuality but by an authoritarian society that condemns sexuality. (Pabst must surely have read Wilhelm Reich, the Freudian Marxist, whose theories about the relationship between sexual and political repression were hotly debated in Berlin at the time.) It is the same society that condemns Lulu. In fact, *The Education of Lulu* would make an apt alternative title for *Lost Girl*, whose heroine emerges from her travails ideally equipped for the leading role in *Pandora's Box*. Her name is Thymiane Henning, and she is the sixteen-year-old daughter of a prosperous pharmacist. In the early sequences, Brooks plays her shy and faunlike, peering wide-eyed at a predatory world. She is seduced and impregnated by her father's libidinous young assistant. As soon as her condition is discovered, the double standard swings into action. The assistant retains his job; but, to save the family from dishonour, Thymiane's baby is farmed out to a wet nurse, and she herself is consigned to a home for delinquent girls, run by a bald and ghoulish superintendent and his sadistic wife.

Life in the reformatory is strictly regimented: the inmates exercise to the beat of a drum and eat to the tapping of a metronome. At length, Thymiane escapes from this archetypal hellhole (precursor of many such institutions in subsequent movies; e.g., *Mädchen in Uniform*) and goes to reclaim her baby, only to find that the child has died. Broke and homeless, she meets a street vendor who guides her to an address where food and shelter will be hers for the asking. Predictably, it turns out to be a brothel; far less predictably, even shockingly, Pabst presents it as a place where Thymiane is not degraded but liberated. In the whorehouse, she blossoms, becoming a *fille de joie* in the literal sense of the phrase. Unlike almost any other actress in a similar situation, Brooks neither resorts to pathos nor suggests that there is anything immoral in the pleasure she derives from her new profession. As in *Pandora*, she lives for the moment, with radiant physical abandon. Present love, even for sale, hath present laughter, and what's to come is not only unsure but irrelevant. I agree with Freddy Buache when he says of Brooks's performances with Pabst that they celebrated 'the victory of innocence and *amour-fou* over the debilitating wisdom imposed on society by the Church, the Fatherland, and the Family.' One of her more outré clients can achieve orgasm only by watching her beat a drum. This ironic echo of life in the reform school is used by Pabst to imply that sexual prohibition breeds sexual aberration. (Even more ironically, the sequence has been censored out of most of the existing prints of the movie.) Brooks is at her best — a happy animal in skintight satin — in a party scene at a nightclub, where she offers herself as first prize in a raffle. 'Pabst wanted realism, so we all had to drink real drinks,' she said later. 'I played the whole scene stewed on hot, sweet German champagne.'

Hereabouts, unfortunately, the film begins to shed its effrontery and to pay lip service to conventional values. Thymiane catches sight of her father across the dance floor; instead of reacting with defiance — after all, he threw her out of his house — she looks stricken with guilt, like the outcast daughter of sentimental fiction. In her absence, Papa has married his housekeeper, by whom he has two children. When he dies, shortly after the nightclub confrontation, he leaves his considerable wealth to Thymiane. Nobly, she gives it all to his penniless widow, so that the latter's offspring 'won't have to live the same kind of life as I have.' Thereby redeemed, the former whore soon becomes the wife of an elderly aristocrat. Revisiting the reform school, of which she has now been appointed a trustee, she excoriates the staff for its self-righteous cruelties. 'A little more kindness,' her husband adds, 'and no one in the world would ever be lost.' Thus lamely, the movie ends.

'Pabst seemed to lose interest,' Brooks told an interviewer some years afterward. 'He more or less said, "I'm tired of this picture," and he gave it a soft ending.' His first, and much tougher, intention had been to demonstrate that humanitarianism alone could never solve society's problems. He wanted Thymiane to show her contempt for her husband's liberal platitudes by setting herself up as the madam of a whorehouse. The German distributors, however, refused to countenance such a radical dénouement, and Pabst was forced to capitulate. The result is a flawed masterpiece, with a shining central performance that even the closing, compromised sequences cannot dim. Brooks has written that during the making of the film she spent all her off-duty hours with rich revellers of whom Pabst disapproved. On the last day of shooting, 'he decided to let me have it.' Her friends, he said, were preventing her from becoming a serious actress, and sooner or later they would discard her like an old toy. 'Your life is exactly like Lulu's, and you will end the same way,' he warned her. The passage of time convinced her that Pabst had a valid point. 'Lulu's story,' she told a journalist, 'is as near as you'll get to mine.'

In August, 1929, she returned to Paris, where backing had unexpectedly been found for *Prix de Beauté*, her last European movie and her first talkie — although, since she spoke no French, her voice was dubbed. The director, briefly surfacing from obscurity, was Augusto Genina, and René Clair received a credit for the original idea. Like so much of French cinema in the thirties, *Prix de Beauté* is a *film noir*, with wanly tinny music, about a shabby suburban crime of passion. Brooks plays Lucienne, a typist who enters a newspaper beauty contest. It's the kind of role with which one associates Simone Simon, though the rapture that Brooks displays when she wins, twirling with glee as she shows off her presents and trophies, goes well beyond the emotional range accessible to Mlle. Simon. Lucienne-Brooks is triumphantly unliberated; she rejoices in being a beloved, fleshly bauble, and she makes it clear to her husband, a compositor employed by the prize-giving newspaper, that she wants a grander, more snobbish reward for her victory than a visit to a back-street fairground, which is all he has to offer. She leaves him and accepts a part in a film. Consumed by jealousy, he follows her one night to a projection theatre in which a rough cut of her movie is being shown. He bursts in and shoots her. As she dies, the French infatuation with irony is fearsomely indulged: her image on the screen behind her is singing the movie's theme song, 'Ne Sois Pas Jaloux.' In *Prix de Beauté*, Brooks lends inimitable flair and distinction to a cliché; but it is a cliché nonetheless.

At this point, when Brooks was at the height of her beauty, her career began a steep and bumpy decline. In 1930, she went back to Hollywood, on the strength of a promised contract with Columbia. Harry Cohn, the head of the studio, summoned her to his office for a series of meetings, at each of which he appeared naked from the waist up. Always a plain speaker, he left her in no doubt that good parts would come her way if she responded to his advances. She rebuffed them, and the proffered contract was withdrawn. Elsewhere in Hollywood, she managed to get a job in a feeble two-reel comedy pseudonymously directed by the disgraced Fatty Arbuckle; her old friend Frank Tuttle gave her a supporting role in *It Pays to Advertise* (starring Carole Lombard); and she turned up fleetingly in a Michael Curtiz picture called *God's Gift to Women*. But the word was out that Brooks was difficult and uppity, too independent to suit the system. Admitting defeat, she returned to New York in the summer of 1931. Against her will, but under heavy pressure from George Marshall, her lover and would-be Svengali, she played a small part in *Louder Please*, a featherweight comedy by Norman Krasna that began its pre-Broadway run in October. After the opening week in Jackson Heights, she was fired by the director, George

Abbott. This was her farewell to the theatre; it took place on the eve of her twenty-fifth birthday.

For Brooks, as for millions of her compatriots, a long period of unemployment followed. In 1933, determined to break off her increasingly discordant relationship with Marshall, she married Deering Davis, a rich young Chicagoan, but walked out on him after six months of rapidly waning enthusiasm. With a Hungarian partner named Dario Borzani, she spent a year dancing in nightclubs, including the Persian Room of the Plaza, but the monotony of cabaret routine dismayed her, and she quit the act in August, 1935. That autumn, Pabst suddenly arrived in New York and invited her to play Helen of Troy in a film version of Goethe's *Faust*, with Greta Garbo as Gretchen. Her hopes giddily soared, only to be dashed when Garbo opted out and the project fell through. Once again, she revisited Hollywood, where Republic Studios wanted to test her for a role in a musical called *Dancing Feet*. She was rejected in favour of a blonde who couldn't dance. 'That about did it for me,' Brooks wrote later. 'From then on it was straight downhill. And no dough to keep the wolves from the door.' In 1936, Universal cast her as the ingénue (Boots Boone) in *Empty Saddles*, a Buck Jones Western, which is the last Brooks movie in the Eastman collection. She looks perplexed, discouraged, and lacking in verve; and her coiffure, with the hair swept back from her forehead, reveals disquieting lines of worry. (Neither she nor Jones is helped by the fact that all the major sequences of an incredibly complex plot are shot at night.) The following year brought her a bit part at Paramount in something called *King of Gamblers*, after which, in her own words, 'Harry Cohn gave me a personally conducted tour of hell with no return ticket.' Still wounded by her refusal to sleep with him in 1930, Cohn promised her a screen test if she would submit to the humiliation of appearing in the corps de ballet of a Grace Moore musical entitled *When You're in Love*. To his surprise, Brooks accepted the offer — she was too broke to spurn it — and Cohn made sure that the demotion of an erstwhile star was publicized as widely as possible. Grudgingly, he gave her a perfunctory screen test, which he dismissed in two words: 'It stunk.' In the summer of 1938, Republic hired Brooks to appear with John Wayne (then a minor figure) in *Overland Stage Raiders*. After this low-budget oater, she made no more pictures.

In her entire professional career, Brooks had earned according to her own calculations, exactly $124,600—$104,500 from films, $10,100 from theatre, and $10,000 from all other sources. Not a gargantuan sum, one would think, spread over sixteen years; yet Brooks said to a friend, 'I was astonished that it came to so much. But then I never paid any attention to money.' In 1940, she left Hollywood for the last time.

The Eastman house stands in an affluent residential district of Rochester, on an avenue of comparably stately mansions, with broad, tree-shaded lawns. When my second day of séances with Brooks came to an end, I zipped up my notes in a briefcase, thanked the curator and his staff for their help, and departed in a taxi. The driver took me to an apartment building only a few blocks away, where I paid him off. I rode up in the elevator to the third floor and pressed a doorbell a few paces along the corridor. After a long pause, there was a loud snapping of locks. The door slowly opened to reveal a petite woman of fragile build, wearing a woollen bed jacket over a pink nightgown, and holding herself defiantly upright by means of a sturdy metal cane with four rubber-tipped prongs. She had salt-and-pepper hair combed back into a ponytail that hung down well below her shoulders, and she was barefoot. One could imagine this gaunt and elderly child as James Tyrone's wife in *Long Day's Journey into Night*; or, noting the touch of authority and *panache* in her bearing, as the capricious heroine of Jean Giraudoux's *The Madwoman of Chaillot*. I stated my name, adding that I had an appointment. She nodded and beckoned me in. I greeted her with a respectful embrace. This was my first physical contact with Louise Brooks.

She was seventy-one years old, and until a few months earlier I had thought she was dead. Four decades had passed since her last picture, and it seemed improbable that she had survived such a long period of retirement. Moreover, I did not then know how young she had been at the time of her flowering. Spurred by the TV screening of *Pandora's Box* in January, 1978, I had made some inquiries, and soon discovered that she was living in Rochester, virtually bedridden with degenerative osteoarthritis of the hip, and that since 1956 she had written twenty vivid and perceptive articles, mainly for specialist film magazines, on such of her colleagues and contemporaries as Garbo, Dietrich, Keaton, Chaplin, Bogart, Fields, Lillian Gish, ZaSu Pitts, and (naturally) Pabst. Armed with this information, I wrote her a belated fan letter, to which she promptly replied. We then struck up a correspondence, conducted on her side in a bold and expressive prose style, which matched her handwriting. Rapport was cemented by telephone calls, which resulted in my visit to Rochester and the date I was now keeping.

She has not left her apartment since 1960, except for a few trips to the dentist and one to a doctor. (She mistrusts the medical profession, and this consultation, which took place in 1976, was her first in thirty-two years.) 'You're doing a terrible thing to me,' she said as she ushered me in. 'I've been killing myself off for twenty years, and you're going to bring me back to life.' She lives in two rooms — modest, spotless, and austerely furnished. From the larger, I remember Venetian blinds, a green sofa, a TV set, a Formica-topped table, a tiny kitchenette alcove, and flesh-pink walls sparsely hung with paintings redolent of the twenties. The other room was too small to hold more than a bed (single), a built-in cupboard bursting with press clippings and other souvenirs, a chest of drawers surmounted by a crucifix and a statue of the Virgin, and a stool piled high with books,

including works by Proust, Schopenhauer, Ruskin, Ortega y Gasset, Samuel
Johnson, Edmund Wilson, and many living authors of serious note. 'I'm
probably one of the best-read idiots in the world,' my hostess said as she
haltingly showed me round her domain. Although she eats little — she
turns the scale at about eighty-eight pounds — she had prepared for us a
perfectly mountainous omelette. Nerves, however, had robbed us of our
appetites, and we barely disturbed its mighty silhouette. I produced from
my briefcase a bottle of expensive red Burgundy which I had brought as a
gift. (Brooks, who used to drink quite heftily, nowadays touches alcohol
only on special occasions.) Since she cannot sit upright for long without
discomfort, we retired with the wine to her bedroom, where she reclined,
sipped, and talked, gesturing fluently, her fingers supple and unclenched. I
pulled a chair up to the bedside and listened.

Her voice has the range of a dozen birdcalls, from the cry of a peacock
to the fluting of a dove. Her articulation, at whatever speed, is impeccable,
and her laughter soars like a kite. I cannot understand why, even if she had
not been a beauty, Hollywood failed to realize what a treasure it possessed in the *sound* of Louise Brooks. Like most people who speak memorably, she is highly responsive to vocal nuances in others. She told Kevin
Brownlow, the British film historian, that her favourite actress ('the person
I would be if I could be anyone') was Margaret Sullavan, mainly because of
her voice, which Brooks described as 'exquisite and far away, almost like
an echo,' and, again, as 'strange, fey, mysterious — like a voice singing in
the snow.' My conversations with the Ravishing Hermit of Rochester
were spread over several days; for the sake of convenience, I have here
compressed them into one session.

She began, at my urging, by skimming through the story of her life since
she last faced the Hollywood cameras: 'Why did I give up the movies? I
could give you seven hundred reasons, all of them true. After I made that
picture with John Wayne in 1938, I stayed out on the Coast for two years,
but the only people who wanted to see me were men who wanted to sleep
with me. Then Walter Wanger warned me that if I hung around any longer
I'd become a call girl. So I fled to Wichita, Kansas, where my family had
moved in 1919. But that turned out to be another kind of hell. The citizens
of Wichita either resented me for having been a success or despised me for
being a failure. And I wasn't exactly enchanted with them. I opened a dance
studio for young people, who loved me, because I dramatized everything so
much, but it didn't make any money. In 1943, I drifted back to New York
and worked for six months in radio soaps. Then I quit, for another hundred
reasons, including Wounded Pride of Former Star. [Peal of laughter. Here,
as throughout our chat, Brooks betrayed not the slightest trace of self-pity.]
During '44 and '45, I got a couple of jobs in publicity agencies, collecting
items for Winchell's column. I was fired from both of them, and I had to
move from the decent little hotel where I'd been living to a grubby hole on

First Avenue at Fifty-ninth Street. That was when I began to flirt with fancies related to little bottles filled with yellow sleeping pills. However, I changed my mind, and in July, 1946, the proud, snooty Louise Brooks started work as a sales girl at Saks Fifth Avenue. They paid me forty dollars a week. I had this silly idea of proving myself "an honest woman," but the only effect it had was to disgust all my famous New York friends, who cut me off forever. From then on, I was regarded as a questionable East Side dame. After two years at Saks, I resigned. To earn a little money, I sat down and wrote the usual autobiography. I called it *Naked on My Goat*, which is a quote from Goethe's *Faust*. In the *Walpurgisnacht* scene, a young witch is bragging about her looks to an old one. "I sit here naked on my goat," she says, "and show my fine young body." But the old one advises her to wait awhile: "Though young and tender now, you'll rot, we know, you'll rot." Then when I read what I'd written, I threw the whole thing down the incinerator.'

Brooks insists that her motive for this act of destruction was *pudeur*. In 1977, she wrote an article headed 'Why I Will Never Write My Memoirs,' in which she summed herself up as a prototypical midwesterner, 'born in the Bible Belt of Anglo-Saxon farmers, who prayed in the parlour and practiced incest in the barn.' Although her sexual education had been conducted by the élite of Paris, London, Berlin, and New York, her pleasure was, she wrote, 'restricted by the inbred shackles of sin and guilt.' Her conclusion was as follows:

In writing the history of a life I believe absolutely that the reader cannot understand the character and deeds of the subject unless he is given a basic understanding of that person's sexual loves and hates and conflicts. It is the only way the reader can make sense out of innumerable apparently senseless actions. . . . We flatter ourselves when we assume that we have restored the sexual integrity which was expurgated by the Victorians. It is true that many exposés are written to shock, to excite, to make money. But in serious books characters remain as baffling, as unknowable as ever. . . . I too am unwilling to write the sexual truth that would make my life worth reading. I cannot unbuckle the Bible Belt.

Accepting a drop more wine, she continued the tale of her wilderness years. 'Between 1948 and 1953, I suppose you could call me a kept woman,' she said. 'Three decent rich men looked after me. But then I was *always* a kept woman. Even when I was making a thousand dollars a week, I would always be paid for by George Marshall or someone like that. But I never had anything to show for it — no cash, no trinkets, nothing. I didn't even *like* jewellery — can you imagine? Pabst once called me a born whore, but if he was right I was a failure, with no pile of money and no comfortable mansion. I just wasn't equipped to spoil millionaires in a practical, farsighted way. I could live in the present, but otherwise everything has always been a hundred percent wrong about me. Anyway, the three decent men took care of me. One of them owned a sheet-metal manufacturing company, and the result of that affair is that I am now the owner of the only handmade aluminium wastebasket in the world. He designed it, and it's in the living room, my solitary trophy. Then a time came, early in 1953, when my three men independently decided that they wanted to marry me. I had to escape, because I wasn't in love with them. As a matter of fact, I've never been in love. And if I *had* loved a man, could I have been faithful to him? Could he have trusted me beyond a closed door? I doubt it. It was clever of Pabst to know even before he met me that I possessed the tramp essence of Lulu.'

Brooks hesitated for a moment and then went on in the same tones, lightly self-mocking, 'Maybe I should have been a writer's moll. Because when we were talking on the phone, a few Sundays ago, some secret compartment inside me burst, and I was suddenly overpowered by the feeling of love — a sensation I'd never experienced with any other man. Are you a variation of Jack the Ripper, who finally brings me love that I'm prevented from accepting — not by the knife but by old age? You're a perfect scoundrel, turning up like this and wrecking my golden years! [I was too stunned to offer any comment on this, but not too stunned to note, with a distinct glow of pride, that Brooks was completely sober]. Anyhow, to get back to my three suitors, I decided that the only way to avoid marriage was to become a Catholic, so that I could tell them that in the eyes of the Church I was still married to Eddie Sutherland. I went to the rectory of a Catholic church on the East Side and everything was fine until my sweet, pure religious instructor fell in love with me. I was the first woman he'd ever known who acted like one and treated him like a man. The other priests were furious. They sent him off to California and replaced him with a stern young missionary. After a while, however, even *he* began to hint that it would be a good idea if he dropped by my apartment in the evenings to give me special instruction. But I resisted temptation, and in September, 1953, I was baptized a Catholic.'

Having paused to light a cigarette, which provoked a mild coughing spasm, Brooks resumed her story. 'I almost forgot a strange incident that happened in 1952. Out of the blue, I got a letter from a woman who had been a Cherryvale neighbour of ours. She enclosed some snapshots. One of them showed a nice-looking gray-haired man of about fifty holding the hand of a little girl — me. On the back she'd written, "This is Mr. Feathers, an old bachelor who loved kids. He was always taking you to the picture show and buying you toys and candy." That picture brought back something I'd blacked out of my mind for — what? — thirty-seven years. When I was nine years old, Mr. Feathers molested me sexually. Which forged another link between me and Lulu: when *she* had *her* first lover, she was very young, and Schigolch, the man in question, was middle-aged. I've often wondered what effect Mr. Feathers had on my life. He must have had a great deal to do with forming my attitude toward sexual pleasure. For me, nice, soft, easy men were never enough — there had to be an element of domination — and I'm sure that's all tied up with Mr. Feathers. The pleasure of kissing and being kissed comes from somewhere entirely different, psychologically as well as physically. Incidentally, I told my mother about Mr. Feathers, and — would you believe it? [Peal of laughter.] She blamed *me*! She said I must have led him on. It's always the same, isn't it?' And Brooks ran on in this vein, discussing her sex life openly and jauntily, unbuckling one more notch of the Bible Belt with every sentence she uttered.

The year 1954 was Brooks's nadir. 'I was too proud to be a call girl. There was no point in throwing myself into the East River, because I could swim; and I couldn't afford the alternative, which was sleeping pills.' In 1955, just perceptibly, things began to look up, and life became once more a tolerable option. Henri Langlois, the exuberant ruler of the Cinémathèque Française, organized in Paris a huge exhibition entitled 'Sixty Years of Cinema.' Dominating the entrance hall of the Musée d'Art Moderne were two gigantic blowups, one of the French actress Falconetti in Carl Dreyer's 1928 classic, *La Passion de Jeanne d'Arc*, and the other of Brooks in *Pandora's Box*. When a critic demanded why he had preferred this nonentity to authentic stars like Garbo and Dietrich, Langlois exploded, 'There is no Garbo! There is no Dietrich! There is only Louise Brooks!' In the same year, a group of her friends from the twenties clubbed together to provide a small annuity that would keep her from outright destitution; and she was visited in her Manhattan retreat by James Card, then the curator of film at Eastman house. He had long admired her movies, and he persuaded her to come to Rochester, where so much of her best work was preserved. It was at his suggestion that, in 1956, she settled there.

'Rochester seemed as good a place as any,' she told me. 'It was cheaper than New York, and I didn't run the risk of meeting people from my past. Up to that time, I had never seen any of my films. And I still haven't — not right through, that is. Jimmy Card screened some of them for me, but that was during my drinking period. I would watch through glazed eyes for about five minutes and sleep through the rest. I haven't even seen *Pandora*. I've been present on two occasions when it was being run, but I was drunk both times. By that I mean I was *navigating* but not *seeing*.' When she watched other people's movies, however, she felt no need for alcoholic sedation. As a working actress, she had never taken films seriously; under Card's tuition, she recognized that the cinema was a valid form of art, and began to develop her own theories about it. In 1956, drawing on her powers of near-total recall, she wrote a study of Pabst for *Image*. This was the first of a sheaf of articles, sharp-eyed and idiosyncratic, that she has contributed over the years to such magazines as *Sight & Sound* (London), *Objectif* (Montreal), *Film Culture* (New York), and *Positif* (Paris).

The Brooks cult burgeoned in 1957, when Henri Langlois crossed the Atlantic to meet her. A year later, he presented 'Hommage à Louise Brooks' — a festival of her movies that filled the Cinémathèque. The star herself flew to Paris, all expenses paid, and was greeted with wild acclaim at a reception after the Cinémathèque's showing of *Pandora's Box*. (Among those present was Jean-Luc Godard, who paid his own tribute to Brooks in 1962, when he directed *Vivre Sa Vie*, the heroine of which — a prostitute — was played by Anna Karina in an exact replica of the Brooks hairdo. Godard described the character as a 'young and pretty Parisian shopgirl who gives her body but retains her soul.') In January, 1960, Brooks went to New York and attended a screening of *Prix de Beauté* in the Kaufman Concert hall of the 92nd Street Y, where she made a hilarious little speech that delighted the packed audience. The next day, she returned to Rochester, from which she has never since emerged.

Interviewers and fans occasionally call on her, but for the most part, as she put it to me, 'I have lived in virtual isolation, with an audience consisting of the milkman and a cleaning woman.' She continued, 'Once a week, I would drink a pint of gin, become what Dickens called "gin-coherent," go to sleep, and drowse for four days. That left three days to read, write a bit, and see the odd visitor. No priests, by the way — I said goodbye to the Church in 1964. Now and then, there would be a letter to answer. In 1965, for instance, an Italian artist named Guido Crepax started a very sexy and tremendously popular comic strip about a girl called Valentina, who looked exactly like me as Lulu. In fact, she *identified* herself with me. Crepax wrote to thank me for the inspiration and said he regarded me as a twentieth-century myth. I appreciated the tribute and told him that at last I felt I could disintegrate happily in bed with my books, gin, cigarettes, coffee, bread, cheese, and apricot jam. During the sixties, arthritis started to get a grip, and in 1972 I had to buy a medical cane in order to move around. Then, five years ago, the disease really walloped me. My pioneer blood did not pulse through my veins, rousing me to fight it. I collapsed. I took a terrible fall and nearly smashed my hip. That was the end of the booze or any other kind of escape for me. I knew I was in for a bad time, with nothing to face but the absolute meaninglessness of my life. All I've done since then is try to hold the pieces together. And to keep my little squirrel-cage brain distracted.'

As an emblematic figure of the twenties, epitomizing the flappers, jazz babies, and dancing daughters of the boom years, Brooks has few rivals, living or dead. Moreover, she is unique among such figures in that her career took her to all the places — New York, London, Hollywood, Paris, and Berlin — where the action was at its height, where experiments in pleasure were conducted with the same zeal (and often by the same people) as experiments in the arts. From her bedroom cupboard Brooks produced an avalanche of manila envelopes, each bulging with mementoes of her halcyon decade. This solitary autodidact, her perceptions deepened by years of immersion in books, looked back for my benefit on the green, gregarious girl she once was, and found much to amuse her. For every photograph she supplied a spoken caption. As she reminisced, I often thought of those Max Beerbohm cartoons that depict the Old Self conversing with the Young Self.

'Here I am in 1922, when I first hit New York, and the label of "beautiful but dumb" was slapped on me forever. Most beautiful-but-dumb girls think they are smart, and get away with it, because other people, on the whole, aren't much smarter. You can see modern equivalents of those girls on any TV talk show. But there's also a very small group of beautiful women who *know* they're dumb, and this makes them defenceless and vulnerable. They become the Big Joke. I didn't know Marilyn Monroe, but I'm sure that her agonizing awareness of her own stupidity was one of the things that killed her. I became the Big Joke, first on Broadway and then in Hollywood. . . . That's Herman Mankiewicz — an ideal talk-show guest, don't you think, born before his time? In 1925, Herman was trying to educate me, and he invented the Louise Brooks Literary Society. A girl named Dorothy Knapp and I were Ziegfeld's two prize beauties. We had a big dressing room on the fifth floor of the New Amsterdam Building, and people like Walter Wanger, Michael Arlen, and Gilbert Miller would meet there, ostensibly to hear my reviews of books that Herman gave me to read. What they actually came for was to watch Dorothy doing a striptease and having a love affair with herself in front of a full-length mirror. I get some consolation from the fact that, as an idiot, I have provided delight in my time to a very select group of intellectuals. . . . That must be Joseph Schenck. Acting on behalf of his brother Nick, who controlled MGM, Joe offered me a contract in 1925 at three hundred a week. Instead, I went to Paramount for two hundred and fifty. Maybe I should have signed with MGM and joined what I called the Joe Schenck Mink Club. You could recognize the members at "21" because they never removed their mink coats at lunch. . . . Here's Fritzi LaVerne, smothered in osprey feathers. I roomed with her briefly when we were in the *Follies* together, and she seduced more follies girls than Ziegfeld and William Randolph Hearst combined. That's how I got the reputation of being a lesbian. I had nothing against it in principle, and for years I thought it was fun to encourage the idea. I used to hold hands with Fritzi in public. She had a little Bulgarian boyfriend who was just our height, and we would get into his suits and camp all over New York. Even when I moved out to Yahoo City, California, I could never stop by a lesbian household without being asked to strip and join the happy group baring their operation scars in the sun. But although I went through a couple of mild sexual auditions with women, I very soon found that I only loved men's bodies. What maddens me is that because of the lesbian scenes with Alice Roberts in *Pandora* I shall probably go down in film history as one of the gloomy dikes. A friend of mine once said to me, "Louise Brooks, you're not a lesbian, you're a pansy." Would you care to decipher that? By the way, are you getting tired of hearing my name? I'm thinking of changing it. I noticed that there were five people called Brooks in last week's *Variety*. How about June Caprice? Or Louise Lovely?'

I shook my head.

Brooks continued riffling through her collection. 'This, of course, is Martha Graham, whose genius I absorbed to the bone during the years we danced together on tour. She had rages, you know, that struck like lightning out of nowhere. One evening when we were waiting to go onstage — I was sixteen — she grabbed me, shook me ferociously, and shouted, "Why do you ruin your feet by wearing those tight shoes?" Another time, she was sitting sweetly at the makeup shelf pinning flowers in her hair when she suddenly seized a bottle of body makeup and exploded it against the mirror. She looked at the shattered remains for a spell, then moved her makeup along to an unbroken mirror and went on quietly pinning flowers in her hair. Reminds me of the night when Buster Keaton drove me in his roadster out to Culver City, where he had a bungalow on the back lot of M-G-M. The walls of the living room were covered with great glass bookcases. Buster, who wasn't drunk, opened the door, turned on the lights, and picked up a baseball bat. Then walking calmly round the room, he smashed every pane of glass in every bookcase. Such frustration in that little body! . . . Here, inevitably, are Scott and Zelda. I met them in January, 1927, at the Ambassador Hotel in L.A. They were sitting close together on a sofa, like a comedy team, and the first thing that struck me was how *small* they were. I had come to see the genius writer, but what dominated the room was the blazing intelligence of Zelda's profile. It shocked me. It was the profile of a witch. Incidentally, I've been reading Scott's letters, and I've spotted a curious thing about them. In the early days, before Hemingway was famous, Scott always spelled his name wrong, with two "m"s. And when did he start to spell it right? At the precise moment when Hemingway became a bigger star than he was. . . . This is a pool party at somebody's house in Malibu. I know I knock the studio system, but if you were to ask me what it was like to live in Hollywood in the twenties I'd have to say that we were all — oh! — marvellously degenerate and happy. We were a world of our own, and outsiders didn't intrude. People tell you that the reason a lot of actors left Hollywood when sound came in was that their voices were wrong for talkies. That's the official story. The truth is that the coming of sound meant the end of the all-night parties. With talkies, you couldn't stay out till sunrise anymore. You had to rush back from the studios and start learning your lines, ready for the next day's shooting at 8 A.M. That was when the studio machine really took over. It controlled you, mind and body, from the moment you were yanked out of bed at dawn until the publicity department put you back to bed at night.'

Brooks paused, silently contemplating revels that ended half a century ago, and then went on. 'Talking about bed, here's Tallulah — although I always guessed that she wasn't as keen on bed as everyone thought. And my record for guessing things like that was pretty good. I watched her packing her douche-bag one night for a meeting with a plutocratic boyfriend of hers at the Elysée Hotel. She forgot to wear the emerald ring he'd given her a few days before, but she didn't forget the script of the play she wanted him to produce for her. Her preparations weren't scheming or whorish. Just businesslike. . . . This is a bunch of the guests at Mr. Hearst's ranch, sometime in 1928. The girl with the dark hair and the big smile is Pepi Lederer, one of my dearest friends. She was Marion Davies' niece and the sister of Charlie Lederer, the screenwriter, and she was only seventeen when that picture was taken. My first husband, Eddie Sutherland, used to say that for people who didn't worship opulence, weren't crazy about meeting celebrities, and didn't need money or advancement from Mr. Hearst, San Simeon was a deadly-dull place. I suppose he was right. But when Pepi was there it was always fun. She created a world of excitement and inspiration wherever she went. And I never entered that great dining hall without a shiver of delight. There were medieval banners from Siena floating overhead, and a vast Gothic fireplace, and a long refectory table seating forty. Marion and Mr. Hearst sat with the important guests at the middle of the table. Down at the bottom, Pepi ruled over a group — including me — that she called the Younger Degenerates, and that's where the laughter was. Although Mr. Hearst disapproved of booze, Pepi had made friends with one of the waiters, and we got all the champagne we wanted. She could have been a gifted writer, and for a while she worked for Mr. Hearst's deluxe quarterly *The Connoisseur*, but it was only a courtesy job. Nobody took her seriously, she never learned discipline, and drink and drugs got her in the end. In 1935, she died by jumping out of a window in the psychiatric ward of a hospital in Los Angeles. She was twenty-five years old. Not long ago, I came across her name in the index of a book on Marion Davies, and it broke my heart. Then I remembered a quotation from Goethe that I'd once typed out. I've written it under the photo: "For a person remains of consequence not so far as he leaves something behind him but so far as he acts and enjoys, and rouses others to action and enjoyment." That was Pepi.'

Of all the names that spilled out of Brooks's memories of America in the twenties, there was one for which she reserved a special veneration: that of Chaplin. In an article for the magazine *Film Culture*, she had described his performances at private parties:

He recalled his youth with comic pantomimes. He acted out countless scenes for countless films. And he did imitations of everybody. Isadora Duncan danced in a storm of toilet paper. John Barrymore picked his nose and brooded over Hamlet's soliloquy. A Follies girl swished across the room; and I began to cry while Charlie denied absolutely that he was imitating me. Nevertheless . . . I determined to abandon that silly walk forthwith.

For me, she filled out the picture. 'I was eighteen in 1925, when Chaplin came to New York for the opening of *The Gold Rush*. He was just twice my age, and I had an affair with him for two happy summer months. Ever since he died, my mind has gone back fifty years, trying to define that lovely being from another world. He was not only the creator of the Little Fellow, though that was miracle enough. He was a self-made aristocrat. He taught himself to speak cultivated English, and he kept a dictionary in the bathroom at his hotel so that he could learn a new word every morning. While he dressed, he prepared his script for the day, which was intended to adorn his private portrait of himself as a perfect English gentleman. He was also a sophisticated lover, who had affairs with Peggy Hopkins Joyce and Marion Davies and Pola Negri, and he was a brilliant businessman, who owned his films and demanded fifty percent of the gross — which drove Nick Schenck wild, along with all the other people who were plotting to rob him. Do you know, I can't once remember him *still*? He was always standing up as he sat down, and going out as he came in. Except when he turned off the lights and went to sleep, without liquor or pills, like a child. Meaning to be bitchy, Herman Mankiewicz said, "People never sat at his feet. He went to where people were sitting and stood in front of them." But how we paid attention! We were hypnotized by the beauty and inexhaustible originality of this glistening creature. He's the only genius I ever knew who spread himself equally over his art and his life. He loved showing off in fine clothes and elegant phrases — even in the witness box. When Lita Grey divorced him, she put about vile rumors that he had a depraved passion for little girls. He didn't give a damn, even though people said his career would be wrecked. It still infuriates me that he never defended himself against any of those ugly lies, but the truth is that he existed on a plane above pride, jealousy, or hate. I never heard him say a snide thing about anyone. *He lived totally without fear.* He knew that Lita Grey and her family were living in his house in Beverly Hills, planning to ruin him, yet he was radiantly carefree — happy with the success of *The Gold Rush* and with the admirers who swarmed around him. Not that he *exacted* adoration. Even during our affair, he knew that I didn't adore him in the romantic sense, and he didn't mind at all. Which brings me to one of the dirtiest lies he allowed to be told about him — that he was mean with money. People forget that Chaplin was the only star ever to keep his ex-leading lady [Edna

Purviance] on his payroll for life, and the only producer to pay his employees their full salaries even when he wasn't in production. When our joyful summer ended he didn't give me a fur from Jaeckel or a bangle from Cartier, so that I could flash them around, saying, "Look what I got from Chaplin." The day after he left town, I got a nice cheque in the mail signed Charlie. And then I didn't even write him a thank-you note. Damn me.'

Brooks's souvenirs of Europe, later in the twenties, began with pictures of a burly, handsome, dark-haired man, usually alighting from a train: George Preston Marshall, the millionaire who was her frequent bedfellow and constant adviser between 1927 and 1933. 'If you care about *Pandora's Box*, you should be grateful to George Marshall,' she told me. 'I'd never heard of Mr. Pabst when he offered me the part. It was George who insisted that I should accept it. He was passionately fond of the theatre and films, and he slept with every pretty show-business girl he could find, including all my best friends. George took me to Berlin with his English valet, who stepped off the train blind drunk and fell flat on his face at Mr. Pabst's feet.'

The Brooks collection contains no keepsakes of the actress whom she pipped at the post in the race to play Lulu, and of whom, when I raised the subject, she spoke less than charitably. 'Dietrich? That *contraption*! She was one of the beautiful-but-dumb girls, like me, but she belonged to the category of those who thought they were smart and fooled other people into believing it. But I guess I'm just being insanely jealous, because I know she's a friend of yours — isn't she?' By way of making amends, she praised Dietrich's performance as Lola in *The Blue Angel*, and then, struck by a sudden thought, interrupted herself: 'Hey! Why don't I ask Marlene to come over from Paris? We could work on our memoirs together. Better still, she could write mine, and I hers — *Lulu* by Lola, and *Lola* by Lulu.' To put it politely, however, Dietrich does not correspond to Brooks's ideal image of a movie goddess. But who does — apart from Margaret Sullavan, whose voice, as we know, she reveres? A few months after our Rochester encounter, she sent me a letter that disclosed another, unexpected object of her admiration. In it she said:

I've just been listening to Toronto radio. There was a press conference with Ava Gardner, who is making a movie in Montreal. Her beauty has never excited me, and I have seen only one of her films, *The Night of the Iguana*, in which she played a passive role that revealed her power of stillness but little else. On radio, sitting in a hotel room, triggered by all the old stock questions, she said nothing new or stirring — just 'Sinatra could be very nice or very rotten — get me another drink, baby — I made fifty-four pictures and the only part I understood was in *The Snows of Kilimanjaro*. . . .' In her conversation, there was nothing about great acting or beauty or sex, and no trace of philosophical or intellectual concern. Yet for the first time in my life I was proud of being a movie actress, unmixed with theatre art. Ava is in essence what I think a movie star should be — a beautiful person with a unique, mysterious personality unpolluted by Hollywood. And she is so *strong*. She did not have to run away (like Garbo) to keep from being turned into a product of the machine. . . . What I should like to know is whether, as I sometimes fancy, I ever had a glimmer of that quality of integrity which makes Ava shine with her own light.

The next picture out of the manila files showed Brooks, inscrutable and somewhat forlorn in a sequinned evening gown, sitting at a table surrounded by men with pencil-thin moustaches who were wearing tuxedos, black ties, and wing collars. These men were all jabbering into telephones and laughing maniacally. None of them was looking at Brooks. Behind them I could make out oak-panelled walls and an out-of-focus waiter with a fish-eyed star and a strong resemblance to Louis Jouvet. 'You know where that was taken, of course,' Brooks said.

I was sorry, but I didn't.

'That's Joe Zelli's!' she cried. 'Zelli's was the most famous nightclub in Paris. I can't remember all the men's names, but the one on the extreme right used to drink ether. The one on the left was half Swedish and half English. I lived with him in several hotels. Although he was very young, he had snow-white hair, so we always called him the Eskimo. The fellow next to him, poor guy, was killed the very next day. He was cut to pieces by a speedboat propeller at Cannes.'

Whenever I think of the twenties, I shall see that flash-lit hysterical tableau at Zelli's and the unsmiling seraph at the centre of it.

From the fattest of all her folders, Brooks now pulled out a two-shot. Beaming in a cloche hat, she stands arm in arm with a stocky, self-possessed man in a homburg. He also wears steel-rimmed glasses, a bow tie, and a well-cut business suit; you would guess he was in his early forties. 'Mr. Pabst,' she said simply. 'That was 1928, in Berlin, while we were making *Pandora's Box*. As I told you, I arrived with George Marshall, and Mr. Pabst hated him, because he kept me up all night, going round the clubs. A few weeks later, George went back to the States, and after that Mr. Pabst locked me up in my hotel when the day's shooting was finished. Everyone thought he was in love with me. On the rare evenings when I went to his apartment for dinner, his wife, Trudi, would walk out and bang the door. Mr. Pabst was a highly respectable man, but he had the most extraordinary collection of obscene stills in the world. He even had one of Sarah Bernhardt nude with a black-lace fan. Did you know that in the twenties it was the custom for European actresses to send naked pictures of themselves to movie directors? He had all of them. Anyway, I didn't have an affair with him in Berlin. In 1929, though, when he was in Paris trying to set up *Prix de Beauté*, we went out to dinner at a restaurant and I behaved rather outrageously. For some reason, I slapped a close friend of mine across the face with a bouquet of roses. Mr. Pabst was horrified. He hustled me out of the place and took me back to my hotel, where — what do I do? I'm in a *terrific* mood, so I decide to banish his disgust by giving the best sexual performance of my career. I jump into the hay and deliver myself to him body and soul. [Her voice is jubilant.] He acted as if he'd never experienced such a thing in his life. You know how men want to pin medals on themselves when they excite you? They get positively radiant. Next morning, Mr. Pabst was so pleased he couldn't see straight. That was why he postponed *Prix de Beauté* and arranged to make *Diary of a Lost Girl* first. He wanted the affair to continue. But I didn't, and when I got to Berlin it was like *Pandora's Box* all over again, except that this time the man I brought with me was the Eskimo — my white-headed boy from Zelli's.'

Brooks laughed softly, recalling the scene. 'Mr. Pabst was there at the station to meet me. He was appalled when I got off the train with the Eskimo. On top of that, I had a wart on my neck, and Esky had just slammed the compartment door on my finger. Mr. Pabst took one stark look at me, told me I had to start work the next morning, and dragged me away to a doctor, who burned off the wart. If you study the early sequences of *Lost Girl*, you can see the sticking plaster on my neck. I hated to hurt Mr. Pabst's feelings with the Eskimo, but I simply could not bring myself to repeat that one and only night. The irony, which Mr. Pabst never knew, was that although Esky and I shared a hotel suite in Berlin, we didn't sleep together until much later, when *Lost Girl* was finished and we were spending a few days in Paris. "Eskimo," I said to him the evening before we parted, "this is the night." And it was — another first and last for Brooks.'

More fragments of Brooksiana:

I: Do you think there are countries that produce particularly good lovers?

BROOKS: Englishmen are the best. And priest-ridden Irishmen are the worst.

I: What are your favourite films?

BROOKS: *An American in Paris*, *Pygmalion*, and *The Wizard of Oz*. Please don't be disappointed.

I: They're all visions of wish fulfilment. An American at large with a *gamine* young dancer in a fantasy playground called Paris. A cockney flower girl who becomes the toast of upper-class London. And a child from your home state who discovers, at the end of a trip to a magic world, that happiness was where she started out.

BROOKS: You *are* disappointed.

I: Not a bit. They're first-rate movies, and they're all aspects of you.

Postscript from a letter Brooks wrote to me before we met: 'Can you give me a reason for sitting here in this bed, going crazy, with not one god-damned excuse for living?' I came up with more than one reason; viz., (a) to receive the homage of those who cherish the images she has left on celluloid, (b) to bestow the pleasure of her conversation on those who seek her company, (c) to appease her hunger for gleaning wisdom from books, and (d) to test the truth of a remark she had made to a friend: 'The Spanish philosopher Ortega y Gasset once said, "We are all lost creatures. It is only when we admit this that we have a chance of finding ourselves." '

Despite the numerous men who have crossed the trajectory of her life, Brooks has pursued her own course. She has flown solo. The price to be paid for such individual autonomy is, inevitably, loneliness, and her loneliness is prefigured in one of the most penetrating comments she has ever committed to print: 'The great art of films does not consist of descriptive movement of face and body, but in the movements of thought and soul, transmitted in a kind of intense isolation.'

As I rose to leave her apartment, she gave me a present: a large and handsome volume entitled *Louise Brooks — Portrait d'une Anti-Star*. Published in Paris in 1977, it contained a full pictorial survey of her career, together with essays, critiques, and poems devoted to her beauty and talent. She inscribed it to me, and copied out, beneath her signature, the epitaph she has composed for herself: 'I never gave away anything without wishing I had kept it; nor kept anything without wishing I had given it away.' The book included an account by Brooks of her family background, which I paused to read. It ended with this paragraph, here reproduced from her original English text:

> Over the years I suffered poverty and rejection and came to believe that my mother had formed me for a freedom that was unattainable, a delusion. Then . . . I was confined to this small apartment in this alien city of Rochester. . . . Looking about, I saw millions of old people in my situation, wailing like lost puppies because they were alone and had no one to talk to. But they had become enslaved by habits which bound their lives to warm bodies that talked. I was free! Although my mother had ceased to be a warm body in 1944, she had not forsaken me. She comforts me with every book I read. Once again I am five, leaning on her shoulder, learning the words as she reads aloud *Alice in Wonderland*.

She insisted on getting out of bed to escort me to the door. We had been talking earlier of Proust, and she had mentioned his maxim that the future could never be predicted from the past. Out of her past, I thought, in all its bizarre variety, who knows what future she may invent? 'Another thing about Proust,' she said, resting on her cane in the doorway. 'No matter how he dresses his characters up in their social disguises, we always know how they look naked.' As we know it (I reflected) in Brooks's performances.

I kissed her goodbye, buttoned up my social disguise — for it was a chilly evening — and joined the other dressed-up people on the streets of Rochester.

The New Yorker: 11th June 1979; *Show People*, 1980

INDEX

makes so many references to earlier films and styles of film-making that it could just as easily, and perhaps more accurately, have been called 'Genre Wars.'

Among other pictures cited by Copeland were Martin Scorsese's *New York, New York*, Brian De Palma's *Obsession*, Don Siegel's *The Shootist*, Marty Feldman's *The Last Remake of Beau Geste*, and Herbert Ross's *Play It Again Sam* (written by Woody Allen), all of which drew their inspiration from celluloid sources. Nor did he overlook the career of Peter Bogdanovich, an extended act of homage to the achievements of other directors. He concluded:

There are dangers involved; the dangers of decadence, of art feeding so completely on itself that it becomes totally cut off from life as lived.

In 1965, in an introduction to Malcolm Lowry's novel *Under the Volcano*, Stephen Spender wrote, 'Someone should write a thesis perhaps on the influence of the cinema on the novel — I mean the *serious* novel.' I should say that there was a more urgent need for a study of the influence of the cinema on the cinema — and I do not mean only the serious cinema. It is self-evident that all the arts live off and grow out of their own past. What is new about film is that it is the first narrative art to be instantly accessible, twenty-four hours a day, in virtually every living room. To immerse oneself in drama, opera, or literature, it is necessary, from time to time, to carry out certain errands, like going to a theatre, an opera house, a record shop, a bookstore, or a library; but to become saturated in cinema you do not even have to go to the movies. They come to you. The lover of stage acting will never know exactly how Sarah Siddons or Edmund Kean performed, or what the theatre in Periclean Athens was really like, but for the movie buff such problems do not arise, since the art of his choice is on permanent record, its whole history an open book, visible at the turn of a switch. This explains why so many contemporary novels and plays, as well as films, are swollen with references to, quotations from, and parodies of old movies. A process of artistic colonisation is going on. Never before, I believe, has one art form exercised such hegemony over the others; and the decisive factor is not intrinsic superiority but sheer availability.

The first generation of children nourished, via television, on films has only recently reached maturity, yet it's already clear how deeply — in their private behaviour, not to mention their work as artists — the movies are imprinted on them. As the amount of exposed and edited film inexorably piles up, its ascendancy will increase, and we may have to cope with a culture entirely molded by cinematic habits and values. Edmund Wilson, I suspect, was hovering over this point as long ago as 1949, when, having seen a pastiche Hollywood musical called *Oh, You Beautiful Doll*, he